ALSO BY NEIL LANCTOT

NEGRO LEAGUE BASEBALL:
THE RISE AND RUIN OF A BLACK INSTITUTION

FAIR DEALING AND CLEAN PLAYING:
THE HILLDALE CLUB AND
THE DEVELOPMENT OF BLACK PROFESSIONAL
BASEBALL, 1910–1932

CAMPY

THE TWO LIVES OF ROY CAMPANELLA

NEIL LANCTOT

SIMON & SCHUSTER
NEW YORK LONDON TORONTO SYDNEY

Simon & Schuster
1230 Avenue of the Americas
New York, NY 10020

First Simon & Schuster hardcover edition March 2011

Designed by Ruth Lee-Mui

Manufactured in the United States of America

3 5 7 9 10 8 6 4

Library of Congress Cataloging-in-Publication Data

Lanctot, Neil.
Campy : the two lives of Roy Campanella / Neil Lanctot.
p. cm.
Includes bibliographical references and index.
1. Campanella, Roy, 1921–1993. 2. African American baseball players—Biography.
3. Brooklyn Dodgers (Baseball team)—History. I. Title.
GV865.C3L36 2011
796.357092—dc22 2010044602
[B]

ISBN 978-1-4165-4704-4
ISBN 978-1-4516-0649-2 (ebook)

IN MEMORY OF MY FATHER,

FRANCIS L. LANCTOT,

AND SISTER,

CAROL (LANCTOT) McQUAID

No one had more courage than Roy Campanella. . . . To me, he was the greatest Dodger of them all.

—PETER O'MALLEY

CONTENTS

PROLOGUE

FOR SOME CITIES, a World Series game is an all too rare event to be savored and debated for years afterward. But for a New Yorker in 1958, the Fall Classic was a predictable part of the October calendar, as humdrum as a Columbus Day sale at Macy's or candy apples at a neighborhood Halloween party.

The great catcher Roy Campanella was a veteran of the October baseball wars. Between 1949 and 1956, his Brooklyn Dodgers had taken on the New York Yankees five times, coming up empty all but once. On Saturday, October 4, Campy was returning to Yankee Stadium for yet another Series game, but everything had changed since the last time he'd set foot in the House That Ruth Built. The Dodgers no longer played in their cozy ballpark in Flatbush but in a monstrosity known as the Coliseum a continent away. And Campy no longer played baseball at all because a January automobile accident had left him a quadriplegic. For the past five months, he had doggedly worked with the staff and physicians at the Institute of Physical Medicine and Rehabilitation on Thirty-fourth Street in Manhattan to learn how to function in a wheelchair. He had now sufficiently progressed to leave the hospital on weekends.

His doctors had encouraged him to accept Yankee co-owner Del Webb's invitation to attend Saturday's game at the Stadium, although Campy was initially not so sure. He had not appeared in public since his accident, nor had he sat on anything except a wheelchair. Nevertheless, he set aside any lingering anxiety to make the early-afternoon car ride to the Bronx, where box seats behind the Yankee dugout had already been set aside for Roy, his wife, two of his children, and a male attendant.

When the family station wagon arrived at Yankee Stadium, Campy could not help but think of the times he had suited up in the locker room in the past. He had never liked hitting at the Stadium, but he had enjoyed his fair share of glory there, whacking a key single in the deciding game of the Negro National League championship game as a teenager in 1939 and a more crucial double in game seven of the World Series in 1955, the year the Dodgers finally bested the Yanks. Today, he would just be another fan.

Campy soon discovered his wheelchair was too wide for the Stadium's narrow aisles. He had no choice but to be bodily carried by his attendant, two firemen, and a policeman. "I felt like some sad freak," he later recalled. "It was the most embarrassing thing that ever happened to me. I felt ashamed."

But the fans whose glances he so desperately wanted to avoid soon began to shout out encouragement. "Hi, Slugger!" one greeted him. "Attaboy, Campy!" yelled another. "Stay in there, Campy, you got it licked." Before long, virtually every one of the 71,566 present realized that the fellow with the neck brace and "tan Bebop cap" being carried to his seat was three-time MVP Roy Campanella. "By some sort of mental telepathy thousands in the great three-tiered horse-shoe were on their feet and when the applause moved, like wind through wheat from row to row, I doubt if there were many there who didn't know what had happened," wrote Bill Corum of the *Journal-American.* "It was a sad thing. Yet it was a great thing too, in the meaning of humanity. No word was spoke that anybody will know. Yet it had the same effect as that moment when a dying Lou Gehrig stood on this same Yankee diamond and said . . . 'I'm the luckiest man in the world.' "

Down on the field, the top half of the second inning took a backseat to the heartfelt hoopla in the stands. With the count 1-1 on Milwaukee's Frank Torre, Yankee pitcher Don Larsen stepped off the mound as the players in both dugouts craned their necks to see what was causing the commotion and then began to join in the ovation themselves. Upon spotting

Campy only a few yards away, Yankee catcher Yogi Berra flipped his mask and waved, while home plate umpire Tom Gorman offered "a clenched fist in a 'keep-fighting' gesture."

Campanella, who had vowed beforehand that he "wasn't going to cry," struggled to keep his emotions in check. He smiled back at Yogi (who "kept looking back and hardly could resist the temptation to run over and shake Campy's hand," said one reporter) and winked at the mob of photographers who gathered at his seat. For the rest of that warm October afternoon, he tried to focus on the game, even trying to eat a hot dog without success, but he could not stop thinking about the outpouring of love he had just experienced. "It's hard to explain the feeling that came over me. I don't believe any home run I ever hit was greeted by so much cheering," Campanella said later.

It was the first time he had received such applause in a wheelchair, but it would not be the last. For the rest of his life, his presence, whether in a major league ballpark or in front of a Manhattan deli, would evoke similar responses. He was no longer just a ballplayer but a symbol of something much more.

1

NICETOWN BOY

ASK A PHILADELPHIAN how to get to Nicetown and you're likely to get a funny look, one that unmistakably says, "Why the hell are you going *there*?" And indeed the North Philadelphia neighborhood, named for Jan and Hans de Neus, Dutch Huguenots who had settled the area centuries earlier, is far from a tourist destination today, its gritty and weather-beaten streets a haven for crime, graffiti, and drugs.

But Nicetown was once a vital cog in Philadelphia's economy, a bustling place where thriving industrial concerns operated plants employing thousands. The neighborhood's abundance of job opportunities would attract a slew of European immigrants in the late nineteenth century, including a Sicilian named Frank Campanella and his family.

Campanella ("little bell" in Italian) and his wife, Mary, had originally settled in western Pennsylvania after leaving the old country in 1886. The family welcomed a son, John, in 1889 and eventually three more bambinos. By 1893, Frank opted to move his growing clan across the state to Philadelphia, then the nation's third-largest city, and settled in Nicetown at 4201 North Fifth Street.

Frank spent his first decade in Philadelphia bouncing from job to job as a grocer, laborer, lighter (probably of streetlamps), and a marble worker.

Mary gave birth to at least three other children who failed to survive, although oldest son John grew to manhood and took a bride at age seventeen. According to family lore, the teenage couple ran away three different times before finally tying the knot successfully in 1907. It was not their youth, perfectly acceptable in the early 1900s, that caused such an uproar, but John's highly irregular choice of a wife—a black woman named Ida Mercer.

For Americans who believed that the recent flood of new immigrants from southern and eastern Europe had irreparably tainted the national gene pool, miscegenation was the ultimate crime against the white race. Southerners in particular were raised from birth to believe that all black males secretly lusted after white women, urges checked only through laws and lynchings. No Pennsylvania statutes prevented John Campanella from marrying a black woman, but the societal pressures were daunting. Even in the North, the young couple could expect ostracism and condemnation from both families, particularly the Campanellas, who virtually disowned John. Their children would almost certainly bear the burden of second-class citizenship. As Booker T. Washington explained in 1905, "It takes 100 percent of white blood to make a white man and only a drop of Negro blood to make a Negro."

Ida Mercer, the young lady who had so turned John's head, had grown up in Cecil County, Maryland, in the northeast part of the state, about sixty miles from Philadelphia. Her parents and grandparents were also Maryland natives, all of whom likely toiled on the farms that provided the backbone for the local economy. By 1900, the Mercers had moved to St. George's Hundred in northern Delaware, a rural community just over the Maryland line, where Ida's father and most of her neighbors eked out a meager living as farmers or sharecroppers. With their future prospects bleak, Ida and several siblings decided to try their luck in the big city to the north less than two hours away, eventually settling in Nicetown, as had the Campanellas a decade earlier.

Exactly how Ida Mercer and John Campanella met is lost to the sands of time. Regardless, the unlikely pair subsequently set up housekeeping in Nicetown at 1535 Rowan Street. Four children followed: Lawrence, Gladys, Doris, and a son who died in infancy or childhood.

Like his father, John tried his hand at a variety of jobs before he finally found his calling after World War I operating a fruit and vegetable stand. With a new sense of stability, the family moved again, renting a nearby row house at 4446 North Colorado Street, on the same block where two other Mercer sisters also resided. The neighborhood was so heavily African-American that a census taker initially wrote a *B* (for "black") next to John Campanella's name in 1920 before correcting it to *W.* A decade later, another census taker made the same mistake.

The fifth and final child, Roy, arrived on November 19, 1921. After he became an established major leaguer, his "baseball age" raised plenty of eyebrows, especially since other former Negro Leaguers were known to have shaved off a few years to improve their chances in the big leagues. "Everybody always laughs when Campy mentions his age," a sportswriter once noted, "although no one has ever been able to disprove his November 19, 1921, birthday." No one ever would, as his Philadelphia school records and other documents verify 1921 as his birth year.

Although baby Roy spent his earliest years on Colorado Street, John Campanella wanted something better for his growing family. In 1928, he purchased his first house, a two-story brick corner row home at 1538 Kerbaugh Street in a Nicetown neighborhood that would today be considered remarkably diverse. Twelve of the other twenty-three dwellings on the 1500 block in 1930 were inhabited by white families, the remaining eleven by blacks. The neighbors were mostly blue-collar, including an African-American steelworker, an Irish butcher, and a Polish auto mechanic. Somehow, everyone managed to coexist peacefully, a life lesson that Roy would take to heart at an early age.

At less than fourteen hundred square feet, the Campanella abode was at times nearly bursting from the strains imposed by the onset of the Great Depression. By 1930, seventeen-year-old Lawrence's wife, their infant son, and Ida's brother were also living with the Campanellas. Roy eventually lucked into a small room of his own at the top of the stairs, unlike his sisters, who shared a bedroom. The main floor featured a fairly large kitchen and a high-ceilinged living room where Roy often tuned to his favorite radio program, *The Lone Ranger*. Down in the basement were Campy's train sets, and woe to anyone who disturbed his elaborate arrangement.

"Now you can stay down here and look as long as you want to," he would tell his cousin Thomas Williams. "But I'm gonna tell you one thing.... Look all you wanna, but *do not* touch anything!"

With money scarce, young Roy soon learned the importance of hard work and discipline. His father rose at 5:00 a.m. each day, loaded his battered old Model T truck with fruit, vegetables, and fish, then drove off to sell his stock throughout the neighborhoods. Lawrence's job as a milkman was just as unglamorous and required even earlier hours. Like many a Depression kid, Roy wanted to contribute something to the family income, and Lawrence eventually gave him his first job, paying him a quarter each day to help with his deliveries. He did other odd jobs such as mowing lawns, selling papers, shining shoes, and hawking a hundred-pound bag of potatoes, always turning over his earnings to his mother, who returned a portion as an allowance.

As Roy walked the streets of Nicetown, he learned quickly that he was different. The neighborhood kids, both white and black, took one look at the boy with the Italian name and the skin darker than the swarthiest Sicilian's and put two and two together. "Half-breed," they taunted him. "Roy's a half-breed. And his daddy's a white man." At first, he didn't quite know what it all meant, but he knew it was not a compliment. More often than not, a fistfight followed. But the fights didn't answer the question that gnawed at him—what did it mean to have a black mother and white father? And why was that such a bad thing?

One day, he finally mustered the courage to ask his mother. Ida Campanella had long been prepared for this moment. "Yes, your daddy's white and I'm colored, and it's nothing to be ashamed of," she said. "You're just as good as anybody else and don't you ever forget it." The insults, she told Roy, were not important. "Remember, your daddy has made me very happy."

Something else remained unsaid but understood between mother and son. In the eyes of American society, it was Ida's heritage that determined Roy's racial identity (even the Philadelphia school district made certain to identify Ida as "negro" on Roy's permanent record). The racial arithmetic of the time dictated that one black parent made Roy and his siblings "colored"; it was as simple as that (and clear to the census taker in 1930, who carefully wrote "Negro" next to Roy's name). That designation immediately shut hundreds of doors to Roy, who would have to learn to navigate Jim Crow America.

As a northern city, Philadelphia was relatively free from the extreme legal segregation of the Deep South. But the city's 219,000 African-Americans coped daily with a depressing barrage of blatant discrimination in employment, health care, and accommodations. Although Campanella often portrayed Nicetown as a sort of color-blind Shangri-la, he was no stranger to discrimination from an early age. The integrated schools he attended were closed to black teachers. The Nicetown Boys Club refused to admit blacks, nor did local Boy Scout troops and swimming pools. Instead, Roy had to hitchhike or walk two miles to the Wissahickon Boys Club, where black kids could swim for fifteen cents. Even the movies he enjoyed each Saturday with sister Doris were an iffy proposition, with some Philadelphia theaters openly rejecting black patrons or herding them into separate sections or the balcony. And his childhood psyche was constantly assailed with negative mass media images and ugly stereotypes.

The young Roy Campanella had precious few black role models in his immediate orbit. Except for his friend Quentin Lee's father, one of Philadelphia's first black motorcycle cops, Roy seldom came into contact with black professional men or women. Like most African-Americans, Roy could expect a life of drudgery in a job available only because the white man found it too disagreeable or low-paying to accept.

With a blue-collar future ahead, education was never a priority. When Roy was a little boy, his father would give him an ice cream cone each time he wrote his name correctly, increasing his waistline more than his interest in academics. When he reached school age, Ida sent him off to nearby Asa Packer Elementary, but for Depression kids such as Campanella, school was something you tolerated until you were old enough to start earning real money.

From an early age, athletics, not books, consumed him. As a solidly built, although not particularly tall, boy, he was in demand for the pickup games played throughout the neighborhood. He spent many an afternoon playing football and basketball, already exhibiting a fierce competitive streak. "Whatever the sport," he later recalled, "I seemed to feel that I *had* to be on top." Like many urban kids, he also dabbled in stickball, using a small red rubber ball and "sawed-off broomsticks that we taped at the handle."

Baseball was far more to his liking. At nine, he was already haunting local ballparks, happy to act as a water boy for the men's games. With baseball then the king of the sports world, it was hardly a surprise that he embraced the game so fervently. But baseball also nourished his competitive drive, allowing him to experience the joy of winning, the thrill of seeing how far he could hit a ball, the elation in throwing it harder and farther than anyone else.

It didn't hurt that his neighborhood was a virtual baseball smorgasbord. Shibe Park, the home of Connie Mack's Athletics, was less than two miles away at Twenty-first and Lehigh, and the Phillies' Baker Bowl was even closer, but the A's greater success (three American League pennants between 1929 and 1931) quickly earned his loyalty. By the early 1930s, Roy's allowance money was regularly going to the Athletics. If he didn't have the fifty cents for a bleacher seat at Shibe, he would pay a quarter to sit on the roof of a building behind right field until the A's built the celebrated "spite fence" in 1935 to halt the practice.

It was a great time to be an Athletics fan. The A's featured future Hall of Famers Lefty Grove, a 31-game winner in 1931; Jimmie Foxx, who crushed 58 homers in 1932; and Roy's particular favorite, the hard-hitting catcher Mickey Cochrane. He also liked the Phillies' switch-hitting outfielder Buzz Arlett, whose big 44-ounce bat and .313 average dazzled fans during his only major league season in 1931. The Yankees were always popular, with the aging but still dangerous Babe Ruth and his teammate Lou Gehrig, who blasted four home runs at Shibe one day in 1932 while Roy and his friends watched in astonishment. But it was the Yankees' less heralded catcher who most impressed Roy. "My hero was Bill Dickey," he said later on, "and I was there, whenever I could be, when the Yankees were in town, just to see him."

To further whet his voracious baseball appetite, there were also dozens, if not hundreds, of white and black semipro and amateur clubs scattered throughout the city's neighborhoods, many of which still had vacant lots available for play. At Twelfth and Luzerne streets, less than a mile from the Campanellas, Nicetown kids could watch the highly competitive all-white Philadelphia League teams in action and their occasional scrimmages against Negro League squads. Whether this was Roy's first exposure to segregated baseball remains uncertain, as Campy barely paid any attention to the Negro Leagues while growing up. "I don't think I went to one game until I played," he later admitted. He did, however, remember seeing the legendary black shortstop John Henry Lloyd, probably after Lloyd had retired from high-level competition.

But it was major league baseball that captured most of Roy's attention. The games were nearby, and it was so easy to follow the progress of his favorite team by radio, newspapers, newsreels, or the monthly issues of *Baseball Magazine*, which Roy never missed. Photographs of his favorite players, mostly white, covered the walls of his room, although he did have a few shots of Satchel Paige and Josh Gibson clipped from the skeletal sports pages of the weekly black press.

Roy ate, slept, and dreamed baseball, even though the major leagues, its most sublime form, excluded blacks. The policy meant little, if anything, to Campy, who would not fully grasp the truth for several years (his Dodger teammate Joe Black remained similarly unaware until he was a high school senior). Organized Baseball, like other aspects of American life in the early 1930s, didn't advertise its color line, nor did it need to do so. It was simply taken for granted and not even worthy of comment or thought by most people. "If I wondered at all about why there weren't any colored players, I just thought there weren't any good enough," Roy later observed.

If young Roy didn't fantasize about a major league career, playing the game consumed him from an early age. In contrast to today's ultraorganized world of T-ball and Little League, boys in the 1930s received their baseball education on the sandlots with no adults present. After school and on weekends, shooed out of the house by exhausted parents, Nicetown kids would congregate at nearby Hunting Park and get up a game that would usually last until dark. "You know we'd get just about any kind of hard ball to play with, an old nickel rocket, they used to call them, and we'd wrap it up with electrician's tape," Campanella later explained. "When the tape would come off we would rewrap it again and the ball would wind up . . . so heavy it would feel like a lead ball or an iron ball but we still played with it until we'd lose it."

His parents did little to encourage their son's growing baseball obsession. John wasn't happy about the cuts and scrapes Roy picked up playing the game and tried to extract promises that he would give up hardball. Nor was he pleased when he caught Roy practicing his throwing by hurling apples and potatoes at a lamppost. The boy needed to understand there were more important things in life. John expected Roy home in time to assist with unloading unsold fruits and vegetables and preparing the truck for the next morning ("Roy should be made to help," a nosy neighbor had already advised the Campanellas). If not, a beating awaited him. And Ida wanted Sundays set aside for the Nazarene Baptist Church and then Sunday school.

Roy still managed to squeeze in plenty of baseball, both with and without his parents' knowledge. He roamed the parks of North Philadelphia looking for a game to join and had no trouble finding one. By the time Roy was eleven, he could already throw harder than most boys his age. Pitching might have been a perfect outlet, but he found himself more drawn to catching, a position that guaranteed him a slot in most games. "The other kids didn't want to. I just wanted to play. I didn't care what I did." Catching not only got him into the game, but he was now "in on every pitch. Boy, was I happy." The only downside was the cumbersome mask, which he refused to wear at first, until a foul tip to the face one day changed his mind.

But casual pickup games no longer satisfied him. What he wanted most was to play on a real team—one that wore uniforms and maybe sent off its game results to the local newspapers. He began to hang around the teenage Quaker City Giants (Giants being a long-favored name for black clubs dating back to the nineteenth-century Cuban Giants, the first black professional team), serving as batboy, unofficial mascot, and warm-up catcher between innings. Occasionally, Roy turned heads with his throwing and prowess behind the plate, but the team's manager wasn't about to allow an eleven-year-old on the team. "Try the Nicetown Juniors," he told Roy.

The Nicetown Juniors, aka Nicetown Colored Athletic Club (NCAC), had debuted in 1933, composed mostly of fourteen- to eighteen-year-olds. At what age Campy joined is uncertain, although *Philadelphia Independent* publisher Forrist White Woodard's decision to sponsor the team at the behest of his newsboys appears to have been the catalyst. Roy, who had been selling the black weekly for years, jumped at the chance to get his first uniform, only to find that his youth still worked against him. The coach only grudgingly gave him a spot, and catching, he was told, was out of the question. If Roy did in fact join the team in 1934, his contributions were minimal, as he does not appear in the handful of NCAC game accounts published in the *Philadelphia Tribune* and *Tioga News* that year.

The following season started out even less promisingly. NCAC official Russell Wilder, a postal worker who hung out with the likes of Josh Gibson and Judy Johnson when they were in town, decided that thirteen-year-olds just didn't belong on a team now looking to recruit players between the ages of seventeen and twenty. As Roy told the story years later, he ran home in tears. Ida, despite her reservations about baseball, picked up the phone and called Wilder. The boy loves the game. Couldn't you *please* find a spot for him? Wilder reconsidered and found a uniform for Roy after all.

But if Campy had truly been a charity-case addition to the squad, it's doubtful that his name (initially "Campanello") would have appeared in Nicetown box scores published in the *Philadelphia Tribune* as early as May. His teammate Dusty Ballard later claimed that an injury to the regular catcher gave Roy his big break. According to Ballard's Wally Pipp–like version, Campy seized the job after gunning down the first three runners attempting to steal that day and then belting a base-clearing double.

Although no record of this game has been found, the local press provides other tantalizing evidence of young Roy's blossoming talents. On June 20, the *Tribune* praised the play of "Confenello in back of the plate" in Nicetown's 9–5 win over the white St. Lawrence team. A week later, Roy batted third and banged out two hits against another white church team. Seeing his name in print just like his heroes must have been a thrill, at least on the few occasions the press got it right. Over the next decade, the black press would find numerous creative ways to misspell his surname.

Despite occasional mentions, Roy took more than his share of lumps. He was, after all, a thirteen-year-old, albeit one "big for his age," facing boys several years his senior, now that the NCAC was playing under the Nicetown Giant moniker themselves and had graduated to "A"-level opponents. Wilder did not hesitate to bench him, although Campy hated being on the sidelines. "Sitting on the bench," he once admitted, "makes me nervous."

Riding the pine fueled his already burning desire to improve. If he could find a willing partner, he would practice catching pop-ups and throwing down to second any chance he got. His teammates, many of them current or former Simon Gratz High School athletes, couldn't help but be impressed (and perhaps a bit amused) by the kid whose throws from the crouching position rivaled Mickey Cochrane's. And he was so likable, always smiling and joking.

By September, it was back to school, this year at the predominantly white Elizabeth Duane Gillespie Junior High, a few blocks from his home. After his first real taste of baseball success that summer, the three R's appeared even less important than usual. More than once, Roy ditched classes altogether, instead heading to Hunting Park, "scuffling and playing ball with any other truants I could dig up."

If Gillespie offered him anything, it was another chance to play organized sports. He soon joined the football and basketball teams and even earned a spot on the track squad. Before long, David Patchell, an enthusiastic young gym teacher who also coached the school's teams, began to take an interest in Roy. Unlike some of the other white faculty members, the "totally colorblind" Patchell paid more attention to ability than race. This Campanella, he recognized, was a remarkable athlete, albeit a bit aggressive at times.

One day, after watching the boy blast a tremendous home run in a gym-class softball game, Patchell asked Roy to meet with him. Your athletic ability, he told him, is the kind that could open up doors for you, like a scholarship or even a professional contract. But Roy needed to keep out of trouble. "Don't get involved in gangs," said Patchell. "Let sports be your out and you will do fine." And he reminded Roy that while aggressiveness was admirable, he should always be sure to "keep it in its place" and not run roughshod over the other kids.

Campanella remembered that brief chat the rest of his life. It was probably the first time that he realized that baseball could be a vehicle out of Nicetown. Although John and Ida loved their son, they had never pushed Roy either academically or athletically to transcend his own roots and strive for something more. Ida's devout Baptist faith had instilled acceptance but not necessarily ambition in Roy. She taught her children to recite the 23rd Psalm ("The Lord is my shepherd; I shall not want") in the face of adversity and that "the good Lord will always find a way." Most of all, she reminded Roy and his siblings to always "be happy for what we've got." But Patchell had opened Roy's eyes.

The next spring, Patchell invited Roy to try out for the Gillespie baseball team. When he arrived at the tryout, Roy noticed Patchell had marked off four circles for prospective infielders, outfielders, pitchers, and catchers to gather. He quickly made a beeline to the catchers' circle after seeing no candidates eager to don the tools of ignorance. "It was the only way to make sure I'd make the team," he later explained. And "that's how I became a catcher." Or so goes the legend.

Campanella told the tryout story repeatedly throughout his life. Occasionally, the details changed slightly (Simon Gratz High School sometimes substituted for Gillespie, although Patchell never taught there), but Roy usually insisted that his catching career began that day. In fact, he once claimed that he had played every position with Nicetown except catcher and that it was Patchell who gave him his first catcher's mitt.

Campy may well have staked out the vacant catchers' circle to guarantee his spot, but he was no novice behind the plate. When he became famous, he loved to entertain his listeners with colorful tales of his baseball career. Through years of storytelling, Roy produced a life script for public consumption, although the details were sometimes exaggerated and even contradictory.

How Campanella fared his first season with Gillespie is unknown. Local newspapers did not cover junior high school games, nor are there yearbooks that might fill in the gaps. But as Patchell had recognized, Roy clearly had something—power, confidence, arm strength—that separated him from the other adolescents on the team. Those attributes were more than enough for a Junior American Legion coach named Bill Welsh to invite Campy to join his Loudenslager Post Number 366 team that season.

Campy was the only nonwhite player on the team. But Welsh, witnessing Campy's ability to "mix" with his white Gillespie teammates and his general likability, figured he was a safe bet, even on a Legion club featuring the sons of two current major league managers, Jimmie Wilson of the Phillies and Jimmy Dykes of the White Sox (one wonders what Dykes, infamous for his segregated local bowling alleys, thought of this integration). Campy never forgot Welsh's refreshing open-mindedness. Nineteen years later, he would leave him tickets to game four of the 1955 World Series at Ebbets Field.

Junior Legion baseball provided Roy with "a pretty good idea of how I could do against boys my own age." He soon discovered that his size, strength, and experience exceeded that of his teammates. Infielders instinctively flinched whenever Campy fired the ball down to second or third, although Welsh, his arm broken by one of Roy's errant pitches during batting practice, could hardly blame them. Even the umpires took notice of the kid, who seemed suspiciously big for Legion ball. One actually stopped a game until Welsh provided proof that the boy was only fourteen.

Junior Legion competition earned Roy his first mention in a white newspaper, the *Philadelphia Inquirer*, which reported that "Campanello" banged out two more hits in a victory over Olney Post. Even more exciting were the local tournament games at Shibe Park and the Baker Bowl, his first appearances on major league turf. Later, he would claim that he homered in both venues, but the local newspapers never covered the games.

In between Gillespie and Junior American Legion competition, he somehow found the time to return to the Nicetown Giants. But Russell Wilder and his coach Pender Hill were still not entirely sold on Campy's defense or offense, the latter hardly improved by a stint hitting left-handed. For the new season, they thought it best to stick the kid in left and bat him eighth, leaving the catching in more experienced hands.

Wilder and Hill had big plans for 1936. For the first time, they entered the team in an honest-to-goodness league, the otherwise all-white Northeast Suburban, obtained a home field at Tenth and Pike streets in Nicetown, and even converted Wilder's cellar into a club room for the boys. The *Philadelphia Independent* marveled at the previously obscure team's "great progress . . . that has pitched the wide awake Tioga Nicetown and lower Germantown community into spasms." According to the *Independent*, crowds of more than one thousand, many of them friends and family, were "not uncommon" at their games, although John and Ida were hardly likely to be among them.

Whether Campy's parents were watching did not particularly concern him. All that mattered was that he was in uniform playing the game he loved nearly every summer day in front of actual fans. There was no money in it, but who cared about that? His immersion in higher-level competition was not only paying dividends in his baseball development but was also continuing to broaden his name recognition.

If the exploits of Campy and his teammates were now the talk of the Philadelphia sandlots, one section of the city remained unimpressed. In South Philadelphia, the Black Meteors had long reigned supreme, led by Clarence "Jim" Thorpe, a twenty-six-year-old who had once pitched for the famous Hilldale Club. So strong were the Meteors that they even occasionally booked Negro League clubs for exhibition games, though the big boys usually won handily. More than once a Meteor player had so impressed the Negro Leaguers that he found himself offered a contract the next day.

Nicetown, eager to topple the Meteors from their throne, brashly agreed to a five-game series in late July. The results were not pretty, as the South Philadelphians handily whipped the uptown upstarts. But Campy, again behind the plate, acquitted himself nicely, his two hits a bright spot in an 11–7 defeat. Maybe he had impressed the Meteors' skipper, Otto Briggs, a former Hilldale outfielder who had managed in the Negro Leagues only eight years earlier.

By the time September rolled around, fourteen-year-old Roy had probably played more than one hundred baseball games on three different teams during the last five months. Maybe John and Ida hadn't seen many (or any) of the games, but their son was obviously not about to "outgrow" his baseball mania anytime soon. They could only wonder where it was all going.

2

THE BIG LEAGUE OF COLORED BASEBALL

AS THE NEW YEAR OF 1937 DAWNED, Americans had been contending with the Great Depression for seven years with no relief in sight. The Campanellas were fortunate that John's fruit and vegetable business had continued to provide a steady, if unspectacular, income. It ensured they would never go hungry (Ida's "Italian salad" was a favorite delicacy of visitors to their home). Perhaps they didn't have luxuries, but the family held on to their house and enjoyed the basic amenities without being forced to go on relief like so many others. And the girls were doing well. Gladys was now in college at Tuskegee, and her younger sister, Doris, was about to graduate from Simon Gratz High in June.

But the baby, Roy—what was to become of him? His older brother, Lawrence, had dropped out of high school, and it appeared likely that Roy was drifting down that path. In an era when only about half of American kids completed high school, quitting was not a disgrace. The problem, at least for John and Ida, was that Roy seemed to be uninterested in anything except baseball. How would he earn a living?

There were, of course, the Negro Leagues, the name given to organized African-American professional baseball, which had been fitfully functioning since 1920 with teams mostly clustered in the black population centers of the North, Midwest, and South. Following the economic crash that had wiped out the leagues of the 1920s, black baseball's future appeared hopeless until Pittsburgh promoter Gus Greenlee picked up the gauntlet in 1933. Within three years, Greenlee's new Negro National League (NNL) would embrace six Eastern franchises, Philadelphia, New York, Washington, Pittsburgh (two teams), and Newark.

Throughout the Depression the NNL barely got by. By 1937, Greenlee, the league's big moneyman, was having serious cash-flow problems, and the Crawfords, his team of high-priced (at least for the NNL) superstars, would have to be sacrificed for whatever he could get. Future Hall of Famers Josh Gibson and Judy Johnson were shipped to the Homestead Grays for two players and $2,500, a not insubstantial chunk of change but not enough to bail out Greenlee. Sixteen hundred miles away, Dominican dictator Rafael Trujillo was assembling the best baseball team that ever played in Latin America. He targeted Greenlee's NNL, where the players were enormously talented, severely underpaid, and bound by only the flimsiest of contracts. The raids that spring would set in motion a chain reaction that would send Roy Campanella to the Negro National League at the age of fifteen.

THE CHRONIC and all too tiresome travails of the Negro Leagues did not particularly concern Roy that spring. With Gillespie, the Nicetown Giants, and the Junior American Legion all vying for his services, the boy the kids now called Pooch (nicknamed after the A's right fielder George Puccinelli) expected to be very busy in the months ahead.

Meanwhile, Trujillo's agents had begun waving wads of cash in the faces of NNL players, luring them (without much effort) to the Dominican summer league. The great Satchel Paige of Greenlee's Pittsburgh Crawfords happily led the parade to Latin America, joined by a reported seventeen others, eight of them Crawfords. Roughly a team's worth of players vanished, leaving the reeling NNL owners scrambling to find replacements.

Tom Dixon, player-manager of the Bacharach Giants, a local black independent team, knew what was coming. By the end of May, the Philadelphia Stars had grabbed two of his young outfielders, Paul Dixon (no relation) and Gene Benson, who would enjoy a solid twelve-year career in the Negro

Leagues. Dixon barely had a chance to find replacements before the Crawfords swiped his catcher Buddy Burbage.

Dixon was thirty-one years old. He had grown up in the Germantown section of Philadelphia and was an outstanding athlete, excelling in golf, basketball, and baseball. Not surprisingly, Negro League teams had come calling, and Dixon had spent the early 1930s catching for several clubs. By 1935, he had tired of blackball's salaries and opted instead to join the Bacharach Giants, at one time an Atlantic City–based league team but now operating independently out of Philadelphia. To Dixon, their schedule of local weeknight games and short two-hundred- to three-hundred-mile trips on the weekends was far more attractive than the normal Negro League grind. He could still keep his regular day job at Passon's sporting-goods store downtown while making a few bucks on the side playing ball.

No one ever got rich playing high-level semipro baseball. The Bacharachs, like most nonleague black clubs, operated on the "co-op" or "co-plan" system where the players received 70 percent of the net receipts and management the remainder. In a good month, Dixon might bring home $100, not bad when compared to the $50 to $75 an NNL rookie might get during the Depression. But the month-to-month prosperity of the Bacharachs depended a good deal on their performance on the field. Too many well-publicized losses killed a team's appeal on the semipro circuit, especially when white fans expected the visiting colored clubs to be substantially better than the local boys. If the Bacharachs could not field a decent squad, financial guarantees would drop, opponents would dry up, and Tom Dixon could kiss that extra $100 a month good-bye.

He needed to find a catcher to replace Burbage, but good catchers were hard to come by. Dixon could only follow the ruthless player-procurement pattern of the big boys in the NNL: reach down and gobble up the smaller fish.

With his extensive contacts among the local black press, semipro managers, and former Negro Leaguers, Dixon had heard of Roy Campanella. "Somebody had told me there was a kid playing with the Nicetown Giants who could hit a ball a mile," he recalled decades later. "I didn't believe it, but I thought I'd better see for myself."

Dixon claimed he first scouted Roy at a Nicetown Giants game, although other accounts suggest the venue was a Junior American Legion contest. Regardless, he was transfixed by what he witnessed that spring day in 1937, "a short, wide-chested, broad-shouldered kid" with "arms big as mine" who was far above his peers. He was big, he was strong, he took charge of the game, and he could hit. And yet he was only fifteen years old.

After the game, he introduced himself to Campanella. The Bacharach Giants, he told him, are looking for a catcher. We know you're young but we'd like you to play with us on weekends and during the week when it doesn't interfere with school. And we'll pay you $25 to make a couple of upcoming weekend trips with us through New Jersey, New York, and Connecticut.

Roy couldn't believe what he was hearing. He knew who the Bacharachs were and what they represented. Maybe they weren't the NNL, but they were darned close to it. And to be paid to do the thing he loved more than anything else seemed almost unreal. The $25 (roughly $375 in today's dollars) was more money than he had ever seen in his life.

Of course he was interested. Yet, there was still the problem of his parents, particularly his mother, who seemed unlikely to consent to his taking this baseball business further.

That evening, Dixon and Malcolm McGowan, the Bacharachs' white business manager, drove up to Kerbaugh Street in two monstrous Cadillacs normally used to transport the team's players. As neighbors gawked, the two men entered the Campanella home to discuss their plans for Roy.

The boy was a natural, they told the Campanellas, a can't-miss prospect and sure to "go places." Fibbing just a tad, they claimed that as a Bacharach, Roy would "eat good food and stop at good hotels" when the team traveled on the weekends. But Ida fretted about the boy's missing church on Sundays. Without blinking, the Bacharach brain trust promised that *of course* the boy would go to church before they played on Sunday. And Tom Dixon, a solid citizen who didn't drink, would be sure to keep an eye on him.

John Campanella was already won over, and Roy sensed his mother was weakening. Best of all, McGowan and Dixon still had one more ace up their sleeve. Roy will be getting $25 to play with us, they told Ida. Her eyes widened in disbelief. The boy was going to be paid that much to play that ridiculous game? Roy could go, Ida finally announced, but he would have to be back in time for school on Monday. And she would take that $25 right now, thank you very much. For a brief moment, Dixon and McGowan considered explaining that players didn't get paid before games were played, but decided not to risk blowing the deal. Twenty-five dollars was sheepishly handed over, and Roy was now a Bacharach Giant.

It was a pivotal moment in Roy's life: the fifteen-year-old boy was now a professional. In the years to come, Campanella dusted off the tale again and again for his listeners, adding and embellishing details as he saw fit for the occasion. Still unknown is the exact date that Roy debuted with the Bacharachs. Available box scores, however, do show that Buddy Burbage, whose defection prompted Tom Dixon's scouting efforts, had left the Bacharachs by May 26. Campanella's first documented appearance (as "Cantenella") was a weeknight game on Wednesday, June 2, against a white team in Lansdale, Pennsylvania, about twenty miles from Nicetown. If this was Roy's debut, he made the most of it, banging two hits in five at bats and scoring two runs in an 11–10 loss.

Tom Dixon watched his young protégé from third base that evening. The boy had shown that he could hit, that was for sure. But his fielding left a bit to be desired. He hadn't made any errors, but the white players had run wild on him, stealing five bases. Some managers might have given him the heave-ho after such a performance. Fortunately for Roy, Dixon, as his nephew George Dixon remembered, "had a lot of patience when it came to sports." Dixon wasn't about to dump Campy based on a single shaky day behind the plate. He would bring him along slowly.

Campy's other new teammates were mostly old-timers in their late twenties and early thirties, many with Negro League experience. To Roy's relief, a few younger players were on hand to keep him company. He was especially glad to learn that his eighteen-year-old pal Quentin Lee was also getting a shot. That their old Nicetown club had been reduced to forfeiting games did not concern either in the slightest.

The school week seemed interminable for Roy, even more than usual. He was never so happy as when Saturday came and he was back on the road in one of the big Bacharach Cadillacs. First stop was the resort community of Beach Haven, New Jersey.

Roy could not help but feel a bit uneasy. He had done all right in the Lansdale game on Wednesday, but that was local. This was a night game, and he had little experience playing under lights. Years later, Campanella would write that he was "never more scared in my life. All of a sudden I began to realize this wasn't Nicetown anymore." In his recounting of the game, he claimed that Dixon started behind the plate but gave way to a nervous Campy after an errant ball "tore a fingernail loose." Campy was then inserted into the game, handled the job capably, and the Bacharachs rolled to a 3–1 victory.

The story bears little resemblance to the account in the *Beach Haven Times*. Dixon played third base. Campy was in the starting lineup, caught most of the game, and went 0 for 3 with an error in a 17–6 win.

Following the game, Roy once again stuffed himself into the Cadillac for a two-hour trip to New York, where the team would be staying overnight. He was starting to feel a bit more comfortable. Maybe he wasn't Bill Dickey, but he hadn't embarrassed himself either. Tom Dixon continued to encourage him. And the others, who had initially eyed the youngster somewhat warily and perhaps jealously, were beginning to come around. Even McGowan had fun with the kid, insisting that he would need a gas mask when they drove through the Holland Tunnel (the charmingly naive Roy then tied a handkerchief around his mouth for protection from the deadly fumes).

Once they reached New York, the Bacharachs had precious few lodging options except for establishments that catered exclusively to the colored trade. Most clubs stayed at the Woodside Hotel (made famous a year later by Count Basie's hit "Jumpin' at the Woodside") at 2424 Seventh Avenue at 142nd Street in Harlem. It was there that Roy would check into a hotel for the first time in his life.

Dixon naturally roomed the two Nicetown kids together but neither likely got much sleep that night. A disappointed Lee had sat on the bench in Beach Haven, and his brief stint with the Bacharachs was about to come to an end. But Roy was intoxicated with the new experiences of travel, hotels, and New York City. When he awoke the next morning, he was amazed when he got his first look at Harlem in the daylight.

In 1937, Harlem had the largest concentration of blacks in the United States. As Roy looked outside that morning, he would have seen a sea of dark faces everywhere, heading to churches, restaurants, and businesses. The block-long Savoy Ballroom, a jazz mecca immortalized by Benny Goodman's hit "Stompin' at the Savoy," was a stone's throw away on Lenox Avenue between 140th and 141st streets. Just three weeks earlier, the

Savoy had been the site of Chick Webb's celebrated victory over Goodman in a "battle of the big bands" competition. On 125th Street was the Apollo Theater, where Louis Armstrong had just finished a stint, yielding his spot this week to Count Basie's band and his young vocalist Billie Holiday.

It was easy for a fifteen-year-old boy such as Campanella to be blinded by glitzy venues and glamorous performers in his first trip to Harlem. He had no way of knowing that the Savoy and Apollo were both owned by whites, as were many other Harlem businesses, and that more than 40 percent of Harlem's black households depended on relief to survive. Harlemites faced the same poverty, unemployment, overcrowding, and discrimination as the folks back home in Philadelphia.

Sunday morning, the Bacharachs traveled to suburban Mount Vernon, where they jumped to a quick 1–0 lead after ex–Negro Leaguer Buddy Sadler banged the game's second pitch over the center-field fence. But the Mount Vernon Scarlets, a much tougher opponent than the pathetic Beach Haven bunch, seemed to take a liking to every pitch Roy called that afternoon, peppering 24 hits and 15 unanswered runs until the Bacharachs finally managed to get on the board again in the ninth. The hometowners led again in the second contest before heavy rain stopped the game.

Dixon realized the team would need some additional fine-tuning if they expected to make a dime this summer. Some of these kids were clearly not ready. Campanella did have 1 of the team's 8 hits, but he was still shaky behind the plate. The Scarlets swiped 5 bases, just as Lansdale had on Wednesday. Ten stolen bases allowed in two games wasn't going to cut it. Yet, the boy was only fifteen, and it was his first trip away from home. . . .

THE WOODSIDE Hotel, black baseball central in New York, had been especially busy during Roy's first trip to Harlem. Besides the Bacharachs, the Washington Elite (pronounced "Ee-light") Giants of the Negro National League were staying overnight prior to a Sunday game in Washington. The Elites had just lost a tight 8–7 game to the Newark Eagles in Paterson that Saturday, and neither the players nor their manager, Raleigh "Biz" (supposedly for "busybody" player) Mackey, were in a particularly festive mood that night.

Mackey was less than two months from his fortieth birthday. Many of those forty years had been spent carving out a professional baseball career, one that would have been far more lucrative had he been white. It began in Texas, where like Campanella he was a wunderkind, pitching for his uncle's team in San Antonio at the age of sixteen and later catching for several black semipro teams. His big break arrived in 1920 when the Indianapolis ABCs grabbed Mackey and several of his San Antonio Black Aces teammates. The young Texan was now a Negro Leaguer and would remain one for most of the next thirty years.

Mackey spent only a few seasons in Indianapolis before joining Ed Bolden's Hilldale Club in the exodus of Midwestern players to the newly formed Eastern Colored League in 1923. As much as the Eastern fans were soon smitten with his switch-hitting and extra-base power, his defensive wizardry turned even more heads. "Biz Mackey was one of the great catchers," says Hall of Famer and former teammate Monte Irvin. "More than anything else, he was smart. He knew how to set up a hitter. He was almost an expert at blocking the ball. . . . He knew all the fine points."

By 1936, the years were beginning to catch up with Mackey, now with the Elite Giants. But Mackey proved there was still plenty of life in his old arm that season, gunning down three Philadelphia Stars attempting to steal in a September 5 game. More important, his veteran presence gave the team a much needed lift. Mackey, observed Homestead Grays official Cum Posey, "was the cog which rounded 'Elites' into a real baseball club."

Mackey had been made the playing manager of the Elites for the 1937 season, but the club was struggling with injuries. Mackey himself had managed to play through a "cracked finger" in May, but a recent spiking by Homestead Grays first baseman Buck Leonard turned out to be more serious than anticipated. His foot became infected, and backup Nish Williams had to take over the catching.

The Elites would need someone to spell Williams should he become injured. Mackey, like Tom Dixon a few weeks earlier, started snooping around for a catcher. A suitable, albeit youthful, replacement turned out to be right under his nose that night at the Woodside Hotel.

EXACTLY HOW Mackey and Campanella connected is uncertain, but despite the haze of seven decades, certain facts remain indisputable. Mackey was hurt and needed a catcher. The best guess is that someone tipped him off to Campanella, and he had a chance to see him during the brief period that Roy spent with the Bacharachs. An initial contact was made, but nothing materialized until the Monday following Roy's Connecticut trip with the Bacharachs.

That Monday, June 14, Mackey and his team were staying in South Philadelphia at the Attucks Hotel, a black establishment favored by most of the Negro League teams visiting the city. It would be a perfect time, Mackey reasoned, to call up that Campanella kid in Nicetown. Ida took the message, wondering what kind of man would have a name like Biz, and informed Roy of the call when he returned home from school that afternoon. After learning that Mackey wanted to see him, Roy told his mother he was heading down to South Philadelphia.

If Mackey had failed to get his prey in an earlier meeting, as Campanella often claimed, he was not about to let him get away this time. He had already taken a liking to the kid, and it didn't hurt that they had similar builds. "Campanella looked like Mackey," noted Negro League veteran Ted Page. "He was little, round, fat, and chubby—just like Mackey." Mackey sat the boy down and talked to him about his own career, how he had started young and made it to the big time. There was no reason, he told Roy, why he couldn't do the same. In fact, they wanted him for the Washington Elite Giants right now. And, they'd pay him $60 a month.

Roy probably wanted to blurt out, "Yes, yes, yes—of course I'd love to play for the Elites!" But he hesitated. He felt a sense of loyalty to Tom Dixon and the Bacharachs, who had, after all, given him that first big break. And $60 didn't seem like a whole lot, particularly when he had just earned $25 playing a handful of games with the Bacharachs.

Mackey was momentarily taken aback. Most black kids during the Depression would have jumped at the chance to get a shot in the Negro Leagues; teams received stacks of letters from youngsters begging for a tryout. But this boy, bless his heart, was going to need more convincing. The Bacharachs, he reminded Roy, were not the big time. The Elites were. "This is only a start," Mackey said. "There's no telling how much you can be making in just a few years." Most important, Roy would be getting a chance to learn the tricks of the trade from a true catching master.

Roy began to waver. When Mackey pulled out an Elite Giants uniform and cap for Roy to try on, all resistance evaporated. Moments later, he was nervously sitting on the team bus in the midst of more than a dozen strangers who dubiously eyed Mackey's latest find. The team could barely field nine healthy players, and now Mackey was bringing in this whippersnapper, who at fifteen might very well be the youngest player in Negro League history.

Mackey had already decided the kid was going to catch tonight, and that was that. The Elites were scheduled to play the white Norristown Professionals. The Professionals had beaten the Bacharachs three weeks earlier, and Mackey figured they would provide a reasonable test of Roy's ability. He also wanted to see how Roy handled the lefty Tom Glover, who would be on the mound that night for the Elites.

Like most semipro clubs, the Professionals regularly booked black teams, who typically drew the most fans on the circuit. Monday nights were not always the best days for attendance but at least there was no competition from the local major league teams, who were idle that day. And what else was there to do on a hot June night in Norristown? Homebodies could tune in to NBC's *Fibber McGee and Molly* and CBS's *Lux Radio Theater*, both Monday-night "must-listen" radio for many Americans. But in an era when air-conditioning was still out of the reach of the typical homeowner, summer evenings were seen as a time to get outside and cool off.

When the Elites' bus pulled in to the parking lot at Roosevelt Field that night, eighteen hundred fans looked on with a mixture of anticipation and curiosity. Thanks to his stint with the Bacharachs, Roy had gradually grown accustomed to playing before white crowds, whose behavior usually varied with the score. As a catcher, constantly within shouting distance of obnoxious fans, he had no choice but to learn fast. He knew that to succeed with the Elites, he would have to tune out the catcalls and insults.

Mackey put Roy in the eighth spot in the lineup. The Elites batted first, and Roy watched his teammates go down quickly against Warren Yerk, the Professionals' twenty-six-year-old pitcher. Roy then strapped on his shin guards and chest protector, adjusted his catcher's mask, and made his way to home plate trying to act casual. Tom Glover, meanwhile, had to wonder if he was going to be in for a long night. Could he trust this pudgy kid to hold on to his best fastballs and curves?

Roy made it through the first inning without any mistakes, but Norristown jumped out ahead 1–0. The lead didn't last long, as the Elites soon unleashed a barrage of hits against the Professionals' overmatched pitchers.

Already, Roy began to recognize what kind of baseball these Elites played. He watched in amazement as center fielder Bill Wright belted two tremendous home runs, the second one landing "on somebody's front porch," according to the *Norristown Times-Herald*. He saw a vengeful Norristown pitcher drill Wright in the sixth, only to pay seconds later when the next hitter, Leroy Morney, bashed one over the fence. He marveled at the craftiness of Glover, who easily mowed down the Professionals after a shaky first inning.

And Roy hadn't done too badly himself. In his first 4 at bats, he singled twice and scored one of the team's 11 runs. Behind the plate, he was rock-solid with no passed balls, no stolen bases allowed, and no errors. Even the most skeptical of his teammates couldn't help but be impressed that the kid had stepped in and done a man's job in his very first night with the team. Mackey could only congratulate himself for being such a shrewd judge of talent. Twenty years later, he still proudly remembered Roy's debut in Norristown and the two hits he laced that night.

Back home on Kerbaugh Street, Ida Campanella sat fuming. It was a school night and her youngest still wasn't home. This baseball nonsense had gone on long enough, and the boy needed a good licking. When Roy finally walked through the door, he saw that Ida, belt in hand, was ready to pounce. What ensued is difficult to say, since Campanella, as usual, provided different versions of the incident. But Ida was furious that her son was out late playing baseball and had ditched his paying Bacharachs gig for something lamely called the "big league of colored baseball," even though he didn't even have a dollar to show for it. The belt soon found its target with surprising frequency and precision, while Roy, in between darting and dodging, tried frantically to explain the events of the past few hours.

After Ida finally calmed down, she placed a call to the Attucks Hotel to get the lowdown from this Mackey character. Fortunately, Biz Mackey knew how to handle angry mothers, or at least how not to antagonize them further. He promised to visit the Campanella home the next day with the team's owner, Tom Wilson.

Wilson almost never traveled with the Elites, but by chance, he had been in Washington with his team on Sunday. Although he had been involved in baseball for at least twenty years, the game was generally of secondary concern to Wilson. He raised hogs and pigs on a large farm near Nashville, dabbled in real estate, and built a successful dance hall. Like many of the other Depression-era Negro League owners, much of his venture capital for legitimate enterprises came from illegal, nonviolent side businesses such as a gambling casino or the numbers racket. But Wilson was no uncouth roughneck. He was heavily involved in local politics, and his parents were both physicians. Like Mackey, he knew that Ida would have to be handled with kid gloves.

For the second time in a month, strange baseball men called upon the Campanella home. Roy, at school, was not privy to the conversation that would determine his future. But Ida Campanella was not a stupid woman. She was not going to block her son's path if there was truly something to this "colored major league" business. Nor was she about to hand him over without some haggling and negotiation. Ida listened as Mackey and Wilson (and perhaps traveling secretary Vernon Green, per one version) explained their interest in Roy and reiterated their offer of $60 per month. "We hesitate about taking a fifteen-year-old boy away from home to play ball," said Wilson as he calmly puffed away on one of his ubiquitous Omar Turkish-blend cigarettes, "but it would be a shame to hold Roy back, since he's ready. Suppose I promise you that I'll look after his associations? Will that be okay?"

It was okay but it wasn't enough. The boy could join the team but he could not take any long overnight trips until the school year was over. And the $60 salary would go directly to her. The family could certainly use the money, and she wasn't about to let a fifteen-year-old handle all that cash. The deal was settled, the two men departed happily, and Roy returned home shortly after to find out that he was still an Elite Giant.

The events of the last twenty-four hours seemed straight out of the hackneyed juvenile baseball fiction that kids like Roy ate up at the time. Teenage boy makes the big time—how could life get any sweeter? His mother had acquiesced, the school year was winding down, and plenty of baseball awaited him, more, in fact, than he could ever have envisioned. As Roy soon discovered, the Elite Giants' schedule was not for the faint of heart, and the team was going to make him earn every bit of that $60. For the first time, he would have to prepare himself for daily baseball on a different diamond almost every night. He would also need to learn how to set aside yesterday's failures, play with nagging aches and pains, and cope with grueling bus trips.

It was an unrealistic burden to place on a fifteen-year-old boy and probably a recipe for disaster in most cases. But Roy, as Mackey and Wilson realized, was an exceptional individual. Not only was he a superior athlete, he was mature for his age, open to instruction, and learned quickly. He had an affable personality and made friends easily. It would be hard for his new teammates *not* to like the kid, at least Mackey and Wilson hoped. What had most impressed the Elites brass was the poise and confidence Roy had shown. Even grown men were a bundle of nerves in their Negro League debuts, but the kid had gone out there and done his job without fuss or fanfare.

Of course, he was still in his comfort zone. The Elites were headquartered in Philadelphia for the week, and none of their scheduled games for the next few days involved too much travel or heavy competition. Roy's second night with the team required only a short hop to Chester to play the Crescents, a black semipro club he had faced just a few weeks earlier as a Nicetown Giant. He managed a hit in four at bats, giving him three in two days, but he also made an error. Rain canceled the Elites' Thursday game against the Mount Vernon Scarlets, who had run so wild on Campy eleven days earlier. On Friday, the team was booked in Belmar, a New Jersey beach community whose residents were eager to see the colored club promoted as featuring "at least six men over six feet tall." Roy, perhaps not sufficiently tall enough to satisfy the white fans, rode the bench that evening while the Elites hammered the locals 11–1.

Still, Mackey had no reason to be displeased with his young protégé. The boy had shown he was at least good enough to handle the semipros, who comprised so much of the Elites' weekday schedule. But the real test, he realized, would be how Roy fared this weekend against *real* competition: the NNL's Newark Eagles. Owned by Abe Manley, yet another mogul who had turned to running numbers as the fastest way to swell his bank account, and his vocal wife, Effa, who was white but chose to "pass" as black, the Eagles that year featured no fewer than five future Hall of Famers, including an eighteen-year-old infielder named Monte Irvin, then playing under the name Nelson to preserve his amateur status.

Years later, Irvin recounted his first meeting with Roy: "I came to Newark and I had heard about him, this hotshot young rookie. I went over to him. 'I understand you're the hottest thing in Baltimore [*sic*]. I want you to know that here in Newark, I'm the main man.' So he said, 'Okay, I have no problem with that.' And from that moment to the moment he passed on, we were friends."

That Saturday, Irvin's Eagles would face the Elites at Parkside Field in West Philadelphia. The local Stars were away on a road trip that weekend, and the league powers that be saw no reason why a good venue such as the Quaker City should be vacant that weekend. For Roy, it was hardly the ideal locale for his first league game. Nobody liked playing at Parkside, where fans and players contended with trains that filled the air with thick clouds of smoke and soot as they approached or departed the nearby roundhouse. Even worse, he would now have to bear the pressure of acquaintances and family members there to see him succeed or perhaps, in the case of the more jealous types, fail.

About thirty-five hundred black fans, many probably grumbling about having to watch a couple of out-of-town teams, paid their way into the rickety old field that afternoon. A general-admission bleacher seat cost all of thirty-five cents, and those willing to cough up another fifteen cents could sit in the grandstand, which provided remarkably close access to the action. Many were regulars who showed up every Saturday for the chance to enjoy two games for the price of one and see some of the best black athletic talent in the country.

The Elites and Eagles put on a good show that day, splitting two games both decided by one run. Unfortunately, no box scores have been unearthed to document the specifics of Roy's NNL baptism of fire. The *Tribune* and *Afro-American* preferred to devote their limited sports columns the following week to Joe Louis's historic victory over Jim Braddock, while the relevant issue of the *Independent* no longer exists on microfilm. The local white press, inconsistent in its coverage of Negro League games, either ignored the doubleheader or never received game information for publication.

Fortunately, Randy Dixon, the sports editor of the *Tribune*, recorded the essentials of Campanella's Negro League debut. As a veteran black sportswriter, Dixon knew well the nightmare of trying to assemble a couple of pages of sports each week with only a tiny budget and minimal personnel. Submitted press releases or wire service stories often had to substitute for on-the-spot reporting, except in the case of local Negro League games and other important events that Dixon deemed worthy of covering in person.

That Saturday, he took his usual seat in the shabby Parkside Field "press box," not expecting to dig up much of anything newsworthy that afternoon beyond some gossip or perhaps a tidbit for his Sports Bugle column. After all, the Joe Louis fight was going to get full play when the *Tribune* came out on Thursday, and he wasn't going to waste more than a few lines on a couple of visiting teams.

But he discovered a remarkable story unfolding before him. The Elite Giants had just signed a local player, all of fifteen, who had played for Randy's cousin Tom Dixon's team a few weeks back but would be getting his first shot in the big time today. This, he recognized, was news. Even in the casual, "everything goes" atmosphere of the Negro Leagues, this was not something that happened every day. Was this some sort of publicity stunt, a way to goose attendance for a game without much local appeal otherwise? Dixon resolved to keep a close eye on this kid, if he actually got into a game, and get the lowdown for his readers.

What he saw astounded him, his excitement still palpable in the column he wrote a few days later. Topping his Sports Bugle column the following Thursday was a simple but prophetic headline: "Roy Campinelli [*sic*] A Future Great":

> Biz Mackey, probably the greatest catcher of all-time Negro baseball, gave Campinelli the once-over last week, liked his attitude to say nothing of his work, and signed him to do duty for the Elite Giants. A kid of 15 summers in the big time. . . .
>
> Roy went on exhibition last Saturday when the Elites and the Newark Eagles cavorted on local loam while the Phila. Stars were out on the road. . . . And what he showed was a revelation. "Your Man" Dixon says without qualification that no one, anywhere, possess[es] a more deadly or accurate throwing arm from home plate to second base than this mere slip of a lad. Ask anyone who was on hand Saturday to see him mow down ambitious base stealers with his rifle pegs.
>
> The ball players marveled, the fans went into delirium. The critics gaped. But Roy just took it all as a matter of routine duty. Once he learns a little more tricks and brushes up a bit, he'll be a star of stars. The only thing

> I don't like about him is the length of his name. Sorta tough on columnists and headline writers to spell correctly. Otherwise he has more earmarks of a future great than any lad his age mine eyes have ever seen.

If John and Ida Campanella still had even the slightest misgivings about a life of baseball for their son, Dixon's words likely changed their minds permanently. Except for births, deaths, or arrests, working-class families such as the Campanellas did not make the newspapers, black or white, yet here was the baby of the family being praised as a "star of stars" and a "future great."

Roy may have been playing like a Negro Leaguer, but he sure didn't feel that he was *living* like one. Summer vacation, he hoped, would change all that. He could finally get out from under his family, go on the road, and get his first close look at Negro League baseball and the vast, sprawling country that was Jim Crow America.

3

MACKEY'S PROTÉGÉ

HAD HE SCRIPTED IT HIMSELF, Roy could not have made a better impression in his NNL debut. Little did he know just how difficult it was to break into and remain in the Negro Leagues.

Established players simply did not take kindly to the presence of eager, fresh-faced rookies. With league teams generally carrying only fifteen to eighteen men, most veterans jealously protected their roster spot. The preferred strategy was to make a newcomer miserable through a relentless campaign of hazing and "riding" until he either flamed out or went running home to his mama.

Fortunately for Roy, Biz Mackey was his manager. And Mackey, although generally laid-back, was prepared to bust some heads to stop any clique that might try to scare Campy off the Elites. Of course, the usual teasing and juvenile practical jokes favored by ballplayers were acceptable, provided they didn't go too far, although Roy was occasionally reduced to tears. The boy was a special case, and his teammates would have to adjust to the presence of a fifteen-year-old.

Roy would have plenty of adjusting of his own to do. He was a kid, albeit a big one, in the midst of grown men. The youngest of his teammates was probably pitcher Jimmy Direaux, who was about twenty or twenty-one, but to a teenager such as Roy, he was just as intimidating as the rest. Most were Southern-born, some with no more than a sixth-grade education. Their attitudes were shaped by their formative years in the rural Jim Crow South, a place Roy had never seen, and they had little in common with the chubby kid from the big city with the Italian name.

At first base was "Shifty" Jim West, a colorful character from Alabama whose propensity for grabbing throws with one hand fascinated both white and black audiences accustomed to the sensible two-handed catch then in vogue. The Kentucky native Sammy T. Hughes held down second, dazzling Roy with his "speed, power, and . . . great pair of hands." Light-hitting Hoss Walker of Texas was the current shortstop but would be replaced by Pee Wee Butts in two years. Rounding out the infield was Felton Snow, another Alabama native, ranked by Homestead Grays official Cum Posey in 1939 as "just about the best all-around infielder of Negro baseball."

In the outfield, the solid yet unspectacular Texan Zollie Wright was stationed in right but was frequently overshadowed by a younger and more accomplished namesake in center. At only twenty-three, the switch-hitting Bill Wright of Tennessee was already a superstar, as Roy quickly learned that first night in Norristown. "Bill Wright," Mahlon Duckett of the Philadelphia Stars recalled, "could do it all. . . . He could run, he could hit, he could field."

Henry Kimbro, another Tennessee native, was the team's left fielder and speedy leadoff man. An enormously talented player despite his diminutive size, he also inspired fear and loathing with his aggressive play and unfriendly disposition. Kimbro, recalled Monte Irvin, was not only "mean" but "evil," which in blackball circles signified players who were particularly difficult, troublesome, and downright ornery. One did not mess with Henry Kimbro, and most players thought it prudent to keep a safe distance from him. But Roy eventually got to know the intense young man, and they became good friends.

Like most NNL teams, the Elites carried five or six pitchers, and Roy would have to learn the idiosyncrasies of each, particularly the staff's current big three. Besides the lefty Tom Glover, whom Roy had caught in his Norristown debut, the Elites relied heavily on the strong right arm of Bill Byrd. Blessed with a good fastball and outstanding control, Byrd also sported a killer spitball, which NNL officials graciously permitted a few select pitchers to throw. Loaded up with slippery elm and tobacco, Byrd's sinking spitter not only gave hitters fits but was known to drive catchers crazy. Fortunately, Byrd believed in encouraging young players, and a grateful Campy quickly dubbed the thirty-year-old "Daddy."

Right-hander Andy "Pullman" Porter's blazing fastball proved just as challenging. Cum Posey claimed that Porter, not Satchel Paige, had the "fastest ball in colored baseball." Even nineteen years later, after eight major league seasons with the Dodgers, Roy still considered Porter the fastest pitcher he had ever caught.

Andy Porter is the only known surviving member of the 1937 Elites. Now approaching one hundred as of this writing, his memories of a young Roy are still vivid. "He was a little old guy, weighed about 145 pounds," recalled Porter. "He looked good as a catcher. And he just felt . . . he *knew* he could catch." His perseverance also impressed Porter. "He was a hustler," said Porter. "He tried hard all the time." Like others, Porter cited the crucial role of Biz Mackey in Roy's development: "Mackey helped him a lot. Mackey was a great catcher too."

Unlike some coaches, Mackey did not try to force his pupil to copy his style. There were different ways of catching, Mackey felt, and each receiver should use the form that worked best for him. However, the boy needed instruction in the mechanical and mental aspects of the position. Roy soon discovered there was much he did not know about catching. After watching Mackey for a few games, he began to wonder whether he knew *anything* about catching.

Mackey hammered home just how much a good defensive catcher meant to his ball club and a pitching staff. He began to work with Roy on blocking low pitches, teaching him the importance of proper footwork and remembering to "always try to keep the ball in the center of your body." It would take time for Roy to master the technique, frustrating Bill Byrd, whose success depended on his catcher's smooth handling of his spitter. "You're going to get that kid hurt back there," he warned. An unconcerned Mackey responded, "Well, he ain't going to learn if he don't catch."

Roy observed the many subtle ways that Mackey helped his pitchers. He watched the way Mackey gave a good low target and "framed" borderline pitches to get a strike call. He noticed how Mackey coddled some pitchers and goaded others. He saw Mackey play head games with hitters, quizzing them about their bat or the fatigue they must surely be feeling from last night's game. Roy also began to learn the rudiments of setting up hitters and calling a smart game behind the plate. "You got to say to yourself," Mackey told Roy, " 'What's this fellow looking for? What's he think the pitcher's going to throw?' "

Mackey quickly grasped that the boy needed some work on his throwing. He might have a gun for an arm, but it took him too long to pull the trigger and he didn't always hit his target. The key, Mackey told Roy, was not how hard you threw the ball but how fast you let go of it. Take a little off the throw, release it quickly without too much arm movement, and you'll be just as successful throwing out runners. And catch with your throwing hand close to your glove to cut a few more moments off your release. Mackey also tried to teach Campy how to handle the double steal, but he was not quite ready for such advanced instruction. "It took me a long while to get it," Roy admitted late in his career.

Actually, it took a "long while" before Roy mastered Mackey's tips and tricks well enough to warrant the "Mackey clone" tag he was later given by so many old Negro Leaguers. More than once, he was reduced to tears as Mackey corrected, pushed, and prodded him. But Mackey seemed to possess an unending supply of patience. "You never did see him get angry," noted Roy. "He would get mad on occasion, but not too often." Besides, Mackey realized the boy was only going to get better with age and experience. In two years, Mackey told a sportswriter that August, this kid will be the best catcher in the NNL.

DURING ROY'S first five weeks with the Elites, he was not yet subject to the Negro Leagues' infamously brutal travel regimen. For the rest of June and much of July, the club bus rambled up and down the 240-mile Washington–New York corridor, stopping at most of the large and medium venues in between. The Elites played so often in the Philadelphia area it's possible that Roy may still have been sleeping most nights at Kerbaugh Street.

To precisely track his performance during these five weeks or any of his time in the Negro Leagues is impossible. The NNL's published schedule of league games provided only a fraction of a club's itinerary, which included a generous helping of white semipro opponents. "We had so many games that nobody kept track and we didn't have time to add it up," Campy later recalled. "Who could follow us? We didn't even know where we were going."

The pages of the African-American press do provide valuable, if somewhat limited, documentation of Roy's Negro League career from its inception. Black newspapers were generally quite good at providing a first-person account and a box score of local NNL games. Still, they were *weekly* entities with only limited space for sports, and none was in a position to cover every game played by the local nine the prior week. Most accounts were unavailable anyway, as league teams were frequently too busy or too understaffed to wire the results of away games to the hometown newspaper. Games scheduled early in the week are especially elusive in the black press: too late for the current week's publishing deadline (usually Tuesday or Wednesday) and too stale to be mentioned in the following week's edition. White dailies varied widely in their coverage, with some offering consistent box scores and others ignoring the NNL altogether.

The existing fragmentary evidence, then, gives us only a skeletal portrait of Roy's performance in his early days with the Elites. With Mackey back in action by early July, Roy was now a third-string catcher, behind Nish Williams on the depth chart. Third-string catchers, particularly fifteen-year-old ones, usually don't play much, and Roy was no exception. "They just carried him around to catch batting practice," Buck Leonard would later claim, "and he learned how to catch that way."

But the Elites were not paying Roy $60 a month just to warm up pitchers. Mackey found opportunities to get him some work against white semipros, where the competition and pressure would be less intense. In four July starts against white New York, New Jersey, and Pennsylvania teams, Roy banged out an impressive five hits in twelve trips to the plate. Once again, he proved he could handle pitchers several years his senior, even on clubs said to be just as good as class A or B minor league teams, at least according to Leonard.

League games were a different story. The kid's debut against Newark had been impressive and all, but Mackey knew that Roy was far from ready to play regularly against NNL clubs, which soon found large holes in the chunky phenom's swing. Roy managed a fluke double "behind some construction work in right field" in a game against the Black Yankees in Paterson on June 26 but did little else in his rare league at bats in early July. And just as Mackey had predicted, runners brazenly began to take liberties on his throwing arm. On July 3 in Philadelphia, Mackey inserted Roy as a defensive replacement after Nish Williams was removed for a pinch runner in the seventh inning. Before Roy had a chance to get settled, he had allowed a stolen base, committed an error, and found himself being pinch-hit for by a *pitcher* in the ninth inning, all before the hometown folks.

It was an embarrassing and ego-deflating performance. Roy was in a frustrating new world, hitting against strange pitchers, trying to grasp the complexities of Mackey's catching clinic, and contending with pangs of loneliness. Worst of all were the long hours he spent on the bench, the interminable weekends where he watched the Elites play two doubleheaders without getting a chance to swing a bat or catch a ball even once. For now, he could only hope he might see a bit more action on the team's upcoming long road trip in late July and early August.

With the Elites not drawing particularly well at Griffith Stadium, Tom Wilson did not hesitate to put his team on the road for a few weeks. The tour would start in New York on July 19, then move through Pennsylvania, New Jersey, Maryland, and West Virginia with additional stops in Columbus and Cleveland. From Ohio, the team would make the grueling (but not atypical by Negro League standards) five-hundred-mile "jump" to Nashville for a weekend series with the New York Black Yankees, then swing back for games in Cincinnati and Columbus. The Elites would then scoot back on their bus and ride another five hundred miles in time to play the Black Yankees at Yankee Stadium on August 15.

Such a wacky itinerary was beyond the comprehension of any white ballplayer, even a class D minor leaguer. Roughly twenty-eight hundred miles would have to be covered, all by a big old bus prone to breakdowns and brake failures (and without the interstate highways, two decades away in the future). But as Roy discovered, this was life in the Negro Leagues in its purest form. "The players must understand," Grays official Seward "See" Posey once blithely explained, "that we must play every game we can get and will have a few long jumps." Posey's own club understood all too well, rambling a whopping thirty thousand miles in 1937 during a 179-game season.

The trip was a seminal moment in Roy's life. It was not only his first prolonged journey away from Philadelphia, but it was also his first chance to get out from under Ida's ever-watchful eye. Maybe he was only fifteen, but now he would be sleeping, eating, and living just like a *real* ballplayer. But he was also about to get a crash course on Negro League baseball and the bitter realities of race in America in the 1930s.

Today, allowing a fifteen-year-old boy to roam the country playing baseball with a bunch of adult men would be unthinkable. But during the Depression, no one seemed unduly concerned. With so many fathers unemployed and home lives bleak, many a teenager hit the road hoping to find something better or at least a taste of adventure and excitement. By 1937, everyone was accustomed to the sight of hordes of unsupervised kids riding the trains or hitchhiking across the country. Compared to these homeless vagabonds, Roy was living the life of Riley.

But once the trip started, he began to appreciate just how utterly exhausting the Negro League lifestyle was. How could athletes be expected to perform at a high level when they were nearly constantly bouncing along the highway to the next venue? Fairmont, Charleston, Columbus, Cleveland—the parks soon became a blur. The routine was the same: play the game, get back on the bus, and above all make it to the next town on time. If that required driving like a maniac all night to make an afternoon game the next day, the players had to grin and bear it. "The bus," Roy would later recall, "was our home, dressing room, dining room, and hotel." Those who complained could leave. After all, bus travel saved the owners precious dollars, and they had no plans to return to using expensive trains just to suit a few swellheaded prima donnas.

Thriftiness had its limits, and for longer stays, traveling secretary Vernon Green had to find some form of lodging for his players. In larger cities such as Nashville or Cleveland, Green booked the Elites into black hotels. The better ones, such as the Dunbar in Washington, provided accommodations as lavish as any white establishment, but too many others were ramshackle, old buildings infested with bedbugs. Even worse were the tank towns whose single hotel was off-limits to blacks, forcing Green to scramble to dig up local black families who might be willing to board a player or two for a night. If that failed, there was no other choice but to herd the sleepless team back on the bus for whatever rest they were lucky enough to grab.

Segregation, Roy discovered, was almost inescapable on the road. He had encountered discrimination and prejudice back home, but this was something entirely different, something far more extreme. Race determined every move the Elites made off the ballfield, even the food they ate. Every restaurant was unique, and Roy's new teammates gave him the lowdown about which places would accept his meager fifty-cent daily-meal money, which ones made the Negroes go around the back, and which ones should be avoided. Usually, the Elites had no time to stop anyway, and it was more imperative to find a grocery store willing to sell the team cold cuts to be hastily consumed on the bus. Even the gas stations were an iffy proposition. Like other players, Roy learned to pick out the red and white Esso signs from a distance. "They were the only ones who would let us use their restrooms," recalled Newark Eagles pitcher Leon Day.

As the bus rambled farther below the Mason-Dixon Line, the stench of Jim Crow became even more pungent. The Elites traveled only as far south as Nashville this trip, but the supposedly progressive "Athens of the South" still exposed Roy to the essentials of American apartheid. Like other Southern cities, each race had its own hospitals and schools, and a recently passed municipal ordinance required that Nashville "Negroes and whites frequenting poolrooms, theaters and other indoor amusements places must be separated by a distinct floor." Even Sulphur Dell, the city's minor league ballpark, made sure to provide "a special section" for white fans who might wish to attend any of the Elites' games scheduled there.

It was a culture shock for a Philadelphia boy, but Roy's mostly Southern teammates knew the situation all too well. Keep your mouth shut, don't make waves, and, above all, don't antagonize any white people. Otherwise, you might find yourself swinging from the branch of a tree. Lynching, although a less frequent occurrence than in the past, was still a very real possibility in 1937.

Roy despised but eventually resigned himself to the absurdities and humiliations of Jim Crow America. But self-pity was not part of the Negro League experience. His teammates, he noticed, might grumble over the travel and other indignities, but they also seemed to enjoy themselves a great deal on the road. Some were smooth-talking Casanovas, always with a different woman in every city. Others preferred the rush of gambling and seemed to be perpetually organizing or participating in a poker or dice game. Andy Porter and Bob Griffith later hatched a plot to use loaded dice to snooker Campanella out of his money in a craps game. Roy had never played craps before, but he dutifully put his money down, rolled the dice, and hoped for the best. When the two dice stopped, Roy saw he had rolled an 11—a win. The older men exchanged puzzled looks. Something was going terribly wrong. Nevertheless, they threw down their dollars again, only to watch the novice gambler roll another 11. With no money left, the would-be scammers beat a hasty retreat. Roy couldn't help but chuckle as he overheard Porter berating Griffith, "I thought you gave him the other dice, you dumb cluck!"

The Elites, like all baseball teams in this era, white and black, also had their share of boozehounds. Most, like Mackey, were able to keep their drinking from interfering with their on-field performance, although some were not quite so disciplined. Bill Harvey, who joined the Elites in 1942, got so plastered one day in 1944 that he began bellowing at the fans, earning him a suspension from the usually lax NNL.

Roy was too young to fit in with the drinkers or the skirt chasers and too poor to do much gambling either. At times on the trip he might have felt he had more in common with the batboy than his teammates. But he was no loner. Mackey was keeping an eye on him, and he could always talk to his roommate, Bill Wright. And on the long bus rides, he sat and listened to the stories, jokes, boasts, and tall tales told by his teammates, who began to include the pudgy kid with the high-pitched, squeaky voice in the conversation. During these bull sessions Roy learned the truth about the Negro Leagues, the leagues that many lumped in the same class with white semipro baseball. "I had this explained to me by the older players," he recalled, "and explained in such a way as to show me that none of the white players in any of the other leagues, major or minor, could play any better than we could."

Once Roy watched the superstar Josh Gibson play a few innings, he knew his teammates weren't kidding. Gibson had gone to the Dominican with Satchel Paige and the others, collected $2,200 for seven weeks of play, then returned to the United States on July 20. A few days later, he was back with the Grays, who barnstormed with the Elites during part of their road trip. Then only twenty-five, but already in his eighth year in the Negro Leagues, Gibson was a man at the top of his game, not yet a victim of the physical and emotional problems that would dog him later.

Although Gibson's reputation as a slugger is undisputed, his catching ability is somewhat less certain. Contemporaries praised his strong throwing arm, but more than a few players and writers noted his weakness in handling foul pop-ups. "Josh is unquestionably a great hitter," remarked sportswriter Sam Lacy in 1939, "but for all-around catching, he's no Dickey." Gibson was no Mackey either, at least according to the old Hilldale shortstop Jake Stephens, who believed "Biz was tops in catching, throwing, and getting the most out of pitchers, and he was always at his best when the going got tough." When recently pressed to give his assessment, Monte Irvin insisted that Gibson "was very adequate . . . might not have been the best defensive catcher, but he was big and strong" with a "rifle for an arm."

Roy got his first look at the man who would overshadow him for most of the next eight years on Saturday, July 24, in Cumberland, Maryland. Gibson had spent most of the last ten days on a ship heading back to New York and had had little opportunity to get his timing or stroke back. The Grays batted him cleanup that night anyway, and Roy, who was catching for a change, probably figured his pitcher, Jimmy Direaux, might be able to keep him in check. But Josh Gibson was no ordinary ballplayer, and the layoff had no effect. From a perfect vantage point behind home plate, Roy watched in astonishment as Gibson's lightning-quick bat connected for two doubles in the Grays' 7–6 win. The following day, Gibson belted a tape-measure home run at Oriole Park in Baltimore, although rain washed the blow from the record books.

For the rest of his life, Roy was an unabashed admirer of Gibson and considered him the greatest player he ever saw. "Big, strong, could run, helluva catcher, and could hit that ball," he told one reporter in 1957. "I wish I could hit like him. He was the baddest son of a gun I ever saw with a baseball bat." But Roy hadn't done too badly himself that weekend, chipping in with a single and a double in Cumberland. And Gibson, "a likeable big lug," according to Lacy, began to take a friendly interest in Roy, at least when he wasn't teasing him with taunts of "little boy" and "little kid." Gibson offered him some throwing tips, warned him about blocking the plate before he had the ball, and suggested a shorter stroke at the plate, although Roy would never abandon his somewhat frenetic hitting style.

If only his friends back home in Nicetown could see him now. Two months ago, Roy was playing Junior American Legion baseball with a bunch of teenagers. Now he was chatting up *the* Josh Gibson, traveling from town to town like the grizzliest Negro League veteran, and earning (well, at least Ida was) $30 every two weeks. And he was no cute fifteen-year-old gimmick or mascot there only to amuse the fans. He was actually contributing, smacking an occasional hit, trying to catch Bill Byrd's spitter, and slowly establishing himself as a bona fide professional player.

Mackey was pleased with Roy's progress. The trip confirmed what he'd sensed from the beginning—the boy not only had freakish talent for his age but had the necessary personal qualities to handle whatever obstacles life threw at him. How many adolescent boys could have coped with traveling the country on a bus with a bunch of older strangers? How many could have hit even a loud foul ball off the worst Negro League pitcher? But the kid never seemed to doubt his ability and never played scared. Plus, he did what he was told, accepted his limited role on the club, and didn't cause any trouble.

By the second week of August, the trip was winding down, and the Elites' bus was creaking its way back home. But before the team hit Yankee Stadium on Sunday, August 15, the Elites would have one last five-game series squeezed into two days in Ohio. Such extreme scheduling was not unheard of in the Negro Leagues, particularly during the Depression, but it was a shocking experience for a rookie such as Roy. The incident left a profound impression, so much so that he would repeatedly tell reporters the story of how the Elites had played two doubleheaders on the same day in Cincinnati and Middletown, Ohio. "And I caught all the games, four of them," he would boast. "I wasn't tired," he told another reporter. "I was young then and I didn't mind."

This colorful tale falls apart on closer examination. Local newspapers reveal that the Elites played a doubleheader at Crosley Field in Cincinnati on Thursday, August 12, beating the Black Yankees 3–2 in game one and tying the Negro American League's Cincinnati Tigers 2–2 in game two. Both were seven-inning games, and Roy caught only game one, going hitless in one official at bat. Moments after the final out, the three teams frantically boarded their buses for the forty-mile drive to the small steel-mill town of Middletown, only to arrive an hour late for a scheduled 8:00 p.m. doubleheader. The waiting fans had to settle for a pair of six-inning games, the Elites participating only in game two, a 1–0 loss to the Tigers with Roy behind the plate. Unbelievably, still another doubleheader was on tap for the same three teams the following day, this time in Columbus, where the Elites earned a split. Whether Campy caught is uncertain, as no box score appeared in the Columbus newspapers.

Although Roy never really caught four games in one day, the tale became part and parcel of the Campanella legend, the indefatigable iron man scornful of days off. "What do I want with rest?" he would repeatedly ask when he got to the majors. "This is a breeze compared to the old days in the colored leagues when I once caught four games in one day and we rode all night in buses."

AFTER RETURNING east, the Elites played out the string, futilely chasing Gibson's Grays while hoping to keep out of the red before the season ended in mid-September. Most NNL owners were hemorrhaging money, and Tom Wilson was no exception. It would take almost three months before Roy would receive his final paycheck, and his parents had to wonder again about the stability of this "major league" of colored baseball.

But another issue besides money preoccupied the Campanella family in the fall of 1937: Roy's scholastic future. The only thing he liked about school—sports—was no longer open to him, as his professional status excluded him from amateur high school athletics. He wanted to quit school when he turned sixteen in November, and John Campanella, satisfied that the boy at least had gainful employment, was not prepared to stand in his way.

Where Roy spent his last weeks of schooling remains a mystery. Simon Gratz High School has always proudly claimed Campanella as an alumnus, likely based entirely on Roy's frequent references to the school in interviews. But Stanley Frank's lengthy *Saturday Evening Post* feature in 1954 notes that a "routine check of official records" revealed that Roy's schooling ended in the ninth grade at Gillespie Junior High School and not at Gratz. The local *Evening Bulletin* subsequently publicized the surprising finding, with no refutation from Roy, who according to Dodger publicist Frank Graham, Jr., was furious when the story surfaced.

Roy's Philadelphia school records are now faded and extremely difficult to read, but they do confirm that he was in the ninth grade in the fall of

1937, and probably still at Gillespie, which housed grades seven through nine. There is no evidence that he actually took classes at Gratz, the plaque at the school front entrance notwithstanding.

Roy bided his time in the classroom until November 19, his sixteenth birthday. On that day, in between celebrating sweet sixteen, he filled out the necessary paperwork to leave school for good. There were no regrets, no fears for the future. What could a colored man in the Depression do with a high school diploma anyway? If things didn't work out in baseball, he could always work on his father's truck, and he didn't need a diploma for that. But the possibility of failure barely entered his mind. He was a professional ballplayer now, and he planned to stay one for as long as possible. Mackey was a baseball lifer, and Roy saw no reason why he couldn't be the same.

But he would pay a price for his limited formal education. Not only do his few surviving examples of handwritten correspondence abound with misspellings, but his grammar and vocabulary made many an English teacher cringe when he later became a public figure (particularly his fondness for words such as *onliest* and *ain't*). Yet Roy was a charismatic speaker throughout his life, learned quickly when a subject interested him, and possessed a quick wit. "He has an amazing memory," marveled Dodgers teammate Joe Black in 1953, "and knows what every batter in the league can and cannot hit."

As he grew older, Roy was increasingly uncomfortable identifying himself as a ninth-grade dropout. Instead, he would often tell interviewers that he spent three years at Simon Gratz and "could have gone to college." "I was gonna be an architect," he told Roger Kahn. "I would have loved that, drawing plans." The architect-instead-of-baseball-player story became yet another fantasy to find its way into the Campanella canon; in fact, Roy's highly fictionalized comic book published by Fawcett in 1950 even depicts him earning an "honor medal in draftsmanship" while proudly graduating from high school in 1939!

Roy did enjoy the limited drafting instruction he received in junior high, or at least found it more tolerable than his other academic subjects. But becoming an architect would have meant more studying, and more studying meant less baseball. And baseball, from the time he was old enough to walk, was his obsession. Old-timers often make the dubious claim they would have "played for nothing," but it was no exaggeration in Roy's case. "I think that if I was working in a steel mill," he remarked years later, "I'd go home every night, get a catcher's mitt, and go out looking for a ball game."

At age sixteen, he had been given the ultimate gift: the chance to make a living doing the thing he loved best. It was a no-brainer. School was out, and the Negro Leagues were in.

4

ELITE GIANT

WINTERS IN PHILADELPHIA were never easy for Campy. It was not so much the cold as the agonizing wait for spring, and baseball, to return. He could hardly stop thinking about what 1938 held in store: a $30-per-month raise, his first spring training, and a full season of Negro League baseball.

In the meantime, Roy went back to the mundane life of an ordinary sixteen-year-old adolescent boy in Nicetown. He hung out with his friends, helped his father, took in an occasional movie, and dutifully attended services at the Nazarene Baptist Church every Sunday. He even tried amateur boxing that winter and "exhibited much promise as a leather tosser," said the *Philadelphia Tribune*. But when his opponent in the local Golden Gloves tournament battered his nose soundly, he quickly hung up his boxing gloves for good.

As Campy prepared to leave for spring training, he might have felt like a rather grown-up young man, but he still had to answer to Ida. She carefully doled out $14.90 for the one-way train fare to Nashville and pressed a brown bag full of sandwiches into his pudgy hands to tide him over during the long trip. She still worried about her boy's soul, particularly now that he would be on the road for months with that Biz fellow and those other rough baseball characters. Before he left, Ida presented him with a pocket-size Bible. The Good Book, she told him, can give you solace and provide clarity in difficult times. She asked him to promise to read from it each day. Even after he became a major leaguer, the Bible remained an essential part of his daily routine. More than once, the normally cynical sportswriter Sam Lacy marveled that Campy "reads at least one passage from the Bible every night before retiring—no fooling."

As the train sped toward Tennessee, Roy had more than scriptural verses on his mind. Once south of Washington, he would have been shuttled into either a separate but inferior "Negro car," with the inevitable "dirty, dilapidated seats," or a "partitioned coach," where black and white passengers were separated by a curtain. But such indignities and humiliations were part of being a black professional ballplayer. He would either have to tolerate them or go back home.

He would also have to learn to accept the Negro Leagues' notion of spring training. Once Roy reached Nashville, he figured he would participate in the same leisurely workouts that major league players performed in Florida and California each spring. But Tom Wilson, like other black baseball owners, expected games to be played immediately to defray the costs of rooming and boarding his team. "The ordinary procedure," complained Halley Harding, a Negro League player turned sportswriter, "is to arrive at camp about Friday, practice Saturday . . . and then play Sunday. From then on, it's a game almost every day."

Before he had a chance to work off the winter fat or stretch his muscles, Roy was in uniform hitting and catching live pitching in exhibition games throughout the South. With Nish Williams now gone and his mentor another year older, Roy expected to see his name scribbled on the lineup card more often this year. But Mackey had decided managing and catching was one job too many and handed the managerial reins over to the veteran George Scales, who had spent much of 1937 in the Dominican Republic. At thirty-seven, Scales still swung a mean bat, but he was a bit of a hothead. Still, Scales was a master teacher, always ready to share his fifteen years of baseball knowledge with Roy or any other player who would listen.

Besides the managerial switch, the Elites would also have a new home in

1938. Two years of playing to empty seats had convinced Tom Wilson that Washington was not a black baseball town. Nor were Nashville and Columbus, both flops as home cities for the Elites in recent years. Fast running out of viable markets, Wilson decided to try his luck in Baltimore, historically a far better bet for Negro League baseball than Washington despite its smaller black population. During the 1920s, local fans had worshipped the Black Sox, faithfully pouring into Maryland Park after church each Sunday to watch their boys play their weekly doubleheader. With the Black Sox defunct, Wilson moved his club to the Monumental City, where they would remain for the next thirteen years.

The relocation did not particularly concern Roy as spring training wound down in early May. The Elites had played in Washington so rarely last year that he would later forget that the team had ever been based anywhere except Baltimore. And with the Elites on the road so much, the chances that he would develop much of a connection to any home city were slim. Like Washington, Baltimore was a segregated town ("just like being in the South," recalled one player), featuring a lively black business and entertainment district on Pennsylvania Avenue, not far from the York Hotel, where the Elites and other league teams stayed. During their limited downtime, players might take in a show at the Royal Theater, enjoy a seafood dinner, or perhaps go to Pimlico to play the ponies. But Baltimore, recalled Monte Irvin, was "really noted for pretty women at that time," and the Elites' skirt chasers were looking forward to the move.

The city's reputation for loveliness did not extend to Bugle Field, the team's rather pathetic excuse for a home field. Although Wilson wanted Oriole Park, the home of the city's International League affiliate, objections from white residents left only Bugle, a wooden facility holding about seven thousand fans. With its inaccessible location, poor lighting, and infield full of ruts, league officials felt Bugle was "not suited for the big time Negro Baseball which Baltimore had long enjoyed." Nevertheless, it was now the Elites' home turf.

Rain and mud nearly spoiled the Elites' Bugle debut on Sunday, May 15, but fans went home happy after their new heroes trounced the Philadelphia Stars 17–8. Roy sat on the bench that day, watching Mackey catch the entire afternoon, even after the game had turned into a blowout. The old reliable showed no sign of fading, rapping a double and even stealing a base.

Second-string or not, Roy knew he was not going to play much, at least in league games, as long as Mackey was healthy. And Scales didn't seem inclined to use the kid, unless the situation absolutely warranted it.

Life as a benchwarmer, Roy discovered, required a mental adjustment. The boy who had once played seven days a week on junior high, American Legion, and sandlot teams was now lucky to get 10 at bats per week, mostly against the semipros. Still, he reminded himself that he was only sixteen and he was damn lucky to be getting that $90 a month as a backup.

Campy never stopped wanting to get better. He continued to pick Mackey's brains about catching. He talked to Scales about hitting. And he began to analyze the NNL that season, trying to comprehend what it would take to be successful in an unorthodox organization vastly different from the white major leagues he knew and loved as a child.

By any objective standard, the NNL seemed to be a league in name only. Close to half of the games were nonleague, and the balanced schedules so essential to white Organized Baseball were nonexistent. Not only did few teams have complete control over their home park, but black fans just didn't have the cash to attend more than one or two games a week. Instead, the NNL usually tried to create a schedule requiring each league team to play each other ten times, but even that modest goal proved difficult to achieve. It seemed rather peculiar, Roy thought, that while his new buddy Monte Irvin's Newark Eagles barely made an appearance in Baltimore that season, the Elites spent entire weeks barnstorming with the Grays and Crawfords.

Other bizarre quirks abounded. Nobody knew his batting average. League teams were supposed to send in the results of each game, but compliance was spotty at best and sank to an all-time low in 1938. With standings or statistics rarely appearing in the black press, Campy had only the vaguest notion of what was going on in his own league. He wondered how players ever got raises without hard data to bring to the bargaining table. A manager's subjective perception, he eventually decided, was the key. "In the colored leagues a player who didn't play didn't get paid," Roy would later explain. "There were no averages to go by. What paid off was being in the lineup. A fellow who was around all the time got the notice."

Getting in the lineup was one thing. Staying there was another. The successful Negro Leaguer, Roy discovered, had to be remarkably adaptable.

Unlike major leaguers, who might face sixty or seventy different pitchers a season, the Elites batted against a much wider variety of pitching. "We saw different pitchers all the time," Roy later recalled. "We traveled quite a bit, and faced pitchers we hadn't seen before, and would never see again." The Elites never knew what to expect from the white semipros. One night Roy might be hitting against some no-name twenty-year-old kid, perhaps the town's former hotshot high school star. The next day, he might be trying to catch up with former Athletic George Earnshaw's high hard one.

Hitting against Earnshaw, now pitching for the Brooklyn Bushwicks, was especially surreal. Just a few summers ago, Roy was sitting in the Shibe Park bleachers watching Earnshaw mow down American League hitters on his way to three consecutive 20-win seasons. Now Roy was actually standing in the batter's box, sixty feet six inches away, futilely trying not to be distracted by the big right-hander's trademark "high leg kick." But Earnshaw was hardly the only ex–major leaguer to pitch against the Elites. More than a few oldsters preferred to work and play semipro ball part-time rather than return to the low-paying minors. Dumped by the Brooklyn Dodgers in May 1938, the veteran former Yankee ace Waite Hoyt quickly signed up with the Bushwicks but found himself on the losing end of a 4–3 decision against the Elites a month later.

Roy didn't hit against Hoyt that day, but he would get plenty of looks at other tough white pitchers that summer. Perhaps the most famous on the circuit was a chunky hurler by the name of Joel Skelton, better known by his professional alias, Jim Duffy. Good enough to pitch minor league ball in the 1920s, Duffy eventually decided he could make more money on the East Coast as a hired gun for the semipros. "He cheated," recalled Jake Stephens, "and they always saved him for some good colored ball club." Besides the conventional spitter, Duffy threw a baffling array of pitches with the aid of a banana peel hidden under his hat and a needle sewn into his glove.

Trick pitches, Roy discovered, were also favored by the NNL's own hurlers. The league had occasionally attempted to phase out the spitter and other illegal deliveries, but enforcement was fairly lax. Roy soon learned that saliva, dirt, emery, and sandpaper made baseballs do strange things, so strange that Cum Posey would insist that there was "not a hitter, living or dead, who can or could successfully hit a 'doctored' ball if thrown by a pitcher who knows how to deliver it." But the Elites had their own way of neutralizing a spitball pitcher's effectiveness. "We used to cross him up," Roy recalled. "We'd get our bat boy to rub up the baseball with dry mustard before the game. The pitcher would get that mustard in his mouth, and it would be hot, and he'd have one hell of a time."

The NNL also had plenty of pitchers who relied on nothing more than a good old-fashioned fastball and curveball. Future Hall of Famer Leon Day of the Eagles threw BBs, once punching out eighteen Elites in a 1942 game. Homestead's Raymond Brown, also later enshrined in Cooperstown, featured a devastating curve that could make even the best hitters' knees buckle. If he could hang in there against Brown and Day, Roy realized, he could do some damage in this league. But sixteen-year-olds do not become outstanding hitters overnight. A halfway decent curveball gave Roy fits, and his batting eye was still a work in progress.

As he watched the stars such as Bill Wright perform at a high level each day that summer, he sensed that success depended on more than just raw ability. In the intensely ferocious competition of the NNL, he would have to learn to play without fear. He could not flinch when opposing pitchers decided to see how the teenager with the funny name would respond to a fastball under his chin ("They'd fire at you like a duck," he once recalled). Nor could he give an inch when players like Homestead's Vic Harris, a notorious "nasty slider," came tearing around third base, salivating at the prospect of separating the kid catcher from his chest protector.

A pushover or patsy was not going to last long, particularly in a league where umpires seemed helpless to maintain even minimal discipline. Fistfights between players were hardly a rarity, nor were outright attacks on the men in blue. Some packed pistols and knives to protect themselves from the league's "bad actors," such as Jud Wilson, who, quipped one writer, was "ready to fight at the drop of a hat, your hat, my hat, his hat, or anybody's hat, it makes no difference." And Roy discovered his own teammates were no choirboys either, watching in amazement one day as Bill Wright and manager Scales teed off on a pair of hapless umps.

Such was life in Roy's first full year in the NNL. "Baseball ain't the old folks home," he would later say, and most battle-scarred Negro League veterans would have agreed. Still, it was not a bad existence for a young ballplayer. With Mackey catching most of the important games, the Elites did not ask a great deal of Roy. Barring an unforeseen injury to the master, Roy figured he would occupy a similar low-profile role in 1939.

But Mackey, now forty-one years old, began to wear down late in the season. Scales had to let the kid catch both ends of an August 21 doubleheader, and Roy responded with three hits in eight trips against the Crawfords that Sunday. A few weeks later, Mackey was so badly banged up that Scales had no choice but to start Roy in the first game of a best-of-five playoff series against Philadelphia. A single, double, and what may have been his first home run as a professional followed as the Elites battered the Stars 13–8.

Rain canceled the next playoff game, and the series was eventually abandoned as too unprofitable to continue. But Roy's performance against the Stars showed everyone, particularly Scales, that Roy was more than just an overgrown teenager with a lot of potential. This Campanella kid, Scales and Tom Wilson began to realize, might be ready a whole lot sooner than they'd thought. And he'd be a helluva lot cheaper than Mackey.

JOHN AND Ida were glad to have their boy home for the winter. Their objections to baseball, such as they were, had long been swept aside in the face of Roy's steady paychecks from the Elites. In fact, Papa Campanella had of late become a devoted follower of his son's career, often turning up in the clubhouse on Sundays laden with bags of fruit while requesting that the older players "look after" Roy when the team hit the road again. But Campy, nearly seventeen, his five-foot-nine-inch frame now packing more solid muscle than baby fat, was no longer the same naive schoolboy who had left home the previous June. In two years he had seen and experienced more of America, both good and bad, than his parents had.

It was hardly surprising that the more-worldly Campy's interests had recently broadened to include women, particularly a lovely sixteen-year-old Nicetown girl named Bernice Ray. "They were neighborhood kids," recalled her brother George, "like when a guy likes a girl when he plays around with her." Their relationship had evolved from playmates to friends and now two teenagers strongly attracted to each other. Before long, the adolescent couple gave in to their hormones. In December, Bernice told Roy that she was pregnant.

In 1938, the options for an unwed teenage mother were limited. Abortion was illegal, although the practice did go on secretly and unsafely in most communities. Family and societal disapproval prevented her from raising the child herself. She could give up the child for adoption, but she would be expected to conceal her shame from friends and family. Philadelphia even had its own "center for unwed expectant mothers," sponsored by the local black women's clubs, where girls like Bernice could wait out their pregnancies away from the frowning faces of neighbors.

Marriage was the favored solution in Depression America, allowing the girl's virtue to remain relatively preserved and the child to be given a name. Roy's parents favored this solution and had already seen their other son, Lawrence, "do the right thing" nine years earlier when faced with a similar predicament. Resigned to their fate, Roy and Bernice were wed on January 3, 1939. Seven months later, Bernice gave birth to a baby girl named Joyce.

Years later in his autobiography, Campy would offer a frustratingly brief discussion of his first marriage, one that conveniently omitted the pregnancy. "I had a job and I was making some money," he explained, "and we both felt that we could swing it." The anxiety that he must have felt, a promising young professional ballplayer suddenly facing marriage and fatherhood, is nowhere to be found. But at seventeen, he was now a man with a man's responsibilities.

THE ELITE GIANTS, despite the move to Baltimore's supposedly greener pastures, had taken another financial bath at the box office. Convinced that drastic changes were necessary for 1939, the team's brain trust of Wilson and Green replaced fiery George Scales with Felton Snow, a move that suited Roy and most of the other Elites. Like Mackey, Snow was calm and relaxed, able to get results without bullying or belittling his players. "They weren't harsh managers to play for," recalled Andy Porter. "As long as you did your job and tried to do it as well as you could, they were satisfied."

But Snow's genial countenance turned sour as he watched the Elites quickly become the league's doormats after losing three starting pitchers to Mexico. Roy was just as frustrated. Not only was Mackey getting most of the starts, but Campy seemed distracted by his impending fatherhood whenever he was in the lineup. At times he looked downright amateurish trying to cut down speedsters such as Jake Dunn of the Stars or solve the offerings of the spitballer and well-known headhunter Neck Stanley. After Stanley handed him yet another 0-fer in game one of a Memorial Day doubleheader in Brooklyn, the normally jovial Roy had reached his breaking point. Only a few moments into the second game, he fumed over a bad call and got himself tossed by umpire Frank Forbes. Fans then sat through a fifteen-minute delay, as Snow, vainly trying to inspire his troops, ranted and raved while making vague threats to pull his team off the field. The Elites eventually finished the game, only to receive a humiliating 14–5 thumping at the hands of the Black Yankees.

Snow had seen enough. If the Elites wanted to salvage their season, reinforcements were needed now. He knew just where to get them. The rival Negro American League's Atlanta Black Crackers had just fallen apart after an abortive move to Indianapolis. Sparked by the addition of two Black Cracker pitchers, a shortstop, a catcher, and a first baseman, the rejuvenated Elites thrashed the Philadelphia Stars four straight games in early July and began to turn their season around.

Snow and Tom Wilson were pleasantly surprised by their talent haul, which included the slick-fielding twenty-two-year-old first baseman Red Moore. Nearly seventy years later, Moore still remembered coming to Baltimore for the first time in the summer of 1939. The city, he recalled, was "more or less" segregated, as was the team's new home at Oriole Park, whose locker room remained off-limits to the Elites. But such indignities were more than offset by a loyal fan base and a "real good" owner, at least by the standards of the Negro Leagues. With Tom Wilson, one "didn't have no trouble with the first and fifteenth." Moore also befriended and occasionally roomed with the club's resident teenage sensation. "He was a very young buck," chuckled Moore, "but he was really an outstanding catcher."

Although Moore was a solid pickup, a then obscure nineteen-year-old shortstop named Tommy "Pee Wee" Butts proved to be the most impressive of the former Black Crackers. Though he had a relatively light bat, his uncanny ability to gobble up anything hit in his direction turned heads. Butts, raved sportswriter Russ Cowans, "goes to the right or left with equal ease, and he's able to get the ball away without having to come to an erect position." Roy was just as impressed by the little guy with the big glove, consistently ranking Butts with another Pee Wee (Reese) as "the best two" he saw in his long baseball career.

Campy and Butts would spend most of the next six years together, but their personalities initially clashed. Snow had decided to room the two teens together, and the more mellow Butts found Roy's chatterbox ways annoying. "He'd say, 'Come on, Pee Wee, let's talk about this,'" recalled Butts. "I'd say, 'Okay, go ahead,' and he would talk me to sleep." Meanwhile, a bantering session got a little too personal for Roy one day. "I think I said something a little wrong, and I repeated it," said Butts. "But I wish I hadn't." Although Butts never disclosed the nature of his comment, it was probably a crack at Roy's mixed parentage, a disturbing flashback to the "half-breed" taunts Roy had heard on Kerbaugh Street as a child. Roy quickly flattened the lightweight Butts, but his anger soon dissipated. "He shook my hand and said, 'All over,' and brushed me off," said Butts. Roy had earned his respect, and the two became friends for life.

With the addition of the ex–Black Crackers, the frugal Elites brass looked to trim the more expensive fat off an already swollen roster. The veteran Jim West was sent packing to Philadelphia in July, and Mackey appeared likely to be the next to go. Old Man River could only roll on for so long, his salary was among the team's highest, and the Elites had no need to carry three catchers. Mackey was dispatched to the Newark Eagles, where he eventually assumed the managerial reins and even continued to catch for another several years.

Roy was now without his mentor, but this was what he had always wanted, to play the game he loved every day, whether it was on the Nicetown sandlots or in the NNL. The catcher's job was his, and no one, he vowed, would ever take it from him.

WITH CAMPY behind the plate, the new-look Elites bounced back in the second half of the NNL campaign, winning thirteen of twenty-one league games. Snow silently groaned at Roy's occasional difficulties with passed balls and wild throws, but he couldn't help but be impressed by the kid's hustle and desire, the way he busted his ass down the line to "beat out a slow roller" against a white team or how he hung in there to homer off Sam Thompson of the Stars. Even local sportswriter Art Carter took notice of "youthful Leroy Campanello," who was "doing a good job, although he still lacks experience."

The Elites finished the regular season with a 25-21 record, good enough for third place and a slot in the first round of the playoffs. Like many white minor leagues during the Depression, the NNL had adopted the rather generous "Shaughnessy" system, allowing the top four finishers to advance to the postseason. The Elites would be matched against the second-place Newark Eagles, while the front-running Homestead Grays would take on the fourth-place Philadelphia Stars.

Despite the NNL's ongoing issues with scheduling and completing playoffs, the first round went on as planned in early September, the Grays besting the Stars in five games, and the Elites knocking off Newark in four. The attendance, to no one's surprise, was miserable. Only 462 fans bothered to show up for the Elites' first game in Newark, and the entire four-game series brought in a piddling $216.79 to the Eagles' owners.

The skimpy box office take did not concern Roy or his teammates. What worried them was getting past the Grays, the league's swaggering bullies, who featured a devastating offense led by Josh Gibson and Buck Leonard (the "black Lou Gehrig"), and a sterling pitching staff anchored by Roy Partlow and Raymond Brown. The Grays were in an especially ornery mood entering the series. They had won 70 percent of their league games this year but had been forced to risk their standing against inferior clubs in the playoffs.

The series opened on Saturday, September 16, in a neutral site, Philadelphia, where Partlow scattered four hits in a 2–1 Grays victory. On Sunday, the two teams completed one game of a scheduled doubleheader in Oriole Park, a 7–5 Elites win, before Baltimore's Sunday curfew law cut short the nightcap. With the series knotted at one game apiece, the playoffs were then put on hiatus for six days to ensure maximum attendance the following weekend.

The Elites had ample reason to be cautiously optimistic as they waited for the series to resume. Not only had they held their own against the Grays thus far, but Gibson had proved to be human. Big Josh went hitless in game one and looked shaky behind the plate in game two, though he did blast one of Jonas Gaines's offerings into the outer regions of Oriole Park. But Campy had contributed virtually nothing to the Elite cause, managing only two measly hits in his last nineteen playoff at bats while committing two errors and a passed ball. Snow thought it best to bench him for a meaningless Wednesday-night game against the Brooklyn Bushwicks, hoping to keep him fresh for what would prove to be the biggest weekend of Roy's young career.

For the second successive Saturday, Quaker City fans were treated to playoff baseball. Why Philadelphia should get two playoff games and Pittsburgh, the Grays' home, none might have baffled some fans, but economics drove such decisions. The Grays didn't draw especially well at Forbes Field, it was expensive to rent, and both teams had a better shot at making a few bucks in black-baseball-crazy Philadelphia. It didn't hurt that Homestead would be starting South Philly resident Specs Roberts against Bill Byrd in game three.

The Elites' own representative from the City of Brotherly Love got his first look at Roberts in the second inning. With Bill Hoskins on third after a triple, Roy whistled a "fiery bingle to left" to give the Elites a 1–0 lead. He scored a moment later on Byrd's double. The Grays quickly cut the lead in half when the rejuvenated Gibson crushed a line shot over the center-field fence. Byrd, his spitter suddenly hittable, began to falter, allowing three runs in the third and fourth as the Grays prepared to put the game on ice.

The Elites had other ideas. Henry Kimbro, he of the "evil" temperament, led off the fifth with a single. Sammy Hughes followed with a bouncer to shortstop Jelly Jackson, who fired to first for what appeared to be a routine out except Kimbro decided to make a break for third. The startled Grays first baseman Buck Leonard then made a desperate heave to Jackson, who landed on the headfirst-sliding Kimbro at third, who was called safe by the umpire in a bang-bang play. Within seconds, Kimbro was living up to his reputation, blindly whaling away at Jackson, who "proceeded to return the barrage of lefts and rights with a vengeance," according to sportswriter Earl Barnes. The brawling pair was ejected, but the incident seemed to spook the Grays. Red Moore singled home Kimbro's pinch runner a few moments later, and Roy tied the score at 4 the next inning with a solo shot inside the left-field foul line.

Campy now had a single, a homer, and two RBIs to his credit, but his day was far from over. Two doubles (or a double and a single, depending on the game account) and three more RBIs followed, as the Elites battered Roberts for six more runs on the way to a 10–5 victory and a 2-1 edge in the series. With the hometown fans watching, Roy had just enjoyed the greatest day of his career to date, one that had matched, if not bettered,

Josh Gibson, whose big bat also launched four hits and a homer in a losing cause that afternoon. The Grays, meanwhile, were in shock. They had underestimated Campanella, who, according to the league cognoscenti, was no threat with the stick and could be fooled with a good curve.

The series then shifted on Sunday from the shabby confines of Parkside Field in West Philadelphia to major league baseball's cavernous cathedral in the Bronx, Yankee Stadium. During the early 1930s, the Elites and other Negro League teams had played only sporadically at the Stadium until a fateful radio interview with Yankee outfielder Jake Powell in 1938 changed everything. Asked by WGN broadcaster Bob Elson how he spent his winters, Powell thoughtfully replied that he was employed as a policeman in Dayton, Ohio, where he kept himself fit cracking "niggers" on the head with his billy club.

Ten or twenty years earlier, Powell's comment might have escaped public recrimination. But black America was now better organized with a stronger press less willing to accept insults without a fight. The groundswell of black protest forced Commissioner Kenesaw Mountain Landis to suspend Powell for ten days, and the image-conscious Bronx Bombers were also pushed into damage control. Yankee officials not only rented out their park for an unprecedented six Negro League promotions in 1939 but also donated a $500 Ruppert Memorial Cup to be awarded to the black team with the best record at the Stadium.

The Elites, up 2-1 in the series and sporting a 3-0 record at Yankee Stadium to date, were now poised to capture two prizes on Sunday: the league championship and the first Ruppert Cup. Although such a high-stakes game seemed likely to sell itself, the NNL's publicity machine did its best to ensure a good turnout, planting the usual stories in the black newspapers and even managing to get some ink in the stodgy *New York Times*. As a further lure for the ladies, it was also announced that Mr. Gibson would "autograph six balls for lucky female fans" after the game.

A decent-size crowd estimated at eight thousand to ten thousand Harlemites trooped into Yankee Stadium that afternoon to watch the Grays and Elites slug it out for a fourth time. Despite his heroics the day before, Campy was still batting in his customary eighth position in the lineup. He had no expectation of another four-hit game, certainly not against Roy Partlow, who had so thoroughly dominated the Elites in game one, or at

Yankee Stadium, murder for hitters in the late afternoons, when the shadows were at their worst. But Mackey had taught Campy that a catcher's greatest value was with the glove and not the bat. His pitch selection, he knew, would probably be more crucial than the three or four times he might hit that day.

Roy and his pitcher, Jonas Gaines, worked in perfect sync the first six innings, holding the Grays scoreless. Unfortunately for the Elites, Partlow was just as good, cruising along with his own two-hit shutout until a sudden string of bad luck in the seventh. With one out, Bill Wright hammered a double into left field, followed by a Dave Hoskins single that ricocheted off Partlow's knee. The rattled Partlow settled down enough to fan Pee Wee Butts for the second out, but was then victimized by an infield error that scored the first run of the game. With runners on first and second, Roy stepped to the plate and promptly "drilled a single to right," plating Hoskins for a 2–0 Baltimore lead that would stand for the remainder of the afternoon.

After the game, the Elites were presented with the Ruppert Cup, but at least one black fan was not impressed. "This is what you'd call throwing a dog a bone," he remarked. "There still ain't no colored players in the major leagues and Jake Powell is still on the New York Yankees roster. So they buy us off with a gold-plated cup." It was hard to argue with such logic, not when the big time and the big money were still off-limits to Roy and his teammates. White major league players would collect shares ranging from $4,282 to $5,614 for their participation in the 1939 World Series. The Elites, meanwhile, would each receive a watch from Tom Wilson for winning their first and what proved to be their only NNL title.

Like most of his teammates, Roy did not brood about the inherent unfairness of baseball apartheid. *This was the way things were.* You had to accept it or you'd go crazy. Instead, he focused on what he had achieved this season. At age seventeen, he was now the Elites' first-string catcher and a major contributor to their championship run. His homer, 6 RBIs, and .353 average in the Grays series had even temporarily knocked Josh Gibson out of the headlines. And maybe, just maybe, the black press would even start spelling his name correctly.

He had passed every baseball test in 1939 with flying colors, but one final exam remained to be taken. After the series, Webster McDonald, the man who always claimed he had discovered Campy for the Philadelphia

Stars, invited him to participate in a barnstorming series in Baltimore against a group of major leaguers including Jimmie Foxx of the Red Sox. Such games had been common for decades, allowing white players the chance to make a few bucks and blacks the opportunity to demonstrate their ability against major leaguers.

The Beast, as Foxx was nicknamed, did not take part in the doubleheader won by the white team by 3–1 and 2–0 scores, although the *Baltimore Morning Sun* reported that he "put in an appearance." He was, however, quite impressed with the colored team's youthful catcher, who was flawless behind the plate and even banged out one of the four hits the Negro Leaguers managed off Pete Appleton of the Washington Senators in the first game. Appleton, to be sure, was only a mediocre pitcher, sporting a 4.56 ERA that season, slightly below the American League average of 4.62. Still, he was an established major leaguer good enough to win 14 games just three years before and pitch in the majors for another several seasons. This Campanella fellow, Foxx realized, could play in the major leagues, if only . . .

5

A RISING STAR

ANOTHER SEASON ENDED, another drab Philadelphia winter. This year, Roy had a wife and child to lift his gloom, although the marriage's foundations already appeared shaky. Bernice and the baby were living with her family while Roy was still with his parents. With Campy away half the year, it made little sense for two teenagers to get a place of their own right now.

The unorthodox arrangement probably did not bother Roy much. He loved Bernice and baby Joyce, but he was eighteen, a time when most young men are far from ready to settle down. Living separately minimized his responsibilities and his commitment to the marriage. He could see Bernice at his leisure (he would see her often enough that she would be pregnant again by January) without the inconvenience of the day-to-day intimacies, obligations, and spats that either make or break a marriage.

In some ways, he was still the same boy he had been a few years back, living at home, eating his mother's spaghetti, and listening to the *Lone Ranger.* Baseball, as always, remained his obsession. The game was not only the young family's sole means of support, but it was also all he had as a black man in Depression America. Never, he decided, would he take that fact for granted, and he resolved to let nothing, family responsibilities included, interfere with his progress up the baseball ladder.

The playoff with the Grays had advanced Roy several rungs up that ladder. His name, despite the inevitable misspellings, was no longer a mystery to black fans and writers. "Ray Camponella," raved Earl Barnes of the *Philadelphia Independent,* "is definitely the best all-around young catcher to break into the Negro national league since Josh Gibson. . . . Camponella (who is still growing) has a deadly throwing arm, is brainy, fast, and developing into a good hitter."

Although Tom Wilson and Felton Snow also loved the kid, they still thought it prudent to pick up the veteran backstop Bill Perkins in a trade. With Perkins too good a catcher (THOU SHALT NOT STEAL was inscribed on his chest protector) and hitter to languish on the bench, Roy braced himself for a return to second-string status. But Snow decided that Perkins, too old to catch every day, would be kept fresh by regular outfield stints, leaving plenty of work for Campy behind the plate.

Snow understandably felt more secure with the experienced Perkins doing the receiving, although he could find no fault with Campanella's aggressiveness. "He had the snap throw," remembered pitcher Ross Davis, who joined the team that year, "and would try to catch guys off base and stuff like that." The problem, even after three years, was accuracy. "He'd throw all the balls into the ground," observed Pee Wee Butts. "He was quick and everything, but his arm just wasn't true." Without Mackey to work his magic on his throwing kinks, word got around fast that the kid could be run on. A white team swiped two bases on Roy on Friday, May 17, 1940, followed by two more by the Grays that weekend. On June 8, the *Chester Times* reported Campanella "threw wild" trying to pick off another white runner. A few weeks later the Black Yankees stole three in a 9–5 loss to the Elites.

Snow remained patient. Campanella wasn't Mackey yet, but other parts of his game had drastically improved, particularly his hitting. Curveballs had long been the kid's weakness, but the cantankerous George Scales, brought back in a trade, made Roy his pet project and proved to be the perfect instructor. Years later, Campy would insist that "no one in organized baseball today could hit a curve ball better than George Scales."

Scales quickly sized up the holes in Roy's hitting approach. "He was a hard swinger," recalled Butts. "If he hit anything it was gone, but a curve ball he'd be off guard. If it was two feet outside, he would swing at it." Campanella, Scales quickly determined, would need to be taught to recognize the spin on the curve, to wait long enough before swinging, and to lay off balls out of the zone. Above all, he needed to stop bailing out when he saw a breaking ball. Day after day, Scales drilled Roy on the curve, even placing bats in front of him in batting practice to keep his feet in place.

Before long, Roy was catching on. The baseball adage that "hitters develop power with age" was also proving true. Grays pitchers needed no convincing after yielding two homers to Roy in Harrisburg on May 18 and another pair in Baltimore on July 14. By August, ten of Roy's nineteen hits in fourteen league games had gone for extra bases, and his average of .359 was second on the Elites only to Scales's .408. That Campanella kid, whispered league pitchers, was really beginning to look like the second coming of Josh Gibson, who spent most of the season playing in Venezuela and Mexico.

Despite Campy's newfound slugging ability, the Elites fell to second place behind the Grays, who began their string of six straight NNL championships. Still, he had taken another giant step forward in 1940. He was also discovering just how much fun it was to play in the Negro Leagues. At eighteen, he found himself enjoying a growing camaraderie with his teammates. He loved the fan recognition, the mentions in the black press, and the often weird and sometimes poignant sights on the road that provided him abundant fodder for stories for years afterward. One day that season Roy saw a bankrupt Jesse Owens, only four years removed from his Olympic triumphs, reduced to running exhibitions after Negro League games. On another, he watched his manager, certain that the brakes on their creaky, old bus were about to fail on a sloping road in Pennsylvania, make a desperate leap out the door, only to see the vehicle stop safely a few seconds later.

Celebrity brought yet another reward: women. The ladies hadn't paid much attention to him when he was a baby-faced second-stringer, but now they wanted to know just who was that cute roly-poly catcher with the big smile and twinkling eyes. He had once been awkward with women, but now they approached him in the black nightclubs and hotels where the Elites congregated. Like many a ballplayer before and after, Roy was unable to resist temptation on the road.

His partner in crime was a young pitcher from Alabama named Bill Barnes, who roomed with Campy in the early 1940s. "We was kids and the rest of the guys was grown men, thirty, thirty-five years old," Barnes recalled. "We did too many crazy things. We liked the girls. They couldn't keep us in the hotel." The two youngsters even came up with a clever ruse to beat Felton Snow's eleven-o'clock curfew. "We'd get in the bed with our clothes on," said Barnes. "He'd come and check us in, and no sooner than he left, we was out of the bed and gone."

Women, travel, baseball, fame—it was a dream come true for an eighteen-year-old. But for Bernice, the situation was far from ideal. Her growing family, which now included a second daughter, Beverly, still had no home of their own, nor would they see much of Roy that winter. He had been invited to play in Puerto Rico, another rung up the baseball ladder, and no way was he going to turn down such an opportunity. The family could use the money, and family life would once again have to come second.

FOR A select group of players, winter baseball, whether in Puerto Rico, Cuba, Venezuela, or even Los Angeles, perfectly solved the problem of off-season employment. Instead of working in some menial job, they could loll in the sun, play a few games a week, and pick up a check comparable to their normal Negro League salary.

Since its formation in 1938, the Puerto Rican Winter League had recruited African-Americans to strengthen the local teams. Each club was allowed to start three imports, mostly plucked from the upper tier of Negro Leaguers. Caguas, an inland city about twenty miles south of San Juan, signed up Roy and his teammate Bill Byrd, along with Lenny Pearson of the Newark Eagles, who left behind a woman scorned. Pearson, it turned out, had secretly been carrying on with the Eagles' married boss lady, Effa Manley, who was furious that he wouldn't be around during the cold winter months.

Some players found the language barrier in Puerto Rico too difficult to overcome. "Most of us will be glad when it's over here," wrote Pearson in a letter to sportswriter Art Carter. "The people here are very nice. They try in every way to make us contented and happy, but we can't speak their language and they are hard to understand." But Roy, despite forgetting most of his junior high Spanish except "huevos y jamón" (eggs and ham), picked up the rudiments of the language relatively quickly. He soon found a great deal to like about Puerto Rico besides the $45 per week and assorted bonuses ($1 for each single, walk, or RBI, $2 for a double, etc.) he was collecting. The workload was minimal, consisting of a morning/afternoon double-header on Sunday. The rest of the week was a paid vacation. "We would fish, go to the beach, sightsee," remembered Monte Irvin, who joined the San Juan club that winter. "There was always a nightclub you could go to dance, sit around, drink beer." Roy's ever-hearty appetite found a variety of exotic foods to sample, including barbecued goat, papayas, and fried green bananas. Best of all, segregation was less of an issue, although the island's best hotels still refused black patronage.

Puerto Rico also gave Roy his first experience with truly *organized* baseball. "The fact that the league is run systematically," noted Art Carter, "without a series of ifs, buts and what nots is doubtless a big factor in the swaying of American players to accept work there." Batting averages were kept, schedules were followed, and every team played forty-two games divided over two halves with the winner of each half meeting for the championship. Discipline was far stronger than in the Negro Leagues, as Satchel Paige discovered when he was fined and suspended for lollygagging between pitches.

With the likes of Paige, Leon Day, Dave Barnhill, Raymond Brown, and Roy Partlow all taking regular turns on the mound, Campy found the going rough. By late January, his .255 average ranked last in the league among the imports. But his buddy Irvin was on even shakier ground after an 0-for-21 skid and wondered whether he might be shipped back to the States.

When Irvin's San Juan team came to Caguas, Roy resolved to help out his friend. "Dude, I see you're in a slump," he told Irvin before the game. "If we get a big lead, I'll let you know what's coming." Irvin was naturally dubious, but when he came to bat later in the game with his team trailing by four, he heard Campy murmur, "Fastball." The startled Irvin watched a perfect heater cut the heart of the plate. He collected his thoughts and stepped back in the box. "Curveball," whispered Campy. The Caguas pitcher obediently heaved a breaking ball, and once again Irvin could not pull the trigger.

By this point, Roy was furious. "Campy was jumping around back there," said Irvin, "wondering what the hell was the matter with me and why I didn't swing." Finally convinced, Irvin slammed Roy's next called fastball over the fence and later clubbed a second homer that day, once again thanks to his friend's advance notice. With the score tightening up in the late innings, Campy decided that his pal was now on his own, but Irvin was always grateful for those two gift home runs. "That's what kept me there instead of catching a boat back to the cold weather in New York," he later recalled.

Like Irvin, Roy would also rediscover his batting stroke. On February 23, he became one of four players in Puerto Rican Winter League history to homer twice in the same inning, prompting awestruck fans to pass the hat as a reward for Señor Campanella. By the season's close, Roy had smacked eight dingers, tying Buck Leonard for the league lead and sparking Caguas to an overall 27-15 record and a playoff berth against Santurce for the championship.

Santurce won three of the first five playoff games and needed only to split the final two scheduled in Caguas on Sunday, April 6, 1941. With his team trailing 2–1 and facing elimination in game six, Campy came to the plate against Luis Cabrera with the bases loaded in the fifth. Cabrera was probably the best of the local pitchers, but Roy had already taken him downtown in game three. As the Caguas faithful nervously watched, Cabrera wound, threw, and Roy promptly deposited the pitch deep over the left-field fence for a grand slam.

The entire park went berserk. His teammates carried him from home plate in triumph, while swarms of happy fans pressed dollar bills into his hands. Meanwhile, shell-shocked Santurce never recovered, losing the game in a 16–4 blowout and eventually the series in the second game that afternoon. Winning another championship was sweet, but Campy was even more thrilled that league officials, swayed by his big hit in the playoffs, decided to award him the Leading Home Run Hitter trophy, tie or no tie with Leonard. The inscription had the wrong year, but Roy treasured the prize, as he would every award he would collect in his long career. He loved seeing tangible evidence of his success, and the walls of his homes would eventually be covered with awards great and small. "A man," he would say, "gets a warm feeling in his heart when he sees them displayed there."

One last validation was still to come. A few months later, he ran into Josh Gibson, who had heard tales of Roy's slugging exploits that winter.

Instead of the usual teasing comments of "little boy" and "little kid," the big man got serious all of a sudden. He looked at Roy with a mixture of bemusement and admiration: "You're growing up to be a man now."

BACK HOME in the States that spring, war was now the topic on everyone's mind. Nazi Germany's successful thrust through much of western Europe in 1940 had forced reluctant Americans to contend with the possibility of involvement in yet another global conflict. Aid to Great Britain had dramatically accelerated, defense plants were humming, and the country's first peacetime draft was now in force. The effects were already being felt throughout the baseball world. Detroit Tigers superstar Hank Greenberg was drafted, and other ballplayers wondered whether they would be next to receive a "greetings from Uncle Sam" letter.

Although Tom Wilson feared that most of his infield might disappear because of their age and lack of dependents, he soon discovered that draft officials had only marginal interest in black servicemen. In the segregated U.S. army, black soldiers required separate training facilities, and the military was not equipped or inclined to handle large numbers of "colored" GIs. Rather than simply integrate, the Selective Service Department preferred to maintain a 10 percent and later 5 percent cap on black draftees, largely sparing the Negro Leagues from the manpower problems faced by white Organized Baseball during the war.

At nineteen, Roy did not yet have to consider the possibility that he might have to exchange his baseball uniform for green khakis and his bat for a rifle. The first draft call had only included men twenty-one and over, and his wife and two children would have deferred him anyway. The army life did not appeal to him in the slightest, not when he was now making $175 per month, a figure he proudly related to his new teammate Charles Biot, who was only making $160. Combined with his Puerto Rican wages, he was pulling in roughly $1,800 a year, much more than a colored kid from Nicetown with a ninth-grade education had any right to expect in 1941. It was not a middle-class income, but enough for Roy and Bernice to finally set up housekeeping in their own Nicetown apartment on 3822 North Smedley Street, a stone's throw away from John and Ida. With everyone under the same roof and Roy spending more time with Bernice, the marriage appeared to be at its most stable.

Black America was also showing signs of stability in 1941. The preparation for war lifted the country out of the decade-long Depression, and African-Americans would eventually benefit from the more robust economy and expanded employment opportunities. With money jingling in their pockets for the first time in years, black fans began to turn up at Negro League games in unprecedented numbers, approaching twenty thousand to thirty thousand in some venues. The Negro Leagues, Roy sensed, were developing into a viable business, and he looked forward to getting a bigger piece of the financial pie in the years to come.

But a fatter paycheck remained elusive as long as his glove lagged behind his bat, especially in an era when most baseball men viewed a catcher's primary function as defensive. Snow still believed Roy's throwing and game-calling needed additional polish and preferred to continue his two-catcher scheme. This year, he partnered Campy with the even more ancient Eggie Clarke, a traditional good-field/no-hit receiver acquired via trade. Like any young player, Campanella chafed under such an arrangement. Part-timers, he knew, could never develop a big enough name or reputation to command a higher-end salary. But Snow, albeit unintentionally, was actually doing him a great favor, lessening the strain on his body now and prolonging his baseball life in the future. Had the Elites worn Campy down as a teenager, the entire trajectory of his baseball career could have changed. Ironically, the games he *didn't catch* as a young Negro Leaguer might well have been just as important as the ones he did.

Campy's torrid bat, however, would soon force Snow to rethink his two-catcher system. After Clarke caught the season opener in Harrisburg on May 10, Roy was back behind the plate in Baltimore the next day, slamming a double and a homer off Homestead's always tough Roy Partlow. What followed was one of Campy's soon-to-be-familiar streaky batting tears where every pitch looked as big as a beach ball and every ball he hit was a bullet off his bat. By the end of May, he was terrorizing NNL pitchers to the tune of a .579 average, forcing even the usually Homestead-centric Cum Posey to take notice. He opened his June 21 weekly *Pittsburgh Courier* column with news of Roy's league-leading hitting and reassurances that "despite his name [he] is one of us."

That Posey felt the need to inform his readers of this fact illustrates the degree of Roy's anonymity, even four years after his NNL debut. For black fans, his name still lacked the cachet of a Gibson, a Paige, or even a Mackey. But he was now on the radar screen of Posey, probably the most powerful official in the NNL and the man who many believed actually ran the league, though Campy's boss, Tom Wilson, was the titular president. And Posey, though Roy didn't realize it at the time, was in a position to dramatically boost a player's public profile.

Unfortunately, Campy's dreams of a breakout season and superstardom abruptly disappeared in June when he contracted a severe case of pneumonia that would send him to bed for weeks. Day after day, he lay in an agonizing wait for his body to rejuvenate, the doctors and Bernice insisting that he stay put. When he was finally allowed to leave his sickbed, he predictably headed to Parkside Field to watch the Elites take on the Stars. Still, he would not be permitted to don a uniform for another two weeks. Even then, he was far from 100 percent, but his desire to play was so intense that he virtually willed himself to withstand any lingering fatigue, just as he would other painful injuries throughout his career.

His bat was embarrassingly slow after the long layoff. The Stars and Black Yankees held him hitless in his first two league games back, as did the white Lloyd A.C. But his stroke began to return as July wore on. On Saturday, July 19, he went 3 for 5 in a 14–3 rout of the Newark Eagles, who let old friend Biz Mackey pitch three innings that day. The next afternoon, Roy drove in three runs against the white Brooklyn Bushwicks, then added two more hits against the Kansas City Monarchs on Monday night in Baltimore. With Josh Gibson in Mexico this year, the revitalized Roy was now emerging as the leading candidate to start behind the plate for the NNL in the upcoming East-West Game at Comiskey Park.

The East-West Game was black baseball's crown jewel. Like the major league All-Star Game (which predated its birth by only two months), it featured the best of both existing leagues squaring off in an annual contest. Unlike the various attempts at black World Series, the East-West Game was perfectly arranged to capture the interest and limited finances of African-American fans: a single promotion on a Sunday in the heart of Chicago's black belt. Record-setting crowds of more than thirty-three thousand had turned up at Comiskey in recent years, including a surprising number of curious white sportswriters and fans.

Player selection, at least according to the NNL and NAL, was based on the major league's original system of fan voting. The black press published weekly results perpetuating the notion that thousands of fans had cast their votes for their favorite players. But black sportswriters in the know viewed the voting as a farce. "It gives you the giggles to read all the stuff about voting and balloting for the East-West game," wrote the *Philadelphia Tribune*'s Ed Harris that July. "I don't know how they do it in the West but here in the East there hasn't been hide nor hair of anything even resembling votes. . . . Nobody is being kidded into thinking that anyone else but the owners are choosing players."

Harris was convinced that Cum Posey did the choosing and vote manipulating in the East. His suspicions are confirmed by a private letter from Posey to Effa Manley in 1943 admitting to "juggling votes so we could get three men off a team and have the public think they were picking them." But the Posey "system," as corrupt as it was, actually benefited Roy in 1941. Posey remembered Roy's red-hot hitting earlier in the season; he needed to take three Elites anyway, and with Gibson gone, the only other viable option was Mackey, who would be celebrating his forty-fourth birthday on the day of the game. Accordingly, fans were informed in late July that Campy "overtook the veteran Biz Mackey of Newark with a sensational spurt" in the voting, and Roy was now an all-star for the first time.

"It was felt in many quarters," Art Carter later noted, "that selectors had made a big mistake in naming Roy." Word on the street suggested that Campanella was "unable to throw well enough to halt the fleet-footed West base stealers" and "his experience wouldn't be any help to East pitchers." Even Earl Barnes, long a Campy cheerleader, preferred to see Mackey behind the plate. "According to gossip in diamond circles," wrote Barnes, "Roy has had extreme difficulty in adjusting his cap to fit the proportions of his thinking facilities lately."

If Campy was bothered by such talk, he gave no indication on the long train ride to Chicago. He shot the breeze with Monte Irvin, who had also been chosen, played some cards, and joined the others in his car as they belted out a new song by Count Basie fittingly entitled "Goin' to Chicago Blues." By this point, he was well accustomed to being underestimated. Fifteen-year-olds, he had been told, can't play in the Negro Leagues. Nineteen-year-olds don't belong in the East-West Game. But every mocking comment and sneering dismissal had stoked the already considerable competitive fires that burned within him. And the chance to perform on black baseball's biggest stage, the East-West Game, would do no less.

Sunday, July 27, was an all too typical summer day in Chicago. By 7:00 a.m., the mercury had already reached eighty-three degrees, perfect weather for baseball. NNL and NAL officials expected a good turnout, maybe 35,000, particularly with local black hotels booked solid with fans from all over the country. But no one was prepared for the hordes that began making their way into Comiskey Park by late morning. Everyone on the South Side, it seemed, was on their way to the big game, many fresh from church, clad in their Sunday best. Three hours before gametime, 5,000 fans had already taken their seats, and thousands more mobbed the ticket booths and turnstiles in the early afternoon. By gametime 47,865 hearty souls had packed Comiskey, "the largest crowd to ever attend a sport event in Negro history," according to Fay Young of the *Chicago Defender.*

It was an unmatched triumph for the Negro Leagues. "Only Marcus Garvey and Father Divine," marveled New York sportswriter Dan Burley, "have attracted so many Negroes to one place and to one event." But the promotion was not without the usual quirks common to black baseball. Pregame ceremonies started late, after Edgar Brown, a member of FDR's informal "black Cabinet," bored the crowd with an interminable "race problem address." A subsequent attempt to introduce each league's players quickly fell apart when the announcer "lost his copy," leaving Roy and his Eastern teammates "stranded on the first base line looking like a lot of statues and feeling greatly embarrassed." And Joe Louis, scheduled to throw out the first ball, was nowhere to be found.

By now, Campy was used to the by-the-seat-of-your-pants style of the Negro Leagues. But neither he nor most of the other Eastern players were fully prepared for the hundred-degree temperature at Comiskey that afternoon. Not only had they neglected to bring sunglasses, but their heavy wool uniforms made conditions worse. Though weighed down with the "tools of ignorance," Roy had his own strategy to cope with the heat. A wet cabbage leaf under the cap was his favored method.

Cabbage leaf or not, the field was a steam bath, and the Western team salivated at the prospect of making the kid catcher's life miserable that afternoon. Roy had barely finished warming up Terris McDuffie before the

NAL decided to test him. With runners on first and third and two outs in the first inning, Jelly Taylor got a tremendous jump and took off for second, hoping to draw a throw. Campanella, the West smugly concluded, was unlikely to gun down Taylor, and his attempt would almost certainly allow a run to score. But Mackey had taught Roy years ago that at times a catcher just had to eat the baseball. As Taylor slid in safely, the only thing Campy could do was keep the ball in front of him and get it back to his pitcher. He breathed a sigh of relief a few moments later when McDuffie retired the hitter on an easy bouncer to end the threat.

The West took another crack at Roy in the second inning. McDuffie, already wilting from the heat, hit Tommy Sampson with a pitch to start the frame. Trailing by only a run, Western manager Candy Jim Taylor ordered a sacrifice bunt from Pepper Bassett, best known for his cute trick of occasionally catching in a rocking chair. Fielding a bunt could be a hair-raising experience for even the most experienced of catchers, and the NAL hoped the kid would botch it. "It's up to the catcher to run the play all the way," Campy later explained. "He has to have that timing to get out and field it if he has to, and if he can't, he has to be just close enough, but not too close, to the man who fields it, to yell directions." This time, Roy only had to follow his own instincts. He pounced on Bassett's bunt without hesitation and fired a perfect strike down to second to nab Sampson.

By the third inning, the already oppressive sun had grown only stronger, baking both teams. "The players who have been in South America," remarked Fay Young, "said they have never suffered with the heat to that extent before." McDuffie bailed out early, as did the West's Newt Allen, who "had to be worked over in the dugout to prevent prostration." In a desperate attempt to win the war of attrition, the NNL squad began submerging some towels in ice and applied them to the sweltering players. But Roy appeared to be getting stronger as the day progressed. He picked up another assist on a nubber in front of the plate in the fourth, nailed Howard Cleveland stealing on a strikeout-throwout double play in the fifth, and ranged to the stands to haul in a foul pop in the sixth.

Campy was putting on a catching clinic, but most fans remained distracted. Why hadn't Satchel Paige, the biggest name in black baseball, pitched? By the eighth inning, with the East now ahead 8–1, the crowd began to shout, "We want Satchel," and Candy Jim Taylor obliged. As Paige loped to the mound, photographers snapped away, including a number of amateurs (among them a "pretty gal picturetaker with . . . yellow pajamas") who left their seats in the stands to get a shot of their hero. Paige, who had taken a pitch to the arm recently, was not at his best, and rumors circulated that he was playing against doctor's orders. But Monte Irvin, sitting on the bench next to Campy and Lenny Pearson, knew better than to underestimate Old Satch. "You know what he wants to do to the first hitter," remarked Irvin. "He wants to strike him out. You know what a crowd-pleaser he is." And just as Irvin predicted, Paige quickly buzzed three past Pearson, punched out Dave Hoskins on a sinker, and then retired the dangerous Buck Leonard on a pop-up as Comiskey went wild.

Satch the showman had stolen Campy's thunder, but the kid would have the last laugh. In the ninth inning, after Paige had set down his fourth straight hitter, Campy came to the plate, determined to break the string. He had faced Paige last winter in Puerto Rico and was well aware of the old master's pinpoint control. The best strategy, he decided, was to go up there hacking. With the count even at 2-2, Roy took a mighty cut at a Paige offering, managing to tap what Irvin recalled as a "swinging bunt" down the third-base line. Still, it was good for a single, the first and what turned out to be the only hit off the great Paige that afternoon.

In the bottom of the inning, the NNL's Bill Byrd dispensed with the first two Western hitters before Jimmy Crutchfield reached on an infield single. Despite a five-run deficit, Crutchfield inexplicably tried to steal, and Campy made him pay with a bullet throw down to second to end the game. The Comiskey Park press box had seen enough. Leonard's homer and Paige's pitching notwithstanding, the kid had had a helluva day behind the plate and clearly deserved the game MVP. One female writer disagreed, instead casting her vote for the West's George Mitchell, the pinch hitter at bat when Crutchfield was thrown out. For Art Carter, such bizarre choices definitively confirmed "the folly of having women in the press box." The ladies, he grumbled, just didn't know their baseball.

As the sweaty but happy crowd exited the ballpark, Roy was presented with his second major award in four months. His national coming-out party to black America was complete, and never again would his name be a mystery to the African-American media (although some journalists persisted in calling him "Campenello"). Four years after his debut, Campy was a star, and he expected Tom Wilson to pay him accordingly in the future. Maybe he wasn't Josh Gibson, whom Posey still ranked above Roy in his annual "best of" list that October. But with Roy only nineteen, ten years younger than his hero, the once enormous gap between the two catchers appeared certain to shrink further in the future.

THAT FALL, Campanella, Gibson, and most of the other big names headed to Puerto Rico for another season of winter ball. This year, it was a family affair for Roy, who took Bernice and the babies for six months of sunshine in Caguas.

Whether due to family pressures or baseball burnout, he could not seem to get untracked. Monte Irvin, rescued by Roy a year earlier, decided it was time to repay the favor. "What you need," he told Campy, "is to come over to San Juan and get away from the kids for a while. We'll go out and do a little dancing." The two pals headed to one of the local clubs, grabbed a table, and ordered drinks. Each time a new song began, Roy got out on the dance floor while Irvin secretly slipped some rum into Campy's Coke, his beverage of choice at the time. By his third dance, Roy was feeling no pain. "I don't know why I feel so good," he told Irvin. His friend smiled. "See, I told you all you had to do was to get away from Caguas out there in the country," said Irvin, "and come over here where everything is happening." By 1:00 a.m., Roy apparently had had enough dancing and fortified Coca-Colas. But before he returned home for the night, he turned to Irvin, his eyes twinkling. "You thought you were fooling me, but I knew what you were doing," said Roy. "Please invite me back again and do the same thing." The rum and Cokes, soon to be his favorite drink, worked wonders, as he began to hit the ball with authority once again.

By November, Campy had settled into a familiar routine: weekdays in Caguas with the family and Sundays at the ballpark. In nearly three years of marriage, he had never spent so much time with Bernice and the girls, nor would he ever again. The marriage, if his willingness to dance with strange women at a nightclub is any indication, had lost its luster. Bernice was a neighborhood girl but he was no longer a neighborhood boy. He was transforming into a black sports celebrity on the verge of outgrowing Kerbaugh Street, Nicetown, and, apparently, his wife.

Bernice, perhaps unaware of her husband's growing disenchantment, may have viewed the Puerto Rico trip as a chance to reconnect. But international events intervened. On Sunday, December 7, Campy was in bed, listening to the radio and pondering his plate approach against hard-throwing Leon Day, scheduled to pitch for Aguadilla in the second game of the day's doubleheader in Caguas. Suddenly, a frantic Spanish voice interrupted the music with a bulletin: "The Japanese have just attacked Pearl Harbor."

6

WAR AND A TRYOUT

THE PEARL HARBOR ATTACK and subsequent full involvement of America in World War II sent shock waves through the black baseball colony in Puerto Rico. "Man, the war scared me so much that I grabbed the first boat out for home," Terris McDuffie told one sportswriter. "I know Puerto Rico is a long way from Manila and Singapore, but you can never tell when those Japs might get a notion to start flying toward the islands, and I'd rather be back home where I know where to hide than down there where you've got to be a tree climber to know what it's all about."

Though justifiably concerned, Roy and most of the other Americans were less jittery, even with blackouts and antiaircraft guns now part of the local picture. After all, three months remained on the winter league schedule, and it seemed foolish to sacrifice an easy paycheck because of the remote possibility of a Japanese attack. Ultimately, Tojo decided his Zeros could be deployed more fruitfully elsewhere than the ballparks of Puerto Rico, and the season went on as planned. Thanks to Irvin's rum and Cokes, Campy brought his final average up to .295, a 32-point jump from his first year at Caguas. But this winter belonged to the unstoppable Josh Gibson, whose freakishly high .480 average and .959 slugging percentage in 1941–42 have yet to be surpassed in the PRWL record book. Strangely,

Campy failed to homer once, perhaps a result of lingering aftereffects from his bout with pneumonia earlier that summer.

After a harrowing boat ride home, Roy returned to the States to find a nation transformed. That April, Hitler was hanged in effigy to kick off a series of war-bond rallies in Times Square as ten thousand cheered. Radios filled the airwaves with a steady stream of corny patriotic tunes such as "Let's Put the Axe to the Axis" and "We've Got to Do a Job on the Japs, Baby." And Americans puzzled over their new ration books, trying to figure out exactly how much (or little) sugar, gasoline, and other necessities they were permitted to buy that week.

At twenty, Roy now found himself eligible for military service under the revised draft law. As a married man with two children, he was eventually classified 3-A, a group not likely to be called. Still, the draft weighed heavily on his mind during the next three years. Local Selective Service officials wanted to be kept informed of his whereabouts at all times, and postcards had to be mailed from each stop on the Elites' itineraries.

Twice during the war he was called back to Philadelphia to take defense jobs. Bendix Aviation, a local firm that had refused to hire African-Americans until recently, put him to work as a porter, a glorified janitorial position commonly given to black men in those days. After two weeks of mopping and sweeping, he could take no more, and the draft board mercifully allowed him to return to baseball. His second contribution to the war effort was a winter position at the Disston factory, which manufactured steel armor plate for tanks. "I was given the job of operating a huge hammer press," recalled Campy, "which pounded slabs of red-hot steel ingots into long, thin strips." After watching a coworker's arm mangled in an industrial accident, he requested a transfer to a position less threatening to his baseball career. The factory agreed, and shortly thereafter draft officials permitted him to return to the Elites for good.

Campanella's brief and unpleasant work experiences during the war confirmed what he already knew only too well. Baseball was a precious gift, one that had rescued him from a life of drudgery awaiting most black men, especially those with limited educations. Even when he became an established major leaguer, he remained genuinely grateful to the game. "I remember what I was doing before I got this break," he remarked in 1950.

"I remember cleaning toilets and scrubbing nuisance waste in a steel mill in the off-season." The cynics, the complainers, and the malcontents in baseball—he could never understand them. They just didn't realize how lucky they were.

THE EARLY days of the war rocked the normally sturdy foundations of major league baseball. Officials fretted that the federal government might shut down spectator sports for the duration until President Roosevelt ultimately decided "it would be best for the country to keep baseball going." Still, the game could expect no special favors. Players could be drafted, night games curtailed, and travel limited, but major league parks could stay open during the war.

Baseball men breathed a sigh of relief. But with the onset of war, the long-suppressed issue of race suddenly resurfaced. The United States was now fighting a war abroad against oppression, discrimination, and fascism. How, then, black leaders argued, could Americans permit such practices to continue in their own country?

The aggressive efforts of black activists and their allies to highlight the hypocrisy of maintaining segregation and discrimination at home forced many whites to reconsider their country's treatment of African-Americans. The "Negro problem" could no longer be swept under the rug, and racial demands ignored in the past suddenly found receptive audiences. In a surprising breakthrough, Hollywood films and network radio, two major pillars of popular entertainment, began to tone down their stereotypes. Although progress was painfully slow at times, the war was succeeding in finally softening the most extreme aspects of American racism.

Activists recognized the favorable climate for eradicating baseball's color line. If discrimination truly damaged the war effort, as some said, how long could a highly public entity such as Organized Baseball continue to get away with its Jim Crow policies? How long could Organized Baseball, its player ranks increasingly depleted by the draft, continue to operate on a segregated basis?

Spring training had barely begun before the first shot in the renewed fight was fired across the bow. A California-based black journalist named Herman Hill decided to bring a couple of obviously talented players to spring training and demand a tryout.

The Chicago White Sox trained in Pasadena in those days, and Hill knew where he could get his hands on two top-notch local players. Nate Moreland was a pretty fair pitcher, good enough to spend 1940 as Roy's teammate on the Elites before jumping to Mexico in 1941. Hill also brought along Jackie Robinson, a multitalented football and basketball star at UCLA. Baseball might have been Robinson's worst sport at the time, but he had played some semipro ball in the past and had shown enough ability to attract the interest of the Elites last spring. Although Robinson eventually decided against coming East, the thought of Campy and Jackie as Negro League teammates several years before their Dodger days remains an intriguing what-if.

White Sox manager Jimmy Dykes was not happy to see Hill, Moreland, and Robinson advancing upon him that March 18. According to Hill, Dykes "refused to pose for pictures with Jackie and Nate," while his players "hovered around menacingly with bats in their hands." Dykes quickly sent the trio on their way, but not before he did some quick buck-passing. "We are powerless to act," he sputtered, "and it's strictly up to the club owners and Judge Landis to start the ball a'rolling. Go after them!"

The mainstream media ignored or was unaware of the Pasadena "try-out." New York columnist Joe Williams later blamed the news blackout on Commissioner Kenesaw Mountain Landis, who supposedly told Dykes to "keep his trap closed," particularly around nosy journalists. As long as the mass-circulation newspapers stayed off the story, integration could remain a nonissue, safely relegated to the pages of the weekly black press. But in the months that followed, the controversial American Communist Party would succeed in finally propelling Jim Crow baseball into the national spotlight. For the first time, major league officials, including Landis himself, would find themselves sweating, squirming, and stuttering over the subject of race.

American communists, attempting to secure black support, had become increasingly aggressive in civil rights causes, including baseball segregation, since the mid-1930s. Not all African-Americans welcomed their support; some remained convinced that communist involvement gave reactionary whites yet another weapon to undermine black advancement. Still, the communists wielded considerable influence, particularly through the unions, and their skills in organizing, picketing, and protesting were unparalleled.

They even had their own newspaper, the New York–based *Daily Worker*, whose sports pages consistently attacked with gusto baseball's color line.

Following the Dykes incident in Pasadena, the *Worker* and its sportswriters launched an assault on segregated baseball. Columns excitedly chronicled the production of twenty thousand buttons labeled SCORE AGAINST HITLER/LIFT BAN ON NEGRO PLAYERS, plans to hand out leaflets at the New York premiere of the Lou Gehrig biopic *Pride of the Yankees*, and support from the eighty-thousand-worker Ford local UAW-CIO in Detroit. Meanwhile, the *Worker* cranked up the pressure on Commissioner Landis, encouraging readers to forward letters and petitions to his office in Chicago.

Historically, Landis has been depicted as the major obstacle to integration, and undoubtedly he had no interest in ending the color line. But the ultraconservative team owners deserve an equal, if not greater, share of the blame. Like most American businessmen of the era, they wanted no part of blacks, and any commissioner they brought in was bound to reflect that attitude. Nor did Landis, lacking any real "rule-making power," have the authority to compel the owners to integrate. "If he had had any such power," his assistant Leslie O'Connor later explained, "there are certainly a dozen or more rules he would have thrown out."

But most baseball fans, rightly or wrongly, perceived Landis as the game's only real authority. The integration issue, he increasingly sensed, was being dumped on *his* lap. The sixteen owners didn't have to deal with the petitions, letters, and telegrams, or the most serious charge of all: that baseball's color line was "spreading disunity" in the midst of war.

After yet another major league manager, this time Brooklyn's Leo Durocher, was quoted in July as favoring integration if permitted by the powers that be, the judge finally cracked. Landis, who had admitted to a reporter that he was "sick and tired of getting hell from various people for barring Negroes from baseball," subsequently issued his first-ever public statement acknowledging the color line: "Negroes are not barred from organized baseball by the commissioner and never have been during the 21 years I have served. . . . That is the business of the managers and the club owners. The business of the commissioner is to interpret the rules of baseball and enforce them."

Landis had neatly tossed the hot potato into the hands of the owners.

Although the *Daily Worker*'s Nat Low was convinced "this ruling will usher in a new era," the widely read columnist Dan Parker of the *New York Daily Mirror* disagreed: "Landis' statement was hypocritical," asserted Parker. "He's a wise old bird, quite familiar with the art of using words and saying nothing. As for the owners, they'll do as they've always done—which means that they'll do nothing."

Parker was right. Washington owner Clark Griffith insisted that now was not the right time, instead suggesting that "colored people should develop their own big league baseball and challenge the best of the white major leagues." Larry MacPhail of the Dodgers even offered the peculiar argument that integration would *hurt* blacks by killing the Negro Leagues and limiting their opportunities to "play professional baseball."

But at least one major league official did not recoil at the thought of integration that summer. It was not Branch Rickey, then winding down his final year as general manager of the St. Louis Cardinals, but a more obscure owner in Pittsburgh, William Benswanger. Over the years, Benswanger had come to appreciate black talent, and once even flippantly offered to buy Josh Gibson. With the Pirates a second-division club, twenty games out of first place, and going nowhere fast, what did he have to lose?

SINCE EARLY summer 1942, even before the Landis statement, Campy had begun to wonder whether something remarkable was about to occur. He had never seriously considered the rather far-fetched possibility of playing big league ball, but now white newspapermen were hanging around asking questions and snapping photos. "I'm sure I could do OK in the majors," Roy told one New York reporter at Yankee Stadium. "As for discrimination from the players, that's bunk. I've played against many big leaguers who have come from the South and have never had anything but the friendliest of relations with them. We'd get along perfectly if we were given the chance."

In early July it appeared that he might get that chance. The hometown Philadelphia Phillies, according to the rumors, were interested, reportedly dispatching a scout to Yankee Stadium to watch Campy whack three hits in a Baltimore victory over Newark on July 4. Twelve days later, the *Daily Worker* fanned the fires by claiming that Roy had worked out with the Phillies at Shibe Park and was then "told to wait till 'something turns up.' " Actually, the Phillies had not the slightest interest in Roy or any other black player. But Campy's actual contact with the team remains somewhat of a mystery, as usual complicated by the multiple versions he provided throughout his life.

A contemporary article by Randy Dixon, chronicler of Roy's splashy NNL debut five years earlier, provides the most reliable account of what actually happened with the Phillies in 1942. Sitting in John and Ida's parlor in Nicetown, Campanella explained to Dixon, "I never worked out with them [the Phillies] in practice, nor has anyone asked me to." He had, however, been in touch with owner Gerry Nugent, who told him that "I was welcome to play with the Phillies if I was good enough and all that I needed was for a scout to recommend me to him or Manager [Hans] Lobert." Roy knew that was nonsense, but his enthusiasm never wavered. "I'd love the chance to see how I'd make out," he told Dixon. "If it ever happened that I was the first Negro to break in the big tent, I realize I'd be on the spot. But the wolves could howl and the fans and players could do whatever they wanted, but the only thing that would stop me would be that I just would not be good enough."

If ever an owner should have jumped at the chance to integrate, it was Gerry Nugent. With the pathetic Phillies on their way to their fifth straight last-place finish and teetering on the brink of financial ruin, signing a black player (particularly a hometown boy) might conceivably have saved his franchise. But like the rest of baseball's owners, Nugent had limited vision, held captive by his prejudices and fears (although he proudly informed the press that he had employed a "colored man and his wife" in his home for years). The National League eventually took over the debt-ridden Phillies a few months later and began shopping the team to interested buyers. Although minor league official Bill Veeck was interested in acquiring the franchise and stocking it with black players, the deal never materialized, and the Phillies would remain lily-white until well into the 1950s.

Most Negro League observers believed that Campanella, because of his unique mix of youth and experience, deserved to be on the short list of major league candidates. A few years earlier, Josh Gibson would have been the consensus pick, but he was now thirty and admitted he was having trouble pulling the ball this year. His growing problems with alcohol and a brain tumor would land him in a psychiatric ward within six months. A few reporters rallied behind Satchel Paige, although the colorful old pitcher didn't appear particularly interested in going anywhere. Paige made an unfortunate statement to the national wire services citing hotels, spring training, and his own high salary as barriers to integration. He did, however, tout "Speed" (!) Campanella as one of his seven Negro League selections for the majors.

The *Daily Worker* sports department had already decided on three can't-miss players: Campanella, his teammate Sammy T. Hughes, and pitcher Dave Barnhill of the New York Cubans. Now all that was needed was for some major league owner to give them a tryout. Nugent obviously wasn't their man, but William Benswanger seemed far more open-minded. "It might be a good thing for the game to add the Negro stars to the various big league teams," he announced in the days following the Landis statement. "I certainly am not against it."

When Benswanger arrived in New York in late July for a Pirates series with the Dodgers and Giants, Nat Low of the *Worker* rang up Benswanger and tried to get a sense of where he actually stood on the race issue. Low suggested Hughes and Barnhill as candidates for the Pirates. Benswanger did not respond immediately. Finally, he said, "I will be glad to have them try out with the Pirates."

The historic development hit the newspapers and national wire services on Sunday, July 26. At Yankee Stadium, where Barnhill's New York Cubans were appearing in an NNL promotion, black fans greeted the announcement with a "thundering roar of approval." But what, the players couldn't help but wonder, did a tryout offer *really* mean? To Campy and Hughes, the word *tryout* conjured up images of inexperienced teenage schoolboys and sandlotters getting a hurried look and an even quicker rejection.

Almost immediately, Benswanger began to lose his nerve. Supportive letters and telegrams poured into his office, but he was deeply concerned by some of the "scathing denunciations" that also crossed his desk. And as a good American capitalist, the communist connection frightened him. By Monday, Benswanger was already distancing himself from the *Daily Worker.* "So far as colored boys playing in the major and minor leagues are concerned, I reiterate that I think they should be allowed to play," he told a *Pittsburgh Sun-Telegraph* reporter, "but I certainly resent any Communist paper telling us how to proceed." He would now, he announced, work with the black *Pittsburgh Courier*, his own scouts, and white sportswriters on the selection of players and tryout dates.

Meanwhile, Campy found himself part of a national media frenzy. To Satchel Paige's bemusement, Fox Movietone News even showed up at Yankee Stadium on August 2 to get footage of the tryout trio for their newsreel audiences. "I've been playing baseball for sixteen years," said Satch, "but I've never seen so much fuss made over Negro teams in all my life." Fifteen photographers were also on hand, including one from the *Daily Worker* who snapped a probably posed photo of Campy reading the communist newspaper. Such a picture might have come back to haunt him during the blacklist hysteria of the 1950s, and Campanella in later years was careful to disavow the radical connection to the 1942 tryouts and even made the dubious claim that he "had no idea at the time that it was a Communist paper." However, he remained friendly enough with Lester Rodney and other *Worker* sportswriters during the McCarthy era to warrant a scolding from the rabid anticommunist periodical *Counterattack* in 1955.

As the days passed, Campanella grew increasingly pessimistic that the Pirates, or any other major league team, would give him a shot. "I don't believe there is a thing to it," Pirates manager Frankie Frisch told reporters. And conservative columnists such as the *Cleveland Plain Dealer*'s Gordon Cobbledick now warned of impending "social problems" if black ballplayers became major leaguers. What about the controversies sure to develop if Campanella was forced to stay at a black YMCA on the road or if a Southern pitcher threw a little too close to him? "The furor gets under Campanella's skin," wrote Cobbledick, "and he goes into a batting slump and Frisch benches him and the *Daily Worker* yells 'Discrimination!' and the first thing you know colored people and white people who formerly got along amicably get to disliking each other and there's hell to pay generally."

Several years later, Branch Rickey would adroitly handle most of these so-called obstacles. Benswanger, however, was no Rickey. His decision to integrate had been spontaneous, with no advance preparation or long-term plan in place. As August wore on, he said nothing further to the press and began to dodge the barrage of phone calls from the *Courier*'s Wendell Smith and the *Daily Worker*'s Lester Rodney badgering him about a tryout date. The persistent Rodney would eventually get a return call from Benswanger's secretary informing him that the tryout was off. "I called and I insisted on speaking to him," Rodney recalled. "He was very curt. . . . He said, 'I'm sorry. I have nothing to say. . . . I can't go ahead with this.' "

What changed Benswanger's mind? Rodney offered the plausible explanation that Benswanger came under enormous pressure from his fellow owners and Landis. Benswanger would later claim that he was swayed by Cum Posey, the NNL's main mover and shaker, who like other black owners was profiting during the war.

The hopes of Campanella and millions of African-Americans had been raised and then cruelly crushed again. In desperation, Roy wrote to Benswanger, who eventually sent back a discouraging letter explaining how he would have to start in the minor leagues and might never make the majors anyway. Campy informed the Pirates owner that he was more than willing to start at the bottom, but Roy knew it was futile. Benswanger's brief flirtation with integration was over.

The failed 1942 tryout bitterly disillusioned Campanella, although he could take some consolation that the mainstream-media publicity had raised his profile still higher. Besides the Pirates and the Phillies, the Boston Red Sox reportedly contacted him, and the Brooklyn Dodgers were also aware of his talents. "Plenty of Negro players are ready for the big leagues," admitted Dodger official Larry MacPhail when apprised of Campanella and other black stars. "In five minutes I could pick half a dozen men who could fit into major league teams." Then why in hell, Roy wondered, didn't they sign them up? War or no war, the big leagues weren't going to budge. It had been silly for him to think otherwise, and he vowed that he would not allow himself to be duped so easily in the future.

BACK WITH the Elites, Campanella discovered that his sudden national celebrity came with some financial benefits. The Pirates may not have been interested, but the three tryout players each had a $200 offer on the table from the Cleveland Baseball Federation to participate in a fund-raiser at Municipal Stadium on Sunday, August 9. No Negro Leaguer, lucky to be earning between $150 and $300 monthly, was going to turn down such a proposal, although the three men dutifully checked with their owners. The Cubans' Alex Pompez gave Dave Barnhill his blessing, and Hughes and Roy expected Tom Wilson to do the same. But Wilson did not take kindly to Hughes's and Campanella's requests for time off, not with the Elites in a pennant race and scheduled to play three games with the Grays in Baltimore that weekend. Be in uniform tonight, he warned them, or expect a big fat fine when you get back.

Campy and Hughes, well aware of the NNL's usual lax discipline, decided Old Tom was just bluffing. Three hours before the Elites squared off with the Grays on Friday, the pair left their hotel to board a train for Ohio. On Sunday, all three tryout players joined the NAL's Cincinnati Buckeyes, who easily crushed a group of white sandlotters before thirteen thousand fans. The umpire halted the 12–0 blowout after six innings, but Campy still had time to collect a couple of hits and pose for wire service photos, which circulated nationally the following week. Overall, it had been a cushy weekend and probably the easiest $200 he had ever made.

Back in Baltimore, Wilson and Vernon Green were seething. Not only had Campanella and Hughes defied them, but the Grays, after beating the Elites on Friday, had pulled into first place. And Wilson, as NNL president, at least vaguely recognized that star players deserting league teams to play exhibition games did not exactly enhance the reputation of black baseball. When the two runaway Elites returned a few days later, Wilson hit them with both barrels: a suspension, $250 fine, and removal from the upcoming East-West Game that Sunday. "They deserve no sympathy," remarked Cum Posey, who blamed the whole affair on the "premature publicity" that made the players get a little too big for their britches.

Campy was shocked that Old Tom, usually a hands-off owner, had taken such a drastic stance. Now Wilson was messing with his money, perhaps the one thing capable of transforming the amiable, happy-go-lucky catcher into a raging rebel. Wilson and his goddamned league, Roy vowed, wouldn't get a cent of that fine, unless, of course, they decided to play hardball and garnish his bimonthly wages. Such extreme measures appeared unlikely in a league famous for imposing punishments and just as quickly abandoning them, particularly when they involved marquee players. Although Roy was kept off the NNL's East-West team (the press reported that Josh Gibson suddenly passed him in the last week of "voting"), the suspension from league games didn't last long and he was back in the Elites lineup by August 21. And the $250 fine might also vanish once Wilson had a chance to simmer down and reassess Campy's value to the team.

But Roy was not in the mood to bide his time. Just a few weeks ago, he had been *that close* to joining a major league club, only to be told, in essence, that it was all a mistake. Such an emotional roller-coaster ride inevitably bred resentment toward the old life he thought he had escaped. He had once been overjoyed just to get the opportunity to play in the "colored leagues," but now he saw them for what they really were: a dead end.

Guillermo Ferrera, an official with the Monterrey club of the Mexican League, was keenly aware of Señor Campanella's problems and his talent. That August, his bosses authorized him to get in touch with Campanella, offer him $100 weekly plus expenses, and get him across the border pronto. Contrary to Roy's account in his autobiography, the Mexican proposition was not completely unexpected. Every Negro Leaguer was aware of the Mexican promoters who skulked around the hotels and parks of late, waving wads of cash and making big promises. The Mexican League had already tried several months earlier to sign Roy, Lenny Pearson, and Monte Irvin, although only Irvin was enticed.

Ferrera found Campy more receptive this time around. Not only was the salary better than what he could make in the States, but he also felt no loyalty to Tom Wilson. Besides, no one knew whether the war might force a shutdown of the Negro Leagues and all American professional baseball next year. As for any guilt for leaving his team in the midst of a pennant race, what difference did it make if the Elites finished first or second? Another watch from Wilson, perhaps?

On Sunday, August 23, Campy singled as a pinch hitter in the second game of a doubleheader in Baltimore against the New York Cubans. Following the game, he returned to Philadelphia, said good-bye to Bernice and the kids, then headed to New York to catch a flight for San Antonio. After five years, hundreds of games, and thousands of sweaty miles, he had closed the book on the Negro Leagues, he hoped for good.

7

MEXICO

WHEN CAMPY ARRIVED IN SAN ANTONIO, he found Ferrera and another man waiting for him in a battered, old jalopy, prepared to drive the roughly three hundred miles across the border to Monterrey. The two Mexicans were bemused by how little the stocky, young *americano* had packed in his duffel bag, but Roy wanted to be able to make a quick getaway if things didn't work out.

About two hours into the drive, the trio pulled in to a seedy roadside establishment outside Cotulla, "one of the crummiest little towns in Texas," according to Lyndon Johnson, who taught there briefly in the late 1920s. Something about Roy's accent and skin color raised the suspicions of their white waitress, who finally demanded to know whether he was Mexican or American. Informed that Roy was "no Mexican," she erupted as if the victim of a cruel practical joke. "If he's an American, he sure ain't no white man. Don't you know we've got laws against niggers eating in a place reserved for whites?"

As a veteran Negro Leaguer, Campanella was no stranger to such indignities, although he would later often choose to downplay or completely eliminate them from his life script. But the Cotulla incident disturbed him enough to include it seventeen years later in his generally Pollyannaish autobiography.

Mexico, he would soon discover, was nothing like Texas. America's neurotic obsession with skin color had not infected its southern neighbor, whose inhabitants were predominantly mestizos of both European and Native American descent. For the first time in his life, Campy could deactivate the internal radar that every African-American relied upon to determine which clubs, restaurants, and theaters were safe to patronize. Even better, the Mexican League covered all living expenses, including maids and even tutors for the players' families.

Although each of the six league clubs was privately owned, the man behind the Mexican baseball miracle was thirty-five-year-old Jorge Pasquel. Pasquel, later described by Monte Irvin as the "George Steinbrenner of Mexico," had the world by the tail: a lucrative customs brokerage business worth millions, powerful political connections, and a highly attuned sense of Mexican nationalism. A man of seemingly limitless ambition, he would spend most of the next five years unsuccessfully trying to raise the Mexican League to the plateau of the American majors. As the first step of his master plan, Pasquel had aggressively been recruiting top Negro Leaguers and then assigning them to teams based on need.

The Monterrey Industrials, desperate for catching and involved in a close pennant race with Torreón, had dibs on Campanella. Located in the foothills of the Sierra Madre Oriental mountains, Roy's new home was less than two hundred miles from the Texas border and retained a strong American influence, so much so that Mexicans considered the city *muy americanizado* ("much Americanized"). Still, playing in Mexico required adjustments that some Americans were not willing to make, particularly the white major leaguers who came over later. But for Campy and most blacks, the Liga Mexicana de Béisbol was nothing short of a godsend, offering decent wages, a manageable ninety-game schedule played only on Thursdays, Saturdays, and Sunday mornings before the afternoon bullfights, and a wildly enthusiastic fan base. "When the fans whistle, they're peeved," explained Harry Donovan, a white minor league umpire recruited by Pasquel. "If they're overjoyed because of some particular play, they'll throw money on the field . . . or even come out of the stands and carry him to the dugout." Some of the more rowdy sort even tried to unnerve the visiting team by tossing a steady stream of firecrackers from the bleachers.

Mexico, Campanella sensed after a few days, would work out just fine, as long as he performed at his usual level. It would not be easy in Monterrey, where the temperatures regularly reached the high nineties and fans willingly paid extra for a seat in the shade. "He'd lose fifteen or sixteen pounds in a game," recalled Pee Wee Butts, who joined his friend in Monterrey in 1943. "But I'll tell you where he would pick it up again—at the table. They had steaks that big—eighteen inches—and he'd eat it all."

The high altitudes, particularly in Mexico City, also gave him fits. "Why, after you hit a double down there, they almost have to call time out so you can get your breath back," Campy later told a reporter. "The air is too thin." It was just as frustrating to watch his pitchers struggle to get their curveballs to break instead of spin in the low-air-pressure environment. Park conditions, except for Pasquel's Delta Park in Mexico City, were remarkably shoddy, with no dressing rooms or showers at most venues. Most notorious was Tampico, which not only lacked clubhouse accommodations but also had train tracks running in the outfield. "Every afternoon the train came through the right-field gate," said Roy, "and exited through a gate in left field, with the game being held up during the run."

Pasquel and the Mexican fans did not want to hear complaints about playing conditions. The imports from America were being paid big bucks and were expected to produce. For the most part, they did, paced by Veracruz's Monte Irvin, who led the league in batting average (.397) and homers (20) in only 63 games. Campy's brief introduction to Mexican baseball was solid but unspectacular. In twenty games for Monterrey, he hit .296 (slightly above the overall league average of .288) with a pair of homers, 15 RBIs, and an OBP (on-base percentage) of .367. His Industrials, meanwhile, finished the season in second place, a game and a half behind Torreón.

Aside from an early tiff with Monterrey's owner over delayed payment on a performance bonus, Campanella had enjoyed his stay in Mexico. He had fun hanging out with apartmentmates Irvin and Quincy Trouppe when he was in Mexico City and even prepared spaghetti for them, at least until Trouppe began terrorizing Monterrey pitching. "Quincy, don't expect me to cook any spaghetti when I come to Mexico City," quipped Campy. "It must have give[n] you extra power."

Financially, Pasquel had taken care of Roy just as he promised. He quickly discovered just how free the Mexican magnate could be with his pesos. Late in the season, Irvin's Veracruz Blues trailed the Industrials by a run in the ninth inning with two outs and one runner on. "Jorge called me over," Irvin recalled, "and *demanded* I hit a home run." Campy knew what Pasquel wanted, and whatever Pasquel wanted, he usually got. But this was Mexico, not Puerto Rico, and Campy wasn't about to give out any freebies this time. Quickly falling behind two strikes, Irvin looked for a strikeout fastball on the next pitch, guessed right, and crushed a game-winning homer. A beaming Pasquel pressed $500 into Irvin's hand when he reached home plate while Campy, "raving and ranting and jumping up and down," watched the proceedings in disbelief. "Gee whiz, Monte," said a still fuming Campy after the game, "you got to be the luckiest SOB." But Irvin finally managed to calm his friend down. Pasquel, he told Campy, had told Irvin to split the $500 with Roy "for calling the right pitch!"

Campanella was happy enough with Pasquel to return in 1943 for a second season. This year, Bernice and the kids would accompany him, perhaps in a last-ditch attempt to save the marriage. Ten other American blacks would also be in Mexico, although Negro League owners tried to stop the defections. Effa Manley reported Newark's Willie Wells and Ray Dandridge to Selective Service officials, only to learn that both were deferred and under no obligation to "stay in essential industry" in America. In Pittsburgh, Homestead official Rufus "Sonnyman" Jackson took a more direct approach after discovering a representative from the Liga Mexicana de Béisbol at Forbes Field trolling for players. He grabbed the unfortunate Mexican, ejected him from the park, and then subjected him to a severe "cussing out."

Back in Baltimore, Tom Wilson merely watched as three of his stars—Campanella, Butts, and Bill Wright—headed south of the border. With the feds now tightening access to gasoline and restricting bus use, Wilson had no desire to get involved in a bidding war with Mexico. He did, however, listen to offers for the Three Amigos from other owners willing to gamble on their eventual return to the States. The Philadelphia Stars' Ed Bolden wanted Campanella, the hometown kid he had missed out on six years earlier. Eventually, a deal was reached sending Roy to Philadelphia, although the specifics were never released to the press.

The Stars notified Roy of the trade, but he had no intention of going anywhere. "This is a very fine country," he informed Art Carter in a handwritten May letter. Already, Campy was not shy about putting his best foot forward with sportswriters. He casually mentioned to Carter in July that he was "leading the league in home runs with 9," and even included an article about the All-Star Game. "You can print it if you want to," wrote Roy, "but please send me a clipping of it." But beneath the boasts and seeming contentment lay subtle traces of homesickness. "I hear that the Elites aren't doing so good," opened one of his letters to Carter. "I wish I was there to help them."

Ultimately, Roy was better off in Mexico, at least from the perspective of his long-term development as a ballplayer. With the day-to-day level of competition far more consistent than in the NNL, coasting was not an option. There were just too many good ballplayers in Mexico, and not only from the United States. Monterrey's best pitcher that season was the Venezuelan Vidal Lopez, who led the league in ERA with a 2.08 mark and also hit .304 as an outfielder. League teams were also strengthened by an abundance of Cuban talent, both black and white. Former major leaguer Mike Guerra caught for Puebla, while the versatile Martin Dihigo, veteran of many a Negro League campaign, managed, pitched, and played the field for Torreón. The homegrown Mexican players, no patsies either, included ex–Washington Senator Chile Gomez and future American League batting champ Bobby Avila.

Most observers felt that Pasquel's league was at least equivalent to the high minors by 1943, although the light weekly schedule allowing managers to use their number one starting pitchers more frequently might skew the comparison somewhat. Still, Mexican League statistics provide at least a crude barometer of how Roy and other blacks might have performed in a more organized setting. As in 1942, NNL expatriates took home most of the major hitting prizes. The triple crown went to Campy's old friend Bill Wright, whose 13 homers, 70 RBIs, and sizzling .366 average led the circuit. But Roy also enjoyed a fine year with Monterrey, which narrowly beat out Torreón for the Mexican League title. He appeared in all ninety games, showing good power with 12 of his team's 27 homers (the entire league hit only 176), 24 doubles (fifth best in the league), 54 RBIs, and a .289 average (league average .271). For a young hitter, he also demonstrated a surprising command of the strike zone, fanning only 28 times in 342 at bats while collecting 46 walks.

Had a white catcher (or a black one light enough to pass) with the added bonus of Roy's deferred draft status put up similar numbers, he would have been on the fast track to the major leagues. Campy only had to look to the other Mexican Leaguers offered deals by war-depleted teams. Guerra, a .313 hitter that season with Puebla, went straight to Washington in 1944, where he hit .281 in 210 at bats. The Senators also went after three of Roy's teammates, Daniel Rios, Alberto Leal, and Epitacio Torres, all of whom eventually decided to stay with Monterrey. And Mexico City's Manuel Salvatierra, the so-called Mexican Babe Ruth whose 12 homers matched Roy's 1943 total, got picked up by the Los Angeles Angels of the Pacific Coast League.

Campanella knew he was as good, if not better, than most of the white Cuban and Mexican players getting look-sees. More than ever, he also knew that he could play major league baseball. "I knew I could make it after I played in Mexico," he would later say. But fixating too long on that realization brought only frustration and bitterness. Nothing had changed concerning baseball's color line since he had left the States a year earlier. Sure, Landis had again publicly stated that no rule barred black players from the major leagues. But that statement, Roy already knew, added up to exactly nothing.

What Roy didn't realize was that a watershed event had occurred in the intervening months. Following the departure of Larry MacPhail, the Brooklyn Dodgers hired Branch Rickey as their president and general manager. The sixty-one-year-old Rickey was a baseball lifer, first as a player, then a manager, and finally a front-office fixture with the St. Louis Cardinals. But Rickey, unlike most of his colleagues, was not wed to the tried-and-true ways of the past. Twenty years earlier, he recognized that his small-market Cardinals could never hope to compete with wealthier franchises for players on the open market. A better solution, he recognized, was for the Cardinals to develop and control their own talent by purchasing minor league clubs and creating a chain from the lowest classification to the highest. Thanks to Rickey's advocacy of what became known as the farm system, the Cardinals became one of the National League's most successful franchises.

Rickey was a visionary but he was also a paradox. His devout Methodism, teetotalism, and well-publicized refusal to attend games on Sunday coexisted alongside a ruthless determination to maximize his profits by paying his players as little as possible. As a coach at Ohio Wesleyan in the early 1900s, he was remarkably empathetic toward one of his black players facing discrimination but had no qualms about refusing to sign Bob Berman a few years later when he discovered the Bronx schoolboy was Jewish. An exceptionally intelligent and well-read man, he also tended to pontificate, and his fondness for multisyllable words did not endear him to the more earthy band of writers who covered his teams.

Foibles aside, Rickey knew how to run a baseball team, and the Dodgers were delighted to get him once he wore out his welcome in St. Louis. After arriving in Brooklyn, he immediately set out to reconfigure the franchise for long-term success. Scouting efforts, he decided, needed to be dramatically expanded, not just domestically but throughout Latin America. "We are going to beat the bushes, and we will take whatever comes out," said Rickey. "And that might include a Negro player or two." The team's board of directors signed off on Rickey's secret plan, and scouts were soon dispatched around the world, including Mexico.

Tom Greenwade, famous for later signing Mickey Mantle, was the Dodgers' man in Mexico in the spring of 1943. His major objective, at least as outlined by Rickey in a confidential April 29 memo, was to locate and sign "good Mexican players," presumably white, for their minor league clubs. But Greenwade, probably with Rickey's encouragement, also began filing reports on the Mexican League's imports from America and Cuba. Greenwade even worked out a special code to maintain the secrecy of his cloak-and-dagger activities. "If the first word of his message started with a letter below *M* in the cable, he was reporting on a player of Latin extraction," sportswriter Tom Meany later recalled. "If it started with a letter above *M* in the alphabet, then 'Negro.' "

One Negro in particular intrigued Greenwade: Mexico City's twenty-eight-year-old Cuban shortstop, Silvio García. The former Negro Leaguer had already impressed Brooklyn manager Leo Durocher during the Dodgers' training trip to Havana a year earlier and was now coming off an outstanding Mexican League campaign. But talent alone, Rickey knew, would not be enough for any black man entering white Organized Baseball. He ordered a complete background check on García, which turned up fairly clean. "Informants state they have never seen him taking strong liquors or making use of drugs," an April 12, 1943, report noted, "although he likes women (but apparently has no mistress)."

Despite passing the Rickey morals test, García never signed with Brooklyn, but what precisely quashed the deal remains unclear. One story claims that the Dodgers pulled the plug once they asked García how he would handle a slap from a white player ("I kill him," he supposedly replied). Greenwade would later offer the explanation that García just wasn't good enough and couldn't pull the ball.

Campanella was probably unaware of Greenwade's stealth mission to Mexico in 1943. Mexican League games regularly drew five thousand to ten thousand fans, and the presence of a single American scribbling notes in the stands would not have attracted much attention, especially when Clark Griffith's Washington Senators were always sniffing for Latin players light enough to pass in America. Years later, García's Mexico City teammate Quincy Trouppe would assert that Greenwade set up meetings with several American black players that year, perhaps to camouflage his real interest in García. But if Trouppe's version is accurate, the story would almost certainly have been leaked by one of the players to the black press or to Campy himself. And Campy, always happy to stretch a story or two for the benefit of his listeners, never once claimed to be scouted during his two seasons in Mexico.

After Campanella became a superstar in the major leagues, various stories surfaced that Greenwade had scouted and recommended Roy to the Dodgers as early as 1943. If he did, the scouting report never found its way to Rickey, who later denied ever hearing of Campy until at least 1945. In any event, Rickey was not quite ready to start signing American black players. His interest in García and references to "good Mexican boys" suggest that he believed Latin players might be a safer bet to break down the color line. For now, he decided to sit tight and keep his mouth shut about any future plans.

FOLLOWING THE close of the Mexican League season, Roy put out his usual feelers for a winter baseball gig. This year, Puerto Rico was out, as league officials decided they would make do without any imports. Instead, he accepted an offer from Monterrey manager Lazaro Salazar to play for the Marianao team in the highly competitive Cuban winter league. The four-team circuit not only featured the island's best black players but also natives such as the Philadelphia A's Bobby Estalella, a "light mulatto" who passed as white in the States.

Marianao, mostly composed of Mexicans, Cubans, and Americans, fared miserably that winter, winning only thirteen of forty-eight games. Although Roy did not quite match his Monterrey performance, he did lead his new club with 27 RBIs while coping with the cavernous dimensions of Havana's La Tropical Stadium, the site of all league games. An even bigger adjustment would involve acclimating himself to his first white American teammates since adolescence. Thanks to an agreement allowing minor leaguers to play winter ball in Cuba, four appeared with Marianao that season: Eddie Popowski, then a Red Sox farmhand and later a major league coach; Ora Burnett, an infielder in the Cardinals' chain; Leon Treadway, a .300 hitter as a Giants rookie in 1944; and pitcher Ralph McCabe, who would later have the tiniest sip of major league coffee with the Indians in 1946. Treadway and Burnett were both Southerners, and one wonders how they responded to an integrated setting during those months. But Roy never said anything about his unique interracial experience in Cuba, and whether the Dodgers were even aware of it two years later remains uncertain.

Though Campanella had no way of knowing it, Cuba was an important preparation for the future. Historians have often cited the significance of Jackie Robinson's background in interracial college football, which gave him a leg up on other potential color-line candidates. But few, if any, are aware that Campy actually played alongside white Southerners as early as 1943. Unlike some Negro Leaguers who could not adjust to an integrated environment, Roy showed no discomfort, outperforming all four of his white Marianao teammates. White, black, Mexican, Cuban—Roy usually managed to win most of the guys over, thanks to the sheer élan of his personality and the wise counsel of Biz Mackey years earlier. Mackey, recalled Monte Irvin, "taught Campy how to get along. How to get along with people, how to get along with other ballplayers. . . . Don't get involved in the politics. Just go out and play. Play and then everything else will take care of itself." It was a lesson that Campy never forgot, although not everyone would be comfortable with its implications.

• • •

PASQUEL WAS eager for Campanella to return to Mexico in 1944. If the league was to maintain its caliber of play, he knew he had to attract and retain the best talent available. He had only recently landed his first big-name white American player, the soon-to-be-forty-eight-year-old Rogers Hornsby, who signed a $10,000 contract to manage the Veracruz Blues. Although Pasquel's infamous full-scale raid on the majors was still two years away, the Hornsby deal hinted that the Mexican promoter might go after bigger fish in the future.

There appeared to be no compelling reason for Campy not to re-up with Monterrey for a third season. Pasquel had been financially square with him from day one and even covered Roy's flight home to Philadelphia. The leisurely March-to-October ninety-game schedule exacted less punishment on his body while allowing him to collect two extra months of salary. His command of Spanish had also steadily improved, and he was able to take full advantage of Mexico's more tolerant society.

But Roy was still a gringo in a foreign country. He was more than willing to come home, at least if the offer was sweet enough. And for the first time, Negro League owners were in a position to match, if not better, Mexican salaries after a banner year of record-setting attendance and grosses. "Our league seems to be in fine shape," NAL president J. B. Martin happily confided to Effa Manley in February 1944. "They all made more money this last year than they ever made in the history of baseball."

The Elite Giants had also done well at the box office but had failed even to play .500 baseball in 1943. Getting Campanella back, Tom Wilson decided, might give his club a much needed boost. Overtures were made, the hatchet was buried, and Wilson and Roy made plans to meet up at an owners' meeting at the Hotel Theresa in New York in early March. In the meantime, the secret trade to the Stars was voided, clearing the path for Campy's return to the Elites.

Campanella had once been in awe of his boss, so much so that he was not prepared to haggle a great deal over his salary. But this wasn't the Depression anymore, and the Elites weren't going to get him for less than the $3,000 he was pulling down in Monterrey. Wilson, aware of the talent shortage due to the draft and Mexico, readily agreed to Roy's demands and even waived the $250 fine still hanging over his head. What Wilson probably didn't know is that the Selective Service had actually denied Campy permission to play outside the United States this year, at least if a brief notation in an unpublished preliminary outline for *It's Good to Be Alive* is accurate.

A *Pittsburgh Courier* reporter covering the league meeting caught a startling glimpse of Roy in the lobby of the Theresa that week. "Campanella," wrote the admiring journalist, "showed up dressed to kill and resembling one of the Mills Bros. now that he has grown a mustache." The transformation from chubby Nicetown nobody to a confident, flashy Harlem man-about-town was complete. He now had money, fame, and a taste for the finer things in life that would only grow in the future.

Bernice, perhaps an unwelcome reminder of his more humble past, no longer fit into the picture. The months spent together in Mexico had failed to strengthen their always wobbly relationship, and the pair would finally separate for good later that year. It was hardly a surprising outcome for a teenage marriage, particularly one strained by two small children and a husband constantly away from home. But Bernice always had a special place in her heart for her first love. She never remarried and kept the name Campanella for the rest of her life. "I think she loved him," said her granddaughter Gale Muhammad, "until she died."

THE ELITES had not changed much in the two years Roy had been away. Felton Snow was still running the club, and other familiar faces such as Byrd, Scales, Kimbro, and Glover were there to welcome Campy back to the fold. A young shortstop turned pitcher from New Jersey named Joe Black was also with the team, at least when he could get weekend passes in between his army duties in New York. Roy soon took a fatherly interest in the former Morgan State college student he dubbed Junior, schooling him on the league's hitters and the pitfalls facing rookies, including women. "Campy was one of the few guys who would take the time and trouble to help you," Black recalled. "He was nicer than most of the guys in a rough league. If you tried to get them to show you how to do something, they'd say it took them six years to learn and you can do the same."

Roy would also cross paths in 1944 with another hard-throwing rookie pitcher from New Jersey: his future roommate and close friend Don Newcombe. The seventeen-year-old Newcombe had dropped out of high school a few years earlier, took a stab at military service until he was discovered to be underage, then did some truck driving while playing semipro ball around his home in Elizabeth. Over the winter, a friend had put him in touch with the Manleys, who took one glance at his husky six-foot-four-inch, two-hundred-pound frame and invited him to spring training.

Newcombe made the team but soon discovered a vast difference between semiprofessional and Negro League baseball. Facing the Elites that season, he was instructed by his manager Mule Suttles to brush back Campy. "Well, I'm only seventeen," he later recalled, "and I don't know anything." In his various retellings of what followed, Newcombe claimed he either "didn't get it in enough" or he threw "the first pitch right over his head." The outcome, however, was the same, as Campy subsequently blasted a Newcombe offering into the nether regions of Ruppert Stadium.

Newcombe's tale of his first encounter with Roy remains unverified. But at least one of their matchups that season is documented, an August 22 night game in Harrisburg. The box score provides an accurate snapshot of the teenage Newk's raw talent: a kid with a golden arm (8 strikeouts) who also hadn't the foggiest notion of where the ball was going (8 walks, 1 wild pitch). The Elites also battered Newk for 7 runs on 12 hits, including a double by Campy, batting cleanup that night.

Newcombe, like most of the other NNL pitchers, was no puzzle to Roy, who slammed twenty-three hits in his first fifty-four at bats back with the Elites. But Snow, as much as he loved Campy's booming bat in the lineup, wasn't sure how to keep it there with defensive wizard Eggie Clarke still on the roster. He decided Campanella would catch most of the time but would go to the outfield on days when Clarke was behind the plate. Snow had already tried the move two years earlier, and likely rolled back at least a few of the thousands of miles on Roy's baseball odometer. While no Joe DiMaggio, Campy acquitted himself reasonably well during his outfield stints over the next two seasons. "He was really fast," Joe Black recalled. "He saved a no-hitter for me one night with four great catches in left field."

As long as Roy was playing every day, he was happy. Still, he would have much preferred to be a full-time catcher, even if some believed he was not fit to wear the mask of his mentor Mackey. Years later, sportswriter Joe Bostic claimed that Snow was never entirely sold on Campy's catching ability. The Negro League Campanella, Bostic wrote, "was always something less than a tactical giant in those days or so Felton Snow always contended."

Complete data on passed balls, errors, stolen bases allowed, and staff ERA that might shed a more accurate light on Roy's NNL catching skills will never be available. But clearly, his slugging and not his defense was earning him most of the ink at this stage of his career. Veteran sportswriter Dan Burley, for instance, ignored Campy entirely in his discussion that year of black baseball's best defensive catchers, naming Clarke and six others. Nor did he mention Josh Gibson. "I don't put Josh Gibson in this class," explained Burley, "because Jolting Josh is in reality a power hitter and not the workmanlike catcher of the type as are Clark[e], Haywood, Radcliffe and Duncan."

Like his hero, Campanella was increasingly perceived, fairly or unfairly, as a hitter first and a catcher second. And as long as Gibson continued to live up to his reputation as the best hitter in baseball, Roy was going to come up the loser in any head-to-head competition. When both were selected to the East-West Game that August, Gibson caught all nine innings for the NNL's team while Campy was dispensed to third base. "I felt pretty funny on third but I only had one chance," he later recalled. "Artie Wilson hit a ball to me and I threw him out at first. . . . I knew Artie would hit it to me. He always hits 'em down that way."

Gibson collected his usual two hits that afternoon, including a mammoth 440-foot double that struck one of Comiskey Park's amplifiers in center field. But it had become increasingly obvious in recent months that something was seriously wrong with the great Homestead catcher. During spring training, his behavior had become so erratic that the Grays unsuccessfully tried to get him to return to Pittsburgh for treatment. Instead, he hit the bottle with a vengeance, despite repeated warnings about "breaking training" (the euphemism used by the press to describe heavy drinkers). After a May incident in Baltimore where he had to be "removed from Bugle Field" and a subsequent arrest for disorderly conduct, Gibson finally wound up in Gallinger Hospital in Washington for observation. Although some players were relieved that Josh was receiving treatment, Negro League insiders wondered "if it is true that Josh has lost his mind."

Miraculously, Gibson was again terrorizing league pitchers within a few weeks. But the Grays now had a Jekyll and Hyde and were no longer certain which Josh was going to show up each night. By the end of the 1944 season, Campanella appeared to be the better bet behind the plate. "This year I rate the young Philadelphia receiver over Gibson," wrote Rollo Wilson, "because his game has advanced while Josh's has declined." Even Gibson's boss, Cum Posey, compiling his annual blackball dream team, agreed: "We placed Campanella over Gibson because Gibson did not stay in shape to play regular, and even with Gibson in perfect shape, it is a close race between him and Campanella."

Gibson's remaining years in baseball would be similarly marred by alternating periods of productive play and growing instability. In 1945, he was hospitalized at least twice, including a stint in Puerto Rico after being found "hiding in the mountains without clothes." At one point Posey desperately tried to interest the Elites in a Gibson-for-Campanella deal, but Tom Wilson would have none of it. Roy, he knew, was almost ten years younger, earned a fraction of Gibson's $1,000-per-month salary, and was in the lineup every day, rain or shine. The Grays had no choice but to hold on to the fading Gibson, who put up good power numbers in 1946 before finally succumbing to a stroke in 1947 at the age of thirty-five.

Roy never forgot the tragedy of Josh Gibson, a brilliant ballplayer too old and too sick to get a shot in the majors once the color line fell. He was only too aware of how the trajectory of his own life might dramatically have been altered had he been born even four or five years earlier. When he reached the majors, Campy did whatever he could to keep Gibson's memory alive. He would not only spellbind sportswriters with Paul Bunyanesque tales of Josh's mighty hitting exploits but also gave thousands of white readers their first introduction to Gibson in a 1954 *Sport* feature entitled "The Best Catcher I Ever Saw." Eighteen years later, Roy did even more to ensure the preservation of Josh's baseball legacy, serving as a member of the nine-man special committee that unanimously elected Gibson to the Baseball Hall of Fame in 1972. "Everything I could do," he would always say, "Josh could do better."

DESPITE GIBSON'S ongoing difficulties, the Grays as usual captured both halves of the NNL race. Some Baltimore fans, tired of being also-rans, began to call for Felton Snow's head on a platter, but the Elites brass was not interested. "Snow did the best he could with the material at hand," explained Vernon Green, "and we can see no reason to change managers."

Green and Tom Wilson also had no complaints about Campanella, whose $3,000 salary turned out to be a bargain. Not only did he carry the team's offense throughout most of the season, but his power displays electrified fans. Larry Luongo, then a high school junior, never forgot seeing Campy in action that summer in an exhibition game in Camden, New Jersey. As workers from a nearby four-story wool factory casually watched the proceedings from a window, they suddenly noticed a tremendous line-drive homer off Campy's bat screaming toward them. Instinctively, the men ducked, just before the ball smashed through the window. Luongo later became a Campanella fan, puzzling some of his less tolerant acquaintances. "I took a big ribbing," he recalled, "because of Campanella's color and his Italian name and my having an Italian name."

Campy's slugging would also turn the heads of Mickey Owen and Whit Wyatt of the Brooklyn Dodgers, who decided to go see a Negro League game one June evening while in town for a Phillies series. After taking their seats in the rickety stands of old Parkside Field, the two men watched Baltimore's catcher slam five straight hits, including a double and an inside-the-park grand slam. The brilliant performance was perhaps motivated by Campy's desire to show the big leaguers what they were missing. He knew damn well that he could outhit Owen, who homered only 14 times in 13 major league seasons and would only manage a .256 average during his brief stay in Mexico in 1946.

Rollo Wilson, covering the game for the *Philadelphia Tribune*, began to think more about which NNL players were the best candidates to jump to the Big Show, should the color bars ever be lowered. Veterans such as Gibson and Buck Leonard, he decided, were too old to merit serious consideration, and talented rookies such as Philadelphia's young Panamanian shortstop, Frank Austin, definitely "needed seasoning." But Campanella, Wilson insisted, was a "sure-fire" big leaguer, ready now, if only the major leagues would wake up.

8

MR. RICKEY

ORGANIZED BASEBALL OFFICIALS had not been asleep during the war. Despite an alarming player shortage by 1945, they had found new and creative ways to avoid signing Negro Leaguers. Beardless teenagers, washed-up old-timers, light-skinned Latins, even one-limbed players—all were thrown into the breach to keep rosters fully stocked with warm bodies.

Campanella and other blackball stars could only shake their heads at the peculiar sights of sixteen-year-old Tommy Brown trying to play shortstop for the Dodgers or the amputee Pete Gray in the Browns outfield. For Roy, it was even more disturbing to see two of his Cuban winter league teammates, catcher Rogelio Valdes and infielder Luis Suarez, make the opening-day roster of the Washington Senators in 1944. Neither had much to recommend them except their skin color. Valdes, Campy's *backup*, had hit .149 in Marianao, only slightly bettered by the slick-fielding Suarez's .196 mark.

African-Americans could claim some small victories during the war: increased job opportunities, growing awareness of discrimination among whites, and more favorable depictions in popular culture. But baseball's color line had not budged. And the Jim Crow units in the nation's armed forces provided perhaps the most visible display of the continued second-class status of blacks, despite all the talk about democracy and freedom. As long as a highly public institution such as the military remained segregated, Organized Baseball officials could conceivably maintain the status quo indefinitely.

Roy was neither surprised nor appalled by baseball's reactionary attitudes. The Benswanger "tryout" fiasco of 1942 had killed whatever hopes he might secretly have harbored about getting in the major leagues, but he wasn't about to brood. Be grateful, Ida had told him long ago, for what you have. As a twenty-three-year-old black man, he was pretty damned fortunate. Playing the game he loved year-round, he was now a star earning $5,000 or more per year, at a time when the median income was only $2,379.

His personal life was also blossoming, thanks to a new lady in his life, Ruthe Willis. He had first met Ruthe as a teenager during one of his early baseball trips to New York. In his autobiography, he claimed that Ruthe was introduced to him by the Pittsburgh Crawfords' batboy during his first weekend with the Bacharachs, although numerous prior accounts place the original meeting at the 1939 World's Fair, perhaps during a basketball game. Campy, always conscious of his public image, may have thought it wise to roll back the date to '37, before his marriage.

Roy was immediately infatuated with the attractive young woman from Harlem. He was delighted to discover that Ruthe was also a tremendous athlete herself, good enough to play tennis with future Wimbledon champ Althea Gibson and to captain the Astor Girls softball and basketball teams. Ruthe found herself drawn to Campy's effervescent personality, which differed so much from her own. "Ruthe was not an outgoing person," recalled her longtime friend Barbara Brannen. "She had been that quiet type of person." Jackie Robinson's wife, Rachel, also remembered Ruthe as reserved: "Not very expressive but she could be fun. I enjoyed her."

The two teens grew closer during Campy's trips to New York, but the relationship apparently fell victim to his family situation in Philadelphia and his budding baseball career. In the meantime, Ruthe married in 1942, gave birth to a son, David, and by 1944 was separated. But Roy had never forgotten her. When he returned to the States, he decided to see if Ruthe was still at 301 West 152nd Street in Harlem. He called her up, they went bowling that night, and before long the two were inseparable.

Ruthe and David became Roy's new family, so much so that he began to present Ruthe as his wife at least three years before the two officially tied the knot. By then, Campy was on the verge of major league stardom and had already begun tidying up the details of his somewhat messy past personal life, particularly a teenage marriage he now considered embarrassing. Sportswriters during his Dodger years would be told that Roy married Ruthe back in 1939, and reference books such as the annual *Sporting News Baseball Register* dutifully printed the info as fact. Bernice, back in Nicetown raising Joyce and Beverly, would seldom be acknowledged publicly except for a brief mention in his autobiography. As part of the charade, David was usually introduced to friends and media as Roy's biological son, the truth not revealed until years later.

In 1945, Roy had no public image yet to craft and protect. All he knew was that he wanted to be with Ruthe and David, who soon began calling him Dad. "They had a wonderful love affair," recalled Brannen. "Things were going very well for them."

WHEN SPRING arrived, Roy headed down to Atlanta for preseason workouts. He was already in pretty good shape, as usual fresh from winter ball in Puerto Rico, where he had put up a .294 average for Santurce in a half season of play.

While Campanella and the Elites barnstormed through the South during the early weeks in April, surprising developments unfolded hundreds of miles away. For the first time, major league teams found themselves forced to offer tryouts to black players.

It all began in New York. With the discrimination issue now more visible, Governor Thomas Dewey signed the Ives-Quinn bill into law in March. The new legislation created the State Commission Against Discrimination, a permanent agency to address and remedy charges of prejudicial hiring and firing in New York. Although the statute would not take effect until July, black photographer Chick Solomon got to thinking as he snapped pictures of Dewey signing the bill. "The law is on our side now," Solomon remarked to friends. "Doesn't mean it's going to make Christians out of these bastards who run the major leagues, but at least there's nothing to prevent any qualified Negro player from walking into a major league training camp and demanding a tryout."

Solomon was aware that the Brooklyn Dodgers were training close to home at nearby Bear Mountain because of wartime travel restrictions. As a photographer who covered the weekly Negro League games in New York, he was also quite familiar with the best black ballplayers and believed Roy Campanella the ideal candidate. Unfortunately, Campy was nowhere near New York, and Solomon soon gave up on the scheme. Whether Campanella, after his crushing experiences with Benswanger and Nugent in 1942, would have gone along with the plan is debatable.

But a Harlem sportswriter, Joe Bostic, remained convinced of the merits of the tryout idea if he could just find a player available immediately and willing to stick his neck out. His search led him to two childhood pals from Mobile, Alabama: Dave "Showboat" Thomas of the New York Cubans and Terris McDuffie of the Newark Eagles. On Friday, April 6, Bostic left his home at 7:30 a.m., picked up the two players, and headed across the George Washington Bridge, hoping to make history.

The Dodger brass, none too pleased by Bostic's unannounced visit, tried desperately to make him go away. First, secretary Harold Parrott passed him on to Branch Rickey's elderly assistant Bob Finch, who turned on the waterworks as an apparent display of his heartfelt concern for the poor, unfortunate colored folks in America. When Finch's crocodile tears failed to move Bostic and his party, Rickey resigned himself to meeting with the aggressive young reporter later that afternoon. Privately, he supported Bostic's ultimate goal. But Rickey had already laid out careful plans to integrate *his way*, and he wasn't at all keen on a bunch of do-gooders and left-leaning activists pressuring him. The Mahatma, Bostic later recalled, "went berserk almost." He went off on a long diatribe, "punctuated with spicy epithets," about how force would never accomplish their goals. When Bostic refused to retreat, Rickey finally agreed to let the Negro Leaguers return for a workout the following day.

Thomas, an outstanding defensive first baseman, and McDuffie, a dependable starting pitcher, could probably have played in the major leagues, especially in 1945, when the talent level was so shallow. But neither had the youth (both were at least in their late thirties, if not older) or squeaky-clean background needed to pass Rickey's muster. Plus, the *Daily Worker* had gotten involved with the tryout, and Bostic's own paper, the *People's Voice*, had communist connections certain to send Rickey into another tizzy. Not surprisingly, the Dodgers politely rejected Thomas and McDuffie, and Bostic's grand plan came to naught.

But baseball's troublesome "Negro problem" was not quite so easy to stomp out this time. A few days after the Bear Mountain incident, Wendell Smith of the *Pittsburgh Courier* announced *another* tryout was in the works, this time in Boston, where the Red Sox and Braves had been threatened with the loss of their Sunday baseball licenses. Unlike Bostic, Smith tried to assemble a more youthful group of candidates, contacting Sam Jethroe of the Cleveland Buckeyes, Dave Hoskins of the Homestead Grays, and Jackie Robinson of the Kansas City Monarchs, who had recently been discharged from the service. Smith also wanted Campanella, and the *Courier* even tried to get permission from the notoriously difficult-to-reach Tom Wilson.

Whether Wilson permitted or denied Roy the opportunity to participate is unknown. Campanella never discussed the incident, and he may quickly have been dropped from consideration once the logistical difficulties of getting him to Boston became apparent. Eventually, Smith lined up Jethroe and Robinson, although the Grays, dubious of the whole scheme, refused to allow Hoskins to go, and he was replaced by Philadelphia's Marvin Williams. As promised, the trio worked out at Fenway Park on April 16, the result identical to Bostic's Bear Mountain escapade. The Red Sox offered no contracts, while the Braves weaseled out of the agreement altogether.

Had Bostic's and Smith's machinations accomplished anything? NAACP official Roy Wilkins believed they had. "We are now up to the tryout stage," he remarked, "which is farther ahead than we ever have been." And baseball's powers that be, now beginning to squirm, began to look for ways to delay the inevitable while placating segregation's critics. In March, twelve of the sixteen major league teams had smugly ignored Sam Lacy's proposal to appoint "a colored man to make a survey of Negro baseball" with the goal of "finding the best way of ironing out the many ramifications" of integration. But just eight days after the Boston tryout, nervous owners agreed to Lacy's plan, subsequently creating a four-person committee to study the race issue.

If the new committee offered some hope to black fans, the concurrent selection of Kentucky senator Albert "Happy" Chandler to replace the recently deceased Commissioner Landis generated little enthusiasm. Like most Southern Democrats at the time, Chandler was no champion of integration. The status quo and the old runaround, most blacks moaned, is all we can expect from this guy, particularly after Chandler claimed no knowledge of "discrimination against Negroes in the big leagues." But other post-election Chandler statements seemed to reflect a more open-minded attitude than his predecessor's. "I don't believe in barring Negroes from baseball," he told one reporter, "just because they are Negroes." Chandler's greatest contribution (despite his own magnified and unsubstantiated claims) over the next year would be his decision not to obstruct integration once it was in motion. Whether this warranted his election to the Hall of Fame in 1982 is something for baseball historians to debate.

Chandler owed his position to the continued goodwill of the owners, who preferred that he keep his big mouth shut. After speaking with the new commissioner, Wendell Smith was convinced he had been "'coached' by someone within the major league executive channels. . . . He is saying, it seems, the things he has been told to say." One only had to glance at some of the commissioner's public statements to recognize the heavy-handed influence of Yankee official Larry MacPhail, who had pushed hard for Chandler's election. "Negro baseball officials and players don't know exactly what they want at present," asserted Chandler in early May. "They may want to play in their own leagues and then meet the major league champion in a playoff game."

MacPhail, although selected to serve on Lacy's committee, wanted blacks to "play in their own leagues." He was intent on perpetuating and even strengthening the current segregated system, which allowed his Yankees to rake in thousands of dollars each year renting out the Stadium and several of their minor league parks to black teams. The "solution" to the current dilemma, MacPhail explained privately to Chandler, was for the major leagues to assist in the "establishment and operation of strong Negro leagues." Such a scheme would keep those annoying do-gooders off their backs, maintain the rental-income gravy train, and delay integration for a number of years. And MacPhail apparently had Rickey in his corner. "A decent, strong Negro

League," Rickey confided to an associate that spring, "may help to solve the problem, which is becoming more and more evident."

Rickey, unbeknownst to MacPhail, actually saw involvement in black baseball as another vital piece of his nearly completed integration puzzle. But Rickey knew that the established black leagues would not welcome his intrusion into their affairs, leaving former NNL honcho Gus Greenlee's newly organized United States League as the only viable option. Greenlee, now in the midst of an ultimately futile struggle with the NNL and NAL for parks, players, and prestige, jumped at the chance to do business with Rickey. An agreement was soon reached for the placement at Ebbets Field of a USL franchise, the Brooklyn Brown Dodgers.

Rickey's press conference that May announcing his connection with the USL baffled most observers. That foxy Mahatma *had to be* up to something. Was he just trying to keep the Joe Bostics of the world out of his hair? Or did the Brown Dodgers actually serve a larger purpose? Years later, Rickey would insist that his interest in the United States League had been nothing more than a subterfuge "to enable me to do open scouting, with experienced men, in the Negro field." As for the Brown Dodgers, they were nothing more than a "mythical team."

Rickey's simplistic version of events has passed into baseball lore despite ample evidence of the existence and operation of the Brown Dodgers and the USL. Undoubtedly, Rickey had more than just scouting on his mind when he teamed up with Greenlee and company. A black team at Ebbets Field, he hoped, might allow the Dodgers to start tapping into that lucrative rental-income stream so important to MacPhail's Yankees. With integration on the horizon, it would also provide a cost-efficient means for Rickey to develop and control his own black talent. Plus, the Brown Dodgers might desensitize Brooklynites to the eventual presence of black players at Ebbets Field.

The USL elicited little more than a yawn from Campy. Even with Rickey's involvement, this new league clearly didn't have much financial backing, not when Greenlee didn't have anywhere near the cash he had had in his Depression salad days. As for the Brown Dodgers, Rickey was crazy if he thought he could make black baseball pay at Ebbets Field. There weren't enough blacks in Brooklyn, and Harlemites were long accustomed to getting their Negro League fix at Yankee Stadium or the Polo Grounds. And why should Roy jump ship now when the NNL and NAL were finally in the black? Sure, things were starting to get interesting, but Roy and most veteran Negro Leaguers sensibly chose to stay put.

CAMPANELLA WAS about to begin his ninth season in professional baseball. Experience had smoothed out most of the rough spots in his game, although his development might have been even more advanced had he followed the traditional path of a comparable white prospect. "I've never had any real coaching," he later admitted. "It's not the fault of the Negro coaches and managers, they tell you the best they can. But none of them has been in the big time and had a chance to pick up the real inside pointers."

The crowds, salaries, and venues of black baseball had improved a great deal since Campy had first donned a Washington Elite Giants uniform. But the lifestyle of the NNL remained a far cry from the most humble of minor leagues. The Elites still traveled almost daily, even scheduling three games at two cities on July 4: a daytime doubleheader in Philadelphia and a night game in Baltimore. Although years of such nonsense annoyed some players, the interminable road trips never bothered Roy much. His teammate Jim Zapp recalled that Campy "liked to sit on the back wheel," which would "bounce up and down" as the old bus creaked its way from town to town. As for Jim Crow, it was not, nor would it ever be, his nature to complain about such things. After all, he was getting paid to play baseball. Everything else was irrelevant. Whatever his team asked was just fine with him.

During 1945, the Elites would have Roy filling a number of roles not normally in his job description. Snow had him at third base on opening day and later continued the left-field experiment, although Campy's judgment of fly balls could be uncertain. But the most impressive display of his versatility came that June, provoked by a teasing crack to the Baltimore pitchers about "how easy their work was." Put your money where your mouth is, they retorted, and Campy, never short on confidence, readily accepted the challenge.

The Elite pitchers sat on the bench the following night in York, Pennsylvania, fully expecting their bigmouthed catcher to get his brains beaten out by the Newark Eagles. Dumb luck, they muttered, as Roy made it through the first inning unscathed. But Roy had a decent fastball, and the lighting at West York Athletic Field wasn't the best. The Eagles scored only twice in the first seven innings, while Campanella helped his own cause with a tremendous three-run homer. Biz Mackey, the old master of versatility himself, probably couldn't help but chuckle as he watched his protégé mow down Newark's frustrated hitters.

In the eighth, it looked as if the Elites' newest hurling sensation was finally going to get his comeuppance. With two men on and the score now 8–3, the dangerous Johnny Davis stepped to the plate. Campy, though dominant with the hard stuff all evening, decided to get cute and show his curve, such as it was, to Davis, who promptly walloped a three-run homer. But Snow made no move for the mound, opting to let Roy work his way out of the jam. He retired the next hitter, then held the Eagles scoreless in the ninth to finish out his 5-hit, 10-strikeout performance.

The *York Dispatch* hailed Campy's "brilliant demonstration of pitching," and Snow was impressed enough to give him another start in September. But Snow had no serious thoughts of converting the league's best catcher into a pitcher. Not only would league hitters not be fooled for long by Campy's one-pitch repertoire, but the mental and physical demands of the position might ruin his throwing arm and damage his hitting stroke. And the Elites desperately needed a productive Campanella in their lineup to have any hope of beating out the Grays.

Despite Josh Gibson's ongoing difficulties and an aging roster, the Homestead mystique remained intact for another season. "The other teams in the NNL," remarked Sam Lacy, "were psychologically unfit to do battle with the Grays rather than physically incapable of stopping them. They flunked their best chance in ten years this season—except in 1939 when the Elites took the title—proving, with little doubt, they just don't have the stuff." For Campy, the Elites' failure to unseat the Grays was more than offset by a career year offensively. According to "official" league stats, he finished sixth with a .365 batting average in 40 games, led the league in RBIs, and whacked 5 homers, 3 behind Gibson's league-leading 8.

With the regular season over by mid-September, Campy had several weeks to kill before winter ball got under way. He was no longer on salary, but he knew he could pick up a few bucks playing exhibition games. There was a good opportunity in Baltimore, where the Elites had already arranged a city series with most of the core of the Orioles' roster supplemented by a few other minor leaguers. Even with most of the Orioles' regular infield absent, locals expected the white team to have little difficulty with the Elites. But the minor leaguers soon discovered that these guys were a lot better than they thought. After jumping out to a 4–0 lead in the first inning of game one, the Elites then romped to six straight victories over the hapless Oriole All-Stars, with Roy slamming six hits in his first eight trips to the plate.

As much fun as Campanella had in the first two games, he did not stick around for the end of the series. Effa Manley had a proposition for him. It was not, despite her reputation as a femme fatale and her fling with Campy's buddy Lenny Pearson, a sexual one. She was promoting a five-game series in Brooklyn and Newark between a group of black all-stars and a team of major leaguers managed by Dodger coach Charlie Dressen. Mackey's going to manage, Manley told Roy, and profits would be divided among the players after she took her cut. Are you in?

Campy did not need to mull over the offer long. The involvement of major league players meant bigger crowds and more money than the Baltimore series. Plus, he was looking forward to playing for Mackey again and was eager to test his mettle against big leaguers. But Manley found it difficult to assemble the remainder of her roster. Satchel Paige, despite a $1,000 offer, wasn't coming, and his Kansas City teammate Jackie Robinson had more pressing concerns. She had also tried to lure Josh Gibson and Buck Leonard, only to discover the Grays' big boppers were already committed to a New Orleans promotion. In desperation, Manley and Mackey eventually pressed seven of their own Newark Eagles into service and eight from the five remaining NNL clubs.

It was not, several black sportswriters later complained, the ideal team to take into battle against a talented group of National Leaguers, even by the war-diluted standards of 1945. Leading off was Brooklyn's pesky second baseman Eddie "the Brat" Stanky, who led the majors with 148 walks. The lineup also featured two .300 hitters: Dodger outfielder Goody Rosen, whose .325 average was third best in the National League, and the hard-hitting third baseman Whitey Kurowski, who launched 21 homers for the Cardinals. As for pitching, Dressen was relying on the strong right arms of Hal Gregg, an 18-game winner for Brooklyn, and his hard-throwing young teammate, nineteen-year-old Ralph Branca.

Sunday, October 7, was a rainy day in New York, so rainy that a number of Brooklyn baseball fans took one look outside and decided to stay home and listen to game five of the Cubs/Tigers World Series on WOR radio. Manley, cursing her bad luck, was certain the games would be canceled. But somehow the ground crew at Ebbets got the field into something near playable condition. Meanwhile, 10,424 hardy souls, about half of them black, showed up that afternoon curious to see if Larry MacPhail's recent disparagement of Negro League talent was indeed accurate.

Playing against major leaguers was nothing special for Campy, but this particular soggy Sunday was a seminal moment in his life. It was not only his Ebbets Field debut but his first time catching Don Newcombe, who had been given the start by Mackey. It may also have been his initial appearance before Branch Rickey, rumored to be lurking on the premises that afternoon despite his well-known refusal to attend Sunday games. And Campy's old mentor Mackey was just a few yards away in the dugout, proud that his teenage find had turned into everything he had hoped and more. Almost by magic, Campy's entire baseball life—past, present, and future—was materializing that day in Brooklyn.

Newcombe was a somewhat puzzling choice for the assignment. Although his crackling fastball was good enough to beat the Elites three different times in August and September, his league-leading 55 bases on balls indicated location problems. He promptly walked the first two major leaguers he faced, one of whom scored after an error by third baseman Murray Watkins. Somehow, he kept the white team at bay until the third, when his right elbow suddenly began to ache. The veteran Roy Partlow was brought in to relieve while Newcombe made the long trek to the Ebbets Field clubhouse. Disconsolate, he fretted about his condition and his future until a middle-age white man named Clyde Sukeforth stopped by his locker for a chat. I'm a scout for the Dodgers, he told Newcombe. And Branch Rickey is interested in talking to you.

Back outside on the muddy ballfield, the game was beginning to become interesting. Trailing 2–0, the Negro Leaguers finally mounted a threat off Hal Gregg in the fourth. Singles by Willie Wells and Campanella along with a bunt by Lenny Pearson loaded up the bases for Monte Irvin with no outs. Hoping to break the game open, the dangerous Newark slugger instead bounced into a double play, but the black team was now on the board. In the seventh, the Negro Leaguers jumped on the fading Gregg for three more tallies, sparked by Frank Austin's key two-run single. With the major leaguers now behind 4–2 and unable to do much with Partlow, game one seemed safely in the bag for the NNL squad.

Unfortunately, Partlow's neck began to bother him in the eighth. After he walked two hitters, Mackey yanked him in favor of Bill Byrd, the Elites' aging but still effective right-hander. Campy, like every other black fan in the ballpark, knew what was coming: the good old spitball that had given Negro Leaguers fits for years. But the white players would have none of it. Maybe you allow that pitch in *your* league, they told Byrd, but the spitter is illegal in the majors. Stripped of his best weapon, Byrd quickly allowed a game-tying single to Frank McCormick of the Reds and the game winner to Eddie Stanky off the glove of Murray Watkins an inning later. The five-inning nightcap that followed was also a nail-biter, the Negro Leaguers once again falling just one run short in a 2–1 loss.

Effa Manley was none too pleased with the sloppy performance of several of her "all-stars," which she chalked up to "stage fright." Watkins, she confided in a letter to Vernon Green, was a defensive disaster at third and "seemed scared to death. In fact all the colored boys did." Never one to mince words, she also questioned her own team's baseball savvy. "The white boys looked so smart, and were constantly doing something to show how smart they were," wrote Manley, "and our men on the other hand were constantly showing how dumb they were." But the great black sportswriter Rollo Wilson thought the Negro Leaguers had performed quite creditably. The Dressen team didn't hit much; in fact, Partlow struck out the side in game one and allowed only a single hit in four-plus innings of relief. Wilson was also impressed with Campanella, who "chased a foul to the stands along third base and made a catch which has perhaps never been equalled on that field by any other catcher."

Roy had done himself proud in the first two games, and the $135 he received from Manley for a few hours of work was just as sweet. He hoped for more of the same when the series shifted to Ruppert Stadium in Newark on Friday night. Instead, the evening belonged to game two's winner, Ralph Branca, who tossed a 5-hit shutout, struck out 10 hitters, and was "almost unhittable," according to Monte Irvin. "He was the best I'd ever batted against," Campy later recalled. In the midst of the 10–0 shellacking, Dressen stopped to talk to Campy between innings on his way to the coaching box. Could Roy meet with him for a moment after the game? Sure, but Campy wondered what the fast-talking little man possibly wanted. Certainly it was nothing of great importance, even if Dressen was a Dodger coach. As long as Campy had been playing, black players loved to joke that big league "scouts" were scrutinizing their games, but Roy never took it seriously.

But he sensed something was different. Dressen was for real, waiting for him as promised after the game. Branch Rickey, he told Roy, wants to see you tomorrow morning at 10:00 a.m. Do you know how to get to the Dodgers' offices at 215 Montague Street? When Roy admitted he didn't, Dressen instructed him to take the A train from Harlem to the Jay Street–Borough Hall stop. From there, it would be a short walk to the Dodger offices.

That night at the Woodside Hotel, the same hotel he had first stayed in during his first frightened days as a professional eight years earlier, Campy pondered the events of the past few hours. Like most fans, he knew who Branch Rickey was and of his recent involvement with black baseball. But he had no idea that Rickey's secret integration scheme was about to reach fruition. Sure, Rickey had recently admitted to a conference with Jackie Robinson, but there had been no talk of signing him for the Dodgers. "That would bring in a lot of problems which I am unable to solve," he told a reporter. His only interest in Robinson, he insisted, was for a black team. In reality, Rickey already had an option on Robinson's services and plans to sign several "other and possibly better players" in the coming weeks before allowing the story to go public.

Roy arose early that Saturday morning, boarded the subway, and soon found himself ushered into Rickey's wood-paneled, fourth-floor office on Montague Street. As he took a seat, his eyes were drawn to a portrait on the wall that he recognized as Lincoln, a crayon illustration of a "fierce-looking pirate," and a blackboard listing the hundreds of players controlled by the Dodger organization. Rickey sat across from him behind a large mahogany desk, omnipresent cigar in hand, which he sometimes chomped rather than smoked. After pleasantries were exchanged, Rickey began to talk and Campy quickly sensed that he best not interrupt.

"He spoke in a profound manner," recalled Lynn Parrott, the son of

Dodger road secretary Harold Parrott, "almost like William Buckley, but not as affected. . . . Everything he said had a sense of importance because of the way he said it."

Rickey, when first interviewing a prospective player, white or black, wanted to get a sense of the fellow's personal qualities. The reports turned in by his trusted scouts told him what he needed to know about a man's baseball talent, but Rickey was just as interested in what the man did off the playing field. Not only were background checks common in the Brooklyn organization, but Rickey often conducted his own unique "test" to determine a candidate's suitability for the Dodger family. Clyde King, a Dodger signee a year earlier, remembered the barrage of questions Rickey fired at him during his initial meeting: "Do you want to get married? Do you believe in God? Do you have a family? . . . Do you think you get nervous before a big crowd?"

Roy dutifully answered the Mahatma's every question, but he soon became convinced that Rickey already knew everything about him. In later years, he would often allude to an extensive report ("three to four inches thick") the Dodgers had compiled on him. "He read it all to me," Campy told Peter Golenbock, "and I was flabbergasted! They had followed me, and they knew everything about me, about my family, my parents, my schooling, everything." But clearly the Dodgers, at least initially, did not dig as deeply as they should have. "Our general opinion, from what we had learned," scout Clyde Sukeforth later explained, "was that Campanella was too old." Fortunately, Rickey had finally gotten the lowdown from Oscar Charleston, the old-time black superstar who had not only managed the Brown Dodgers for a spell but provided valuable info on Negro League prospects. "That boy's not too old," he told Rickey. "He started early." Nevertheless, Rickey would later ask to see a birth certificate.

After dissecting Roy's weight, habits, and personal qualities for what seemed to be an eternity, Rickey finally made his intentions clear. Would Campanella like to play for him? Roy was not entirely surprised by the question. The bushy-eyebrowed, bespectacled man had, in the conversation, mentioned the infamous Brooklyn Brown Dodgers more than once. Whether Roy knew that the team had already flopped at Ebbets Field in 1945 is uncertain, but he knew enough that he didn't want to go there. "I told him right off the bat that I was with an established Negro team,"

Campy later recalled, "and I wasn't taking no chance on a new one." With the conversation at an impasse, Rickey asked about Roy's winter plans, requested that he not sign any contracts before talking to Rickey first, then bade him farewell.

Considering the events that followed, it seems peculiar that Rickey didn't level with Campanella that morning. "We want you for the Dodgers," he might have said, "but keep your mouth shut until we're ready to announce it." But as of that Saturday, October 13, Rickey still planned to delay his integration announcement for at least another month and perhaps longer. Better that Campanella be kept "on the string" for now, rather than clue him in and worry that he might blab to reporters prematurely.

Press leaks were soon the least of Rickey's worries. With New York elections only weeks away, Mayor Fiorello La Guardia was eager to manipulate the integration issue to the advantage of his would-be successor, Newbold Morris. The mayor planned during his weekly radio broadcast on October 21 to trumpet the supposedly influential role of his recently created Committee on Baseball. The Mahatma, unhappy that baseball's color line had become an "election football," persuaded La Guardia to keep mum for at least another week while Rickey planned his next move. He eventually decided that Robinson's signing would have to be announced almost immediately, *before* the mayor once again took to the airwaves and tried to use the issue to swing a few votes.

In the meantime, Campy remained in New York after his meeting with Rickey. The second Sunday doubleheader was on tap at Ebbets with the major leaguers, although the results were only nominally better than the first weekend. Virgil Trucks, fresh from beating the Cubs in game two of the World Series, handcuffed the Negro Leaguers in the opener on four hits, one of them a single by Campy. Mackey's men finally snapped their losing streak in the second game, managing a 0–0 tie in a five-inning affair, but the real star of the game was an obscure pitcher by the name of "Leftwich," who punched out four major leaguers in his five shutout innings of work. Black fans and writers in the know recognized the mysterious Leftwich as Homestead Grays pitcher John Wright, who thought it best to keep his real name out of the newspapers while still doing a stint in the navy.

After the doubleheader, Campy collected his $57 share for the day and headed back to the Woodside. Within a few days, he expected to be on the move again, this time to Venezuela for an exhibition series with a group of Negro League stars managed by Felton Snow. This team, Roy realized, had a lot more punch than the one that had just done battle with the big leaguers. This time, solid professional hitters such as Quincy Trouppe, Gene Benson, and Buck Leonard were on the squad, accompanied by base-stealing threats Sam Jethroe and Frank Austin. And Kansas City's Jackie Robinson, no slouch himself at bat or on the bases, was also booked for the trip.

Campy knew Robinson slightly. Their paths had crossed in August when the Monarchs had made a brief stop in Baltimore. Campy remembered how Jackie and some of his teammates, suspicious that the scoreboard had failed to record at least a few of their runs, tried to check with the so-called official scorer, only to discover he had already left the park. The pair had also appeared on opposite sides in the East-West Game in July, although Jackie went 0 for 5 while Roy had two hits.

Roy discovered that Robinson, along with most of the other players slated for the South American tour, was staying at the Woodside. With the trip now delayed because of a coup in Venezuela, there was little to do but hang out at the hotel, shoot the breeze with the guys, and maybe play a little cards. Before long, Roy found himself in a game of gin rummy with Robinson. As the two men looked over their hands, the subject turned to Branch Rickey. That Campy had been down to Montague Street was no secret to Jackie. He had already been through the same thing himself and wondered about the outcome of Roy's meeting with the Mahatma.

The conversation with the old windbag, Campy told Jackie, didn't really amount to much. I think he wanted me for that Brooklyn Brown Dodgers team they're always talking about. Robinson smiled. He had believed the same thing when he first heard of Rickey's interest. As the card game continued, Jackie began to tell his own story while Campy's eyes widened in disbelief. Yes, he had signed with Rickey, but not for the Brown Dodgers. He was going to join the Montreal Royals, the Dodgers' International League affiliate. In the meantime, Roy was sworn to secrecy, at least until the formal historic announcement on October 23.

In hindsight, Rickey's choice of Jackie Robinson appears nothing short of brilliant. Certainly, few, if any, black ballplayers could have improved upon Robinson's remarkable performance as the key figure in the obliteration of baseball's color line. Yet this decision might just as easily have blown up in Rickey's face. Robinson, as baseball fans would discover, was an impatient, restless man who possessed a fierce pride, a hair-trigger temper, and what Sam Lacy would label "a biting tongue." Could such an individual be expected to tolerate Rickey's insistence on a "turn the other cheek" philosophy?

There was also the question of experience. Robinson was twenty-six years old with only a single year of professional baseball under his belt. He had done reasonably well as a Monarchs rookie, earning a spot on the East-West team and slamming seven straight hits against the Grays one Sunday afternoon. But wouldn't a more established player with a proven track record have been a safer bet? A number of Negro Leaguers would later insist, with some justification, that plenty of better men were available in 1945.

Rickey was well aware that Robinson's black baseball credentials lacked the pizzazz of those of a Paige or Gibson. But Rickey recognized that Jackie had the talent to succeed, along with the perfect background to present to a potentially dubious press, public, and teammates. He was an intelligent, articulate army veteran who had attended UCLA (without graduating) at a time when relatively few Americans, white or black, pursued higher education. Plus Robinson already had the experience of playing alongside whites in high-level competition.

After Robinson became a legend, several writers perpetuated the notion that no other black player could have filled his role as "pioneer." Yet Rickey, under different circumstances, could easily have gone in an entirely different direction. Longtime Dodger executive Buzzie Bavasi claimed that Don Newcombe, seven years younger than Robinson and with more professional experience, had some support within the Brooklyn organization. Whether a nineteen-year-old high school dropout such as Newk had the maturity to withstand the enormous publicity and pressure is something we'll never know.

Many Negro League officials had long believed that Monte Irvin was the ideal candidate to break the color line. He not only had the intellect, the polish, and the college background (Lincoln University) prized by Rickey but was also a few weeks younger than Robinson with years more experience. Unfortunately for Irvin, he had been drafted in 1943, *after* his brilliant season in Mexico and *before* Rickey's scouting efforts began. When he finally returned to the Eagles in the summer of 1945, he was slow to return to his old form as he grappled with the lingering effects of "war nerves." It's doubtful that Rickey's scouts knew or cared much about Irvin until the October postseason series, when they watched him crack 4 hits in 8 trips against major league pitching.

What about Roy? Gus Greenlee pushed Rickey to make Campy his first signing, according to Greenlee's brother Charles, although Carl Rowan's *Wait Till Next Year*, written with Robinson, claimed that "some scouts raved; others were not overimpressed. Rickey took a personal look and thought Campanella had great potential, despite the fact that he seemed to take his eye off the ball at the last second . . . causing him to strike out a great deal." But how much the Dodgers had actually scouted Campy before the fall of 1945 remains unclear. According to Rickey himself, "Campanella was never mentioned to me by Wendell Smith or anybody else," and Rickey became aware of Roy only after "incidental observation" by his assistant Bob Finch.

Undoubtedly, most contemporary Negro League observers in 1945 regarded Campanella, by virtue of his superior experience, as a better bet than Robinson. But Roy, unlike Jackie, was a man of limited education. Perhaps even more problematic was his biracial ancestry and Italian surname. The darker-skinned Robinson, his biographer Arnold Rampersad contends, "was probably far more Rickey's idea of what the first Negro player should look like—and what he thought black Americans would want the first to look like—than Campanella." Indeed, a story from Campy's Dodger days humorously illustrates the ambivalent feelings his mixed parentage sometimes elicited. Facing Robin Roberts one day, he fell behind 0-1. "C'mon you, Roy," shouted a group of black fans. "Let's knock it!" Roberts then got a second strike. "Please, Roy . . . mash that ball!" But when Campy struck out seconds later, his cheering section suddenly turned hostile. "You goddamn dago, you couldn't hit that ball anyhow."

There was also the matter of temperament. Robinson's feistiness, Rickey likely believed, would be of greater value to the fight than Campy's more placid nature. And Roy's position may have played a role. Rickey was genuinely concerned (and with good reason, as it turned out) that white pitchers would not take orders from a black receiver. The issue had already been broached during their first conversation, although Campy was quick to inform Rickey that he had "handled white pitchers in Spanish down in Mexico!"

Roy was delighted to see Jackie get a shot at the big time. Still, he naturally felt more than a few pangs of jealousy. If Bill Benswanger or Gerry Nugent had had backbones, he could have been in the same position three years earlier. But Rickey was no spineless jellyfish and welcomed the slings and arrows from all sides. "I knew I was right, and when a man is right he cannot do wrong," thundered Rickey, who seemed to be enjoying his martyr status. "I anticipated the adverse reaction that has been expressed by certain people but I had the shield of right and I wasn't afraid."

Rickey meant business. "It was a pleasant shock," future major leaguer George Crowe recalled. "When they signed Jackie to play in Montreal, everybody's hopes went up." But Campy's own status was in limbo at the moment. His earlier meeting with Rickey, he now understood, had actually been about a major league opportunity, although nothing had been resolved except a promise not to sign with any other team. He now wished that he had jumped at Rickey's offer, vague as it was at the time. "I knew I could play in the big leagues, but I wondered if I'd ever get the chance again," he wrote in his autobiography. "I had had it once—and I muffed it."

Campanella's various retellings of this episode similarly stress his anxiety over his initial failure to sign with Rickey and his long, painful wait until his next contact with the Dodgers several months later. The actual story may be less dramatic. A document in the Branch Rickey Papers indicates that Campanella actually returned to Montague Street on October 25, two days after Robinson's signing. On that day, Campy signed a preliminary agreement, calling for a bonus of $1,500 and monthly salary of $400, to play "for the Brooklyn Brown Dodgers or any other club the Brooklyn organization might designate." Newcombe, whose first meeting with Rickey probably predated Campy's by a few days, apparently agreed to a similar deal a few moments later. Both players were ordered not to go public with the news, although rumors surfaced in the *Brooklyn Eagle* that Roy had already signed.

Strangely, Campanella never once mentioned the October 25 agreement after reaching the majors, and he likely forgot its existence. Always proud to have been among the first black signees, he would almost certainly have disclosed an incident that placed his own signing within hours of Robinson's. He did, however, often intimate that he might have signed before Jackie had he fully understood Rickey's intentions, although Campy was probably unaware that Rickey had been in contact with Robinson well before he had ever met Roy.

The issue of who signed first would flare more seriously in the future and already provoked some friction in Roy's budding friendship with Robinson. After Jackie returned from Montreal that fall, he brought his fiancée, Rachel, around to the Woodside to meet Campy and Ruthe. Twelve years later, the Robinsons still remembered the conversation. "Campy said that someone in the organization . . . had approached him earlier, before he approached Jack," Rachel Robinson related to Carl Rowan. "This is his point . . . that he had the opportunity to be the first, and I think that's in the back of his mind all the way along, that he should have, or could have been." His attitude did not surprise her. "Campy knows nothing but baseball," she remarked. "Having played baseball since he was nine or so, I guess he did feel that he should have been the first."

9

NASHUA

ROBINSON'S SIGNING had drastically transformed the baseball landscape. Exactly how much, no one was quite sure. Would Rickey now launch a full-scale raid on the Negro Leagues? And who were the mysterious "several other Negroes" he was supposedly interested in signing?

The Robinson news deeply disturbed most Negro League officials, whose control of their players had always been remarkably tenuous. A surprising number of teams, including the Elites, didn't even bother with contracts, preferring more informal oral or written arrangements that minimized their own obligations should a player fail to perform up to snuff. Gentlemen's agreements among the owners, rather than Organized Baseball's infamous reserve clause, kept players from jumping their clubs. But Branch Rickey, it turned out, was no gentleman. The Monarchs never signed Robinson to a contract? Then they shouldn't expect to get a single penny out of him. And they never did.

Tom Wilson sensed that he would soon be in the same boat as the Monarchs' owners. Campanella, he guessed, was about to bolt. Why else would he have paid off a $200 advance as soon as he reached Venezuela without writing so much as a word of explanation? Wilson, unlike his colleague Cum Posey, who was in a near frenzy that John Wright (aka Leftwich) was

him. Better for Campanella to be too good for the league than to fail miserably and set the whole plan back. Rickey directed Finch to see if Danville would take Campy and Don Newcombe as a package deal. Newcombe, he believed, had a bright future but would need to be carefully handled, ideally with Campy and not "some inexperienced youngster."

Campy sat squirming, trying to remain calm while Finch made the call to the less-than-enthralled Danville president, Kish Bookwalter. Rickey was a friend and all, but he had to be out of his mind if he thought a small coal-mining town on the Illinois/Indiana border was the place to send two Negroes. Besides, the club was building a brand-new ballpark, financed by selling stock at $10 a share. Why jeopardize its success on a risky move almost certain to kill local goodwill? Tell Branch to try another ballclub. Years later, Newcombe would claim that president Tom Fairweather threatened to shut the 3-I League (Indiana, Illinois, Iowa) down if forced to integrate, but the decision appears to have been made solely by Danville.

Rickey now only had one card left to play. It was to be Nashua or Roy might be getting fitted for a Brooklyn Brown Dodger uniform after all. The Dodgers owned Nashua outright, and Rickey hoped the team's young general manager, Emil "Buzzie" Bavasi (so nicknamed as a child because he was "always buzzing around"), would be able to find a spot for the two men. Bavasi, a native New Yorker back in baseball after two years in the army, had no objections. Plus, he doubted that the town itself, heavily populated by French Canadians with a "pretty good reputation for accepting things"—and happy to have minor league baseball after a thirteen-year absence—would pose much difficulty. In the meantime, he would schmooze with the necessary local big shots to make sure that potential difficulties had been ironed out by the time the two arrived in late April.

Nashua and the New England League was to be Roy's destination, but there was still the little matter of money to decide. With class B team payrolls capped at $3,000 per month, a measly $185 a month was all the Dodgers could offer him, along with a $2,400 signing bonus. Some big leagues, he thought. For a moment he wondered whether the friends who told him he was a fool to take a pay cut to play in the minors weren't right. Ruthe, however, knew better. "It's been practically your life's dream," she told him. "Money is not the important thing, now." Still, Roy was relieved that Rickey managed to find a clever way around the salary cap by hiring him as a rather pricy $500-a-month Negro League scout for the Dodgers in the off-season.

The official announcement of the Campanella and Newcombe signings, numbers three and four on Rickey's integration list, hit the afternoon papers on April 4. But the Nashua news was overshadowed by the ongoing saga of Robinson and Wright. Roy, like everyone else, was desperate to see them make good. On April 18, he headed down to Jersey City to watch Montreal's opener and witness the historic end of Organized Baseball's color barrier. Although Wright was not in the lineup, Robinson did not disappoint, collecting four hits in five trips while stealing two bases. The Great Experiment was off to a flying start.

Campy's turn was coming soon. A few days after Jackie's debut, he left Harlem for Nashua, a textile-mill town on the New Hampshire/Massachusetts border about which he knew next to nothing. He initially thought the Dodgers were assigning him to *Nashville*, although he doubted that was likely to happen anytime soon. He did know, though, that few blacks lived in Nashua; the 1940 census had only recorded thirty-seven in a population of nearly thirty-three thousand.

Campanella and Newcombe could not help but feel a bit apprehensive as they waited for their new teammates to arrive from spring training. The search for food and lodging would be the first litmus test of local racial attitudes. Arriving at a motor inn outside of town, they braced themselves for the worst. Instead, Newk remembered, "they gave us two beautiful log cabins outside." They were a bit cold, but Campy "kept saying things were going to get better. We had to start somewhere." When the two men went to get a bite at the nearby Howard Johnson, they were treated like any other patron. "Hey, Newk, this town may be all right," said Campy, grinning, as he munched on fried clams, a New England staple.

In the days that followed, Roy began to feel himself quite fortunate to be in Nashua. The team's strapping player-manager, Walter Alston, seemed like a decent sort, albeit a bit quiet. After bouncing around pro ball since 1935 with only a single major league at bat (a strikeout) to his credit, he had turned to managing, although a high school teaching gig back in Ohio still paid the bills in the winter months. To Campy's surprise, Alston informed the team that Campanella, by virtue of his vast Negro League experience, would take over the club anytime Alston was thrown out of a ball game. If any players objected, they kept their mouths shut. "You didn't fool with him," pitcher Larry Shepard recalled. "He had a look that if you wanted to start anything, he was available."

Roy was also grateful that Buzzie Bavasi was handling things off the field. Campy quickly gathered that Bavasi had his back at all times and would be certain to squelch any clubhouse racial turmoil. Besides, in an era of no guaranteed contracts, any troublemaker could expect to be shipped out almost immediately. "Campy was one of my favorites," Bavasi remarked sixty years later. "My first impression was everlasting. Finally found a player who actually loved the game . . . motivated by pride, not money."

With Campy and Newcombe on board, Bavasi was certain that Nashua would at least be competitive. But Nashua was a tiny market, even by New England League standards. A winning club was absolutely essential, not only to draw fans but to relax some of the pressure on the two Negro fellows. Fortunately, Rickey's recent aggressive scouting efforts had generated players to stock Nashua and other clubs in Brooklyn's extensive minor league chain. Most farm systems had a sudden embarrassment of riches, thanks to hundreds of returning servicemen, many of whom would land in the New England League. "They had a lot of talent up there," recalled Nashua pitcher Bernard Reinertsen, himself a recently discharged vet. "It was not a crummy league."

As they waited for the season to get under way, Campy and Newk began delicately feeling out their new teammates. Rickey had already lectured the two in his usual schoolmaster fashion on the essential need to shut up, play ball, and avoid incidents. Beyond that, they were on their own. But an integrated professional baseball team was uncharted territory. How, Roy wondered, should they proceed? As a catcher, he knew (as did Rickey) that it was particularly critical for him to build camaraderie with his pitchers. Should he try to make friends immediately? Take an active leadership role? Keep a low profile off the field? Hang back and wait to be included? Or should he, as Mackey had taught him, follow his instincts and just try to get along with everybody?

Amazingly, the Nashua roster was free of racism that season. Whether by design or coincidence, most, if not all, of Roy and Newk's teammates were Northerners—men who had not been programmed since birth to believe in the segregation and inferiority of blacks. Some, hailing from small New England towns like Nashua, where blacks were virtually nonexistent, were oblivious to the issue of skin color. Roy's backup, Gus Galipeau of Woonsocket, Rhode Island, had lived twenty-six years without even *meeting* a black person. But Galipeau soon befriended Roy, who shared an occasional hot betting tip with the veteran French-Canadian catcher. A year later, Galipeau even roomed with Newcombe, perhaps the first example of an interracial living arrangement in Organized Baseball.

Roy's genuine friendliness, boyish nature, and wry sense of humor quickly won over the rest of his Nashua teammates. Many still remember him warmly six decades later. "You couldn't find a nicer guy," recalled pitcher Donald Chartier. "I'd pick him for a friend anytime." Shortstop Billy DeMars agreed, "He was a great person . . . just a funny guy." And Roy found himself enjoying the interracial setting. "Everything is swell here," he wrote black sportswriter Dan Burley in late April. "All the players on the team are fine fellows."

With the race issue—Rickey's biggest concern—seemingly neutralized before the season had even begun, Roy was brimming with confidence. "We're going to make good up here," he told Burley, "so we can be seen that much sooner in Brooklyn. Catch on?" His enthusiasm waned somewhat when he got his first look at Holman Stadium, Nashua's massive home park. With no outfield fence, only evergreen shrubs placed at rather discouraging distances of at least 450 feet from home plate, he could forget about home runs. The considerable outfield gaps did offer an inviting target, but many of Roy's hardest-hit balls that season fell harmlessly into the gloves of opposing outfielders, who quickly learned to play the Negro slugger extraordinarily deep.

Alston, unconcerned with any potential power loss, still wanted Campanella batting cleanup when the team opened its season on May 8 in Lynn, Massachusetts. That evening, Roy hopped on the Nashua bus for the one-hour ride to Lynn, a manufacturing town of ninety-eight thousand famous for its shoe factories. He was a long way from Kerbaugh Street. Ten years ago, he was playing on the sandlots of Nicetown. There was no place in baseball for the colored man, everyone told him, so he should find himself a job and stop this foolishness. Now he was in the minor leagues playing with the white boys, and he was sure he wouldn't be there for long. "I have my mind set on making this work," he told one reporter. "If we have the stuff, we'll go to the top." He had long since set aside any remaining doubts about the New England League's salary scale or caliber of play. When old friend Jorge Pasquel offered him a three-year, $15,000, all-expenses-paid deal to return to Mexico, Roy was not interested.

Lynn, a Red Sox farm club, and its fans were waiting to watch Roy fall flat on his face in his debut. "I don't ask for the sensational kind of day Jackie had, that's expecting too much," he remarked. "All I want is a couple base hits." On the mound for Lynn was Roger Wright, a Tennessee native and yet another ex-serviceman trying to revive his career after three years away from the game. Despite winning 17 games for Lynn that season, Wright would spend the next twelve years bouncing from city to city, never once getting a call-up to the Big Show.

Campy knew nothing about Wright except that his brother Ed pitched a few short miles away in Boston for the Braves. But Roy was used to facing strange pitchers cold and quickly adjusting to their repertoire. No sooner had Wright retired Roy on a grounder in his first minor league at bat than the pendulum began to shift. Eager to atone for an earlier wild heave into center, Campy reached on an infield single in the fourth, "whaled a whistling single into center" in the seventh, then capped off the day with a tremendous two-run homer in the ninth. Lynn took the game 7–4, but the 3,939 fans shivering in the early-May New England night couldn't help but be impressed by what they had just seen. Nashua's colored catcher, they agreed, was a pretty darned good ballplayer.

SOLVING WRIGHT'S offerings proved to be rather simple. Adjusting to Nashua, Roy discovered, would not be quite so easy. He had mostly lived in large, ethnically diverse areas his entire life—Philadelphia, Baltimore, Harlem, even Monterrey—and now he was stuck in the middle of a virtually all-white town where French was still spoken among many residents just a few generations removed from their Quebec homeland. Except for a few movie theaters, not a whole lot was going on in Nashua. "It is," noted Wendell Smith, "a typical New England town, quiet, liberal and staid in its ways."

Roy was grateful to have family around to buffer the initial shock of small-town living. Ruthe and David came up from Harlem regularly to join

Campy at the Laton Hotel and soon became regular fixtures at Holman Stadium. "We used to put Campanella's kid up on a milk crate," recalled Billy DeMars, "and let him play the pinball machines." Meanwhile, Ruthe did everything she could to advance her man's career, comfortably mixing and making nice with the white ballplayers' wives. She did, however, draw the line at being photographed with the other gals, supposedly because of fears that "too much publicity" would affect their children. More likely, she and Campy worried that the public might somehow find out they were still legally married to other partners.

His adjustment was also aided by his deepening friendship with the always mercurial Don Newcombe. One moment joking and laughing noisily, another pouting and aloof, Newcombe could be a difficult young man to handle. But Campy knew exactly which buttons to push to get the big fellow back on track. "Campy kind of looked after him and took care of him," said Larry Shepard.

Family and friends aside, Newcombe and Campanella both clearly understood that the white townspeople would largely determine their experience in Nashua. As far as they could tell, Nashuans didn't seem particularly hung up on race, as they experienced no explicit hostility, with no angry letters to the local newspaper denouncing their presence or hastily called meetings of citizens demanding their banishment. Instead, a genuine sense of curiosity prevailed. "We had never seen black people before, but that didn't matter," remembered Lucille Roy, then ten years old. "We got to see baseball, and that's all we cared about. It didn't matter to us that they were black."

What mattered was their baseball talent, so striking that even ambivalent locals were soon won over to their side, especially when the team began winning. Before long, townspeople began inviting them over for dinners, offering them the use of their car, and picking up the tabs for their meals. Nashuans even made Newcombe an honorary fireman, as Campy discovered one day as he watched a fire engine speed past him on the way to the park. "Who should I see sitting right up in the middle but Newk," he later recalled, "wearing a fire hat, laughing and waving his arms like mad. . . . He looked like he was having the thrill of his life."

In short, it was a lovefest, one that Rickey could not have scripted better himself. "They just about own the town," reported the *Nashua Telegraph* in June, "and are the two most popular members of the Nashua team." For Campy, it was particularly surreal to find himself surrounded by hordes of white children demanding his autograph. Was America really changing? "Sure they're Negroes. So what?" one fan told a visiting reporter. "Plenty of white ball players wish they had their ability. You know, if those two fellows aren't treated right, we fans will go down there and punch the guilty on the nose."

With Nashua so exceptionally hospitable, Roy could concentrate less on racial issues and more on baseball, although daily league games would require some adjustment. On the other hand, the travel was cushy by blackball standards, with most games played within a hundred-mile radius of Nashua. Longer trips, such as the two-hour jump to Portland, Maine, were still no fun, but Campy and Newcombe kept their teammates in stitches on the bus warbling a saucy number entitled "When Rufus Raised the Roofus."

Alston, who initially felt that Roy was "reluctant to assert himself with white boys," watched his catcher's confidence growing by the day. He was particularly impressed by the way Campy handled the club after Alston was tossed from a game in Lawrence, Massachusetts, on June 15 for arguing balls and strikes. With no visitors' clubhouse, Alston was forced to cool his heels in the parking lot. "We were losing by one run and had a man on when it happened," Campy later explained. "The first thing I did was to put big Newk in to pinch-hit. He hit the ball into a river that ran behind the outfield for a home run."

In the years that followed, Campanella and Newcombe were fond of recounting the tale of the dramatic homer and shrewd managing that night in Lawrence. But the *Nashua Telegraph* indicates that Alston was actually ejected *after* Newcombe homered. Newk's two-run blast, Alston believed, might have been good for three if umpire Bernie Friberg hadn't blown a recent 3-0 call on Billy DeMars, who was eventually retired instead of walking. Friberg quickly sent the fuming Alston on his way, while Campy assumed the reins in the top of the seventh with Nashua now trailing 4–3. Besides bringing in the hard-throwing Mike Nozinski to relieve, Roy actually didn't have too many managerial moves to make. His teammates Bob Kellogg and Harvey Porter made him look like a genius by belting round-trippers in the eighth and ninth innings to give Nashua the 7–5 decision.

If Campanella hadn't actually sent Newcombe to pinch-hit that night, he had otherwise handled the job with aplomb. Impressed by his ability, baseball knowledge, experience, and approach to the game, Campy's white teammates found themselves respecting a black man for the first time in their lives. But at least a few opposing players were openly hostile to Nashua's colored battery of Newcombe and Campanella.

With the modest breakthroughs during World War II, many African-Americans hoped for continued progress in peacetime. Baseball was now integrated, professional football would follow suit by the end of the year, and strides in employment, housing, and education seemed likely to follow. Still, Campy had no illusions about the persistence of American racism. "I doubt if things will ever change," he once told a black reporter. Disturbing news stories in 1946 of lynchings, attacks on returning servicemen, and the renewed determination to squelch black voting in the South seemed to justify his cynicism.

Nashua may have been a safe haven but Roy and Don knew that the New England League, despite its location, had its share of bigots. Years of playing against white semipros had thoroughly prepared Roy for the usual racial slurs and insults. He was not, however, quite ready for what he encountered one night in Nashua against the Manchester Giants.

The game was fairly uneventful until Manchester's catcher Sal Yvars stepped to the plate. Yvars, then twenty-two, was a native New Yorker, a fellow *paisano* in his first year of professional baseball. Before entering the batter's box, he grabbed a handful of dirt and then just as casually tossed it directly into Campy's face. The Nashua crowd erupted in a fury. "I thought they were going to go down there," remarked one fan, "and ruin that Manchester player." That is, if Campy didn't get to him first. He wanted to break every bone in Yvars's body. But he knew fighting, shoving, or even arguing was out of the question. All he could do was wipe the dirt off his face and summon every ounce of self-control he possessed. "I called time right away," Roy later recalled, "and told him if he ever did that again, we were going to tangle right there at home plate. He didn't say a word."

Yvars always claimed the dirt was meant for Campy's shin guards, but Newcombe suggests Yvars had actually thrown dirt on Campy twice that evening before Roy finally reacted. "Yvars was a dirty goddamn baseball player then," said Newcombe, "and when he got to the New York Giants, I never forgot and tried to bust his ass many times when he came to the plate." Ironically, Yvars's involvement in two other incidents would profoundly shape the course of Brooklyn Dodger history. That same year, he crashed violently into Alston, who was straddling the first-base line attempting to snag a pop-up. Although Alston thrashed the living daylights out of Yvars in the one-sided fight that followed, the collision effectively ended Alston's playing career and forced him to concentrate on managing. In 1951, Yvars would play a key role in an elaborate sign-stealing scheme that helped the Giants overtake the Dodgers for the National League pennant.

Yvars's antics proved easier to squelch than an ongoing feud with the Lynn Red Sox, a team that seemed to mirror the long-standing racist attitudes of the parent club in Boston. Their manager, Thomas "Pip" Kennedy, went so far as to threaten to "drive those two colored boys out of the league in a week's time," and most of his players followed his race-baiting lead. "They had some real crackers on that team, real rednecks," recalled Newcombe. Filling the bill were two future major leaguers: pitcher Walker Cress and catcher Matt Batts, both of whom thought it cute to follow the ancient racist custom of rubbing a Negro's head (in this case, Roy's) for good luck.

Beneath Roy's genial facade, such indignities infuriated him. But Rickey wanted cheek-turning, not fisticuffs, so Roy's bat would have to do the talking. Facing Cress on June 28 in Lynn, Roy belted a key two-run blast to help spoil the sidearmer's otherwise brilliant fifteen-strikeout performance. Afterward, Cress and Kennedy were seething.

The simmering racial tension with Lynn finally erupted one night in Nashua. The principals in the incident—Bavasi, Newcombe, Campy, and Alston—would each tell a slightly different version later, but certain facts are undisputed. On this evening, Kennedy had been exceptionally vicious in his race-baiting. "Wanted to know if we were sleeping with them and stuff like that," recalled Alston. After the game, Alston and Bavasi resolved to confront Kennedy in the office while he waited to collect his share of the gate. The Lynn manager, annoyed by Bavasi's intentional stalling, began to drop a few choice four-letter words, oblivious to the presence of the wives of Bavasi and Alston. In 1946, one was not supposed to swear in front of a lady. "Don't you talk that way in front of my wife and Mrs. Alston," barked Bavasi, "or I'll knock you on your fanny."

Kennedy was hardly intimidated. "The guy told Buzzie he was pretty brave," said Alston, "talking like that when he had me there to back him up." But Bavasi, still fuming over the treatment of Campy and Newcombe, walked outside and challenged Kennedy with the entire Lynn team watching from the bus. "Why don't you say to me right now what you said to them and I'll kick your ass," said Bavasi. "Go ahead and say that to me." At that moment, a single word or move by Kennedy might have provoked a fistfight or even a full-blown free-for-all between the two teams. But Kennedy, perhaps aware of the damage Alston had inflicted on Yvars, thought better of it. He meekly boarded the bus and headed home to Lynn. "We had no more trouble with Pip Kennedy," Bavasi later wrote.

Fittingly, Nashua would be matched against Lynn in the best-of-seven championship playoff in September. Thanks to the black talent so despised by Kennedy, the Dodgers took the series in six games. Newcombe stopped the Red Sox on ten hits in game five in his only start, while Campy, recently dubbed Mr. Murder for his torrid bat, hit .364, homered, and drove in 7 runs. But Campy somehow remained grounded and unaffected. "Here he is, the hitting hero of the series, and all these people are trying to congratulate him," recalled Marshall Cobleigh, then a sixteen-year-old kid responsible for scoreboard duties at Holman Stadium. "But here he's sitting there with . . . [Ruthe's son] David, making a rabbit out of his handkerchief. He was just a sweet human being."

Humbleness aside, Roy knew that he had accomplished a great deal in 1946. After a slow start, he hit .305 in his last 292 at bats to finish with an overall .290 average and a solid .393 OBP. He drove in 96 runs, second best in the league, and hit 13 of Nashua's 53 homers, each smash earning a prize of one hundred baby chicks per a peculiar promotion by a local farmer. Most remarkably, he thrived in an alien environment despite an inordinate amount of pressure. "You know, people expect us to do better than any other players," Campy admitted in August. "Why, unless I hit two home runs in every game, my friends are heartbroken. Sure, we carry a great responsibility. We know that. But, heck, we're no supermen. We're ballplayers like the other fellows."

Back in Brooklyn, Rickey was generally pleased with the results of the first year of his Great Experiment. Jackie Robinson, with whom Campy corresponded during the season, had a monster season in Montreal. Newcombe and Campy had acquitted themselves rather nicely in Nashua. But

John Wright and the newest signee, Roy Partlow, had not fared nearly as well, eventually finishing the season in class C ball. "From all appearances," Rickey told one black reporter, "they suffer a terrible inferiority complex when they are facing white boys." For Wright, who was released following the season, the bigger problem was his inability to adjust to an integrated environment. "He wasn't comfortable around white people, the word got out," says Monte Irvin. Wright would later claim that Herman Franks, his catcher in Montreal, tipped off his pitches to opposing hitters.

Rickey was not fazed by Wright's failure. Nor was he fazed after reading a recent secret preliminary report mostly authored by Larry MacPhail hysterically warning his fellow owners that integration might negatively impact MLB's bottom line. If anything, the Mahatma was more determined than ever to expand the scope of the Great Experiment, dispatching Campy to scout the Negro Leagues only a few days after the New England League campaign ended. Roy proved to be ideal for the job, not only making the obvious recommendations of Irvin and Larry Doby, but also raving about Joe Black and an obscure NNL rookie named Junior Gilliam. "The young boy Gilliam," he wrote Dodgers officials, "has the making of a good player. He is one of the youngest players in the league. He is very apt and has good habits."

Baseball still consumed Roy. Within days after completing his scouting duties, he was back in uniform barnstorming with Jackie, then left for Puerto Rico for another winter ball season. Taking a break never occurred to him. Money, of course, motivated Campy, but a more powerful force lured him back to the diamond day after day, month after month, year after year. He simply never felt more alive or more content than on the ballfield. Campanella, Robinson would later note, often thought about little else than baseball.

The Dodgers were quite happy with Campy's performance in class B ball. "Very good receiver, hits ball where it is pitched with power," wrote Jake Pitler in a September 1946 scouting report. "Uses good judgment." Rickey was not surprised. "Roy is much too good for that league," he told Sam Lacy.

Obviously, Campy would not be returning to Nashua, but his 1947 destination remained uncertain. Although Hy Turkin of the *New York Daily News* speculated that Campanella might be the "first Negro regular of majors," Rickey had other plans. If anyone was going to integrate the Dodgers, it would be Robinson, who had had a better season in a higher classification (one wonders whether Rickey might have considered Roy for Brooklyn in 1947 had Robinson struggled in Montreal). Besides, the Dodgers had no real need for a catcher. Bruce Edwards, a youngster from California, had drawn raves since his recall in June, and most observers believed the job was his for the foreseeable future.

Montreal, the Dodgers decided, would be Campy's next stop. In his heart, he knew he was ready for the majors now. But he had been patient for ten years, and a year in Triple A sure wouldn't kill him. "I just left everything to what Mr. Rickey talked to me about," he later recalled. "That was all."

IN LATE February 1947, Campanella said good-bye to Ruthe and David and hopped a plane for Havana, Cuba, for his first spring training with the Dodgers. After the racial problems last year in Florida, the Brooklyn brass had decided that the Dodgers and their top minor leaguers would fare better in the land of cigars, sugar, and Mafia-controlled casinos.

Campanella and the other three blacks in camp would not be staying at the Dodgers' opulent headquarters at the Hotel Nacional. Nor would they be staying with the other minor leaguers at the more humble dormitories of the still-under-construction Havana Military Academy. Rickey worried the "new fellows" on Montreal might rebel against the presence of Negroes, and the last thing he wanted right now was an embarrassing incident. With so much at stake, Campy, Jackie, Newk, and Partlow had no choice but to yield to a segregated living arrangement, at least for now.

The four men, all Negro League veterans, were used to Jim Crow accommodations. But the Hotel Los Angeles in downtown Havana put the *flea* in *fleabag*, a place so disgusting that Newcombe became violently ill after watching a cockroach crawl out of his vegetable soup. Meanwhile, Sam Lacy was shocked by the "suite" Campy and Jackie shared: "a room sans sunlight, but with ample ceiling leaks and toilet facilities which left no doubt as to their purpose for being there." Among the numerous other Cuban humiliations, Ernest Hemingway reportedly invited the Dodgers to his home but "specifically requested" the exclusion of the black players. Not surprisingly, Campanella later deliberately kept the story of Papa

Hemingway's prejudices from his son Roy, Jr., who became a fan of the macho novelist as a teenager. "He didn't want to discourage me from reading Hemingway or any other authors."

Havana, after Campy's happy Nashua experience, was a rude slap in the face. Still, his determination never once wavered, not even when the indefatigable Jorge Pasquel turned up offering him $5,000 and then $10,000 annually to return south of the border. You'll never play for Brooklyn anyway, he told Campy. Why stay here? But Roy implicitly trusted Rickey. The old man had kept all his promises so far. He wasn't going to run out on him now.

Robinson, meanwhile, was facing an undercurrent of resentment ranging from muttering over his use of a drinking cup to a petition signed by several players to keep him off the Dodgers. Hoping to ease his friend's mounting stress, Roy challenged Jackie to an occasional game of checkers and kept him laughing with his usual quips and stories. But privately Campanella was coping with his own anxiety in Havana. His right arm was sore, his throws to second lacked their usual zing, and some whispered about his weight.

Montreal manager Clay Hopper (dubbed Clod by his detractors) was keeping a close eye on the man who was supposed to be his number one catcher in 1947. Hopper, a good old boy from Mississippi famous in baseball lore for once questioning Rickey whether he truly believed the "nigger's a human bein'," had since made his peace with the Great Experiment. From all reports, Hopper had treated Robinson fairly in 1946, recognizing that his handling of black players might determine whether he got a shot managing Brooklyn. Still, he had serious reservations about this latest Negro Rickey had sent his way, at least until the end of spring, when Campy finally began to live up to his press notices. Hopper's jaw dropped as he watched a now healthy Roy casually fire rockets down to second base, blast a 410-foot homer in Panama, and streak from first to third on an errant throw.

Hopper also discovered that his new colored catcher was a bit of a card. After a particularly bad call at home plate one day that spring, Hopper roared out of the dugout barking obscenities and gesturing angrily. The Cuban umpire quickly prepared to give the Montreal manager the heave-ho until he saw Roy approaching. "Don't throw him out," Campy pleaded in

Spanish. "He's not angry, he's praising you!" Seeing the ump's puzzled expression, Campy continued. "He's saying that was a fine call; and he wishes American umpires were as good as you. . . . He says he's going to get you a job in the States umpiring." The flattered Cuban arbiter allowed Campy to haul his manager back to the dugout without punishment. "What did that blind man say?" Hopper asked Roy. "He said you were absolutely right," said Roy, his eyes twinkling. "He said he missed the play and wants you to know he's sorry."

By the time Montreal had left Cuba and headed back to the States for a series of exhibitions with Brooklyn, Campy was again in his comfort zone. He had hoisted his preseason average to .323, but the real star was Robinson, who had slammed 29 hits in his first 56 at bats that spring. "I'm convinced now," Roy told the *Afro*, "that both Jackie and I can hit major league pitching."

Jackie was about to get his chance. During the fifth inning of the twelfth and final exhibition game between Brooklyn and Montreal on April 10, Branch Rickey's assistant Arthur Mann distributed a one-page news release to the gathered sportswriters in the Ebbets Field press box. The message was simple but profound: "The Brooklyn Dodgers today purchased the contract of Jackie Roosevelt Robinson from the Montreal Royals." No announcement was made over the public-address system, but Campy, as friend and roommate, probably already knew that Jackie was going to the Dodgers. Roy naturally was ecstatic: for Jackie, for black America, and also for himself. It would be his turn soon, as long as he took care of business in Montreal and Jackie did the same in Brooklyn.

The press box, abuzz with the Robinson news, had long since stopped paying attention to the action on the field by the time Jack Banta retired the last Dodger hitter to give Montreal a 4–3 victory that afternoon. Campy congratulated his pitcher and then headed to the clubhouse accompanied by Jackie and the other Royals. Spring training was almost over, but a whole new ordeal was about to begin.

BEFORE DEPARTING for Brooklyn, Robinson had thoroughly briefed Campy on what to expect in Montreal, a predominantly white city of about a million English- and French-speaking inhabitants. The fans, he told him, are not only color-blind but incredibly supportive, as Roy soon discovered.

"Gosh, Homey," he wrote Jackie, "you've given me a hard road to go. These folks up here all call me 'Jackie' and I'm expected to follow in your footsteps. Next time, don't make your prints so big."

Campy's task would not be easy, especially with the support system that had sustained him in Nashua no longer in place. He had no other blacks to kibitz with on the Montreal roster; Roy would be the only Negro in the entire league. Partlow had been let go in spring training, while Newcombe, whom Rickey privately considered "troublesome" because of salary-advance issues, had been shipped back to Nashua. And Ruthe and David were in Harlem, leaving Roy to share a room with Herb Trawick, a Pittsburgh native who had recently integrated the Canadian Football League.

Campanella also was well aware that the International League was a huge jump from the New England League. Most rosters were chock-full of familiar veteran major leaguers such as Babe Dahlgren, Chet Laabs, and Luke Hamlin, along with hotshot can't-miss prospects such as Billy Pierce, Sherm Lollar, and Gus Zernial. But *intimidation* was never a word in Roy's vocabulary. "He can take it with a smile," remarked Fay Young, the Midwest dean of black sportswriters. "He has the guts and his disposition is such that he'll never crack under the strain."

If Campy did not crack in the early days of the season, he didn't show a whole lot at the plate either. He managed only 4 hits in his first 29 at bats, although the weather wasn't particularly conducive to hitting. Not only was the team's opener in Syracuse played in frigid conditions, but two inches of snow forced the Royals' home debut to be postponed for several days. And Delorimier Downs, even after the snow melted, was no place for a right-handed pull hitter like Roy. The left-field wall was "officially" 341 feet away (some players believed it was at least 350), topped by a 24-foot fence. Not surprisingly, Campy would hit only two homers before the hometown fans that season.

He would also have to adjust to a racial environment far more hostile than in the New England League. The Newark Bears heaped racist insults upon Campanella during their first trip to Montreal, and other clubs followed suit. "It was just as bad as Robinson," recalled his teammate Butch Woyt. "He took all that N-stuff. . . . It was hard to sit on the bench and hear the crap coming out of those guys." But Campy, Woyt noted, never gave an inch. “He’d come out, straight-faced, he wouldn’t complain or nothing, just went out and played the ball game.”

Sam Lacy, the Great Experiment’s devoted chronicler, saw firsthand Campy’s remarkable ability to withstand and even transcend the most venomous of taunts. Sitting in the stands in Baltimore one evening, Lacy could no longer tolerate the ugly remarks that Oriole fans rained down upon Campanella as he stepped into the batter’s box. “Hey, pal, give me one,” he shouted encouragingly in pidgin Spanish. Campy, trying to oblige his friend, belted George Hooks’s next offering for home-run distance but foul into the left-field stands. “Bring it over to the right,” Lacy called out, again in Spanish. “As though the shot were called perfectly,” Lacy later wrote, “Campanella lifted the next pitch into the tenth tier of the stands for a homer, much to the dismay of the red-faces. It would have been hard to believe if I hadn’t seen it.”

Campanella almost never acknowledged the degree of racial animosity he faced in the International League. Disclosing such difficulties was just like complaining, and he was assuredly no complainer. Besides, Rickey had constantly reiterated the importance of avoiding conflict, even when provoked behind the plate. “Some of those older players,” Montreal first baseman Ed Stevens recalled, “they’d really try to take him out and see how they could rough him up.” But Campy, despite the encouragement of Stevens and others, refused to retaliate. “If some guys think they can get fun out of life by trying to pick on us and get us mad, it’s okay,” he told one reporter. “We don’t get mad, it’s strictly small-time stuff with them, we’re not joining in.”

Campanella did not experience any open intolerance from his own teammates, who knew better than to obstruct the Mahatma’s wishes. But Campy kept a low profile on and off the field in the early weeks of the season, determined not to “push” himself on any reluctant white player. Like Jackie in Brooklyn, Campy intentionally took his postgame shower after the whites had finished, perhaps on orders from Rickey, well aware of Southern taboos against close interracial contact. Afterward, he usually retired to his room to read the Bible his mother had given him years earlier or to listen to the radio.

His teammates, however, warmed to him quickly. Campy, as always, not only knew how to get along with people but was hard *not to like* with his laid-back but quick-witted ways. His personality, the Montreal players and sportswriters discovered, bore little resemblance to Robinson's. "Jackie always struck us as being deadly serious and conscious at all times that he was the guinea pig," remarked Dink Carroll of the *Montreal Gazette*. "If he had any light moments, they came when we weren't around." But Campy was "just another ballplayer," subject to the same insults and practical jokes as everyone else.

Robinson himself noticed the difference when he came to Montreal with Brooklyn for an exhibition game in July. No sooner had he set foot in the clubhouse to greet his old roomie than the Montreal players gave him the lowdown "about some of the pranks pulled on Roy and made fun of his high-pitched falsetto." Campy, his voice excitedly rising another octave, tried futilely to stop the good-natured mocking, but no one paid any attention. Such a scene, sportswriter Sam Maltin remarked, was unthinkable with Jackie a year earlier.

By the end of the season, Campy had developed close friendships with several white Royals. But he forged his most important relationship with a thirty-one-year-old catcher from Connecticut named Mike Sandlock. Praised by Rickey as "one of the best" defensive receivers around, Sandlock had been in pro ball since 1938 and had had a couple of brief go-rounds with the Braves and the Dodgers. Although expected to challenge Campy for the starting job, he saw his role as friendly instructor rather than cutthroat competitor. "We used to walk the streets and everything and talk baseball," Sandlock remembered. "He was very easy to get along with . . . not hard to explain things to."

Among the topics discussed was Campy's persistent habit of winding up when throwing down to second, which not only cost him precious moments but often led to rushed and hurried throws to compensate. Sandlock, Campy later explained, "had me do nothing but throw. I learned to get the ball off quickly and without a windup." Sandlock also shared his encyclopedic knowledge of International League batters until Roy could recite from memory which hitter was a sucker for a 3-2 curve and which one couldn't hit a good fastball on the fists worth a damn.

Thanks to Sandlock, Roy's ten-year evolution from a raw amateur catcher to topflight, polished receiver was now virtually complete. "I have improved a lot," he told one reporter. "I can feel it myself. I can actually see it." His arm, so inconsistent in the past, now ranked among the best in professional baseball. In 1947, he would cut down an impressive 65 percent of enemy base stealers, second in the International League only to his mentor Sandlock's 67 percent in part-time play.

Montreal's pitching staff, like Nashua's, grew more comfortable with Campy behind the plate as the season progressed. "His judgment is great," raved the hard-throwing Jack Banta. "I rarely shake off the pitch he calls for." Although some whites might privately have resented taking orders from a black man, Roy consciously worked to win them over. "A catcher," he later explained, "has to make people like him, no matter what. . . . I knew I had to take charge when I was out there on that field. . . . I had to make everyone on the team work with me."

Hopper, pleasantly surprised by Roy's sterling work behind the plate, was not concerned about his early-season plate struggles. "He's gonna give out a lot of headaches when he starts hitting that ball like he can," he announced in late May. And Roy was certain his luck would change once the weather warmed up. "I don't find the pitching in the league puzzling," he insisted. "I see those balls coming, they look easy, and then I find myself walking to the bench, hitless." By July, he was rapping the ball at a .305 clip while the Royals built a commanding lead in the International League standings.

Campy's solid start in Montreal was overshadowed by events back in Brooklyn. Robinson, despite facing vicious racial slurs from the Philadelphia Phillies, a threatened strike by the St. Louis Cardinals, and hostility from some of his own teammates, was performing beautifully with the league-leading Dodgers and looked like a shoo-in for Rookie of the Year. Not only were white Brooklynites crazy about Jackie, but black fans, many sporting newly purchased Brooklyn caps, were now packing Ebbets Field. Meanwhile, the Cleveland Indians and St. Louis Browns signed their first black players in July, destroying any lingering hopes among some owners that integration might be a Brooklyn-only phenomenon. The Great Experiment, Rickey's critics had to concede, had been an unqualified success.

With four black players in the majors by August, three without minor league experience, Campy had to wonder how long Rickey intended to keep him in Montreal. "What else has he got to do?" wrote Lloyd McGowan of the *Montreal Star.* "His hitting has improved. He has power. He can throw." Even opposing managers expected Campanella to be Brooklyn-bound soon. Paul Richards of the Buffalo Bisons considered Campy the "best catcher in baseball," while Rochester's Cedric Durst pronounced him a superior prospect to Robinson. But Rickey believed that Campanella needed at least one and perhaps two years of AAA ball under his belt. Besides, one Brooklyn official observed, the Dodgers already had a catcher, "the best in the league—Bruce Edwards."

Rickey, famous for profiting off excess talent, seemed perfectly positioned to pull the trigger on a Campanella trade. "Maybe Campanella is the Negro player and Detroit the ball club Branch Rickey referred to," the syndicated columnist Dan Parker speculated in late June, "when he said recently that another major league team was making inquiries about a colored star." Campy himself took the rumors seriously enough that he informed a black sportswriter in September that his sale to Detroit was imminent, although the Tiger organization would remain lily-white for another six years.

Whatever remote chance Roy had for a major league call-up abruptly vanished thanks to a late-season slump dropping his final average to .273. Although a reporter later cryptically alluded to Campy being "a troubled boy" in Montreal, the obvious culprit was overuse by Hopper, who had him catch a league-leading 126 games, including 26 straight at one point. That Campanella might put up better numbers with a few strategically placed days of rest or even an occasional stint in the outfield never dawned on Hopper, or, for that matter, most of Roy's managers later on in Brooklyn. Campy himself would certainly never dream of asking for a day off, regardless of a chipped bone in his right hand or the forty pounds that catching melted off him that summer.

As Campy slumped in August and September, so too did the Royals. By the last day of the season, a once seemingly insurmountable lead of 14 games over the Jersey City Giants had been frittered away to a single percentage point. To win the pennant that would mean an extra $400 per man, Montreal needed to either sweep its final doubleheader against the last-place Toronto Maple Leafs on Sunday, September 7, or split and hope for a Jersey City loss to Baltimore.

The season's largest crowd of 19,953 packed Delorimier Downs that afternoon, cheering happily as the Royals took a 5–3 lead into the last frame. Since Jersey City had already won its game, Montreal had to shut down the pesky Maple Leafs in the ninth, then beat them again in the second game to prevent a collapse of epic proportions. Campy, still in his offensive funk, hadn't contributed much to the cause thus far, but he did save a run in the sixth when he "held the ball in a vise-like grip" during a nasty collision at home plate.

The entire season now rested on the left arm of Johnny Van Cuyk, who had held the Maple Leafs scoreless since relieving Banta in the fifth. But Van Cuyk, who had just thrown a complete game on Thursday, appeared to be tiring. He dropped a pop-up to start the inning, then allowed a single one out later to put runners at the corners. With the right-handed Matt Batts, formerly one of Pip Kennedy's henchmen at Lynn, up next, Hopper called for the righty Chet Kehn, who retired Batts on a lazy infield pop-up.

Len Kensecke, a .245 lefty hitter with 2 homers, was now the Maple Leafs' last hope. The obvious move to everyone in the park, including Mike Sandlock in the bullpen, was to bring in the southpaw Al Gerheauser for a better matchup. But Hopper opted to stick with Kehn, who was supposedly tough on lefties.

Kensecke only saw two pitches from Kehn. The second one he promptly clouted over the right-field fence to put the Maple Leafs ahead 6–5. As the crowd fell deathly silent, a tearful Kehn got the third out, but the shell-shocked Royals failed to score in their half of the inning. Improbably, the Jersey City Giants, thanks to a furious .684 pace since July 4, had won the International League pennant. To complete the nightmare, the Syracuse Chiefs then swept the now second-seeded Royals four straight in the first round of the playoffs.

Campy, like the rest of his teammates, was devastated. "Every once in a while, I still see that ball Kensecke hit go flying over the screen," he wrote to Al Campanis that winter. "I still don't believe we lost that pennant after being so far in front. There'll never be anything like that again." The unhappy ending also spoiled his otherwise solid year at Montreal. He had not, it was true, matched Jackie Robinson's Montreal offensive performance. But his catching had been sensational, good enough to earn him a near-unanimous selection to the International League all-star team (the dirt-throwing Sal Yvars was the only other catcher to receive a vote). "I regard him a surer shot than Jackie was when he was under me," remarked Clay Hopper. "He's ready!"

Back in Brooklyn, Branch Rickey's season had also ended in disappointment. The Dodgers fell just short to Joe DiMaggio's Yankees in a hard-fought World Series, losing in seven games. Still, the Great Experiment had been an unparalleled triumph so far. Robinson was not only a tremendous ballplayer but most of his teammates had come to accept him. What more could he have asked for?

Rickey's plans for Campy remained uncertain. The Dodgers already had two blacks on the roster, thanks to the late-season purchase of Negro League pitcher Dan Bankhead from the Memphis Red Sox, and a third appeared risky. Campy, sportswriter Harold Burr observed, "definitely won't be brought up if Dan Bankhead makes the grade." But Bankhead, wild and hittable in his few outings, seemed likely to be ticketed for the minors.

Jackie Robinson was confident that Rickey would promote Campy to Brooklyn. He was just as certain that his friend had the ability and drive to succeed in the majors. "He is a real worker," Robinson noted. "He wants to be the best player in the league and is not going to let anything stop him. Roy has his eyes set on the majors and it is all he lives for. Maybe next season we will be together again."

10

BROOKLYN

AS USUAL, Campy gave no thoughts to a restful off-season. The Vargas team of the Venezuelan winter league wanted him as their player-manager, offering $1,000 per month, 20 percent of the gate, and the option of bringing along his pick of American players. The money, probably nearly double his monthly International League wages, was too good to pass up, but the challenge of managing was even more irresistible. Catchers, constantly involved in field decisions and strategy, usually believe they can manage, and Campy was no exception. Plus, his near fluency in Spanish ensured no communication difficulties with Vargas's native players, including the team's shortstop Luis Aparicio, Sr., whose young son Luis, Jr., a future Hall of Famer, often hung around the park.

Like Pasquel and other Latin promoters, the Venezuelans expected the Americans to produce or get out (one owner even had Tiger farmhand Saul Rogovin briefly jailed that winter for not "trying" hard enough). The thought of coasting would never have occurred to Campy, but his hard-nosed style nearly did him in one day against Rogovin's Venezuelan team. Perched at second base, Roy saw a perfect opportunity to score on a hit to the outfield, only to spy Luke Easter, the Homestead Grays' giant slugger, blocking his path at third. Never slowing down, Campy sent the hulking

Easter flying—but not for long. "All of a sudden I can hear him chugging along behind me," he recalled later. "I crossed the plate and kept right on going." Fortunately, Campy had an ace in the hole: his equally menacing pal Don Newcombe, one of his American recruits for Vargas. "Take care of him, Newk," he shouted when he reached the dugout, and Easter decided to back off.

The story was long part of Campy's repertoire, but he usually skipped over the less humorous conclusion. After the game, the still enraged, nearly six-foot-five-inch, 240-pound Easter was waiting for him. "Wait a minute, Luke," Roy sputtered. "You don't think a little guy like me is going to hit a big guy like you. I ain't that dumb, man." Never at a loss for words, Campy convinced Easter to forgive and forget.

Back home in Harlem, Ruthe had some startling but wonderful news. She was pregnant and due in June. Their marriage, put off for three years, was now necessary, and divorces had to be secured. Campy's divorce proceedings against Bernice, initiated a year earlier, were finalized in Philadelphia on December 1, 1947, on the grounds of "desertion." But Ruthe faced an uphill battle in New York, where adultery was the only acceptable grounds for divorce. Instead, she headed down to Virginia, presented herself as a state resident, and received her divorce a week after Campy's. Four months later, on April 30, Roy and a very pregnant Ruthe would secretly wed, the details never revealed to the public.

With another child on the way, Campanella began to think more seriously about his future. He was now twenty-six years old, he had yet to play a moment in the major leagues, and Brooklyn was already loaded with catching. Bruce Edwards, despite a shaky performance in the recent World Series, was expected to return, as were his two backups: the veteran Bobby Bragan and a promising youngster from Indiana, Gil Hodges. And Cliff Dapper, who had had a nice season in AA ball, was also expected to get a look-see in spring training. Dubious about his prospects, Campy could only wonder whether the Brooklyn cap that he proudly wore that winter in Venezuela (courtesy of Jackie Robinson) might be the lone part of a Dodger uniform he would don in 1948.

Rickey, as usual, not only had his own ideas, but already had the Dodger spin machine hard at work that winter. "Dodgers Planning Outfield Shift for Roy Campanella, Their New Negro Catcher," blared the headlines of Dodger beat writer Harold Burr's November 19 article in the *Sporting News*. Rickey, according to Burr, believed that Campy would perfectly fill a need for a right-handed-hitting outfielder, particularly since lefty-swinging Dixie Walker had been woeful against southpaws. Actually, the Mahatma was planning to ditch the aging but still popular Walker, one of the leaders in the petition movement against Robinson the previous spring. And Rickey also wanted fans and the press to see Campanella as an outfielder. Just exactly why would not be revealed until spring training.

Campy had no reason to believe that Rickey might be intentionally misleading the press. Robinson had been moved to first base last spring, and there was now talk of giving the oft-injured, wall-crashing outfielder Pete Reiser a shot at first. Roy, to his credit, was game, even querying his teammate Al Campanis whether he might have "a better chance to make the club this season if I tried the outfield?"

With some work, Campy might have developed into a serviceable corner outfielder. "He has a great arm and I hear that he didn't drop a foul fly all last season at Montreal," Brooklyn manager Leo Durocher remarked. "That must mean he's a pretty fair judge of fly balls." But other baseball men could not understand why the Dodgers would want to mess with the best catcher in the International League. "They know their own business over there, of course, but I wouldn't," observed Newark Bears manager Bill Skiff. "This Campanella can run and hit, and he is as quick and has as strong a throwing arm as you'd want to see."

Rickey was also aware of Bruce Edwards's shortcomings behind the plate, his fourth-place finish in the National League MVP vote notwithstanding. In February, a few hours after he had set off a firestorm by disclosing how his fellow owners had supported MacPhail's reactionary preliminary 1946 report on integration, Rickey found himself discussing Edwards with Fay Young on a flight back to Chicago. Campanella, he told Young, might prove to be a superior receiver to Edwards. Why, then, did Rickey want to stick him in the outfield? As usual, Rickey kept mum. All would be revealed in good time.

THE CAMPANELLA situation was only one of Rickey's growing concerns that spring. Despite nearly winning the World Series, the Dodgers were in the midst of a roster shake-up. As predicted, Rickey had sent

Dixie Walker to the Pirates as part of a six-player deal in December that brought over pitcher Preacher Roe, infielder Billy Cox, and infielder Gene Mauch. Eddie Stanky, the club's regular second baseman in 1947, would be next to go, shipped to Boston for cash and a sore-armed first baseman named Ray Sanders, whom Rickey eventually returned to the Braves. The departure of the popular Walker and Stanky did not sit well with Dodger fans, but Rickey was unapologetic. "Did you ever hear the story of the man who jumped out the thirtieth-story window?" he asked one reporter. "As he passed the fifteenth-story window, he shouted to his pals, 'I'm perfectly all right; there's not a thing wrong with me.' Well, I don't want to be like the man who jumped. It was too late for him to make any move."

Rickey's embattled manager, Leo Durocher, presented an even bigger headache. Back after a season-long suspension for supposedly associating with gamblers, Durocher knew he was on a short leash and that the slightest infraction would mean the ax.

The Dodgers' upcoming spring training season promised to be intriguing, if lacking the Robinson-fueled drama in Cuba a year earlier. Once again, the team would be basking in an exotic locale, this time the Dominican Republic, which reportedly offered Rickey a $60,000 guarantee and swanky accommodations at the Hotel Jaragua ("a slightly more impressive structure than the Taj Mahal," quipped one writer) in Ciudad Trujillo. The small Caribbean nation also offered a more tolerant racial atmosphere without the "undercurrent of white superiority" present in Cuba.

After guiding his Vargas club to a second-place finish in the Venezuelan winter league, Campy reported to the Dominican in late February. Still Montreal property, he would not be staying at the lush Jaragua but in a more humble hotel room about twenty miles away in San Cristóbal, the hometown of the dictator Trujillo, whose raids on black baseball had set Campy's career in motion eleven years earlier. Although Roy would never meet Trujillo, Rickey and a few other Dodger officials were introduced to the Dominican strongman at his palace, where a photographer coaxed him into posing with a Brooklyn cap.

Within a few days after Roy's arrival, Rickey summoned him to his room at the Jaragua. Roy figured the outfield switch would be the old man's topic of discussion, sandwiched between the usual fatherly advice. It might also be a good time to ask about Brooklyn's plans for him, but

Campy knew by now that most Rickey conversations were monologues and not dialogues.

Rickey beckoned Roy to take a seat and then began to speak. He knew very well that Campy was no outfielder and that he was more than ready to catch for the Dodgers. Noting Roy's baffled expression, Rickey explained that the American Association, one of three AAA-level minor leagues in Organized Baseball, needed to be integrated by the "right person." Would Campy be willing to bite the bullet and join the Dodgers' American Association affiliate in St. Paul? Rickey then outlined his scheme, how Roy would make the Dodgers out of spring training, then be sent down to St. Paul after he "failed" as an outfielder.

Campanella was stunned. Rickey was asking him to sacrifice his career, albeit temporarily, for the good of the Great Experiment. But Campy couldn't help but remember how Rickey had "stuck his neck out" by signing blacks in the first place. Besides, he later recalled, "you don't talk back to Mr. Rickey." He had no choice but to go along with the plan and keep the press out of the loop. For his part, the normally frugal Rickey would add $1,500 to Roy's $5,000 minimum major league salary he would receive once he was placed on the Brooklyn roster.

Rickey had not consulted Durocher about the decision to farm out Campanella. The Dodger skipper would learn of the scheme only when he tried to present his own ideas about revamping the Dodgers' lineup. Why not put Hodges at first and let Edwards, Campanella, and Bragan handle the catching? The Mahatma frowned. Bragan was at the end of his career and ticketed for a minor league managerial position. Campanella was going to St. Paul. Case closed. Durocher protested but his own position was too precarious to make a public stink. The best he could do was extract a promise from Rickey to recall Campanella at midseason if necessary.

Rickey then went to work on the press. On March 7, he announced his plans to promote Campy to Brooklyn before spring training ended. "I've requested Clay Hopper," he told Harold Burr, "to play Campanella in the outfield in our exhibitions with Montreal here and over at San Cristóbal. You know it has been our ambition to make a right-handed-hitting outfielder out of Roy." Three days later, Roy found himself in left field in a scrimmage against Brooklyn at Ciudad Trujillo, misplaying a Hodges liner into an inside-the-park home run.

Rickey's ploy appeared to be working perfectly. So perfectly that the outfield experiment was abandoned after a single week. There was no need, apparently, to embarrass Campy any further. Except for one brief fling at third base, he would be allowed to return behind the plate that spring, although his playing time would be reduced. The press would, naturally, then infer that Campanella wasn't quite good enough to stick with Brooklyn. In the meantime, Durocher would praise Hodges every chance he got. "I wouldn't trade Hodges," he gushed, "for any two catchers in baseball."

By this point, Rickey's devious machinations had probably begun to wear on Roy. But ballplayers generally did what they were told in those days. If Mr. Rickey wanted him to stand on his head and wear his uniform inside out, he would have done that too. For now, he could do nothing except continue his workouts with Montreal in San Cristóbal and hope for the best.

In between the daily workouts and exhibition games, Campy talked baseball for hours at breakfast with Mike Sandlock and the other Montreal catchers. He frolicked in the hotel swimming pool with Sandlock and Chuck Connors, then a Montreal farmhand but better remembered today as the star of the long-running television series *The Rifleman.* A local driver named Juan Barrett also provided regular excursions for Montreal players from San Cristóbal to Ciudad Trujillo. One Sunday, Campy arranged for Barrett to take him into the Dominican capital. At the last moment, Roy decided against it, fearing he wouldn't make curfew. It proved to be a fateful decision, as Barrett's station wagon overturned four miles from its destination, killing Barrett.

A few weeks later, Roy had another near miss, this time on a DC-4 plane heading for Dodgertown, Rickey's new minor league spring training base at Vero Beach, Florida. After about ninety minutes in the air, one of the plane's engines died and a second began to sputter. As the players exchanged uneasy glances, the pilot decided to turn around rather than tempt fate any longer. "I kept looking down at all that water," Campy remarked. "I can't swim, you know."

On March 31, the Dodgers announced that Campy had been purchased from Montreal and was now on the Brooklyn roster. Roy's dream, so long deferred, was finally a reality, and he would later remember that day was "the happiest . . . of my life." His exhilaration, however, was fleeting. Once the twenty-five-man cut-down date arrived on May 20, he knew he would be headed back to the minors.

For now, Roy was glad to finish spring training as a Brooklyn Dodger. Before leaving the Dominican Republic, Durocher had split the squad, assigning Campy to the A team that would barnstorm through Texas, Oklahoma, North Carolina, and Maryland before heading home to New York for opening day. Jackie Robinson would also be joining him, and the two friends looked forward to once again rooming together and resuming their pinochle feud.

Robinson was having a rough time after his triumph of 1947. He had hit the banquet circuit hard that winter, so hard that he reported to spring training close to thirty pounds overweight. A furious Durocher, his job on the line, vowed to sweat the blubber off Robinson, but the results were disappointing. "Robinson seemed indifferent and bitter about being expected to do the same work everyone else was doing," the usually supportive Sam Lacy remarked. "Whether this was a mental attitude brought on by too much public acclaim cannot be ventured here."

Robinson eventually worked himself back into shape, although he never forgave Durocher for his heavy-handed weight-loss tactics. Rickey, meanwhile, was worried about his young star, who frankly seemed a "mess" when he reported and was now about to embark on his first-ever preseason barnstorming tour through the South as a member of the Dodgers. The crowds were certain to be phenomenal but Rickey fretted that "Robinson's admirers" might "take it upon themselves to hold special days or celebrations" and "put us back a hundred years in what we are trying to do."

Campanella had already seen the adulation of Southern blacks even before his squad left Florida. In his first game in a Dodger uniform on March 31, he watched three thousand black fans pour into Ebbets Field No. 2, Brooklyn's brand-new ballpark at Vero Beach. They were then herded, rather roughly, into a roped-off segregated section in the outfield, but their ardor never dampened. An enthusiastic outburst greeted every ball Jackie caught or hit that day, including a home run that "sent the Negro portion . . . into ecstasy," according to a *New York Times* reporter. Campy was also welcomed warmly, although he caught only the final three innings, about as much as Rickey would allow.

The jaunt through Texas, Oklahoma, North Carolina, and Baltimore followed a similar script of huge crowds, segregated seating, and emotional fan responses. In Fort Worth on April 3, whites cheered after Robinson was thrown out stealing. Two innings later, black fans let out an even louder roar when Campy swiped second. Both men predictably contended with "racial epithets . . . that carried plenty of sting" at each game, along with Jim Crow living arrangements afterward. But Wendell Smith also noted the genuine curiosity and courtesy exhibited by some white Southerners, particularly the kids who clamored for their autographs.

With opening day fast approaching, the catching situation was suddenly in flux. The incumbent, Bruce Edwards, was now doubtful, thanks to a flare of his chronic sore arm. Durocher, however, continued to follow Rickey's script perfectly. If Edwards went down, Hodges would be his catcher. "It would be bad for Hodges's morale if I didn't catch him," he offered weakly. "How would it make him feel if I suddenly told him Campanella was my catcher?"

Always suspicious of Rickey's smoke screens, Dick Young of the *Daily News* sensed there was more to the story. "Why not Roy Campanella?" he asked as the tour neared its completion. "Durocher won't explain that one, but a good guess is that you don't waste time playing a man you're planning to sell." The Detroit rumor surfaced again that spring, although Campy knew he wasn't going anywhere. Wait, try to stay sharp, and keep his mouth shut—that was all he could do until spring training ended.

After the Dodgers romped to their twenty-fifth straight preseason victory (all against non–major league competition) on April 12, Campy and Jackie left their segregated Baltimore hotel together. Ruthe, David, and Rachel Robinson had come down from New York in Jackie's Cadillac, and the five would be driving back together.

Roy was glad to see his family but he knew their reunion in Harlem would be brief. "As things now stand all I can do is stand," he remarked to an *Afro* reporter. "I can't sit down. I can't relax. I can't even unpack. They've got me living in my suitcase." Still, he kept mum about Rickey's St. Paul scheme.

FOR THE moment, Campy was a Brooklyn Dodger, and playing in Brooklyn, he would discover, was an experience like no other.

Technically, Brooklyn was part of New York, at least since the "Great

Mistake of 1898" had ended its glory days as an independent city. But to its 2.7 million citizens, Brooklyn would never have much in common with worldly Manhattan, a few miles away across the East River, or the rest of the city. Its neighborhoods were remarkably diverse, heavily populated by Jews (roughly 50 percent of the population), Italians, Irish, and a growing number of blacks. Most of Brooklyn's citizens were solidly working or middle class, many owning their own modest homes. "I like Brooklyn," remarked Branch Rickey soon after his arrival in 1942. "It is not New York. . . . It is homefolks."

A select few civic institutions knitted the otherwise disparate groups of "homefolks" together. There was the Brooklyn Bridge, an unprecedented feat of engineering when it opened in 1883. Coney Island's beaches, amusement parks, and hot dogs were world-famous. The *Eagle*, Brooklyn's last remaining daily newspaper, kept borough residents abreast of local happenings. But the Dodgers and Ebbets Field, their idiosyncratic ballpark in Flatbush, were the unifying force in the community. "Around their battered standard," writer David Boroff observed later, "Brooklynites always rallied."

Admittedly, the Dodgers, so named in the late nineteenth century because Brooklyn residents were said to be always "dodging" trolley cars on local streets, had often tried the patience of even their most loyal rooters. After two World Series appearances in 1916 and 1920, the franchise crashed and burned, finishing in the second division fourteen of the next eighteen years. While the Yankees grabbed the headlines with regular championships and the likes of Ruth, Gehrig, and DiMaggio, the Dodgers' ineptitude became a national joke. Sportswriters gleefully reported (and embellished) wacky tales of the "Daffiness Boys," such as Babe Herman, who fielded balls off his skull and once doubled into a double play. Local fans could only wince at the parade of "bums" wearing Brooklyn uniforms those years, prompting *World-Telegram* cartoonist Willard Mullin to create the plump, shabbily dressed, unshaven, cigar-smoking "Brooklyn Bum" in 1937. Mullin's drawing quickly caught on, and "Dem Bums" became the Dodgers' unofficial second nickname.

The franchise was in deep trouble by the late 1930s. Ebbets Field was in atrocious shape, the team thousands of dollars in debt to the Brooklyn Trust Company, and the farm system nearly barren. Fortunately, the

Dodgers' fractured and constantly bickering ownership group finally made a smart decision in 1938. They hired Larry MacPhail, a dynamic, progressive-thinking baseball man (except when it came to race), who immediately went to work transforming Brooklyn into a legitimate baseball organization again. After obtaining working capital from Brooklyn Trust, MacPhail spruced up Ebbets Field, began investing heavily in player talent, and handed the managerial reins to Leo Durocher. The new and improved Bums jumped to third place in 1939, second in 1940, and finally the National League pennant the following season. And Brooklynites, a record 1.2 million strong in 1941, began pouring into Ebbets Field as never before.

By the time MacPhail departed a year later, the once pitiful franchise was now ranked among the National League's elite. Still, it would be Rickey who would oversee the final stage of Brooklyn's makeover. His headlong plunge into the black-player market while other teams dithered on the sidelines would eventually give the Dodgers a tremendous competitive advantage in the years to come. For a team that had only recently begun to turn a profit, this risky move might have antagonized a devoted fan base. But Rickey knew the "homefolks" of Brooklyn were a different, more tolerant breed, used to mixing with different cultures and ethnicities. They had accepted Jackie, and there was a good chance they would accept Campanella, at least if they ever got a chance to see him in action.

TUESDAY, APRIL 20, 1948, was another routine workday for most New Yorkers. The major topic of discussion around office watercoolers throughout the city was Mayor O'Dwyer's plan to end the five-cent subway fare in place since 1904. Beginning July 1, locals would have to pay a dime—*a dime!*—to ride the subways.

In the meantime it still cost only a nickel to get to the Polo Grounds, where the Giants and the Dodgers were set to renew their age-old rivalry and inaugurate New York's baseball season that day. As 48,130 happy fans took their seats and waited patiently for the game to begin, some noted the changes in the Polo Grounds, particularly the lack of advertising on the outfield walls and the mostly grassless outfield, yet to be resodded after football season. A few clicked on their "portable" radios, tuning in to Brooklyn's Red Barber and Connie Desmond on WHN, sponsored by Old

Gold cigarettes ("It's A Treat!"), or the Giants' Frankie Frisch and Maury Farrell over at WMCA. But everyone paid attention when Babe Ruth, cigar in hand and clad in a "long cream-colored camel's hair coat and a matching cap," entered the park around 2:00 p.m. with his wife and daughter. The Bambino, his body wracked with cancer, had less than four months to live. He received a thunderous ovation as he took his seat near the Giants' dugout.

Over in the Dodger dugout, Campy sat drinking it all in. He was not in the lineup, but he felt a surge of pride just participating in the usual opening-day parade of the two ball clubs to the flagpole, the formal raising of Old Glory, and the playing of the national anthem. He might have been even prouder had he known that the great Mel Ott, now the Giants' manager, had been watching him intently during pregame infield practice. "This is the first time I've seen him," Ott remarked. "They tell me he is quite a catcher." And Ruthe was in the stands cheering Campy on, sitting with Rachel Robinson, whose husband would lead off the game in a few minutes against the Giants' right-hander Larry Jansen.

The crowd, exhausted by the hours of pomp and anticipation, breathed a sigh of relief when Robinson finally stepped into the batter's box. Jansen, a 21-game winner as a rookie in 1947, retired Jackie, and the season was under way. For Campy, that meant exile to the bench with the rest of the second-stringers and unproven youngsters, such as the Californian Edwin "Duke" Snider, who had spent much of spring training receiving special instruction on the strike zone.

For the first six innings, Jansen mowed down the Dodger hitters with ease while clinging to a 3–1 lead. In the midst of a four-run Brooklyn rally in the seventh, Gil Hodges was lifted for a pinch hitter, forcing Durocher to weigh his catching options. Edwards wasn't 100 percent, but Bobby Bragan was still on the roster and available. And then there was Campanella, the man he wasn't supposed to use. Durocher decided to test Rickey. He would put in Campanella and see what happened.

Campy, surprised and excited to get the call, found himself working with the veteran reliever Hugh Casey, a Georgian whose racial views were straight out of the old Confederacy. Robinson had already been subjected to Casey's casual announcement of his remedy for bad luck in poker: procuring "one of those big black nigger women." But Robinson later recalled that he "got along wonderfully well with Casey," whose life would end in suicide three years later.

Campy's relationship with the Southerner would not be quite so congenial. Casey, he discovered, was not keen on taking orders from a black catcher. All Campy could do was put the signal down and let Casey decide. "If he didn't want to throw it," Campy later recalled, "you throw what you want to, then." Casey threw what he wanted, but his pitch-calling was decidedly amateurish that afternoon, the Giants cuffing him for 3 hits, 2 walks, and 3 runs in 3 innings of relief.

The racial issues that confounded Campy's catching would also surface in his first major league at bat. In the top of the eighth, he came to the plate against Giant reliever Ken Trinkle, who promptly drilled him in the ribs on the first pitch. Although Trinkle's control was not the best, it was likely a purpose pitch to a rookie and a Negro one, to boot. "Loosening up" a hitter was part of the game in those days, and Roy had seen enough high, hard ones in his career not to get too upset. But he soon discovered the unprotected skulls of black players were a favorite target for certain major league hurlers, who "let the ball talk for them."

Despite Casey's shaky relief work, the Dodgers held on to win the opener 7–6. Rickey, sitting near the Dodger dugout with his wife and movie star Laraine Day, otherwise known as Mrs. Leo Durocher, was pleased except for the three innings a certain pudgy catcher had played that afternoon. "I told you not to play Campanella," he told Durocher. The next day, Leo toed the line. He used a record twenty-four players in a 9–5 loss at the Polo Grounds. Campy was not one of them.

Over the next five games, Roy played exactly two innings of baseball. The Dodgers, meanwhile, were slumping, losing two of three to the Phillies, followed by a shutout by Boston. Durocher decided his lethargic bunch needed a shake-up for the second game of the Braves series on April 27. Reiser would get his first start in center field, Spider Jorgensen would go to third, and sore-armed Bruce Edwards, who was bouncing his throws down to second base, would be benched in favor of Campy. The new-look Bums collected a total of six hits that chilly afternoon, falling to Boston by a 3–2 score.

Durocher knew what was coming. He had not only defied Rickey but the team had *lost*. Campy hadn't done much, going 0 for 3 with a walk, but Rickey was apoplectic. "You better not play Campanella again," he warned. Durocher, by now certain the old man cared more about the Great Experiment than the Dodgers' current record, finally gave in. Campanella, he told Rickey, would not be used under any circumstances.

Campy sat on the bench for the next sixteen days as the team made its way through Philadelphia, St. Louis, Chicago, Pittsburgh, and Cincinnati. "I just want to play ball," he told Sam Lacy. "I don't care where it is. That's why you see me catching batting practice every day. Nobody has told me to do that. I just do it voluntarily. If I don't do anything, I'll go crazy."

Away from the cruel punishment of the bullpen and the bench, he could at least enjoy his new lifestyle. Big leaguers, he discovered, received \$5 to \$6.50 per day in meal money on the road, a far cry from the sixty cents he earned with the Elites back in 1937. The accommodations were an amazing upgrade from the rat traps he had known in the past, "the best thing about being in the major leagues," he once observed. But some hotels still openly refused black patronage even after a year of major league integration. In St. Louis, Campy and his roommate, Jackie, were shuttled off to a Negro hotel while the rest of the club stayed at the plush Chase.

Roy's friendship with Jackie had continued to blossom during the road trip. He invited Jackie and Rachel to spend the weekend with him at his parents' house on Kerbaugh Street during the Dodgers' stop in Philadelphia. In Chicago, the two men went to the Elmer Ray/Ezzard Charles bout with Lacy and Fay Young. To Young, Campy and Jackie "get along like two brothers," although Jackie appeared to be the dominant sibling. Robinson, Young noticed, not only argued about who would win the fight but teased Campy after Ray, his favorite, was KO'd in the ninth round. But Roy took it all in stride. If anything, his respect and affection for Jackie was growing after witnessing the abuse his friend still encountered.

Despite Durocher's constant lineup shuffling, the Dodgers were still bobbing along at the .500 mark at the end of the trip. And the catching question had yet to be settled. Bruce Edwards was swinging the bat reasonably well but now had a sprained thumb to go along with his sore arm. Why, then, writers wondered, did this Campanella continue to gather splinters on the bench day after day? "Everyone's wondering what gives with Roy Campanella," wrote Dick Young. "Looks like he's ticketed out, without having been given much of a chance to show his stuff. If that's so, why did the Brooks bring him up from Montreal in the first place?"

Rickey winced. "What is all this mystery of why Durocher hasn't been catching Campanella?" he thundered to a group of writers. Durocher only needed three catchers, Rickey explained, and one obviously had to go. Edwards wasn't going anywhere. Nor was Hodges, a future MVP according to the Mahatma. Then why not Bobby Bragan? "If you should put it to a vote among the thirty-four Dodger players, I venture to say that thirty-three of 'em would cast their vote to keep Bragan." The American Association scheme was conveniently ignored.

No one was surprised when Campy's demotion to St. Paul was finally announced before gametime on May 17. "I hated to see him go, but that's the life of a baseball player," a philosophical Jackie Robinson remarked. "I'm sure Roy will come back to the big leagues. Maybe he won't make it this year because after they see him at St. Paul they won't want to let him go. But he'll be back next season and I'll bet he sticks."

AFTER BEING in limbo for nearly three months, Roy relished the chance to hit and catch live pitching again, even if he had to stay at St. Paul for the rest of the season. Rickey was paying him well to play AAA ball, and he might attract the interest of another major league club in the meantime.

The prospect of integrating the American Association did not particularly concern him. As the only black in the International League last season, he had already heard every moronic insult. This year, he had Ruthe and David along as a buffer. After arriving in St. Paul, the young family quickly set up housekeeping in rented rooms in a private home at 707 Rondo Street in the city's largest African-American neighborhood.

Walter Alston, his own career on the upswing, was now managing the Saints and wasted no time getting Campy into the starting lineup on Saturday, May 22, in Columbus against the Red Birds. The local fans who witnessed American Association history that afternoon were not impressed by St. Paul's Negro catcher. A rusty Roy made a throwing error on a pickoff play and struck out twice against a young left-hander named Harvey Haddix. He continued to struggle as the team moved through Toledo, Louisville, and Indianapolis, managing only 4 singles in 20 at bats. Worst of all, the Jim Crow accommodations made him feel like a Negro Leaguer again. He stayed in a black hotel in Indianapolis and had to enlist his old manager Felton Snow to find him a private room in Louisville.

With the Saints 2-8 since Campy's arrival, St. Paul fans wondered why the Dodgers had sent them this .167 hitting catcher instead of Duke Snider, recently shipped out to Montreal. But as soon as Campy returned to Minnesota soil, his bat began to heat up. In his first Twin Cities appearance on Sunday, May 30, at Nicollet Park in Minneapolis, he clubbed two homers against the Millers. The following morning, he homered, tripled, and drove in three runs at St. Paul in the first game of a two-venue Memorial Day doubleheader. When Alston sat Roy down in the afternoon affair at Nicollet, a beer-addled white fan was unable to hide his disappointment. "There was a colored man out here yesterday who hit two home runs," he mumbled to no one in particular. "Where ish he?"

The colored man eventually made a pinch-hitting appearance that game. The first pitch Roy saw from the Millers' Mario Picone sent him sprawling in the dirt, but as usual he said nothing. "I keep one thing in mind," he told a reporter a few days later. "A colored ballplayer has to be a gentleman." Rickey had reiterated this lesson and Campy was determined to abide by it, regardless of the circumstances.

Picone retired Campy, but most pitchers would not be so lucky in the next few weeks. The notoriously streaky Campanella was now locked in at the plate, the ball jumping off his bat. He was pleased to discover that Lexington Park in St. Paul, thanks to a 315-foot left field, was a right-handed hitter's paradise. In his first seven games at Lexington, he hit .538, slammed 8 homers (few of them cheapies), and drove in an amazing 24 runs. The once-derided Campy was now drawing comparisons to Ted Williams, whose American Association slugging exploits had wowed Minnesotans ten years earlier.

Carl Rowan, later one of the most prominent African-American journalists of his generation, was covering the Campanella story as a young reporter for the black *Minneapolis Spokesman*. The white fans, he marveled, were now head over heels in love with their new catcher, pleading with him to "park one" each at bat and passing their scorecards to the batboy for Roy to sign. Campy, meanwhile, told Rowan that there had been "no incidents" except for segregated hotel accommodations, and his teammates were "a great bunch of fellas."

For now, everything seemed perfect for the Campanella clan, which was about to welcome a new member. On Father's Day, June 20, Ruthe presented Roy with a gift: a seven-and-a-half-pound son named Roy, Jr. Around friends and family, he would often be known as Little Roy.

Meanwhile, the situation at Ebbets Field had gone from bad to worse. The team lost eight straight home games in late May. The still chunky Robinson had not only cursed out the *Mirror*'s Gus Steiger for writing about his weight but had also been placed on waivers. The roster, so promising preseason, had been decimated by injuries and peculiar roster moves that left Durocher at times with only seven serviceable pitchers. Leo himself was catching hell from fans impatient with the team's struggles. "Hey, Hollywood," screeched one Brooklynite, "why don't you go back to your flower garden!" Others pointed to Rickey, who, it was whispered, was now the real manager of the Dodgers: "He masterminds too much with the lineup."

By the end of June, the National League's defending champion was not only wallowing in sixth place, six games under .500, but had become, in the words of one writer, "fodder for radio comics." Durocher now begged for reinforcements from the farm, only to encounter resistance from the Dodger brass. Three of their four top minor league affiliates were owned outright by Brooklyn, and Rickey knew that it was bad business to cherry-pick their rosters during the regular season. Still, he had no other option, barring simply writing off the season as a disaster.

With the Bums last in the league in hitting and seventh in homers, Durocher knew exactly whom he wanted: George Shuba, a .389 hitter with AA Mobile, and Campanella, who had bashed thirteen homers in six weeks with St. Paul. Rickey reluctantly agreed. To free up roster spots, Don Lund was placed on waivers and little-used Bobby Bragan was sent to Fort Worth to become player-manager. Shuba's and Campanella's promotions were then announced on June 30, shortly after the Dodgers had absorbed a 13–4 pummeling by the Phillies.

Campy was in Toledo when Alston gave him the startling news after a Wednesday doubleheader. His elation was tempered by concerns about whether Ruthe and a ten-day-old baby could make the trip to New York.

Calls were hastily made to Brooklyn officials, who arranged for Ruthe to see a St. Paul physician on Thursday while Campy frantically packed. After the doctor gave his blessing, Campy, Ruthe, and Little Roy boarded a New York–bound plane the next morning, leaving behind David and Campy's mother-in-law, Fannie, to ride back by train. Thankfully, the flight was uneventful, and a friendly stewardess even warmed the baby's bottle.

The plane touched down at LaGuardia at three thirty, just enough time for Roy to get Ruthe and the baby situated at her mother's place in Harlem. From there, he hopped the subway for Ebbets Field, where the Dodgers had a night game against the Giants. Exhausted but excited, he was looking forward to reuniting with Jackie as he made his way into the clubhouse. Instead he was greeted by a sarcastic voice belonging to Dick Whitman, a part-time outfielder and teammate of Campy's last year in Montreal: "Campanella's here. We're saved."

While still pondering Whitman's comment, Campy was welcomed more enthusiastically by Durocher, who had decided that Campanella was going to be his catcher. "How can you keep a fellow who has hit twelve homers in such a short time out of the lineup, even if he has to lead off," he told one reporter. Hodges had already been moved to first base earlier in the week. Bruce Edwards, sore arm and all, would be tried at third, giving the Dodgers a peculiar three-catcher lineup tonight.

After John Griffin, the team's obese, cigar-smoking equipment man, gave Campy a locker and number 39 (he had worn 56 earlier that year), Roy took a closer look at his surroundings. The aging yet intimate thirty-four-thousand-seat park oozed idiosyncratic charm in every nook and cranny. Newcomers quickly noted the Schaefer Beer sign on the scoreboard in right-center field, whose *h* and *e* letters doubled as "hit" and "error" symbols. At its base, hitters were invited by Abe Stark's clothing store to HIT SIGN, WIN SUIT, although its placement nearly four hundred feet away made the prospects for new threads remote for most players.

The ballpark's most famous fan was a stout, fifty-year-old racetrack-concessions employee named Hilda Chester, who had parlayed her cowbell, banner (HILDA IS HERE), and leather lungs into national recognition as Brooklyn's Number One Fan. Adding to the fun or chaos was the Dodger Sym-Phony, a band of merry musicians whose whistle tweets, trumpet blasts, and cymbal crashes noisily punctuated each game.

Even the organist and the public-address announcer, forgettable or unknown in most parks, left lasting impressions. Gladys Goodding was famous for her lightning-quick, soprano rendition of the national anthem, her version of "Chiapanecas" (the Mexican hand-clapping song) in the seventh-inning stretch, the fox terrier who sat beside her, and her fondness for liquid lunches. She even took requests from the players, often favoring Pee Wee Reese with "Apple Blossom Time" and Carl Furillo with "O Sole Mio." Then there was John "Tex" Rickards, who announced each game from, of all things, "a metal bridge chair resting on a couple of empty soda-pop boxes" near the Dodger dugout. Rickards, sniffed one out-of-town writer, "sounds like a train-caller with laryngitis," but his Brooklynese and ungrammatical warnings to fans ("Don't throw nuthin' from the stands!") were music to their ears.

As he took batting practice at Ebbets that night, Campy also took note of the field's quirky dimensions. Left-handed sluggers loved to take aim at the short right-field porch only 297 feet away. But a right-handed power hitter, he quickly realized, could also do plenty of damage here. Rickey had brought in the left-field fences recently from 357 to 343 feet, and center field was a reasonable 393. Maybe Ebbets wasn't a homer haven like Lexington Park, but it sure wasn't Delorimier or Holman, where it took a cannon to clear the fence.

A large crowd of 33,104 made its way into the park that Friday evening, including Rickey, who emerged from his sickbed to see his new three-catcher combo in action. The results, at least initially, seemed to offer encouragement that the season might still be salvaged. Aside from a catcher's interference call, Campy was almost perfect, banging out a double and two singles, nailing Buddy Kerr stealing, and making a brilliant grab of a foul pop outside the Dodger dugout. Shuba chipped in with two hits in three trips. Bruce Edwards, however, looked baffled at third base, and the Giants bunted on him mercilessly. Worst of all, the Dodgers blew a 4–3 lead in the ninth inning, lost their sixth straight game, and fell into the National League cellar. As the team quietly dressed afterward, Durocher hurled his spikes against the clubhouse wall.

The Durochermen, having apparently bottomed out, suddenly came to life during the weekend. On Saturday, they finally snapped their losing streak after scoring five runs in the seventh inning to overcome a 5–2 deficit and holding on for a 7–5 win. The holiday finale on July 4 was an even wilder affair, featuring thirty-seven different players, lead changes galore, Robinson's three bunt singles and steal of home, and Leo's ejection in the fifth inning. The biggest thrill of all came in the bottom of the ninth when the Dodgers, trailing 12–9, pulled off an amazing comeback, tallying four times to beat the Giants 13–12.

But the real story was Campy, who had just completed a fairy-tale return to the Big Show. In thirteen plate appearances during a series he later described as the "greatest . . . of my life," he reached base ten times on nine hits and a walk. Twice he went deep on Sunday, the second a gargantuan shot off Monty Kennedy into the upper deck in left field, supposedly "a region untouched by a Brooklyn batter in years." His work behind the plate was just as impressive, particularly his skill in handling Willie Ramsdell's knuckleball. "The Negro is by far the best receiver Brooklyn has had since Al Lopez," Mike Gaven of the *Journal-American* observed a few days later. "He should have been the first-string catcher on opening day."

Few would have disagreed, but Campy was not one to fixate on past injustices. If Rickey's manipulations had cost him a couple of months of his major league career, so be it. Number 39 was now his and he was never going to give it up. "They're gonna have to cut this one off me," he would later insist. "Do you realize how long and hard we worked to get into one of 'em. . . . Once they put one on you, never take it off."

Beyond the uniform, Roy had also earned his first taste of real celebrity, far beyond what he had experienced in the Negro Leagues. Fans, kids, even cops began to recognize him outside the ballpark, wanting to shake his hand or get his autograph. He would meet Lena Horne, who would present him with his first car, a Buick Super 8, on a day held in his honor late in the season at Ebbets. He even picked up a small endorsement deal, appearing alongside jazz chanteuse Ida James in a cereal ad running in the black press ("Get Hep to Post's Cereals—They're Tops!").

The local beatwriters and columnists also wanted a piece of him. New York had no fewer than ten daily newspapers in 1948, eleven if one counted the communist *Daily Worker*, and their columns needed to be filled with interviews and stories. The *Daily News*' Dick Young, Roy would come to discover, was the most persistent of the bunch.

Young was only thirty years old but was already the preeminent sportswriter in New York. Unlike most of his colleagues, who covered the game and little else, Young went into the locker rooms after the game, probing, prodding, and questioning. His readers ate it up. "Dick Young was a great reporter and a perfect writer for a tabloid," *New York Times* columnist Dave Anderson recalled. "He was *the* baseball writer of that era. . . . I learned the business in self-defense because of Dick Young."

For all of Young's undeniable gifts, some found him obnoxious and overbearing. Lynn Parrott remembered watching Young cut in front of a bunch of players on a waterslide in Havana. "They let him do it," Parrott recalled, but the incident epitomized Young: "brash, fast-talking, full of his own self-importance." Still, Young was not easily categorized. Ideologically liberal as a young man, his later columns of the 1970s and 1980s were often fuddy-duddy rants about the new breed of athlete and the perceived moral decay of American society. But at the same time the aging Young offered unqualified support to the first generation of female sportswriters.

Young was sympathetic to the first wave of black ballplayers. "I had always respected Dick for being a newspaperman that went out and got stories and wrote them," Jackie Robinson later noted, "regardless of whether or not they were going to hurt anybody as long as they were truthful." Campy would also come to recognize Young's talents and influence, and the two soon became pals, culminating in Young's authorship of Roy's 1952 biography. But Young later soured on Jackie, whom he perceived as too "militant" and too outspoken. Unwittingly, Campy would be caught in the middle of their squabble, learning too late a painful lesson about the media, one that he would impart to his adult son years later. "White people," he told Roy, Jr., "will use you to attack other blacks."

WHILE ROY basked in his new celebrity, Leo Durocher sat waiting for the ax to fall. Two of Rickey's partners, Walter O'Malley and John Smith, apparently wanted Leo gone, and the Mahatma himself lacked the will to protect him any longer. In the midst of the heroic July 4 comeback at Ebbets, Rickey had dispatched press secretary Harold Parrott to the clubhouse to ask for Durocher's resignation. "Hell, no, I won't resign," barked the Lip. "He's going to have to fire me and he's going to have to do it man-to-man." Instead, Rickey waited, while the Dodgers reeled off six wins in eight games prior to the All-Star break.

Over at the Polo Grounds, Horace Stoneham was also looking to switch managers. The Giants weren't going anywhere under Mel Ott, and Stoneham decided to ask Rickey for permission to talk to Burt Shotton, who had managed Brooklyn during Durocher's suspension the previous year. Shotton, Rickey informed him, was off-limits. But then someone, either Rickey or Stoneham, depending on the version, suggested Durocher instead. Within a day, a surprising deal was put together. Durocher would take over the Giants, while Shotton would return to the helm of the Dodgers.

Giant fans shuddered when they heard the news. Hire their hated archrival's manager? "That's horrible," wailed one. "Absolutely horrible!" Brooklynites, meanwhile, were glad to see Leo go. "Durocher was too much of a loudmouth for his own good," remarked a fan. "I even feel sorry for the Giants a little." Somehow, Leo resisted the urge to fire a departing blast at Rickey and company. "I want to let bygones be bygones. But I will tell you this: We didn't get started at Brooklyn until I insisted and insisted that we get Campanella. He was the difference."

Burt Shotton, Campy would discover, was nothing like Durocher, personally or professionally. The Lip was a fast-talking city slicker who wore expensive suits, doused himself in cologne, and was borderline obsessive-compulsive about cleanliness. As a manager, he drove his players mercilessly. "If you missed a signal," Gene Hermanski recalled, "don't bunt when you're supposed to, man, he'd jump on your ass." "Nice guys finish last" was Durocher's famous credo, although he later clarified his position. "I don't say a fellow has to be no good to win ball games or a pennant," he explained. "I like to associate with nice people too. I'm talking about fellows who come to the field in a jolly mood, not caring whether they win that day or not."

Shotton, nearly sixty-four, was far from a firebrand. With his glasses, bow tie, white hair, and paunch, the "Old Sourdough from Ohio" looked more grandfather than baseball manager. Unlike Durocher, he did not crave the spotlight. He refused to wear a uniform and so never budged from the bench ("like an embalmed cucumber showing nothing," sniffed gossip columnist Dorothy Kilgallen), delegating his coaches to argue with umps and pull pitchers. His players found him laid-back almost to a fault. "I tell 'em what to do and if they don't do it—well, I don't lie awake nights." As for his managerial philosophy, it was simple yet refreshingly candid: "When I have players who can do what I want done, I am a good manager. When they can't, I am a bad manager."

Despite Shotton's nonthreatening demeanor, writers were surprised to discover that the Brooklyn manager could be "crabbed and hostile in a grumpy old man's way," even once challenging Dick Young to a fight for questioning the guts of the Dodger pitching staff. Rickey, however, was comfortable with the Old Sourdough, a fellow Midwesterner he had known for more than thirty years and called his "best friend." Shotton, according to the Mahatma, was "a great manager," although some players believed him to be little more than "Mr. Rickey's puppet."

Robinson, who had come to detest Durocher, was pleased with the change. Shotton, except for an unfortunate reference to "nigger rich" ballplayers, for which he later apologized to Jackie, had handled the Great Experiment well in 1947. But Campy was not so sure he was going to like his new manager, who was already praising Hodges as a "great young catcher" and suggesting Campy needed some rest. Still, Shotton decided Campanella and Hodges would stay in the lineup in their current positions, although the struggling Billy Cox would get a shot at third. Carl Erskine, a friendly, clean-cut young pitcher from Indiana, would be recalled from Fort Worth.

With Shotton now in command, the Dodgers began to make a run at the league-leading Boston Braves. Meanwhile, Campy experienced the usual highs and lows of a rookie trying to adjust to the depth and consistency of major league pitching. As his average began to plummet, he sought the advice of the veteran Arky Vaughan, a former National League batting champion winding down his career with the Dodgers. Vaughan suggested that Campy "stay ready for a pitcher's fast pitch," then adapt to whatever else he might offer. "I think that was the soundest advice I'd ever got about hitting," Roy later observed.

Other Dodger teammates were not so friendly or forthcoming with assistance. "It is not difficult to sense which of them still have private reservations, still cling to conditioned prejudices," wrote Jack Sher in *Sport* that October. "It isn't in what they say, but in their attitude, the fear and suspicion in their eyes when you question them about Robinson." There was no surefire way to determine whether a fellow liked or disliked playing with Negroes. For every bigoted Southerner like Hugh Casey, there was a Pee Wee Reese, the Dodgers' Kentucky-born shortstop who befriended Jackie and would become one of Campy's closest Dodger buddies.

As a catcher, Campy simply could not wall himself off from his teammates, regardless of their racial attitudes. If some of the veteran pitchers such as Casey didn't respect his pitch-calling, it was Campy's job to win them over with his ability, enthusiasm, and encouragement. Fortunately, it did not take long for most to come around. All they needed to do was watch Campy's smooth handling of the hard-throwing but erratic Rex Barney. "Barney was always afraid to let up," remarked Dodger coach Clyde Sukeforth. "He'd never throw his curve in the tight spots. And that's where Campanella has worked his miracle. He keeps calling for half- and three-quarter-speed pitches, for fast curves and slow ones. He allows Rex to show just enough of his fastball to keep the hitters looking for it."

At times, Barney thought he knew a bit more about pitching than his battery mate. A year later, Barney was sailing along with a no-hitter at Wrigley Field one September afternoon with no outs in the eighth and the dangerous Phil Cavarretta at the plate. Campy called for a curve, but Barney, believing that Cavarretta would take the first pitch, shook him off. Instead, he fired a fastball, which Cavarretta promptly rifled for a single for what turned out to be the only hit he allowed that day. As he left the field, Barney turned to hear Campy's high-pitched voice angrily calling to him, "Don't you ever shake me off again. You know I'm smarter than you are. And I've always been smarter than you are. And I'll always be smarter than you are. Pitchers don't know a Goddamn thing. They's why they have catchers."

By September, the now red-hot Dodgers had caught the Braves, and Brooklyn fans were thinking pennant. But the Bums' miracle renaissance was nearly overshadowed by another story. Jackie Robinson, after suffering silently for nearly two seasons under Rickey's orders, had apparently struck off his shackles on the ballfield. Writers reported breathlessly how the "Negro ace threw his cap on the ground and went into a rage of disagreement" on August 2 against the Cubs and got himself tossed in Pittsburgh by a prejudiced umpire and former Dodger named Butch Henline three weeks later. To Branch Rickey, another important milestone had been reached. "It's good! It's healthy! It proves Robbie's still a team man."

Campy was uneasy about Jackie's new behavior. With only four blacks in the major leagues, a single mishap could conceivably set back the entire movement. "It may take ten years to go ahead but you can fall all the way back in one," he once insisted. "You got to walk a chalk line all the time." Concerned that his friend might be falling off the "chalk line," Roy expressed his concerns to Jackie, saying, "It's nice up here. Don't spoil it."

Or so goes the moth-eaten legend. Robinson thought the story originated with Dick Young, although its first mention may have been in a 1950 article in the *Sporting News*. In any event, the "it's nice up here/don't spoil it" tale in its various incarnations became a favorite of white sportswriters to highlight the difference between the Dodgers' black stars. Jackie, according to the papers, was the aggressive hothead, always "popping off." Campy, meanwhile, was passive, grateful to be in the major leagues.

As the story continued to make the rounds during the 1950s, Robinson grew increasingly annoyed with its implications. Late in his career, an umpire made the mistake of mentioning the incident again to Jackie at an airport. Robinson was furious. "I would like to take five newspapermen and throw this question at them and have them put down on paper the time—I don't mean the day or the week, but I would like for them to give me the *year* when this incident was supposed to have happened," he complained. "And I would like them to tell me where it happened, what city it was in, and I would bet you that I couldn't get two answers the same from these five newspapermen, because for one thing I never remember the incident." In fact, *Wait Till Next Year*, his 1960 collaboration with Carl Rowan, would flatly claim that "no such conversation ever occurred."

Whether the story originated with Campy is unclear. It seems more likely that Young or some other reporter might have invented a conversation after seeing a worried Roy commiserating with Robinson after his first major league ejection. And Roy was perhaps justified in his anxiety. The Great Experiment was still young, he had been in the major leagues for only a few months, and Rickey had until recently constantly reinforced the absolute necessity for blacks to behave as "gentlemen" on and off the field. Robinson had deviated from that standard, and Campy expected the proverbial shit to hit the fan.

It didn't. Jackie would only grow more confident, outspoken, and aggressive in the years that followed. But Roy never quite shook the fear that a wrong move or an unpopular statement might jeopardize the Great

Experiment. "Everything we did stood out so much then," he told historian Jules Tygiel years later. "You couldn't afford to make a mistake . . . because you stood out like a sore thumb."

THE DODGERS faltered in September, in no small part due to Leo Durocher's Giants, who beat them six times in eight meetings down the stretch. The recently released Hugh Casey blamed the third-place finish on the inexperienced roster assembled by Rickey. "They just weren't aggressive or hustled like Brooklyn teams always have. Why, they'd munch candy bars on the bench, laugh, and kid around. You don't win pennants with that approach." Rickey, however, was confident that things would be different in '49: "I like my team . . . I really do."

Rickey viewed Campy as an important part of the Dodgers' future. He had performed reasonably well in his rookie campaign with a .258 batting average, .345 on-base percentage, 9 homers, and 45 RBIs in 279 at bats, respectable numbers for a National League catcher at that time. But his throwing game set him apart from his peers. In 1948, he gunned down 23 of 34 runners, including the last 12 who attempted to run on him.

Still, he was not yet a star or especially well known outside of Brooklyn or black America. He didn't receive a single vote for Rookie of the Year, which went to Al Dark of the Boston Braves. Nor did he earn selection to the *Sporting News*' Freshman All-Star Team. He had cleared the biggest hurdle, it was true, but he still had a great deal to prove.

11

OUT OF THE SHADOWS

FOR THE FIRST TIME IN YEARS, Roy faced the unsettling prospect of an off-season without baseball. As a major leaguer, he was no longer eligible for winter ball, although his black celebrity status quickly created two job opportunities. During the evenings, he would make appearances and serve as night manager at the Regent Theater, a Brooklyn movie house catering to the large black community in the Bedford-Stuyvesant section. His days would be spent with Jackie Robinson at the Harlem YMCA, where the two men would hang out with the kids and serve as athletic instructors.

Their young charges were initially too awestruck to speak. "A lot of the younger kids didn't believe who we were," Campy remarked. "They kept asking grown-ups, 'Is that really Jackie Robinson and Roy Campanella?' " As the days passed, the big-shot big leaguers became simply "Campy" and "Jackie," two swell fellows who refereed their basketball games, played a mean game of checkers, and sometimes even shot pool with them.

Quietly and unobtrusively, Robinson and Campanella were serving as role models, long before the term had become a cliché. "Those kids seeing Jackie and Roy in the flesh will have a constant reminder that making the grade IS NOT IMPOSSIBLE for a Negro boy or girl who has the ability and guts to plug," enthused sportswriter Joe Bostic. And Campy understood and embraced his influential position among black youth. He not only helped to arrange athletic scholarships for some Harlem Y kids, but spent thousands on trophies. "I've always thought a trophy or an award of some kind makes a youngster try harder," he explained.

Like millions of other young couples after World War II, Campy and Ruthe were looking to buy a house. The burgeoning postwar suburbs, the Campanellas quickly discovered, did not welcome black families. Levittown, the massive development on Long Island about to open in March, refused sales to blacks. But the path to suburbia was less daunting than it had been a few years earlier. Thirteen days after Campy's major league debut, the Supreme Court had ruled that the restrictive covenants limiting house sales to "Caucasians" could no longer be enforced by law.

In New York, the decision had an immediate impact in the Addisleigh Park section of St. Albans in southeast Queens. A few affluent blacks had moved into the residential neighborhood in recent years, only to encounter hostility from several white families, who filed a successful lawsuit arguing that sales to blacks violated the original housing agreements. Thanks to the Supreme Court decision, Addisleigh Park was now open to black homebuyers.

Campy and Ruthe had their eye on a white clapboard house at 114-110 179th Street in Addisleigh Park. It had a good-size lawn, a two-car garage, and plenty of room for the growing family. Everything was perfect, except for the price. Campanella did manage to extract a raise (up to $8,800) out of Rickey, but the always paternalistic Mahatma sent someone to investigate the property. Campy, he thought, was a little too free with his money. "You're always going to be in debt, Roy," he scolded. "The day will come when we'll have to hold an exhibition game for you! You won't live within your income."

Despite Rickey's warnings, the Campanellas moved into their new home in January 1949. Encouraged by Roy, the Robinsons relocated to the neighborhood six months later. The two friends, separated by only a few blocks, could now carpool together to Ebbets Field each day and looked forward to spending time at each other's new home.

In most communities, the presence of two major leaguers, one of them already a legend, would leave local residents starstruck. But Addisleigh Park was not a normal neighborhood. Lena Horne, Count Basie, Cootie Williams, Duke Ellington's son, Mercer, and one of the Mills brothers already lived there, soon to be joined by other black celebrities, many more from the jazz world. Over the next twenty-five years, Addisleigh Park functioned as a sort of Beverly Hills East for black America, a place where one might see Ella Fitzgerald walking her dog or Billie Holiday stepping into a car with her abusive paramour John Levy.

Despite his own humble beginnings, Campy fit in quite well among the giants of black entertainment and society. "He was wonderful as a neighbor and a friend," recalled Barbara Brannen, who lived a few houses down. "Campy would drive through the neighborhood. . . . He would wave to the children. . . . He'd get free cornflakes and he would give that out to the kids." The inevitable autograph requests never seemed to bother him. But Jackie, decidedly less outgoing, soon grew tired of the lack of privacy. "I don't think he was all that close with the people out there in St. Albans too much," remarked Delores Patterson, a close friend of the jazz saxophonist Illinois Jacquet's family, who resided near the Robinsons and the Campanellas. The two men's experiences in the same neighborhood highlighted one of their fundamental differences. Campy, Buzzie Bavasi later explained, "enjoyed being a big wheel among his people." Jackie, Bavasi felt, did not.

CAMPY HAD little time to get settled in his new digs in Queens before it was time for spring training. This year, there would be no journey to an exotic tropical locale. The Dodgers, major and minor leaguers alike, would hold their preseason workouts at Dodgertown in Vero Beach on the eastern coast of Florida.

Dodgertown was a typical Rickey stroke of genius. The Mahatma, Red Barber recalled, "dreamed about having everybody in one central place where he could see everything and everyone" and believed that "by forced teaching, training, and closer observation," player development would be accelerated. When an abandoned naval training station in Vero Beach became available, Rickey saw a perfect opportunity to realize his ambition. The opening of Dodgertown followed in 1948, although mostly limited to lower-level farmhands initially.

This spring, Roy and the rest of the Dodgers would participate for ten days in what one reporter called "assembly line baseball at its fantastic best." Hundreds of players arose in the early morning to the sound of "police whistles," followed by breakfast at the mess hall, then a Rickey baseball lecture, note-taking expected. From there, players participated in calisthenics before assignment to intrasquad games or drills that bore the usual Rickey stamp of innovation: sliding pits, "new-fangled batting tees," and other "Buck Rogers gadgets," including an automatic pitching machine. The Mahatma himself was there to oversee the whole shebang, correcting, scolding, and praising. "We do not claim that we can develop a synthetic ballplayer here," he admitted. "We can help a batter improve himself by revealing his faults to his complete satisfaction."

Campy couldn't help but be impressed by the ambitious scope of Dodgertown. But Rickey's dream came at a severe price for the organization's black players, who would contend with rampant segregation. Don Newcombe later described Vero Beach as "one of the worst hellholes a man could go to." Newk and other blacks seeking a nearby alternative to mess-hall cuisine or entertainment beyond the pinball machine, jukebox, and other camp fare were out of luck. The Dodgers would later attempt to address the problem by adding a golf course and a lake stocked with fish, but local segregation remained the rule until the 1960s.

Rickey was acutely aware of the racial situation in Florida. Dodgertown officials, according to Sam Lacy, not only were privately told to "keep on the alert for any untoward incidents," but were also prepared to move the camp to San Juan if serious difficulties emerged that spring. Routine segregation, however, was another matter altogether. Jackie Robinson might not like the hundred-seat Jim Crow section allotted to blacks at the main Vero Beach ballpark, but the Dodgers were not prepared to do anything about it. Nor were they likely to battle bigoted roadside proprietors, a problem that Campy and Jackie experienced all too often in Florida.

How the two men handled spring training restaurant segregation later became another way to accentuate the differences between the "fiery" Robinson and the "passive" Campanella. Harold Parrott, an admirer of Robinson's, would offer in 1976 the by then standard tale of Campy hungrily devouring a meal Parrott carried to the bus while "pleading" with a "seething" Jackie to "avoid a scene." But Roy would tell an entirely different story in 1964, a time when black protest was commonplace. "I spoke up the first time I rode in a Dodger bus and couldn't go in a restaurant in West Palm Beach," he boasted. "From now on," he told Parrott, "make arrangements so I can get a car so I won't be embarrassed sitting in a bus while the others eat. I'm not sitting in any kitchen to eat, either!"

Which is the real Campy: the Uncle Tom or the freedom fighter? Two contemporary and more reliable accounts from 1950 say neither. Jackie Robinson told a reporter that year that he and Campy had both recently refused an offer to "go around back" to be served at a Florida restaurant, instead preferring to hail a black cab to get food in a "colored neighborhood." Meanwhile, Roscoe McGowen's *Baseball Magazine* profile of Campy recalled a similar spring training incident at a roadside stop. The female proprietor, informed by Parrott that the Dodgers "had a colored boy with the club," nevertheless agreed to serve Campy, who declined. "Look," he told Parrott. "That woman is just being nice. If I should go in there and eat, it would make trouble for her if some people found out about it, as they sure would. She might be boycotted and lose her business. No, I'll just stay out here in the bus. I don't mind."

The Robinson and McGowen anecdotes illustrate Campy's essentially moderate approach to Jim Crow practices. Although he refused to submit to the degradation of eating "around back," he was not comfortable disclosing to anyone just how much segregation bothered him. Grin and bear it, don't whine. That was Campy's credo. "It is practically impossible," a reporter once remarked, "to get Campy to admit that any phase of his life was especially difficult or unpleasant." Dave Anderson agreed: "Publicly, there was always a smile on his face and everything was fine."

Something else would continually inhibit Campy from taking a more assertive stance in similar situations in the future. Protests, confrontations, and arguments made some people uncomfortable. Robinson never cared much if an unpopular position cost him a few friends or admirers. But Campy was happiest when he was on everyone's good side, and he would consciously shape his public persona to achieve that goal.

THE BROOKLYN squad that congregated in Vero Beach that spring differed little from the third-place club of 1948. Except for trading the once-promising Pete Reiser to the Braves for outfielder Frank McCormick,

Rickey had barely fussed with the roster, certain its current configuration was good enough to contend.

Shotton was also confident, although he worried about his catchers. Campy, after a winter of Ruthe's home cooking, reported overweight at 203. Despite cutting out soda ("Roy is a Coke addict," quipped one reporter), starches, even liquids, the pounds were slow to melt. Bruce Edwards, meanwhile, was dogged by a knee calcification and his all too chronic sore arm.

To Roy's dismay, Shotton seemed intent on handing the catching job back to Edwards, his fair-haired boy of two years earlier. "I'd be willing to bet right now," the Brooklyn skipper announced in March, "that Edwards catches one hundred games." When pressed by reporters about Edwards's excruciating arm pain and bouncing heaves to second base, Shotton was unconcerned. "Sure, he made a bad throw. But so has Roy Campanella on occasion."

Campy, by now accustomed to the whims of the Dodger brass, remained silent. But he knew he had at least a few things in his favor. Edwards, no matter how much Shotton and even Rickey tried to build him up in the press (perhaps for a trade for the aging slugger Johnny Mize), could no longer throw properly. According to writer Tom Meany, Edwards also appeared a bit blasé about reclaiming his job and "somehow gave the impression that it made little difference whether he played or sat on the bench."

Roy, his starting job in jeopardy, followed his usual eager-beaver approach that spring. If Shotton still wasn't in his corner, he'd make a believer out of him. He watched intently one day as his boyhood hero Bill Dickey provided instruction to the Yankees' struggling young catcher Yogi Berra. "I couldn't hear what they were saying," he recalled later, "but I got a good look at the throwing lesson and Dickey showing Berra how to shift his feet." Within minutes, Roy had added another weapon to his throwing arsenal.

While Campanella waited for Shotton to make up his mind, his buddy Don Newcombe was having his own problems that spring. Newcombe, a 17-game winner at Montreal in 1948, was already attracting six-figure offers from other big league clubs. The Dodgers, however, remained concerned about his immature and petulant behavior. In the last year, he had squabbled with manager Clay Hopper, threatened to quit Montreal after a tough loss, ignored the Dodgers' request that he not play winter ball, and then got himself released by two different Cuban teams. This spring, he had picked a fight at Vero Beach with Mike Guerra, his Cuban winter league manager ("in the midst of seven or eight Dixie cops," marveled Sam Lacy). The brawl became ugly, as a white fan yanked a picket from a fence, tossed it to Guerra, and urged him, "Kill that nigger!" With rumors spreading that the Negro had "attacked a white man," Rickey apologized to local officials and ordered Newcombe not to stray beyond Dodgertown for his own protection.

Newcombe, hopeful about getting a shot with Brooklyn, had sealed his own fate. The Dodgers had too much talent to put up with the shenanigans of a still unproven black player who didn't have a particularly impressive spring to begin with. "I think he can pitch in the majors," Shotton remarked, "but he might undo everything these other two fellows have accomplished." Even the *Baltimore Afro-American* fretted about how the "fine records" of Jackie, Roy, and Cleveland's Larry Doby might be "endangered by off-color behavior on the part of a single one of these future baseball stars. Too much is at stake."

That Newcombe, the youngest and least experienced of Rickey's five original African-American signings, might have needed to be handled with kid gloves apparently did not occur to anyone in the Brooklyn hierarchy. Instead, he was branded a moody troublemaker, a label neither Roy nor Jackie felt he deserved, his penchant for calling whites "blue-eyed bitches" notwithstanding. To Carl Erskine, Newk was admittedly "a little belligerent. . . . He was a scared kid. He didn't know how to act."

The Dodgers eventually shipped Newcombe back to Montreal. Emotional as ever, Newcombe refused to report, but finally headed back to Canada for his fourth minor league season. Then late in spring training, Shotton announced that Edwards wasn't ready and Campanella would be behind the plate on opening day in Brooklyn.

Campy still had to survive the unpleasant final lap of spring training: a two-week barnstorming jaunt through Texas, Oklahoma, Georgia, North Carolina, and Maryland. For Rickey, the crowds and the chance to further acclimate the South to the Great Experiment were too irresistible to pass up. Jackie and Roy, however, could expect a steady stream of segregation and verbal abuse.

They were not disappointed in Beaumont, Texas, their first stop. "Undoubtedly," wrote Sam Lacy, "this is the most backward town—from a race relation standpoint—the Dodgers have played in their two years of Spring barnstorming. . . . Booing, filthy name-calling, and insults . . . have greeted each appearance of Jackie Robinson and Roy Campanella." Adding to the ugly scene was Tiny, the public-address announcer, who referred to the two men as simply "the niggers." Nevertheless, hundreds of black fans, many of whom traveled considerable distances and then waited in "colored" ticket lines for hours, not only cheered Jackie and Campy but stood patiently in the rain afterward to get their autographs.

For downtrodden Southern blacks in Beaumont and elsewhere, Robinson and Campanella were monumentally important symbols of integration. In their own lives, the pace of racial progress appeared glacially slow. It was a time, Lynn Parrott recalled, when "a black family would get off the sidewalk and into the street to let the white people walk down the street. . . . It was accepted as the way things were in the South." But every appearance of the Dodgers in Dixie challenged age-old notions of white supremacy. Whether it was Edwards telling off "a young smart aleck who passed a racial epithet" in Tulsa or a Campy homer in Dallas eliciting a spontaneous seat-cushion shower from elated black fans, the racial status quo was being undermined.

Atlanta, the tour's ninth stop, loomed as the biggest challenge. For the past three months, debate had raged locally about whether the Dodgers should be allowed to break the normal taboo against interracial athletics. Although the majority of Atlantans seemed to accept that a three-game series with the Southern Association's Crackers would not seriously harm their cherished way of life, a hard-core group of bigots felt otherwise. Their leader was Samuel Green, a fifty-nine-year-old physician who doubled as Grand Dragon of the state Ku Klux Klan. "As long as they stay in their place, we get along fine," he told New York columnist Jimmy Cannon. "You call Negroes *mister* to their faces and don't feed them. We look after them. I don't care how you feel. God made people white for a purpose and black for a purpose."

Their purpose, as far as Green was concerned, almost certainly did not involve playing baseball with white folk. Rumors surfaced that there would be "trouble," perhaps even violence, if the two Negroes appeared in

Atlanta. Years later, Campy would even claim that he and Jackie received a telegram from the Klan promising to "shoot you out on the field." According to Campy, the telegram was turned over to Rickey, who then contacted Martin Luther King, who encouraged the Dodgers not to back down. "When we got to Atlanta," Campy asserted, "we went to Dr. King's home and had dinner with him and stayed with him just about the entire trip."

But King was then a twenty-year-old student at the Crozer Theological Seminary outside Philadelphia. Perhaps Campy was actually referring to King's father, Martin, Sr., an influential local minister, although Robinson never mentioned meeting him. As for accommodations, Sam Lacy reported, "We are lodged at the Royal," a black hotel on Auburn Avenue.

Regardless of where Campy and Jackie stayed in Atlanta, they both were aware of their vulnerability once they stepped onto the field for the opening game on April 8. Robinson had already mapped out his survival strategy. The black fans, he knew, "had come out there well prepared and loaded to take care of me if they had to die in the meantime." If something happened, Jackie resolved "to head right for center field and get right in the middle of them; in fact, even lead the charge!" Campy was less confident. "You've got it made," he told Jackie. "You're playing second base. All you have to do is run into center field, and you'll be safe. I have to run all the way from home plate."

Neither Jackie nor Campy would need to make any desperate sprints across Ponce de Leon Park that weekend. Except for the extensive national media coverage and record-breaking attendance, the series was uneventful. The Klan, despite Green's ominous threats, failed to make an appearance. A few whites did try to boo Robinson in his first at bat, only to be overpowered by the combined cheers of both black and white fans. "It should prove," said Cracker owner Earl Mann, "that the South is perfectly capable of working out its own social problems."

Campy was also warmly greeted by the crowd on Friday night for what would be his only appearance in Atlanta. He singled off Dick Hoover in the second and later caught Chet Hajduk's foul pop-up to end the game. As he walked off the field, he tossed the ball to a white youngster, one of many who besieged the two black Dodgers for autographs after the game. But it was Robinson, a *Courier* writer noted, who was "the center of every eye every minute he was on the field" that weekend. And Jackie did not disappoint his admirers, cracking four hits against the Crackers and even stealing home. "The nigger there," a local reporter remarked to Shotton, "is pretty good, eh?" Shotton did not follow his racist lead: "Robbie is quite a ballplayer and a real gentleman."

Robinson's star, already high, was on the rise. "He has become the Babe Ruth of his people," mused Harold Burr, and few would disagree. Campy, meanwhile, was glad to be leaving Atlanta and the South in one piece. In five days he'd be back home in St. Albans, and soon after that his first full major league season would finally get under way.

IT IS easy to view postwar baseball through the soothing, nostalgia-drenched impressions of HBO's *When It Was a Game* or Ken Burns's *Baseball* series. Film clips of the Campanella era reveal sights hopelessly quaint to modern eyes: mostly smallish players, baggy uniforms, gloves left on the field between innings (until 1954), and minimal head protection at the plate. The game, the old-timers claim, was somehow simpler, purer, and more innocent in those days. For one thing, it was baseball's last drug-free era, although reports would surface by 1957 about the use of amphetamines and tranquilizers in sports. There were no radar guns, only DuMont's crude "cathode ray oscillograph," which clocked Joe Black's fastball at 93.2 miles per hour in a one-shot exhibition at Ebbets in 1953. The only computer most fans had heard of was IBM's amazing "electron calculator," which was "fed a wealth of baseball statistics" and declared Willie Mays the National League's best player in 1954.

The players, so goes the old-timers' argument, were also a different breed. The pampered and overly sensitive stars of today would have wilted in an era of brushbacks, no pitch counts, and no-holds-barred bench jockeying, where arrests, paternity cases, mental breakdowns, and physical deformities were all fair game for dugout loudmouths. "That doesn't exist today," observes Dave Anderson. "Nobody says a word now in the dugout."

The shockingly meager pay of the postwar era also contributes to perceptions of the era's purity. The minimum salary in 1949 was $5,000 (about $45,000 today), eventually boosted to $6,000 in 1954. By the mid-1950s, an established regular might be lucky to reach $20,000 a year ($160,000 today), bigger stars commanded roughly $30,000 to $45,000, and the elite—such as Mays, Musial, Mantle, and Williams—fell within the

$50,000-to-$100,000 bracket. No Brooklyn player would ever top $50,000 during Campy's career, although the Dodgers' $500,000-plus annual payroll was among the highest in the National League.

With so few getting rich in those days, it is all too easy to swallow the clichéd notion that the postwar players "played for the love of the game." In reality, the major leaguers of that era loved money as much as the so-called greedy ballplayers of today. They simply had the misfortune of being trapped in a system with no free agency (Rickey believed opponents of the reserve clause had "communist tendencies"). Worst of all, players had only the vaguest idea how much their colleagues actually earned. At contract-signing time, they would simply mumble to reporters that they were "satisfied," but the published salary figures were nothing more than sportswriter guesstimates. "The strange thing to me is that the player has been bulldozed into going along with this," wrote Dick Young in 1955. "Through the years he has been convinced that it is to his best advantage to keep his salary secret, and besides 'it's nobody's business.' "

The owners not only held all the cards but also bullied their charges into docile submission. "Sign it or stay home" was a frequent warning that usually succeeded in prompting a nervous ballplayer to grab the nearest pen. "We were like kids going into war with a popgun," recalled Pee Wee Reese, describing his Brooklyn salary negotiations. A star like Reese could at least threaten a holdout, but most players feared antagonizing their all-powerful employers. Even the modest step of hiring labor lawyer J. Norman Lewis in 1953 to advise on pensions and other issues left more than a few major leaguers uneasy: "We cannot get the owners mad."

With its relentless player exploitation, baseball in the 1940s and 1950s was hardly as innocent as some still believe it to have been. Nor do those years represent the last vestige of baseball's supposed golden age before rampant commercialism and expansion permanently transformed the sport. Instead, the era is more accurately characterized as a transitional period, a time when baseball was laying the groundwork for the modern game of today.

THE OLD-TIMERS of Campanella's era were certain that *their* baseball had changed, and for the worse. The modern players, they insisted, were barely competent, in Ty Cobb's words, without their "phony fences . . . moved in" and "jack rabbit" ball. Why, most of these fellows couldn't even stay in the lineup every day, thanks to this harebrained "two platoon system" now in vogue. Even Leo Durocher, an active player as recently as 1945, was convinced that major leaguers were overly coddled by the umpires, who had cracked down on brushbacks and takeout slides. "The way the game is being played now," he complained in 1955, "they should call time in the fourth inning every day and let everyone circle around the mound. Then they should serve tea and crumpets."

The apparent declining virility in the game particularly applied to starting pitchers, believed by the ancient Cy Young to be "babied too much." Why else couldn't major league pitchers finish games anymore? But some baseball men understood that major league pitching, regardless of the dip in complete games, was actually *better* than in the days of Ruth and Gehrig. "Today, eighty percent of the pitchers in the National League, and probably the American League, have a variety of stuff the old-timers never saw, much less tried to hit," Dodgers manager Charlie Dressen remarked in 1952. "They throw knucklers, screwballs, sliders, sinkers, forkballs, and palm balls. Even rookies throw curves at two or three speeds."

The most significant change in pitchers' repertoires was the increasing use of the slider, or what some still called the nickel curve. Most of the old-timers didn't like it. "A slider is an unnatural pitch," insisted Phillies coach Cy Perkins in 1949, "and I'm sure a lot of the arm operations that have become necessary are the result of throwing this accursed pitch." But Dressen and Casey Stengel both recognized its undeniable effectiveness, as did Ted Williams, who claimed in 1956 that "the slider has made pitching at least twenty-five percent better."

Besides the slider, most of the oldsters never had to cope with the growing number of games under the arc lights. By the end of Campanella's career, the Dodgers were playing nearly half of their games at night, and some players found it difficult to adjust. "It ruins your whole day," observed Pee Wee Reese in 1955. "You lie around in your room and eat in the middle of the afternoon. It's a mixed-up life." Baseball's tried-and-true travel routine was also undergoing a transformation as air travel became safer and more cost-efficient. The Dodgers began to reduce their reliance on the railroads, returning from Midwestern trips by plane except for a hard-core group of nonflying players and writers. By 1956, the NFL, NBA, and NHL had all but abandoned the trains, and MLB would soon follow.

For baseball, an even more important postwar technological breakthrough was television, which almost overnight became the focal point of virtually every American family's living room. Despite fears that TV would diminish the live gate, major league teams were quick to hop on the gravy train. In Brooklyn, WCBS handled the telecasts for a few years before WOR took over for good in 1950 with a crew of Red Barber, Connie Desmond, and a twenty-two-year-old youngster named Vincent Scully. Although some franchises cautiously limited their telecasts to occasional home games, the Dodgers were airing more than a hundred games a season by the mid-1950s and raking in the National League's highest TV/radio rights fees. Already, some fans complained that commercials were at least partly responsible for the growing length of games.

For Campanella and other players, television brought instant celebrity. Ironically, as the video age dawned, major leaguers themselves became increasingly bland in their public personas, indistinguishable in their looks and conservative in their attitudes. In a 1955 *New York Times* piece fittingly entitled "Mighty Robot at the Bat," John Lardner described the modern player as an automaton who carefully followed the rules and seldom thought of disobeying his manager. "'Color,' or eccentricity," wrote Lardner, was in remarkably short supply beyond Sal Maglie "wearing his sideburns long," Ted Williams "wearing his pants long," Willie Mays's basket catches, and Ted Kluszewski "cutting his sleeves short to show his muscles." Still, writer Gay Talese believed the typical ballplayer was like the rest of postwar America: "security-conscious, unwilling to risk a comfortable future by being tabbed as a clown, bad actor or non-conformist."

To achieve the cherished "comfortable future," major leaguers eagerly accepted any endorsement deals, commercials, and appearances that came their way, although the fees were pitiful by today's standards. Gene Hermanski recalled getting $850 for a Gillette endorsement and TV commercial, "and I grabbed it." An appearance on Ed Sullivan's nationally aired CBS television program was good for $100. Dodger players picked up $50 for appearing on WOR's postgame show. Perhaps worst of all was the Topps baseball card company, which paid the players in merchandise. Not until the emergence of Frank Scott as baseball's first real agent did Campy and other elite players begin to see change. A former Yankee employee who saw an opportunity when Yogi Berra was paid in watches for appearances, Scott built a stable of ninety-two major leaguers by 1956, including Roy.

Campy would eventually land a few major endorsements with Gillette, Wheaties, and RCA but his deals with Lucky Strike, Coca-Cola, and Beech-Nut gum were primarily for the Negro market. Much of corporate America, still fearing Southern backlash, was not eager to use blacks as spokesmen. Camel cigarettes, for example, ran full-page ads in New York daily newspapers in 1952 featuring nine Yankees and Dodgers, all of them white.

Although Madison Avenue may have lagged behind, baseball was changing rapidly after World War II. The expanded commercial opportunities, improvements in pitching, night games, airline travel, and television all signified a new order in the game, one that Campy could hardly have imagined when he first became a professional back in 1937. But the most dramatic transformation was the presence of black players in major league uniforms. And Campy was only too glad to be among them.

THE DODGERS opened their 1949 season at Ebbets Field on April 19. Few Brooklyn fans realized that Shotton's starting lineup was to become one of the most famous in baseball history. Campy was behind the plate. Hodges, Robinson, Reese, and Cox held down the infield positions. Young Duke Snider, still an unknown commodity, was in center field, flanked by the rifle-armed Carl Furillo in right, and the rookie Cal Abrams in left. Abrams would soon give way to Gene Hermanski and a parade of other aspirants who could never quite lock up the position. The record-setting opening-day crowd of 34,530 fans watched the new Shottonmen thrash Durocher's hated Giants 10–3. Robinson, healthy, happy, and newly installed in the cleanup slot, thanks to a suggestion by team statistician Allan "Slide Rule" Roth, led the attack with three hits and a homer. But Campy provided the key blow: a three-run blast into the left-field seats that put the Dodgers ahead for good in the fourth.

The homer was an important first step in permanently quashing a lingering belief in Dodger circles that Campanella would never outhit Bruce Edwards. By this time, everyone knew that Campy could catch. "But what we need is that long-ball hitter," Pee Wee Reese insisted in spring training. "Edwards can do it and I want him in the lineup somewhere." Shotton agreed: "We need his bat."

The specter of Edwards and his .295 batting average two years earlier was not going to disappear unless Roy generated more offense. From the moment he reported to Vero Beach, he had worked at improving his batting eye and avoiding bad pitches. One of Rickey's new atomic-age gadgets, the batting tee, proved particularly valuable. "I discovered there," Campy explained, "that I'd be swinging too hard, trying to ride the ball out of the park on every pitch." He also sought help from George Sisler, who convinced him to level his swing and further altered his batting stance. Last year, Arky Vaughan had encouraged Roy to open up his stance and use his "foot in the bucket" technique to get a better handle on outside pitches. Under Sisler's tutelage, Campy kept a similar approach but now moved his legs in closer, bent his back knee just a bit, and shifted his stance so that he was almost directly facing the pitcher.

Though uncomfortable at first, the new stance quickly paid dividends. In the Dodgers' first fifteen games, Campy went 23 for 49, belted 4 homers, and drove in 15 runs, more than enough to convince Shotton. "The Lord . . . made him a good catcher," he gushed in a *Time* magazine piece fittingly entitled "Burt's Catcher." "He'll be another Bill Dickey someday." Shotton was so impressed that he moved Campy to the fifth slot in the order by late April despite his old-school conviction that the catcher should always bat eighth.

No longer a rookie clinging to a roster spot, Campy was now an accepted and integral part of the Dodgers. Like Jackie, who announced that spring that he "should be able to play and think as anyone else," Campy now felt more free to reveal his true personality. His dealings with his pitchers reflected a more aggressive, take-charge attitude, and his chatter behind the plate became more animated. "How do you like this one, boy?" he would call to the mound. "Don't like it, eh? Well, here's another. How do you like that? All right, we'll try it."

The umpires also noticed a change in his demeanor. On April 27, after taking a game-ending called third strike from Dave Koslo at the Polo Grounds, Campy began squawking to plate umpire Bill Stewart. Ironically, Robinson played peacemaker, pulling Campy away from Stewart, who warned that "one more word" would mean a fine. Four days later, at Ebbets, Campy would run into similar trouble with the same umpiring crew. "I've played in leagues where they paid the umpires two bucks a game and their sight was better than yours," he muttered to Jocko Conlan after another third-strike call. Conlan promptly gave Campy the heave-ho, his first in Organized Baseball.

Roy recognized that Berra or Edwards would probably not have been ejected for such a statement. "I didn't curse him," Campy explained to reporters afterward. "I never do, but since I had that argument with Bill Stewart at the Polo Grounds, it looks like I am forbidden to talk." Indeed he was. Only a year earlier, American Association umpires had warned their colleague James Clegg "not to take anything" from the league's new Negro catcher.

But the incident also demonstrated that Campanella, despite his nice-guy persona, was no pushover. "The big Philadelphian always was a real competitor, the kind of guy whom you have to defeat," observed Joe Bostic. "He isn't a ruffian, or never was, but neither was he ever a shrinking violet. . . . So, if they're looking for a Caspar Milquetoast, they'll have to dig up another candidate . . . Robust Roy definitely isn't their man."

Despite Robust Roy's spark, Rickey and Shotton were not happy with the club's .500 record in the first month. They decided it was now or never for Don Newcombe, who had posted a 2.65 ERA in five starts in Montreal. "I think he has decided to keep his mouth shut," remarked Shotton. The still dubious Old Sourdough quickly gave Newk his first chance in relief at Sportsman's Park on May 20, only to watch the Cardinals pepper him for three singles and a bases-clearing double.

To his credit, Shotton handed Newk the ball again two days later in Cincinnati. This time, Newk's fastball and curve were working beautifully, so beautifully that the Reds began complaining that the "giant Negro" (the description favored by most white sportswriters) was throwing spitters. Jocko Conlan, apparently still smarting over his recent tiff with Campy, was also suspicious. "What are you talking about?" asked Roy. "He's a kid, twenty-two years old. What does he know about throwing spitballs?" Somehow Campy managed to keep Conlan at bay that afternoon while Newcombe calmly shut out the Reds on five hits. "This kid's going to be a great pitcher," raved Jackie Robinson. "He can win the pennant for us."

Newcombe's arrival succeeded in kick-starting the Dodgers' sluggish season. More important for Rickey, it represented another breakthrough for his Great Experiment. With Campy, Jackie, and Newk (mistaken for the Nat King Cole Trio by a confused white woman) now in Brooklyn uniforms, the Dodgers became the first major league club to carry three black players. More than a few snide comments greeted the increasingly integrated look. How would Brooklyn fare, a Boston reporter asked Shotton in July, without Campanella, Robinson, and Newcombe? Shotton remained unfazed: "What would happen if any three players on the team were put out of action?"

Despite their undeniable contributions, the three black Dodgers remained an entity apart from their white teammates. Although Robinson would later emphasize the need for the blacks to "spread out," their lockers in the late 1940s were intentionally clustered together. Showers also remained a problem. "Sometimes, the guys on our own team, they didn't want to take showers with us," recalled Don Newcombe. "They had us off in one corner of the clubhouse." Not until 1951 would new manager Charlie Dressen finally halt the practice. On road trips, no one ever considered pairing up a black player with a white one. Campy and Jackie rotated as Newk's roommate, and the three, usually accompanied by Sam Lacy or another black reporter, might play pinochle or take in a movie after a game. "I didn't socialize with the white players on the Dodgers," Newcombe recalled. "The wives didn't sit together in Ebbets Field, and their husbands didn't socialize in the early stages of integration."

Not surprisingly, Ruthe Campanella was not part of the elite Dotty Reese clique that every Dodger wife aspired to. Nor were the Campanellas likely to be invited to any of the white Dodgers' homes for Sunday dinner, at least in 1949. But Campy's outgoing personality and quick wit made it easier for him to reach out across racial lines than Robinson or Newcombe. Even the most reluctant convert to integration couldn't help but chuckle when Roy bantered with the pitchers or even the Mahatma himself. "Judas Priest, Roy, you're as fat around the waist as I am," remarked Rickey one day after encountering Campy under the Ebbets Field stands that season. "But I bet I can carry it around the bases faster than you" was Roy's quick comeback. "Roy was always very sociable," Newcombe explained. "He was raised in an integrated life and knew how to act and react. A lot of time people didn't like how Roy did it so easily, but that was his way."

THE DODGERS entered the All-Star break in first place with a 47-31 record, a half game in front of the Cardinals. Campy, after his early-season tear, had tailed off considerably to .266 with 11 homers, a decent first half but not good enough to beat out the Phillies' Andy Seminick in the All-Star balloting. Still, his second-place finish and million votes collected revealed that he had become a "name" player, although some fans remained puzzled about his racial origins. "Kingdom Brown wants to know whether or not Roy Campanella is a Negro or white," wrote Swig Garlington in the *Amsterdam News*. "Truth of the matter is, I don't know. . . . It's what the folks say one is, and is without a clear-cut definition."

Such matters did not trouble National League manager Billy Southworth, who named Roy to the All-Star squad as a reserve. But to black fans, the selection of Roy, along with Robinson, Newcombe, and Doby, was of historic significance. For the first time, black players would appear in an All-Star Game, fittingly to be held at Ebbets Field on July 12.

Except for Robinson's double in his first at bat, it was mostly a disappointing afternoon for the former Negro Leaguers. Doby was hitless in his only at bat, Newcombe was the losing pitcher, and Campy went 0 for 2 with an error. In fact, All-Star Games were usually an exercise in futility for Roy, who managed just 2 singles in 20 lifetime at bats. Rickey was more concerned with the National League's seventh defeat in the last eight games. "It seems to me," he sighed, "that the nationwide fans' voting idea is not the best one to select the team."

Rickey had weightier matters on his mind that afternoon. Just a few days earlier, the powerful House Un-American Activities Committee, a permanent congressional body responsible for ferreting out domestic communism, had requested Robinson's presence to answer black singer Paul Robeson's recent comment that American blacks would not take up arms against the Soviet Union. Although some of the Brooklyn brass advised against it, Rickey pushed Robinson to appear. A fervent anticommunist himself, the Mahatma also recognized the value of placing Robinson on the "right side" of an issue that frightened much of America.

Jackie agreed to testify. Robeson, he felt, had no right to speak for black America. "I want my kid to have the things I have," he told reporters. "Campy and I would fight any aggressor—the Russians or any other nation." But what Roy actually felt about Robeson and HUAC remains unclear. Many years later, his son would claim that Campy had also been asked to testify but refused, preferring to stay out of politics. No other source has ever confirmed this story, and it seems unlikely that HUAC would have been interested in a ballplayer who was neither a superstar yet nor particularly well educated.

If Campanella did decline to testify, he may have made the right choice. Although Jackie's much-publicized appearance before HUAC on July 18 received almost unanimous praise from the mainstream media, some blacks were uncomfortable with his decision. "When Paul Robeson said he is not willing to fight against Russia, he is not thinking about himself," editorialized the *Baltimore Afro-American.* "He is thinking about millions of colored people in the South who can't vote, who are terrorized by mobs at the least provocation, and cannot get a decent job or a decent education. Our advice to Jackie Robinson, as much as we admire him, is that he put away his pop gun and put on his baseball uniform." Robeson himself believed that Jackie had made a mistake by testifying and legitimizing HUAC "and I feel someday he'll recognize and regret it."

Late in life, Robinson admitted that he would "reject such an invitation if offered now." Still, the HUAC appearance succeeded in further elevating Robinson's already exalted status. He was already in the midst of a career year, currently leading the league in hits, RBIs, average, and stolen bases. And in every Harlem record shop, the celebrated author Langston Hughes observed, "loud-speakers are blaring the new Buddy Johnson record about Jackie Robinson hitting that ball!" It was hardly surprising, then, that Sam Lacy cryptically alluded to a "slight trace of jealousy creeping into the Brooklyn Dodgers' locker room."

THE DAY after Robinson's testimony, the Dodgers beat the Pirates 4–3 for their sixth win in seven games, to extend their lead over the Cardinals to a season-high 3½ games. Within five weeks, the bulge had been squandered. After dropping three of four to the Braves, two by shutouts, the Brooks trailed the Cards by two and were fading fast. "They just don't do anything right," the Old Sourdough ranted after the excruciating 7–6 finale in Boston on August 22.

But Shotton's throwback ways were also to blame. Convinced "every player should be an unbreakable, untiring, uncomplaining mechanism," he rode his regulars mercilessly ("they're better hurt than any of the others well" was his philosophy). Even after a collision left Campy's right shoulder "swollen to twice its normal size," Shotton stubbornly continued to write his name in the lineup until the lead-footed Frank Baumholtz swiped two bases on him. Nor would Shotton rest Campy and Jackie, both ailing, during the disastrous Boston series, with the two going 3 for 31.

Shotton, his ice-cold team now facing a doubleheader with the Cardinals at Ebbets, still remained calm. "I've just washed my face and combed my hair, and if we can win a ball game, I'll be practically human again," he remarked. But the Red Birds took game one to open up a three-game lead, as horrified Brooklyn fans braced for the worst in the nightcap. With the score knotted at three in the eighth inning, Campy whacked a clutch double off Howie Pollet and scored the game-winner on a Snider double. The following afternoon, Roy homered, Newk shut out the Cardinals, and the Dodgers were back in business for the stretch run.

Over the next eighteen days, the rampaging Bums won fifteen of twenty, paced by the reunited Nashua black battery. Newk tossed two more shutouts on his way to a 32-inning scoreless streak while Campy bashed the ball at a .371 clip with 4 homers. Unfortunately, Eddie Dyer's Cardinals refused to crack, picking up another half game after their own sizzling 15-4 run. Now down a game and a half with sixteen to play, Brooklyn faced an uphill struggle. The Red Birds were heading home for two weeks while the Dodgers would play their next ten on the road, including three in St. Louis, and at less than full strength. Reese was questionable after a Larry Jansen fastball caught his elbow. Robinson's legs were beginning to tire. Hermanski and Cox were banged up, and Shotton had no faith in their replacements.

The trip began uneventfully at Crosley Field on September 13 with a 6–3 win behind Carl Erskine, who picked up his eighth straight victory since his recall in July. But the next day in Cincinnati presented a nasty situation that threatened to derail the Dodgers' pennant train. Each white Dodger regular received a letter signed by an "Ardent Fan." "You're some man," it read, "to play with a bunch of 'niggers.' Wonder how it must feel to have everything you do overshadowed by Jackie Robinson, Campanella, and Newcombe." The rest of the letter contained more racist rants.

Such letters were nothing new, nor were their origins a surprise. Cincinnati's racial attitudes reflected the city's close proximity to Kentucky and the land of Jim Crow. Its Netherland Plaza Hotel forced the black Dodgers to take their meals in their rooms. Its best-known sportswriter, Tom Swope of the *Post*, was an unapologetic bigot.

Ironically, it was a Kentuckian who quickly acted to defuse what might have become an ugly situation. Pee Wee Reese was only thirty-one, but no one questioned his authority as captain. An All-Star shortstop beloved by the Brooklyn faithful, Reese also possessed a remarkable ability to keep the Dodger ship from running aground. "If a player needed to be consoled, Pee Wee would console him," Vin Scully recalled. "If a player needed to be kicked in the fanny, Pee Wee would do that too."

Reese had already demonstrated his public support of the Great Experiment by famously placing his hand on Robinson's shoulder in the midst of a volley of enemy racial insults. But this situation, he realized, needed to be handled in a more subtle manner. On the team bus headed to Crosley Field that afternoon, Reese pulled out the letter and began reading it out loud, adding his own humorous editorial comments. His teammates were soon convulsed with laughter, the letter's hateful message all but forgotten by the time the bus had reached Crosley. The relaxed Dodgers whipped the Reds 4–2 to stay 1½ behind with fourteen to play.

Campy rapped two more hits that afternoon. In his season and a half in the major leagues, he had gone through his usual streaky periods but never one this long. He was looking forward to the Dodgers' next stop, Pittsburgh, where Newk would be matched in the opener against Bill Werle, a sidearming lefty who gave up a lot of hits (Roy had doubled off him when he last saw him in July).

Werle was taking no chances with Campanella this time. His first offering that Friday evening headed directly toward Campy's unprotected skull. Roy tried to duck but instead ducked directly into the sailing pitch. As the crowd of 28,202 gasped, Campy fell to the ground unconscious and showed no signs of movement as he was carried off the field on a stretcher. Back in the clubhouse, trainer Harold Wendler grew concerned when

Campy barely responded to a lit match before his eyes. A cold towel proffered by Newk finally roused him. The first face Roy saw was the bushy-eyebrowed, bespectacled visage of Rickey. "Roy! How are you, Roy? Do you know who I am? Who am I?" Campy, though still foggy, replied, "Mr. Rickey, you feelin' all right?"

It was a typical Campanella moment: disarming humor in the midst of crisis. But there was nothing funny about what had just happened. "This was the worst I've ever seen," Wendler told reporters. "I saw Joe Medwick get hit in the head, and Frenchy Bordagaray, but they snapped out of it almost right away. Roy was a long time coming around, and he didn't look too good to me when he left for the hospital." Thankfully, the beaning turned out to be less serious than it appeared. Campy had suffered only a mild concussion (although he would complain of headaches for several months) and within an hour had recovered enough to listen to the end of the game in his hospital bed.

Sam Lacy, like most of the Dodgers, wondered whether the pitch had been intentional. "He was crouching over the plate and I tried to push him back," Werle explained. "I didn't try to hit him." But Werle usually had good control, averaging only 2 walks per 9 innings in 1949, although he walked five hitters and also clipped Robinson with a pitch that night. Whether the beaning was racially motivated is debatable, but Werle had already hit Campy once before (and would do so again in 1950) and would hit Robinson in 1951 with a pitch that Jackie was certain was deliberate.

Robinson, like Campy, had been thrown at from the moment he entered Organized Baseball, his fantastic reflexes always keeping his noggin out of harm's way. Still, he was shaken up by the sight of his friend crumpled in a heap at home plate. He ran to Campy's side, called the hospital for reports on his condition, and was ready to contact Ruthe had the situation deteriorated. Robinson also wisely decided to reconsider the issue of head protection. Without fanfare, he began to wear the late-1940s version of a helmet, "two plastic strips reinforced with sponge rubber, sewn into either side of the cap."

Like most players of his era, Campy had usually scorned helmets as sissy stuff. "You can't hit much worrying about whether you'll get hit," he explained. The Werle beaning would permanently change his macho viewpoint. In the days that followed, he would also be fitted for a helmet, opting for a more heavy-duty model that sat atop the skull under the cap. By today's standards, much of his head was still frighteningly vulnerable. "It's bound to take away some of the force of the blow if the ball hits you in that part of the head," Roy insisted. "If you wear one, you feel a little more confident."

The beaning dealt a near deathblow to Brooklyn's already precarious pennant hopes. The Pirates roughed up a troubled Newk for six runs that night while the Cards beat Boston to extend their lead to 2½ games. The following morning, Campy was released from Presbyterian Hospital, harboring secret thoughts of playing that day, but Shotton knew Campy was in no condition to catch. Instead, he spent the afternoon on the bench watching the Dodgers lose again to the sixth-place Pirates.

With the disastrous Pittsburgh series at an end, the Dodgers headed to Chicago, hoping the last-place Cubbies might prove easy pickings. Less than forty-eight hours after a serious beaning expected to sideline him for ten days, Roy was back in the lineup. "I'm not trying to be a hero," he insisted. "I admit I don't feel perfect but I am thinking of that World Series money. . . . I've got four kids, remember, and I've got a mortgage on that house in St. Albans." His return was less than inspiring: a passed ball, a strikeout, two pop-ups, and a single. But in the next two games, he batted .500, picked Roy Smalley off at first, caught two shutouts, and sparked Brooklyn to a three-game sweep.

The rejuvenated Campy and the Dodgers were now ready for their three-game showdown with St. Louis, who still clung to a 1½-game lead with ten to play. The series loomed as a symbolic racial struggle between the forces of integration and segregation. With their strike threat in 1947, the Cardinals had soundly rejected the Great Experiment. Their fan base extended far beyond St. Louis throughout the Jim Crow South. Their park continued to informally segregate black patrons. And their hotel was inflexible in its refusal to accept black ballplayers. While Reese, Snider, and other white teammates relaxed in the splendor of the plush, air-conditioned Chase, the Dodgers' tan trio—the key to their season—sweltered in the St. Louis heat in a shabby black hotel. The noise was equally oppressive, as Newcombe, scheduled to pitch the opener, had to contend with the din of a "constantly screeching" jukebox directly below his room.

But Newcombe held the Cardinals scoreless for the first eight innings of the first game of a Wednesday twin bill. In the bottom of the ninth of a taut 0–0 thriller, Newk got two quick strikes on the leadoff hitter, Enos Slaughter. The next pitch looked just as good, except to plate umpire Bill Stewart—the same Bill Stewart with whom Roy had clashed earlier that season—who called it a ball. The Dodgers went bonkers, especially Jackie, who shouted to Newcombe and Campy while grabbing for his own throat. Robinson would later claim that he was simply telling Campy "not to let Newcombe choke up," but everyone in Sportsman's Park knew what the gesture really meant. Within a few moments, Slaughter had doubled, Robinson was ejected, and the Dodgers were on the short end of a heartbreaking 1–0 loss. "He accused me of choking up," Stewart told reporters. "I won't take that from any man." Whether a white man would have elicited the same reaction from the ump remains questionable.

Later, Stewart's own boss, National League president Ford Frick, admitted that the ejection had been unduly hasty, and even some Cardinal fans thought that he had blown the Slaughter call. That their beef was clearly legitimate offered no consolation to the Bums, now three games out in the loss column with only eight to play. The nightcap, and the season itself, now rested on the thin shoulders of Preacher Roe, the junkballing control wizard who also threw a pretty nifty spitter. Campy loved working with Roe, the man he would always credit as the best pitcher he ever caught.

After the lanky Arkansan stopped the Cards on two hits to earn a doubleheader split, the Dodgers erupted for nineteen hits the following night, bludgeoning the Cardinals 19–6. Thrilled by Jackie's two hits and Campy's twenty-first homer, more than a few of the many black fans watching "got very loud . . . including one group of four women who often shouted at them, 'You're our boy.' "

Winners of seven of ten on the eventful road trip, a relaxed Dodger team boarded a LaGuardia-bound DC-6 the next morning. At 93-55, they were now only a half game behind the Cardinals, who were fighting a sudden rash of injuries. Everything now seemed to be going Brooklyn's way. On Saturday, September 24, Shotton started Newcombe against the Phillies on only two days' rest. Newk threw a four-hitter, while Campy chipped in with his twenty-second homer, the eighth he had hit in Newcombe's twenty-nine starts.

Sunday's game, the Ebbets Field regular-season finale, began promisingly enough. Ralph Branca, rarely used since early August and recently released from Shotton's sizable doghouse, was sailing along after seven innings with a 3–1 lead, thanks to a two-run single by Campy. Tex Rickards then made a strange announcement: Branca had a blister and would not pitch the eighth. In came Jack Banta, who promptly yielded four runs to put the game on ice for the Phillies. With the Cardinals beating the Cubs for the second straight day (the bad news was intentionally kept off the Ebbets scoreboard until the fans were exiting), the Bums were in deep trouble: two games out in the loss column with four to play, all on the road. Aware of the gloomy outlook, the frustrated Brooklyn fans roughed up the Phillies as they hastily made their way to their bus.

Almost immediately, the fingerpointing began. Branca insisted the blister was nothing but a cover story by an incompetent Shotton, whom he claimed yanked him "before I even showed it to him." The Old Sourdough begged to differ. Campanella had told him "unsolicited" after the seventh that Branca had "lost his stuff," and Branca himself had then voluntarily displayed the raw skin on his right index finger. As for Branca, "if he doesn't like me, I am sorry, but that won't make any difference to the club."

His manager and pitcher publicly bickering was too much for Rickey in the midst of the final week of a pennant race. "I choose to believe that both men are honest," he soothingly told reporters. But the "facts," per Rickey's understanding, suggested that it was Campy, concerned about the blister, who had advised Shotton to pull Branca.

Roy was not at all happy at being placed in the middle of a public dispute. Shotton had asked him a question and he had merely answered it. He had not volunteered anything. At least that was Campy's story. "This is the first time I've ever had a manager try to pass the buck to me," he complained. "Shotton still manages the ball team and no catcher can tell him when or when not to remove a pitcher." But in his eagerness to avoid conflict, he had already shown a tendency to retreat from controversial statements, such as a February comment to Dick Young critical of the Negro Leagues that kicked up a mini-fuss in the black press. Even Sam Lacy got a hint of the pitfalls involved in quoting Campy. In the days that followed, he heard "several different versions" of the blister story, which all "came from one person . . . Roy Campanella."

Idle until Wednesday, the Dodgers now needed help from the sixth-place

Pirates, who had played the Cardinals tough all season and had kept the dangerous Stan Musial at bay at Forbes Field. On Tuesday in Pittsburgh, Campy's adversary Bill Werle held Musial to a single in five trips as the Cards lost 6–4. The Dodgers now trailed by a single game with four to play, the exact same scenario as in the American League, where the Red Sox and the Yankees were duking it out in a better remembered, but no more compelling, pennant race.

Rain on Wednesday favored Brooklyn. The Cards would now have to face Murry Dickson, the Pirates' tough right-hander, who had already beaten them four times this year, on his normal three days' rest on Thursday. Before a slim crowd of 9,573 mostly concerned with Ralph Kiner's fading assault on 60 homers, Dickson continued his mastery over his former team, which managed only six hits in a 7–2 defeat.

Back in Boston for a crucial doubleheader, the Dodgers contended with the previous season's celebrated duo of Warren Spahn and Johnny Sain. Spahn, seeking his twenty-first victory, took a beating in a soggy game one, while Sain was chased in the first inning of game two after surrendering five unanswered runs. As the rain continued to fall, the Braves intentionally missed double plays, issued intentional walks, and even built a bonfire in front of their dugout while Connie Ryan donned a raincoat in the on-deck circle. The stalling techniques did not amuse the men in blue. Ryan was ejected, Newk was told to "just keep pitching," and the Dodgers eventually took the rain-shortened game 8–0.

Now in first place for the first time since August 20, Campy and his teammates romped noisily in the Braves Field clubhouse. "Cancel those 50 World Series tickets," Rickey gleefully wired Cardinal owner Fred Saigh. With St. Louis in the midst of a monumental collapse, an even bigger celebration seemed imminent. On Friday afternoon at Wrigley Field, the Red Birds lost their third straight to fall one game off the pace with two to play. A Dodger victory or Cardinal loss would clinch at least a tie for the pennant. "A week ago I'd have settled for the playoff," Shotton told a reporter as he prepared to board a Philadelphia-bound train that evening. "But now—but now! . . . I won't settle for that. We've gotta win."

Saturday was a big day for the Dodgers, but an even bigger one for Campy, who would be honored by the hometown folks before the game. He couldn't help but feel a bit embarrassed by the pile of gifts he received or the presence of black song stylist Savannah Churchill, who crooned her 1947 hit "I Want to Be Loved (But Only by You)" especially for him. But he was proud that his family was there to share in his recognition, along with other friends who still remembered him as the chubby Kerbaugh Street kid who loved to play baseball.

With the festivities over, the Dodgers turned their attention to Phillies starter Ken Heintzelman, owner of a glittering 5-0 record against Brooklyn this year. The left-handed Heintzelman was looking for win number 18, although he had no interest in 20, he told one reporter, since his bonus would mostly go to taxes, "which would only go for somebody on relief." The Dodgers sent him to the showers in the fifth, but the Phillies eventually overcame a 3–0 deficit to come out on top 6–4. Even more disturbing were the Phillies' continued casual racist taunts two years after they had made Robinson's rookie season a living hell.

The only good news came from Chicago, where the Cardinals lost again. The best the Red Birds could now hope for was a tie and then a playoff series with the Dodgers for the second time in four seasons. "Well, if we win tomorrow, it won't make any difference what the Cards do," Campy observed. "So let's do it."

The man chosen by Shotton to carry the Dodgers into the promised land that Sunday was Newcombe, once again working on two days' rest. After three innings and five unanswered runs, the Dodgers were ready to pop open the champagne. But the overworked Newk, Campy noticed, was not getting his pitches down. In the fourth, he threw one high pitch too many to Willie Jones, who deposited a 3-run blast into the left-field seats. Moments later, Newk was out of the game, the deficit cut to 5–4. And in Chicago, the Cards had finally awakened from their slumber, building a 6–0 lead by the fourth. Unless their margin held, the Dodgers faced a long trip to St. Louis for playoff game one on Tuesday.

In the fifth, Brooklyn once again threatened. Hits by Furillo and Hodges put runners on second and third with no outs and Roy up. The Phillies had given him little to hit so far, walking him in four of his seven series plate appearances. Expecting the same from new pitcher Jim Konstanty, he quickly fell behind 0-2 before working the count to 2-2. On the sixth pitch of the at bat, Campy ripped a double into the left-field corner for two runs. The lead, back at three, now looked safe.

The Phillies, still fuming over their treatment in Brooklyn last weekend, would not die easily. Bill Nicholson doubled home Del Ennis in the bottom of the frame to cut the lead to two, and run-scoring hits by Granny Hamner and Ennis tied the score at seven an inning later. Dodger fans, devastated by the double whammy of a blown 5–0 lead and an insurmountable Cardinal lead in Chicago, let out a collective groan in the general direction of their radios.

The next three innings only worsened the Brooklyn faithful's torture. Campy again came up with Furillo and Hodges on in the seventh, but this time skied out to Richie Ashburn. The Dodgers blew another scoring chance an inning later when Duke Snider was nailed in a rundown between second and third. Only Jack Banta's clutch relief pitching kept Brooklyn alive.

In the tenth, Dem Bums finally broke through. Heintzelman, beginning his fourth inning of relief after starting on Saturday, yielded a single to Reese, who went to second on a sacrifice by Eddie Miksis. Snider, despite his supposed aversion to lefties, then slammed Heintzelman's first offering into center field to put Brooklyn up by one. A single by Luis Olmo brought home the Duke for a precious insurance run a few moments later.

Back in Chicago, the Cardinals clustered around a radio in the Wrigley Field clubhouse, praying for another Phillies miracle comeback. They cheered excitedly when Mike Goliat singled with one out off Banta, who had now suffered a torn nail on his right middle finger. But this was not to be a repeat of the infamous blister game of a week earlier. After falling behind the dangerous rookie Ed Sanicki, who had walloped three homers in his first twelve major league at bats, Banta struck him out swinging. Working carefully to Ashburn, Banta found himself in a 2-0 hole. Shotton then sent Clyde Sukeforth to talk to the young pitcher, who had no intention of yielding the ball. Three pitches later, Ashburn lofted a harmless fly to left field to end the game.

At that moment, Shibe Park abruptly transformed into Ebbets Field. "Hysterical Brooklyn rooters," wrote Philadelphia sportswriter Stan Baumgartner, "danced on the dugout, tossed confetti, pounded strangers on the shoulders and formed impromptu parades about the stands." The ensuing scene in the visitors' clubhouse was just as chaotic. Don Newcombe toted a resistant Shotton through the dressing room while shouting, "Pinch me and make sure I'm not dreaming." Preacher Roe grabbed a pair of scissors and began snipping wildly at any available necktie. But an emotionally drained Reese was in no mood for frivolity: "I could sit down and cry right now, even though we won." Nor was Robinson. "That was the hardest game of my life—football or baseball," Jackie told a reporter. "Nothing ever took more out of me."

Campy was already dreaming about his first World Series. "The Yankees might be tough, but I don't see how they can be any tougher than those Phils were today. Man, they really made us sweat."

CASEY STENGEL'S Yankees had just pulled off a miracle of their own, beating the first-place Red Sox two straight to win the American League pennant by a single game. But some National League observers thought that the injury-plagued Bronx Bombers, despite their historic October magic, were vulnerable, especially with their biggest star, Joe DiMaggio, fighting a nasty virus and "looking more like a scarecrow than a baseball player." "This is the worst-looking Yankee team I ever saw in a World Series," muttered Rogers Hornsby.

Even with the Yanks at less than full strength, the upcoming clash offered plenty of story lines far beyond the obvious subway-series angle. The Bums were hoping the third time was the charm after Yankee victories in 1941 and 1947. Stengel was triumphantly returning to Brooklyn, where he began his career thirty-seven years earlier and later failed in his first managerial stop. And journalists predictably scrambled to make the inevitable contrasts between the "homefolks" of Ebbets Field and the Manhattan swells and corporate types who supposedly patronized Yankee Stadium. The celebrated gossip columnist Dorothy Kilgallen preferred the comforts of Flatbush. "The crowd is noisier, the atmosphere more gala, the spirit more evident than it is in the Yankee Stadium," she wrote that October. "Ebbets Field has a gemütlich quality, like a cozy little neighborhood bar as compared with the grand ballroom of the Waldorf-Astoria. It is a much better place for letting your hair down, so they do."

The race issue provided the starkest contrast between the two clubs. The Yankees had finally gingerly stuck their toe into the integration waters earlier that year, signing a few Negro Leaguers mainly to beef up attendance for their Newark affiliate. No one, however, actually expected to see blacks in pinstripes anytime soon. The Yankees, after all, had screeched "all kinds of filth and race remarks" at Robinson in the '47 series. Their top reliever, Joe Page, was given the dubious title of the "most prejudiced" pitcher in the American League by Larry Doby. Some also whispered about DiMaggio and his San Francisco restaurant, "where Negroes can't even call on the phone for a sandwich and have it handed to them on the sidewalk."

With the battle lines clearly drawn, interest in the Series was feverish in the forty-eight hours before game one at the Stadium on Wednesday, October 5. Everyone seemed to want to forget, at least temporarily, the recent frightening news that the Russians now had the A-bomb and of the thirteen-person killing spree of a vet gone berserk in New Jersey. In Brooklyn, locals cheered as Roy and the other Dodgers motored down Flatbush Avenue in a parade of open cars. "The Yankees should only break their leg," remarked one lady fan. "That's how I hate them Yankees." At Yankee Stadium, choice seats were harder to buy than a ticket to the current Broadway smash *South Pacific*, and bleacher lines began to form a full day before gametime. An old-timer, one reporter noted, "had someone hold his place in line while he walked up and down haranguing the fans about what a great baseball team the Chicago Cubs were in 1906." "Today, what are baseball players?" the oldster asked scornfully. "Bunch of hams."

At Sing Sing, inmates were granted permission to listen to the Series in the prison yard over an amplified radio hookup. A Long Island junior high school planned to pipe the broadcasts into classrooms over the PA system. But Beth-El Hospital took an opposite approach, removing all table radios from cardiology patients, who might become overly stimulated from one World Series thrill too many.

Some fans viewed radio or bleacher seats as an inferior substitute for the newest technology sweeping the nation. A record fifty-one television stations would be carrying the games, including six of the seven New York channels. "Television has grown up in the past year," wrote columnist Dan Parker. "What with superimposed shots of base runners while the main camera was covering the battery, not to mention the head-on views of the batter from a camera located in center field."

Although only 6 percent of American families owned a set in 1949, an enterprising fan could easily get his TV fix in a bar, tavern, or even an appliance store. In an experimental move, the Series was also simulcast on the full screen of six movie houses nationally, including the forty-one-hundred-seat Fabian-Fox in Brooklyn. For $1.20, the Flatbush moviegoer was entitled to a double feature ("a dog picture and a violent Cagney opus," sniffed one reporter), TV coverage of the game, and the full ballpark experience, complete with vendors peddling food.

Unfortunately, the much-hyped Series proved to be a letdown after the thrilling conclusions of the regular season. The opener at Yankee Stadium was exciting enough, a scoreless nail-biter between Newcombe and an orange-juice-fueled Allie Reynolds, won by the Yankees in the bottom of the ninth on a Tommy Henrich homer. In game two, Preacher Roe used 136 pitches, at least two of them spitters to fan DiMaggio and Johnny Lindell, to whitewash the Yankees on six hits and even the Series at one. Following the final out, an emotional Rickey threw his arms around Roe and planted a flurry of wet ones on the startled hurler, all with an unlit cigar still in his mouth. When asked about the lovefest the next day, Rickey denied it had ever occurred: "I never kissed anybody in my life."

The Yankees then calmly won the next three 4–3, 6–4, and 10–6 to take the Series in five games. In the days that followed, shell-shocked Brooklyn fans pointed to Carl Furillo's injury (his "groining" as he called it), Snider's pathetic .143/8-strikeout performance, and Shotton's peculiar managerial moves, particularly starting Newcombe on two days' rest twice. Rickey was also bitterly disappointed. "There have been pennants I wanted to win as much as this one, and perhaps even more," he said afterward, "but never, never before did I yearn to win a World's Series as much as I craved this one." He was especially furious with Roe, the former object of his affection, who was unwilling to pitch game five with what turned out to be a broken index finger that he could not fit into a glove.

Former Dodger Dixie Walker had his own take on the Dodgers' frustrations, an explanation eerily familiar to contemporary ears. "The Yankees are a lucky team," he insisted. "They're great, they force the breaks because they are good ballplayers. . . . But no team can win without luck and they have generally been lucky." Lucky or not, the Yankees had the big prize again while the Dodgers were developing a reputation as World Series chokers. "You know, I'm beginning to wonder if I'm ever going to play on a series winner," mused Pee Wee Reese. "I've been in three of them now—and I don't know."

• • •

THE SERIES proved to be a pivotal moment in Campanella's career. When he first drove up to Yankee Stadium with Jackie for game one, the pressure of a huge crowd, media everywhere, and the general hoopla were inescapable. "I was nervous before my first Series," he said years later. "I was nervous before every Series." The butterflies disappeared as soon as he caught Newk's first pitch. Over the next five games, he quietly put on a brilliant show that would not soon be forgotten.

Although Campy reached base in seven of eighteen plate appearances and belted one of Brooklyn's four homers, his fielding attracted the most attention. Sportswriters raved about his aggressive chatter with the pitchers, his "amazing pickup" of a near wild pitch, and his bullet throw that caught Henrich napping between second and third. Most memorable was Campy's fourth-game pickoff of Phil Rizzuto, who had thought Roy a fellow *paisano* until he saw him in person. "*Que pasa?*" Campy affably greeted the diminutive shortstop the next day. "What's cooking yourself, and stop picking me off third. What ya trying to do—get me fired?"

The national press was universal in its praise. "A graceful and solid receiver of pitches, a dangerous batter, an excellent thrower and a nimble-witted cat behind the mask, the Negro hustler was magnificent in his team's defeat," wrote Franklin Lewis of the *Cleveland Press*. "Campanella," asserted Stan Baumgartner of the *Philadelphia Inquirer*, "stood out like a giant, proving that he is one of the best, if not the best catcher in the major leagues." Even the normally cranky Joe DiMaggio was effusive. "Brooklyn showed me the greatest catcher, hitting excluded, I had seen in my experience. That Campanella is a wizard. His accurate arm, his alertness, his freezing you to the bat, his pickoffs—well, there's my idea of a receiver."

But the most meaningful accolades came from his two childhood heroes: Bill Dickey and Mickey Cochrane. "From what he showed in the World Series and in the few games I did see him play," Cochrane told Sam Lacy, "I'd say he might be one of our 'great' catchers." Dickey, who had watched him at close range from the Yankee dugout, was even more certain of Campy's elite status. "He's easily one of the smoothest receivers of his generation, has an excellent arm and is very strong with a bat," he remarked. "It makes me feel pretty good to have him say he learned something from me."

Campy's World Series heroics completed his movement out of the shadows. He was not Jackie Robinson, but his name and face were becoming recognizable far beyond Brooklyn and black America. For the first time in his Dodger career, he had no postseason worry about where or how much he would be playing next season. His only real concern was whether Rickey might start paying him something close to what the "best catcher" in the major leagues deserved.

12

THE SPLIT

LESS THAN SEVENTY-TWO HOURS after the Series had ended, Roy was back on the road again, this time with Newk and Larry Doby as part of Jackie's postseason barnstorming tour through the South. If the usual Jim Crow conditions were no fun, the payday was, a $3,500 guarantee plus another $1,500 if the tour managed to get in at least fifteen games and two Sunday promotions. Campy's Series share was only $4,272.74, so $5,000 to hang out with his pals and play ball for a month must have seemed like a steal.

The tour began uneventfully in Newport News on October 12. About thirty-five hundred mostly black fans showed up that afternoon to watch the Robinson All-Stars beat up on a group of Negro American Leaguers 7–3. The four major leaguers then hopped in a car to drive the twenty-three miles to their evening game in Norfolk. What greeted them at High Rock Park exceeded their wildest expectations: a huge crowd of twelve thousand fans, more than quadruple the number who normally attended local minor league contests.

Robinson was ecstatic. "The first week we could see this was going to be one of these fabulous tours—we had them standing on top of one another . . . everybody was going standing room only practically every place we went," he later recalled. But Campy, Newcombe, and Doby were not as pleased when they discovered Jackie had a percentage deal: $5,000 up front plus a third of anything earned over $70,000. Robinson stood to make three, even four times as much as Campy's $5,000 and Newk's $4,500 shares. That Doby had cut a better deal—$5,000 guarantee, an extra $25 for games one to twenty, plus 5 percent of the gross after expenses—did not lessen his annoyance with Jackie.

The three ballplayers seriously considered leaving but instead confronted Jackie while driving together to a venue. "If you guys feel I should have made your deal for you, I am in favor of calling this tour off right now," an unapologetic Robinson told them. "I don't like what you are inferring here—I made my deal—you made your deal—and I can't be responsible because you are going to get five thousand dollars." His words, while correct, did little to soothe their resentment, nor did his offer to turn over his share of a few extra games later added to the schedule.

Lester Dworman, who promoted Robinson's Southern tours, offered a slightly different recollection when interviewed nearly sixty years later. Robinson's barnstorming jaunts, he recalled, were not always easy, plagued by crooked promoters and oppressive Jim Crow laws. Still, the tours usually did "fantastic. We made a fortune." As for the participants, he admired Robinson, remembered Doby as a "prince," and claimed Newcombe was "nice . . . but all he cared about was getting laid."

Campy was a different story. "Jackie and I were partners. . . . Campy saw the first night . . . that the audience was jammed. . . . So Campy said, 'I want a better deal.' " But Dworman, a signed agreement from Roy in hand, would have none of it. "Jackie and I said go screw, go home, get the hell outta here and good-bye. . . . So Campy was gonna leave, but he decided there was nothing he could do so he might as well play."

As the tour proceeded through the Deep South, some fans began to sense something was wrong. In Nashville on October 19, locals complained that Jackie was "unapproachable and appeared lackadaisical," while others felt Doby was "hostile." Despite his own growing anger, Roy went about his business as usual. "Campanella played hard and apparently tried," wrote Sam Lacy, "and the fans were quite pleased with his affability." As for Newk, he was already preparing to leave the tour early for another, and presumably better-paying, barnstorming gig on the West Coast.

After three weeks, an impressive 148,561 fans had already watched the Robinson team in action, almost 50,000 more than expected. But Jackie decided to pull the plug with four games left on the schedule. A cold had turned into the flu, and he returned home in early November reportedly $15,000 richer. The following week, despite the promises of one writer to vote only for whites, Robinson was elected Most Valuable Player of the National League.

Just a few weeks earlier, Campy would have been elated for his friend's good fortune. Now, the bad taste left from the tour had changed everything. How much, it is difficult to say, since he never publicly spoke of the 1949 barnstorming incident. Still, money was always important to Campy, and even more so once he became a major leaguer. He simply could not comprehend how a close friend for four years could look the other way while a slick promoter lowballed him. Although Newcombe eventually got over the episode and Doby came to agree that he should have cut a better deal, Roy's feelings for Jackie had permanently changed.

Had he wished, Robinson could easily have asked Dworman to rework Campy's agreement. That he did not was partly due to his conviction that regardless of friendship, his only obligation was to himself, but also to Robinson's belief that he deserved the lion's share (three years earlier, he had delayed a San Diego promotion "by holding out for a larger hunk of the proceeds"). "Where he plays, Robby has a pulling power comparable to Babe Ruth's," Milton Gross of the *New York Post* marveled in September. Campy and Newk undoubtedly had "intensified the draw. But there is little doubt that Jackie, now approaching something of a Superman's status among his people, can pack the parks on the road alone."

Years later when he began to take his own team on the road, Campy consciously pursued a different financial arrangement. "Roy instituted everybody getting the same share, whether you were playing in the major leagues or the minor leagues," recalled George Crowe, part of the '49 tour as a Boston Brave farmhand. "And that was a real boost for the guys that were playing in the minor leagues."

For the next few months, the public had no inkling of the widening breach between Campy and Jackie. The two returned to the Harlem YMCA for a second year, appeared at local schools, and attended the inevitable postseason sports banquets, sometimes uncomfortably seated together. They were still neighbors in Addisleigh Park, their wives now both pregnant. Seven-year-old David went to Jackie Jr.'s third birthday party in November, although within three years Roy would reportedly forbid his children to attend similar Robinson functions.

Sam Lacy, close confidant of both men, finally broke the story of their estrangement on the front page of the *Afro-American* after planting several hints in prior columns. Campy and Jackie, he reported, were now "barely on speaking terms" off the field and had resisted efforts by Lacy and Newcombe (strangely described as "thoroughly satisfied" with his barnstorming cut) to bring them together, although Robinson appeared more receptive than Roy. Further confirmation from the celebrated Broadway columnist and radio star Walter Winchell was still not enough to convince some black journalists, who were critical of Lacy's "sensationalizing." In the coming months, Lacy would suggest the relationship had improved somewhat, and there was even talk of the pair rooming together again. The damage, however, proved to be irreparable.

In retrospect, their friendship was destined to fail. Except for a common racial heritage and shared baseball experiences, Robinson and Campanella had almost nothing in common.

From an early age, Campy was outgoing and quickly put strangers at ease with a quip or amusing anecdote. Jackie was introverted and less comfortable with the hordes following his every move. More than a few black fans could not understand why their hero "ignored their questions and acted aloof" in public.

The contrast between Robinson's and Campanella's public personas had recently surfaced during the World Series. On the way to Yankee Stadium, Campy and Jackie had stopped at Smalls' Paradise, the famous Harlem nightspot. While Campy went inside for a brief meeting, a black fan named Harold Douglas walked up to Robinson, offered his hand, and wished him good luck in the Series. "He took my hand as if it were a fish and mumbled something about, 'Okay, all right,' and kept on reading his paper as if I had never said a word to him," Douglas complained. As Douglas turned away, he saw Campy, who responded to a similar greeting in his usual enthusiastic manner. "I can excuse a guy who has a lot on his mind, but Joe Louis has gone down the aisle for many a championship fight and he's never been too busy or occupied to return a fan a civil answer," Douglas related to journalist Dan Burley. "I didn't like it one bit and neither did the fellows who saw what happened."

Robinson's behavior that day was not surprising. His controversial 1948 *Ebony* article, "What's Wrong with Negro Baseball," revealed his solidly middle-class orientation in its criticisms of the conduct of his fellow Negro Leaguers and their fans. Even as a major leaguer, Robinson blanched at the often overly enthusiastic rooting of some African-Americans. During one game in 1948, Jackie became so embarrassed by an "overly raucous" black woman that he "unobtrusively drifted near her and told her please to be quiet, because she was making a spectacle of herself."

Robinson's ultracompetitive nature fueled his greatness on and off the ballfield. "He plays just as hard to win a no-stake pinochle game with teammates on a property trunk as he does to win the last game of a World Series," noted trainer Harold Wendler. But such passion inevitably rubbed some players the wrong way. Moments after the Dodgers lost the '49 World Series, Joe Bostic watched Robinson inform Doby he would outhit him every year they played in the majors. "Being able to excel at all the things that he did, he just figured he was number one," Monte Irvin recalled. "It seemed like he thought he was just a little bit better than other players." And his self-assuredness sometimes gave way to an overbearing, and sometimes tactless, sense of self-righteousness. "Jackie spoke like he wanted to speak," Campy later explained. "He didn't care what you thought about it."

For those who moved in the same circles as Robinson and Campanella, their differences were striking. To Lynn Parrott, Robinson "was more business," "focused" in a "coiled-spring kind of a way . . . in everything that he did. . . . He had a sense of purpose about him that you just look at him walking towards you and you go, 'This guy's on his way to do something.' " In contrast, Campanella "forever had a big smile, laughed easily, was loved by everybody. He was just an instinctively, intuitively, pleasant happy person to be around."

Even their interests outside baseball failed to overlap. Although Campy liked movies and later became a tropical-fish and model-train hobbyist, everything came a distant second to baseball. He loved to play it, he loved to talk about it, and he wanted to stay in it for the rest of his life. On the other hand, Jackie's college background allowed him to more easily cultivate a life outside the game. "You don't find companionship on a big-league club," Robinson once explained. "You work together on the field, but off the field you look for people you have things in common with." For Jackie, baseball was a job, one beneath his considerable mental capacity. He had no sooner been voted MVP than he announced, "The sooner I can get out of baseball, the better."

Robinson's extracurricular activities would eventually include involvement in the burgeoning civil rights movement. Soon after winning the MVP, he announced that every "self-respecting person" supported the civil rights platforms of both major parties and should push for passage of congressional legislation. In contrast, Campanella would consciously embrace the largely apolitical nature of most athletes, white or black. "He was the quintessential jock," his son later observed.

If Campy held any strong political views, he kept them to himself. Politics meant disagreements, conflicts, and controversies, all of which he disdained. Such a stance guaranteed widespread acceptance and acclaim from the public and the press, particularly in postwar America, when consensus and conformity were highly valued. But this attitude destroyed any chance of a permanent friendship with Robinson, who came to agree with Paul Robeson's contention that black celebrities "just can't play ball and sing, we've got to speak out for our people."

Had Jackie's and Campy's personality and philosophical differences been somehow overcome, one other issue could still never be resolved. Campanella, Sam Lacy would later insist, was fundamentally jealous of Robinson, as were a number of other black players who followed him in the 1950s. "For the most part, they felt they could do the same things Jackie was doing, but he was commanding the headlines." Robinson agreed. Campy's complaints about his barnstorming cut, Jackie believed, were simply a more overt expression of envy that had already surfaced following Jackie's signing in 1945. Within a few years, however, it would be Robinson who would occasionally resent Campy's growing popularity while his own public approval waned.

Both men were careful to keep their feud from the eyes and ears of their teammates. "I never saw one thing in the clubhouse that spoke like they had a breach," noted Carl Erskine. "It was not obvious at all." But Erskine, who was close to Campy and Jackie, keenly appreciated their differences perhaps better than anyone else. "I say they're both right. Because if you had been Campanella living in poverty in Philadelphia and you got out of that through playing in the Negro League and winter baseball and finally being allowed to play in the major leagues, think of that in Campy's situation. Jackie had a mother that saw that he was a disciplined kid and he went to school and stayed in school, went to college. . . . Campy was relegated to 'I'm black and I'm poor and that's where I'm at.'

"They came from two different directions, and because of that, Jackie was never satisfied that just playing big league baseball was much of an accomplishment, with all the rest that had to be done. Campanella says, 'Man, look what I got to do. I got to be a big league player. How big is that in my life?' . . . And Jackie felt like, you know, just making the big leagues was not even close to why he was there."

For Campy, the barnstorming fallout meant the loss of a dear friend, one who had been almost like a brother to him. "They were so respectful and admiring of each other," Rachel Robinson recalled, "and had so much fun together." Now there would be no more shared rides to Ebbets Field, no more visits to each other's home. Instead, their interactions would be marked by a polite but distinct coolness. But on the playing field, it was as if nothing had ever happened. As far as anyone could see, the Dodger foundation appeared as strong as ever.

IN THE weeks before spring training, the baseball world watched curiously to see how the wise old Mahatma would handle the 1950 salaries of his three black stars. Robinson, the new MVP, was supposedly asking for $50,000, eventually settling for what the press guessed to be $35,000. Newcombe, recently named Rookie of the Year, was boosted to $13,000. As for Campy, Rickey handed him a blank contract and told him to fill in a reasonable amount. Campy took pen in hand and wrote down $12,500. "That's about what I figured Roy would ask for," Rickey chuckled. "It's a fat salary, but he's worth twice that much. He'll get what he wants."

In reality, Roy's "fat salary" was precisely the same as that of Andy Seminick, who had a lower batting average and on-base percentage, committed more errors and passed balls, and caught twenty-nine fewer games. Some sportswriters, most notably the *Daily News'* Jimmy Powers, who had already christened Rickey "El Cheapo," felt Campy, Robinson, and Newcombe were drastically underpaid. But Roy, the bad old days of the Negro Leagues never far from his mind, would have none of it. "Maybe they aren't paying what we're worth in the present baseball market," he admitted. "But they are paying us a darned sight more than we'd ever get in another job . . . and we're all lucky we didn't come along . . . five or six years earlier." As for staging a holdout, Campy was dubious. "Should we quit if we didn't get it? . . . Little Roy isn't ever going to quit . . . if he can hobble out of a wheelchair and get up there, that's what he will do. . . . Little Campy's gonna draw his Social Security right at home plate if they'll let him."

Little Campy did not look so little when he reported to Vero Beach twenty-one pounds overweight that spring. "Three times around Campanella and you've done a day's work," quipped one teammate. Even Shotton joined in the fun: "How are you gonna get to first base—roll?" The Dodger brain trust prescribed a diet until Roy contracted the flu. A hospital stay might have sped his recuperation, but Campy was not eager to be sent to a Southern medical facility, where the usual Jim Crow conditions would prevail.

Florida still seemed hopelessly stuck in a time warp in its race relations. After learning that Campy, Newk, Jackie, and Sam Lacy had borrowed Harold Parrott's rental car, the rental agency angrily demanded its return. Campy had an equally unpleasant experience returning from a game at West Palm Beach. Hoping to avoid another embarrassing roadside segregation incident, he had decided to stay behind, have dinner, then catch a train back to camp. When he arrived in Vero Beach at 2:00 a.m., he found no car waiting and no white cabbie willing to pick him up. Instead, he wearily covered the two and a half miles to Dodgertown on foot.

Such occurrences did not surprise Rickey, who knew the Great Experiment still had many obstacles to overcome. The Dodgers had been grappling with one of their own: whether Brooklyn fans would tolerate a lineup with four black players. The issue had surfaced in 1949 with the emergence of Sam Jethroe, a speedy .326 hitter at Montreal now ready to take over left field. A "highly secret meeting of some forty representative Brooklyn citizens, Negro and white" that August assured Rickey that their only interest was in a winning team. Still, Dan Burley claimed the Mahatma remained rather sensitive to "any suggestion that he has an 'Uncle Tom's Cabin' at Ebbets Field." Rickey had bristled at Yankee GM George Weiss's sly, but not altogether inaccurate, insinuation that the Dodgers' success was not the product of a well-stocked farm system but of brilliantly executed "raids" of the Negro Leagues.

Although Jethroe was shipped to the Braves in October in a deal involving cash and several players, another African-American hurler was about to join the Brooklyn pitching staff: Dan Bankhead, a minor leaguer since his brief stint in Dodger blue back in 1947. A 20-game winner and .323 hitter at Montreal, Bankhead seemed poised to become Brooklyn's next breakout black star, at least if he could keep his behavior in check. To Rickey, Bankhead's problem was a lack of confidence. "He doesn't have the friendly jocularity of a Newcombe, or the lovable personality of a Campanella, or the sense of a Robinson." Later, he would more bluntly suggest that Bankhead, the only real Southerner of the bunch, was burdened by what he called a "slave complex."

Despite organizational misgivings, Bankhead would become the fourth black Dodger. But Robinson remained the quartet's indisputed leader. Jackie now had his own radio show on ABC. He would soon be on the cover of *Life* magazine. A film treatment of his life, *The Jackie Robinson Story*, had just been shot with Jackie in the title role. A Robinson doll was being manufactured, and his name was also appearing on "miniature bats, gloves, candy bars," and clothing. Sportswriters guessed that he might clear $135,000 through various deals in 1950.

Robinson's growing celebrity came at a predictable cost. His phone never stopped ringing, and nuisance lawsuits began to dog him. "He has less privacy than a gold fish in a glass bowl," observed journalist Alvin White after spending time at the Robinson home. Sam Lacy even wondered whether Jackie might be headed for a breakdown. Not surprisingly, Rachel Robinson had already begun to broach the subject of retirement with her husband.

Robinson was not in his comfort zone that spring, reporting late because of film work and twelve pounds overweight. That Rickey granted him extra time to finish his movie probably did not sit well with some already envious Dodgers, nor did his supposed "indifference toward training." Lacy even alluded to an "open flare-up" with "one of the Bums' regular outfielders." Robinson's feud with Campy, now public knowledge thanks to Lacy, only added to his stress.

Jackie, as usual, worked himself back into shape by the end of spring, as did Campy. Their workouts might have been far more bearable had they enjoyed each other's support, laughter, and companionship as they had in the past. But Roy was also beginning to see the benefits of separating himself from Robinson. He was no longer the other, less important Negro Dodger, mostly ignored during spring training last year. Now, thanks to his World Series heroics, white and black Southerners increasingly recognized him and wanted his autograph. And there was no question about his acceptance by his white teammates. Rickey himself claimed that Campy was the "best liked guy" on the club.

His popularity assured, Roy set his sights on two goals for 1950. After a taste of the World Series, albeit a bitter one, he wanted a championship. He also hoped to boost his power numbers. In 1949, he had hit 22 homers. This year, Roy told reporters, he was shooting for 30.

BROOKLYN ENTERED the new season heavily favored to repeat as National League champs. Who could match big boppers such as Hodges, Campanella, and Snider, on-base machines such as Robinson and Reese, and the one-two, righty/lefty punch of Newcombe and Roe? And the Brooks looked even stronger this year with the addition of infielder Bobby Morgan, the International League's MVP in 1949, and the hard-throwing Bankhead.

The Dodgers got off to a quick start, playing .623 ball through June 20 while clinging to a razor-thin margin atop the National League. As expected, the Cardinals were breathing down their necks, but Eddie Sawyer's scrappy young Phillies, nicknamed the Whiz Kids, were also in the thick of the race. For Shotton and Rickey, everything was going as planned. Robinson was hitting .360, Snider .333, and Newcombe and Roe had already racked up 15 of the team's 33 wins.

The biggest surprise was Campy, who was not only hitting .306 but was in the midst of an eye-popping power surge. Between May 24 and June 17, Roy belted ten round-trippers in a mere seventy at bats, culminating with a five-game home-run streak. The catcher whose bat had been a question mark only a year earlier was now tied with Ralph Kiner for the National League home-run lead with fourteen. Remarkably, his first twelve homers were hit while batting eighth. The Old Sourdough finally moved him up a notch after realizing that Campy was not going to get a thing to hit as long as he had an automatic out following him.

Roy's 22 homers in 1949 had earned him slugging credentials, but no one seriously believed he had Kiner power. There was considerable talk that the ball was juiced this year ("a jackrabbit—with Benzedrine," one wag claimed). The National League and American League would both set new home-run records in 1950, although the Spalding people predictably denied any change in materials or manufacturing. Roy had also likely tailored his swing to take full advantage of the friendly dimensions of Ebbets Field, the site of 29 of his first 45 major league homers. But his own body provided the real explanation for the power burst. "If you had ever seen his forearms, they were like tree trunks," recalled his teammate Don Zimmer. "What a pair of arms he had."

Defensively, Roy was as smooth as ever in the early months of the season, on his way to nailing a phenomenal 62.5 percent of the base runners foolish enough to run on him that year. Still, some sportswriters could not accept that a black man was not only running the game from behind the plate but running it *well.* "Not long ago," wrote Roscoe McGowen, "a baseball writer (who charitably shall remain unnamed) delivered an impromptu lecture . . . the central theme of which was that Campanella 'has no mental ability.' The point, barely discernible, seemed to be that Roy had great mechanical skill but didn't know how to handle pitchers, what pitches to call for, et cetera." Shotton, by now a full-fledged Campanella supporter, promptly put the misguided scribe in his place. And Campy, with every game he played, would permanently destroy the racist stereotype that blacks could not handle a thinking man's position such as catcher.

Campanella and the Dodgers' other three black faces remained an anomaly in the major leagues. Only five other blacks appeared on big league rosters that June, spread out over three other clubs—the Giants, Indians, and Braves. All could expect plenty of racist garbage from bench jockeys, the second-division Cincinnati Reds and their ringleader, Walker Cooper, among the worst. As a catcher, Roy was especially vulnerable but willed himself to tune them out. "I didn't hear a whole lot of things. If I did, I wasn't concentrating on what I was doing." If things got particularly nasty, he could always rely on Newk to send the bigmouth sprawling to the dirt his next time up.

Brooklyn's ongoing success was the most effective way to silence the bigots. In late June, another trip to the Series didn't seem out of the question. Maybe the Mahatma was a genius after all.

RICKEY WAS pleased with the club's fast start. Nevertheless, he fretted about the pitching staff. "Roe and Newcombe," he told Arthur Godfrey on a June 28 CBS television appearance, "that's all we have as far as pitchers are concerned."

No sooner had Rickey spoken than the Brooks promptly dropped six straight games, including three to the hard-charging Phillies at Shibe Park. The following weekend, the confident Whiz Kids took two more at Ebbets before dropping the finale on Sunday, July 9, the last game before the All-Star break. The formerly unstoppable Dodgers were now nestled uncomfortably in fourth place, 4½ games behind the Phillies, Cardinals, and Braves. "Things just aren't breaking right for us," Campy told Joe Louis, who was just as puzzled by the Dodgers' woes as the rest of black America. "When we get good pitching, we don't hit. When we hit, the pitching seems to be terrible."

The Dodgers somehow managed to stay in the thick of the four-team race following the break, but something was missing. Whether it was Snider "tossing his bat into the air when popping up" or Newk's comment of "guess we better write off this season as a dead loss," the Dodgers appeared to be a flat, dispirited bunch. "They're not hungry enough," smirked one Phillie. But the real problem, insiders whispered, was underlying dissension. As usual, Campy managed to keep his wry sense of humor in the midst of crisis. "Dissension? We got no dissension," he told reporters. "What we haven't got is pitchers."

Shotton was not so amused. His staff was pathetically thin, burdened by sore-armed Rex Barney, inexperienced kids such as Joe Landrum and Chris Van Cuyk, and little-used Billy Loes, a bonus baby who could not be farmed out again without risking his loss through waivers. There were also signs that Shotton was losing control of the Bums. "There's going to be more hustle on this club or you'll be seeing different players in the lineup," he warned. "I am not going to get beat with players who don't run out hits and who want to 'give up' as soon as things don't go so well."

Like sharks smelling blood in the water, the New York press corps began to encircle Shotton. Most of them had never warmed to the cross Old Sourdough, and the feeling was mutual. "He has developed a contempt for newspapermen," wrote Arch Murray of the *Post* after the '49 Series, "that is little short of incredible." Now it was payback time. The *Journal-American* began sponsoring an "If I managed the Dodgers" contest, offering cash prizes and box seats for the best letters in one hundred words or less addressing the Bums' current woes. Over at the *Daily News* (which had sarcastically dubbed him "Kindly Old Burt Shotton"), Dick Young blasted away, quoting "a star player, not a malcontent," who believed his manager was "often 'two plays behind' in making decisions."

The press attacks on Shotton, Rickey knew, were also meant for him. Young thought Rickey a manipulative phony but also resented the Mahatma's unwillingness to curry his favor. Rickey had no choice but to defend his beleaguered skipper. "He has done a magnificent job," he told reporters on August 2 in a predictable burst of hyperbole. "He has made mistakes, but he has taken blame for the mistakes of others too."

A week later, Rickey appeared far less enthusiastic. A few hours after the Dodgers had dropped their second straight game to the Phillies and fourth in a row to fall 6½ games off the pace, Rickey spoke at a banquet at the Hotel St. George in Brooklyn. Usually the picture of unperturbed omniscience, the Mahatma demonstrated a rarely seen impatience and exasperation. "The Dodgers of a year ago were the result of this organization when the players sweated and toiled," he told the surprised gathering of 350. "The Dodgers of 1950 are what is left of a team with complete satiety and where complacency has set in." That some of his own players had already left the function before his speech to see a Sugar Ray Robinson fight in Jersey City gave credence to his words.

If Rickey had hoped to fire up the troops, he was in for a disappointment. The Dodgers headed to Boston, where they were no-hit by Vern Bickford on August 11, then committed an embarrassing seven errors in a 10–2 loss the following day. Even Campy, whom Mike Gaven felt was not part of Rickey's recent indictment, seemed in a fog, committing two errors and getting picked off second by Warren Spahn. "The Brooks are playing as though they realize they are through," observed Dick Young, "and don't give much of a damn from here on in."

With the season apparently lost, everyone expected changes for next year. Robinson, mired in a horrible August slump, thought he might be playing his last games in Brooklyn. "Jackie's not the only one who's thinking that," Campy told Milton Gross. "There's a lot of fellows on the club don't figure they're going to be back." The public speculation on next year's roster annoyed Rickey. "Right now, we are concentrating on the 1950 pennant," he explained, "and it is sorely disappointing to me to hear that our players are talking about anything other than winning this year's pennant."

No sooner had the Robinson trade rumor been quashed than the Dodgers began showing signs of life. They swept Durocher's Giants at the Polo Grounds. Carl Erskine, recently recalled and for good this time, beat the Braves at Ebbets. A three-game sweep of the Pirates at Forbes Field followed. And Roy, rejuvenated by the recent birth of his son Tony, was beginning to heat up again, slamming six hits, including an opposite-field homer, during the Pittsburgh series.

The newly resuscitated Brooks then headed to Cincinnati for the second leg of their Western swing. The seventh-place Reds dropped the first three games of the series to extend Brooklyn's winning streak to nine. Hoping to cool off the red-hot Dodgers, Reds manager Luke Sewell sent left-hander Ken Raffensberger, 12-14 on the season, to the mound on Saturday afternoon, August 26.

Raffensberger was a junkballer, always around the plate with an outstanding slow curve, but he was no mystery to Campy, who had taken him deep once already this year. "I'd get up at five in the morning to hit against that guy," he once bragged. In the second inning, he got his first look at Raffensberger with Hodges on first and the Dodgers trailing 2–0. Ahead 0-2, the Reds' lefty tried to slip a third strike past Campy, but Roy sent a screamer over the left-field wall at Crosley Field and onto the roof of a nearby laundry building.

By the time Roy came up in the fourth, the Reds were again up by two runs. With Hodges on first with a bunt single, Raffensberger was facing the same situation he had bungled in the second. This time, he managed to get a strike before Roy belted a tremendous moon shot over a fifteen-foot beer sign on top of the laundry roof, estimated by one observer to have traveled 460 feet. In the sixth inning, Raffensberger finally wised up. With two runners on and the score tied at four, he walked Campy on a 3-2 pitch.

Raffensberger was still out there when Roy stepped to the dish in the eighth with the score unchanged. Hodges, following the script perfectly, was again perched at first base. With .222-hitting Bobby Morgan and the pitcher to follow, an intentional walk or pitch-around would not have been unreasonable. But Raffensberger admirably, or perhaps stupidly, went right after Campy. The first pitch was a strike, and Roy crushed it over the left-field wall, where it caromed "against a screen guarding a laundry window." His perfect day ended with three homers, six RBIs, and the Dodgers' tenth straight victory. Over twenty-one at bats in 1950 and 1951, Raffensberger allowed eight hits to Roy, seven of them homers. "Love that boy," Campanella said, grinning.

The Dodgers' streak ended the next day in St. Louis, although Campy blasted another home run. He now had twenty-eight on the season, third best in the National League and tops on the Dodgers. "His total is somewhat amazing when it is considered that he has been to bat only 354 times," observed Mike Gaven. "Because he is at the bottom of the batting order and is often passed intentionally, he has had from 50 to more than 100 fewer swings than other home run hitters of note."

Gaven also made the inevitable comparison with Robinson, whose average had tumbled from the .370 range to .330 and who appeared to have "lost that step to his right" in the field. Campy, meanwhile, looked as if he might break the Dodgers' home-run record of thirty-five held by Babe Herman, a feat Gaven believed "would steal a lot of thunder from Robinson." "Roy wouldn't begrudge Jackie or anyone else in this world anything," he noted. "But he's making that big bat, probably the heaviest in the league, speak for those five little Campanellas out on Long Island and his 1951 salary will be a lot closer to Robinson's than it is this year."

THE LATE-AUGUST spurt provided a much-needed adrenaline rush to the discouraged Brooklyn faithful. The Dodgers now had a firm grip on second place and had pulled within four of the Phillies. With eight meetings on tap between the two clubs in September, the Bums expected to make the Whiz Kids sweat down the stretch.

But the maddening inconsistency that had driven Shotton batty all season reappeared. Ten straight wins were followed by seven losses in the next ten games. After losing to the Giants 8–5 at Ebbets on September 5, the Dodgers once again found themselves 7½ games behind, exactly where they stood when their streak began a few weeks earlier. Even Rickey appeared to have given up. On a West Coast scouting mission to watch the Hollywood Stars, Brooklyn's shorts-clad Pacific Coast League affiliate, he was asked whether his team still had a chance. "That," the Mahatma remarked, "would appear to be a pretty difficult assignment."

The Dodgers trooped into Philadelphia on Wednesday, September 6, for a potentially season-ending doubleheader. Roy usually enjoyed coming home and kidding his father, who had developed into a Phillies fan in his old age. Campy did not, however, enjoy playing at Shibe Park, where too many white fans, already angered by local blacks who rooted for the Dodgers, spewed racial hate.

Newcombe won game one, spinning a three-hit shutout to pick up his seventeenth win. But with Newk needing only 106 pitches, Shotton came up with a typically old-school idea. Why not start Newk again in the nightcap? Shotton had always believed that major league pitchers, even in 1950, were still capable of what used to be called the "iron man stunt" of handling both ends of a doubleheader, certainly "a big, strong boy like Don." Although the feat had not been accomplished since 1926 or even attempted since 1940, Newk obligingly took the ball for a second crack at the Phillies.

Newcombe, often criticized by Shotton for his supposed "laziness" and unwillingness to pitch through pain, fared surprisingly well. He heaved ninety-one more pitches before departing for a pinch hitter in the eighth inning, trailing 2–0. In the bottom of the inning, Shotton called for the disappointing Dan Bankhead, who had struggled with various ailments all year. On Bankhead's second offering to Willie Jones, the Phillies' third baseman just got a piece of the ball, sending a foul tip toward Campy.

Roy's two-handed catching technique usually allowed him to catch or at least block most foul tips. This time, he had no chance. The ball struck him squarely on the right hand, and he knew by the excruciating pain that it was bad. His thumb was not only bleeding profusely but he saw bone poking through the skin. "That's the only day I ever looked at my hand and got sick at the sight of it," Campy recalled later. He walked off the field to show the damage to trainer Harold Wendler, who took one look at Roy's mangled thumb and thought him done for the year.

With Bruce Edwards hastily pressed into service, the Dodgers eventually pulled out the second game, thanks to a three-run rally in the ninth. Now trailing by 5½ games and only three in the loss column, the Bums were very much alive. "They wrote us off too quick," Shotton roared gleefully. The Dodgers received more good news when X-rays revealed that Roy's thumb, despite its gruesome appearance "as big as a delicatessen sausage," was only dislocated, rather than broken. With stitches, penicillin, and rest, Campanella was now expected to return in ten days.

On Thursday, Erskine outdueled Robin Roberts to send the Phillies to their fifth straight loss. The Whiz Kids, who had managed just four runs in their last five games, appeared to be choking. "They're shivering over there now," chortled Gene Hermanski. "They're plenty worried." Meanwhile, the supposedly dissension-ridden Dodgers were remarkably loose. "Each day, now, as the Brooks ride to the ball park in their chartered bus," wrote Dick Young, "they sing a little thing entitled, 'The Fading Phils,' a parody on the official Whiz Kid march, 'The Fighting Phils.' "

The Fading Phils managed to stave off an embarrassing four-game sweep at home by taking the series finale on Friday. Even more crucial to the pennant race, they succeeded in disabling Jackie Robinson, whose desperate dive for a smash to his right resulted in a torn thumb ligament, a cast, and an expected three-week recovery. Although Jackie was scornful of the prognosis, he was soon gloomy about his prospects.

Shotton now had no choice but to move Billy Cox to second, insert Bobby Morgan at third, and keep Edwards and his .160 average behind the plate. Such a weakened lineup would not win for long. The battered thumbs of his star catcher and second baseman, he knew, would have to heal quickly for the Dodgers to have any chance of catching the Phils. During Saturday's game against the Giants, the two ballplayers sat in the same row at the Polo Grounds, both in civies and strategically separated by a few seats.

While Campy and Jackie recuperated, the Dodgers lost five of eight and found themselves trailing again the following Sunday, September 17, to the Cubs, 3–1 in the seventh. A desperate Shotton called first for Robinson, who promptly singled in his first at bat in nine days. Next, he sent up Campy, his six stitches now removed, to hit for pitcher Ralph Branca. Gripping a special rubber sponge fashioned to the handle, he poked a single, sending the Ebbets Field crowd of 13,023 into delirium. Robinson eventually scored on Reese's hit, but Bob Rush stopped the Dodgers cold the rest of the way.

With the loss to the seventh-place Cubs, the Brooks fell into third behind the Braves. More than ever, Shotton knew he needed Campy and Jackie for the season's final two weeks. At least Campanella, who had caught the last two innings, seemed almost ready, although Jackie still couldn't play the field. "It doesn't hurt too much," admitted Roy. "Sure, it's sore and you can see that the gash still hasn't healed, but I think I can play and I'm going to try it."

Shotton let Campy catch the final three innings of Monday's game, yet another defeat to the lowly Cubs. Barring a miracle, the season was just about over. After four straight losses, the Dodgers were now nine games out with seventeen to play. The Phillies merely had to win seven of their remaining thirteen games to eliminate the Bums, who now had the red-hot Giants breathing down their neck for third place. The supposedly überfaithful Flatbush fans had given up as well. Only 5,569 (2,051 paid) showed up that afternoon; Ebbets attendance would crack 10,000 only three times in the remaining eleven home dates. "It was different in the old days when we were usually in the second division and anything we did in the way of winning came under the heading of a surprise," observed Babe Herman, one of the original Daffiness Boys and now a Pirate scout. "Now they've gotten used to winning and it's all or nothing."

To his credit, Shotton did not throw in the towel. If he was going to go down, he was going to go down with his best. On Tuesday, September 19, in the first game of a twin bill against the Pirates, he wrote Campanella's and Robinson's names in the starting lineup for the first time in almost two weeks. Campy and his still swollen thumb managed to make it through seven innings, Jackie four, but their absences had little effect on the game or the series. The Dodgers swept the doubleheader, then took the remaining pair to finish their season 19-3 against the hapless Corsairs.

Shotton, ever the optimist, was now convinced that his Dodgers were destined to win, even with the deficit still a healthy seven games. Brooklyn fans were not yet ready to believe. Campy and Jackie were finally almost 100 percent, but the Phillies would have to be monumental chokers to blow such a large lead with only eleven to play. Still, most Brooklynites were curious to see how their frustrating Bums would fare in the first of a two-game set in Philadelphia on Saturday afternoon. When they tuned in to WMGM at 1:25 p.m., shocking news greeted them: Branch Rickey was selling his 25 percent interest in the team for $1.025 million to William Zeckendorf, a forty-five-year-old real estate developer famous for acquiring and later selling the land on which the United Nations headquarters in New York was built.

The public had no clue this was coming. Rickey's contract was up in October, but no one seemed to suspect that he would not be back in 1951. Behind closed doors at Montague Street, it was a very different story. Following the July death of part owner and former Pfizer executive John L. Smith, his widow had turned over her voting rights in the corporation to Walter O'Malley, who now controlled 50 percent of the shares. O'Malley wanted Rickey gone. He was certain the old man and his expensive ideas were a liability, especially with attendance sagging and expenses rising. His bad relations with the local press didn't help matters either. Rickey also got a piece of every player sale, which irritated O'Malley to no end.

Rickey could have held on to his 25 percent stake in the club and chosen to stay the course, but he knew he could not peacefully coexist with O'Malley. He also desperately needed money, as he had borrowed to finance his original stock purchase years earlier. Although O'Malley had already made him a lowball offer for his shares, the Mahatma had an ace up his sleeve. Under the current ownership agreement, if any of the three principals sold shares to an outsider, the others would have the opportunity to match the sale price. With Zeckendorf apparently willing to pony up $1 million, almost three times what Rickey had originally spent, O'Malley would have no choice but to match it. Otherwise, his 50 percent control might become meaningless if Zeckendorf and his 25 percent teamed up with the Mulvey family, who still owned the remaining 25 percent of the franchise.

It soon became apparent that Zeckendorf was not simply a disinterested party. He was a friend of Pittsburgh Pirates owner John Galbreath, who knew that Rickey wanted out of Brooklyn and hoped to hire him to save his own struggling franchise. The Zeckendorf offer, arranged through Galbreath, extricated Rickey from Brooklyn with a tidy profit, freed him to accept a position with Pittsburgh in November, and put $50,000 in the pocket of Zeckendorf for his trouble. Everyone was happy, except for O'Malley, who was certain the deal was bogus, particularly when he later saw Rickey's signature on the $50,000 canceled check to Zeckendorf.

Among the Dodgers, the response to Rickey's imminent departure was mixed. Ralph Branca thought that money "should be a little looser around here" under a new regime. But for Jackie Robinson, the departure of Rickey was devastating. "I'm losing a great personal friend. There's no telling how much he has done for me." Campy felt the same. He had always enjoyed a special bond with the Mahatma, an old backstop himself who loved to discuss catching with Roy. "It seemed that Mr. Rickey was playing the game through me," he recalled. "I was that close to him."

In time, Campanella would become just as friendly with O'Malley, a man whom Robinson came to despise. It would be yet another issue to drive a wedge between Roy and Jackie.

THE RICKEY announcement had no apparent impact on the rejuvenated Bums. Newk picked up his nineteenth win on Saturday afternoon, followed by an Erv Palica two-hit, 11–0 shutout on Sunday before thirty-two thousand horrified Shibe Park fans. The Whiz Kids' lead was now down to five games. "They're through," said one frustrated Philadelphian. "They've run out of gas. Maybe they won't win another game."

The Phils still had a comfortable lead with only a week to go. But they looked disturbingly shaky. Their pitching staff was in a shambles. Curt Simmons was no longer available after his National Guard unit was called up because of the recent outbreak of the Korean War. Bubba Church had only recently returned after missing nine days thanks to a Ted Kluszewski smash off his face that required plastic surgery. Bob Miller was iffy with a bad back. And their final nine games were on the road, while the Dodgers would play their last eleven at Ebbets.

The Bums were glad to be home, but their task would not be easy. Because of earlier rainouts, they faced a nightmarish week: doubleheaders on Monday, Wednesday, Thursday, and Friday. Their only consolation was the three doubleheaders the Phillies faced on their way to the finish line. The impending grind recalled Roy's old Negro League days, but he was no longer a teenager. Campy and Edwards split catching duties in the first twin bill against the Giants, although Edwards's error and passed ball did not win him any new fans. After the smoke had cleared, the Dodgers had managed to take two of three on Monday and Tuesday. The Phillies did the same in Boston. Status quo.

Billy Southworth's Boston Braves then arrived in Flatbush on Wednesday for a grueling six-game ordeal over three days. Trailing the Brooks by only three games, the Braves had no intention of lying down, not when second-place money meant something in those days. Southworth went with his best, Warren Spahn, while Shotton countered with Newk in the opener. Neither was around at the finish. The Dodgers cuffed Spahn around for eight hits in six innings, including Campy's first homer since August 27, and held on to win 9–6. Roy, his left wrist freshly spiked by Sam Jethroe, sat out game two, a 4–2 loss at the hands of Johnny Sain. Over at the Polo Grounds, the Phillies, about to be swept by the Giants, breathed a sigh of relief when they learned the outcome. Their magic number was now 2 to clinch and 1 to tie. Surely they were safe now.

The Whiz Kids, however, seemed intent on making the season's final days as excruciating as possible for their fans. Another doubleheader sweep at the hands of the Giants followed on Thursday. But the Dodgers again could do no better than split with the Braves. Coughing and sputtering to the finish line, the floundering Phillies had backed their way into at least a tie. And the Bums were frankly a long shot for a miracle. Somehow, weary pitching staff and all, they had to sweep the Braves on Friday while the Phillies were idle, then beat the Whiz Kids twice that weekend.

Campy at least was finally back to normal. Shotton had let him catch both games on Thursday and Roy had responded with four hits. He was eager to get another crack at the Braves on Friday if the weather would cooperate. Showers were forecast for New York that day. If one or both games were rained out, there would be no makeups, and the final weekend against the Phillies would be meaningless.

At gametime Friday afternoon, the skies over Ebbets Field were cloudy, but no rain was falling, and the temperature was in the high sixties. Preacher Roe, looking to reach 20 wins for the first time in his career, was the man of the hour in game one. Facing him was a "jumbo-sized," twenty-eight-year-old Rhode Islander named Max Surkont, an August pickup by the Braves, who had never faced the Dodgers in his brief career. Roe pitched well enough, allowing seven hits and three runs in seven innings, but the

Dodgers did even less with Surkont's unfamiliar offerings. After the Braves tacked on two more in the eighth, the Bums found themselves trailing 5–2, their season down to six outs.

Surkont got two of them quickly, retiring Hodges and Campy in the eighth after a Furillo walk. When Cox kept the inning alive with an opposite-field double, the Old Sourdough sent up the lefty Cal Abrams, mostly inactive since his June 30 recall, to pinch-hit for Bankhead. Though hitting just .212 after an 0-for-15 start, Abrams always had good plate discipline and this time succeeded in drawing a walk.

In today's baseball, Surkont would be gone by this point, but Billy Southworth had little faith in relief pitchers, his Braves leading the majors in complete games that year. Instead, he let Surkont go after Pee Wee Reese with the bases loaded and two outs. The move appeared sound when Reese sent a feeble checked-swing grounder to first baseman Earl Torgeson, "a chance," wrote Dick Young, "your six-year-old son could have handled." But Torgeson bobbled the ball, everyone was safe, and the score was now 5–3. Given an extra out, Brooklyn scored four more times, then held off the Braves in the ninth for a lucky 7–5 win.

The Dodgers had cleared the first of four hurdles on the way to the promised land, but reality soon set in. Adrenaline-fueled or not, Roy and his teammates were about to play their ninth game in five days. They had failed to sweep any of the week's three previous doubleheaders. They were up against Vern Bickford, who had no-hit them in August and had beaten them three other times this season. Shotton, running out of serviceable arms, was gambling with rookie Chris Van Cuyk, a midseason callup whose most memorable major league moment had been his spring training tiff with Jackie the year before.

Van Cuyk, idle for the past thirteen days, was no miracle worker. The Braves pounded him for four quick runs before Shotton replaced him with another rookie, Brooklyn native Jim Romano. In the fourth, Campy finally reached his preseason goal of thirty homers with a titanic two-run smash to center that cut the lead to one. Unfortunately, a throwing error by the usually sure-handed Billy Cox allowed the Braves to pick up two more unearned runs, and the Dodgers found themselves trailing 6–3 when they came to bat in the sixth.

For the second time that Friday, the Braves proved incapable of holding a three-run advantage. Hodges started the sixth-inning rally with a single. Campy then hammered a pitch into the right-field corner for a run-scoring, opposite-field double, his third hit of the game. Moments later, the Dodgers had not only rallied to tie the score at six but went up by one in the seventh on Jackie Robinson's fourteenth homer. Erskine then mowed down the Braves the rest of the way, and after five hours of baseball, the miracle Dodgers had two more crucial wins under their belt.

It was like 1949 again in the Ebbets clubhouse. Shotton, resplendent in casual checked shirt and usual Windbreaker, happily threw his arms around Campy and Jackie while flashbulbs popped noisily. "Hello, Mama," the suddenly touchy-feely Old Sourdough greeted his wife on the phone. "Do you still love me?" Several Phillies had been on hand to watch the games, only to find themselves the target of paparazzi eager to capture their despondent responses to the Braves' meltdown. The always volatile Russ "The Mad Monk" Meyer, who had taunted the Ebbets fans when the Braves took their early lead, issued a warning to photographer Bert Brandt: "If you snap me again, I'll smash your face." When Brandt kept on snapping, Meyer (who would tangle with Jackie in 1951) went after him before an usher stepped in.

Across town at the Commodore Hotel in Manhattan, Eddie Sawyer sat in his room, head in hand, intently watching the doubleheader on TV. When it was all over, he put on a brave face for reporters. "It's better that we win for ourselves," said the Phillies skipper. "You can't expect another team to win your battles." Besides, the pressure was still on the Dodgers. "One defeat and they're all through."

A playoff, unthinkable a few days ago, now seemed almost inevitable. On Saturday, a coin toss determined that the Dodgers would get game one in Brooklyn, followed by the remaining two, if necessary, at Shibe. The arrangement suited Pee Wee Reese just fine. "I'll take the first game at home and hope to win it."

There was still the two-game weekend series with the Phillies. Erv Palica was starting the opener on Saturday. Campy had always believed that Palica "had more stuff" than the other Dodger pitchers, and he was glad to see the hard-throwing twenty-two-year-old from California finally fulfilling his potential. Since July, he had been a staff ace, winning twelve games, including a pair against the Whiz Kids. Opposing Palica was Bob Miller.

The borough still had surprisingly large pockets of ambivalence about the Dodgers' fate. Only 23,879 showed up on Saturday afternoon, although Mike Gaven called it "an old-fashioned Brooklyn crowd that booed every visiting play and applauded every Dodger move." In the early innings, the fans had little to cheer. Miller was tougher than expected, holding the Bums scoreless through four, and even made Roy "look mighty sick on three curves" to start the fifth. A few moments later, his stuff had vanished. Cox and Abrams singled, Reese whacked a triple to right, and Eddie Sawyer hastily called for his barely warmed-up bullpen ace Jim Konstanty to face Duke Snider. The overworked Konstanty, making his record seventy-fourth appearance, had not been sharp of late. He promptly grooved a pitch that Snider belted onto Bedford Avenue to put the Dodgers up 4–0.

The Phillies were not dead yet. In the sixth, they pushed across three runs, the third thanks to a yellow-sweater-clad "bobby-soxer" who interfered with a ball still in play. Bobby-soxer and friend were ejected from Ebbets, but Palica appeared to be unnerved. With one out, he walked Willie Jones. Jones, never a base-stealing threat, then took off for second, perhaps on a botched hit-and-run play. Campy had been inconsistent since his injury, throwing out only two of seven runners, far below his normal success rate. This time, he fired a strike down to Jackie, nailing Jones and killing the rally.

Although Palica settled down and handled the Phils in the seventh and eighth, the 4–3 lead felt far from safe, particularly with Jones and his 25 homers scheduled to lead off the ninth. The Flatbush faithful, nervous and nail-biting, came to life when Robinson and Furillo reached base with no outs in the eighth. Shotton, following the book as usual, ordered Gil Hodges to lay one down. Hodges bunted the ball back to Konstanty, who whirled and fired to third for a fielder's choice. (Hodges, despite his 32 homers, actually had 11 sacrifice hits in 1950. He would have a total of 3 in the next three seasons.)

Had Hodges been successful, Konstanty would almost certainly have intentionally walked Campy, as he had already done once before. Instead, Sawyer now hoped that Campy would bang one of Konstanty's infamous palm balls into an inning-ending double play. On a 1-0 count, Konstanty tried to fool him with a slider. The pitch hung and Campy drilled it over the 393-foot sign in center field for three runs. The Phillies, their backs broken, went down easily in the ninth. Left for dead a week ago, the Brooks now had to win just one more to force a playoff against a shell-shocked, beaten-up ball club that had lost its last five and eight of its last ten to earn the new nickname of Fizz Kids.

After the game, Campy headed into the locker room, accompanied by Little Roy, who had proudly watched his daddy in action that afternoon. A boy who had caught Campy's home-run ball wanted to know if he wanted it. Two baseballs, Reese suggested, would be a fair trade. For the second straight day, the photographers gathered at Campy's cubicle. Over the past six days, Campanella had been simply sensational, hitting .400 with 3 homers and 11 RBIs.

Around 6:00 p.m., the lighthearted mood abruptly changed. A stranger walked up to Don Newcombe, tomorrow's starter, handing him a piece of paper as he left Ebbets. It was a summons, and Campy had been given one as well. Both were being sued for breach of contract by Lester Dworman, the man who had promoted Robinson's 1949 barnstorming tour.

After last year's debacle, Roy, Newk, and Doby had been determined not to barnstorm again with Jackie. Their postseason plan was to do a separate tour with Alex Pompez, the owner of the soon-to-be-defunct New York Cubans, who had worked with Dworman in '49. Dworman, however, had options on their services for 1950, and after last year's windfall he would have been a fool not to exercise them. Dworman dropped the lawsuit when the recalcitrant trio agreed to team up again with Jackie.

For now, Campy and Newk had to focus on the Phillies, first place, and the playoff. The blackboard in the clubhouse said it all: "Let's Go!! Tomorrow is It!"

NEWCOMBE, THE man upon whose arm the season rested, had not been the same pitcher since his failed attempt at the iron-man stunt. In seven appearances, five of them starts, he had gone 2-2 with a 4.82 ERA, allowing 43 hits in 37.1 innings. He had already pitched three times this week, twice in relief and a no-decision against the Braves. On the other hand, his counterpart, Robin Roberts, was even more exhausted, making his third start of the week. The two men had more than fatigue in common.

Both were twenty-four years old. Both wore number 36. Both had 19 wins. And they had been matched up five times already this season, including on opening day. The Phillies had won four, the Dodgers only one.

Dubious Brooklynites finally came out in force that Sunday. The largest crowd of the season, 35,073 strong, elbowed their way into Ebbets while another 10,000 were turned away. At eighty-two degrees, the weather was unseasonably warm for October in New York. With the heat and two tired pitchers, a slugfest seemed likely.

Instead, a classic pitchers' duel unfolded, as neither side managed to break through in the first five innings. In the sixth, the Phillies drew first blood. With two outs, Dick Sisler, son of Hall of Famer George, whose instruction had proved invaluable to Campy, singled past Gil Hodges into right field. Del Ennis followed with a seemingly catchable fly ball that fell "just a foot in front of" Snider in right center, sending Sisler to third. Willie Jones then jumped on Newk's first offering for a single to put the Whiz Kids up 1–0. Before the Flatbush fans had a chance to panic, the old reliable Reese tied the score with a freak home run, a "looping slice to right field that hit the screen about five feet inside the foul line, slid straight downward and wedged between two metal bars at the point where the screen and wall join." A young fan eventually "risked life and limb" to retrieve the ball, perched precariously atop the ESQUIRE BOOT POLISH sign ("For the Shine of Your Life").

Both pitchers tossed two more goose eggs in the seventh and eighth. In the ninth inning, Newk appeared to be weakening. Granny Hamner started the inning with a solid smash to left field, snared nicely by Cal Abrams at the wall. Andy Seminick kept up the attack with a single off Billy Cox's glove. Eddie Sawyer then inserted Putsy Caballero, best known for making his MLB debut at age sixteen in 1944, as a pinch runner. Caballero immediately set off for second, only to be cut down on another fine Campy throw. A few moments later, Newk retired Mike Goliat on a fly to center to end the inning. The Dodger fans exhaled, mopped their brows, and relaxed, at least for a moment. One run was all that was needed. And the top of the order was coming up in the bottom of the ninth.

Roberts had been extremely tough so far, yielding only three hits, two by Reese and a single by Roy in the eighth. Abrams, again showing a good batting eye, walked on a 3-2 pitch to start the ninth. Shotton then called on Reese to bunt. The Little Colonel fouled two off before banging a single into left center for his third hit of the day.

Up next was Duke Snider, whose single off Ken Heintzelman had put the Bums in the World Series a year earlier. Another sacrifice attempt might have crossed the Old Sourdough's mind, but Snider didn't like bunting and the Phillies were expecting it. The Duke was told to swing away.

Working from the stretch, Roberts threw one pitch to Snider. The Duke turned on it and drove it solidly into center field. Dodger Nation, listening on their radios or watching on television, screamed with joy while Philadelphians felt their hearts leap to their throats. As Abrams wheeled around third with the potential winning run, Richie Ashburn was up and throwing. He had been playing Snider surprisingly shallow. "I've heard it said I was backing up second for a pickoff play or backing up second for a possible bunt by Snider," Ashburn later explained. "Both wrong, even ridiculous . . . I had shortened up a couple of steps as all outfielders shorten up with the winning run on second in the bottom of the ninth inning."

The Dodgers had run on Ashburn freely that year. This time, as Dick Young would write, he "would uncork perhaps the best peg of his big league life," a perfect one-hopper to Stan Lopata, who had to wait to tag out Abrams. Although Roberts still had to contend with Reese and Snider on second and third with one out, the Ashburn throw was a momentum killer.

Robinson was up next, and Sawyer and Roberts wanted no part of him, issuing an intentional walk to load the bases. To the fans' horror, Carl Furillo, never known for his patience at the plate, then hacked at Roberts's first pitch and sent a harmless foul pop to first for the second out. Gil Hodges, the last chance to salvage the once promising inning, momentarily raised hopes by cracking a long drive that right fielder Del Ennis appeared to lose in the sun briefly. The ball bounced off his chest, Phillies fans gulped, but somehow Ennis managed to hang on. The fates, it seemed, were now turning against the Brooks.

At 4:25 p.m., the Ebbets Field lights were turned on. Shotton sent Newcombe out for his tenth inning of work, his longest outing of the year. Despite allowing only one run, his stuff had been spotty at best. He had not set the Phillies down in order since the first, but Shotton hoped for three more outs before Newk batted in the bottom of the inning.

With Roberts leading off the tenth, Sawyer momentarily considered pulling his pitcher for pinch hitter Dick Whitman. After assuring his skipper that he was "fine," the .109-hitting Roberts surprised everyone by singling to center. Eddie Waitkus, whose shooting by an obsessed Chicago girl had rocked the baseball world in 1949 ("Only one girl ever fell in love with me," he once observed, "and she was nuts"), tried to bunt him to second before blooping a single into center. With two runners on, Ashburn, the next hitter, was sacrificing, and everyone in the park knew it. Newk was off the mound at the crack of the bat, scooping up the bunt and firing to Cox for the force.

Dick Sisler was up next. Newcombe's steady diet of sliders and curves had failed to stop the lefty-swinging Sisler, who had banged out three straight singles to right field after striking out in the first. Campy reiterated the simple advice he had given Newk all day: "Keep the ball in on him, and he doesn't hurt you."

Newcombe quickly went ahead 1-2 on Sisler, the man whose stuttering was a favorite target of Dodger bench jockeys. Newk then made a perfect pitch, high and tight, but Sisler fouled it off. The next pitch was not nearly as perfect: high, outside, and right where Sisler liked it. The stammering Sisler connected for an opposite-field drive that soared over the head of Cal Abrams, the goat of the day, and into the stands for a three-run homer. "Campy just stood there and shook his head," Newk would later recall.

Newcombe managed to retire the next two hitters, but the disheartened Ebbets crowd knew the end was near. Roberts got Roy on a long fly to left, Jim Russell struck out, and Tommy Brown popped to first base. The Dodgers had finally run out of comebacks.

Campy, like the rest of his teammates, was in near shock as he made his way into the clubhouse. "The place was a deathly dungeon," wrote Dana Mozley of the *Daily News*. "Few players were ready to talk for several minutes, most of them just sitting and staring at their lockers." A reporter asked Shotton whether he'd be back next year. "That's a hell of a question," barked the Old Sourdough. "How would I know?"

Few, if any, of the Dodgers were ruminating at that moment about their manager's future. Instead, the Bums and their legions of followers endlessly replayed the missed opportunity in the ninth and what might have been. How, they asked, could Abrams get himself thrown out on such a play? In the days, months, and even decades that followed, a good deal of blame was assigned to "Abie," who, it was said, was never a good base runner, didn't get a good jump from second ("I never saw a guy run so slow," complained one fan), and took too wide a turn around third base. Abrams had his own alibi. By late in life, he had perfected a strange tale of third-base coach Milt Stock "halfheartedly waving me in with his left hand, while biting the fingers of his right hand," Ashburn's "bad throw that didn't come close to the plate," and his own manful attempt to hit the catcher "as hard as I could" to score the winning run. But game film shows Stock clearly waving in Abrams, a perfect throw to the plate, and only the most minimal collision at home, where Abrams didn't even slide.

Milt Stock, long a faithful Rickey man (and the father-in-law of Eddie Stanky), would also wear the goat horns. Stock's coaching abilities had already been questioned a year earlier when his decision to hold Furillo at third cost the Dodgers a key run during the famous Branca "blister" game. But Stock offered a seemingly logical explanation of the Abrams play: Abie was quick, the Dodgers had been running on Ashburn all year, and Reese was already on his way to third and might have run into Abrams had he been held. "The way Roberts was pitching in a 1–1 game, ninth inning, you had to play it that way," he insisted.

In a less meaningful game, Stock might have had a justifiable case for sending Abrams. But here where a single run meant first place and a playoff, the gamble was foolhardy at best, particularly with Ashburn in so shallow (whether Stock was aware of Ashburn's positioning is another matter). Assuming that Stock had held Abrams and Reese got back to second safely, Roberts would have been facing a near-impossible situation: bases loaded, no one out, and Robinson, Furillo, and Hodges to follow. Still, Shotton refused to blame Stock. "Whitey Ashburn just wasn't playing good baseball to play Snider so close, and he'll never make another throw like that as long as he lives."

Although the Sisler homer was a devastating end to the 1950 season, Roy felt he had put together his best year to date as a major leaguer. His late-season injury was frustrating, but he still finished fifth in homers, sixth in slugging, and eighth in OPS (on-base plus slugging percentage). To Jimmy Powers, Roy's "superb handling of the pitching staff and his big bat driving in countless runs," particularly in the lower depths of the order, made him the true MVP of the Dodgers.

The Bums, Campy knew, would have an entirely different look next season. Rickey was out, and no one knew who else might be joining him. Before his departure, the Mahatma offered some parting words of praise for his Dodgers: "It's a marvelous club. If it doesn't win the pennant next year by ten games, I'll be amazed."

13

A YEAR TO REMEMBER

THE SHOCK OF THE SISLER HOMER had barely subsided before Roy had to return to the barnstorming wars again. His heart was not in it. "The undersigned citizens would like to know who in the h____l Roy Campanella thinks he is. . . . He stouty [*sic*] refused to sign autographs in the dugout during the game," four Daytona Beach fans complained angrily. "We think success has gone to his swelled head." Although Negro American League president J. B. Martin rushed to his defense, Roy clearly wanted the tour, and his legal obligation with Dworman and Jackie, to end as quickly as possible.

For a change, he wanted to forget about baseball. Ironically, so did Jackie. Both men planned Latin American vacations in November with their wives. A year earlier, the two couples might well have vacationed together. This time, their paths did not cross, although Roy and Ruthe arrived in San Juan only hours after the Robinsons left.

Back in Brooklyn, heads were rolling on Montague Street. Out were Rickey's son and several scouts, who loyally followed the Mahatma to Pittsburgh. In were O'Malley and two new vice presidents: Campy's old friend Buzzie Bavasi, appointed de facto general manager, and Fresco Thompson, the farm system director. The O'Malley regime had also begun "de-Rickeyfication." "He [O'Malley] had a rule," Bavasi recalled. "Anyone mentioning Mr. Rickey during lunch in Room 40 at the ball park was fined $5.00. . . . Later on Walter added Marvin Miller to the list."

Two Rickey men, press secretary Harold Parrott and statistician Allan Roth, escaped the O'Malley hatchet. They soon found that their new boss was almost nothing like his predecessor. The forty-seven-year-old O'Malley, a "portly, jowly, florid" fellow with an oily charm, had joined the Dodger family years earlier not as a baseball savant but as a corporate lawyer. Nor did he have Rickey's pretensions for being a "great man" or martyr for any social cause (although he always insisted that his own role in the Great Experiment had been shortchanged). Above all, he was a remarkably savvy businessman whose primary concern, bordering at times on obsession, would always be the bottom line. "Nobody who ever ran the Dodgers," Dick Young once observed, "has cared less about winning for winning's sake than does Walter O'Malley."

O'Malley looked at the books and frowned. Ebbets attendance had plunged from a league-leading 1.633 million in 1949 to 1.185 million in 1950. Although bad weather, radio/TV overexposure, and the Korean War had slashed major league gates by 13.6 percent, the Brooklyn brain trust searched for more local explanations. Some in the organization questioned, again, whether too many Negro players and fans had scared away whites. But O'Malley suspected a bigger problem might be a negative press, long alienated by Rickey's distortions and general know-it-all attitude. An easy first step was to make nice with Dick Young and pacify him with plenty of scoops. "Dick Young was a guy that the Dodgers were always afraid of," Jackie Robinson later mused. "The NEWS, I guess, and the power of the NEWS."

Then there was the issue of the manager. Shotton's press relations were atrocious, particularly with Young, whom he detested. He was colorless and refused to budge from the dugout. "Fans like to see a manager, they like to cheer him and jeer him, and suffer with him," O'Malley observed. "They can't see him if he isn't in uniform." Nor was he much of a strategist, although nowhere near as inept as some critics described him. Robinson later assessed Shotton as a "good, sound baseball man: he was quick." Campy also thought him competent, albeit a bit predictable at times.

Most of all, Shotton was a Rickey man, close enough to affectionately call him Rick. For that reason alone, he had to go, as did his beleaguered third-base coach Milt Stock, who ended up performing the same job for Rickey's Pirates in 1951 (and was not "run out of baseball," as some legends have it). The Old Sourdough, still convinced that he might have kept his job had the Dodgers pulled out the infamous Abrams game, went home to Florida and never managed again.

The short list of potential replacements included team captain Pee Wee Reese, who was uninterested in becoming a player-manager; Bill Terry, who had not managed in the majors since 1941; and two ex-Dodgers currently piloting AA clubs: Bobby Bragan and the former Flatbush favorite Dixie Walker. That Bragan or Walker, both unapologetically opposed to the Great Experiment back in 1947, might be at the helm of the Dodgers four years later did not excite black fans, although Jackie himself publicly announced his willingness to play for Walker.

O'Malley ultimately decided to go in another direction. He handed the job to Charlie Dressen, a fifty-two-year-old former Dodger coach who hadn't done much in an earlier managerial stint with the Reds in the 1930s but had just guided the Oakland Oaks to the Pacific Coast League pennant. For O'Malley, Dressen was the ideal choice. He was everything that Shotton was not, a brash and pugnacious little fellow, not quite five feet six inches, who loved the limelight and never quite knew when to shut up.

Dressen, even by the undeniably quirky standards of the day, was rather eccentric. He was well known for his "ear piercing whistle," a bizarre theory that "no incubator baby could go nine," and surprising facility in the kitchen. The would-be gourmand not only liked to whip up a mean batch of chili but also enjoyed gnawing on raw onions (Dressen, one sportswriter later marveled, "ate onion sandwiches like others eat ham or cheese sandwiches"). He surrounded himself with an odd collection of hangers-on who stroked his considerable ego whenever necessary.

Despite his various idiosyncracies, Dressen undoubtedly knew the game well, although perhaps not quite as well as he thought. His major problem was an almost neurotic need to demonstrate his brilliance, to the point of overmanaging with needless squeeze plays and other "fancy stuff." Nor was he at all shy about hogging credit, so much so that many around baseball thought him a narcissistic windbag. But sportswriter Bill Roeder believed Dressen's "egotism is more effervescent than aggressive. . . . He likes to talk about himself and his triumphs, but as often as not the boast is accompanied by a boyish smile."

If Dressen was a bit of an egomaniac, he was not a bigot. Roy could expect to get along quite well with his new manager, whose devotion to baseball rivaled his own. "Dressen and Campanella are the two men I know who think about baseball every day of their lives," Jackie Robinson once observed. "I think all Campy ever wants for Christmas is some new way to fool the other team. Dressen is like that, too."

Soon after his hiring, Dressen was interviewed by a black writer eager to learn how the Negro Dodgers might fare under the new regime. The bubbly little skipper, never at a loss for words, claimed Jackie was going to run more, there'd be no more iron-man stunts for Newk, and Bankhead would be scrutinized in spring training "to see if I can't get him going." As for Campy, Dressen wanted no repeat of his late-season injury problems. He already had an idea to keep Roy healthy, although his plan would not be disclosed until spring training.

FOLLOWING HIS return from Latin America, Campy settled back into the life of a typical suburban father. In between his usual hours at the Harlem Y, he played with David and Little Roy, doted over baby Tony, and enjoyed his first prolonged stay at home in months.

One Tuesday evening in January, Roy and Ruthe came home around 6:00 p.m. to discover the Campanella abode was without hot water. A trip to the basement revealed the pilot light was out, so it would be a simple matter to simply relight the flame.

Roy struck a match while Ruthe held the spring door at the base of the heater open. He was unknowingly playing Russian roulette. Escaped gas had settled in the base, meaning one wave of the match in the wrong direction could blow the heater, the basement, and the Campanellas to kingdom come.

Within seconds, the match had ignited the odorless gas, generating a tremendous explosion that sent Roy staggering backward. "I'm burned!" he screamed. "My face is burned!" His mother-in-law, Fannie, tried to apply butter to his scorched nose, succeeding only in pulling off a layer of skin. More disturbing were his eyes, a blistered mess.

In the chaos that followed, Ruthe frantically tried to reach Roy's physician, Lyndon Hill, without success. Finally, a neighbor drove them over to Hill's home, where Hill did some quick first aid, then sent them on to Jamaica Hospital. There, a specialist named Arthur Minsky reassured Campy that his eyes and cornea were not as bad as they initially appeared. Topical ointment and bandages would take care of things, and his vision should not be affected. The facial burns were only second-degree and would heal without residual scars.

With Campy no longer in danger, the media swooped in to cover the dramatic tale. Still, he insisted that at least one eye be uncovered temporarily for any pictures, lest his public grow too concerned about his condition. "I sure was lucky," he admitted. "The only thing that bothers me now is this nose of mine. It's the worst spot that got burned, and, man, it's sore."

Privately, Roy was more worried than he let on. Both eyes would have to be bandaged for three days, and only then would he find out whether Minsky was right. "I was scared," he later admitted. "Never so scared in my life." In times of crisis, he turned to prayer, just as his mother had taught him. He also thought more seriously about his future. If he was done in baseball, at age twenty-nine, how would Roy Campanella, a ninth-grade dropout, support himself and his family?

When the bandages finally came off, Roy was relieved to discover that he was not blind. His vision, imperfect at first, soon returned to twenty-twenty. He felt even better a few days later when he signed his 1951 contract for $18,500, a $6,000 increase. But Roy had not entirely forgotten his recent anxiety. Never, he decided, would he put himself in such a vulnerable position again. He would open a liquor store to ensure that his family would always have a source of income. "I prayed to God again," a melodramatic passage in his autobiography reads, "and made Him a solemn promise that if He allowed me to see again, I'd do my best to get into some kind of business."

Campy may well have decided to get into the liquor business while in Jamaica Hospital, but the idea was hardly new. He had already been thinking about a business since at least the previous March and had even discussed his plans with Rickey. The Mahatma, a hard-line prohibitionist in his youth, tried to steer Roy toward a more respectable enterprise, but Campy stood firm. "I told Mr. Rickey the field for colored persons in their own business was limited. He not only agreed with me but said he never had thought about it." Besides, Campy reminded Rickey, "my people drink. They'll make better customers for whiskey than for sporting goods."

O'Malley made Campy's dream a reality. He not only agreed to advance Roy the necessary start-up capital but also pulled some strings. With package-store licenses currently capped at about twenty-five hundred in the metropolitan New York area, one could enter the liquor business only by purchasing an existing establishment. Profitable stores in attractive locations fetched exorbitant prices, so the easiest path for a novice such as Campy was to buy a loser business and then move it to a more favorable area. When a store in Flushing became available, Roy acquired the license and later transferred it to the southeast corner of West 134th Street and Seventh Avenue, only a block from the Harlem YMCA.

That the State Liquor Authority did not object to the transfer to "Alcohol Alley," already home to "eight liquor stores within a two to four-block radius," was probably the work of O'Malley, who had likely called in a few political favors and greased a few palms. Business got done that way in New York in those days; package-store graft became so rampant that the state finally launched a formal investigation in 1955 and even called in Roy to testify. Although published reports suggested that up to 90 percent of liquor-store-license transfers were fueled by bribes, Campy steadfastly insisted, "There were no payoffs and there was nothing under the table." Still, the subsequent crackdown made it nearly impossible for Monte Irvin and Willie Mays to pull off a similar license transfer from Brooklyn to Harlem.

From the moment he acquired the Harlem license, Campy threw himself into renovating the building, which had more than its share of history. A former owner of the old Bacharach Giants, Barron Wilkins, had once operated the Exclusive Club there, only to be gunned down in front of it in 1924. More recently, Monroe's Uptown House occupied the spot, hosting Billie Holiday, Dizzy Gillespie, and other jazz greats. By the time Campy's store opened in September, the battered, old nightclub was almost unrecognizable: a "gleaming structure of marble-like stone . . . it stands out among the drab clutter of neighboring Harlem buildings." No one could miss the somewhat garish neon sign—ROY CAMPANELLA LIQUORS—out front, although the ever-frugal Campy was not happy with the final cost of some of the interior upgrades. "The bronze trimming inside," he later complained, "cost me almost five hundred dollars. That's what comes from letting your wife pick out things."

Inside, patrons basked in the suitably masculine environment of dark mahogany wood, baseball murals, and plenty of booze for sale, eventually including Roy's own signature-brand whiskey: Campy's Old Peg. But the biggest lure was Roy himself. When Campy parked his big Cadillac out front, everyone in Harlem seemed to make an instant beeline to his door. "So long as they walk out of the store with a package, that's all I care."

Jackie Robinson couldn't help but be impressed by Roy's business acumen, although selling hooch certainly did not appeal to him. Dick Young later claimed that Robinson rejected a "lucrative liquor business" offer "because he believed that wasn't the sort of enterprise for him, as an example to the kids who worshiped him." Instead, he tried to pursue more socially uplifting entrepreneurial opportunities. In 1952, he took a stab at opening a new department store on 125th Street in Harlem featuring his own line of clothing and his name in neon à la Campy. His hope, he told reporters, was that local blacks could get quality, reasonably priced goods without having to go downtown. Unfortunately, as his wife, Rachel, would later recall, "It just didn't work. So he was out of that very shortly after."

In contrast, Campy's store was reportedly grossing close to $400,000 annually within a few years. Perhaps selling liquor in an already booze-besotted neighborhood would not win him any humanitarian awards, but Campy was practical enough to realize that the liquor business probably offered him the best chance for long-term success. And for the next twenty-seven years, Roy Campanella Liquors would remain a Harlem fixture, a place where the owner himself could often be found behind the counter or just talking baseball with customers.

AMONG CHARLIE DRESSEN'S numerous quirky beliefs was his insistence that overeating had ruined many a budding baseball career. The decline of Bruce Edwards, for example, was easily explained: "He got fat and his arm went bad." Dressen was also certain that overweight players tended to wear down in the waning stages of the season. Since Robinson had admitted to fatigue last September, Dressen prescribed a special winter diet to ensure that Jackie would be in tip-top form come spring training.

Campy, a hefty 218 pounds on reporting, naturally attracted Dressen's critical gaze in Florida. "I want you like you were when I first saw you catching at Newark," barked Dressen, referring to that fateful October 1945 day. Almost immediately, he subjected Roy to baseball's tried-and-true slimming techniques: a rubber tube around his sizable tummy and a grueling exercise called Hi-Lo. "This is a game," wrote Sam Lacy, "in which Dressen drops a ball at Campy's feet; he must catch and toss it shoulder high to Dressen, who drops it again just as soon as Roy straightens up." Within minutes, Roy was huffing, puffing, and soaked with sweat. "I see why they call this Hi-Lo," he quipped. "You're feeling high, and I'm feeling low." Afterward, he couldn't resist singing, "Bring back, bring back, bring back 'Ole Barney' . . . to me."

But Ole Barney Shotton was not coming back, and Dressen was far from finished with his Campy makeover. He decided that Roy would also benefit from the Mayo diet, the same weight-loss plan Jackie had undertaken. The diet had nothing to do with the Mayo Clinic, which did its best to disavow any association. Rather, it was a then popular method for shedding pounds quickly through heavy consumption of high-protein foods (similar to the Atkins diet), particularly eggs.

Campy was not thrilled with Dressen's brainstorm or his concurrent order to Campy to curb his beer drinking. He had always played his way into shape every spring and saw no reason why this year should be an exception. Eventually, he went along with the plan, albeit with a great deal of complaining. "Eight eggs a day, broiled, scrambled, poached, scalloped," he later fumed. "At night I could eat steaks, lamb chops, all the meat I wanted, but for breakfast and dinner nothing but eggs and salads and no bread, no butter, no potatoes." But just as Dressen had hoped, the surplus pounds began to melt away, although Campy fretted that his power might disappear along with his waistline. He was so pleased by his new svelte self (a remarkably trim 198 at one point) that he ran out and purchased four new suits.

Other than Dressen's attempt to turn the camp into a glorified fat farm, spring training was relatively tranquil. During downtime, Roy did a little fishing and relaxed with Ruthe, David, and Little Roy, who joined him in Miami, now serving as Brooklyn's second base of spring training operations. The two young Campanellas found a ready playmate in Jackie, Jr., and even later appeared together in a polio-awareness-campaign photo spread. Their fathers, both victims of Dressen's egg diet, remained cordial but distant.

Spoiling Campy's carefree mood was yet another round of injuries, this time a bruised knee and a chip fracture of his already battered right thumb that sidelined him for a week. Though less than 100 percent as the Dodgers made their final swing north, he insisted on catching the entire opening game in Atlanta for the thousands of blacks sure to be in attendance. "I just want to stay in until I get one hit for these people," he told Dressen. Instead, black fans shivering in the forty-four-degree weather that Friday night had to be satisfied with Robinson's two hits.

By Sunday, Roy was beginning to feel more comfortable. Hitless in his first seven at bats in Atlanta, he finally singled off the old Dodger Kirby Higbe, now pitching for Dixie Walker's Crackers. On Monday, he homered twice in Asheville, followed by a 4-for-4 performance in Greensboro the next day. His thumb healed, his weight ideal, and his eyes perfect, Campy deemed himself ready for the new season.

EXCEPT FOR Dressen, the acquisition of veteran outfielder Hank Edwards from the Cubs, and the promotion of several unproven farmhands, the Dodgers were essentially the same club that had flirted with mediocrity for much of 1950. Still, most observers viewed the Brooks' chances as far better than those of the defending-champ Phillies, who had been tarnished by a four-and-done World Series performance against the Yankees. In a preseason United Press poll of 168 writers, only 18 predicted another pennant for the Whiz Kids, less than a third the number who thought the Dodgers would return to the top. But most of the so-called experts polled favored another New York team: Leo Durocher's Giants.

In his two and a half years at the Polo Grounds, Durocher had been no miracle worker. Despite his professed desire to build "his kind of team," the Giants had finished fifth in 1948, fifth again in 1949, and were languishing in sixth place at the All-Star break in 1950. Two moves saved their season and Durocher's job. The Giants claimed pitcher Jim Hearn on waivers from the Cardinals and plucked thirty-three-year-old Sal Maglie from the bullpen. From July 17 on, Hearn went 11-3 with a 1.94 ERA in 16 starts, Maglie 13-1 in 15, and the Giants played close to .700 ball to finish third, only three games behind the Dodgers.

With both clubs now contenders, the historic Giant/Dodger rivalry, somewhat muted during much of the 1940s, when Brooklyn and St. Louis were one-two in no fewer than five different races, was heating up again. Much of the feuding in recent years had centered around Durocher and Robinson, both skilled bench jockeys who loved to get the other's blood boiling. Last June at Ebbets Field, Robinson finally found a way to shut Leo up, at least temporarily. "Are you wearing your wife's perfume tonight, Leo?" he taunted, mocking Durocher's famous yen for sweet-smelling colognes and toilet water.

As bench jockeying hardly fit Campy's style, he had no involvement in any of the classic knock-'em-down/drag-'em-out struggles with Durocher, who genuinely liked and respected Roy anyway. But other Dodgers detested the Lip as much as Robinson, particularly Carl Furillo, the victim of a bad beaning from Sheldon Jones the day after Jackie hurled his sly perfume remark. Certain Leo and his infamous "stick it in his Goddamn ear" philosophy were to blame, Furillo was ready to square off with his old manager at the Polo Grounds five days later before umpires and teammates stepped in.

Although the bad blood was unmistakable in 1950 (Leo was the first to call to congratulate Eddie Sawyer after the Dick Sisler game), the hiring of Dressen added an entirely new dimension. Dressen had been one of Durocher's loyal lieutenants in Brooklyn before moving to the Yankees after the 1946 season. In recent years, he not only resented that Durocher was unable to get him a similar coaching gig with the Giants, but he also came to believe that he had been denied appropriate credit during his earlier stint under Leo. Now, he wanted nothing more than to wipe the smug smirk off Durocher's Hollywood mug and show everyone who the real master bench strategist was.

The new season was not even a week old before sparks were flying, and this time Campy would be involved. The Dodgers were at the Polo Grounds for a three-game set after splitting their opening series with the Phillies at Ebbets. Brooklyn took the first game on Friday but trailed 3–2 when Roy faced Larry Jansen to start the fifth on Saturday afternoon.

Campy sensed what was coming. His pitcher Chris Van Cuyk had just brushed back Hank Thompson a few moments before following a Giant home run, and baseball code deemed that an opposing player would have to go down. As expected, Jansen buzzed Roy once, and Campy accepted the chin music without comment. But when a second pitch again sent him sprawling, he could no longer keep silent. "I've been hit on the head and I know what it is," he explained afterward. "Some of these guys who do the throwing never got it. Maybe if they did, they wouldn't think it's such a damn joke." Seconds later, catcher Wes Westrum, disdainful of Campy's insinuations, was in his face giving it right back to him. Before Campy's first major league brawl (an interracial one, to boot) could ensue, Dressen and umpire Augie Donatelli performed the obligatory peacemaking roles. Giant and Dodger fans already sensed that this season was going to be a doozy.

The Dodgers bounced back to win that afternoon and took the finale on Sunday to sweep the series. The following weekend at Ebbets, they withstood another volley of beanballs to beat the Giants twice more. "Jockeying," wrote Arch Murray of the *Post,* "was brutal," with Newk's "eat your heart out" taunts reportedly leaving Durocher "white and shaking with rage."

Eleven straight Giant losses, five to the Dodgers—it couldn't get much better for the hordes of Leo haters in Flatbush. A packed house of 33,962 showed up Monday night eager to see the noose tightened further. But when the Dodgers fell behind quickly 6–0, everyone's attention turned to a smoldering feud between Robinson and Sal Maglie.

Maglie never needed prodding from Durocher to throw inside, particularly at a team whose loudmouthed manager had publicly scorned his fastball. His usual strategy was simple: loosen 'em up with the high, hard one, then get 'em on the big curveball. Robinson, weary of dodging bullets aimed at his head, resolved to even the score that Monday night. After homering in the first, Jackie tried to lure Maglie off the mound in his next at bat with a bunt up the first-base line. Although the ball rolled foul, Robinson plowed into the man they called the Barber anyway. The crowd held its collective breath awaiting Ebbets's first interracial brawl, but no punches were traded.

Campy, one of Maglie's favorite targets, couldn't help but admire Jackie's daring, Ty Cobb–like maneuver. Less enamored were National League president Ford Frick, who warned Bavasi that he would "step in" if the Dodgers didn't keep Robinson in line, and Durocher, who predictably labeled it "bush." "Then you're a bush league manager," Jackie fired back, "because you taught me to do things like that." Even Sam Lacy felt Robinson "shouldn't try to take matters into his hands. . . . He loses friends that way, and he's bound to be the greater loser in any personal flare-up."

By 1951, Robinson was no longer concerned with making friends. In four years, he had completely shed his passive-rookie persona to emerge as a ferociously competitive figure who always seemed to be in the middle of everything. Although Brooklynites loved Jackie, his hard-nosed style and now razor-sharp tongue irritated many opposing fans and writers not ready for such behavior in a black man. Three weeks after his collision with Maglie, he would receive death threats in Cincinnati. The baseball establishment itself also seemed determined to put the now "controversial" Negro and his "God complex" (as one black physican labeled it) back in his place, from Frick to the *Sporting News,* which warned Jackie to "Stop, Look and Listen." Even the umpires had grown weary of his constant questioning of their decisions. "I'm not blind to the fact that certain umpires are out to get me," Jackie observed. "Anything I do, they'll give me the worst of the breaks."

Campy drew lessons from Jackie's ongoing trials and tribulations. Roy had never been one to "pop off" to the press anyway, but the growing anti-Robinson feeling around baseball (even at Ebbets, where Jackie recently heard his first boos) seemed to confirm that Campy's more subdued approach was a better way to win friends and influence people. Lacy agreed. "Jackie talks entirely too much," he wrote. "This may be no fault of his. . . . In his anxiety to become 'just another ball player,' Robinson doesn't realize that this can never be. . . . Unlike the other ball players . . . Robinson stands to be quoted every time he opens his mouth. . . . His is still a fishbowl existence, much as he would like it to be otherwise."

DESPITE THE decisive thumping of the Giants, the Dodgers had not shown a great deal of luster against the rest of the National League. After twenty-one games, the Brooks were sitting in fourth place with an 11-10 record, only three ahead of the Giants. Roy had contributed little, hitting only .222 with a single homer in his first 63 at bats. Maybe Dressen's egg diet had sapped his strength after all. Cholly himself seemed to be losing patience, dropping Roy from sixth to seventh in the lineup, but Bavasi was unconcerned. "He'll snap out of it. . . . I know what he's doing wrong and I'm absolutely sure he'll start to unload any day."

Whether Bavasi straightened him out is debatable, but Roy suddenly began to regain his touch at the plate in early May. After hammering a long double in St. Louis on May 18 off Al Brazle, a soft-tossing lefty in his favored Ken Raffensberger mold, Campy was pleased. "That's the first one I've hit really well all year. I was beginning to think I'd lost my power." A week later, he put together two straight four-hit games against the Braves at Ebbets, boosting his average above .300 for the first time since the season's first week.

Historically, when Campy went on one of his tears, the Dodgers won, and this was no exception. Between May 9 and June 14, Brooklyn took twenty-three of thirty-one to vault into first place by a comfortable six-game margin over the Giants. Roy, meanwhile, bashed the ball at a phenomenal .411 clip, slamming 46 hits in 112 at bats. His every move on the ballfield seemed instinctively correct, whether restraining Jackie from belting Phillies pitcher Russ Meyer on May 31 at Ebbets following a collision at home plate (and Meyer's utterance of the insult "nigger motherfucker") or brilliantly picking off two Cardinals at second *in the same inning* on June 14.

The Dodgers were rolling but Bavasi was not completely satisfied. With the June 15 trading deadline approaching, he wanted to beef up left field, the team's recurrent Achilles' heel, where Gene Hermanski, Cal Abrams, Tommy Brown, and rookie Don Thompson had all been tried and found wanting. Bavasi coveted Andy Pafko, the veteran Cubs slugger who had cracked 36 homers to go along with a .304 average in 1950. The Cubs, mired in seventh and going nowhere as usual, were willing to deal. "Anytime I want a free meal, I just walk into a lobby, drop my bag, and shout, 'Who wants Pafko?' " quipped Cubs manager Frankie Frisch. "Everyone wants to buy me dinner to talk it over."

Bavasi offered Hermanski, little-used infielder Eddie Miksis, and pitcher Joe Hatten, whose contributions had been minimal since 1949. Bruce Edwards and his balky arm were also thrown into the deal at the request of Frisch and Cubs official Wid Matthews. In return, Brooklyn would get Pafko, former Dodger-killer Johnny Schmitz, second baseman Wayne Terwilliger, and a new backup catcher, Rube Walker, whom Bavasi preferred to Chicago's initial offer of good-hit/no-field Smokey Burgess.

Durocher was aghast. Brooklyn had picked up Pafko from his old manager and pal Frisch without letting go of a single player of real value.

Worse, the Giants had offered what Durocher considered to be a far more attractive package, including Bobby Thomson, only to be told a week earlier that Pafko wasn't going anywhere. "It was the worst double cross a guy ever got from a friend," the Lip fumed. "It was a lousy thing to do to me and I'll never forgive him for it."

The rest of the baseball world was just as baffled by the deal, which seemed remarkably stupid. Bill Corum labeled it "the worst trade ever made in the history of baseball," while others likened it to the one-sided Red Sox/Yankee deals of the 1920s. (Had the Cubs reached Rickey, often called by other general managers to assess Dodger offers, the deal almost certainly would not have gone through.) Cardinals president Fred Saigh even worried that the Dodgers might build such a big lead that "they won't draw and neither will anybody else."

Dressen was unconcerned. He had outflanked Leo ("without spending a cent," he smirked) and Brooklyn now looked unbeatable. "I've been on some good clubs in my time, but this is the best," Campy remarked. "When this club makes up its mind that it's going to win . . . it'll win, believe me."

FOLLOWING THE "Big Steal of 1951," as the *Sporting News* creatively dubbed the Pafko trade, the Dodgers finished their western swing and returned to New York for a showdown with the second-place Giants. With the two clubs scheduled to square off six times in nine days, Durocher was hoping to slice off a chunk of the Brooks' six-game lead.

The Giants were not the same demoralized bunch so easily crushed earlier in the season. They had won twelve of their last seventeen and had added a sensational new center fielder: twenty-year-old Willie Mays. Since his late-May call-up, the former Negro Leaguer had hit .316, stroked 6 homers, and wowed fans with his spectacular speed, defense, and arm.

Around baseball, everyone wanted to know how the Dodgers, historically the destination of top Negro talent, had missed such a phenom. Arthur Daley of the *New York Times* alluded to "rumors that both Robinson and Roy Campanella had turned thumbs down on Willie Mays," but both men dismissed such a notion. They claimed they had barnstormed against him back in 1948, liked what they saw, "but some scout said he couldn't hit a curve ball." Years later, Campy would adamantly state that he recommended Mays to the Dodgers, but "the scout they sent down didn't like us colored fellas much, so he didn't say nothing good about Willie." Meanwhile, Branch Rickey, Jr. ("The Twig"), announced that a Birmingham official, Eddie Glennon, had tipped off the Dodgers. The Mahatma supposedly dispatched two scouts (both still working for Brooklyn, according to the Twig), who were unimpressed with Mays.

Mays appeared determined to show the Dodgers every ounce of talent they had missed. In his first-ever at bat against Brooklyn on June 26 at the Polo Grounds, the hot-hitting rookie belted a double off Preacher Roe and scored the game's first run a few moments later. At that moment, Campy recognized that it might take more than a steady diet of inside fastballs to neutralize the Say Hey Kid. Distraction, he decided, would be his strategy.

The next time Mays stepped into the batter's box, Campy was ready. "What do you say, Willie?" Campy started. "When you going to get married? You getting much?" Mays, his eyes widening, said nothing. A tight pitch from Roe then sent the youngster sprawling. "That's nothing. You better get your hits today, because tomorrow Newcombe's pitching, and he don't like young niggers." Mays, by now a frazzled bundle of nerves, did little the remainder of the series, managing only 1 hit in his next 10 at bats. Eventually, he sought advice from Durocher, who recommended a strategically tossed handful of dirt as the most effective way to silence Brooklyn's talkative receiver.

Mays's early brushes with Campanella would become a part of baseball lore, although Campy himself felt that his reputation as a chatterbox behind the plate was exaggerated. "I don't believe in that," he later explained. "I've got too much concentrating of my own to do." But Mays, he felt, required special handling. "When I was his age . . . I couldn't get into the majors. I had to learn the hard way. This kid walks right in, and he's gonna have to learn the hard way too." Nevertheless, Roy grew quite fond of Willie, who shared Campy's fervent love of baseball and aversion to controversy.

Despite Mays's struggles, the Giants took two of three from the Dodgers at home. By the time the two clubs met again in Brooklyn for a July 4 twin bill, the Dodgers' lead had been cut to 4½ games. With Maglie pitching and the Giants up 4–0 in the eighth inning of game one, the Dodger lead appeared likely to shrink further. Inserted as a pinch hitter, Campy promptly clouted a two-run homer to cut the Giant lead in half (the Barber's brushbacks never bothered Roy, who finished his career with a .287 average and 6 homers against Maglie in 94 at bats). From that moment, nothing went right for Durocher, who watched in disbelief as the Dodgers knocked out Maglie, swept the doubleheader, then beat the Giants a third time the following night. Throughout the final game, Roy gleefully tormented poor Mays, who discovered that Campy wasn't kidding about Newk's contempt for the younger members of his race. "Oh, Donald! How could you?" he quipped in mock dismay as he watched Willie hit the dirt again and again.

With Brooklyn now up by 7½, Jackie Robinson was already prepared to break open the bubbly. "The Dodgers will win the National League pennant," Robinson announced. "We've got more spirit and more balance than any other club in our league, and I think the tremendous spirit will offset any danger of overconfidence catching hold to us." Lacy, sighing that Jackie as usual "couldn't stay unquoted," wasn't so sure. In 1942, the Bums had squandered a 9½ game bulge on August 16. Four years later, a 7½ game advantage in early July wasn't enough.

But this club, Brooklyn fans convinced themselves, was different. After sweeping the Giants, the now red-hot Dodgers took three more in Philadelphia to enter the All-Star break with a 50-26 record, the best in baseball. "You can order your World Series tickets now," wrote one reporter. "If the front office sends the dough back, keep mailing it to them. Brooklyn's a cinch."

LIKE MOST of the Dodgers, Roy was pleased with his first-half performance. Not only had he stayed healthy, but his .326 average, fifth best in the National League, reflected a more mature approach at the plate. "He's a better hitter now than he ever was," remarked Clyde Sukeforth. "He's making the pitcher give him the ball he wants to hit. He has a much better knowledge of the strike zone." His home-run production was down slightly, but Campy expected to do some catching up during the long home stand that would open the second half.

The Dodgers picked up where they'd left off, beating the Cubs twice to extend their winning streak to eight, only to drop six of the next seven. The team had hit their first real patch of adversity, leaving Dressen clueless how to proceed. Rather than boost his pitching staff's flagging confidence, he publicly ripped Erv Palica, cuffed around by the Pirates, as a choker and a malingerer. Fan reaction to the comment was strongly negative, and O'Malley and Bavasi, who had hoped to keep Dressen under control, were also none too pleased. Nor were they happy with Cholly's subsequent premature announcement of his rehiring for 1952 or his sly explanation for the Dodgers' success thus far in '51. "Maybe my methods are different than Shotton's and Rickey's. Maybe they're better."

Dressen, eager to put the Palica mess behind him, quickly claimed all was forgiven: "We took a shower together after the game and used the same piece of soap." Still, doubts almost certainly would have intensified at Montague Street had the Dodgers not abruptly reeled off ten straight wins, seven on the road. The key, almost everyone agreed, was Campy.

The power that had been missing suddenly reappeared. He hit his thirteenth homer against Max Lanier at Ebbets on July 20 and added a pair against the Cards two days later. On the western swing that followed, he opened the trip with two more homers in a three-game sweep of the Cubs. At the Dodgers' next stop in St. Louis, Campy produced a game-winning three-run blast off his "cousin" Al Brazle on July 27, his second off Brazle in five days.

Campy had seven homers in eight games. Ten in July, a new Brooklyn record for a month. Though still hitting sixth in the order, Campy was now emerging as the biggest threat in the Dodger attack. "Ice up the beer," his teammates now shouted when he strode to the plate in the late innings, anticipating another key hit and another case of brew provided by Dressen after every win (Rickey, ever the moralist, had banned beer in the Brooklyn clubhouse).

FOLLOWING THEIR 10-3 road trip, Brooklyn returned home for three more with the Giants on August 8 and 9. Now up by 9½, there appeared to be little at stake beyond Durocher and Giant pride.

The Dodgers, showing no sign of the "complacency" Rickey had warned about last year, went about their jobs with cold-blooded efficiency. They swept Wednesday's doubleheader to extend the deficit to 11½ games. On Thursday, Campy would almost single-handedly administer the last rites. He homered off Larry Jansen in the second. He singled and scored in the fourth. In the seventh, he greeted relief pitcher Sheldon Jones, who had dusted him off yesterday, with a tie-breaking solo shot. And in the ninth inning, he somehow managed to hold on to Jackie's relay despite a nasty collision with Whitey Lockman, who was trying to score the tying run from first on a Mays double to right center. With Mays advancing to third on the throw, Dressen then violated conventional baseball wisdom by ordering an intentional walk of the potential go-ahead run, Bobby Thomson. Wes Westrum then bounced into a game-ending 5-4-3 double play.

Afterward, the Dodger dressing room rivaled a Mardi Gras celebration. "Eat your hearts out, you blankety bums—you're through," Jackie bellowed at the door separating the home and visitors' clubhouses. Dressen, meanwhile, happily boasted of the brilliance of his intentional-walk strategy (he did *not*, however, utter his famously ungrammatical "The Giants is dead" until 1953).

Campy was more subdued. Lockman had hit him like a Sherman tank ("the hardest I was ever hit"), and his body still ached. "It was like taking a punch from Joe Louis," he admitted. But Dodger fans now loved him more than ever, even more, it seemed, than Jackie. "Campanella," Jack Lang of the *Long Island Daily Press* noted, "now gets the biggest ovation given any Dodger player since the days of Dixie Walker." A Brooklynite holding court at a local bar summed up his appeal: "Look at him. He does everything. Hits like a fool. Catches all day, every day. . . . Where you gonna find a better one?"

BY SATURDAY afternoon, August 11, the Dodger lead stood at an almost unfathomable 13½ games. Nothing to do, Brooklyn fans smiled, but relax for seven weeks and wait for those World Series tickets to go on sale. Even the ultracompetitive Robinson felt secure enough to take a few days off for a minor operation.

Durocher and the Giants had other ideas. Almost overnight, they began to win. The Dodgers did not concern themselves at first, even after being swept three straight at the Polo Grounds. But when the Giant streak reached nine, every heart in the borough skipped a beat, though not Dressen's. "We've still got an eight-game lead and I've still got the same guys who built it up. Why get panicky?" Durocher, meanwhile, was now the picture of confidence. "Sure we got a chance, a good chance," he told a reporter. "What the blank do you think I come out here every blanking day for? Because I want to lose?"

By the time the smoke had cleared, the Giants had ripped off an amazing sixteen straight victories, shaving the Dodger lead to an uncomfortably close five games. In recent years, the Giants' surge has been linked to an elaborate sign-stealing scheme using a telescope in the center-field clubhouse at the Polo Grounds and a buzzer to signal the pitch (fastball/curve) to the bullpen, which in turn telegraphed the pitch to the hitter. The story had been a well-kept baseball secret for decades, although columnist Milton Gross accurately alluded to the Giants' 1951 sign-stealing the following May with no apparent reaction.

Precisely how much the signs benefited New York remains uncertain. From July 20, the point at which the sign-stealing supposedly began, the Giants actually hit better on the road than at home for the rest of the season. Their pitching, not hitting, improved most dramatically. Others question the actual effectiveness of the Giant system. What about sliders, changeups, and other pitches? Could the information be signaled fast enough to benefit most hitters? "Stealing signs is dangerous if you don't know for damn sure that the one giving the sign is getting it correct," observed Don Thompson, who didn't know of the Giants' shenanigans. "Because you can get killed . . . looking for a curve and getting a fastball."

During the Giants' streak, Brooklyn went 9-9, hardly a collapse, but enough to let Durocher and company back into the race. And Campy, like the rest of the Dodgers, suddenly seemed human again. After smashing his twenty-fifth homer on August 13, raising his average to .336, he hit only .209 the remainder of the month, and even his usually sterling defense began to suffer. The speedy Sam Jethroe challenged Roy three times in eight days, each time sliding in ahead of his throw.

The Lockman collision, which had left Roy unable to bend his left elbow, was at least partly to blame. Although a Dodger doctor suspected a possible bone break, Campy was not interested in getting an X-ray or resting. Bad elbow or not, he was not about to start sitting out games now with only a month left. He had another motivation to stay in the lineup. Campy and Newk had already requested and received an advance from Bavasi on their anticipated World Series shares. Newk had spent his dough on a new Cadillac.

With the lead back up to seven on the last day of August, even the most pessimistic Brooklyn rooter suspected their Bums would pull it out in the end. Some even began to request World Series tickets. "I wish folks would stop trying to jump the gun," complained one official. "We can't accept any orders yet." But the Dodgers themselves were already preparing to begin scouting potential American League opponents, and Dressen was certain the worst was over. "Every game we win," he told Dick Young, "they've got to win two."

THE FINAL month opened with a big weekend series at the Polo Grounds. If Brooklyn swept both, the Giants were just about done. Instead, the Dodgers found themselves buried twice under an avalanche of seven homers, almost certainly aided by Leo's secret spyglass. Roy's signs were not hard to decipher, thanks to the tape he often applied to his fingers for pitchers unable to see his black fingers. Although Campy later claimed that he normally changed his signals "anywhere from two to three times a ball game," Pee Wee Reese felt that Roy was not always sufficiently diligent. "Sometimes with a runner on second Campy [would] just go down and give II, hoping that the runner wasn't looking. A lot of times I was on second base hoping that the guy would do that, so when I saw Campy do this, I thought they must be getting it too."

Unaware that his signal calling was being compromised, Roy was more concerned with his still ailing left elbow, which had begun to lock up at inopportune moments. Fearing the worst, he finally submitted to an X-ray, which revealed bone chips or what the press called "joint mice." Surgery could be deferred until the winter, but he could expect ongoing discomfort for the remainder of the season.

Campy was relieved. He could always play through pain, and he was more determined than ever to catch both ends of the doubleheader scheduled that same day at Ebbets against the Braves. As the Labor Day crowd watched in awe, he singled in the second, clubbed a grand slam in the third, homered again in the sixth, and doubled in the seventh. So much for the bone chips affecting his swing. In game two, Dressen moved him into the cleanup slot, where he added a single and a double before the Braves finally retired him on a pop-up in the fifth. The Dodgers won both games, but the real story was the gritty performance of "Superman Campanella." "He seems indestructible," marveled the *World-Telegram and Sun*'s Joe King.

After extending their winning streak to four with two over the Phillies, the Bums were feeling loose again. The pennant was theirs for the taking. Beat the Giants this weekend at Ebbets and it was all but over.

Newk, shelled by the Giants in the Polo Grounds the last weekend amid cries of "choker," took the mound on Saturday, September 8. The big right-hander had shown signs of impatience with Campy last time out, even tearing the ball from his hands at one point, but Roy was unconcerned. "He's just a kid. He hasn't grown up." This afternoon, the kid was brilliant, tossing a two-hit shutout, as the Dodgers widened their lead to 6½ games. Ironically, the desperate Giants were now convinced that Dressen, a master sign thief himself, was up to something sinister at Ebbets. "They seemed to suspect a phone hookup between the Brooklyn dugout and a spotter in the stands," wrote one reporter, "and Alvin Dark and Herman Franks were discovered snooping around the bench afterward trying to trace phone wires."

On Sunday, September 9, 34,004 fans crowded into Ebbets hoping to see the Bums administer the death blow in the final regular-season meeting of the two clubs. But Sal Maglie, the Giants' own Superman, beat the Dodgers 2–1 for his twentieth win. Campy spent most of the afternoon on the bench, fighting yet another nagging injury, this time a painful right hip bruise from a slide the day before. Although he singled as a pinch hitter and caught the last two innings, he knew he was not right, even after the Dodger medical staff drained an accumulation of fluid after the game.

Nevertheless, Campy was on board the Cincinnati Limited the next day with the rest of the Dodgers, although he was not expected to play. Leery of his usual claim that he was "feeling fine," the Dodgers had already called up ex–major leaguer Mickey Livingston from Fort Worth for catching insurance. "We've got to make sure that Campy is tip-top for the Series," explained Bavasi. "So we're not going to take any chances with his condition." Rube Walker did the catching in the Tuesday opener, rookie Clem Labine shut out the Reds, and the lead was now six, eight in the loss column. With only fourteen games to play, time was running out on the Giants, and the Dodgers knew it. "Players who never before in their lives had any conception of what a 'combination number' meant, are now tossing around figures like a bunch of young Einsteins," wrote Dick Young.

Campy still couldn't move well but Dressen wanted him catching on Wednesday, especially with Ken Raffensberger scheduled to go. Surprised to see Roy playing, Reds manager Luke Sewell was determined to match

Dressen move for move. He not only gave Raffensberger a quick hook in the second but brought in the big sidearmer Ewell Blackwell, normally a starter, who had just worked on Sunday. And if Raffensberger was Campy's bosom cousin, Blackwell was his evil twin. Roy could simply not touch Blackie, "the baddest man I ever faced," managing only two hits in thirty-two lifetime at bats. Three times, Blackwell faced Campy with runners in scoring position, and each time Roy went back to the bench muttering to himself.

The Dodgers had to settle for a split in Cincinnati before heading to Pittsburgh for two with Rickey's last-place Pirates. "You've got the pennant, now go out and get the World Series," Rickey told Roy. "You can do it if you watch your weight." Campy couldn't resist talking up his new liquor store, which his old teetotaler boss had disapproved of earlier. "We deliver anywhere, Mr. Rickey."

The pesky Pirates divided a pair with Brooklyn on Friday and Saturday, while the Giants swept the Cubs in Chicago. With the lead at five, the Dodgers marched into Wrigley Field to start another two-game set on September 16. Crew-cutted Clem Labine, suddenly emerging as the staff ace, whipped the Cubbies on Sunday for his fourth straight win. With each start, Campy grew more impressed with the young French Canadian from Rhode Island. "Clem's got a sinker that's real heavy—the ball just jars you."

Monday's Wrigley finale began uneventfully. Starters Turk Lown and Newk both retired the side in order in the first. After Jackie flied to center to start the second, Campy stepped to the plate, hoping to get back on track after managing only three hits in fourteen at bats on the road trip. And Lown, a former Dodger farmhand sporting a 3-8 record and an ERA over 5.00 in his rookie season, was no Cy Young.

Campy had drilled a game-winning homer off Lown in June, but he would have no chance to tee off on him this time. Nearly two years to the day of the Werle beaning, he once again ducked into a fastball. The flimsy plastic liner that he had donned since 1949 provided no protection, as the ball struck him below the cap against his left jaw and ear. Still conscious but with blood oozing from his lacerated ear, a shaky Roy was carried off the field on a stretcher, then rushed to Illinois Masonic Hospital by an ambulance called by a group of nearby firemen watching the game on TV.

Like the Werle beaning, the damage proved to be less serious than feared. X-rays revealed no fracture, but the doctors wanted Roy in the hospital at least overnight, with Bavasi deputized to keep him from bolting. Although the beaning appeared to be unintentional, Sam Lacy wondered why "tan" stars seemed to be victimized far more often than their white counterparts.

Dodger fans received even more bad news that afternoon. Newcombe, who always seemed to be pitching during Campy's crises, was breezing along after six innings with a two-hit shutout and a 3–0 lead. After the Cubs pushed across two runs in the seventh, Dressen called for sore-armed Clyde King, who promptly yielded a two-run pinch-hit homer to old friend Gene Hermanski. The Dodgers eventually went down to an agonizing 5–3 defeat, the lead was down to four, and Gil Hodges experienced what he later described as "my first real fright" concerning his team's pennant hopes.

While Hodges and his teammates grimly headed on to St. Louis for the last leg of the trip, Campy was left behind in Chicago, with plans to send him home to rest. Likely he wondered why the baseball gods appeared intent on maiming him each September. Still, he insisted that his jaw wasn't really hurting and he would be back in the lineup by Friday. "I ate a big breakfast. What more proof do they need that I'm all right?"

Roy, despite his seemingly miraculous recuperative powers, was not all right. "His equilibrium suffers whenever he moves," noted Bill Roeder, "and it is painful for him just to get through the day; he says it's like a gun going off in his head when he chews, coughs or blows his nose." Roy felt even sicker when the Dodgers dropped the opener in Sportsman's Park, his replacement, Walker, botching a double steal and striking out twice. Fortunately for the Brooks, Roe and Erskine silenced the Cardinal bats in the next two games. Flying home from St. Louis, the young Einsteins calculated the new magic number as 5 with ten to play.

On Friday, September 21, a decent crowd of 23,753 settled in at Ebbets to watch the Dodgers begin their final home stand. Campy again wasn't playing, Jackie's groin was bothering him, and Cox and a couple of the other nonfliers were late for the opening pitch thanks to a delayed train heading back from St. Louis. Still, Dodger fans felt relatively secure as the

Giants had lost yesterday. The defending champion turned fifth-place Phillies, losers of twelve of sixteen to the Bums thus far, were in town. And Labine, 4-0 with a 1.00 ERA in his first four starts, was on the mound.

But the Dodgers, the fans discovered, badly needed Campy. In the first inning, a botched pickoff throw by his replacement, Rube Walker, with one out put runners on second and third. To set up a force, Dressen then ordered Labine to walk Bill Nicholson and then go after Willie Jones, the Phillies' leading slugger. Labine got two strikes and then hung a curveball that Jones promptly blasted for a grand slam. Within one inning, Labine was gone, the score was 7–0, and the game was out of reach.

Jones's homer landed Labine squarely in Dressen's doghouse, from which he would not emerge for nine critical days. Walker also received plenty of blame. The Ebbets crowd booed him mercilessly that night, and Dressen was quick to pile on the beleaguered catcher afterward. Walker, Cholly claimed, didn't know the hitters. If he had only seen Dressen's sign, there wouldn't have been a grand slam. "I wanted him to throw a sinker. Walker didn't understand my signs."

Dressen now decided that Campy, despite ongoing headaches and dizziness, had to catch the remaining weekend games. The initial results weren't pretty. On Saturday, Roy went 0 for 5 and left 7 runners on base, the Dodgers falling again 7–3. The following afternoon, his head felt no better, and ice packs between innings provided only limited relief. "It was so bad the first five innings that I didn't think I could stand it." But somehow Campy managed to crack four hits, including his thirty-second homer, to spark Brooklyn to a 6–2 win. "It's a funny game," he remarked later. "Some days you feel right and you get nothing. Other times you're not right and boom."

At the close of the weekend, the Dodgers still led by three with seven to play: four in Boston and three in Philadelphia. Just four wins meant the pennant, even if the Giants somehow managed to win all five of their remaining games.

On Monday, the Giants came from behind to beat the Braves 4–3 at the Polo Grounds to cut the lead to 2½. Brooklyn was idle but Dressen was still confident, talking of calling up an extra pitcher for the Series. And Boston, he recalled, was the scene of the Dodgers' clinching in 1941.

There would be no Dodger celebration at Braves Field that Tuesday. Boston soundly thrashed the Bums twice, while in Philadelphia the Giants won their fourth straight. The lead was now down to one game, and Dressen, who had earlier in the week announced that "the pressure is all on the Giants," was now facing a must-win game on Wednesday, September 26. Before the game, Dressen gave the boys a pep talk, and the speech appeared to work wonders. After Campy slugged Max Surkont's first offering in the first for a bases-clearing double, the Brooks waltzed to an easy 15–5 win.

The ship now apparently righted, the Dodgers liked their chances on Thursday with Preacher Roe on the hill. "It will be Roe, Roe, Roe to the pennant," quipped Dressen. Just a few days earlier, there had been talk that Dressen would not use Roe the final week to protect his National League–record .917 winning percentage and 22-2 mark. Now, with the Giants refusing to lose, Roe had to start.

The Preacher pitched reasonably well the first seven innings. In the eighth, with the score tied 3–3, Roe appeared to be tiring, yielding successive singles to Bob Addis and Sam Jethroe. With Earl Torgeson up, runners on first and third, and nobody out, the Dodger infield moved in. Dressen made no move to the bullpen, although the scenario was made to order for Labine's sinker ball.

What followed was an unforgettable moment in the '51 race. It began routinely enough with Torgeson bouncing a grounder to Jackie, who immediately fired home. With the plate apparently blocked by Roy and the throw in plenty of time, Addis appeared to be a dead duck. "Campy spun him off," recalled Carl Erskine. "He never reached the plate." But umpire Frank Dascoli, a thorn in Dressen's side all season, called Addis safe. The throw, he claimed, was "off to the right. Campy had to reach out and then back."

From his earliest days as a professional, Roy had generally accepted umpires' calls—good, bad, or indifferent—without much protest. But this time he was not quite so calm. "Campy jumped up and down like a meaty yo-yo," wrote Dick Young, "and screamed in that piping voice of his." Not only did he jump and scream, particularly after Dascoli turned away, but he flung his catcher's mitt to the ground in disgust. Seconds later, Dascoli tossed Campy out of the game. It was only Roy's second ejection in two seasons, both at the hands of Dascoli, who worked in law enforcement in the off-season but really wanted to be a "cowboy actor."

Dascoli was not done yet. He ejected coach Cookie Lavagetto, but then sent most of the Dodger bench to cool their heels in the clubhouse.

Although Roe escaped without further damage, the Dodgers now had to score in their last at bat or face losing another half game to the idle Giants. Reese doubled down the line to start the ninth and then advanced to third on Robinson's grounder. At that moment, Dodger Nation was cursing Dascoli. Campy would have been due next and sure to bring the run home. He had already hit two deep fly balls today (in his three remaining career plate appearances against Chet Nichols, he would walk once and homer twice). Instead, Nichols had to contend with Wayne Terwilliger, sent up to hit for Rube Walker. Terwilliger, aka the Twig, had barely played in the last month and had not had a hit since August 14. After getting ahead 2-0, he tapped a "feeble hopper" with Reese holding at third. Nichols then fanned Pafko and the game was over.

Dascoli and the rest of the crew beat a quick retreat to their dressing room, only a few uncomfortable feet away from the Dodger lockers. On the way, they encountered Campy, still raging, four-letter words flying fast and furious. "Everybody was hollering and screaming and calling these guys everything under the sun," Jackie Robinson later recalled. "Gutless incompetent" and "choker" were among the more polite terms reserved for Dascoli. Meanwhile, the usually mild-mannered Roe, his record now gone, kicked in the umpires' dressing-room door, although Robinson predictably got the blame.

Undoubtedly, Dascoli was not the best of umpires. Since his debut in 1948, he was known mostly for his size (six feet two inches), his overly demonstrative style (a "TV umpire," sniffed some), and his unbelievably quick thumb. The National League would eventually tire of his confrontations with players and managers, finally canning him in 1961. Still, he may well have called the Addis play correctly. "I thought I went underneath his glove," says Addis. "It was a very close play but I thought I got my foot in there." Several writers watching from the press box were inclined to agree, while Dick Young would simply state, "It was close—very close."

Almost everyone believed, however, that his ejection of Campy was indefensible. "I didn't cuss him and I didn't touch him," Roy claimed. "I never said anything but 'Frank, how can you call that man safe?' " One might ask whether race was a factor, as Roy always believed that umpires gave black players a much shorter leash on squawks. But no one ever suggested that Dascoli was a bigot, just overly touchy (he had led the majors in ejections in both of the last two years). Dascoli believed his decision was appropriate. After all, Campy threw his glove. "If I don't throw him out of there then, the next guy will try to throw the center-field fence."

In the aftermath, writers speculated that a few Dodgers would be suspended for their door-kicking antics, but Ford Frick had no stomach for wrecking the Brooklyn roster for the season's final weekend. Instead, he fined Campy, Jackie, and Roe and reportedly bawled out Dascoli "for having been 'too hasty' in ejecting Campanella."

Like many of his teammates, Roy came to believe the Dascoli game may have cost Brooklyn the pennant. Still, grudges were usually not his nature. When he next saw Dascoli, he greeted him "just like nothing happened," although the Brooklyn fans were feeling far less charitable toward the men in blue.

FOR MONTE Irvin, his friend's ejection confirmed that Brooklyn was doomed. Durocher agreed. "The Dodgers now must win their remaining three games to clinch it, if we win our remaining two. I don't think they can do it. They are screaming at the umpires. Pretty soon they will be screaming at each other. Pennant pressure can give even the steadiest of pros the yips. They've got the yips."

The "yips" were also apparent to Sam Lacy, who headed to Shibe Park on Friday to watch the Dodgers begin their last series. "The bravado they displayed as they went through their pre-game paces . . . was definitely feigned. . . . This club was tight, as tight as my long-oval hatband." Although Campy belted his thirty-third homer to give the Dodgers an early 3–0 lead, the Phillies rallied in the late innings, eventually winning in the ninth on another backbreaking hit by Willie Jones. After 152 games, the Dodgers and Giants were now tied.

Along with several teammates, Roy sat shell-shocked in the lobby of the Hotel Warwick the next day while waiting for the night game ahead. "I just can't believe it . . . just can't believe what's happened to us." Like many fans, he was ready to turn to a higher power. "I'm a believer in prayer. I'm going to ask everybody on this team to say just one little prayer, before the game." Unfortunately, the Giant fans were praying just as fervently for *their* team, who beat the Braves that afternoon for their sixth straight win.

The Dodgers needed a savior and Don Newcombe would have to do.

"Hum that pea, big boy!" Campy shouted, and Newk was only too happy to oblige that evening. Working on only two days' rest, he shut out the Phillies on seven hits, besting his nemesis Robin Roberts. For the third straight year, Brooklyn's fate would be decided against the Phillies on the final Sunday of the season.

Dressen gave the start to his ace Preacher Roe, still stewing about the Dascoli game. Almost immediately, Roy sensed that the Arkansas Cornstalk, pitching on two days' rest with an iffy arm, didn't have it. Four runs chased him in the second, and the Dodgers soon found themselves down 6–1 after three. With the Giants leading in Boston, O'Malley even began thinking about drafting a congratulatory telegram, while some fans went to their church to pray.

Campy was not ready to give up. In the fourth, he crushed a Bubba Church pitch into deep right-center and saw a chance for his first triple of the season. As he headed to third, Roy suddenly experienced the all too familiar sensation of stabbing pain, this time in his right thigh. As usual, he shook it off and even scored a few moments later on an error. After withstanding burns, bone chips, and a beaning this year, a mere muscle pull wasn't going to keep him out now.

Despite a quick taping of the thigh, he was almost immobile the remainder of the game. But his teammates' inspired play that afternoon made him forget his discomfort. He marveled how the Dodgers, after learning of the Giants' victory in Boston, fought back to tie the score at eight in the eighth inning. He thrilled in Big Newk's clutch performance, hurling 5.2 innings of shutout relief only a day after throwing a complete game. And like much of America, he was amazed by Jackie Robinson's brilliant heroics: a game-saving catch in the twelfth (although some, including Reese, would later suggest he trapped the ball), and what proved to be a game-winning homer in the fourteenth.

While the Brooklyn faithful at Shibe celebrated happily (and dodged tin cans heaved by angry Phillies and Giants fans), the Dodgers romped in the clubhouse. Campy's mood was more introspective. A best-of-three playoff was starting tomorrow, and he would not be at his best. Still, he had much to be proud of, unlike several of his teammates who had slumped badly down the stretch. Since August 12, the start of the Giant comeback, Roy led the team in homers (11), RBIs (36, tied with Pafko), average (.320), slugging (.633), and OPS (1.008). Maybe Brooklyn's detractors might still label them a bunch of chokers, but Campy most certainly was not.

THE DODGERS had, for the third time in six years, already won the coin toss for the playoff. Unlike 1946 and 1949, Dressen opted to yield home-field advantage for the chance to get the jump on Leo by playing game one at Ebbets on October 1 (he later claimed the Dodger brass made the choice, preferring the Polo Grounds' "greater seating capacity").

Campanella, after praying he'd "be able to walk when I woke up," was in the lineup against the sinker-balling Jim Hearn that Monday afternoon. But his leg had barely improved in the past twenty-four hours, despite Ruthe's rubbing alcohol and an injection of novocaine. The true extent of his infirmity became painfully clear in the fourth, when he came up with runners on first and third, one out, and the Giants ahead 2–1. On a hit-and-run, Campy cracked a grounder to Al Dark, who flipped to Eddie Stanky to begin an apparent inning-ending double play, spoiled by a horrible throw pulling Whitey Lockman far off the bag. Relieved the Dodgers had at least tied the score, the crowd was shocked to see Campy tagged out barely halfway down the line. "Any other runner, or even a sound Campanella, would have beaten it out," observed Jack Lang.

The Dodgers never threatened again and went down to a 3–1 defeat. With Bavasi and Dressen both publicly alluding to Roy's bad wheels as a factor in the loss, Campy began to wonder whether he should be playing. His balance was off while hitting, the Giants infielders were now playing him on the outfield grass, he couldn't move fast enough to back up plays, and he was virtually a statue behind home plate. And the Dodgers now faced the unenviable task of trying to beat a club that had won thirty-eight of its last forty-five and was going home. Despite the inescapable atmosphere of doom and gloom, Roy somehow remained upbeat. "We've beaten them before at the Polo Grounds and we can do it again."

It would not be with Campy's help. Even after a last-ditch attempt to freeze the pain with ethyl chloride on Tuesday, he still could not run. Though frustrated that his body would not obey his commands, his sense of humor remained intact. "Wotta year . . . never was hurt so much. Guess

I should have been hit on the head this time, instead of the leg getting hurt. I can keep playing if my head hurts. I get dizzy, but I've been dizzy all my life anyway."

His absence mattered little in game two. Emerging from Dressen's doghouse, Labine whitewashed the Giants on six hits to deadlock the series. Rube Walker had a fine game, clocking three hits including a gargantuan homer over the right-field roof. But Dressen kept a close eye on Campy's replacement all day, warning Walker to change signals after he suspected Bobby Thomson was tipping off Mays from second, and even calling every pitch in the ninth.

Bobby Thomson's historic walk-off home run off Ralph Branca in the deciding game is an oft-told tale that need not be recounted. Campy spent the fateful afternoon on the bench, occasionally retreating to the cramped bathroom in the dugout to say a quick prayer. "Sink, you devil, sink!" he shouted as he watched Thomson's blast sail into the left-field seats.

In the years that followed, Campanella, like most of the Dodgers, would offer his own version of what had occurred on October 3, 1951. Late in life, he would insist in some interviews that he "begged Charlie Dressen to let me play . . . but he wouldn't let me." But Campy made no such claim at the time; his comments during the series reflect a grim awareness that he was physically incapable of playing. Nor did any sportswriter, all of whom had seen Campy's pathetic attempts to run in game one, feel compelled to question Dressen about Roy's subsequent benching. Still, in the last three innings of game three, on at least four occasions a healthy Campy might have made a difference.

In the bottom of the seventh, Irvin led off with a double. Trailing 1–0, Durocher called on Lockman to sacrifice, and the play fell to Walker. Walker, wrote Dick Young, "in an atrocious moment of misdirection, fired the ball to third—long after there was a possible chance of heading off Irvin." Instead of a runner on third with one away, Newcombe was now facing a first-and-third/nobody-out situation. Although Bobby Thomson then brought home Irvin on a sacrifice fly, Newk may very well have pitched to him differently with one out instead of none.

Working with Campy almost always made Newk a better pitcher. Roy, along with Robinson and Reese, prodded and scolded a weary Newk into going out for the eighth inning. But during the fatal ninth when Newk began to unravel, Campy was not there to soothe his roomie, although Durocher actually feared the Dodgers "might bring Roy Campanella in . . . for the last two outs . . . as a psychological stunt to inspire Newcombe to stay in there and fight," and Dressen at least considered the possibility.

Dressen's choice of Ralph Branca to relieve Newk that inning may also have been partly driven by Campy's inability to catch. He wanted no part of Carl Erskine, supposedly bouncing his curveball in the bullpen. "I think if he envisioned a wild pitch and Walker is slow as molasses, he processed that real quick and said let me have Branca," says Erskine. "That's pure speculation, but I think that might have been a time where Campanella would have made a difference."

And then there was Branca's crucial pitch sequence to Thomson. Branca's first pitch to Thomson was frighteningly hittable, but neither Walker nor Dressen made a move to the mound. "If Roy Campanella is healthy, and catching that game, he stops the game right there and goes out to tell Branca to keep the ball low," said Dressen a few days later. "But Roy is lame, on the bench with me. So Branca throws the next one high and it goes for a three-run homer."

Monte Irvin would offer the most telling description of a healthy Roy's impact on the 1951 playoff. "Campy was the brains. We didn't fear anyone as much as we did Campy."

14

ACHES, PAINS, AND A COMEBACK

NO SOONER HAD THOMSON touched home plate than the Dodger switchboard was jammed with near-hysterical callers screaming, "Lemme talk to that blankety-blank O'Malley [or Dressen or Bavasi] or anyone else." Others channeled their frustrations into creating effigies of Dressen to be abused appropriately by passersby.

Campy could barely bring himself to leave the Polo Grounds that afternoon. "It was the biggest disappointment of my life in not being able to play," he sighed. "I just can't get around to realizing that we lost it." O'Malley himself believed Campy's late-season injuries probably cost the Dodgers the pennant. But Roy recognized that the entire team was culpable, even chiding Reese for remarking, "I guess the good Lord just didn't want us to win it." "Don't say that, Pee Wee. Don't go blaming the Lord for what we should have done."

After voting on their second-place shares, the Dodgers went home to lick their collective wounds until spring. Campy and Jackie, however, had their usual barnstorming commitments to fulfill. That the two men were now leading separate all-black clubs ("voluntarily fostering the very thing it took several lifetimes to break down," scolded Sam Lacy) confirmed conclusively what many had initially been reluctant to believe.

Jackie, his name still box-office gold, proved to be the stronger draw throughout the South. But Campy managed to trump Jackie in a more dramatic way that fall. On October 31 he was informed that he had been elected the National League's Most Valuable Player. "He was practically yelling, he was so overjoyed," Ruthe told Lacy. "I think Campy . . . had just about given up any thought of it after they . . . lost the pennant."

Campanella's 1951 season was undeniably impressive. Despite spending most of the season hitting sixth or seventh, he finished fourth in average (.325), third in slugging (.590), third in OPS (.983), third in homers (33), and fourth in RBIs (108). He was just as superb controlling the running game (admittedly limited in those days), cutting down 34 of 49 runners attempting to steal for a 69 percent success rate, far above the 37 percent average of other National League catchers. And his league-leading 140 games (out of 154) behind the plate reflected an almost unbelievable durability.

Not everyone was thrilled with his selection. One writer, likely more concerned with race than performance, left Campy off the ballot. Others suggested that runner-up Stan Musial, with his usual sterling offensive numbers, was more deserving. Even Jackie Robinson thought Musial would have won the award hands down if the Cardinals had contended. Nevertheless, he admitted that Campy "deserves every honor he can get. . . . I am convinced that Campanella is the best catcher in baseball today."

Privately, Robinson had mixed emotions. He had put together what he considered to be his best season: 19 homers, a .338 average, and a league-leading .992 fielding percentage at second base with only 7 errors. Yet he had finished only sixth in the voting. Although he admitted Roy "had done a fantastic job," Jackie later claimed that a white sportswriter told him, "If you ask any impartial observer who is the guts of that Brooklyn team and made it tick this year, nine out of ten people would tell you 'Jackie Robinson.' " But Jackie's "controversial" qualities, the writer explained, cost him when it came time to cast votes.

That Robinson included this story in his biography betrayed at least a trace of envy. Still, he insisted that he was merely trying to highlight the "small-minded hypocrisy" of the press, hardly a debatable contention, then or now. Jackie's outspokenness and occasional abrasiveness likely cost him some votes, but he was unwilling to make nice with the writers just to get an award. "I had made a vow to myself," he later wrote, "to be more proud of being respected than being liked."

With the exception of Milton Gross at the *Post* and Roger Kahn during his brief stint at the *Herald Tribune*, Robinson's relationship with much of the New York press corps would deteriorate in the years to come. Frank Graham, Jr., who became the Dodgers' public relations director in 1952, saw firsthand how Robinson became increasingly irritated by the slightest dig or a perceived slight. "I remember once when Mike Gaven of the *Journal-American* heard that Jackie was unhappy with something he had written; Mike asked me if I would talk to Jackie and try to explain that he wasn't really criticizing him. I went to JR and told him that Mike was contrite that he had offended him, but Jackie turned away and said testily, 'Fuck him.' "

IN AN era when baseball was still the unquestioned king of all sports, winning the MVP meant celebrity status in America. Roy was now a national figure, his name as recognizable as Liberace, Brando, and Doris Day. But exactly what, some wondered, made this half-Negro/half-Italian fellow so special? What set him apart from the pack?

At first glance, he looked nothing like an athlete, his chunkiness further highlighted by the baggy uniforms then in vogue. But once the game began, fans found it hard to take their eyes off him. The man opposing players called Fatso could do almost anything on the ballfield.

Watching Campy hit was almost worth the price of admission. Up to the plate he would plod, big bat (as heavy as 37 ounces by 1955) loaded with "grippy beeswax" in hand, furiously chomping his gum or tobacco. Once settled in his usual foot-in-the-bucket stance, he would hack away, like "a kid in gang fights wielding a sock full of sand," wrote Milton Gross. "I never saw a guy who could swing like he could," recalled his teammate Glenn Mickens. "He ended up on that back leg . . . his knee catching the ground." But he usually managed to whack the ball hard somewhere, though he was very much a guess hitter. He ran surprisingly well for a catcher and could even steal an occasional base (as many as eight one year). "He always scored from second on a base hit," Carl Erskine insists. "He just had good instincts."

He was just as compelling behind the plate. Most pitchers loved throwing to Campy, who would offer three to four different targets, all while squatting lower to the ground and closer to the hitter than most of his contemporaries. Shifting the center of his body to receive every pitch, his ability to block balls was legendary, despite using what he called a "firm glove," with only a little olive oil added to soften the leather. "He's the one and only guy that I ever saw take a glove out of the box and catch with it in the game," recalled Dodger teammate and fellow catcher Dick Teed. "It was unbelievable to me. How in the world can he do this?" Even if a ball happened to pop out of his mitt, Campy was so quick and his arm so deadly that few runners tried to advance. "He did things that I never saw another catcher do."

But what ultimately distinguished Campy from other elite jocks was his personality. Here was a celebrity who was anything but bland and who exuded color from every pore. How many ballplayers looked like a "dusky, whiskerless Santa Claus" but could hit like Joe DiMaggio? How many had such a high, squeaky voice that everyone seemed to make fun of, even his own teammates? ("Why don't you catch cold and talk like a man?" Reese teased one day.) And most important of all, how many superstar athletes were never at a loss for words?

Despite his ninth-grade education, Campy's capacity for language was extraordinary. "I don't want to miss a word he says," remarked Reese. "He's funnier than Bob Hope. He's always coming up with an expression that eases the tension in a tight game." In the Campanella dictionary, the "express" was a fastball, "local" or "public enemy number one" a curve, "jelly leg" a nervous hitter, and "long left leg" described a batter with his foot in the bucket. He seemed to possess an inexhaustible supply of wise and witty sayings, ranging from "a baseball doesn't have any sense" to his most famous and enduring comment: "You have to be a man to be a big league ballplayer . . . but you have to have a lot of little boy in you too."

He was always ready with a quick comeback that usually had his teammates roaring. One day at the Polo Grounds, a few drunken fans in the upper deck began fighting. "Hey, Campy," said Gil Hodges, "it looks like a couple of your customers are going at it up there." "No, sir," answered Roy, his eyes twinkling. "I don't sell any of that fighting liquor. I only sell *happy* liquor." On another occasion, a writer asked how he had handled former college basketball sensation Johnny O'Brien in his first major league at bat.

"We just hooked him, that's all. . . . I don't care how many points that kid scored in the Garden and elsewhere last winter, you can't curve a basketball."

Even rival players, though they might hurl an occasional fat insult in his direction, found him difficult to resist. They remembered not only his affability, but the little gestures, the way he sent a telegram to Giant catcher Bill Sarni after a heart attack or made sure that the Cubs' Gene Baker still got a full barnstorming share after illness forced him to leave a tour early. Johnny Temple never forgot Roy's words of encouragement at the 1956 All-Star Game. Sensing resentment from Jackie Robinson about his controversial selection along with four other Cincinnati Reds, a disheartened Temple retreated to the Griffith Stadium locker room. "As long as I live, I'll be thankful to Campy for what he said: 'You wouldn't be here, boy, if you didn't deserve it.' "

The writers were also generally fond of Roy, at least early in his career. He was easy to interview, extremely accommodating, and always willing to "give you that extra moment," said Lester Rodney. Although Roy's cooperative press relations partly reflected his essential congeniality, shrewd calculation was also involved. Unlike Robinson, Campy was not only determined to have the media on his side but to use them to present an image designed to gain as wide acceptance as possible.

Campy, wrote Frank Graham, Jr., "consciously created a role for himself . . . a high-voiced, good-humored, homey philosopher" or something akin to Will Rogers in a catcher's mask. The writers and the public ate it up. Already a master storyteller who loved an audience, he became particularly skilled as a speaker, spinning a never-ending supply of tales from his extensive baseball travels. Graham, who saw Roy assume his "lovable old Campy" persona more than once, couldn't help but detect "a lot of ham. . . . This is not to suggest that Roy is a phony. He is a kind man, eager to be liked, very much in love with life and entirely deserving of the affection in which he is so widely held. But there is a little bit of the actor in each of us, and Campy's cheery enthusiasm sharply underlined the thespian in him."

Roy's image as "homey philosopher" was strengthened by the media's fascination with his religious attitudes. Dick Young's 1952 biography, which succeeded in crystallizing the Campy persona for the masses (and future writers, who cribbed from it mercilessly), was careful to note Roy's devout faith, as would most future profiles ("Bible Belter" was the title of one). By the mid-1950s, a Cincinnati preacher even cited Campy as "a true Christian," although one congregant questioned how a liquor salesman could be anything but hellbound.

Campy was not concerned about the supposed sinfulness of the booze business. He was nowhere near as religious as the media often chose to present him. He did read the Bible and pray daily, but he rarely attended church away from home. "A man doesn't have to go to church to be a good Christian," he once observed to Don Connery, although the controversial statement (at least for 1950s America) never made it into print. Connery, who worked on a lengthy *Time* magazine cover story on Campy in 1955, understood Roy's beliefs better than most other journalists. "He just does what comes naturally and lets the Lord do the rest. Yet because of his greater fame, and possibly his color, it is he whose name is being sounded from pulpits as the Bible-reading exemplar."

Roy did not discourage the media's occasional tendencies to portray him as Billy Graham in a baseball uniform. Nor did he discourage his growing reputation as an "all-wise, all-powerful catcher." He did, however, object to writers undermining his image by publishing an offhand comment that stirred up trouble. His usual strategy, to deny the statement, did not exactly endear him to the press corps as his career progressed. By 1956, Ed Linn suggested that Campy, for his refusal to stand behind his quotes, "is probably the least liked" among the Dodger beatwriters, who also complained that "he saves his best stuff for the writers he thinks can do him the most good."

The writers seldom disclosed the other sides of Roy beneath the well-scrubbed public image. The friendly teddy bear of a fellow was actually an exceptionally powerful man with a ferocious desire to succeed. "Roy Campanella was much more competitive than he looked," noted his teammate Ben Wade. "He seemed happy-go-lucky, but he was tough." He was also no shrinking violet on the bench. Campy, wrote Oscar Ruhl in 1951, "though many think he is a deadpan Joe—can ease into the opposition as effectively as any bench jockey."

His tastes and interests were simple. He loved a good cigar, Cadillacs (with a ROY39 license plate), and expensive clothes ("a terrific dresser," recalled a friend). Unlike many Dodgers, he was not into cards, usually preferring to spend his free time on the road watching movies or television and reliving the last game. "He'd talk baseball, baseball, baseball," recalled Don Newcombe. "You'd come back upset after a game and he'd settle you down." Except for Newk, Reese, and Bavasi, he was not particularly close to any of the Dodger family off the field. "Roy was pretty much a loner," said Bavasi.

Campy had a genuine fondness for children, and his own boyish nature made it easy for him to relate to them. Happy Felton, the stout host of the Dodger pregame show where local boys competed for a chance to meet their favorite Bum, noted the winners often chose Roy, who loved to joke with the kids. "You want to be a ballplayer, son?" he asked one. "Then you gotta take a chaw outta this," offering the shocked lad a hunk of chewing tobacco. He was as genuinely excited for the awestruck youngsters as they were themselves. "A kid on a big league ballfield. Can you imagine that?"

It was no different with his own children. He loved to run his elaborate model-train setup (so elaborate that Lionel gave him an endorsement deal) in the basement with David, Little Roy, and Tony. Later, the trains were replaced by an equally impressive collection of six hundred tropical fish housed in twenty tanks. "They really made my children follow me around," Campy explained, "when I took care of them." On Sunday afternoons during the off-season, he would take the kids to the movies. He liked westerns; after meeting Gene Autry in 1953, he turned to Joe Black: "When I tell my kids I shook hands with Gene Autry, they'll never believe me."

Around the home, he epitomized the typical postwar suburban father constantly involved in DIY projects. He not only constructed the mini-aquarium in the walls of his basement, but he also built furniture, including a bookcase filled with baseball literature. "He could work with concrete, wood, cars, landscaping," recalled his son Tony. "It was just amazing." He liked to cook, even teaching Ruthe how to prepare spaghetti, and was known to whip up pastries in his spare time.

Most of all, he loved being Roy Campanella, and it was obvious to anyone who met him. Paul Reichler, whose father, Joe, helped ghostwrite Campy's autobiography, remembered Roy as "one of the most approachable 'stars' I ever encountered. . . . He made you feel comfortable immediately. A big engaging smile, quick to laugh. He seemed happy to be who he was, doing what he was doing, and he radiated his happiness to others."

• • •

OVER THE winter, Campy's liquor store swarmed with customers eager to keep the hot stove burning with talk of his MVP selection or Bobby Thomson. And then there was Newk, who had just been drafted into the army. "That was a tough break," Campy remarked. "This was going to be his greatest year, the first season he would have some real money. . . . But that's life, that's the way things go."

The front office was after Roy to take care of the four bone chips still floating in his left elbow. He put them off in December, citing the Christmas rush at the store, but finally agreed to a January 7 date with the surgeon. But when Dodger official Lee Scott arrived to pick him up, Campy stoutly refused to go, even after frantic calls to Bavasi and O'Malley. "Why have your arm cut if it's all right," Roy asked. "There's no sense in going in there and cutting me up and maybe causing all sorts of complications. The elbow doesn't hurt me at all and I know it won't affect my batting."

Bavasi was baffled. Campy had complained about discomfort only weeks earlier. "He had a month to think it over. . . . Sure we're miffed about it." Ed Sinclair of the *Herald Tribune* suspected there was more to the story, maybe Roy trying to force the Dodgers into bumping his salary into the Jackie Robinson/Yogi Berra high-$30,000 range. "It also was learned," wrote Sinclair, "that a number of Campanella's teammates have expressed surprise and concern over his unwillingness to submit to the operation."

Before the media could run wild with the latest "dissension on the Dodgers" story, Bavasi did damage control. Campanella, he claimed, had already signed his contract in December for around $25,000 without any objections or mentions of surgery. "I don't see how in the world a guy could write a story like that," Campy fumed to Milton Gross. "I don't care how much money Robbie [Robinson] makes. He can't play my position. I hope every player on the club gets all he can. . . . I won't have the operation because I don't think I need it. They could offer me a mint to do it and I still wouldn't. I'm just not the type to ask for money that way." Gross himself suggested that Campy was hardly about to blackmail O'Malley, the man who had just made his lucrative liquor business a reality.

Campy's scalpel-dodging antics did not sit well with Dressen, brought back in 1952 on the same salary and on a short leash. Nor was he happy to see Roy report to spring training at a husky 221 pounds. Once again, he put Campy on the Mayo diet as soon as he reached Florida. The sickening prospect of another spring of eggs morning, noon, and night horrified Roy, who wondered again whether Dressen's wacky diets sapped his power.

Campy stomached another go-around with Dressen's protein-rich menu that spring. He also swallowed the usual bitter pill of grinding segregation, although his patience and good humor were beginning to wear thin. He was tired of scrambling for a black cab to pick him up at the airport and staying at private homes in little towns such as Bradenton that lacked Negro hotels. He bristled when he heard that Bradenton's mayor was nervous that Campy and Jackie might not appear for a potentially lucrative local exhibition game. "If that mayor wants us so much, why won't he let us stay in his hotel?"

The final trip north from St. Petersburg to Baltimore, described by Sam Lacy as "the worst the tan Dodgers have experienced," showed how little the South had changed. At most stops, the black Dodgers and Boston Braves accompanying them depended on tips from "red caps and cab drivers as to 'the best place in town to eat,'" a crapshoot at best. In one Alabama town, the supposed "best place" featured "flies and roaches meeting customers at the door," prompting two players to opt instead for take-out chicken procured by a porter, according to Jim Crow protocol, from the back door of a diner. "The salary I get," observed Jackie, "should always include some kind of monetary reward for the humiliation and inconveniences that come to me."

Campy was inclined to agree, although he was determined not to let segregation affect his play. He forced himself to block out the ugly racial taunts heard in Mobile ("Hit him in the head," fans screeched at Robinson) and tried to concentrate on his preseason preparations. "Campy is all business," Dressen enthused happily at the end of spring training. "He is belting the ball hard and anxious to catch. He swears that, if I'll let him, he will catch 154 games this summer. Naturally, I don't want that, but you can't beat that kind of spirit."

SPIRIT ASIDE, no one was quite sure how the Dodgers would recover from the soul-crushing events of last season. The taunting had already begun. "Hello, Charlie," greeted one sportswriter, "how big a lead will you need this year?" Dressen, inwardly seething, claimed to be unconcerned. "I hear the Giants are laughing at us. . . . Let 'em laugh. Let 'em holler at us. Let 'em holler at Ralph Branca. I hope they do."

The Dodgers showed no signs of lingering aftereffects, winning eight of their first nine while throttling the Giants twice in three meetings. Campy, now installed in the cleanup position behind Robinson, was also off to a hot start with 3 homers and 13 RBIs in his first 38 at bats. He found that he enjoyed hitting behind Robinson, whose running game generated more fastballs in Roy's wheelhouse.

With Campy once again among the league leaders in average, homers, and RBIs, another MVP season appeared to be in the making. Instead, he would be dogged by an almost continuous string of nagging injuries.

The aches and pains began at Wrigley Field on May 3 when former Dodger farmhand Toby Atwell, Campy's replacement at St. Paul back in 1948, stupidly tried to score on a shallow fly ball to the rifle-armed Carl Furillo. Out by a good "ten feet," Atwell hurled himself into Roy "with a Bronko Nagurski charge," sending him crashing to the earth, ball still in hand. Campy was ready to take a poke at Atwell until a teammate hauled him away. He managed to finish the game but within three days his aching back and shoulders forced him to the bench.

No sooner had Roy recovered than he was on the receiving end of another bruising collision, this time with Gus Bell of the Pirates on May 16 at Ebbets. Bell, according to one report, hit Campy "so hard . . . that his spike cut through the nail on the backstop's big right toe." As a catcher, Roy was no stranger to contact, but this really did seem more football than baseball. Still, the Pirates were not done yet. Less than twenty-four hours later, rookie pitcher Ron Kline drilled Campy in the left wrist, probably unintentionally, but enough to sideline him for five more days.

Dressen felt no need to rush Roy back. At 20-7, the Dodgers had the best record in baseball and were riding a five-game winning streak. Not until Thursday, May 22, did Campy pronounce himself ready to return against the Reds at Ebbets. Hitless in his first three at bats, he belted a three-run, game-tying blast in the eighth for his first homer in a month. The Dodgers went on to win 8–7, thanks to a fine relief performance by the team's latest Negro addition, Roy's old teammate Joe Black, who earned his first major league victory.

With Roy's confidence again on the upswing, he joked with writers before Friday's game at Shibe Park about the vitamins he was now taking ("You'd be surprised . . . the power that's in these little eggs"). And the "little eggs" appeared to be working. Not only did he slam the first pitch he saw from Karl Drews that night into the upper deck, but an inning later he crushed a grand slam that sailed nearly over the left-field roof. With 3 homers and 8 RBIs in his last 3 at bats, Roy couldn't help but feel that the worst was over.

It wasn't. That same night, the Phils' Jackie Mayo came tearing around third base trying to score on a single by Drews. The relay from Andy Pafko was in plenty of time, and Mayo, like Atwell and Bell before him, tried to dislodge the ball by plowing headlong into Campy. Once again, Roy held on but got the worst of the collision: another spiking and a damaged right thumb that would require a cast and keep him out of the lineup for the next twelve days.

Dressen had seen enough. Campanella, he complained to reporters, was "too darn polite. . . . He just stands there and lets those guys come charging into him. I keep telling him to stick it in their mush. Give it to 'em once and they won't come barging in anymore." Campy, meanwhile, dismissed all talk of his supposed courtly behavior, likely instilled by Rickey years earlier. "Me polite? . . . I ain't polite. I'll tag them fellows."

Campanella was not the only catcher with problems on collisions. Within days of Dressen's comments, Casey Stengel was also urging Yogi Berra to be more aggressive around the plate. But if Campy had an Achilles' heel, it was tag plays, and even Pee Wee Reese would later suggest that "he didn't block the plate like Westrum or Del Rice or Walker Cooper." Dressen, ever the know-it-all, felt the problem was easily solved. "He should step up the line, blocking the path, and swing away as he makes the out. . . . Campy told me he waits because he is afraid they will slide. I told him if he is up the line they would have to slide too soon and he has them blocked anyway."

The thumb cast, Campy's first in more than fifteen years of catching, finally came off in early June. Once again, Roy seemed to be getting on track. He put together a nine-game hitting streak, raising his average to .284, and was now third in the NL in RBIs. On June 19 he caught what he believed to be the first no-hitter of his long career: a one-walk masterpiece by Carl Erskine at Ebbets against the Cubbies.

Campy (far left) with the Nicetown Giants, circa 1936. (*Sporting News*)

Campanella, age sixteen, in his second year with the Elite Giants. This photograph originally appeared in the September 25, 1938, *Philadelphia Tribune,* which misidentified Campy as "George Campanella." (John W. Mosley, Blockson Collection, Temple University Libraries)

A 1942 shot of Campy, probably taken around the time of his aborted tryout with the Pittsburgh Pirates. (Larry Lester/Noir Tech)

Campy never forgot Branch Rickey's role in the Great Experiment. Here the two men pose for the signing of Campy's 1950 contract. (Larry Lester/Noir Tech)

Dodger manager Leo Durocher with his new three-catcher lineup, July 1948. From left to right: Bruce Edwards, Gil Hodges, Durocher, Campanella. (*Sporting News*)

Campy and Jackie Robinson at the Harlem YMCA, November 1948.
(University of Minnesota Libraries)

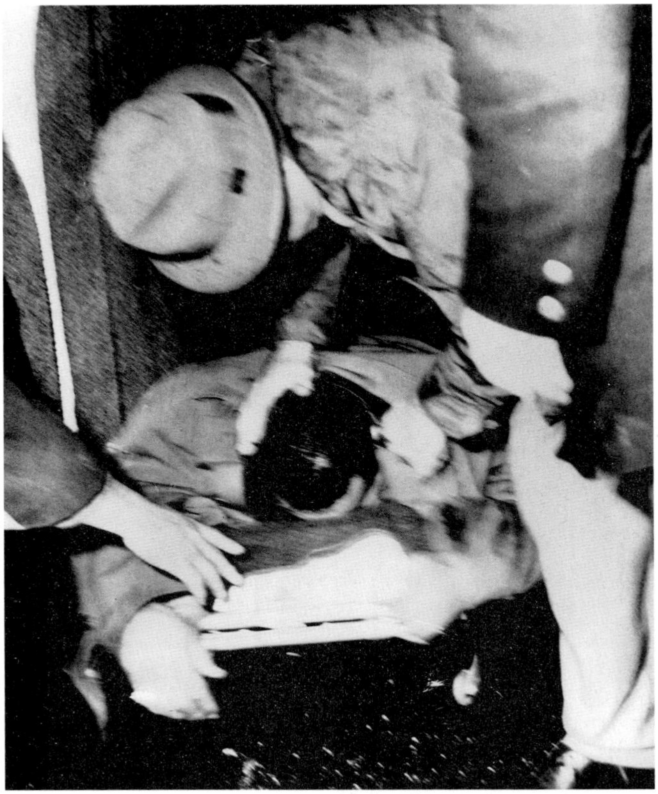

Campy is placed in an ambulance moments after his accident, January 28, 1958. This photo is the only known shot of Campanella taken that night. (*Sporting News*)

The Chevy rental car Campanella drove on the night of the accident. (John Drennan, Nassau County Department of Parks, Recreation & Museums, Photo Archives Center)

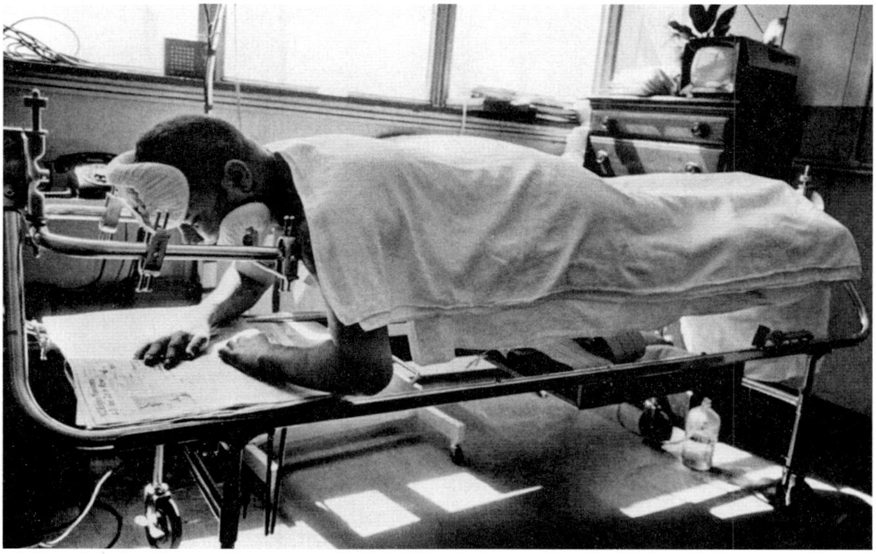

Campanella, his body immobile in a Stryker frame, reads the sports pages at the Institute of Physical Medicine and Rehabilitation, New York, May 1958. (George Silk, AP/Wide World Photos)

Campy with Dr. Howard Rusk, attendant Leroy Newson, and Dr. Edward Lowman at his first postaccident press conference, held at the Institute of Physical Medicine and Rehabilitation, New York, September 1958. (National Baseball Hall of Fame Library, Cooperstown, NY)

A family portrait taken shortly after Roy's hospital discharge, November 1958. Despite the smiles, Campy's quadriplegia had already begun to affect his marriage. (John Drennan, Nassau County Department of Parks, Recreation & Museums, Photo Archives Center)

On May 7, 1959, 93,103 fans honored Campanella at the Los Angeles Coliseum, an attendance record that stood for forty-nine years. (*Sporting News*)

Campy in a rare shot with his daughter Joyce from his first marriage and granddaughter Gale, July 1959. Years later, Gale attempted to reach out to the grandfather she never knew. (John W. Mosley, Blockson Collection, Temple University Libraries)

With the publication of *Baseball Has Done It* in 1964, Jackie and Campy publicly mended fences at Roy's liquor store. (Bettmann/Corbis)

Campy in 1980 with his third wife, Roxie, who brought much-needed peace and stability to his life. (*Baltimore Afro-American*)

Campy speaks to the crowd at his Baseball Hall of Fame induction ceremony in 1969, while Commissioner Bowie Kuhn looks on. (National Baseball Hall of Fame Library, Cooperstown, NY)

Jackie, Campy, and Sandy Koufax together for their uniform retirement ceremony at Dodger Stadium, June 1972. Less than five months later, Robinson was dead at the age of fifty-three. (Harry Adams, Institute for Arts & Media, California State University, Northridge)

Despite Campy's uneven start, the Dodgers rolled into the All-Star break five games ahead of their 1951 pace with a major league best 51-21 record. Except for Hodges and Furillo, the vets had performed capably, and the pitching staff appeared stronger than in '51, thanks to the clutch contributions of Billy Loes and Joe Black. Still, Durocher's Giants trailed only by 4½ games, even after losing Irvin to a broken ankle and Mays to the army for two years. "If Willie gets any better," a relieved Campy quipped, "I don't want to see him."

Roy, his various bumps and bruises just about healed, was hoping for an injury-free second half. But the Dodgers had barely played two games before he was again writhing in pain. On Friday, July 11, Campy tried to pick off Gene Hermanski at first base in the eighth inning of a tight game at Wrigley Field. As he followed through on his throw, his hand struck the bat of the current hitter, of all people his recent nemesis Toby Atwell. Although Roy refused to leave the game, he was in no shape to play the next day.

The hand felt no better at the Dodgers' next stop in St. Louis. By Monday morning, the normally doctor-phobic Campy was desperate enough to stop at Homer G. Phillips Hospital, the local Negro facility, for X-rays. "I knew I was doing the wrong thing the minute I walked in the door and got a whiff of that ether. But I'd gotten that far so I went ahead." The diagnosis was not good: a fracture of the second metacarpal bone of his right hand. Casting was recommended but Campy declined, at least for now.

When he arrived at Sportsman's Park a few hours later, he learned of another crisis in Dodgerland. Jackie Robinson, informed that his wife had been hospitalized for emergency surgery (for what proved to be a benign breast lump), had just left the park "in tears" and had hopped a flight to New York to be at her side. Campy then went to Dressen and asked to play. "A lot of people are here to see Robbie and me, and they're going to be disappointed if both of us are out," he explained. "Maybe I can help the club." Barely able to throw or grip the bat, Roy amazed everyone by catching all nine innings of a Carl Erskine shutout and punching a run-scoring single to right.

Roy continued to play throughout the remainder of the road trip, although Dressen made Campy promise he would see Dodger physician Eugene Zorn when he returned home. Zorn confirmed the diagnosis and put Roy in a cast for the second time that season. He would not appear in the lineup again until the end of July.

In all his years of catching, he had never experienced such a nightmarish season, and he could no longer contain his frustration. Mr. Happy-Go-Lucky was now given to brooding about his misfortunes while exposing a seldom-seen surly side. "Like to see one of you fellers in the press box come down and try to hit Robin Roberts with sore hands," he complained. He also took it personally when Roger Kahn wrote of a lack of spirit on the Dodger bench following a George Shuba home run. "I can't clap. My hand's broke," he barked. "I ought to punch you right in the jaw." Roy eventually simmered down, but Dressen later warned Kahn, "You shouldn't rile Campy. . . . He's worried about himself."

The anxiety was just as noticeable on the field. Umpires were shocked to discover that the supposedly "gentlemanly" Campy's fuse had suddenly grown remarkably short. Now he was seen throwing his bat after taking a called third strike and "tore off his glove, his cap and maybe some of his hair" on a contested call by an incompetent ump named Augie Guglielmo, who lasted only a single year in the National League. By the end of the season, the "happiest man in baseball" had been ejected a league-leading three times. Rickey's shackles were, at long last, off.

The team's success was his only consolation. Despite injuries and sore arms galore, the Dodgers began the final month a full nine games up on the Giants. Dressen, by most reports, had done a reasonably good job thus far. He had not overused his regulars (except perhaps Campy, who caught twenty-seven straight games including eight doubleheaders at one point), and he had generally kept his big mouth in check.

The Giants, true to form, were not about to go down without a fight. Monte Irvin's return in late July had not only helped to kick-start the offense but gave the club an emotional lift. Maglie, apparently over midseason back woes, was again resembling the pitcher who had shut out the Dodgers in his first three starts. Then there was Durocher's penchant for sign-stealing. Although author Joshua Prager has suggested that the Giants retired their telescope in 1952, both the Phillies and the Braves were convinced "something funny went on during their games" at the Polo Grounds that year.

Telescope or not, the Giants went on another furious tear, winning fourteen of eighteen and slicing the lead to 3½ games by September 12. The accursed "Creeping Terror" of 1951 was back for an encore. "If they lose the pennant this year," remarked one Brooklyn fan sadly, "I'll never watch them again. It's like someone in your family getting operated on every day. I just haven't that much emotion to invest." Durocher envisioned a more extreme scenario: "I know one thing. If we ever should beat them now, there'd be one hundred thousand suicides over there in Brooklyn."

The borough's mounting anxiety was intensified by two concurrent developments. In the midst of the Giants' surge, Dressen's *Saturday Evening Post* article (ghostwritten weeks earlier), fittingly titled "We Won't Blow It Again," appeared on the newsstands amid much snickering from the non-Brooklyn public. Even more distressing to Dodger fans was Jackie Robinson's talk of quitting after an altercation with umpire Larry Goetz and a subsequent $75 fine from NL president Warren Giles ("the most incompetent man," according to Jackie). Once again, Robinson began to hear boos.

Giles also slapped a $100 fine on Campy, ejected by Frank Secory only minutes before Robinson's brouhaha with Goetz. "He told me to shut up and I said, 'Listen, Frank, this is no schoolroom. I'm a grown man. I can talk to you.'" Campy wondered whether race factored into Giles's punishments, citing Wes Westrum's lesser $50 fine last year for pushing an umpire, albeit with a three-day suspension attached. Still, Campy paid up without formal complaint, setting up more inevitable comparisons with Jackie.

Despite Leo's dreams of another miracle, the Giants never got closer than three games. On September 23, the Dodgers finally nailed down the pennant that had eluded them in 1950 and 1951. Three days later, the Yankees clinched their fourth straight American League flag. For the fourth time in twelve seasons, the Bronx Bombers and Bums would be squaring off for all the marbles.

This year's Brooks appeared likely to put up a better fight than Shotton's 1949 version, at least if Dressen had anything to say about it. The Yankees, he defiantly announced, are "not a great club." "As I told my players . . . there are no DiMaggios, Henrichs, and the others up there to scare you anymore." Robinson agreed, "We are ready for them this time, both mentally and physically." Even the Brooklyn official press buttons, unused leftovers from last year's disaster, conveyed an air of optimism, boldly proclaiming THIS IS NEXT YEAR.

Campy was less confident. He had missed more time recently, thanks to a "neglected hangnail" turned serious left-arm infection. His right hand had never quite recovered, and his production down the stretch had been minimal. "The hand is bad," sighed Dodger physician Eugene Zorn. "And it will stay bad for a while. . . . He won't be able to grip the bat." But Roy gave no thoughts to sitting. "I want to play in this series bad. All year I been thinking about playing in it."

Dressen decided on a bold stroke to start the Series. In the last week of the season, he had moved rookie sensation Joe Black out of the bullpen and was now handing him the ball in game one at Ebbets. Black attributed much of his success this year to his old Negro League mentor. "Campy's smart," he explained. "Because of him, I'm breaking my curve better, and because of him, I'm mixing it in with a little fast stuff. . . . Watching him, no one can possibly know how much he means to a team and to a pitcher, the way he gives you confidence, sets up the hitters and all that."

Roy had simple advice for Black against the Yanks. "I told him, relax and feel free. . . . You can't throw the ball where you want it every time. Stop aiming the ball." Black obliged, scattering six hits in a 4–2 complete-game victory over the defending (and still all-white) world champs. "I killed them both," a near-euphoric Dressen crowed afterward. "I killed the magazine article . . . and the others . . . who were going to second-guess me for starting Black." "EXPERTS: DROP DEAD," happily proclaimed the headline of the *Brooklyn Eagle*'s late edition that day.

But the always indomitable Yankees quickly bounced back to take game two, thanks to a three-hit, 131-pitch performance by Vic Raschi. Preacher Roe then returned the favor in game three at Yankee Stadium, heaving 156 pitches to subdue the Bombers 5–3. In game four, it was all Allie Reynolds, who punched out ten Dodgers, including Robinson three times and Campy twice, in a brilliant four-hit shutout. "I was kidding Larry Doby the other day about not being able to hit Reynolds," remarked Roy. "But I know why now. And it ain't funny, up there swinging at something darting at you outa those Yankee Stadium shadows."

With the series tied at two, 70,536 fans jammed Yankee Stadium on Sunday, October 5. Among them was a young senator from California named Richard Nixon, who just twelve days earlier had saved his place on the Eisenhower ticket with a manipulative but effective nationally telecast speech invoking his family's dog, Checkers. Nixon was in full campaign mode that afternoon, munching on hot dogs and drinking soda pop like an average Joe and making a point to meet Campy and Jackie. Ever the politician, he declared he would favor neither club. "I'll cheer all the good plays, and I'm for the best team."

Nixon saw a fantastic yet strangely forgotten game that day. The Dodgers took a quick 4–0 lead off Ewell Blackwell, now an American Leaguer, only to fall behind 5–4 in the fifth following Johnny Mize's three-run homer off Erskine. At that moment, Dressen again gambled, allowing "Oisk" to stay in. The fates suddenly began to turn against the Yankees. Erskine set down the next nineteen hitters, the Dodgers tied the score in the seventh, and umpire Art Passarella killed a potential Yankee rally by calling out Johnny Sain on an obvious infield single in the tenth. In the eleventh inning, with one out and the Dodgers up by one, an apparent game-tying home run by the always scary Mize fell harmlessly into Furillo's glove. "I didn't want to see it," said Campy afterward. "When disaster is staring me in the face, I find it very easy to turn my back." Berra then struck out, and the Dodgers now led the series 3-2, with games six and seven to follow at Ebbets.

With just 3 hits in 20 at bats, Roy had not done much the first five games. Still, he had thwarted three of four Yankee base-stealing attempts while handling the pitching staff with aplomb. In game six, he would be working with the talented but eccentric Billy Loes, who had already publicly predicted that the Yankees would win in six. "I wish I was making two hundred dollars the rest of my life and not working for it," he once observed. "I'd like to be a gigolo. I'd like to be a movie star." Such musings often elicited guffaws, but Campy genuinely liked the kid. "Billy may not be a genius on the street, but when he's pitching, he's smart."

Loes looked plenty smart for the first six innings, holding the Yanks scoreless while the Dodgers clung to a 1–0 lead. In the seventh, however, the would-be gigolo suffered a sudden meltdown. He allowed a homer to Berra, committed a bizarre balk, then took a smash off his leg ("the sun blinded me," he famously claimed) that caromed into right field for the go-ahead run. After the Dodgers went down to a 3–2 defeat, even the usually supportive Campy had lost patience. "Whatever possessed you to throw that ball to Berra?" he griped.

Tuesday, October 7, was a chilly day for a deciding game. "Topcoat weather," said Mel Allen on the NBC telecast. For the second straight game, Ebbets was strangely not sold out. Dressen went with Joe Black for the third time, Stengel with Ed Lopat.

Campy soon realized that Black, working on two days' rest for the second time in four days, had nothing. Mickey Mantle's solo homer and Mize's single chased him in the sixth, and the Yankees tacked on another in the seventh to go up 4–2. Lopat, meanwhile, had not survived the fourth, but Reynolds, relieving for the second time in two days, once again stifled the Dodger bats.

The Bums had one last chance in the seventh. In a peculiar move, Stengel brought in the previous day's starter, Vic Raschi, who promptly loaded the bases with one out. With Duke Snider, who already had four Series homers, up next, Casey called for lefty Bob Kuzava. Snider worked the count to 3-2, while Dodger fans, aware of Kuzava's control problems, dreamed of a walk or something better. Instead, Snider popped harmlessly to third, leaving it up to Jackie Robinson. After a long foul sent the crowd's hearts fluttering momentarily, Robinson blooped a shallow pop-up near second base that no one seemed to want to catch. At the last moment, Billy Martin ("that fresh kid I got at second," remarked Stengel) raced in, his cap flying off, to save the day with a fine shoestring grab. The inning was over, the Dodgers went down easily in the eighth and ninth, and the Yankees, for the fourth straight year, were champs.

As the mournful fans departed Ebbets, organist Gladys Goodding dug deep into her repertoire for appropriate fare, offering "This Nearly Was Mine" and "You Got Me Cryin' Again," among other chestnuts. Dodger Nation, once again processing another defeat, pointed to Robinson (.174), Campy (.214, 1 RBI), and particularly Hodges, who went 0 for 21 after ending the season 0 for his last 10. Then there was that damned Yankee mystique. "Why do the Dodgers always have to lose?" asked Jimmy Cannon. "Why couldn't they get one little break?"

Campy, packing his gear and heading home to St. Albans, could only hope that the Dodgers' fortunes, along with his own, would be better in 1953. "They'll come through eventually," wrote Bob Considine. "If no other good provider appears, St. Law of Averages must give them an eventual benediction."

• • •

ALONG WITH the rest of the Brooklyn brain trust, Walter O'Malley sat down after the Series to assess the recent campaign. The club had performed well on the field, and its 1.088 million attendance led the National League. Still, he wondered what had happened to the 1.8 million who had shown up five years earlier. Why were Series games six and seven, both potential clinchers, not sold out? Certain that "the fans are no longer as emotionally attached to the ball club as they once were," he blindly groped for answers in the months ahead. A more colorful team. "Metered" (pay) television. Above all, a new park.

O'Malley also set out to light a fire under his chubby catcher, whose tummy appeared to be expanding faster than his batting average. Did Campy want to stay in baseball after he was through playing, perhaps as a Dodger coach? Then he would need to make a more concerted effort to stay in shape. "I want him to set an example to the others," said O'Malley. "Before he learns to handle other men, he's got to be able to handle himself."

Campy was not surprised by O'Malley's critique of his conditioning. He was getting older, and Dressen remained obsessed about his weight, especially after an injury-riddled season. Campy liked the idea of coaching, a job he found far more appealing than managing, at least right now (his stint as a winter-league pilot, he told a reporter, "didn't improve his rest and peace of mind"). "Mr. O'Malley has offered me a great opportunity . . . and you can bet I'm not going to flub it. . . . To me baseball is more than a game. It's a religion."

His devotion to his chosen faith was never more obvious than during that winter. Following his usual barnstorming gig, this time with no competition from Robinson, too busy with his new department store, he returned home determined to cut down on the fried foods and starches he loved so much. As he wrestled with the inevitable hunger pangs, he turned to his model trains for distraction. "When I played with the trains, I wouldn't think about eating. So I ate less. Kept my mind busy and I lost weight."

To further melt away the pounds, Campy headed to Hot Springs, Arkansas, in February with Ruthe and the kids for pre–spring training workouts and to sample the resort's famous baths. The soothing waters had jump-started his 1951 MVP campaign, and he hoped for a similar result this time around.

Future NFL Hall of Famer Bobby Mitchell, then a Hot Springs teenager, recalled the thrill of mingling with Roy and other elite black athletes who came into his town each year. "I was crazy about Campy. He'd try to play basketball with us, but no basketball playing for him." Mitchell chuckled. "Always had that smile. Now, he could get pissed off. . . . He wanted you to be good. He'd get upset with any of us if we wasn't putting it out."

One day, Roy went to watch a local Negro high school basketball game and noticed that Mitchell was not in uniform. "I got to work," the teen explained. "I got to get a suit for graduation."

Campy would have none of it. "Nah, you meet me downtown."

Campy provided the money for Mitchell's suit and told the youngster to get back on the court.

Mitchell did, graduated, and then went on to college and stardom in the NFL. He hung on to that suit "forever," a reminder of Campy's willingness to serve as a mentor and role model. "If anything happened within our community and he wanted to do something about it, he could have," Mitchell recalled. "He had that kind of influence."

THE HARD work that winter paid off. Campy reported to Vero Beach eighteen pounds lighter than last spring, although not quite slim enough to win the hat Bavasi had promised him if he went below two hundred. The press was fascinated with his new look, particularly the mustache he now sported thanks to a shaving holiday during the barnstorming season. Sportswriters wondered whether Campy would crack the current major league mustache barrier, but Roy stuck with it just long enough to win a bet with Reese, who doubted he would report with the offending facial hair. In the future, Pee Wee would have the honor of shearing Campy's winter growth each spring.

Among the Dodger beatwriters, Campy's Clark Gable–like appearance soon took a backseat to a bigger story at Vero Beach: the plans for last year's International League MVP, a promising Negro youngster named Jim Gilliam. Years earlier, Gilliam had served as batboy for Campy and the other Elite Giants during their visits to Nashville. The Elites eventually signed Gilliam, later selling him, along with Joe Black and another prospect, to Brooklyn for $10,000, one of the best deals the Dodgers ever made.

Dressen quickly determined that Gilliam was good enough to push

Jackie off second to third and relegate Cox to a utility man. While Robinson was not exactly thrilled, Cox was so incensed that he heaved his duffel bag out of a ninth-floor hotel window. The real issue, the press soon gathered, was race. "Some of the white players," Robinson later explained, "felt it was unfair to remove Cox in order to bring another colored player into the infield." The Dodgers in question, among them Preacher Roe and Bobby Morgan, openly made their feelings known through wisecracks about blacks "taking over." "Pretty soon now they'll have to be getting special hotels for us," quipped another.

With the controversy now press fodder and threatening to spiral further out of control, spin doctor Bavasi had to act fast. "We have never had any dissension on the club and never will," he announced. Typical media exaggeration, that was all. To further reassure nervous fans, a photo of Jackie and Cox shaking hands appeared in the *Journal-American*, always eager to toe the Dodger party line. But the *Post*'s Milton Gross was not so easily appeased. "Negro baiting remarks were made, not all in jest," he observed. "Why and how could this have happened on a team which served as the classic demonstration that whites and Negroes can work side by side, not with tolerance, but with respect?"

The Great Experiment had succeeded beyond Rickey's wildest dreams. But an undercurrent of resentment still existed, even though such feelings rarely flared openly. "Unlike what was often reported, the Dodgers weren't always unified," Don Newcombe later recalled. "There was a lot of infighting that went on, much hate and animosity. . . . We were going to take away someone's job." It was Bavasi, according to Campy, who kept racial tensions under control. "If Buzzie saw something coming, he'd call a player in and just say a few words, and it would be all over."

Gilliam's superior defense, batting eye, and speed soon erased any doubts about his addition to the Brooklyn infield. Campy and Jackie also did their part to smooth his transition to the big leagues, briefing the youngster on appropriate behavior for a Negro Dodger. Although the generally reserved Gilliam never took a formal side in the current Campanella/Robinson cold war, it soon became obvious that the rookie was in Robbie's corner, particularly when he began to room with Jackie. "He and Jackie got along fine," noted Monte Irvin. "He didn't have any problem because he would go along with whatever Jackie wanted to do."

• • •

GILLIAM WAS only one part of the reconfigured Brooks roster for 1953. Obliging Dressen's wish for another starter, Bavasi swung a three-way deal with the Phillies and the Braves, picking up Russ Meyer, the same hothead who had nearly come to blows with Robinson in 1951. A young left-hander named Johnny Podres, whom Dressen had futilely campaigned for last spring, would also round out the staff. Andy Pafko and his $30,000 salary had been traded to the Braves, leaving a gaping hole in left field. The usual suspects—Don Thompson, Dick Williams, and George Shuba—would briefly be trotted out as replacements, but Jackie would eventually volunteer to play left, freeing Cox's return to third.

Phillies skipper Steve O'Neill was not impressed by the roster shuffling. "Brooklyn will never—never, I say—have another year like last year," he announced. Certainly, they would never repeat their 54-11 record against the league's bottom-feeders. But Campy liked Podres a lot ("that boy—he's got it"), and he had faith in the rest of the much-maligned Dodger pitching staff. His only concern was himself. "I'm just praying that I don't get hurt this year," he sighed. "If I don't, I feel pretty confident I'm going to have a real good year."

The 12,433 fans who shivered through forty-degree weather at the Dodgers opener on April 14 left Ebbets that afternoon convinced that Campy was going to have a "real good year." He cracked three hits in the first five innings, including a three-run homer off Murry Dickson, while the Dodgers beat up on the Pirates again. The old Roy, 1951 vintage, appeared to be back. "My hands," he explained later, "they're in good shape."

As he continued to tattoo the ball, it became clear that something else was going on. Roy had changed his stance, moving closer to the plate, although he tried his best to keep it a secret. Even without the video available today, National League pitchers were soon onto Campy's attempt to expand his plate coverage. "They don't pitch me the way they used to," he mused. "I used to know what to look for when I went up there, but now they throw me all different stuff in all different spots."

Fastball, slider, curve, screwball—it made little difference. By the morning of May 13, he was leading the National League in hits (34), home runs (10), RBIs (40, 19 ahead of his nearest competitor), average (.395), and slugging (.826). Pressed for an explanation, Roy refused to overanalyze his success. "I'm just trying to meet the ball. . . . I'm swinging smooth. I'm swinging easy."

He was also carrying the Dodgers as never before. Twice in May he crushed walk-off homers, including a dramatic three-run blast to beat the Giants on May 27, although Jolly Cholly couldn't help but take a little credit for that one. With two on, two outs, and the Dodgers trailing by one, Dressen called Campy over and told him to look for the curve from Jim Hearn. "And that's exactly what Hearn did, he threw me a curve, and I hit it upstairs in the bleachers." "Didn't I tell you?" Dressen roared as Campy circled the bases.

As his offensive numbers continued to skyrocket, the press began to dig into the record books. Campanella's blast off Hearn gave him 16 homers and 51 RBIs after only 35 games, better than Babe Ruth's 1927 home-run and Hack Wilson's 1930 RBI record-setting paces. Not surprisingly, the national media came calling. *Life*, the mass-circulation, glossy-picture newsmagazine, put Roy on the cover of its June 8 edition with the caption "Baseball's Greatest Catcher." Eleven shots of Campy on the field, at his liquor store, and at home with his family (including Ruthe, whose pregnancy was probably intentionally obscured) accompanied the piece. "They shot pictures of me in so many different angles you would have thought I was a shooting gallery and they were trying to hit the bull's-eye," he quipped later.

His star was undeniably on the rise. Gilbert Millstein, whose review of *On the Road* in 1957 made Jack Kerouac famous, profiled Campy in the *New York Times Magazine*. He was invited to appear as the mystery guest on CBS's popular *What's My Line,* although the blindfolded panel had no trouble identifying the gum-chomping Campy ("You sound so rugged," cooed Dorothy Kilgallen). Gordon & Gordon, twin black comedians, recorded a song about him for Capitol Records. Business at the liquor store, along with autograph requests, went through the roof.

By June, Browns owner Bill Veeck told Jimmy Cannon that Campy, along with Robinson, were the two "guys with the greatest personal followings in the game." Somewhere, Branch Rickey was smiling.

DESPITE CAMPY'S superhuman heroics, the National League race was no runaway early on. Winners of nineteen of twenty-two by mid-June, the Dodgers still found themselves in a dogfight, not with the Giants, but the Braves, now Milwaukee-based thanks to the first major league franchise shift in fifty years. Roy had cooled off, his average dipping below .300. His futility became so pronounced that an old woman stopped him on 125th Street in Harlem one day, set down her bag of groceries, and gave him batting tips.

But before long, his stroke returned. By the break, he was in the midst of an eleven-game hitting streak that would bump his average to .305. He even managed to get his first-ever All-Star hit, poking an eighth-inning single in Cincinnati off the Ageless One, forty-six-year-old Satchel Paige of the Browns. Roy couldn't help but think back to their 1941 East-West confrontation. Who among the thousands present that day could have foreseen that no fewer than five former Negro Leaguers would be appearing in a major league All-Star Game just twelve years later?

Baseball, in its own sluggish fashion, had changed in unexpected ways. Even bigoted fossils such as Ty Cobb had shown signs of mellowing. "I see no reason in the world why we shouldn't compete with Negro athletes as long as they conduct themselves with politeness and gentility," the Georgia Peach drawled in 1952. Cobb was particularly impressed by a young minor league hitter named Henry Aaron and also admired Jackie's talents. "Cobb once told me," Dressen later related, "that he got more kick out of watching Robinson play than any other player in the majors."

Another Negro player would catch his eye that summer. After the break, Wendell Smith interviewed Cobb at a Dodgers/Cubs game at Wrigley on July 29. Which player on the field, Smith asked, "impressed him the most?" Cobb pointed to Campy. "That fella's a great catcher. . . . The very best in the game. He reminds me a little of Roger Bresnahan. If he can stick around for five or six more years, they'll have to put him alongside the game's all-time catchers."

That the legendary Cobb, who had little use for most modern players, white or black, had praised Roy so effusively was another feather in his cap. But he received an even bigger thrill that same day: news that his wife had given birth to a daughter, named Ruthe, who would quickly become known as Princess. With three boys in the household, Roy and Ruthe were delighted with the arrival of a girl this time around (Joyce and Beverly did occasionally visit from Philadelphia but were seldom publicly mentioned).

The proud papa was soon photographed diapering his new daughter and even gave tips to new dad Ralph Kiner on the fine art of baby-changing.

Everything that had gone wrong in 1952 was now going right. Meanwhile, the Dodgers had begun to put some distance on the pesky Braves, taking three of four at Ebbets in late July to build a 7½-game lead. While not yet approaching Dodgers/Giants standards, signs of bad blood between the two clubs had begun to surface. Campy exchanged harsh words with Johnny Antonelli after a knockdown pitch, while Robinson nearly came to blows with Lew Burdette, who called him a "black bastard" for daring to bunt in a run.

Burdette, a West Virginian known for his "adolescent sense of humor," had a history of racial altercations. As a Yankee farmhand, he had badly beaned Jim Pendleton, then a Dodger minor leaguer at St. Paul (and now, ironically, Burdette's teammate), in a rainstorm, sending him to a hospital. Robinson had been Burdette's sworn enemy ever since Jackie stole home off him in the blowout game of the final Boston series in 1951. Since then, Burdette had never failed to take his revenge with brushbacks and even a tag that Jackie thought disproportionately hard.

Burdette was on the mound when the Braves and the Dodgers next met, this time in Milwaukee on August 3. With Robinson out of the lineup that night, a repeat of the near fisticuffs at Ebbets the previous week appeared unlikely. Instead, the large Monday crowd of 32,739 was transfixed by a scoreless pitcher's duel between Burdette and Russ Meyer, finally broken by the Dodgers in the top of the seventh. Trailing 1–0, the Braves failed to score in their half of the inning as rain began to fall.

In the eighth, Snider led off with a homer. According to baseball custom, the next hitter could expect chin music, but Hodges popped out without seeing anything unduly close. Instead, Burdette saved his firepower for Campy, hurling the first pitch at his head. Roy said nothing and worked the count to 2-2, only to find himself on the receiving end of a second beanball. On the next pitch, he struck out swinging.

Burdette didn't like the hostility he saw in Campy's scowl. "Black nigger bastard," he shouted. At that moment, Roy completely lost it. Bat still tightly in hand, he headed straight for the mound, prepared to give Burdette the thrashing of his life, at least until Del Crandall and Furillo somehow restrained and disarmed him. Meanwhile, the dugouts emptied, with Eddie Mathews heading for Roy, only to be tossed aside by the mighty yet gentle Hodges. Strangely, umpire Tom Gorman ejected no one, claiming afterward that he didn't hear Burdette's remark. Campy would tell a different story. "Why did you call him that," Gorman supposedly scolded Burdette, "and start all this?"

Ironically, the rain washed the eighth inning, and Campy's fateful strikeout, from the books. But the story of the "near riot" at County Stadium did not immediately disappear. The media, intrigued that Mr. Congeniality had uncharacteristically lost control, breathlessly pumped him for an explanation. "I never said a word to the man," he announced. "I was walking back to the dugout and he called me a name. If I'd of got to that man, I'd of broken the bat across his head." As the writers' jaws dropped, Roy quickly reverted to his Lovable Old Campy persona. "No, I wouldn't," he said with a smile. "The bat—I just didn't have time to get rid of it." As for Burdette's claim that pitching inside was his "bread and butter," Roy was dismissive. "My head ain't his bread and butter."

Although Campy complained that Burdette "would like to have killed me with that ball," the bigger issue was the N-word, which was becoming increasingly frowned upon as baseball's integration accelerated. Not surprisingly, Burdette's three black teammates confronted him about his racial remarks.

For the first time, Campy found himself being labeled "controversial," a word anathema in postwar America. The Milwaukee fans were merciless for the remainder of the series, hurling cushions and eggs initially and then booing his every appearance. "It seems funny to hear Campy booed," noted one Dodger official. "It has never happened anywhere else in the league." Only after a thirteen-year-old Milwaukee girl named Margaret wrote him a sympathetic and well-publicized letter did the tide begin to turn.

The boos would dissipate but the story of Campy's altercation with Burdette would live on in baseball lore, with the predictable distortions over time. By the end of his life, Burdette would claim that his "smile" following the strikeout provoked Campy. Roy, who developed a soft spot for Burdette after he visited Campy following his accident, similarly downplayed or ignored the racial aspect of the incident to some interviewers. He would also boast that he homered off Burdette in his next at bat, although it was actually on his seventh try.

The Burdette affair revealed that Campanella, despite his reputation as nonconfrontational, was very much aware of the racism that still surrounded him. His usual strategy throughout his life was to ignore or avoid it. At times, however, he simply could not.

DURING THE remainder of August, the Bums bludgeoned their opponents into submission, reeling off thirteen straight victories while building a double-digit lead over the Braves. As for Leo and company, six straight losses to the Dodgers confirmed Dressen's earlier "Giants is dead" declaration. His grammar caused a good deal of snickering, although the *Brooklyn Eagle* and the New York Board of Education leaped to his defense, arguing "the term Giants refers to an entity, a single body," as in the *United States.*

Roy was also on fire, reaching base eleven straight times at one point. During the Dodgers' August surge, he hit a torrid .407, slugged 8 homers, and drove in 32 runs to give him 124 RBIs for the season, a new National League record for catchers. The rest of the Brooklyn lineup was just as deadly. Snider and Hodges had both amassed more than 100 RBIs by the end of August, Furillo was in the midst of a career year, and Robinson and Gilliam were almost always on base. The pitching, as Campy had predicted, had been surprisingly decent, anchored by Erskine, on his way to his first 20-win season.

The fans, and most of baseball, were certain that the Bums could not be beaten this year. Even the frightening news of the Russians' successful H-bomb test failed to dampen borough spirits. "We'll worry about that," observed one Brooklynite, "after we take the Yanks in the Series." Unlike the last four Septembers, there was little drama in the final weeks of the season. The only question now was how many games the Dodgers would win (Dressen's wish was 100) and how soon the team would clinch.

Campy had more personal goals in mind. As his RBIs continued to pile up, he broke the Dodger record of 130, then surpassed his hero Bill Dickey's major league mark for catchers of 133. On September 6, his thirty-eighth homer, a second-inning smash off Ruben Gomez at the Polo Grounds, set a new major league record for catchers, one that would stand for forty-three years. Unfortunately, the historic blast was overshadowed by what followed moments later. Gomez drilled Furillo, who then decided it was time, at long last, to take care of Durocher. In the ensuing free-for-all, someone—Durocher, Irvin, or Jim Hearn, depending on the telling—broke Furillo's pinkie, sidelining him for the remainder of the regular season. Poor Furillo didn't even get off a good shot. "I'd pay a thousand dollars if I'd hit him. It would be worth it."

Even without Furillo, the Dodgers clinched their second straight National League title six days later in Milwaukee. In the postgame hilarity, hats were destroyed, some of the Brooklyn brass were pushed in showers, and booze flowed freely. "I shoulda had that order," Campy kidded to O'Malley, motioning to the bubbly. "How do you think I'm gonna keep my liquor store if the Dodger business is going somewhere else?" The Big O reassured him that if the Dodgers won the Series, he'd "double the order," get more at Christmas, and require the manager and coaches to buy from Campy's store. "I guess that'll get it," said Roy, beaming, "but you didn't say I could help 'em drink it. How come?"

The Yankees' Phil Rizzuto, a veteran of too many clinchings to remember (and still another on September 14), scoffed at the televised Brooklyn celebration as "tame" and predicted the Bums wouldn't be partying for long. "If those Dodgers couldn't beat us last year, then they never will beat the Yankees in the World's Series." But old-timers such as Rogers Hornsby felt 105 wins could not be taken lightly. "This is the Dodgers' best club," he insisted. "If they go into the series with confidence, they should win easily." If not, they "ought to slit their throats."

Jackie agreed. "If we don't win it this time . . . we'll never win it." Skeptics still pointed to iffy Dodger pitching, but Campy insisted his staff could handle the Yanks. "Look," he told a reporter, "they can be beaten. Most teams have folded and run for cover at the mere mention of their name. But we're not going to roll over and play dead for them. They've won four series straight, but they'll win the fifth over my dead body."

The Yankees had won those four without a single Negro player and appeared unlikely to change anytime soon. They were particularly perturbed last winter when Robinson had dared to implicate the Yankee brass in his response to a question about the team's racial attitudes on NBC's *Youth Wants to Know*. "I think the members of the Yankee team are fine sportsmen and wonderful gentlemen," he began, "but there isn't a single Negro on the team now and there are very few in the entire Yankee farm system." The words stung the baseball establishment. "Robinson Should Be Player, Not Crusader," a *Sporting News* headline scolded. Reporters then solicited responses from other Negro players, including Campy, whose wishy-washy comment, like Doby's, did not sit well with Jackie. "He [Robinson] was just trying to give an honest opinion, but I wouldn't want to be in that spot . . . considering all the confusion."

With most of black America in their corner and favored by more than half of the writers polled by the United Press, the Dodgers waltzed into Yankee Stadium on Wednesday afternoon, September 30, determined to take care of business this time around. Nearly seventy thousand fans and millions more on a record 119-station television network watched eighty-six-year-old Cy Young throw out the first ball and then settled back to enjoy another subway series.

Campy led off the second, the Dodgers already trailing 4–0 thanks to Erskine's fit of wildness. After getting ahead 0-2, Allie Reynolds uncorked a pitch so high, hard, and tight that Roy was forced to throw up his hands to protect his head and face. The ball struck his right hand squarely. "The pain was almost unbearable," wrote Wendell Smith, "so excruciating, so agonizing . . . that he was compelled to burrow his pudgy nose in the earth and dig desperately, like a terrified mole, for relief, while the umpire and his fellow-players tried to console him."

Another racial beanball or merely an attempt to neutralize a dangerous Dodger hitter? No one hazarded a guess, although Roger Kahn says Reynolds always believed chin music the best weapon against black hitters. Roy somehow willed himself to stay in the game, a 9–5 Dodger loss, and later refused to get X-rays. "If it's broken, I don't want anybody to know it until the Series is over, including myself." Instead, Harold Wendler tried to freeze the pain before game two with ethyl chloride, while Campy applied a rubber sponge to his bat handle. Neither did much good. Still in intense pain, he grounded out four times against Ed Lopat, who stopped the Dodgers on nine hits.

To be useless again while his team struggled was the cruelest punishment of all. "You scuffle all year to get in the Series," he complained, "and the first time up—it fixed me. I should send one of my sons up there. They can swing better than me." Looking down at his swollen hand, the knuckles now "indistinguishable," he muttered bitterly, "Thank you, Mr. Reynolds." Few expected he would play in game three on Friday at Ebbets.

Just as in the '51 playoffs, Campy now had to decide whether to play or sit. Freezing agents and whirlpools had done nothing to alleviate his discomfort. On Thursday night, Roy and Ruthe decided to try a home remedy: a poultice of antiphlogistine. The pain was still there the next morning, but the heat application somehow allowed him to get a much better batting grip. After banging a few homers in batting practice, he pronounced himself ready to play. Dressen agreed, although not before scolding Roy for some of his press statements. "Don't tell the sportswriters one thing and me another," he barked. "I didn't say you had to catch, remember that."

Roy was taking a considerable risk catching that afternoon. The Dodgers were not only facing a must-win game, but Roy was scheduled to appear live that night on the debut of Edward R. Murrow's new CBS interview series, *Person to Person.* Irving Rudd, the Dodgers' promotions man, had recommended Roy to Murrow weeks earlier as an ideal guest thanks to his "pleasing personality and warm family background." And Rudd, along with Murrow, had already casually mentioned how nice it would be for the show if Campy homered in today's game.

His performance in the early innings probably did not excite CBS executives dreaming of a ratings bonanza that night. In the second, his delay in chasing a wild pitch allowed Berra to reach second on a walk, and his first two at bats off Vic Raschi produced a strikeout and an infield out. By the sixth, Dressen was desperate enough to ask Campy, the team's leading RBI man, to lay down a sacrifice bunt for the first time all year, only to watch him pop to the pitcher. Thus far, his sole contribution was his usual capable handling of Erskine, pushing him to throw the curve more and more as Oisk's fastball lost velocity by the fifth. "Bury it, Carl," Campy yelled. "Don't you hesitate, I'll get it."

Erskine had been almost unhittable, punching out twelve Yankee hitters, but the score was tied at two when Roy came to the plate in the eighth. Raschi had handled him on fastballs, some rather close, all day. This time, Stengel's strategy was all too explicit. "Stick one in that nigger's ear," he yelled from the bench, jamming his finger in his own ear so there would be no confusion. Raschi, however, would have no opportunity to follow

Old Case's orders. On the first pitch, he fired another fastball, but this time Campy, bum hand and all, got all of it. The drive cleared the ten-foot left-field wall and landed seven rows in to give the Dodgers a 3–2 lead. In the ninth, Erskine finished his masterpiece, striking out two more Yankees, to set a new World Series record of fourteen.

At ten thirty that evening millions of Americans turned on their televisions to watch Murrow spend the next thirty minutes with Campy and the conductor Leopold Stokowski. "Now this is really an ordinary studio in midtown Manhattan," Murrow began. "We have nothing that is generally referred to as a gimmick but we do have a device. The device is that window and we hope to make it something of a long-range window in order that you may look out of that window and into the homes of some interesting people." The viewer was then taken to St. Albans, where the Campanella family, except for the baby, was introduced to America. Campy, relaxed and smiling, then gave CBS its money's worth. He gave a tour of his home. He showed off his trophies. He told a funny story about a fishing trip gone sour and even shook a toy Eight Ball to see who would win tomorrow ("Cannot predict now"). Ever the politician, he even managed to slip in a reference to Bible reading. The nation loved every minute.

The next day, he was back at Ebbets for game four. The Series was beginning to get interesting. The press had picked up the story of Stengel's beanball order, although the "nigger" comment never made it into the sports pages. "Crybabies," stormed Casey. "Imagine them crying after they win a game." But the Dodgers would shed no tears that Saturday. Not only did they whip the Yankees 7–3, but the last play of the game provided a little bit of payback to the hero of last year's Series. With the bases loaded and two outs in the ninth, Billy Martin tried to score on a Mantle single over Reese's head into left field. Don Thompson pounced on it quickly and fired a perfect one-hop strike to Campy. The "fresh kid" was out by a mile, and Roy, finally heeding Dressen's advice, slapped the tag on the scrawny Martin with every ounce of force he possessed. "He threw him," said Thompson. "Turned him a flip." "What the hell was he thinking about when he tried to score?" Campy asked later. "He tried to run over me, he tried to knock me down, but I tagged him good and he didn't knock anybody down but himself."

The Series was now tied, but Brooklyn's bliss did not last long. On Sunday, the Yankees knocked out young Johnny Podres in the third on the way to an 11–7 victory. Back at the Stadium on Monday, the Yankees moved in for the kill, putting three quick runs on the board off Erskine. Down to their last twelve outs, the Bums got one back off Whitey Ford in the sixth, and then tied the score in the ninth on the still-ailing Furillo's stunning opposite-field two-run homer off Reynolds.

But the Yankees, being the Yankees, were not about to let the Dodgers back into the Series. Hank Bauer worked Clem Labine for a walk to start the ninth, then advanced to second on Mantle's one-out infield single off Cox's glove. Next up was Martin, a .257 hitter during the regular season who had somehow raked Dodger pitching for eleven hits in his first twenty-three at bats (Dressen naturally blamed his pitchers for failing to pitch him "close in," as per his impeccable instructions). Campy called for a sinker, Labine threw a good one, but Billy the Kid perfectly placed it into center field for a Series-ending single.

The Dodgers' October failures were becoming a national embarrassment. "It is almost incredible how Brooklyn keeps on losing," wrote Fred Lieb. "The Dodgers are the Dodgers," sneered the obnoxiously cocky Martin, "and if they had eight Babe Ruths, they still couldn't win."

While the Yankees romped, Campy sadly headed for the clubhouse. For a man with a near-useless right hand, he had performed admirably, stroking five hits in his last eleven at bats and throwing out four of six runners attempting to steal. Still, it gave him no consolation. "It was a wonderful season. . . . But it ended up in a heap of nothing."

15

IT HURTS UP HERE

ALTHOUGH THE DODGERS would have preferred that Campy rest his hand that fall, barnstorming commitments came first. With a far-flung itinerary on tap, including stops in Hawaii and the West Coast, Roy had assembled a star-studded cast featuring Doby, Black, Gilliam, and a recently furloughed Newk. He also took along former Negro Leaguer Othello Renfroe, late of the independent ManDak League, who never forgot how Roy made sure that he received the same share as the big leaguers. "His going to the major leagues," he recalled later, "never changed his attitude."

Jackie was also back on the circuit, but the tour's promoters had trouble recruiting several players who preferred Roy's "share and share alike" philosophy. "That's why some of us turned down guarantees to go with Jackie Robinson's team," explained Black. "We like Campanella's plan. Everybody gets the same." Still, the Robinson team had something that Campy's didn't: an integrated roster featuring three white major leaguers.

For Roy, the tour was a perfect way to forget about the unhappy conclusion of his Dodger season. In between baseball, he relaxed with Ruthe in Honolulu, renewed his friendship with Newk, and even saw his old mentor Biz Mackey, now residing in Los Angeles. His team even managed to outdraw Jackie's integrated club, which predictably ran into trouble in

Birmingham. Rather than challenge local segregation laws, Robinson opted to bench his white players. Forcing the issue, he later explained, would have jeopardized the imminent repeal of Birmingham's segregated-sports ordinance and strengthened local extremists such as Police Commissioner Bull Connor.

Jackie's decision did not go over well with the black press, which he felt "beat my brains out without ever trying to get my side of the story." Amid the criticism were persistent rumors that he was through with the Dodgers. "Some claim Robinson is too aggressive for his own good," remarked Sam Lacy, "that even his Brooklyn bosses are beginning to tire of his frequent outbursts against what he considers underhandedness." Lacy doubted Jackie was going anywhere, but Robinson disclosed that he would play only in New York and would be "willing [but] not happy to play with the New York Giants."

While Jackie dodged brickbats that fall, Campy accepted still another bouquet: his second National League Most Valuable Player award. Although today's sabermetricians would probably wince at his selection over Duke Snider or Eddie Mathews, both superior in nearly every offensive category, contemporary sportswriters preferred to look at the overall picture. Campanella, they recognized, had just put together one of the best catching seasons ever: 41 homers (3rd in the NL), 142 RBIs (1st), .312 average (10th), and 1.006 OPS (4th). Defensively, he led the league in innings caught, putouts, and runners caught stealing. "What more can a man ask?" he told reporters gathered at his liquor store on his thirty-second birthday. "It was a great thrill to have won it once. I just can't tell you how I feel about winning a second time."

With two MVPs under his belt, Campy's already healthy celebrity took a quantum leap forward over the winter. Another network-television appearance materialized, this time on NBC's *Name That Tune*, where he won $417.50 despite misidentifying "Yankee Doodle Dandy" as "Happy Doodle Dandy" ("Just couldn't say 'Yankee,'" he quipped). A producer was considering a biopic of his life. A film role even fell into his lap, playing himself in *Roogie's Bump*, the tale of a boy with a magic pitching arm who joins the Dodgers (Hollywood had been on a baseball-fantasy kick of late, churning out flicks about a team-owning cat and a bat-repellent-inventing professor). Shot on location in New York, the film suffers from cringeworthy dialogue

("Holy jumping jeepers"), a child lead who had apparently never thrown a ball before in his life, and rock-bottom production values. But Campy hammed it up appropriately, even donning a giant catcher's mitt to catch Roogie's fast one. The film flopped upon its release in late summer 1954 and is remembered today chiefly for its shots of Ebbets Field and cameos by four Dodgers.

The picture's failure mattered little to Campy. Getting a chance to act in a movie, low-budget or not, was just another wonderful perk of being famous. There seemed no reason why the fun should ever end. "I don't know why I can't go on catching for years and years," he told a reporter. "Maybe even ten or twelve years, if I don't get hurt." His life, it seemed, was just about perfect.

OVER AT Montague Street, the situation was considerably less tranquil that off-season. Dressen's contract was up for renewal, and the gabby little skipper and his wife, Ruth, had thoughtfully taken the liberty of drafting a three-and-a-half-page letter to O'Malley requesting a raise, a three-year deal, and a $10,000 tax-free expense account. Above all, Dressen craved vindication, especially the multiyear security of Durocher and Eddie Stanky that Charlie believed would protect him from the chorus of critics who questioned his every move. "It was nerve-racking as the dickens to hear some radio or TV commentator say, 'Dressen is about to be replaced,' after the Dodgers had lost a tough game or to read in the paper, 'The Skids Are Greased for Dressen,'" he sighed. (One wonders how the thin-skinned Dressen would have fared in a world of 24-7 sports radio, Internet bloggers, and ESPN pundits.)

O'Malley took one look at the letter ("All I can say is that it was a pip") and decided it was time to bid Cholly bye-bye. As Buzzie Bavasi later recalled, Ruth Dressen, the prime mover behind the fateful note, "didn't realize that Walter was in baseball for not the love of the game, but for the love of money. And it was his money she wanted." But O'Malley's disenchantment went beyond the letter. The front office believed that some of Dressen's call-ups had not only been unjustified but had also affected farm system profits. There was talk that he had screwed up Joe Black last year by trying to teach him a new pitch. Dressen still talked too much, overmanaged at times, and liked the limelight a little too much for O'Malley's tastes. Most important, he had failed, three times, to bring a championship to Brooklyn. Although Dressen quickly realized he had miscalculated and voiced a willingness to sign a one-year deal, O'Malley had already made up his mind. "I feel a good manager is worth saving . . . but not for an eternity."

A number of Dodgers were not sorry to see the Dressen era end. "He didn't hesitate to tell a man off," noted Fresco Thompson. "He wouldn't wait to talk it over calmly when the player's feelings wouldn't be hurt." Nor was he above ripping his players for the writers' benefit, even Campy. "If the team was going badly, Charlie got critical after a few belts," Roger Kahn recalls. "From time to time Dressen said caustically that Roy was 'a high school catcher,' i.e., he called curve, fastball, curve, fastball, etc." Cholly had even belittled Campy's signals to his face during a clubhouse meeting late last season. "What are you doing with your fingers?" he barked.

Roy was furious. "What has Cholly got against me?" he asked Dick Young later. "I tell you he's got something in for me. It's a damned shame. I felt like crying." Their relationship, Young noted, was never the same.

Dressen's departure was soon overshadowed by conjecture about his replacement. There was no shortage of eager applicants, including one gentleman who had "recently guided a neighborhood team to a championship and feels ready to run the Dodgers. He would accept a one-year contract." But the people's choice, if fan letters were any indication, was captain Pee Wee Reese, long the heir apparent. Jackie Robinson, despite Young's claims that he could not coexist with Reese as manager, loved the idea, as did Campy.

O'Malley and Bavasi preferred that Reese stick to shortstop for now but felt obliged to check, halfheartedly, whether the thirty-five-year-old Little Colonel wanted the job. They were relieved to discover that he didn't. The hassles of being a player-manager did not appeal to him, nor did the prospect of distancing himself from his teammates. Managing, one writer observed, would have forced Reese to "get tough with his friends—the guys he has played with for years; and played cards with; and gone to the movies with; and played golf with; and sucked up a few beers with." Although Durocher thought Pee Wee "crazy not to take it," Reese would never show any interest in managing.

Once Reese was crossed off the list, the Dodger brass chose to go in an entirely different direction. Rejecting the usual preference for well-worn, retread managers, they promoted from within, handing the job to Walter "Smokey" Alston, who had just guided Montreal to victory in the Junior World Series against the Yankees' Kansas City farm club. The hiring of the obscure skipper, who had been to Ebbets Field exactly twice in his life and had never seen a World Series game, hardly excited the fan base. "Dis guy is gonna manage th' Dodghuhs?" asked one Brooklynite incredulously. "He ain't gonna be here very long. . . . I don't like him awreddy."

But Alston was exactly what O'Malley and Bavasi wanted: a manager who was the "antithesis" of Dressen. Unlike Cholly, who never read a book in his life, Alston was a former high school teacher who shocked writers by using words like *deltoid*. He was a Midwesterner through and through, once stating that he wouldn't "trade ten feet" of his backyard in Ohio "for all of New York." And unlike the perpetually babbling Dressen, he didn't have a whole lot to say. "Real square," sighed Dick Young.

Campy was pleased with the choice. He had never forgotten how fairly Alston had treated him in Nashua and St. Paul. "He's a great guy, a nice guy, and a good baseball man," Roy told reporters. "Walt helped me quite a bit with my hitting, and I'll do my best to help him. I surely think the world of him."

ROY REPORTED to spring training a happy man. His salary had been boosted into the $30,000 range, still less than Yogi Berra's, but more than enough to keep the Campanellas comfortable. His right hand was just about back to normal. His weight, despite a slew of winter banquet invitations, was now at a trim 194 pounds. Rather than dip into the diet pills like Jackie and the recently discharged Newk, Campy had shed the poundage by again cutting back on the starches and desserts. "I'm going to beat out some of those infield hits this season," he said, grinning. "Yeah, I'm going in for speed, some bunting, and some stealing of bases."

Roy had no sooner arrived in Vero Beach than he set out to put his new manager at ease. "Skip, don't worry about anything, we'll make it," he told him. But Alston already had plenty on his plate. Robinson had kicked up a mini-controversy by hinting of retirement by next year, only to quickly backtrack. "When I get started talking, I just keep on going and this is what happens," Jackie admitted. And the Dodger beatwriters were restless, irritated with the "tall, taciturn" Ohioan's cautious approach to press conferences.

Where was the dirt, the feuds, the off-the-record remarks that made Leo and Cholly so much fun to cover? "He seems to be suffering from stage fright, like any rookie," wrote Dan Parker, "and he certainly finds it much harder handling the public relations part of his job than running the ball club."

While Alston coped with the media glare, Campy found himself battling the old injury bug yet again. It began with a Willard Nixon pitch that caught him on the right forearm on March 12. Nine days later in Miami, he jammed his left wrist while sliding into second against the Yankees. After resting a day, he returned to the lineup on March 23 and belted three hits.

Within a day, however, his left hand began to ache so much that he could barely pack his luggage. When a few games on the bench failed to produce much improvement, he was sent for X-rays in Tampa. The films showed nothing terribly concerning, perhaps a bone bruise, easily treatable with rest and bandages. "He wanted to play every day but I had to fight him to keep him out," Alston remarked later.

He wasn't always successful, not when Southern blacks still wanted to see their favorite Negro players in action. In Birmingham, which had recently voted to permit interracial athletics (albeit only temporarily, as it turned out), black fans made up at least half of the crowds for a two-game Dodgers/Braves series. Campy started the second contest on April 3, contributing three hits, but he was disillusioned by the continued intolerance of the Deep South. "I never heard such filth in my life," recalled Hank Aaron, then about to start his rookie season. "They wasn't giving it to us, they was giving it to Jackie and Campy and Newcombe." After the game, the abuse continued while the Dodgers boarded the bus until Russ Meyer, whose own racial views had once been suspect, had had enough. "Russ leaped out of the bus," recalled Jackie, "and told them all where to go."

The usual Jim Crow hospitality prevailed throughout the rest of the Southern tour, but Campy was more concerned with his hand, no better despite the prescribed rest, bandages, and whirlpool treatment. Desperate to play, he kept his discomfort to himself since the X-rays had shown nothing anyway. Alston, however, forced him to sit most of the last week of spring training before finally letting him start in the final two preseason games against the Yankees at the Stadium. Campy responded with three hits that weekend, but his two errors and two passed balls suggested something was seriously wrong with his catching hand.

As far as Alston knew, his MVP catcher was just shaking off the rust. He'd be ready, as always, for the opener on Tuesday at the Polo Grounds.

THE ONCE-WHITE-HOT Dodgers/Giants rivalry had been rather ho-hum in 1953. Good old Cholly Dressen (now back with Oakland in the Pacific Coast League) had been right; the Giants "was" dead last year, finishing fifth. But Willie Mays was back for opening day this year, and Sal the Barber was on the hill.

Roy, installed in the fifth slot by Alston, led off the second inning. Maglie threw one pitch, and Roy promptly deposited it into the upper deck. Two innings later, he added another solo shot. When he returned to the dugout following the second blast, he turned to a young rookie named Tom Lasorda, roaring, "Look out, Babe Ruth, here I come!" Although the Giants shut him down the rest of the afternoon (a feat they attributed to their new strategy of "getting him angry" through bench jockeying), Campy was relieved that his hand had passed its first real test. Two more hits and a third homer on Thursday further reassured him that the worst was over. His hand still hurt but at least he could play through the pain.

By the weekend, he was no longer as optimistic. The discomfort had become so intense that he made an appointment on Saturday to see his physician, Lyndon Hill. Hill, a general surgeon, had treated his share of hand injuries thanks to a stint at Harlem Hospital during the 1943 riots. He x-rayed the left hand again, using several different angles, unlike the physician in Tampa. Hill discovered a fracture of the tiny hooklike hamate bone at the base of the ring and little fingers, a common golfing injury easily overlooked on normal X-rays. Even worse, the bone chip was causing damage to the ulnar nerve.

Campy decided to sit on the unhappy news for now, although he confided to Bavasi before Sunday's game that his hand was not right. "It was the first time in eight years Campy ever told me anything hurt him," Bavasi later remarked. "It'll work out," Roy reassured him. Instead, Maglie made matters worse that afternoon by drilling his bad hand in the first inning. The Dodger medical staff, having seen enough, then scheduled two appointments for X-rays on Monday and Thursday. Roy kept neither of them.

Instead, he doggedly kept playing. Hill had told him it would not get worse but that activity would further delay the healing. As the 0-fers began to pile up with alarming frequency, Roy decided to disclose his woes to his sportswriter friends, who were sworn to secrecy lest National League pitchers exploit his hand pain. But when Campy's average sank to a pathetic .163 after a 1-for-20 run, the press would no longer keep silent.

Campy still had no intention of sitting down. On April 27, the same day the story broke, he doubled, singled, and hit two long flies in St. Louis. "I don't care," he said scornfully. "I'm still in there playing. Let them take a million of them." But his bravado was less apparent the next day. He not only went 0 for 5 but the Cardinals had begun to take advantage of his suddenly shaky defense. In the bottom of the tenth, Dick Schofield stole second when Campy "juggled the ball for the dozenth time," then scored the winning run on a single moments later. "You can't minimize the importance of Roy Campanella's injured left hand," wrote Dick Young, "not as long as it is contributing to Dodger defeats."

Alston would force the issue to its unhappy conclusion. After watching Campy manage only a single in three games in Cincinnati, he announced that Rube Walker would catch during the Milwaukee series. It was too much for Campy, who finally phoned Bavasi and told him to book a hospital room.

Roy was contrite in his explanations to the press. "It's my own fault. By playing, it made people think that the ball club didn't want me to get fixed up, and that's not so. I guess I was hardheaded." Hitting, he revealed, had become almost impossible. "I couldn't 'break my wrist' right when I swung hard, and I couldn't hold back on a swing when I wanted to. I tried different handles and even light and heavy bats, but nothing helped."

On May 4, Dr. Herbert Fett removed the offending bone chip, about one inch long, during a procedure at Long Island College Hospital. According to Campy, Fett told him that the chip "had become so entangled with the nerve that if I had waited any length of time, the hand might have become paralyzed. He said I was gradually losing the use of the hand."

How long Campanella would be sidelined remained uncertain. Fett had been somewhat evasive, and there had been talk of a two-month recuperation, although Bavasi suggested twenty-five days should be sufficient. Campy, as usual, was philosophical. "The doctors can cut. But it's up to the good Lord and my wrist when it heals."

• • •

IF ROY hoped for a quiet convalescence, he was in for a disappointment. Only days after surgery, he found himself smack in the middle of another controversy, this time involving Jackie Robinson and the Chase Hotel in St. Louis.

Roy's relationship with Jack had remained frosty at best. As usual, there were no open flares, although Dodger announcer Connie Desmond later alluded to a near fistfight in the clubhouse stopped by Gil Hodges. Such incidents never made it into print, but subtle barbs did appear from time to time. Arthur Daley related a spring training conversation that March where Robinson's teammates were teasing him about receiving an honorary doctor of laws degree from a black college. "I guess I'm now qualified to be a clubhouse lawyer," Jackie joked. "That merely makes it official," Campy replied. "You always were a clubhouse lawyer." Just a few months earlier, the *Pittsburgh Courier* had reported that "a certain Negro star was more than a little agitated because Campanella won the MVP award a second time."

Whether Robinson was the "certain Negro star" is uncertain. But Jackie certainly had ample reason to resent Campy. For the past three years, much of the press had torn Robinson to shreds for being "controversial," while lavishing Roy with praise. "The antis still hate Robinson because he refuses to 'stay in his place,'" Joe Bostic observed. "And the complement to this is the exaggerated fawning over Roy Campanella as the fellow everybody loves . . . a vehicle to use as proof there was no race feeling involved. . . . He, of course, would be a fool not to go along with the gag since he profits so handsomely from it."

The issue of segregation at the Chase Hotel in St. Louis destroyed whatever little remained of their relationship. What went down at the Chase is a familiar tale. The usual rendering suggests that Robinson decided to take a stand, courageously forcing the Chase to accept black players, while the timid Campy preferred to stay behind at the local Negro hotel.

The real story, however, is far more complex. In the mid-1950s, several major league hotels, mostly in the upper South, still practiced some form of segregation. Some, such as the Netherland Plaza in Cincinnati and the Edgewater Beach in Chicago, admitted black players but required them to take their meals in their rooms. Others, such as the Chase and all Baltimore facilities, refused to admit blacks at all.

The Chase, with some prodding, had begun to liberalize its policies. In

1953, the Giants were the first team to be lodged there, albeit with a slew of conditions: no use of the bar, dining room, or pool. During spring training, Sam Lacy announced that the Dodgers would follow suit in 1954, and the newly integrated Pirates also planned to board their rookie infielder Curtis Roberts there.

When the Dodgers arrived in St. Louis on Monday, April 26 (the same day that news of Campy's hand injury reached the press), the team's six black players—Jackie, Campy, Newk, Black, Gilliam, and the newest addition, Sandy Amoros—were offered the option of staying at the Chase but with the usual limited access. Jackie did not hesitate to accept. Half a loaf, he reasoned, was better than none. Once black ballplayers got their foot in the door, the Chase's other barriers would almost certainly disappear in time.

Roy was not interested. Nor apparently were Black, who supposedly discouraged the Giants from staying there, or Newcombe, despite his later misleading attempts to place himself on the "right" side of the infamous Chase story. "A lively argument," Dick Young reported, "ensued in the clubhouse—Robby against Newk and Campy." Young, like Jackie, never forgot Roy's words. "I'm no crusader," he said. "I'm a ballplayer. And I'm happy right where I am." After a frustrated Robinson left in a huff, Newk was seething. "He thinks we owe him something 'cause he was first. We owe him nothing. If he hadn't been first, some other guy would have been."

Robinson marched over to the Chase, the others heading to the Adams, a black-owned hotel. "He checked in, but they made him take his meals in the room," Jackie's teammate Don Thompson recalled. "The very next morning I was sitting with Carl Erskine in the dining room at breakfast. I think Jackie had his own self paged. 'Paging Jackie Robinson.' Everybody looked around." Robinson's presence, however, had no immediate impact on the Chase's policies. When the Pirates arrived later in the week, Curtis Roberts made the mistake of trying to get served in the dining room. After futilely waiting to be acknowledged for forty-five minutes, Roberts finally gave up, checked out, and booked a room at the Adams.

Within a few days, the situation at the Chase had become a national story in the black press. Why, many wondered, had Campanella and others chosen to stay in a Jim Crow hotel? "They didn't want us down there for seven years," Roy initially explained. "So, as far as I'm concerned, they can make it forever." (Ironically, Robinson had employed similar reasoning when reportedly rejecting an offer to stay at the Chase on his second trip to St. Louis back in 1947.) Later, Roy denied ever making such a statement, instead emphasizing the restraints imposed by hotel officials. "We felt that if we were to be Jim Crowed inside the hotel, it would be just as humiliating as being Jim Crowed altogether."

Roy's stance did not lack its supporters. "Everybody knows that Campy is right and Jackie Robinson, who's gotten awful swell-headed lately, is wrong," observed one letter writer to the *Afro*. "Why continue to submit to humiliation and indignities at the Chase when it's possible to be welcomed as a human being at other hostelries?" Martha Howard of Milwaukee agreed. How could anyone, she asked, support Jackie "in his strange role of an Uncle Tom?"

But others felt Campy was the "handkerchief head." "It's so clear," wrote Ralph Galloway of Delaware, "I am puzzled over why Campanella and the other players are not able to see what is at stake." The journalist James Hicks, later famous for being beaten by an angry white mob during the infamous Little Rock 9 crisis in 1957, more forcefully articulated a similar position: "If no colored players stay at the Chase Hotel now, tomorrow the Chase will go back to its policy of no tan guests. . . . Campanella, for whom we all have done so much, should hide his head in shame."

Campy's stated argument—that he would not accept accommodations with racial strings attached—was not without its merits. But in reality he *had* consistently accepted them in Cincinnati and even last spring in Washington when the Shoreham insisted that he and Jackie take their meals in their rooms. Why not, then, in St. Louis? The real reason, some whispered, had less to do with what the Chase didn't offer than what the Adams did.

The owner of the Adams had always taken good—some said *too good*—care of Campy and company. "On our arrival," Buzzie Bavasi recalled, "the Adams . . . had a superstretch limo pick up the black players, usually with a blond or two in the backseat." There were also fat, juicy steaks to enjoy, unlimited use of the owner's car, and other assorted freebies, all conveniently out of sight of the Dodger bosses. "Everybody on the avenue," remarked one black St. Louis resident, "knows they don't want to stay at the Chase because the team manager would know what time they come in and everything else that goes on." Robinson apparently agreed, though he never said so publicly. Campy, Newk, and the others, he believed, preferred the Adams "to beat the curfew."

The black press's hints of shenanigans at the Adams infuriated Roy, whose squeaky-clean public image had taken its first real hit. "The things they've written are pretty serious, and, believe me, somebody is going to answer for it," he warned. "This is our job, this playing baseball, and I, for one, am determined to protect it." In the meantime, Robinson and Brooklyn officials pressured the Chase into an important concession: access to the hotel dining room. The Dodgers subsequently decided that the entire roster would be lodged under the same roof during future trips to St. Louis. Still, the bar and the pool remained off-limits to blacks as late as 1957.

Ironically, during the same month the Chase controversy unfolded, the *Brown* decision ending school segregation was announced. In the context of such a monumental step forward for blacks, Roy's apparent preference for a segregated hotel, whatever his reasons, appeared all the more reactionary. But he was also proud of his own contributions to the civil rights movement. Lester Rodney recalled asking Campy a few days post-*Brown* about baseball's role in the historic ruling. "Baseball was the main thing," he told a surprised Rodney. "All I know is baseball is the first one to have guys together on the trains in the South, the first one where we didn't have to get food in the back of the restaurant." However, when asked point-blank by Mike Wallace five years later whether the "Supreme Court made the right decision," Roy would simply say, "I'm no judge."

Campy's unwillingness to take a more aggressive civil rights position was hardly surprising. He was a member of the executive board of the New York NAACP and had even boycotted a distillery that refused to hire a black salesman, but he was not prepared to go much further than that. Like most black major leaguers in the 1950s, he considered himself extremely fortunate and thought it best not to upset the applecart. "Where else could I have gotten all this?" asked former Negro Leaguer Harry Simpson. "In what other profession could I have been given the same chance?"

Such attitudes made Jackie Robinson cringe. But he knew what he was up against in McCarthy-era America. "At times I have felt that it has become a mark of American society for people to run from controversy 'like the plague,'" he sighed. "Everybody wants to conform." And nonconforming rabble-rousers such as Jackie were not prized highly, even by his fellow black players, several of whom scorned him as a holier-than-thou prig. "Through the early and middle fifties, many of Jackie's contemporaries bristled at mention of his name," Sam Lacy later observed. "Some referred to him as 'The Black Prince.' . . . Others saw him as 'Lord N . . . . r' . . . still others in four letter words usually prefaced with a title of royalty—King, Duke, Baron, etc."

Jackie's "militancy" would be vindicated within a few years as activists began to successfully challenge age-old segregation throughout the South. By 1964, Monte Irvin regretted that he had not pursued a more aggressive path as a major leaguer. "We weren't concerned with our civil rights; we were concerned with our comfort. We should have tried to correct injustices as they arose." But confrontation of any kind would never be Campy's way. "I don't believe in going no place where I'm not wanted. . . . There's no sense in making people do something they don't want to do in their hearts. They got to change out of their own free will. You can't force them."

WHILE BLACK America debated the Chase issue, Roy endured nearly four weeks of recuperation, the longest he had ever been inactive as a professional. He knew the Dodgers, winners of only twelve of twenty-three in his absence, needed him back in the lineup. Rube Walker was an acceptable backup, but his .164 average with no homers since taking over proved that he was no starter.

As soon as his stitches came out, Roy was itching to get back on the field, but Alston held him off. "When I play Campy, I want him to be able to play regularly," he explained. "I don't want him in for a couple of days, then out for a couple of weeks." Finally on Sunday, May 30, Alston relented. Wearing a dress glove at bat, Campy went 0 for 4 in a 5–3 victory over the Giants. The next day, he looked more comfortable, singling, homering, and throwing out a runner in another win.

With Campy back behind the plate, the Dodgers suddenly began to resemble the team that had terrorized the National League in 1953. Heading out West, they took two straight from the Braves and four more from the Cubs to extend their winning streak to nine, eight since Roy's return. Gunning for number ten in St. Louis on June 7, the Bums took a 5–2 lead thanks to Roy's sixth homer, only to see a late Cardinal rally send the game into extra innings. But in the twelfth, Campy again took center stage. Perched on third base with the bases loaded, two outs, Clem Labine up, and the Dodgers now up by one, he suddenly broke for home. The startled Cardinal pitcher, Al Brazle, threw high and outside to Del Rice, who got the worst of the collision at home. "He was in the way," Roy explained later. "It's no more than what anybody would do to me."

Campy's first—and only—steal of home sparked the Dodgers to their tenth straight win. Although the Cardinals snapped the streak the next day, Brooklyn was now sitting atop the National League. Perhaps this Alston fellow, the Flatbush fans murmured, wasn't so bad after all. And Roy was beginning to heat up. Between June 24 and July 2, he homered five times in twenty-nine at bats, including a blast off Harvey Haddix at Ebbets one pitch after the Cardinals' lefty had knocked him down. So much for Dressen's belief that a well-placed brushback could neutralize Campy.

The good times did not last long. The Giants, playing as if it were 1951 again, subsequently whipped the Brooks six straight times, thanks to the new Dodger killer Willie Mays, who clubbed an amazing nine homers in his first twelve games against Brooklyn that season. By early July, the Bums had fallen 6½ games off the pace, sending the fans into a near tizzy. After watching the Giants massacre the Dodgers again, the celebrated builder William Levitt (of Levittown fame) dashed off a letter to O'Malley on July 8 recommending that Dressen be rehired. He was hardly alone in his sentiments, though Cholly, savoring every moment, had not endeared himself to the Dodger brass by recently predicting a Giant pennant. "Why doesn't he learn to keep his mouth shut?" grumbled Jackie.

Campy was having his own struggles. The left hand was already giving him problems again. Squeezing a rubber ball or making a fist helped the stiffness somewhat, but his play had begun to suffer. "It is obvious that he can't control the bat the way he should when he hits," observed Jimmy Cannon. He was also having trouble holding on to pitches. Even Dick Young, normally a Campy cheerleader, criticized Roy for making a remarkably poor and costly throw into center field against the Giants: "the worst play . . . in his entire and magnificent career."

The surgery that had cost him a month had apparently not solved the problem and had perhaps, he feared, made it worse. To his horror he noticed that he now had almost no control over his ring and little fingers or the muscle between his thumb and forefinger. He frantically made another appointment with Dr. Hill, who now suspected severe nerve damage. If so, Campy's career, and even the use of his hand, might be in jeopardy.

This time, Roy decided he would make no attempt to hide his condition. "It is much worse than it ever was before," he announced before a game with the Phillies at Ebbets on Friday, July 9. "The hand just isn't normal anymore." Wearing a "worried, almost terrorized expression," he intimated that the All-Star Game on Tuesday might well be his last. That Campy subsequently doubled and ripped a game-winning homer in the tenth inning led some to wonder whether he was being melodramatic. "That was a helluva performance he put on with a bum hand," remarked Bavasi.

Nevertheless, arrangements were made for Roy to see Dr. Fett on Monday. "I just want to find out if this hand is ever gonna feel right again. . . . It don't hurt me much when I hit the ball, but when I swing and miss . . . oh, man." He was expecting the worst, maybe an order to stop playing or to get additional surgery. Instead, the news was surprisingly positive. The numbness and paralysis, Fett informed him, was caused by "compromise" of the ulnar nerve during surgery and was neither progressive nor permanent. "It's time—not rest—that will make his hand sound again," explained Fett.

Campy was delighted that he could still play. "I feel so great about the news that I'm going out there and hit a homer in the All-Star Game tomorrow," he announced. Maybe his .215 average wasn't exactly All-Star material, but there was no reason he couldn't turn things around soon.

THE DODGERS, still trailing the Giants by 5½, began the second half with a thirteen-game Western road trip. The hoped-for quick Campy revival failed to materialize. He came up fourteen times in the first series in Milwaukee with only a "sad-looking single" to show for his efforts.

In Chicago, Roy once again showed flashes of his old self, homering in successive games on Sunday and Monday. "It doesn't appear to be as numb as it was. Maybe that's my imagination, but that's the way it feels." His optimism proved to be premature. On Tuesday, he went 0 for 4 while the Cubs swiped an embarrassing three bases off him despite pitchouts. A hitless, two-double-play performance followed the next night at Crosley Field.

The loyal Dodger fans did their part to get Campy started. Encouraging letters, "prayers, good luck charms, liniments, etc.," poured in, although nothing seemed to work. Baseball was no longer fun, and by the end of the road trip, his pre–All Star break despair about his future had returned. Once again, he informed the press that the hand had not improved. This time, he criticized the front office for waiting so long to call in a neurologist.

Bavasi and O'Malley decided on a two-pronged approach to their Campanella problem after the Dodgers returned home. Roy would see more doctors and an attempt would be made to raise his sagging spirits. Maybe some of his problems were in his head. The press noted the new "Let's Help Campy" campaign, with batting tips, encouragement, and praise from Alston and team captain Reese. "You've got to admire him for his hustle," remarked Pee Wee. "It's easy to go out there and be alive every day when you're hitting .350, but that poor guy is having such a bad year and yet he never stops hustling."

The rah-rah treatment, though somewhat humiliating for a former MVP, initially seemed to work. He homered off Dave Cole on July 28 at Ebbets and was even encouraged by a long foul ball he hit later that game. Meanwhile, a medical bulletin released to the press that day was also reassuring. A Brooklyn neurologist named Edward Dombrowski had examined Roy and agreed with the Dodger medical staff that the nerve damage was not permanent. Roy could continue playing, but he was warned that it might be five to seven months before the hand was back to normal. "Man," he groaned, "that's over a half a year!"

Privately, he still agonized about his condition. Hill had given him a list of ten to fifteen physicians, and Campy made arrangements to see all of them. The neurosurgeon Samuel Shenkman was the strongest advocate for a second operation. On his exam, Shenkman noticed that Campy "was barely able to abduct or adduct the fingers on the left hand. He had marked weakness of flexure of the left thumb." The culprit, he believed, was scar tissue from the first operation, and immediate surgery was absolutely essential "to prevent any further atrophying of the small muscles of the hand, which might prove irreparable."

Drowning in a sea of medical opinions, Campy had no idea how to proceed. On Monday, August 2, Roy went hitless again. He was now 4 for his last 47, his average a puny .196. Alston, who thought Campy "looked worse today than I have seen him all year," decided it was time for another rest. Before Tuesday's game, Roy saw yet another neurosurgeon, Bronson Ray, whose grave prognosis further muddied the waters. Ray believed Campy's continued catching "has not only prevented recovery of function but has served further to traumatize the nerve." But additional surgery, he stressed, should be a last resort, only if a prolonged period of nonbaseball activity failed to produce recovery.

Although Ray's report remained confidential, Campy resorted to his usual ways to clue in the media. After the Dodgers beat the Cardinals that night at Ebbets, Roy told the press that his pain was "like a toothache" and clearly aggravated by catching. But the brass, he hinted, didn't really believe him. "I read where somebody said that maybe I should have my eyes examined instead of my hand. Well, I'd just like to see the guy who wrote that go up there and swing a bat with one hand and the right hand at that."

Bavasi and O'Malley decided it was time for a heart-to-heart with their unhappy receiver. First, they asked him to keep his mouth shut about his hand. The second question was more serious. Did Roy want to go on the disabled list? It was what Dr. Ray had advised: stop playing and the hand would eventually return to normal.

Campy was not interested. The team trailed the Giants by only five games with about eight weeks to play. Even if he hit .050 the rest of the way, he felt he could still contribute something defensively. "If you used statistics as a guide, I would say Campy makes our pitching staff fifteen to twenty percent better," Newk insisted. Clyde King agreed. "He could make me think I was a Warren Spahn or Clemens or somebody. . . . He was a great motivator."

Once Campy had made his decision to keep playing, a much-relieved O'Malley pursued a more soothing approach. "Nobody doubts your pain," he told Roy. He didn't have to see any more doctors right now. He assured him, somewhat questionably in view of Shenkman's and Ray's recent assessments, that the nerve might take longer to recover if he played but it would not get worse. To seal the deal, he ordered a case of whiskey from Campy's liquor store.

Alston, who like Dressen was less than thrilled with Campy's tendency to communicate his ailments through the press, was not entirely sold on the idea. He gave Walker three straight starts and even talked of platooning his catchers. But he reinstated Campy, now taking vitamins and "electro-impulse treatments," in time for a big 3-game series August 13–15 with the Giants at Ebbets.

The Dodgers swept the series, boosted by Campy's key two-run single in game two. For the first time in weeks, baseball was fun again for Roy, who couldn't help but start thinking pennant again with the Giants' lead now down to half a game. "Both the Giants and Braves," he announced, "are going to have a tough time getting that thing out of our hands."

FOLLOWING AN 18-7 run, the red-hot Dodgers were poised to overtake the Giants as the final month dawned. Instead, the defending champions abruptly imploded, dropping eight of ten, and fell into third place, six games off the pace, by September 9. Once again, calls for Alston's scalp were heard in Brooklyn.

Most of Alston's players were not impressed by their rookie skipper. His personality was drab, the spark was missing, and the emotional-roller-coaster-like rush of playing for an egomaniac such as Dressen or Durocher had disappeared. Nor was Alston much of a strategist. Billy Loes nicknamed him Pebbles for his habit of fiddling with small stones (à la *The Caine Mutiny*'s Captain Queeg and his steel balls) in the dugout absentmindedly during the game. "All of a sudden he would see the situation," recalled Jackie Robinson, "and he tries to do it, but it's too late then. . . . We couldn't tell what he was thinking about: he was flipping those pebbles. . . . Nobody had any respect for Walt as a manager."

Robinson had been an irritant to Alston all season. From the outset, Jackie was convinced that Alston was threatened by Robinson's still unwavering loyalty to Dressen. Alston, meanwhile, viewed Robinson as a bit of a prima donna, who viewed himself as too good to show up on time for practices or keep silent during team meetings. "The first year Jackie and I had it out several times," Alston later observed.

The friction flared openly on September 1 at Wrigley Field in the midst of the crippling ten-game string that virtually sealed the Dodgers' fate. In the third inning with the Cubs up 4–1, Duke Snider cracked an apparent two-run homer to left-center field, except umpire Bill Engeln called it a ground-rule double. Although Robinson came tearing out of the dugout to argue, Alston failed to budge from the third-base coaching box. Jackie, forced to skulk back to the bench alone, was incensed. "If that son of a bitch didn't stand out on third base like a wooden Indian," he muttered, "we would get something." The "wooden Indian" insult eventually found its way back to Alston, who filed it away for later use.

After eight seasons, Robinson appeared to be nearing the end of the line in Brooklyn. Not only was his relationship with Alston rocky, but O'Malley had labeled him a "publicity seeker" after he objected to a $75 league fine for an earlier blowup. And at least some of his teammates besides Roy had soured on him. A waiter overheard five Dodgers talking rather nastily about Jack during a late-night boozing session and reported the incident to Dick Young. When the brass quickly got involved in the ensuing controversy, Jackie realized the story was more than just idle gossip. Bavasi slapped the drunken quintet with fines, while Alston apologized to Jackie for their behavior.

Robinson was surprised but not especially concerned by the animosity of some of his teammates. After all, his race, intellect, stardom, and occasionally prickly personality were bound to make enemies. "This is a business with me," he reiterated, "and nobody has to be in love with me.... Naturally, it is for the best when everyone gets along, but it doesn't matter to me if nobody likes me—so long as they're in there trying to win." But with the now thirty-five-year-old Robinson apparently unable to get along with players, owner, and manager, it seemed a given that he would be sent packing in the off-season. Young believed it would be a mistake. "Robby, even if he can't play regularly, is better than anything the Brooks have on their bench," he wrote. "He's worth keeping, no matter how you look at it."

Campy's future with Brooklyn appeared just as questionable. The hand pain had flared again during the stretch run, and he talked openly of getting a second operation. "In four months it oughta get better," he griped, "if it's gonna get better." Still, he remained ambivalent about going under the knife, especially when his bat began to show signs of life. Over an eleven-game span between September 5 and September 16, he hit .371 with five multiple-hit games, raising his average to .218. "I might fool a lot of people at the plate before the season ends. I ain't such a big out anymore."

His mini-spurt was not enough to save the Dodgers. On Monday, September 20, at 10:40 p.m., Sal Maglie retired Roy on a bouncer to end the game and Brooklyn's two-year reign as National League champs. Afterward, Campy was somber. "It hurts up here," he announced as he gestured to his heart. "Nobody hurt this team more than I did." Injuries can happen to anyone, a reporter told him. "This was more than just an injury," he replied, repeating the words a second time. His old boss Branch Rickey agreed. "It is an entirely different team without him, and it would have been an entirely different story with him."

The season's meaningless final games attracted only the most hard-core of Dodger devotees. On Friday afternoon, a mere 751 fans showed up at Ebbets, among them Cholly Dressen, who had lunched with O'Malley earlier that day. "Hey, Chuck, give us a whistle," they shouted. Dressen obliged. "We win 110 with Charlie," yelled another, much to Alston's discomfort.

Roy was not in the lineup that day. He ended the season hitless in his last twenty-two at bats, dropping his average to .207. Somehow, he kept a stiff upper lip, even throwing a clubhouse party after the Sunday finale, though he knew that everyone present wondered what had happened to him this year. "No one can be certain," observed Bill Roeder, "whether the factors behind Campanella's decline were entirely physical, entirely mental, a combination of both or neither, in which last case the only answer could be that a player only 32 years old lost his touch practically overnight."

ROY'S PRIDE had taken a beating. The benchings, the "Let's Help Campy" campaign, and the drop in the batting order were concrete proof of his rapid descent from superstar to barely ordinary player. He had even begun to experience embarrassment around his own family. "How can a grown man hit .198?" he asked. "When I go home and the kids say, 'Daddy, what are you batting?' I can't tell them I'm batting .198!"

Playing after surgery, he realized, might have been a costly mistake, particularly since the Dodgers finished second anyway. Had he sacrificed his career by trying to be a hero the last two months?

Campy had much to ponder that fall, in between the obligatory Southern barnstorming, the last he would ever undertake (Jackie had already stopped, as television had significantly reduced the profitability of postseason tours). Roy limited his participation to managing only, at least when he was not flying back to New York during the week to see more doctors. "They're not going to pay to see me—a .180 hitter—play," he said with a sigh.

Among the medical men, the consensus was that Campy's left hand had improved only marginally, if at all. Nerve damage was still present, although some sensation in his pinkie had returned. The question again arose whether he should give it more time or opt for the uncertainties of a second surgery that could conceivably make things worse. "They cannot guarantee me that an operation will restore life in the fingers," he complained. "I have made up my mind nobody's cutting me no more."

Nevertheless, on October 14 he returned to see the neurosurgeon Samuel Shenkman, who had strongly recommended a second operation back in July. Campy was growing desperate. The front office had already begun to speak of a contingency plan should he be unable to play in 1955. He told Shenkman that his career was in danger "unless something could be done." Shenkman, trying to lighten the mood, suggested Roy could always play in the minors. "He became a little indignant," recalled Shenkman, "and he said he would never go back to the minors; if he was through in baseball, he was through."

Shenkman then got down to specifics. The nerve, he explained, was either "cut across, badly contused," or now entrapped in scar tissue, and this could only be determined through surgery. If scar tissue was the culprit, as he suspected earlier, then the chance for a good outcome was relatively high. Such a complicated procedure, Shenkman informed him, would cost a rather pricy $9,500, but Campy decided to go ahead.

On the morning of October 20, Roy underwent a four-hour procedure under general anesthesia at Queens Memorial Hospital. Shenkman carefully dug out the considerable scar tissue and adhesions present, freeing the ulnar nerve and, he hoped, restoring normal function. Although it would take weeks, if not months, before Campy would know whether the operation had been a success, he almost immediately began to notice improvement. "I've been trying it," he excitedly announced, "and there's some life in the fingers. It's very encouraging." In the days that followed, he discovered he could now tie his shoes, button his shirt, and fish change out of his left pocket again. Whether he could swing a bat or catch a ball at a major league level was another matter altogether.

Campy was confident. Just twelve days after the surgery, he placed a call to Dodger offices. Bavasi couldn't help but smile when he heard a familiar squeaky voice declare, "This . . . is the Most Valuable Player of 1955 calling."

16

REDEMPTION

OVER THE WINTER, Roy administered a series of tests to the left hand. In December, he tried swinging a bat for the first time. The discomfort, he noted, was no longer present. A few weeks later, he began an informal physical-therapy program in the basement of his liquor store, taking regular swings with a heavy forty-ounce bat and soaking his hand in a whirlpool recently installed by the Dodgers. He even did a little catching, warming up Joe Black at the Harlem YMCA. "It feels *good*," he announced. "I can't wait until I can swing a bat at a pitched ball." Once again, he predicted an MVP for 1955, this time in a letter to his sister Gladys, now residing in Germany.

The Dodger brass, well aware that Campy's claims of "feeling good" were often wishful thinking, continued to prepare for the worst. They did sign Roy to what the press guessed to be a no-cut/no-raise $35,000 contract, but also recalled two minor league catchers for a look-see in spring training while quietly considering trade possibilities. Hoping to snag Jim Gilliam, the Cincinnati Redlegs (*Reds* now deemed undesirable in an era of anticommunist hysteria) dangled catchers Ed Bailey and Hobie Landrith before Bavasi, who decided to wait. Roy, a tad miffed, continued to insist, "They ain't gonna need no catcher."

All would be revealed in spring training, which promised to have no shortage of story lines. Could Loes and Newcombe bounce back from their arm woes? Would the Dodgers promote the highly touted Chico Fernandez and Charlie Neal to swell the club's black contingent to eight? "I honestly don't believe major league baseball is ready for that step right now," remarked Dick Young, who proved to be correct. Most important, could the Dodgers recapture their winning swagger or were they again destined to be also-rans behind Leo's world champion Giants?

Alston was under the gun this year, and he knew it. The press had roasted him alive as the team faltered last September, even suggesting that coach Billy Herman was really calling the shots. Alston became so angered by a column questioning his managerial authority that he threatened to get violent with one beleaguered writer. "You're just sore," he barked, "because I don't kiss your cheek or buy you drinks. If you were younger, I'd punch your nose in." This was hardly what Bavasi and O'Malley had in mind when Dressen was dismissed. Another year of bickering with the media and another second-place finish would almost certainly mean the end of Smokey's brief tenure in Brooklyn.

Alston realized things would have to be different this spring. He was more communicative with the writers and even demonstrated occasional traces of humor. He appeared more forceful on the ballfield, running his players ragged in the hot Florida sun and cursing an umpire during a meaningless Grapefruit League game. The still lingering shadow of Dressen also spurred his transformation. Cholly, though recently handed the Washington Senators job, still seemed to be pining for all things Brooklyn. He not only informed reporters that he would have guided the Brooks to first place in 1954 but later offered (with some prodding) his predictions on Dodger roster cuts and Alston's opening-day lineup.

Of Alston's projected starting nine, Campy remained his biggest question mark. "Roy's the best catcher in baseball if his hand's right," remarked Leo Durocher. "Let's see if it's right. Let's see if this is Campy of 1953 or Campy of 1954." Early reports were encouraging. At his first look at live pitching on March 1, he hit several balls solidly to the outfield at Holman Stadium. "There's no pain," a much-relieved Roy assured reporters. "I can grip the bat and I can tell when I hit the ball good." Although an ecstatic

Campy was soon described as the "happiest guy in camp," Alston was not quite ready to crown him MVP. "Everything I saw at Vero was favorable," he noted, "but I'd still like to wait and see."

Roy continued to test his hand under Alston's watchful gaze. He threw himself into his usual mother-hen role with the pitching staff, which included a promising crop of hard-throwing young hopefuls. Campy was especially impressed with the lefty Karl Spooner ("the greatest young prospect I've ever seen"), who struck out twenty-seven hitters without allowing a run in his two late-season starts in 1954. He also liked eighteen-year-old Don Drysdale, who had only a few months of class C ball under his belt. "Camp, what do I have to do to pitch in the majors?" the youngster asked that spring. "Son, you don't have to do anything more than you're doing right now. Just throw strikes and let old Campy take care of you."

The wise words of "Old Campy" would also benefit one other youthful fireballer in camp. Sandy Koufax, then nineteen, had been signed as a bonus player in the off-season and could not be farmed out. "This boy," Roy marveled, "has more natural speed than any kid I've ever caught." Unfortunately, Koufax's control was so bad that much of the Dodger varsity refused to face him in batting practice. Campy began to work with him on getting his dominating fastball over the plate.

Campy showed no outward signs of any hand problems in the early weeks in Florida. Still, doubts persisted among some writers, who wondered why he wasn't pulling the ball with authority in exhibition games. Talk of a possible trade for a catcher resumed, this time to the Phillies for Smokey Burgess. O'Malley even pulled Roy aside and informed him that a trade was imminent. "I want you to know that you can always manage somewhere in our farm system if your hand cuts short your playing career. Now tell me, should I make the deal?"

Roy was somewhat taken aback by the club's rather lukewarm confidence in his comeback. "Go ahead and make it if you want to," he told O'Malley, "but the catcher you get will wind up on the bench because I'm going to go right on playing." His answer sufficiently placated the Dodger brass, as did a three-hit game, including a double, against the A's on March 23. A few days later, trade talks with the Phillies were called off. Just as they had the past seven years, the Dodgers would sink or swim in 1955 with Campanella behind the plate.

• • •

THE RESOLUTION of the catching conundrum left Alston with one other unresolved problem, a certain cantankerous veteran black infielder. Robinson, despite rumors of trades (Dressen had said he'd take him "if he'll take off fifteen pounds") and retirement, was still with the club and had even expressed a desire to "get back in the good graces of the fans." His vastly improved conditioning from last year was turning heads in Florida. "He's been working hard and I think he's going to have one of the greatest seasons of his career," remarked Roy. "If Jackie decides he wants to burn up the league again, he can . . . and he's been working out like he intends to do just that."

Alston, however, had no immediate plans for Jack. Last year, Robinson had managed to start 115 games, mostly at third and left field. With Billy Cox traded to Baltimore, the hot corner was presumably his for the taking, except Alston seemed to be bending over backward to give Don Hoak every opportunity to win the job. "I can't sit around being a sub," Jackie fumed, "and they won't pay me the kind of money I'm getting to sit on the bench as a pinch hitter and utility man."

By early April, Robinson was still unhappy with his lack of playing time and his inability to communicate with Alston. Benched again in Chattanooga, he took his troubles to Dick Young, who naturally spread the controversy to his millions of readers the next day. Alston was furious. In a subsequent clubhouse meeting, he ranted about Young, players who bitched through the press, and a certain "wooden Indian" insult. Jackie, silent initially, soon sassed him right back, and the two appeared on the verge of trading punches. "I'm sure if I had said one more word, we would have come to blows," Jackie later remarked.

At that moment, Gil Hodges stepped in to prevent an incident, at least according to Jackie's account in *Wait Till Next Year.* But in his original unedited interview with Carl Rowan, he noted that "I think Campanella too" was involved, an admission that perhaps intentionally never made it into the final manuscript. Furillo, meanwhile, suggested that Campy, not Hodges, was the central figure in keeping the peace. "The guy who stepped in between was Campanella. 'When are you guys going to grow up?' Campy said. 'We came here to play ball, not fight each other.' And that sort of cooled things down."

The near fistfight would prove beneficial. Robinson not only returned to the lineup, but he later suggested the fracas "cleared a lot of air." For Alston, the altercation was another step in asserting his control over the Dodger veterans, many of whom privately agreed with Jackie about their skipper's "bush league" lineup shuffling that spring. To the press and players, Alston appeared a changed man from the hesitant front-office puppet some labeled him in 1954. "He could be the strongest man on the club, not excepting Gil Hodges," marveled Reese. "Who'd be crazy enough to challenge Walt?"

IN BETWEEN the various blowups, Campy's spring had been relatively fruitful. He had hit only .235 with a single homer down South, but he had proved his hand was sound. "I'm just waiting to hit in parks with fences around them," he insisted. "I don't care what I hit in practice games. They don't mean anything."

Alston remained unconvinced, even after Roy whacked a couple of homers in the annual preseason tune-up against the Yankees at Ebbets. Campanella, Alston announced, would bat eighth in the opener, yet another blow to Roy's already wounded pride. Now it was Campy's turn to lose his cool. "I ain't no fucking . . . eighth-place hitter," he fumed. "I got no right hitting down there when I'm healthy. . . . I'm being wasted hitting just ahead of the pitcher." The press, startled by his unusually passionate outburst, warned him to simmer down, but this time Roy refused to retract his comments. "The only thing worse that he can do is have me hitting tenth. He can't do that unless he has me sit on the bench." But Alston was not about to be lured into another controversy, particularly one he believed largely press-generated. "Let him show me a few good days and he will be moved up."

Campy was now more determined than ever to show Alston and the other doubters that he hadn't lost a step from his MVP form. The initial results on opening day at Ebbets were not encouraging: a foul pop-up, a bouncer to second, an infield grounder scored as a single when it struck Jackie, and a harmless fly to center. But the following afternoon at the Polo Grounds, he homered off the fading Sal Maglie. Three days later, he ripped two doubles and another homer in the first game of a twin bill in

Pittsburgh. Pleased by Roy's progress, Alston kept his word, moving Campy into the seventh slot the next night in Philadelphia.

Around baseball, the Campanella revival was overshadowed by Brooklyn's sizzling 8-0 start. "I've been playing nineteen years and I never started a season in my career with a winning streak like this," remarked Roy. "You go out one game and one guy does it. The next game it's another." Meanwhile, O'Malley and company licked their chops anticipating the hordes of Flatbush fans sure to turn up when the Dodgers returned home on April 20. "If they can't draw them now after eight straight victories in the most sensational start by any team in more than a decade," wrote Jack Lang, "Walter O'Malley and his backers are in trouble."

Lang was alluding to the growing anxiety that the Dodgers, unhappy with their attendance-drop in '54, aging facility, and limited parking, might consider leaving Brooklyn. The concern appeared increasingly justified after only 9,942 showed up on an admittedly frigid Wednesday night to watch the Dodgers win their ninth straight. The turnout was even worse on Thursday when a mere 3,874 witnessed the Bums break the modern major league record for best season start. Was it television? The weather? "I can't understand this town," remarked Jackie. "They can hardly avoid moving us to some other city if the attendance doesn't pick up." Duke Snider, upon hearing the announcement that the hearty fans present would receive a special souvenir for their dedication, offered a wry but prophetic comment: "You know what the announcement should have been? . . . This franchise has been sold to Los Angeles. It will be televised coast-to-coast tomorrow night. Watch it."

With the Giants in town next, the front office held its breath, hoping the rivalry would pull in the cash customers as in days of old. They were not disappointed. The three-game series drew eighty-one thousand fans, who got more than their money's worth that weekend. Although the Giants snapped the streak in the opener, Saturday's game against Maglie was a classic. The Barber, up to his old tricks that afternoon, drilled Amoros in the butt in the second and then "low-bridged" Jackie and Campy moments later. As usual, the Dodgers then looked to Robinson for retaliation (although batboy Charley DiGiovanna implored Jackie to "let someone else do it for a change"). In the fourth, Jackie tried to lure Maglie off the mound with a bunt with the plan to knock him silly. Instead, Whitey Lockman pounced on it and tossed to Davey Williams. The little second baseman caught the ball but also caught the full force of Jackie's powerful shoulder. The next inning, former LSU football star Al Dark paid the Dodgers back with interest, crashing violently into Jackie using "his own version of a football block" while trying to stretch a double into a triple.

It was good, old-fashioned, hard-nosed Dodgers/Giants baseball, and the fans loved it. Not only did the Bums win, but Maglie didn't dare throw another duster the rest of the game. Robinson had proved to any remaining doubters that he was far from ready to be put out to pasture. "Damn, Jackie, nice going," Alston said afterward, beaming. "Give me five."

With Robinson and Alston now at least cordial again and the club romping, everything appeared serene in Dodgerland. There was, however, one unhappy camper: Don Newcombe, who had hoped to come back strong in '55. "You've got to be serious after you have a bad year," he remarked. "You can't take a cut and ride around in a big car and wear fancy clothes." But he had struggled in his first three April starts, allowing 4 homers in only 18 innings while posting a rather ugly 5.50 ERA. Alston had finally decided to keep him on ice for a while, although Newk expected to get another start when the Dodgers reached Philadelphia on May 6.

The day before, the now 17-2 Dodgers were at Ebbets for an afternoon meeting with the Cards. That morning, Alston's pitching coach, Joe Becker, told Newcombe to throw batting practice. "Wasn't I supposed to be starting in the next few days?" asked Newk. Informed that he was now being held until next week, he stormed off the field in a huff. Alston, once again confronted with a rebellion (and Newcombe's second refusal to throw BP), acted swiftly. "I won't argue with you, Newk. Take off your uniform and go home." A few hours later, Bavasi called a press conference, announcing Newcombe's suspension and fine.

Newk went home and played golf while the Dodgers won again despite Tom Lasorda's record-tying three wild pitches in the first inning. "I was under the impression," Newk weakly explained, "that me and Campy was gonna help win the pennant. Campy's doing okay, but they won't give me a chance." His roomie was not particularly sympathetic. "I don't know what your problems are and I don't want to hear them . . . but in this game you don't never take off your uniform," Roy scolded. "That's your bread and butter. Once you take that off, you are on your way to starvation."

By late that night, a chastened Newk was frantically trying to get in touch with Bavasi, who agreed to see him the following morning. After letting him sweat outside his office for nearly an hour, Bavasi agreed to reinstate Newcombe, but not before he apologized to Alston. Not surprisingly, Newk faced plenty of teasing ("mostly by his roomie," noted one reporter), but the Dodgers were glad to have him back. Alston's stature, meanwhile, had taken yet another leap forward thanks to what the press called "The Great Newcombe Rebellion." "We were all a bit shocked at this because we had rarely seen this side of Alston before," recalled Carl Erskine. "Nobody ever questioned Walt's authority after that."

ALMOST IMMEDIATELY, Newcombe turned his season around. He threw two shutout innings in relief that night. On Tuesday, he one-hit the Cubs, followed by wins in his next six starts, five by complete games. By early June, Newk had already racked up a major-league-leading ten wins without a single defeat.

His roommate was faring even better. Roy was not only driving the ball with authority again, but was also getting more than his share of opposite-field hits, enough to raise his average to a torrid .359 by May 17. By the end of the month, Campy was leading the league in homers (13, tied with Ted Kluszewski), RBIs (46), and slugging (.650). Alston, now a believer, moved him to the sixth slot and then finally cleanup for good.

The left-hand woes of '54 were now a faint memory, although the apparent career-saving procedure had yet to be paid for. O'Malley, despite publicly stating back in September that the Dodgers "will be glad" to reimburse any surgery recommended by a "reputable man," was in no hurry to pony up a whopping $9,500 for an operation that some still believed might have been unnecessary. After fruitlessly pursuing Campy and his bosses for several months, Dr. Shenkman slapped Roy with a lawsuit in late May. "That man must be out of his mind," Campy complained. "Heck, if he had even mentioned money like that to me, he'd have to treat my head."

Roy's denial, contradicted by his own doctor, Lyndon Hill, would fail to convince a jury, which awarded Shenkman $5,000 nine months later.

O'Malley not only had to pay that bill but eventually had to cough up another $15,000 in 1957 to settle a concurrent slander suit. The litigious Shenkman had objected to O'Malley's public insinuations of needless surgery and his quip (stolen from Fresco Thompson) that the surgeon "thought he was operating on Roy's bankroll" instead of his hand.

Around baseball, Shenkman's lawsuit prompted plenty of good-natured ribbing. "How's your $9,500 hand?" asked Willie Mays. "The hand's all right," replied Roy, "it's the bill that's screwy." But if Mays or the Giants had hoped that legal troubles might cool off Campy's thunderous bat, they were wrong. A thirteen-game hitting streak in early June raised his average to .346, second in the league only to Richie Ashburn's. He also managed to catch every inning of the Dodgers' first forty-eight games, a mind-boggling (yet perhaps foolish) display of durability for a thirty-three-year-old catcher coming off hand surgery.

The miraculous comeback predictably became popular media fodder as the season wore on. In June, the *Sporting News* resurrected the age-old debate of who was baseball's best catcher: Campy or his crosstown rival Yogi Berra? Dueling columnists weighed in with the pros and cons of each receiver, both of whom had won two MVPs, while readers were invited to cast their votes for their favorite. Although Campy outpolled Yogi by 161 to 117, the two men, who admired each other tremendously and remained friends to the end of Roy's life, never had any serious personal rivalry. "What difference does it make?" asked one fellow *paisano*. "They're both Italians."

Even *Time* magazine wanted to do a cover story on Campy, who was only too glad to oblige, at least until reporter Don Connery began to dig into matters he deemed a bit too personal, especially his first marriage. "Campy became extremely upset about the possibility of our printing anything other than the present truth that he is married and has six kids," Connery informed his bosses. "When we couldn't give him a flat assurance that nothing would be said, he became more upset, insisting on seeing the story before anything is printed, and sounded very much like a man who would not cooperate on story checkpoints." Much to Campy's relief, *Time* eventually decided not to mention Bernice. By the time the issue hit the newsstands in August, Roy was more concerned about the cover, particularly since *Life* had just published an embarrassing nude shot of him entering a whirlpool. "Tell me one thing," he asked Frank Graham, Jr. "Have I got any clothes on?"

No sooner had *Time* wrapped up its prepublication research than the old injury bug bit Campy again. It was not his hand this time but his left kneecap, struck by a foul tip in St. Louis on June 19. He was still able to swing the bat well enough to collect four hits in Chicago two days later, but he soon found it nearly impossible to squat or even run. In a disturbing case of déjà vu, the doctors could not seem to agree on a diagnosis and treatment, although Campy quickly brushed off talk that he might be stepping into another medical quagmire. "Don't confuse this with my trouble last year. That was a nerve."

The Dodger medical staff eventually diagnosed Campanella with a broken bone spur, easily treated with bandages, rest, and a break from any baseball activity. Still, he missed being around the ball club, even for a day. "I just can't take these games by radio and television," he remarked. "It just kills you to look and listen when you're not there to do anything about it." He was also disappointed that he could not play in the All-Star Game, despite polling more votes than any other player, even more than Yogi, Mickey Mantle, and Ted Williams.

This year, there was no pressure for him to rush back prematurely. By the All-Star break, the Brooks not only held a commanding double-digit lead over the second-place Braves but were 15½ ahead of Leo's floundering Giants. The defending champions, Jackie Robinson asserted, were "showing no desire. . . . Leo Durocher doesn't act like the same manager." Although Durocher sarcastically retorted, "My players and I appreciate Mr. Robinson's expert advice," Jackie was not far off base. Durocher resigned at the end of the season, the first in a series of deathblows to the great Dodgers/Giants rivalry.

In the early summer of 1955, the Dodgers had no thoughts yet of a world without Leo or the twenty-two battles at the Polo Grounds and Ebbets each season. What consumed them was the pennant and the chance for redemption. "They want to nail it down quick," remarked reserve catcher Dixie Howell. "They want it bad."

CAMPY, RECENTLY outfitted with a "special foam rubber insert" for his left shin guard, was pronounced ready to play after the break. "The knee doesn't hurt when I run, when I squat, and when I hit," he happily informed anyone who would listen. "I think it's fixed for good." Trainer Harold Wendler was not so sure. "I doubt if that knee will be right until he has an operation to remove that spur. . . . He says he feels fine, now. He said the same thing after a couple of days' rest last month. Then the knee got worse."

In reality, Roy was not 100 percent, nor would he ever be again. Shenkman's "miracle" operation might have improved the functionality of his left hand, but the damage from last season was apparently permanent. He was still unable to move the ring and little fingers, although he was able to get them around a bat handle. He also dropped more pitches than before, albeit relatively few with runners on base.

Jackie Robinson was also showing signs of decline. His .275 average at the break was far below his usual standards, and the boos had grown increasingly persistent at every National League park, even Ebbets. His body, ravaged by his college football years and eight no-holds-barred seasons with the Dodgers, had begun to break down. Like Campy, his left knee was giving him fits, and only the lure of a bigger pension if he could hang on another season kept him from seriously considering retirement.

If Jackie and Campy were contending with persistent aches and pains, so too was the pitching staff, with Erskine, Podres, and Loes all complaining of various arm maladies as the second half began. But fresh reinforcements from the still lush Dodger farm system soon came to the rescue. Recalled from St. Paul and Montreal in July, Don Bessent and Roger Craig went a combined 13-4 the rest of the way with a sparkling 2.75 ERA.

With the Dodgers winning sixteen of their first twenty-three after the break to extend their lead to 15½ games, Brooklyn baseball had reached its zenith. Perhaps happiest of all were the comeback kids, Campy and Newk. Last year, the good times were few and far between, their conversations depressingly focusing on doctors' appointments and ailments that never seemed to improve. Now their hotel room was party central. "The phone's always ringing now for me and my roomie," Newk observed. "People are calling us from London, Los Angeles, and Australia." Roy, ever the comedian, loved screening the incoming calls. "Campy would answer the phone and then tell me, like a butler, 'Mr. Winston Churchill wants to know if we can make it for dinner tonight.' Or he might say, 'Cairo, Egypt, is calling Mr. Don Newcombe.' "

The seemingly insurmountable lead in August inevitably conjured up unhappy memories of 1951. The cautious Alston, nervous that his boys might get complacent, even posted a reminder in the Ebbets clubhouse: "You all know what happened. Let's have no repetition." But no one seriously believed the Brooks would falter this year. "The Dodgers will finally turn on their old Yankee tormentors and win it all in the big show next Fall," Arch Murray wrote. "They're too good to blow it this time."

Behind the scenes at Montague Street, however, the club's park situation was causing considerable angst. O'Malley envisioned a new facility at the corner of Flatbush and Atlantic Avenue, only to encounter ongoing opposition from the city's powerful planner Robert Moses. On August 16, a day after O'Malley was again rebuffed by Moses, the Dodgers made a shocking announcement that sent shivers up the spines of most Brooklynites. Next season, the team would play seven home games in Jersey City, the former home of the Giants' now-defunct AAA affiliate.

The *Jersey City* Dodgers? Was this the beginning of the end? Jimmy Cannon thought so. "It is only a matter of time when the Dodgers will abandon Ebbets Field. They may stay in Brooklyn. It is possible they will go to Los Angeles or San Francisco." But most of the Dodger players were somewhat blasé about the plan. "If you expect to get paid, you gotta figure the club has to make money," remarked Campy. "I think other clubs should do something like that, too. . . . Maybe major league clubs ought to play some games in other big parks around the country. If it's a league game, it counts, no matter where you play."

The prospect of future home games in (shudder) New Jersey may have affected the Dodgers more than they let on. Not only did they drop eight of their next eleven, but they began to show disturbing signs of panic as the Braves sliced 5½ games off the lead. After the Redlegs swept a doubleheader at Ebbets on August 25, Alston appeared to be at his wit's end. "I wish to hell I could find something to laugh about," he snarled at a group of giggling players. "I can't see anything funny with what's been happening on this ball club."

Duke Snider was also in a foul mood that night. He was embroiled in a horrible slump, his average had dropped 30 points in the last month, and the crowd had booed him after he muffed a fly ball. Without prodding, he launched into a postgame tirade against the local fans. "They're the worst fans in the league," he insisted. "They don't deserve a pennant winner. That's why the owners are talking about playing those games in Jersey City next season."

As soon as the story hit the papers, the Dodgers braced themselves for a violent backlash. But the response was surprisingly gentle the next night, although Snider's three hits probably helped. Even Jack Lang, the writer who had broken the story, was sympathetic. "Time and again I have heard players put the rap on the fans . . . but Snider had the courage to say what he feels and allowed himself to go on record." The Brooklyn fans, noted Lang, had not exactly distinguished themselves this season by their poor support.

With players, writers, and fans feuding, the Dodgers had assumed the character of a second-division club almost overnight. Desperate to get the Brooks back on track after three straight beatings, Alston handed the ball to young Sandy Koufax on Saturday, August 27. Campy had worked with Koufax only twice before, but he knew the kid had great stuff. Two days earlier, he'd watched Sandy blow away the first two hitters he faced on six pitches.

Koufax looked just as good in his second major league start that afternoon. His fastball and curve were both working well, but Campy kept calling for the hard stuff. "Finally, he asked me if I wanted to see any of his other pitches," Roy later recalled. "I told him, 'No, just try to keep ahead of the batters.' " The strategy proved effective, as Koufax threw a two-hit shutout, the first of his career, while punching out fourteen hitters.

Koufax's masterpiece provided Brooklyn with a much-needed surge of adrenaline. The Dodgers abruptly returned to their early-season form, winning ten of their next eleven to build the lead back to sixteen. Once again, Campy was the man of the hour, slamming 4 homers, driving in 12 runs, and hitting .483 during the streak. With his latest tear, the batting title, one prize he had never won, was within his grasp. "I don't figure to be that kind of hitter," he cautiously told one reporter. "My best year I hit .325."

On the morning of September 8, Campy, at .331, trailed Richie Ashburn by a single percentage point. That afternoon, the Dodgers were in Milwaukee looking to nail down the National League flag. In the first inning,

Campy faced the right-hander Bob Buhl with one on and two outs. Buhl came in a little too close, and Roy felt a familiar stinging pain as the ball clipped his right wrist. It was his sixth hit-by-pitch of the season (second highest in the league) and second in three days, both knocking him out of games. Intentional? Buhl had hit only six batters in three seasons. Two of them were Roy, both times in the hand and wrist, although he did later call to apologize. "He hits you and then he asks you if it hurts," griped Campy.

Like Campy, Buhl did not survive the first inning. The Dodgers tallied four times on their way to a 10–2 rout and their third pennant in four seasons. The usual raucous clubhouse celebrations, some spontaneous and others more contrived, followed for the benefit of the TV and newsreel cameras. Players liberally doused each other with beer, though Newcombe was incensed when his new straw hat was ruined by a shower of suds. Meanwhile, a grinning Campy assured reporters he'd be ready for the Series. "But, man, I sure have been hit on the hands a lot this year," he admitted. "Always on the hands. I've been keeping Johnson & Johnson in business." (Johnson & Johnson, grateful for the free publicity, later gave him a year's supply of Band-Aids.)

The batting title was still on his mind when he returned to the lineup three days later. But it was not to be. Whether it was the latest wrist injury or simply a late-season slump, he managed only one hit in his next twenty at bats while the surging Ashburn raised his average to as high as .345 by September 20. A 2-for-3 performance in the finale brought Campy up to .318, good enough for fourth in the league behind Ashburn, Mays, and Musial.

Years later, Campy admitted that he wanted to win the batting crown in 1955. "It was about the only thrill I never got in baseball." But his fantastic comeback represented a far greater accomplishment. He had proven to the fans, the writers, and even some of the Dodgers that he was still the best catcher in the National League, if not all of baseball.

THE AMERICAN LEAGUE race had been tight this year. The White Sox, Yankees, and defending champion Indians were all still alive in mid-September, until a 10-2 run in the final two weeks vaulted the Bronx Bombers into the Fall Classic yet again, and with home-field advantage this year, to boot.

Roy was not disappointed to see the Yankees win. His team, he knew, would be labeled losers and chokers forever unless they somehow found a way to shake loose fourteen years of World Series frustrations. As usual, the task would not be easy. The Yankees, Casey Stengel noted, "always take care of the Series." After losing their first two back in the early 1920s, they had won sixteen of their next eighteen. "There is no getting around the fact that they are a terrific money ball club," Campy acknowledged. "They make you play your hearts out and then you find that isn't quite enough to beat them."

Stengel was bringing a very different Yankee team into battle this year. For one thing, he finally had his first black player, the former Negro Leaguer Elston Howard. For another, the pitching staff that had so consistently handcuffed the Dodger bats for years had undergone a considerable makeover. Ed Lopat had been traded, Vic Raschi sold, and back problems had forced Allie Reynolds to retire. "They used to murder us," Campy sighed. "Without Reynolds and Raschi, they're going to find it a lot tougher."

The Yanks would also find it tougher with a barely mobile Mickey Mantle, now nursing a torn right thigh muscle. It was another encouraging sign for Roy, who was so confident that he told Ruthe they would buy a new home with their winning share.

The Dodgers had their own question marks, namely Jackie Robinson and his knee that had "popped" so inopportunely back in July. Told by Alston to save himself for the Series, Robinson soon squawked about his infrequent playing time. "How can I get ready for the Series if I'm not playing?" he asked in September. Unfortunately, Robbie had looked every bit his thirty-six years whenever he managed to crack the lineup, finishing with a career low .256 average and only 16 extra-base hits. The Dodgers had even discreetly placed him on waivers at one point, pulling him back after at least three teams showed interest.

Robinson's status was just one of the issues local fans passionately debated in the days before the Fall Classic opened. For most Gothamites, the subway series would take center stage for a week, eclipsing the news of President Eisenhower's heart attack, the nuptials of Eddie Fisher and Debbie Reynolds, the "very favorable" reports on the Salk polio vaccine, and the recent brutal murder of a fourteen-year-old Negro boy named Emmett Till in Mississippi. As usual, diehards waited patiently in line (or *on*, in local parlance) for hours for first crack at bleacher tickets. This year, a Chicago carnival worker named Ralph Belcore was first "on" line at Yankee Stadium, only to discover the hard way that it wasn't a good idea to leave his valise unattended in the Bronx. "Why, in St. Louis I left the bag open one night and nobody touched a thing," he moaned. His only consolation, a reporter noted, was that his "stock of salami and cheese was left untouched."

With wet weather on the morning of Wednesday, September 28, the opener at Yankee Stadium, the scene of Rocky Marciano's successful heavyweight-title defense against Archie Moore a week earlier, seemed destined for postponement. But the rain stopped before gametime, and 63,869 fans settled in their seats to watch a couple of good pitchers, Newk and Whitey Ford, go to work.

Newcombe had not been particularly sharp since August, winning only twice while posting an ERA just under 4. His arm, he later admitted, was bothering him again. The Yankees, sans Mantle, raked him for six runs before Billy Martin's triple chased him in the sixth. With the score now 6–3, Campy's instructions to new pitcher Don Bessent were simple: "Watch that boy. He's got a notion."

Roy was perhaps being overcautious. Surely, Martin was not nutty enough to try to steal home with two outs, a right-hander on the mound, and a left-handed hitter (Eddie Robinson) up. Martin was no speed demon anyway, with ten stolen bases in twenty-six career attempts to date. Still, Campy had never forgotten Billy the Kid's reckless baserunning exploits two years earlier. He was also aware of Martin's recent comment that Campanella was still "spike shy" around home plate.

Martin, true to form, took off on the second pitch. The play was surprisingly close; the official World Series film suggests that Martin's foot might have caught the plate a nanosecond before Campy's tag, and Pee Wee Reese himself thought Martin made it. But the collision at home was far more intriguing than Bill Summers's questionable out call, featuring Campy's resounding tag to the neck and Martin's not-so-subtle attempt to throw an elbow in Roy's direction. The two eyed each other menacingly before retreating to their respective dugouts.

The heart-stopping conclusion of the Yankee sixth failed to spark the Dodgers, who went down meekly in order in the seventh. With time running out, Jackie Robinson decided to take matters into his own hands. "I was worried about the way things were going, and I thought that if I could just do something maybe a little bit different, there might be a change in the feeling of the ball club." Robinson got his chance in the eighth, making his own mad dash for home with two outs and the Bums now trailing by two. Like the Martin attempt, the outcome was a toss-up, but once again Summers saw things Brooklyn's way. In the days that followed, roughly half of the baseball world excoriated Jack for such an idiotic play with his team behind, while the other half (including Ty Cobb) praised him for unnerving the Yanks.

The Dodgers had one more chance in the ninth. With one on and one out, Campy came up to the plate to face reliever Bob Grim. Hitless against Ford, Roy was happier to take his chances with Grim, last year's American League Rookie of the Year, since plagued by a sore arm. He smacked a Grim offering solidly to deep right field, only to watch Hank Bauer snare it just in front of the 344 sign. Furillo then struck out, and the Dodgers had lost game one, again. "Watching the opener," one writer sighed, "was like seeing an old movie for the third or fourth time. If you don't remember you sensed what was coming."

Afterward, Campy's frustrations were all too apparent. He ranted about Martin to anyone who would listen, although the press, as was the custom of the day, carefully edited out the choice obscenities. "Anytime that [delete] thinks he's gonna run over me, little as he is, I'll break every [delete] bone in his [delete] body. . . . Just let him take two steps toward me and I'll take care of that little [delete]. He's been too damned snotty for too long." Over in the Yankee clubhouse, Martin boasted that he "might have punched him . . . if it wasn't the World Series."

Game two was more of the same, the Brooks managing only five hits off Tommy Byrne in a 4–2 loss. Roy, whose cleanup contributions consisted of a walk, two pop-ups, and a flyout, had done almost nothing to help the cause. "The goat's horns in the World Series are suddenly beginning to sprout on Campy," wrote Jack Lang. "I think some guys are getting a better line on how to pitch to Campanella," observed one National League official. The trick, some believed, was to pound him with changeups in pitcher's counts.

Just as in 1953, the Dodgers were down 2-0 and heading home to Ebbets for three games. No team had ever come back from a similar deficit to win the Series in its best-of-seven format. Even more depressing, the Yankees had beaten them with two lefties, usually easy pickings for the Bums, and without Mantle taking a single swing.

Before Friday's game, there was no shortage of individuals proffering remedies and counsel to halt the carnage. Clubhouse man John Griffin dug out his special "sponsor's sombrero . . . decorated with a pack of cigarettes, a can of beer and other embellishments" worn during the ten-game winning streak back in April. Alston and NL president Warren Giles rallied the boys with rah-rah pep talks, while Frankie Frisch tried to light a fire under Roy.

"Why aren't you hitting, Campy?" he barked. "Doggone it, Frank . . . what do you think I'm trying to do?" Campy replied.

But Campy had an even bigger responsibility than hitting: starter Johnny Podres, who had just turned twenty-three that day but had pitched only twelve innings in the last four weeks because of injuries. After seeing just two pitches in the first inning, Campy could tell the kid had good stuff. "He threw a changeup," Campy observed, "and I knew he had it going for him. Man, it was a dandy."

For the third straight game, the Dodgers drew first blood. With Reese on and the count 0-1, Campy blasted a two-run smash over the GAS HEAT RATES REDUCED AGAIN sign in left center, his first hit of the Series and first homer in a month. After the Yankees quickly tied the score in the second, Roy decided it was time to throw away the scouting reports warning against "slow stuff." Let's take our chances, he told Podres, with that changeup.

Of the 107 pitches Podres threw that afternoon in an 8–3 victory, at least a quarter were changeups. Baffled and befuddled, the Yankees managed only four hits and a single run over the last seven innings. Suddenly they began to look vulnerable. Mantle, who homered in his first at bat of the Series, was so shaky in center field that he asked to be moved to right after only one inning. The rejuvenated Jackie Robinson had a great game, his daring baserunning inducing a bases-loaded walk in the second and Elston Howard's desperate heave to the wrong base in the seventh. Campy, meanwhile, did himself proud with three hits and three RBIs. "I had to break out of my slump," he said, smiling. "It's about time, isn't it?"

The good times in Brooklyn continued in game four. Campy drilled three more hits, including his second homer of the Series, as part of an eight-run/fourteen-hit attack that tied the Series at two. "The Yankees now have an aroused Campanella to contend with," warned Dan Daniel. "The guy is washed up?"

Newcombe, who had worked less than six innings on Wednesday, was the logical candidate for Sunday's game five. But with Newk's arm and back balky again, Alston decided to go with the kid from North Carolina, Roger Craig. The day before, Roy had thoroughly prepped the rookie for his assignment. "He talked about the Yankee batters," Craig noted, "then he talked to me and gave me confidence. He told me that I could beat 'em." Craig, now poised and ready, allowed only four hits and two runs in six-plus innings, before Clem Labine slammed the door in the final three frames. At least some of the credit, Craig admitted, belonged to Roy, who "really had the Yankees off-balance the way he changed his calls that they might have expected."

With the Yanks now in free fall, the impossible was looking possible to the legions of Brooklyn fans. The Bums themselves were just as excited. Just pack one pair of socks, they shouted giddily to one other in the clubhouse. That's all we'll need. Meanwhile, a reporter asked Duke Snider, game five's star with two solo shots, whether he still believed the fans "deserve a world championship." The Duke's sour views of the locals had not appreciably changed since August. "The players do," he replied.

Stengel, glad to be escaping the "rat trap" (as Hank Bauer had so kindly dubbed Ebbets), now depended on Whitey Ford, game one's winner, to stave off elimination at the Stadium on Monday. Alston countered with the fireballing but erratic Karl Spooner for what would prove to be the last appearance of his brief, injury-plagued major league career. It soon became apparent there would be no celebrations in Brooklyn that night. The Yanks jumped on Spooner for five runs in the first and held on to win 5–1.

The Series was tied and the game seven odds seemed to favor the Yankees. Not only was dastardly Dressen now providing Stengel with free Dodger-beating advice, but Jackie could not play because of a heel injury, and Snider, who had tattooed Yankee pitching for four homers, was questionable after wrenching his left knee. Then there was Yankee Stadium, where the Dodger lineup continued to struggle, even at full strength. "They don't swing the same way here as they do over in Brooklyn," observed Frankie Frisch. "Over there, they go up to the plate and swing for the fences. Over here, they stand with their bats on their shoulders." To Campy, now sporting a .100 average in 40 lifetime Series at bats at the Stadium, the problem was not a lack of aggressiveness but the shadows. "On a bright afternoon this is the toughest park I ever saw for hitters."

But he knew the shadows would not matter if starter Johnny Podres threw the ball as well as he had in game three. "Just get that changeup over like the other day," Campy told him. "Get it over, you got nothing to worry about. That'll set 'em up for the other pitches." Podres, a party-boy extraordinaire who loved booze, babes, and horses almost as much as baseball, did not lack for confidence. "I'll get it over. Get me some runs and I'll win."

True to his word, Podres held the Yankees scoreless through three, although Tommy Byrne was just as tough on the Dodgers. In the fourth, Campy finally snapped out of his Stadium funk, banging a double into the left-field corner for what he would later call "the biggest base hit I ever got." One out later, Hodges singled him home to give the Dodgers a one-run advantage.

The Bombers quickly battled back. Yogi Berra led off the fourth with a probably catchable double that fell between Gilliam and Snider. With Hank Bauer up next, Campy went out to reassure Podres. "Throw hard now," he told him. A fly to right followed, Berra declining to run on Furillo's arm, although Skoonj caught the ball at a somewhat awkward angle. Now the power-hitting first baseman Bill Skowron had to be handled. "Shake me off once," Roy instructed. "Get him guessing." Skowron guessed wrong, bouncing to second. After Bob Cerv popped up to end the threat, both teams began to sense that Podres was going to be hard to beat that day.

Just a few more runs, millions of Dodger fans and Yankee haters pleaded. In the sixth, the Bums did their best to oblige, putting runners on first and second with no one out and Campy up. Alston, ever the book manager, was not about to play for the big inning. He ordered Roy to sacrifice, then Hodges's fly to right center brought in the second run a few moments later: 2–0 Dodgers. Twelve outs to go.

They would not come easily. Martin walked on four pitches to start the Yankee sixth, followed by a Gil McDougald bunt single down the third-base line. With the dangerous Berra up next, Alston conferenced with Campy and Podres. "He's got good stuff, Skip, good stuff," Roy assured him. "He'll be all right."

Stengel, unlike his more conservative counterpart in the Dodger dugout, had no thought of bunting. Yogi was up there hacking, and he belted a long fly to the left-field corner that looked good for two bases at least, particularly with Sandy Amoros playing him to pull. But Amoros never stopped galloping across the vast Yankee Stadium outfield, not only managing to somehow snare the ball but also doubling up McDougald. Campy, watching the play unfold from the mound, later claimed he was certain Amoros would run it down ("because it was high enough"), although he may have been the only one in the park so confident.

For the last three innings, all eyes were on Podres and his catcher, now in sync as if sharing one brain. Not once did Podres shake off Campy, who increasingly called for the hard stuff instead of the changeups the Bombers had come to expect. The Yanks again failed to score in the seventh and eighth. "Campanella was calling the greatest game of his career," Podres later observed. Billy Herman agreed: "Those Podres games, the third and seventh, were two of the finest I've ever seen called by a catcher."

After the Dodgers went down in the top of the ninth, Podres's teammates peppered him with last-minute advice. Campy, who had silently been uttering a few prayers himself, shooed them away. "Dammit, let him alone!" he barked. "Don't everybody tell him how to pitch! He did all right for the first eight innings!"

Three hitters now stood between the Dodgers and the promised land. Skowron began the ninth by bouncing to Podres, who nearly caused coronaries all over Brooklyn when he momentarily struggled to get the ball out of his glove. Cerv flied harmlessly to Amoros for the second out. After Podres got ahead 0-1 on Elston Howard, Campy tried to slow him down a bit. "He was trying to throw that fastball too hard . . . I didn't want him to throw it away."

The count went to 2-2. Campy called for a fastball. For the first and only time that afternoon, Podres shook him off. Instead, his 144th pitch was a changeup tapped by Howard, fittingly, to captain Reese. His throw to Hodges was shaky, but good enough to retire Howard for the final out. The Bums, at long last, were champs.

The reaction in the Dodger clubhouse was a study in contrasts. The younger players quaffed copious amounts of beer and champagne while engaging in the usual rowdy post-victory horseplay. Don Newcombe beered himself this time and serenaded Podres with a parody of the recent hit "Ballad of Davy Crockett." But Campy, Reese, and other veterans were more subdued, some even in tears. "I wasn't the only Dodger crying a little," remarked Reese, "and not the only one thanking God for a prayer answered."

The responses among Brooklynites were just as varied. Some romped happily through the streets, threw confetti, tooted their horns, or jammed the phone exchanges twisting the knife into Yankee friends and relatives. A fan named Carlos Marchand, however, made his way to the Dodger ticket office, got down on his knees, and said a five-minute silent prayer. "I pray—that now that we won, I could die in peace," he explained to an inquiring reporter. "I thank my Lord that he let me see this day."

Campy, like most of Brooklyn, was on cloud nine for the rest of that historic day. He was swarmed by fans at his liquor store and even began passing out bottles to aid in the revelry. When he returned home to St. Albans, he began juggling eggs to the delight of his children. Ruthe was not pleased when he dropped one of them. "What do I care?" he replied. "We just won the World Series."

Later that night, Roy and the rest of the entire Dodger family congregated in Brooklyn for a bash at the Bossert Hotel. The surrounding streets were soon packed with well-wishers, some carrying signs reading YANKEE FANS, GET OUT OF BROOKLYN BEFORE SUNDOWN! Even the cops had gotten into the spirit, telling arrivals at the Bossert to park anywhere. "We're giving out no tickets tonight."

Everyone, it seemed, was a Dodger fan that night, and the future of the franchise was never brighter. "The Dodgers won the title at the most opportune time in the history of the club," observed Dan Daniel. "I dare say Bob Moses is not likely, now, to oppose the wishes of the people of Brooklyn as regards that new ball park Walter O'Malley wants to build at Flatbush and Atlantic avenues." But O'Malley was less certain. When asked by a reporter whether the victory meant the Dodgers would stay in Brooklyn, he simply replied, "I sure hope it does."

17

THE LUCKIEST MAN IN THE WORLD

THE THRILL of Brooklyn's first championship had barely worn off before Campy received more exciting news. Just as he had flippantly predicted a year ago, he was named the National League MVP. "So many great things just couldn't happen to me in one great year," he exclaimed. "I have perfect health after having feared my hand was paralyzed. I had a good season and we won the World Series. . . . A man doesn't rate more than that."

Campy's third MVP was not without controversy. Only five votes separated him from runner-up Duke Snider, who topped Roy in virtually every offensive category except batting average. A screwy ballot from a Philadelphia writer, deputized to fulfill the dying Stan Baumgartner's voting duties, probably cost the Duke what turned out to be his best chance to win the award. The replacement voter mysteriously left Snider entirely off the ballot when a simple fifth-place vote or higher would have made him MVP.

Roy could certainly sympathize with Snider, but he was not about to give back the MVP. As a three-time winner, he had now joined a super-exclusive club that included only Jimmie Foxx, Joe DiMaggio, Stan Musial, and Yogi Berra, who had just won *his* third a few days before. Campy was also looking forward to the usual award-associated fringe benefits. Business at the liquor store skyrocketed, so much so that he was able to purchase the entire building. Another network television appearance materialized, this time with Yogi on ABC's *Masquerade Party*, a rather peculiar game show where a panel had to identify outlandishly disguised celebrity guests. Although decked out in drag as a "buxom damsel" and maintaining a "perfect feminine soprano," Campy was unable to fool the panelists for long.

A few weeks after his *Masquerade Party* capers, the front office disclosed that Roy would receive the highest salary in Dodger history. The press guessed his new contract was in the low-$40,000 range, although the actual amount was closer to $50,000, at least if Bavasi's and Campy's later recollections are correct. That Yogi still earned plenty more did not particularly concern Campy. With his baseball salary, endorsements, and liquor-store profits, Roy was now pulling in $60,000 to $70,000 annually, roughly equivalent to $500,000 today, and he saw no reason why the gravy train should ever stop. "Next year I hope to get more," he announced. "That's because I expect to have an even better season."

Campy was not one to squirrel away his windfall for a rainy day. Life, as he saw it, was for living and money was for spending. First on tap was a bigger home. The Robinsons had moved to Stamford, Connecticut, a year earlier but the Campanellas decided to stay on Long Island. Roy fell in love with Salt Spray, a comfortable waterfront ranch house located on an island once owned by J. P. Morgan and now part of the affluent Nassau County town of Glen Cove. The prospect of a Negro neighbor, regardless of his fame or wealth, did not sit well with some residents of the mostly white community. Campy would soon discover that the North Shore of Long Island could be as reactionary as the Deep South. Years later he bitterly recalled the family being turned away from a Port Washington restaurant under the pretense that he didn't have a reservation. "I can see there are plenty of vacant tables and I know you don't need reservations," he remarked. "Maybe Jackie would have tried to force his way in. I couldn't do it."

Despite scattered objections, Salt Spray's current owner found it impossible to say no to a $58,000 offer, and the Campanellas moved into their new home in early February 1956. Just a few weeks earlier, Campy had shelled out another $28,000 for a forty-one-foot Richardson double-cabin cruiser that slept eight and was eventually equipped with a television, a telephone, and a shower. Like his earlier forays into the world of tropical fish and model trains, Campy soon grew equally passionate about his newest hobby and learned all he could about the intricacies of navigation. That a yacht (dubbed *The Princess* for his youngest daughter) might be a bit extravagant never entered his mind. "I play harder when I'm in debt," he explained. "To me it's really living."

At thirty-four, Roy had seemingly achieved the American Dream. "I'm the luckiest man in the world," he remarked that February. "I've got everything in my life a man could want.... It's wonderful just being alive." And the hero worship never seemed to stop, with even his parents now giving him the superstar treatment. Their Kerbaugh Street home was a virtual Campy shrine, adorned with portraits, newspaper clippings, and other paraphernalia. "He's the most important thing that's ever happened to us," his father admitted. "We love all four of our children, but Roy and his success have naturally been something special." So proud was John that he would pass out slips of paper with Campy's autograph at the neighborhood barbershop.

Such adulation only further inflated Roy's already large ego. Friends and family members began to notice personality changes, some subtle and others not so subtle. A blue pennant flew from his new yacht, loudly proclaiming his achievements (MVP 1951-53-55) for all to see. He began to insist that he be addressed as "Mr. Campanella." Flashes of arrogance even surfaced during his periodic returns to Nicetown. "He was like a god when he would come on the block," recalled Wilson Pettus, Jr., the nephew of one of Campy's close childhood friends. One day, Pettus was surprised to see Campy puffing on a sizable stogie and asked him whether athletes were allowed to indulge in such vices. Campy laughed scornfully. "When you make as much money as me, you can afford these big cigars too."

His marriage was also under growing strain. Campy, by some reports, not only could be a bit of a control freak, but his penny-pinching ways with respect to household expenses were the source of more than one argument. Moments after visitors to their home departed, he would count how many bottles of liquor had been consumed. But if Campy had changed, so too had Ruthe. "Ruthe was a fine young lady, but I think the bright lights of the

Major Leagues had an effect on their marriage," Bavasi later recalled. "It was steadily going down. Both at fault."

The months that Campy spent away from home only added to their difficulties. Like most baseball wives, Ruthe was well aware of the temptations on the road. "We called the girls who hung around baseball players 'Queens,' " recalled Del Ennis. "They were at train depots, at the ballparks, and in hotel lobbies, challenging players to take them on." The Dodgers, recalled one writer, were often serviced by a group of lovely ladies known as the Varsity. Although the front office usually maintained a "boys will be boys" attitude, O'Malley drew the line at interracial couplings, fearing, above all, "an incident." When a few of the "regulars" began to pursue Joe Black, the brass immediately ordered $500 fines for anyone who dared even to talk to the amorous groupies.

Roy, though the product of a successful mixed marriage himself, realized that interracial sex was still dangerous in 1950s America. Years later, he told a friend of an encounter with a white woman that he was certain was a ploy to generate exactly the kind of incident O'Malley dreaded. The woman brazenly opened the passenger door of his Cadillac, sat down, and seductively told him, "I just want to be in this car." Campy, no fool, turned off the ignition and got out. "Well, then you can have it," he told her. "Good thing she left. Or I would have lost me a Cadillac."

Interracial couples, he believed, were generally "not a very good idea. Too many problems." But there was no shortage of black women eager to throw themselves at a three-time MVP. "Jolly and juvenile, he has a definite appeal to the latent mother in all women," wrote Evelyn Cunningham in a *Courier* piece entitled "Male Types That Excite Women." "And as much as they'd like to administer to his colds and charlie-horses and pamper him, they are acutely aware of his virility." How faithful Campy was on the road is merely conjecture, but a private letter from Jackie Robinson suggests that Roy occasionally strayed, just as he had done in the Negro Leagues. "It seems Campy has a girl here," Robinson wrote his wife one spring training in the mid-1950s, "and the fellows keep kidding him about her and it has gotten under his skin. . . . Camp is always kidding the other guys but can't take it himself."

The same letter's other choice comments ("The more you see of Camp the less you like him. To me he's like a snake ready to strike at the best possible moment") revealed just how far their relationship had deteriorated. By 1956, the two men had moved from cordial tolerance to open disdain, all too apparent that spring training when a black youngster showed up asking for a tryout. Since the kid was a catcher, it was suggested that he talk to Campy, but Roy was not particularly interested in doing much. I'm not running the camp, he said, but if I did, "Robinson would be the first son of a bitch to get rid of." The comment made its way back to Jackie, who not only confronted Campy without resolution but also asked to be traded "if this thing was going to develop into a real problem." Told by Bavasi to "forget it," Jackie admitted nearly two years later that he hadn't "forgotten it yet."

Robinson was certain that he understood the root of Campy's growing hostility. "I talked to Newcombe and Gilliam about it and they told me that Camp's boat, Campy's home, all of the fine things he is doing, he is trying to outdo me," he related to Carl Rowan a year later. Campy, Robinson believed, was still jealous that Jackie was first and of the opportunities that came his way. "My being the first, he feels, is the only stumbling block against his moving into a better position in the Brooklyn organization, and that nothing would make him more happy than if I was off the . . . club and he would be the number one man."

Whether Jackie's interpretation was based in reality or merely reflected his own insecurities is difficult to say without hearing Campy's side. Unfortunately, he remained largely silent about the Robinson feud throughout his life. By 1956, however, it appeared that the Dodger organization was no longer big enough for both of them. But on the ballfield, everything seemed as harmonious as ever.

THE PUBLIC remained unaware of Campy's ongoing problems with Jackie and Ruthe. All they knew was that it was spring training again, and the Dodgers looked good enough to repeat. Previously deferred World Series hero Johnny Podres had been drafted (not coincidentally, according to Ted Williams, who ranted about "gutless draft boards, politicians and sports writers") but the addition of Cubs third baseman Randy Jackson and his twenty-one homers salved the wound somewhat.

Unlike last spring, the mood in Vero Beach was relatively calm. There was no anxiety this preseason for Campy, who reported at a trim 206 pounds and confidently professed himself ready to catch another ten years. Robinson, despite publicly ranking Alston last among his four major league managers, was staying out of controversy and playing with renewed determination to retain his third-base job.

Much had changed for Jackie and Campy since their first spring training together back in 1947. "Everywhere baseball is played there have been improvements," Robinson admitted. "However, after ten years of traveling in the South, I don't think the advances have been fast enough." White hotels, restaurants, and cabs remained off-limits, and vicious insults continued to pour from the stands in cities such as New Orleans and Mobile. Although the success of the ongoing Montgomery, Alabama, bus boycott raised hopes for a new day in Dixie, the black Dodger contingent (which now included infielder Charlie Neal) remained subject to the irrational whims of Jim Crow. "You can have this South, all of it," muttered Campy as the preseason neared its close.

Ironically, the success of the Dodgers increasingly hinged on dark faces, five of whom appeared in the opening-day lineup at Ebbets on April 17. The joyous occasion in Flatbush that afternoon included a parade to Ebbets, the ceremonial raising of the championship flag accompanied by Gladys Goodding's rousing rendition of "Heart" from the Broadway smash *Damn Yankees*, and the presentation of World Series rings. Campy not only picked up his third MVP before the game but also proved himself worthy of the honor by clubbing Robin Roberts's first pitch in the fifth for a homer.

Lurking beneath the revelry was a growing uneasiness about the Bums' future. Strangely, only 24,236 fans bothered to show up for what was clearly a seminal moment in Brooklyn history. "If I knew why Dodger baseball isn't better attended at home, why it draws 50 per cent better on the road," a puzzled Dick Young mused, "I could make more dough than if I had the explanation and cure for baldness." But the front office continued to believe the major reason was lack of parking for the growing number of suburban fans. "Our situation in Ebbets Field is economically impossible," a team official remarked. "We'll be out of there for sure by the end of 1957. It's just a matter of where we move to."

Would it be Jersey City? The mere mention of the new second home elicited an angry chorus of boos on opening day. The Dodgers themselves were hardly thrilled with the prospect of playing at Roosevelt Stadium, where the infield was substandard, fences distant, lighting poor, and the locals hostile, although Campy as usual somehow managed to find a silver lining. Jersey City, accessible by water, would give him an ideal opportunity to give his new yacht a workout. Besides, "you can't let a park worry you. . . . This is more like Milwaukee. You just got to hit that son of a gun and forget what kind of park you're in."

The Dodger debut in Jersey City on April 19 was not what O'Malley had anticipated. The weather was chilly, and fewer than thirteen thousand turned out, most of whom spent the game booing the Brooks (and perhaps the saccharine crooner Eddie Fisher, who sang the national anthem that afternoon). Although the Dodgers beat the Phillies in ten innings, most of the players were in a foul mood afterward, openly ranting about the park, the fans, the lack of hot water, and the front office for cooking up such a stupid scheme. As usual, the press fixated on the comments of Robinson, who bore the brunt of the ensuing public backlash.

The Jersey City controversy would be overshadowed by a more shocking development a few weeks later: the May 15 purchase of the much-despised Dodger killer Sal Maglie from the Cleveland Indians. The thirty-nine-year-old Maglie, an amazing 22-6 against Brooklyn between 1950 and 1954, had done little to convince anyone that he had much left in his tank after being set adrift by the Giants last July. But a sharp four-inning relief effort in a recent Jersey City exhibition had turned Dodger heads. "I can't understand how the Giants ever let that man go," Campy insisted afterward.

Maglie's first moments in the Dodger clubhouse were expected to be uncomfortable. Most of his new teammates—particularly Furillo and Campy—had spent the past several years dodging his well-aimed fastballs, although Maglie always claimed he held no personal animosity toward Roy. Campy, Maglie explained, was a guess hitter who often went for the first pitch, and it was good strategy to loosen him up.

The much-anticipated initial meeting proved surprisingly benign. Within a few weeks, Maglie was sharing barbecued ribs with "Paisan Furillo" in his hotel room. As for Campy, Maglie was now one of his boys, to be fussed and fretted over just like the others. Within a short time, Carl Erskine would witness what he later called the "strangest sight he ever saw in baseball": Campy and the Barber "walking arm in arm off the diamond."

The acquisition of Maglie, who would win thirteen games, three by shutouts, gave the Dodgers a much-needed boost. The defending champions had not looked especially impressive in the early going, Campanella least of all. After posting a creditable .267 average with 5 homers through May 22, Roy abruptly stopped hitting. As his average plummeted into the low .200s by early June, Alston dropped him in the order, hoping to "get him mad" again and briefly benched him.

In desperation, Campy tried different bats and stances, but nothing seemed to work. "I'm pressing," he admitted. "I'm swinging at bad pitches. My head is flying out, and my butt is flying out, and I don't even see the ball I'm swinging at half the time." Still, he exuded his usual confidence, at least outwardly. "Don't you worry about daddy. He's far from finished." True to his word, he belted a pair of three-run homers a few days later on June 21 against the Cardinals. "Thank God, I'm out of that," he chirped. "I guess I just ran out of outs."

If Campy expected the homer spree to kick-start one of his trademark tears, he was in for a disappointment. His average remained stuck in the low .200s, Alston relegated him to the dreaded eighth slot, and pitchers now openly challenged him. Just as in 1954, his hand was the culprit, but it was the right hand this time. X-rays revealed that bone chips from an old injury (possibly one that had "never healed properly") had developed in his thumb, which made gripping the bat painful. Immediate surgery, with at least six weeks of recovery, was the ideal treatment, but neither the Dodgers nor Campy was eager to go that route. Instead, he chose to gut it out, hoping that sponges and a thicker-handled bat might get him through the season, although the pain on contact was so intense at times that he could barely run out a grounder.

Alarmingly, his left hand was also giving him fits. "They don't know what is wrong with it," he sighed. "It just keeps getting weaker all the time." He found it harder to hang on to pitches and began to compensate by allowing the ball to strike his mitt and then fall in front of him. The technique annoyed more than a few Dodger pitchers, who believed it cost them called strikes.

In just a few months, his skills had begun to dramatically erode. Hand injuries were a major factor but aging was another. Campy was a soon-to-be-thirty-five-year-old catcher with a tremendous amount of mileage. Since becoming a professional in 1937, he had probably caught, at minimum, close to twenty-five hundred games. The Dodgers, often unduly focused on short-term goals, had not done nearly enough to look out for his future as he grew older. Just last summer, no one in the organization appeared to recognize that it might not be a good idea for Roy to catch all twenty-three innings of a meaningless August doubleheader. With such reckless overuse, his body was bound to break down.

Every once in a while, the old Campanella would reappear. On July 26, a rookie Redlegs pitcher named Tom Acker sent him sprawling with a knockdown pitch. "There's only one answer to that—a home run," shouted a fan. After dusting himself off, Campy promptly clocked the next pitch into the left-field seats. The same remarkable resiliency was on display eight days later when he volunteered to play despite an infected leg. Fortified by sheer willpower and a few shots of penicillin, Roy caught all twelve innings of a four-hour game, contributing two hits and two RBIs.

But such triumphs were few and far between. The achy right hand, now resembling "a clump of twisted, bloated bananas," and the virtually useless left were simply too far gone for him to perform effectively behind the plate. In twenty-four games in August, he committed four errors and three passed balls, while nailing only three of the eleven runners attempting to steal on him. "Campy's trying to do a job with two fingers nature intended him to do with 10," remarked Milton Gross. "He's giving the Dodgers 100 per cent . . . but considerably less in the box score."

CAMPANELLA'S DECLINE was only part of the Dodgers' ongoing struggle that summer. Not only were the Bums unable to catch the upstart Braves, but a mutiny appeared to be brewing against Alston, who had not won any friends by reportedly blasting his players as "gutless" and "choke-ups" in the midst of a five-game losing streak. The incident made the papers, thanks to a leak by the indefatigable Dick Young (who got the "look of the leper" for breaking the story). A devastating column by the *Post*'s Leonard Koppett a few days later further fanned the flames, suggesting that a number of players considered Alston inept and incapable of relating to his men. "Dressen was often disliked," an anonymous player remarked, "but his baseball knowledge was respected. This man is the subject of jokes."

Mr. Anonymous Dodger may well have been Robinson, but he denied any involvement. Sidestepping one controversy, Jackie found himself ensnared in another a few weeks later after firing a baseball at Lew Burdette for making cracks about "watermelons" and number 42. Amazingly, no suspension followed, and the two sworn enemies actually buried the hatchet later.

In between the Alston and Robinson explosions was another bizarre episode. Duke Snider punched a fan in the mouth for calling *him* "gutless" (apparently the cruelest insult of all in 1950s America), breaking two false teeth. But strangely, this Bums team seemed to thrive on turmoil. "Every time we have it," Robinson observed, "we start playing better." Entering September, the Brooks had pulled to within 2½ games of the Braves, most of whom had never experienced the gut-wrenching, late-season pressure of a tight pennant race before.

Campy, bad hands and all, remained in the lineup down the stretch. "They want me in there," he explained. "We're trying to win something." Still, he was realistic enough to begin wondering about his future, particularly with another operation on tap in the off-season. The eternal optimist who had hoped to play ten more years now admitted, "There just isn't any way I can even guess how much longer I can catch."

Though no longer a superstar, Roy demonstrated his still considerable value in the season's final week. On Tuesday, September 25, he not only cracked his nineteenth homer but caught Maglie's no-hitter, preserving the gem in the ninth with an outstanding catch in the Dodger dugout. His contribution the next day was subtle but no less important. After a tough 7–3 loss to the Phillies dropped Brooklyn one game back with three to play, Campy went over to console Sandy Amoros, whose key error and several misplays had enraged Newcombe and several other Dodgers. Roy, one of the few American major leaguers, if not the only, fluent in Spanish, then invited the distraught Cuban to his home in Glen Cove. "We jollied him and talked about the 1955 World Series," Campy later recalled. "Pretty soon, Sandy's head started comin' out of the soup. He wanted to turn in his suit when we left the park. But 'bout one a.m. he was laughin' and I saw he was relaxed."

Thanks to an off-day and a rainout, the Dodgers were idle until a crucial Saturday doubleheader at Ebbets against the Pirates. Amoros smashed a two-run homer his first time up to give the Brooks a 3–2 lead, which they would never relinquish. Campy, meanwhile, rose to the occasion in game two, blasting his twentieth homer and even beating out an infield hit in a 3–1 victory. The doubleheader sweep, coupled with the Braves' second straight loss, gave the Dodgers a one-game lead and clinched at least a tie for the pennant. On Sunday, the rejuvenated Amoros belted two more homers to spark the Dodgers to an 8–6 win and the National League flag.

Roy's deft handling of Amoros suggested that he would be a perfect managerial candidate when his catching days were over. But retirement was far from his thoughts as the team celebrated. Even the usually dour Alston "whooped and . . . hollered with the frenzy of a fan."

"Thank God I could hang in there and play," Campy told reporters as he popped open a beer. His hands, the writers noticed, were still an unsightly mess, but maybe, just maybe, enough was left in them to do some damage in the Series.

THE YANKEES had continued their annoyingly effortless dominance of the American League, winning their eighth pennant in ten years. Their chances to knock the upstart Dodgers off the throne appeared better than average. Not only was their youthful nemesis Johnny Podres in navy blues nearly four hundred miles away at Portsmouth, Virginia, but Mickey Mantle had just won baseball's Triple Crown and was healthy and raring to go. The Mick, whose fruitless assault on Babe Ruth's home-run record had Yankee fans atwitter all season, was now a full-fledged media sensation. "I Love Mickey," Teresa Brewer's gooey ode to the young slugger, had just hit the top 100, featuring a monotone Mantle who mercifully did little more than periodically utter his own name.

Mantle's drinking buddy Billy Martin was still with the Yankees and eager to show the Brooks a thing or three. He had stolen home three times this year "practicin' for Campanella. Does he still tag 'em high on the pants?" Brash Billy, however, assured the world that he was "not trying to stir up trouble. . . . I'm thinkin' of my future in baseball. . . . I wanna be a manager someday. An' I'm gonna make it."

The Series opened on Wednesday, October 3, at Ebbets. Up for reelection in a month, President Dwight Eisenhower showed up to throw out the first ball. Campy, saddled with the unenviable task of somehow trying to catch Ike's heave with his view obstructed by a plethora of photographers, nevertheless made a nifty bare-handed snare. Ever the politician himself, Roy was effusive in his praise of the presidential toss afterward. "It was a good pitch, just above the knees and what would have been on the inside corner to a right-handed batter. It had a little bit of a curve on it too."

The Dodgers took the first two at home, only to run into their usual troubles in the Bronx that weekend. Whitey Ford beat them 5–3 on Saturday, and Tom Sturdivant's six-hitter the following afternoon tied the series at two. On Monday, Don Larsen shocked the world by setting down all twenty-seven Brooklyn hitters in order for the first and thus far only perfect game in World Series history. Like the rest of the lineup, Campy was unable to solve the no-windup deliveries of the man nicknamed Gooney Bird. He struck out on four pitches in the third, popped up on the first pitch in the sixth, and tapped to second in the ninth after hammering a long foul. Larsen, Roy later admitted, "had real good control," although Campy remained convinced that Yankee Stadium's glare and shadows had aided Larsen's historic performance.

The return to the comfy confines of Ebbets for game six on Tuesday failed to revive the suddenly frigid Dodger bats. The Brooks managed only four hits but still beat the Yanks 1–0 in ten thanks to Clem Labine's seven-hit masterpiece. For the third time in five years, the nation braced for a thrilling game seven between the crosstown rivals. This year, there was no Johnny Podres to gallantly ride to the rescue. Instead, Alston handed the ball to Newcombe, a 27-game winner during the season but hardly the ideal man for the assignment. He had become increasingly despondent over criticisms that he couldn't win big games, so much so that he socked a parking-lot attendant who called him "gutless" (that insult again!) after being knocked out of game two. And unbeknownst to the Dodgers, his right elbow had been aching since he started the season finale. The Yankees quickly tattooed him for five unanswered runs and romped to an easy 9–0 victory.

The Brooklyn fans, who had just witnessed their heroes amass a grand total of seven hits and one run over the final three games, trooped sadly out of Ebbets, momentarily distracted by a wild brawl between a lady spectator and a vendor. Back in the somber Bums locker room, Campy was equally frustrated. After a strong start of four hits in his first twelve Series at bats, he went hitless in his remaining ten. The vast national television audience had also witnessed the continued erosion of his catching skills, particularly at a crucial point in game seven. With the score 2–0, two outs and two strikes on Yogi Berra in the third, Roy failed to hang on to a foul tip that would have ended the inning (Carl Erskine suggests that actually "it was not a foul tip . . . but it looked like it because it went in the glove and popped out"). Two pitches later, Berra clouted a two-run homer to put the game on ice.

Though badly in need of a rest, Campy still had more baseball left to play. Less than twenty-four hours after Robinson struck out to end the Series, most of the Dodgers were on a plane headed for Japan, a trip that few were eager to undertake, even for $3,000. Although Roy later claimed that a personal entreaty from Eisenhower at game one forced him to reconsider his own opposition, the story is probably apocryphal. Before the Series began, Campy had already told a reporter that he was "definitely" going, and Sam Lacy claimed that the contract with Japanese promoters required that Jackie, Campy, and Newk appear.

The early days in Japan had all the makings of an unmitigated disaster. Newcombe was barely able to function, bombed on scotch and saki. The drinking problem he had hidden from everyone, even Campy, was now out in the open. And the Dodgers, exhausted and jet-lagged, lost two of their first three to their surprisingly tough "Nipponese" (as the *Sporting News* called them) hosts. "We went over there with the typical American misconceptions," Vin Scully observed. "We expected the local teams to be stocked with little yellow, buck-toothed men wearing thick eyeglasses."

The Dodgers, spurred by O'Malley's order to "remember Pearl Harbor," quickly righted the ship and soon began to enjoy the local color. "Those Japs treated us like we had won the World Series," Campy remarked, "and every morning when I woke up, I got to wondering if they had found out different." With his pockets bulging with one hundred thousand yen in expense money, he loaded up on souvenirs, silks, and pearls for Ruthe and the kids. In between the spending spree and his usual catching duties, Campy found time to counsel and motivate another young outfielder, this time the rookie Gino Cimoli. After watching Cimoli score from second on a sacrifice fly, Roy invited him for a postgame chat at the Imperial Hotel in Tokyo. "Back in the States you been giving the impression you couldn't do nothin', that you were lazy and didn't want to play," Roy told Cimoli. "When spring training starts, you do the same way you're doing here in Japan. Stop popping off, stay out of trouble, and play." A grateful Cimoli, who became an All-Star in 1957, later admitted that "in one little talk . . . Campy did more than anybody to make me a big leaguer."

ON NOVEMBER 12, in the Dodgers' final game in Tokyo, Campy and Jackie Robinson both homered in a 10–2 rout over a Japanese all-star team. It would be Robinson's last home run in a Brooklyn uniform. Less than four weeks after the Dodgers returned to American soil, Robinson was informed that he had been traded to the Giants for the much-traveled lefty Dick Littlefield and cash.

Stunned fans jammed Dodger and newspaper switchboards with demands for confirmation. Robinson was not only an icon but a productive player who had improved in 1956 with 10 homers and a .275 average in part-time play. But Jackie barely tolerated Alston, and his relationship with O'Malley (whose "favorite player" was Roy, according to O'Malley's daughter) had been rocky from day one. From a purely baseball perspective, it was not unreasonable to move a soon-to-be-thirty-eight-year-old player commanding a high salary.

But why now? Rumors of a Robinson trade had been circulating for *years*. Monte Irvin suggests that a confrontation with O'Malley over accommodations in Japan might have been a precipitating factor, although Rachel Robinson remembers no such incident. "I thought the blowup between he and O'Malley occurred before," she recalls, "in spring training when Jack was hurt and O'Malley called him a prima donna for not coming out to an exhibition game."

Buzzie Bavasi offered a far different explanation. The Robinson deal, he later observed, was one of the few occasions during his Dodger tenure when O'Malley ordered him to trade a player. "He and Walter never got along, but the reason for his trade to the Giants [was] warranted. Sorry to say this as I respected Jackie as a man and a player. Never saw anyone with his competitive spirit. Going no further, never will. . . . Walter was correct in demanding a trade." When pressed, Bavasi refused to provide more specifics, except to offer the cryptic comment: "Just say that Jackie wasn't afraid of having a good time."

Robinson had no intention of playing for the Giants. Moments before being informed of the trade, he had secretly accepted an executive position with the Chock full o' Nuts restaurant chain, a company with a roughly 75 percent black workforce. For now, he kept mum about his plans, at least until the biweekly *Look* magazine, which paid him handsomely for the exclusive account of his retirement, could get the story to press in early January. The story, however, was leaked to the New York papers on January 5, 1957, a few days before *Look* hit the newsstands.

A firestorm of criticism followed that Robinson had misled the Giants, the Dodgers, and the media. "That's typical of Jackie," sneered Bavasi. "Now he'll write a letter of apology. . . . He has been writing letters of apology all his life. . . . He tells you one thing and then writes another for money." The insinuation deeply wounded Robinson, who announced that there was no chance that he might reconsider.

Campy was genuinely shocked by Jackie's trade and subsequent retirement. He believed, as did Branch Rickey, that Robinson still had some baseball left in him. "But Jack is grown and Jack knows what Jack wants to do," Roy told a black reporter. "We'll miss Jack. His appearance on the field and his brand of baseball will be missed. But we'll play and we'll be all right." Any personal feelings about Robinson, ambivalent or otherwise, he kept to himself.

That is, until the New York press corps dictated otherwise. On Friday, January 18, Milton Gross of the *Post* spent the day with Robinson in Stamford informally discussing plans for a possible book. Campy was among the topics covered. "I think he's about done," Jackie observed. "I don't think he can come back off last season's record and have another great one like he did twice before. After a while so much of what you have goes. I hope not, but I think it's gone with Roy." Although Robinson thought his comment was off-the-record, Gross published the statement in his column on Monday.

Apparently, Campy did not read the *Post* that day. Not until Dick Young thoughtfully brought it to his attention later in the week did full-scale hostilities ensue. "I'd be surprised if Jackie didn't say something like that about me," he angrily told Young. "He has been shootin' off his mouth about everybody. And most of the time he doesn't know what he's talking about." For the first time, Roy did not hold back in his assessment of

Robinson. "He always believed I was older than he is, but that ain't so. . . . A guy like Jackie should have gone out of baseball with a lot of friends. Instead, he made a lot of enemies. He was always stirring up this stuff in the clubhouse too, making a lot of trouble." And Robbie, Campy insisted, was not sufficiently appreciative of baseball. "Everything he has, he owes to baseball. . . . Does he think those Chock full o' Nuts people would have had anything to do with him if he had never played baseball?"

When Young's account appeared on January 26, Campy was horrified. Like Jackie, he thought his words were off-the-record, although by this point Roy should have known what to expect from an agent provocateur such as Young. Still, he did not retract his statements. "You can play with a guy but not want to live with him," he explained. "I always steered clear of him when he was doing that popping off in the clubhouse." Jackie, glad that the gloves were now off publicly, soon got in a few digs of his own. "He's always been envious of me, that I was the first Negro in baseball," he told a St. Louis reporter. Later in a prepared statement, he denied saying that Roy was washed-up. "I could say why my relationship with Campy was cool, as he said, but it would accomplish no good for me to do so."

In the days that followed, the nation's sportswriters, both black and white, weighed in on baseball's most famous teammate feud since Gehrig and Ruth. Gross marveled at the reactions of "regret . . . shock . . . disbelief. . . . If they dislike each other and say so, now what the hell's the big deal about it?" But Sam Lacy, still friendly with both, felt each had erred, Robinson perhaps more so. Jackie, he once again lamented, "talks entirely too much at times. . . . He made a serious mistake in mentioning Campy at all. . . . It is no secret that Roy is an extremely sensitive individual . . . and even more so now that he is facing a comeback test."

With the dispute still raging, Campy found himself scheduled to appear with Jackie at a Harlem YMCA function. "That oughta be interesting," he wryly remarked. Somehow, they were cajoled into awkwardly shaking hands for the gathered cameramen, but then quickly sat as far apart from each other as possible. Even a buffer was "discreetly placed" so that Ruthe and Rachel Robinson would not have to speak to each other that evening.

The bad blood would only intensify in the weeks ahead, once again thanks to Dick Young's machinations, intentional or otherwise. In early March, Young asked Campy to comment on news reports that White Citizens Councils in Miami were stockpiling dynamite for use in a future race war over integration. "I don't like that stuff, not one bit," he observed. The column's next sentence, however, claimed that Roy "believed much of the current agitation to be caused by compulsory integration." "You can't make a man see things your way by banging him over the noggin with a stick," Campy (described by Young as "level-headed") supposedly remarked.

Robinson, whose growing involvement with the NAACP placed him on the cutting edge of the civil rights movement, was incensed. "To me this was Uncle Tomism of an intolerable sort," he later wrote. "I felt he was big enough, that his position in baseball was secure enough, for him not to have to go around lapping at the rears of prejudiced sportswriters and baseball executives in order to provide decently for his family." Robinson quickly contacted NAACP officials, who suggested a response in an upcoming appearance in Richmond.

Campy pursued his usual strategy when one of his comments kicked up a fuss. "I never made such a statement to Dick," he insisted to the *Afro-American*. "I'm in favor of any move that gets us our rights as quickly as possible." Although the condemnation of "compulsory integration" may well have reflected Young's views rather than Campy's, the "noggin/stick" reference was vintage Campanella: a man who disdained confrontation in racial matters and believed individuals had to "change out of their own free will." He had already made similar statements to Don Connery in 1955 and would again to Mike Wallace in 1959.

To critics of his conservative philosophy, Roy always had a ready answer: "It's been all right to me." Indeed it had. That his experience as a celebrity ballplayer differed considerably from that of the vast majority of blacks in 1950s America did not appear to occur to him. "I'm a colored man," he told Gross a few weeks after the Young controversy. "A few years ago there were many more things I couldn't do than I can today. I'm willing to wait."

Such words made Robinson wince. But most black ballplayers were simply not ready to follow his aggressive lead. Robinson was appalled that Larry Doby sent him a supportive note after his retirement but specifically requested it be kept private. He was even more annoyed that only three of about twenty black players (Hank Aaron, Elston Howard, and Monte Irvin) invited to a $100-a-couple NAACP fund-raiser honoring Branch

Rickey and Duke Ellington bothered to attend (Campy, however, did send a $100 check). The cautious attitude was just as prevalent in other sports, as 1957 Wimbledon winner Althea Gibson took a beating in the black press for her conscious "refusal to turn my tennis achievements into a crusade for racial equality."

To Roy, such "crusades" in baseball were unnecessary. He could simply point to the fifty-five blacks in spring training camps this year, a mere decade after Jackie's major league debut. By outperforming his peers, winning respect, and making friends, he believed he had advanced the cause sufficiently. Robinson felt otherwise. "There isn't a single Negro player in the game today who is aggressive enough to ensure that the Negro will continue to make progress in the game," he sneered. "The trouble with most of them is they don't want to rock the boat."

AN AURA of uneasiness, difficult to detect but nonetheless present, pervaded Brooklyn's first spring training without Robinson since 1945. With much of the Dodger core in their thirties, fans wondered how many championship opportunities the team had left. More disturbing was the Ebbets situation, which had gone from bad to worse over the winter. Still unable to make any headway with Robert Moses, O'Malley had recently acquired the Triple A Los Angeles Angels, an important step toward an eventual move to the West Coast. A few weeks later, Roy found himself posing in photographs with Los Angeles mayor Norris Poulson, who confidently informed him that he would be playing in California next year.

Whether Campy would be playing at all next year remained far from certain. As expected, he had gone under the knife over the winter to remove the right thumb bone chips, one of which proved to be compressing a nerve. He was convinced that everything was now back to normal. "There ain't no cause for anybody to worry about me," he boasted. "I already hit some balls better down here than I did all last year." Besides, 1957 was an "odd" year, so another comeback seemed almost predestined.

Bavasi was not expecting an MVP season from Roy, identified by *Sport* as one of the National League's "Four Big Question Marks." "If Campy can have just a good year, not a great one," he remarked, "I think he'll make the difference." Still, Bavasi knew that it was time to begin grooming a successor. His leading candidate was twenty-three-year-old Johnny Roseboro, whose 25 homers in Montreal had put him on the fast track for Brooklyn. Just like Biz Mackey twenty years earlier, Campy imparted his vast catching knowledge to the youngster that spring, instructing him on shifting his feet properly and throwing. "Get your rear end moving," he barked. "You throw with your butt."

Years later, Roseboro suggested that Campy's most valuable lesson was not catching mechanics but in showing a raw black rookie how to adjust to major league life. Roy had willingly assumed the task for years, even for non-Dodgers. "He was like a godfather," Hank Aaron marveled. "He just taught us how to live." Campy took Roseboro in hand, advising him on press relations ("telling them the truth short of making a teammate look bad"), five-star restaurants, and the proper look. "Kid, you're a big leaguer now and you better begin to dress and act like one" was his command.

The avuncular facade Roseboro found so endearing concealed Campy's growing anxiety. Except for a single four-hit game, the surgically repaired hand did not respond well in spring training. As his failures at the plate mounted, Southern fans began to taunt him with reminders of Jackie's bleak assessment of his prospects for 1957. Even his old manager George Scales flatly insisted to a reporter, "Campy is washed-up."

Like most aging athletes, Roy was not prepared to admit that the end might be near. But an uncharacteristic show of bitterness on a train that spring revealed that the thought was not far from his mind. Riding alongside a young white pitcher whining about the quality of the air-conditioning, Campy could take no more. Try traveling on a Negro train from Mobile to Nashville if you don't like it, he snapped. And you're damn lucky to be getting a shot in the first place. What would *my* career have been like, Roy asked, "if they'd signed me to a contract, even a class D contract when I was eighteen. . . . I'd a liked to have the chance you got, kid."

Campy knew that his spring had not been the best, but there was no thought of easing him out of the starting lineup. Alston was not about to entrust the staff to Roseboro, sent to Montreal for more seasoning; perennial backup Rube Walker, who had never hit enough to play regularly; or any of the fresh-faced farmhands posed with a visibly uncomfortable Campy in a spring training photo. The only other option was twenty-seven-year-old rookie Joe Pignatano, a .295 hitter in Triple A last year, added to the roster as insurance in case Campy and Walker went down.

Roy was behind the plate as usual for the Dodgers' opener at Connie Mack Stadium. It was another frustrating evening for Campy: 0 for 5 with a passed ball. Three more passed balls and an error followed in his next eleven starts, and the whispers that he was done grew louder. But his defense soon stabilized, and he even began to look his old self at the plate, perhaps thanks to a switch to lighter bats with thinner handles. By June 17, he was hitting a surprising .286 with 9 homers in 133 at bats. Another magical comeback no longer seemed quite so far-fetched.

Campy's spurt attracted little attention. Desperate Brooklyn fans were more consumed with the distressingly precarious fate of their beloved Bums. "Let's Keep the Dodgers in Brooklyn" was the rallying cry throughout the borough, seen on buttons, signs, and even the title of a new song by the comedian Phil Foster.

When prodded, most of the Dodgers had little to say about the various relocation scenarios. "We haven't got to the point where we have to feel anything about it," Campy explained, but that was about to change. O'Malley had met privately in April with Moses, who informed him that Brooklyn was out as far as a new ballpark was concerned, instead offering the old World's Fair site at Flushing Meadows in Queens as an alternative. The location and potentially expensive lease did not thrill O'Malley, particularly with Los Angeles officials prepared to offer him much better terms. National League owners cleared the path to a move by voting on May 28 to authorize relocation by the Dodgers and Giants to the West Coast. "I think they're goners," predicted Jimmy Cannon.

Roy was shocked. "Up to now I never thought it could happen," he admitted. He loved Ebbets and cherished the local fans, who had embraced him so wholeheartedly from the very start. But he had been around the game long enough not to hold any romantic notions that baseball was anything but a business. "If they go, I'll go. It won't be the first time I've packed my bags."

As talk of the move intensified throughout the summer, Campy's performance again began to tail off. At times, his bat appeared pathetically slow, and he looked every bit the grandfather he now was (Joyce had recently given birth to a baby girl named Gale). In a series at Connie Mack Stadium, usually one of his favorite haunts, he struck out 6 straight times, the last two embarrassingly with Jackie Robinson in attendance. By the end of July, his average had dipped to .223 following a nightmarish 16-for-109 span. Now waiting impatiently in the wings was the recently promoted Roseboro, who Alston promised "would see a lot more action in the future."

But even in his decline, Roy continued to work his magic with young pitchers such as Danny McDevitt, who credited his first major league shutout to Roy's astute handling. And opposing managers such as the Phillies' Mayo Smith discovered that even an aging Campanella could still be dangerous in the clutch. With the Phils up 4–3, one out, and runners on second and third in the eighth at Ebbets on July 5, Smith ordered Robin Roberts to pitch to Campy. "I knew if we put Campy on that they'd send [Elmer] Valo up to hit for [Don] Zimmer, and I respected Valo more," explained Smith. "I don't respect Campanella. You can strike him out." Campy responded to the slight by clocking the 241st homer of his career. Facing a similar situation three weeks later in Cincinnati, Roy again laced a key hit. "Ol' Camp may not be what he used to be," he chuckled, "but he still isn't that easy."

He still played the game with reckless abandon and passion. When Raul Sanchez of the Redlegs persisted in knocking down Dodger hitters that summer, particularly the black ones, Campy was furious. "That Cuban blankety-blank," he muttered. "I'll fix him." He would get his chance a few weeks later when Jim Gilliam and Sanchez began slugging it out after a collision at first. Not only was Roy one of the first Dodgers on the field but he was soon getting his licks in, though he later claimed he was acting as "peacemaker" and "didn't punch nobody."

That Campy and other black ballplayers felt free enough to participate in an interracial baseball rumble reflected the progress made in a decade of the Great Experiment. Only a few years earlier, some feared that "even a frown" by Jackie would set back the cause. On the other hand, such violent brawls would never have occurred if black players were not constantly forced to dodge so many brushbacks. The beanball remained a weapon of racial intimidation. Even as late as 1957, more than a few white major leaguers genuinely and openly feared that the African-American players were "taking over" the game.

AMID THE rumors, anxiety, and turmoil over the move, the Dodgers had somehow managed to win twenty-two of thirty-two to pull within 1½ games of first place on August 2. Within a week, reality had set in. The

Braves took two of three in Milwaukee, the Giants grabbed three of four at Ebbets, and the Brooks fell five games off the pace. "Slowly, stubbornly, silently, but irrevocably," wrote Leonard Koppett, "the Dodgers are dying."

The mighty core that had steamrolled that National League for a decade was a shell of its former self. Pee Wee Reese and Carl Erskine were ready to be put out to pasture. Newcombe, through drink or his own insecurities, which now included a fear of flying, had descended into mediocrity and despair, even spitting angrily at a booing Jersey City crowd. "The team needs a little more oomph," observed Jackie Robinson, "and I don't know where they're going to get it."

Robinson, some believed, was the missing "oomph," but he expressed no regrets about his retirement. In between his new duties at Chock full o' Nuts, he had moved far beyond baseball, hobnobbing with the likes of Eisenhower and Martin Luther King, Jr. Though still rooting for his old teammates, he remained bitter toward the Dodger organization. "I too have given up on the club but refuse to let it upset me," he wrote a friend that August. "As for the front office it serves them right and if something happens that they don't win I'll not worry at all."

Campy could do little to stop the bleeding. His left hand, according to Milton Gross, was now "completely paralyzed in the fingers. The Dodger catcher has no control over them and the condition will get worse because the muscles are atrophying." But once again, Roy silenced those who believed him washed-up. A day after Gross's bleak report, he cracked four hits against the Pirates at Ebbets, including his first homer in six weeks, a two-run smash off Ron Kline. "The ball don't care whether you're twenty-five or forty-five," he observed somewhat testily. "We're not old. We're experienced. The ball hit Johnny Roseboro on the hand the other day. It hurt him. He's not old. But if the same ball hits me, they say it's 'cause I'm old."

Campy may not have viewed himself as a senior citizen, but Alston no longer believed he was an everyday player. "I don't know why the man keeps restin' me," Roy grumbled. "When I'm through, I'm gonna be restin' a long, long time." But nagging injuries continued to dog him, and his recovery time from bumps and bruises was now days rather than hours. He would start only thirteen of the final twenty-eight games of the season, as the Dodgers fell out of the race for good. His celebrity that he had come to cherish also took a distinct hit. "Man, this is awful," he joked to Newk.

"Nobody calls us. I left a ten-o'clock wake-up with the hotel operator this morning and even she didn't call. I guess that means we are really lousy."

There was already talk that Campy might transition to a player-coach position in 1958 with perhaps eventually a shot at handling one of the Dodger farm clubs. "Campy has the best potential of all the [black] guys," Jackie Robinson admitted. "He knows the game. He loves baseball. If he wanted to coach—there's not a lot of money in it—Roy certainly could do it and I don't doubt that he could get it."

The baseball establishment predictably wanted no part of Robinson, who received no managerial or coaching opportunities except for a half-hearted offer from Vancouver of the Pacific Coast League. "If Robinson weren't such a provocative person, I'd say he'd make a good manager," Cardinals general manager Frank Lane observed. "Lord knows he knows baseball." Others, such as Bavasi, believed Jackie, a "perfectionist," would have difficulty relating to players who lacked his ferocious drive and phenomenal ability.

Campy liked the idea of coaching ("It's baseball, isn't it? And it's the big leagues") but he was not interested in retiring just yet. Even in the season's final week, old number 39 was just as eager to play as the day when Biz Mackey first spotted him. On Tuesday, September 24, he was in the lineup for the sparsely attended finale at Ebbets, appearing in the first four innings before departing. Afterward, while fans roamed the field, some running the bases, others scooping up soil, Campy served crab fingers in the clubhouse, complete with his special sauce. "Lord, how he loved those crab fingers!" Roseboro recalled. "Lord, how he loved to have fun!"

The Dodgers' final weekend was spent in Philadelphia, where Campy's baseball journey had begun two decades earlier. On Friday, Campy set a new National League record by catching at least one hundred games for the ninth straight season. He was back on the bench the rest of the weekend, although Alston asked him to pinch-hit for Roger Craig in the eighth inning on Sunday. Facing rookie left-hander Seth Morehead with nine-year-old Little Roy watching anxiously from the sidelines, he flied to center field. Moments later, the season was over.

His reduced role was likely to continue in 1958. Defensively, he was still adequate, finishing fifth in the league in innings caught, third in assists, and first in fielding percentage. His offense, however, remained spotty, especially away from Brooklyn. For the second straight season, he failed to crack .200 on the road, hitting only .192 with 3 homers, well below his Ebbets line of 10 homers and a .294 average. "He can still help us in the No. 2 spot, but if we are going to get back on top, we've got to get a No. 1 catcher who can drive in runs," Bavasi explained.

Whether Campy's battered hands could even make it through another season remained questionable. "I don't think he could have played a heck of a lot longer," his teammate Don Zimmer speculated. "I don't know if there was enough in that hand left for him to do any good." Roy felt otherwise. National League catchers as a group hit only .243 with an OBP of .313, nearly identical to his own marks of .242 and .316. Bavasi himself admitted that if they released him, "six others would pick him up." And next year, Campy vowed, would be better. "As long as I have my health and strength, I don't worry about how I'll do."

TO THE surprise of virtually no one, O'Malley accepted the Los Angeles offer just nine days after the season ended. The Brooklyn Dodgers, the storied Bums of yore, were no more. Some fans wept, while others would spend the rest of their lives cursing O'Malley for his perceived treachery. More objective observers understood the decision, if not necessarily approving of it. "From a business standpoint, the move from Brooklyn was a smart one," observed Jackie Robinson. "The Dodger management isn't interested in making friends—just money." Even Branch Rickey was somewhat sympathetic: "If I had owned the Dodgers, I wouldn't have moved them, but if I had been in Walter O'Malley's shoes, I don't know what I would have done."

The new Los Angeles Dodgers had no shortage of decisions to make that off-season. Alston, on thin ice after a shaky season and more rumors of "dissension," was retained, but would be assisted by the shocking return of Dressen as coach. The club also reluctantly made plans to move into the Coliseum, a massive, not-ready-for-baseball facility whose 251-foot left-field fence and 42-foot screen made purists cringe. Right-handed pull hitters such as Campy were expected to have a field day, but Roy warned that the stadium might not prove quite so homer-friendly. "Nobody's played at the

Coliseum yet, but they've all got something to say," he grumbled. "The batter will have to pull the ball right quick and sharply to get it down the line and over the forty-foot wall."

Like most of his teammates, Campy would have preferred to stay in Brooklyn. But as a quintessential company man, he did what the team asked of him, even after Bavasi forced him to take a pay cut for 1958. Roy made two trips to Los Angeles, first for a function at the Statler Hotel on October 28, then again a few weeks later for a TV appearance on an Ethel Barrymore special. He began to look for a place to live, eventually settling on a furnished house in the Victoria Park section, although the site still awaited Ruthe's final approval.

Campy was not scheduled to return to Los Angeles until early February for a coaching clinic. In the meantime, he kept a close eye on his liquor store, put his yacht up for sale, and enjoyed the first major snowstorm of the season with the kids. He also made the usual winter appearances, including another awkward meeting with Jackie Robinson at a charity basketball game for the Harlem YMCA on January 16, 1958. The five hundred lucky fans at the Renaissance Casino that night watched Campy coach Doby, Gilliam, Newk, and a bunch of other black major leaguers while a chubby Jackie officiated.

The last weekend in January was busy for Roy. On Saturday, he gave a long-distance interview to Vincent X. Flaherty of the *Los Angeles Examiner.* Lovable old Campy made certain to turn on his considerable charm, just as he had with the New York writers for the past decade. "I'm looking forward to a real good year," he told Flaherty. "A real good year!"

Sunday night brought the annual New York chapter of the Baseball Writers Association of America dinner at the Waldorf-Astoria, usually good for a laugh. In between the usual tiresome speeches and awards presentations, the writers always put on a corker of a musical show, this year a full-blown parody of the recent shenanigans that had left New York short two teams (the Giants had agreed to move to San Francisco). And if that wasn't enough, Vice President Nixon was in the house that night, cracking jokes about the Coliseum and urging expansion to Denver, San Diego, and Minneapolis. Bill Corum, who noted the veep looked better in person than on TV, couldn't help but think ahead to 1960. "As a Democrat, Mr. Nixon scares me."

Campy sat at one of the Dodger tables, enjoying the proceedings with Hodges, Drysdale, and Koufax. During the evening, the sportscaster Harry Wismer sidled up to Roy with a request. Wismer had a local show on WABD, Channel 5, on Monday nights following the conclusion of boxing from St. Nicholas Arena. Was Campy interested in doing a guest appearance around 10:45 tomorrow evening to promote the ongoing Harlem YMCA fund-raising drive? Sure, said Campy, ever obliging. He'd be there.

18

DOSORIS LANE

THE MORNING OF MONDAY, JANUARY 27, meant the beginning of another school week for the Campanella kids and another day at the liquor store for their dad. For a New York winter's day, the weather was mild, approaching forty-two degrees by the late afternoon.

Roy's day was already planned: work at the "juice joint," then head to the studio at East Sixty-seventh Street for his appearance on WABD. First, however, was a detour to Curry Chevrolet at 133rd and Broadway to drop off the family station wagon that Ruthe's brother had banged up. Informed it would not be ready until tomorrow, Campy opted to rent a 1957 Chevy sports sedan. From there he proceeded to the liquor store, where he spent most of the day.

Around 9:00 p.m., the phone rang. It was Wismer. Let's postpone your appearance until next week, he said. That way, we can promote it better and get a bigger audience. Campy agreed. Next Monday was fine.

The tragic events that unfolded over the next several hours have been part of the Campanella canon for the past five decades. According to Roy, he didn't budge from the store until between about 1:30 and 2:00 a.m. Because of a recent snowstorm, the drive back home took ninety minutes instead of the usual sixty.

But contemporary news accounts contradict his story in several crucial areas. His employees informed the press the next morning that Campy had actually left at twelve thirty. From there, eyewitnesses, including sportswriter Art Rust, placed him a block away at Smalls' Paradise on 135th Street (the great trombonist J. J. Johnson and his quintet were on the bill that night). Roy remained at Smalls' until 2:00 a.m., waiting for a friend to return with Roy's rental car, which the friend had borrowed to drive the blind singer Al Hibbler to a TV show. The temperature was about thirty-eight degrees with no substantial local snowfall since January 16.

His next stop has been a well-kept secret. When questioned, the ever-discreet Buzzie Bavasi admitted that Roy had told him in "strict confidence" that he was doing "something he shouldn't have been doing," and not Dodger-related promotional work that O'Malley hoped would be covered by insurance. Bavasi would concede only that Campy "was visiting a friend." Several other interviews confirm the "friend" was actually a lover or a pickup whose identity remains unknown to this day. Some writers, including Roger Kahn, knew the truth but chose to remain silent, hardly surprising in an era when salacious political or celebrity scandals often never saw the light of day.

From the mysterious lady's boudoir, Roy got into the Chevy and headed for the Northern State Parkway. After exiting at Glen Cove Road, he motored through the quiet and deserted streets before reaching Dosoris Lane, whose treacherous S-curve had been the scene of more than a few accidents. It was now 3:34 a.m. Rain had begun to fall. In five minutes, he would be across the bridge to Morgan Island and home. Was Ruthe waiting up? If so, an argument and accusations probably awaited.

Roy headed north on Dosoris and approached the S-curve at a leisurely pace of about thirty miles an hour. According to Roy, he suddenly encountered "big ice patches" as he tried to negotiate the curve. The rented Chevy, not equipped with the snow tires used by most cars in those days, began to skid helplessly toward what was later identified as Pole Number 25 of the New York Telephone Company. "I tried furiously to swerve and felt a chill in my spine when I saw I couldn't," he later wrote. "The brakes were useless." At the last second, he managed to yank the wheel enough to avoid "hitting the pole dead center, but not enough to miss it altogether."

For the rest of his life, Campy would emphasize the road conditions, weather, and the absence of snow tires as the key factors in his accident. But the real cause was something more basic. "Maybe he went to sleep," remarked a Dosoris Lane resident interviewed later. "He said he skidded on wet pavement, but he never went into the S-turn at all." Bavasi stated that Campy "fell asleep at the wheel," and the Glen Cove police theorized as much. It is not hard to imagine that a man without rest for close to twenty hours, drained by work and a recent roll in the hay, would succumb to exhaustion. Whether alcohol from his stop at Smalls' may have contributed is unknown, although Roy was never a heavy drinker, and the policemen and doctors who attended him noticed no liquor on his breath.

The "artillery-like" sound of the crash only yards away awoke a fifty-four-year-old gynecologist named W. Spencer Gurnee and his wife, Betty. Clad only in pajamas and robe, Gurnee raced to the car to administer Demerol while his wife called the police.

Three minutes later, Glen Cove policeman Roger Welden arrived on the scene. The Chevy, he noticed, had apparently struck the pole, spun around, then turned over on its right side. Except for a "dented right fender, a broken right window and some minor body dents," the car looked surprisingly intact. Perhaps its occupant would be equally unscathed.

Welden soon discovered that Glen Cove's most famous resident (Whitey Ford was perhaps a close second) was in that overturned Chevy, "doubled up like a pretzel" and wedged tightly under the dashboard. A later analysis by the Cornell University Auto Crash Research Center revealed that the collision had propelled Campy to the right, "his chin striking the instrument panel before he was thrust under it." The same analysis revealed that a seat belt—unfortunately only optional in American cars until 1964—would have almost certainly prevented serious injury.

The car radio was still playing. "Roy, could you turn off the radio? How are you doing?" Campy, still conscious, went to reach for the dial. His arms would not move. He had already tried futilely to turn off the ignition. "I don't seem to be able to move my arms and legs," he responded. Welden's heart sank.

In the minutes that followed, four more policemen and a wrecker from Freddie's Gas Station appeared. Before Campy could be extricated from the wreckage, the Chevy had to be turned upright, a risky move considering his condition, but there seemed to be no alternative. A patrolman named Frank Poepplein squeezed into the car, covered Campy with a blanket, and did his best to brace him while the wrecker did its work. Working with crowbars, the cops then freed Campy from the Chevy and carried him without trying to "straighten him out" (according to later news reports) to the ambulance that had already arrived at 3:45. Thanks to Dr. Gurnee's appropriation of the police radio ("This is Roy Campanella!" he bellowed. "This is Roy Campanella!"), the emergency room at the Community Hospital at Glen Cove was not surprised by the familiar face peering anxiously from the stretcher that rolled in at 4:12 a.m.

The unenviable task of informing Ruthe was left to Welden. Her response, he noticed, was strangely flat and unemotional. "She couldn't have give a shit less," he later recalled. Was Ruthe in shock? Or did her peculiar reaction reflect the disgust and anger of a wife whose husband was out in the middle of the night again, probably with another woman?

Though only semiconscious, Campy recognized something was drastically wrong. Not only was his back in agony, but his legs continued to feel strangely disconnected from the rest of his body. Meanwhile, a steady stream of ever-frantic doctors, nurses, and interns buzzed around him, poking, prodding, and x-raying. The diagnosis was alarming: paralysis from a broken neck with spinal-cord compression. An immediate cervical laminectomy was ordered to relieve bone pressure on the cord with the slim chance that recovery might follow. But as Dr. William Staas, Jr., an expert on spinal cord injuries, explains, "The canal of the spinal cord is so tight that even a little bit of bony displacement does severe damage to the cord," damage that is often "irreversible."

By this point, Ruthe had arrived and had been fully briefed about her husband's condition. "My back hurts, honey," Roy moaned. "Car skidded." As he was wheeled into the elevator in preparation for surgery, Ruthe overheard Campy ask a heartbreaking question: "Doc, what happened to me?"

It was now 8:30 a.m. The doctors sent Ruthe home to wait, but it would not be a solitary vigil. The media, which had pounced on the story only minutes after the crash, were already camping out at Salt Spray. Inside the house, Milton Gross noticed that everything seemed almost normal. Tony and Princess, both too young to know what was going on, were distracted by the family's Scottish terrier, Bonnie, while Little Roy had insisted on going to school. Their mother somehow retained "a sad strained smile" despite her mounting panic. "You never know, do you?" she asked Gross. "One day, one minute, there's nothing to fear and the next . . ."

As Tuesday morning wore on, the hospital switchboard was flooded with callers who had learned of the accident from the front pages of the daily papers or the *Today* show. Speculation that Campy had died persisted, although Dodger officials now on-site did their best to quash the unhappy rumors. Finally, at 12:50 p.m., Dodger attorney Harry Walsh approached the swarm of newspapermen eager to file their stories before deadline for the evening editions. "Campy is alive," he announced, "and we believe the operation is a success." A few minutes later, a much-distressed O'Malley arrived, cigar in mouth. "I'll have something for you shortly, boys," he told reporters. "Campanella is one of the most wonderful persons I have ever met."

At the press conference that followed, Campy's youthful neurosurgeon, Robert Sengstaken, took center stage. Roy, he explained, was actually a lucky man. "He suffered a fracture—dislocation of cervicals five and six of the vertebrae, at the neck line. . . . If it had been cervicals three or four, an inch or two higher, Campanella would not be here." During the surgery, prolonged because of Roy's bulky neck musculature, Sengstaken and his team first drilled holes into his skull for the Crutchfield tongs needed to keep his head in traction and then "reduced the fracture dislocation by putting the affected pieces back in place." Whether the paralysis would dissipate he did not know, although Sengstaken gave Campy a fifty-fifty shot of returning to normal. In any case, it was still "too early to tell."

If Campy recovers, the reporters asked, can he get back on the field? Sengstaken, though apparently not much of a baseball fan, viewed such a scenario as highly unlikely. "He won't be able to play baseball before a year, and it would be foolish if he tried to continue to play after that." Later, after the press conference had ended, he offered a bleaker prognosis to Jack Lang and a few of the other newsmen still lingering: "I don't think he will ever catch again."

OVER THE next several days, Campy received the saturation media coverage usually reserved for presidents and kings. For much of America, he was not just a ballplayer but a cherished friend they had come to know personally in a way hardly conceivable just ten years earlier. Thanks to television, everyone *knew* Roy Campanella. They had seen him star in the World Series, shave in Gillette commercials, wisecrack on game shows, and chat with Edward R. Murrow. Now they wanted him to get better, devouring the frequent, but unrevealing, medical bulletins issued by the hospital.

Ruthe, despite the staff's chipper promises that "everything is going to be all right," knew that Roy was in bad shape. Her husband, now shaved bald and still heavily sedated, was a mass of tubes, tongs, straps, and sandbags. "He's in such pain I have everything to do to keep from crying when I look at him," she admitted.

Pain was soon the least of his worries. On Thursday, doctors noticed that Campy, though now fully conscious (he had casually greeted O'Malley with "Hello, boss"), had contracted bronchial pneumonia and was having difficulty breathing even with the assistance of an oxygen tent. As Campy lay motionless gasping for breath and fighting his growing claustrophobia, Dr. Charles Hayden poked his head under the tent to have a word with him. Though a longtime Yankee fan, Hayden greatly admired Roy, whose size, background, and drive mirrored his own. "I knew I was in trouble when I was lying there," Campy later told Hayden's son Eric, "and I looked up into your father's eyes and I saw him crying."

Hayden explained to Roy that his situation was dire. The only option remaining was a tracheostomy, meaning that his throat would be incised and a tube inserted to aid in clearing secretions and breathing. After Campy nodded his consent, the procedure was performed under local anesthetic only. In the hours that followed, Campy once more turned to his faith, repeating the 23rd Psalm in his head again and again, but he would later admit, "I thought I was a goner."

Whether through divine intervention or the wonders of modern medical science, Roy survived that night and was soon breathing comfortably again. Within a week, the infection had cleared, and subsequent bulletins announced that he had moved from intravenous feedings to strained and then solid food. But the scraps of information hardly satisfied the media mob clustered in the hospital lobby, all of whom had only one question: would Campanella walk again?

Not one reporter, not even Dick Young, had been allowed to see him. Still, they grasped that Roy would not be back in uniform anytime soon.

Despite the bulletins' peculiar claims that Campy was "cheerful" and had experienced some sensation to the abdomen, the grim and persistent references to "no new improvement in the sense of feeling" and "legs remain paralyzed" were too obvious to ignore.

By mid-February open speculation had begun ("Dodgers Fear Campy Will Not Walk Again," read one headline), fueled by an anonymous physician's widely quoted admission that he had "never heard of a case where a patient's progress stopped, then suddenly resumed." Although Sengstaken quickly announced, "Campanella's progress hasn't stopped completely," his own pessimism was all too apparent. "He may still walk, but the chances are less than when he was admitted to the hospital."

Campy, though still in traction and seeing virtually no one but his wife and the medical staff, soon got wind of the rumors. Ruthe had recently brought him a radio, a decision she came to regret when Roy overheard a broadcaster blathering on about his possible paralysis. "How can they say that?" he sputtered. "How can anybody think a thing like that?" He was certain, he told Ruthe, that he'd "make a liar out of the docs."

But the almost superhuman recuperative powers that had brushed aside a blistered eye, dislocated thumb, and mangled hands now failed him. Hour after hour, he lay like a corpse, his legs useless, his arms that could be extended but able to do little else. His world was limited to his special Stryker bed (known as the "rack" by some patients), a device that allowed him to be turned over every few hours, "like a piece of ham between two pieces of bread," to prevent the development of decubitus ulcers (bedsores).

With the gradual realization that his plight might be permanent, a profound, unremitting depression set in. He insisted that his room be kept dark with the blinds drawn. He wanted to hear none of the thousands of letters of encouragement he had received and tolerated no discussion of baseball. Even his deep religious faith offered no consolation. When Bavasi visited him on February 25, just four weeks after the accident, he was shocked by Roy's condition and state of mind. "Why did it have to be me?" Campy asked bitterly. "Why me?" "I think if Campanella hadn't been a baseball player or hadn't been with the Dodger organization, he might have taken his own life," Bavasi later recalled.

Junius Kellogg, a former Manhattan College basketball star similarly paralyzed four years earlier, tried to reach out to Campy. "They told me

I'd have to accept it," he wrote Roy. "If it turns out you can't play baseball, there are so many other capacities in addition to player. You could still work with kids." But only a firm scolding from Sengstaken broke through Roy's despair. Yes, he had had a bad break, but self-pity, the doctor told him, would get him nowhere. Though Roy couldn't see it now, his life was not over.

The tough-love approach did not entirely convince Campy, but his suicidal thoughts did begin to dissipate somewhat. He made an effort to interact with people and baseball again, even seeing his first visitor outside the family and the front office on March 17, a former Dodger employee named Frank Slocum, who now handled insurance issues through the commissioner's office. Briefed in advance by Ruthe, Slocum was startled to see Campy listening to a Yankee exhibition game and offering insights on how to pitch the hitters until his attention waned. "Maybe he was thinking too much about how he'd like to be playing," remarked Slocum. Still, the revived baseball interest, the corny joke he cracked about the foul-tasting cranberry juice he now drank to prevent urinary infections, and his genuine appreciation of Ruthe's home-cooked meals brought to his room daily suggested that maybe Old Campy had turned the corner.

Other good news arrived as the spring weather turned warmer. The painful Crutchfield tongs finally came off, and his tracheostomy tube was removed. Less ashamed about his appearance, he allowed his children to visit for the first time. Although Ruthe had done her best to explain things, Little Roy was shocked by the sight of his father, "lying prone, looking face down, in a kind of Dr. Frankenstein contraption." In time, the Campanella children, just like their mother, would grow accustomed to the world of hospitals and the strange medical devices within.

Thoughts of the Dodgers, so repulsive to him a few weeks earlier, now surfaced again and again. His once-unshakable sense that he had "let the club down" had given way to a very real desire to reconnect with his former teammates. On April 15, he sent a telegram wishing the Dodgers well in their opener against the Giants ("I'm still with you," it read). Two days later, he addressed the team directly through a long-distance hookup at a televised Dodger function at the Biltmore Bowl. "I've had a tough break," he told host Art Linkletter, "but I've got lots of willpower and I think it will come out all right." The sound of his disembodied voice elicited more than a few tears, but Campy, true to form, got off a joke or two about pitching to Willie Mays lest things get too maudlin.

It had been only eleven weeks since his accident. Mentally, he had returned to the land of the living. His neurological progress, however, had been negligible; he was "essentially a quadriplegic," said Sengstaken. Now that Roy had stabilized medically, Community Hospital had little else to offer him.

On May 1, a specialist named Howard Rusk was brought in to evaluate Roy in preparation for his transfer to another facility. While Rusk examined Campy's body, still "unresponsive as stone," Ruthe waited outside. "It's hopeless, isn't it?" she asked a physician. No, he told her. If anyone could do something for Roy, it was Howard Rusk.

LIKE MILLIONS of other Americans, Rusk had closely followed the Campanella saga over the past few months. His interest was not that of a fan distraught over the crippling injury to his favorite player. Instead, Rusk was certain this man could benefit tremendously from a program of physical rehabilitation.

Rusk, fifty-seven, had been a driving force (some said *the* driving force) in the development of the new field of rehabilitative medicine. His stint in the air force during World War II had exposed him to seriously wounded and disabled servicemen, who were typically discharged after treatment and then dumped into the hands of the Veterans Administration. "They would simply lie around," recalled Rusk, "getting custodial care with nothing to do . . . waiting for some kind of infection or disease to carry them off." The situation was especially dire for paraplegics, who suffered "terrible bedsores, developed kidney and bladder problems, and simply lay in bed, waiting for death" (the words *quadriplegic* or *paraplegic* were then foreign to most Americans, since few such patients lived beyond a short time).

Rusk was convinced that these men need not become charity cases. For one thing, newly developed antibiotics could now keep the often fatal infections at bay. More important, he believed that a comprehensive rehabilitation program, one that encompassed "emotional, social, educational and occupational needs," could produce useful and productive citizens.

Although the military was soon won over, Rusk was frustrated by the postwar resistance he encountered from the medical establishment, which believed his ideas were unrealistic. Eventually, he found a receptive audience at New York University, attracted additional funding from Bernard Baruch and other wealthy philanthropists, and then set out to create the kind of rehabilitation program he had always envisioned. It began with two units at Bellevue Hospital but eventually evolved into the Institute of Physical Medicine and Rehabilitation on Thirty-fourth Street on the east side of Manhattan, the first facility of its kind in the United States.

Within a short time, Rusk's once-radical ideas won increasing acceptance. Physicians began sending him the paraplegics, stroke victims, and other physically disabled individuals they had once deemed hopeless—and were shocked by the results. His patients, many now able to feed themselves, drive, and work, dubbed him Dr. Live-Again.

For anyone even remotely interested in physical rehab in the 1950s, the institute was unquestionably the place to be, a bustling hub where eager young doctors were trained, cutting-edge research papers written, and new assistive devices invented. "It was an incredible place to work," recalls physical therapist Janet Jeghelian. "It was the mecca of rehabilitation." But the most astonishing sights were patients such as Gilbert Provencher, a paralyzed young man from New Hampshire who not only learned to paint using a brush "strapped to his left elbow" but was soon producing works reminiscent of those of Grandma Moses. "We have one rule at the institute," explained Rusk. "No one can tell a patient what they can't do."

Bobbi Wailes, then a teenager recently struck down by polio who today acts part-time in between her duties as program director for people with disabilities at Lincoln Center, remains grateful to Rusk and the institute he helped create. "If it wasn't for him, I don't know how the disabled community would have fared," she says. "I think because of his thinking, we were able to come out of the closet."

EVEN AFTER meeting Rusk and agreeing to be moved to Manhattan, Campy was not yet interested in emerging from behind the curtain. "I'm all right," he halfheartedly insisted to the gathered media awaiting his arrival at the institute on May 5. As proof, he demonstrated his limited function, although he refused to be photographed. "I don't want my kids to see me the way I am."

The ambulance attendants wheeled him into room 107, where famous radio sportscaster Ted Husing had recently rehabbed after a brain-tumor procedure. While Roy tried to get used to his new surroundings and the dozens of other disabled suddenly in his midst, the three men who would oversee his care came calling. He was introduced to Drs. Donald Covalt, "a little ball of fire" who had served under Rusk during the war, and Edward Lowman, a South Carolinian who was rumored to have dated Marilyn Monroe. And Roy reacquainted himself with the towering figure of Rusk. "Rusk was the type of person that if he stood in front of a group and recited nursery rhymes, they would all listen to him," recalled physical therapist Pat Therriault. With his eloquence, Midwestern background, fondness for cigars, and reputation as a shrewd negotiator, Rusk appeared to be cut from the same cloth as Campy's old boss Branch Rickey.

That such an enviable rehabilitation dream team was now working in his behalf did not cheer Campy in the slightest. He was what the doctors called a C5 on C6 quadriplegic, an utterly dependent prisoner of the Stryker bed, with no control of his bowels or bladder. "Can't you give me something?" he pleaded. "I feel like a baby this way."

The doctors assured him he would be taught techniques and strategies to minimize incontinence as part of a general program to achieve "independence through wheelchair self-sufficiency." For now, the first step was to get Campy out of bed. A device known as a tilt board now became part of his daily routine, allowing him to gradually acclimate to a vertical position while promoting blood circulation and protecting against bone decalcification and kidney stones. Although most bedbound patients usually fainted on their first tilt-board "ride," even at a thirty-degree angle, Campy's tolerance was better than most, and he soon built up his time to thirty minutes a day.

By the end of May, he was ready to graduate to a wheelchair, happy news after four months in bed. "If I could sit, I could learn to manipulate the chair. If I could move around, there was no telling what I could do next." But Roy was already discovering that the quadriplegic's "life . . . is a series of complications." After only a brief trial, the wheelchair experiment was halted when a painful contusion developed on his buttocks. Eventually, Campy took another shot at the chair, and this time succeeded. "It always amazed me," remarked physical therapist Bob Bartlett, "that he really sat so well in a wheelchair with such limited motor power in his trunk."

With the help of Bartlett and other therapists, Campy was fully immersed in the institute's program. The major goal, Janet Jeghelian explains, was "to try to strengthen whatever he had and make it functional. . . . He didn't have very much muscle tone left. He could elevate his shoulders, hunch his shoulders up. He had some shoulder motion. But it's like almost a flailing kind of motion. And some wrist extension." Range-of-motion exercises and weight lifting became part of his daily routine, although the wimpy eight pounds he was initially asked to hoist was yet another depressing reminder of his diminished strength. Nevertheless, with the use of a special device, he not only managed to raise the load from his waist to his chin repeatedly, but eventually worked up to twenty-five pounds per hand.

As spring turned into a typically sticky Manhattan summer, his adaptation to life as a quad continued. He had to learn how to be transported back and forth from bed to chair, a seemingly routine task but hardly simple for quadriplegics at Campy's level. "They lose the musculature, a lot of it in their trunk," recalls Therriault. "They also lose their sense of balance. So they have to relearn that. And we would do a lot of matwork and sitting and leaning . . . just relearning their base of support again." Roy would also need instruction in the activities of daily living (ADLs in medical lingo), the mundane yet essential tasks of everyday existence, most of which he would never again perform without assistance. Eating was extraordinarily difficult, especially with no control over his fingers, although the occupational-therapy department eventually fitted him with a special gadget that held a utensil strapped to his wrist.

The grueling, almost boot-camp-like environment produced more than its share of agonizing challenges and frustrations. But Campy, despite his private mental anguish, withstood them all with the same resilience that had served him so well in baseball. Fifty years later, his therapists still marveled at his remarkably cooperative nature and faithful dedication to the program. "He was a gracious man, a man that I thought put a great deal of effort into getting better," Bob Bartlett recalls. "He never had a sour attitude that he was plucked in the prime of his life." His dogged example became a source of inspiration to other patients, the same patients he had recoiled from when first admitted. Now he found himself wanting to reach out to them, hear their troubles, and exchange words of support and encouragement. "One of the things that really impressed me, here's a man with a great deal of notoriety," says Bartlett. "And he came in, as severe off as he was, he was always there to speak to other patients."

The ongoing saga of Roy's "recovery" was never far from the public eye that summer. Besides the regular newspaper reports, he appeared on the *Today* show on June 4, the cover of *Life* magazine on July 21, and as the subject of a two-part *Saturday Evening Post* feature less than a week later. The sight of a once-burly Campy strapped to a tilt board, arms withered and neck still rigid in a brace, elicited pity in some and admiration in others. But his lavishly documented story also resonated in a more profound way by promoting greater awareness of physical disability and rehabilitation. Americans, unaccustomed to seeing celebrities in wheelchairs (Franklin Roosevelt, for instance, had carefully hidden the true extent of his paralysis from the public), began through Campy not only to grasp the enormous difficulties the disabled faced but also would eventually come to appreciate their largely untapped potential.

Just a few months after first meeting Roy, Rusk already sensed his famous patient's symbolic significance to what was then called the "handicapped" or "crippled" community. "I honestly believe that Campy's contribution to this life has been far greater since his accident, and will continue to grow greater, than anything he could possibly contribute to it through baseball."

IN LOS ANGELES, the Dodgers were faring miserably in their new home. The Coliseum proved to be as bad as expected, the shock of leaving Brooklyn still lingered, and the continued graying of the roster took its inevitable toll. But for Carl Erskine, it was Campy's absence that hurt the most: "Things just aren't the same without him. Alston said the first day we'd miss his bat and his catching but we'd miss his spirit most. He was so right. Nothing's the same without him." Newcombe, a lost soul without his roomie's guiding hand on and off the field, agreed: "He was the team's morale builder. He kept all of us in good spirits. He knew when to be serious and when to make a funny remark. He kept us loose and laughing all the time."

Campy, though often exhausted by his rehabilitation classes, did his best to keep up with the Dodgers' sagging fortunes. He listened to the radio for scraps of news, read the sports pages with the aid of yet another specially designed tool, and even donned prism glasses so he could watch televised baseball while still flat on his back. The man who had always found spectatorship a frustrating punishment was now overjoyed by the unprecedented glut of televised baseball. Channel 11 had the Yankees as usual, channel 9 was showing Phillies games, and channel 13 carried Dodgers or Giants appearances in Pittsburgh and St. Louis for any locals who might still be carrying a torch for the dearly departed.

Even through the distorted haze of prism glasses and fuzzy black-and-white images, Campy could tell that the Dodgers had nothing this year. As the club plunged headlong into the second division, he became increasingly distraught. "Skip, they can't be in last place," he tearfully insisted to the visiting Leo Durocher. "It don't seem possible. How can they be in last place?" Determined to do *something*, even from a hospital bed, he drafted another telegram to his boys and placed a long-distance call to Charlie Neal to talk him out of a slump. He also did his best to straighten out the shell-shocked Newk over the phone, but his old friend, winless and now sporting a near-8.00 ERA, was beyond repair. Bavasi finally gave up, shipping him to Cincinnati, and within three years, Newcombe's once-promising major league career was over at the age of thirty-four.

The long-distance conversations, executed through a speakerphone, proved less emotionally taxing than his first face-to-face meeting with a teammate postparalysis. Fittingly, it was his friend Erskine who took the train from Philadelphia after a rainout on May 25. As Oisk walked into room 107, he saw his confident old batterymate lying facedown, now alarmingly vulnerable. "When we saw each other, neither one of us could speak. . . . I had a big lump in my throat. I think when Roy saw me, he must have seen the whole team."

Campy, as was his wont, quickly lightened the mood by enthusiastically describing his Charles Atlas–like weight-lifting prowess and other rehabilitation strides. But thoughts of Roy haunted Erskine when he took his warm-ups at Connie Mack Stadium the next day. He just *had to win* that game for Campy. "I can visualize him watching every pitch from that bed facedown. I'm telling you, it just gave me something extra." And Erskine, just "like a corny movie," whipped the Phillies on a two-hitter, the last complete game of his career.

The ice now broken, subsequent teammate encounters were far less traumatic. When Reese, Hodges, and Rube Walker visited on June 17, Roy was glad to see them but now found it difficult to listen to the usual bitching and moaning that inevitably surfaced in gatherings of veteran ballplayers. "Fellows," he told them, "don't ever gripe about nothing. If you've got to live like this, there's nothing else to gripe about." Branch Rickey also stopped by, as did O'Malley, who assured Campy that a job in the organization awaited him.

For Pat Therriault, Walter Alston's visit was especially memorable. "I was in his room one night adjusting some equipment," he recalls. "Campy was talking . . . 'You pitch that kid, Skip. Because if he gets his control, he'll win you some ball games.' And Alston said, 'Okay, Campy, okay.'" After Alston departed, Therriault learned the identity of the promising yet erratic youngster. "We've got a kid on our club that can put a ball through a brick wall, but he's not real sure which wall it's going through," Campy told him. "His name is Sandy Koufax."

Baseball, like a well-worn, comfortable old shoe, was still there for Roy, as it had always been. But the reminders—his feeble attempts in physical therapy to catch a volleyball from eight feet away and even the reunions with his old comrades-in-arms—were almost too much to bear. "I know they're feeling sorry for me, and it hurts me," he admitted. Dick Young sensed as much when he went to visit his favorite catcher in August. Campy, he noted, now "looks away when he talks to you. . . . He beats you to the punch in the cheering-up bit; he thinks you are appalled, and need it more than he. And when you leave, he tries to reassure you. 'I'm not as sick as they think I am.'"

LIKE THE rest of the Bums, Jackie Robinson was devastated by the accident. "Whether I liked him or disliked him doesn't enter into this. I'm praying for him." Though contending with his own medical crisis (a recent diagnosis of type 1 diabetes), he called the hospital immediately and later sent Roy a supportive note. But whether he was part of the parade of well-wishers to Campy's room is uncertain, as neither the press nor Roy ever documented his presence. "I don't know how often Jack visited," Rachel Robinson admits. "I think that he did care a great deal and was sick when Campy got injured."

Robinson, however, quickly grew annoyed with the subtle insinuations of the voluminous postaccident tributes and would-be eulogies. In a typical comment, Fresco Thompson noted that Campy "has done a tremendous job for his race, through merely being himself, rather than through an apparent effort to lead some campaign." Even more explicit, at least to Jackie, was Joe Reichler's Associated Press feature, which resurrected the infamous "it's nice up here" tale that Robinson detested so deeply. Jackie, now certain he was being made a "patsy," chose to go on the offensive. In an interview with Mike Wallace less than a week after the crash, he reiterated that his differences with Roy centered around "racial matters. So therefore we had nothing to do with each other. We just didn't speak." Asked whether Roy could manage, Jackie made no attempt to sugarcoat his opinion. "Frankly, I don't think he has the personality or leadership ability that is required of a manager." Of course Jackie wanted Campy to recover, "but I doubt if we'll be friendly even when he *does* get well, because we have nothing in common."

Jackie's comments, made with Campy's life still hanging by a thread, appeared ill-conceived and tactless. But the issue continued to consume Robinson, even prompting a scathing letter to Reichler, whose widely circulated story, Jackie believed, made him look like a "troublemaker" who was "bad for the game." He particularly objected to a mention that Campy's "one regret" was "that Robinson, and not he" broke the color barrier.

Shocked by Jackie's extreme reaction to a piece that did little more than recycle thrice-told tales, Reichler tried to smooth things over in a lengthy letter. The well-worn "don't spoil it" and "I'm no crusader" anecdotes, he explained, were not meant as criticism but as an illustration of Campy's "don't make waves" persona. "Roy always has looked out for Roy first, he's never done anything that would tend to get him involved, or disliked, or in a position where he had to take sides. . . . I've said to you more than once that he works at being a politician." But even with his foibles, Campy was essentially "a real good guy." "Isn't it possible for me to be a friend of Campanella's as well as a friend of Robinson's even though they are far apart in thinking, ideals, outlook, etc.?"

Jackie apparently did not think so. Accident or not, the feud was still on.

BY THE end of the summer, Campy's stay at the institute was winding down. He was now adept enough in the wheelchair to be permitted weekend home visits, albeit with plenty of help from staff and his attendant, Leroy Newson. The return to Glen Cove after seven months was bittersweet, but Roy refused to let self-pity sabotage his rehabilitation. Eric Hayden, who tagged along with his father to Salt Spray on many a Saturday afternoon that fall, was astonished by Campy's perseverance. "Over those weeks that we used to visit," Hayden recalls, "he just made remarkable progress. . . . He was determined that he was going to raise that hand. He was going to raise that spoon that was taped to his hand. And he was so happy when he got it to his mouth and he didn't spill the food."

Pleased by his gains, Rusk and the other doctors also recognized the value of getting their celebrity patient—a larger-than-life advertisement for the wonders of rehabilitation—before the public eye. At Roy's first postaccident press conference, held at the institute on September 10, Rusk proudly announced that Campy had shown "phenomenal functional improvement." Roy himself was only too glad to share his recent triumphs—the new battery-powered wheelchair, the switch to a lighter neck collar, and his recent mastery of the fork and spoon.

Although the optimistic tone of Campy's coming-out party heartened some of the media present, others left the institute that afternoon troubled and depressed. They were shocked by his nearly sixty-pound weight loss, his pathetically thin arms, and the thirty minutes of oxygen a day he now required to help with breathing and speaking. And in between the rosy reports of progress, Rusk had dropped the Q-word—*quadriplegic*—a term that disturbed the gathered reporters.

To be displayed like some sort of circus freak for a gawking mob of reporters, photographers, and TV cameras was physically and emotionally draining for Campy. Quadriplegics, he later noted, were often "ashamed to have people see them. . . . In public you're afraid to face normal people in a wheelchair. You feel that you don't belong." But he had already decided that he would never be one of those quads who became prisoners of their curtain-drawn rooms. Nor would he let his appearance go, as he noticed some patients did, instead vowing to "look as neat as possible every day." Years later, he still refused to leave the house until his pants legs and feet were arranged exactly the way he wanted.

Over the next month, the public saw more and more of the always nattily attired yet disabled Campanella. Besides the dramatic World Series appearance at Yankee Stadium, he was the subject of NBC's popular protoreality show *This Is Your Life* on October 1. Just as he did each week (although the usual element of surprise was obviously impossible in Campy's condition), Ralph Edwards recounted his celebrity guest's life through a parade of reminiscing family and friends, among them Roy's old Elite Giant teammate Bill Wright and Nicetown Giant coach Pender Hill. But some viewers felt the sentimental half hour, with neither Rickey nor O'Malley present, fell short of expectations. Several writers believed Robinson, despite the feud, should have been there, although Dick Young claimed Jack was not invited.

The well-orchestrated media appearances and the weekend trips home that fall had gradually nudged Roy toward something approaching normal life again. Still, he remained somewhat ambivalent toward the impending prospect of discharge. In six months, he had grown comfortably secure in the institute's self-contained universe of "cripples" ("like one big family," he later recalled), who perfectly understood one another's struggles as no outsider ever could. "The public is hardly aware of such people," he sighed. "There was a time when I didn't know about this either. . . . I didn't even know what a *quad* meant." In the months ahead, he would do his best to build awareness of his fellow patients. "They want help, not sympathy," he told a banquet audience. "They can do certain work, and more than anything else, they worry about getting employment. I hope you can help them with jobs."

On Friday, November 7, Campy said farewell to his special group of wheelchair buddies. A celebration that night at the trendy Copacabana as a guest of Nat King Cole followed, but Roy found it difficult to relax in his first days back at Glen Cove. Just getting out of the car into Salt Spray was an ordeal, involving a sliding board and the formidable hoisting skills of his now live-in attendant Leroy Newson. Sleeping in his own bed was just as complicated, and he had to be strapped in for the night.

His children, he happily discovered, would ease the often difficult transition from hospital to home. Five-year-old Princess, he recalled, "wouldn't let me out of her sight. In fact, she even stayed in bed with me until I was able to get up." Fully prepared by Ruthe, the kids never failed to treat Campy as the same doting dad he had always been. "They don't feel as though anything is wrong with me," he later explained. "I am just as normal as anyone else, but they really make me feel that way."

• • •

ROY'S SECOND life had begun. Even if he had been so inclined, he knew he could not vegetate in his ranch house (ideal for his new condition) for long. Maybe he was a quad now, but quads still had mortgages and bills to pay. For one thing, his $10,000 insurance coverage had barely made a dent in his hospital costs, rumored to be in the $35,000 range. When Erskine had visited in May, Campy implored him to push for a better plan. "Ersk, you're our player representative," he told him. "The insurance we got is not good enough."

Though Campy's medical debts and ongoing rehabilitation expenses were staggering, he was still far more fortunate than most of his institute pals. Not only had the Dodgers paid him his full $42,000 salary in 1958, but his liquor store continued to be a cash cow. And his name was still highly salable. The *Saturday Evening Post* had paid him $10,000 for his story, the Hearst syndicate hired him to cover the World Series, and *Jet* gave him a ghosted weekly column ("The Way I See It"). But his most profitable new gig was *Campy's Corner*, a daily five-minute sports interview program on WINS in New York, syndicated to fifty affiliates by mid-1959. Assisted by Chris Schenkel, Roy proved to be surprisingly adept behind the microphone, concluding each show with a heartfelt "hoping the game goes well with you."

The radio show became part of Campy's daily routine, which now included outpatient classes at the institute and occasional time at the liquor store. With handicapped-accessible ramps, sidewalks, and restrooms decades away, every new experience—the first car ride at night or first wheelchair visit to Madison Square Garden—was anxiety-provoking. "You wonder how you'll face it," he admitted, "but you do."

Outwardly, Roy appeared to be handling his plight rather admirably. His devout Baptist upbringing continued to bring him solace, and he refused to blame God for his condition. "Things like this happen in life. . . . If things like this didn't happen, then we wouldn't have a life." He had every reason to be thankful, he insisted, for surviving the accident and still being able to earn a living. He was especially grateful to the Dodgers, who had offered him a $25,000 job as a scout and special spring training coach. And he was not about to give up on walking again. "If you don't believe you will, undoubtedly you won't."

But lurking beneath the vintage Campanella smiles and cheerfulness lay real anxieties about his future. Occasionally, he let a comment slip that offered a far more revealing window into his psyche. "Once in a while," he admitted, "I wonder how long this might go on. It all might come back someday, but it might go on for life." His self-described cure for the blues was to "get such thoughts out of my head quickly. You got to keep thinking good thoughts. Otherwise you could go nutty."

With suicide far from uncommon among recent spinal-cord-injury patients, going "nutty" was a justifiable concern. But Campy, like most men of his time, preferred to battle his inner demons alone. Dr. Leonard Diller, a psychologist assigned to Campy as part of his rehab, recalled him as "sort of a nonverbal guy . . . an athletic type with a very calm manner of dealing with what had happened to him." During their sessions, he found it impossible to tap into any raw emotions that Roy might be experiencing. "He didn't talk freely about these feelings, but I had the impression he was the kind of guy who could sort of face reality well. He wouldn't duck it. But he also wouldn't confide about it."

Diller was not surprised by Roy's therapeutic resistance. Most patients in the early months following their injury are not yet ready to confront the permanent reality of their situation. "You sort of want to push back the feelings," he explains, "and you want to push back thinking about the future." For now, Campy preferred to focus on the positive. He was alive, he was home, and the worst year of his life was over. "By next year," he announced, "I'll have this thing whipped."

THE NEW year began tranquilly enough with a return to Edward R. Murrow's *Person to Person* on January 2. Following Murrow's interview with Borscht Belt comedian George Jessel, millions of viewers watched Campy talk about his rehab, his children, his model trains, and his preference to coach rather than manage. Asked about his resolutions for 1959, Roy expressed a desire to "carry on as I am . . . and take care of my family as I've always done."

But Campy's simple hope for a peaceful status quo proved unattainable. Less than three weeks after his Murrow appearance, he was returning home on the Horace Harding Expressway after his normal Monday rehab classes and radio work. Without warning, an air-compressor trailer suddenly broke loose from a dump truck heading toward the city, cleared the divider, clipped a light pole and a station wagon, then plowed "with the impact of a huge cannonball" into Campy's new charcoal gray Cadillac. As the trailer burst into flames a few feet away, the Cadillac's three other occupants—his two attendants and his mother-in-law—all instinctively feared for Campy's safety and his wheelchair. "Get me out!" he yelled. "Forget the chair!"

A later accident analysis revealed the collision to be "by far . . . more violent" than the Glen Cove crash of almost exactly a year earlier. This time, Campy's seat belt and neck brace protected him, and he emerged from the totaled car virtually unscathed (Harlem's gambling folk proceeded to play his license plate and year—ROY39 '59—and were overjoyed when 395 hit). Mentally, however, he was a bundle of nerves for weeks after another near-death experience. "I just don't know what else could happen to me."

Unfortunately, another problem was festering under his own roof, involving David, now sixteen. As far as the public knew, David was Campy's biological son. (David himself did not learn the truth until he was about ten.) Roy had always treated David as if he were his own. "There was no difference," recalled family friend Barbara Brannen. "David was considered as much his child as the others."

As David reached his teens, his relationship with Roy grew increasingly distant. With his own interest in baseball minimal despite Campy's prodding, David came to despise his life as a celebrity kid and the incessant question of whether "he was going to be like his dad." The move to Glen Cove had only intensified his alienation. By the time Eric Hayden got to know him as a fellow YMCA counselor one summer, Hayden could tell something was seriously wrong. "He was a guy who was looking for a friend," Hayden recalled. "And I remember spending time with him and talking and thinking how this guy is really screwed up."

Already, the street-smart David was dabbling in drugs and gang life. His only salvation was his undeniable musical talent, which had blossomed as the only black member of a harmony quartet known as the Del Chords. Even then, David could not escape his father's shadow. "People would come up to him at gigs and tell him how much they admired and respected his father, Roy," recalled fellow Del Chord George Kafcos. "After they would leave, David would utter words that were not the words of a loving son."

The Del Chords soon proved to be more than a cut above the dozens of other groups playing the sock-hop circuit. There was an appearance on the Martha Raye telethon; David soloed on the *Jack Paar Show*; and Kane Records eventually released a Del Chords single that did quite well in certain regions. Each surprising breakthrough allowed Campy to feel a little less uneasy about his troubled son's future. "He was very nice to us," says Kafcos, "and I think genuinely happy that David was focused on something that could be his ticket to success."

But music failed to curb David's rebellious streak or solve his emotional problems. Less than a month after Campy's second accident, David and his friend George DeLemos accidentally broke the glass door of an Auburndale drugstore one night while horsing around. When cops failed to respond to the alarm, the two teens eventually returned for plunder. While DeLemos "grabbed a bunch of cigarettes and things like that," David went for the drugs behind the counter. More trouble followed nine days later when David goaded his buddies and fellow Del Chords into forming a gang and then challenging another group to a rumble. Before the brawl got far, cops swooped in and arrested everyone in sight, including DeLemos and David, both already under suspicion for the drugstore caper.

Though David was only sixteen, the Campanella name was too big to be kept out of the press. The local media immediately jumped on the story, soon joined by the likes of *Newsweek* (complete with photo) and Walter Winchell. Juvenile delinquency was then a hot-button issue, but the public, just as today, was particularly fascinated with the sordid tale of another celebrity kid gone bad. There had been quite a few lately, with the children of Lana Turner, Bing Crosby, and Edward G. Robinson all recently picked up for offenses ranging from drunk driving to murder.

The news of the arrest, initially hidden from Roy, was yet another blow to his increasingly fragile psyche. "This is the worst of all," he sadly told a reporter. "I've spoken to lots of kids who have been in trouble. Now, I've got it right in my own family." To further add to his misery, he was soon forced to disclose two long-hidden secrets—that David was his stepson and that he had married Ruthe much later than 1939. "My first reaction was—how much does one guy have to face?" wrote black journalist Jimmy Hicks. "How much *can* one man stand?"

Campy stood by his eldest boy. "Dave says he got mixed up with some wrong kids and got untracked. I believe him." He was placed on probation with counseling recommended, but his downward spiral was just beginning. The years ahead would bring more scrapes with the law, escalating hard-drug use, and an early death at the age of forty-one.

TYPICAL OF Campy's luck of late, the David saga unfolded at exactly the moment he was preparing to leave for spring training and his long-awaited return to the Dodgers. After a bit of prodding, he finally boarded a plane for Vero Beach on February 28 with two of his attendants, although reporters noticed that Campy wouldn't answer questions and "looked haggard." He was also understandably fretful about his first flight as a quadriplegic and his first time outside New York since the accident.

When Roy arrived in Florida, he found it impossible to hold back the tears before the crowd waiting in the rain for his arrival. His mood soon brightened when he spotted some familiar faces. He "winked slyly" at Pee Wee, now a Dodger coach, and kidded Duke about his recent appearance on *The Rifleman*. And Roy announced that John Roseboro would be his special pupil this spring. "John was scared to death last season of pitchers like Podres, Erskine, Labine, and Drysdale because he thought they knew more baseball than he did. Well, he has to lose that attitude . . . and Campy will see that he does."

As Campy happily talked baseball, lectured the hapless Roseboro, and sported his new Dodger Windbreaker and cap (with an LA instead of a B, he wistfully noted), he could almost momentarily forget his problems that spring. But other instances—a boy asking him for an autograph he couldn't sign or his simple inability to join his buddies on the field again—painfully reinforced how his life had irrevocably changed. The "bad thoughts" that Campy tried so desperately to keep at bay then came flooding back. "I get the feeling often, 'Why did this happen to me?' " he admitted. "Then I have to tell myself, 'Don't be silly, boy, it could happen to anyone. You've got to occupy your mind with something else. Anything. Just don't dwell on it. This is the picture and you're not gonna change it.' "

The entire organization, from the batboy to Bavasi, did its best to make his Dodgertown stay as happy as possible. But his old boss did the most to lift his spirits. Working behind the scenes, O'Malley had arranged for the Dodgers and the Yankees to play two benefit exhibition games for Campy, the first at the Coliseum on May 7 and the second at Yankee Stadium in

1960. Campy, unaware of the ongoing negotiations, was genuinely touched when he learned of O'Malley's plan, a remarkably generous move far beyond the Dodgers' call of duty. Even Jackie Robinson and still bitter New York writers were grudgingly forced to admit that O'Malley was perhaps not quite such an evil ogre after all.

The residents of L.A., still excited by their new major league status, were just as thrilled by the prospect of a historic game on their turf. By the end of March, Dodger business manager Harold Parrott was predicting a possible draw of one hundred thousand fans, and within three weeks the box and reserved seats were already sold-out. As much as Campy's story had touched and inspired the public, the phenomenal ticket demand was inexplicable, particularly for a game honoring a man most fans had never before seen in person. The real lure, some said, was the Pinstripes' first trip to the coast in eight years. "As much as we admire Campy, there's no use kidding anyone," observed Long Beach sportswriter Dave Lewis. "Everyone will be going to see the Yankees."

Roy's face became more familiar to the locals in the weeks leading up to the game. They soon succumbed to his still intact charm and considerable capacity to schmooze. "I'm really and definitely considering moving here," he announced soon after his West Coast arrival on April 11. "The weather's nice." Two days later, his emotional speech at the annual Dodger Dinner left the Beverly Hills Hilton audience, which included Dinah Shore and Frank Sinatra, grabbing for their hankies. "I know I'm crying right now," he began, "but you can understand that . . . I don't want you to pity me. I'm doing great. Sometimes I pity myself, but I know I can take what happened to me."

The next night, Campy was at the Coliseum for the Dodger home opener, a dry run for the benefit coming up in three weeks. Once again, he wowed the crowd, this time by throwing out the first ball using an underhand flip technique certain to have made Dr. Rusk and the institute staff proud. "There have been three memorable days in the history of baseball," Vin Scully told his KMPC listeners. "Babe Ruth's good-bye, Lou Gehrig's good-bye, and now, Roy Campanella's 'hello.' "

Scully would soon witness a fourth historic evening. As fans continued to gobble up tickets for the upcoming exhibition, the Dodgers knew that something special was about to occur. By the morning of May 7, a crowd of eighty-two thousand was already assured, and another twenty-five thousand showed up a few hours later to try to snag one of the ten thousand general admission tickets going on sale at 6:00 p.m. The mob of Angelenos, the men clad in "gaily florid sports shirts," their fair ladies fashionably decked out in "fur capes over slacks," grew increasingly ornery as they watched only two ticket windows futilely struggle against the tide. Some climbed atop a ticket booth, while hundreds more broke down a gate until nightstick-wielding police arrived on the scene to restore order. Eventually, 93,103 made it into the Coliseum legally that night, a record attendance for a major league contest, exhibition or otherwise, that would stand for forty-nine years. Each, from Clark Gable to Frank Sinatra, received a ticket stub stamped with the words I WAS THERE THE NIGHT THEY HONORED "CAMPY."

Few fans would forget the magical yet poignant tribute that unfolded that evening. With a lump in their throats, they spied Pee Wee Reese carefully wheeling Roy toward second base a few minutes before eight o'clock, prompting a rousing three-minute standing ovation. After presentations of commemorative trophies to both teams, introductions of the family (no David), and the usual platitudes by baseball and municipal officials, it was Campy's turn to speak. The inconceivable turnout left him, for perhaps the first time in his life, virtually speechless, but he soon regained his composure. "I want to thank each and every one of you from the bottom of my heart. This is something that I'll never forget, as long as I live. It's a wonderful tribute and I thank God that I'm here. Thanks a million."

The Dodgers, exhausted after an afternoon game in San Francisco, then took the field. With the Yankees up 2–1 after five, play was halted, and the evening's focus shifted back to Campy, who was again wheeled out to the infield. This time, there were no speeches. After the lights were dimmed, the public-address announcer commanded the crowd to pretend they were "lighting candles for a cake for Roy." On a count of three, thousands of lighters and matches ignited, "like swarming fireflies," bathing the Coliseum in an almost supernatural glow.

The Yankees went on to win 6–2, but no one, except Yankee manager Stengel, who was itching to beat the Dodgers before the huge crowd, particularly cared. The big shots in baseball were more distracted by the nearly one hundred thousand tickets sold for an exhibition game. Maybe Hank

Greenberg's suggestion of midseason interleague play wasn't so absurd after all. But to black journalist L. I. Brockenbury, the startling outpouring of love for a black man was far more meaningful than the historic gate. "I wondered if somehow some real good had been accomplished," he observed, "and that somebody in the throng did not go away with a little less hatred in his heart for his fellow [man] who might happen to be of a different race."

Such tolerance did not extend to the Sheraton West on Wilshire Boulevard, where the Campanella family stayed during the trip. The hotel's swimming pool, they discovered, was off-limits for blacks. "My parents were livid," recalled Roy, Jr. After getting nowhere with the Sheraton's manager, Campy took his case to O'Malley, who agreed to take his business elsewhere in the future. "My father's style may not have been combative, but it was not passive," his son noted. "He initiated change."

The Sheraton fiasco put only a slight damper on Campy's euphoria afterward. "It really gets you. Just think—ninety-three thousand people! You know something? That's my playing number, 39, in reverse." Just about everyone was dying to see how much Roy would get, although the Dodgers, amid much criticism, refused to issue a public accounting of the receipts. "Whatever a father does for a son, so to speak, is something between them," O'Malley announced. "No one wants any public credit for such things. This is a 'dignity of man' thing and not to be exploited."

The undignified writers on both coasts speculated that Roy's cut ranged from $50,000 to $75,000, figures that seemed somewhat low considering the record gate and $0.80-to-$3.50 ticket prices (he would take home even less from the all but forgotten second benefit a year later at Yankee Stadium). Years later, Campy would claim that he received a lump-sum payment of $50,000, a figure that jibes with Bavasi's 1960 explanation that Roy's share was about $70,000 minus a considerable $17,000 tax bite.

Bavasi, like many of O'Malley's numerous detractors, was convinced his boss could have been more generous. "The city was good to the fund, reduced their rental fee for that game," he recalled, but "for some reason or other a few bucks remained in O'Malley's pocket." But Roy never voiced the slightest complaint about his share. Maybe the folks back in Brooklyn wanted O'Malley to roast eternally in the fiery pits of hell, but to Campy he was, and would always be, a great man.

• • •

AFTER A month of Campanella stories and sightings, the public's interest in Roy had seemingly been exhausted. "Fans, judging from my mail, grew tired of the constant public pity heaped upon this man," wrote Long Beach sportswriter Bob Kelley. "Being lionized by broadcasters and writers is fine—up to a point. I just think we overdid it."

Campy was not about to disappear anytime soon. He still loved the limelight, even as a quad, but he also recognized the importance of his continued visibility. "Wheelchair embarrasses a man. His natural instinct is to stay home and hide. If I get around, maybe I'll encourage others to do the same, and this would be doin' some real good." In the next five months, national television audiences not only saw him at the World Series, won by the rejuvenated Dodgers, but also as the guest star of a *Lassie* episode, playing himself as Timmy's wheelchairbound Little League coach. "I don't know if you could call it acting," he explained. "It probably helps too that I have a little ham in me. Doesn't everybody?"

But it was the publication of his autobiography that fall that propelled him even deeper into the national consciousness. The book deal had materialized a year earlier on the heels of his much-read *Saturday Evening Post* pieces ghosted by Joe Reichler. "Having read the SEP articles, having talked to people who have seen Campy on the Dave Garroway show from his hospital bed, and having followed the course of this story in the press, I think it can be very BIG," Little, Brown's J. Randall Williams enthused. The Boston publisher felt confident enough to offer a then substantial $25,000 advance to be divided among Campy, his business agent Frank Scott, Reichler, and veteran sportswriter Dave Camerer.

Advance publicity consciously magnified Campy's role, as salesmen were instructed to "never mention . . . that the book will be written by David Camerer and Joe Reichler." Instead, the autobiography was to be marketed as a Campanella production with the "spirit of Campy's talk and way of thinking out loud . . . retained as far as possible" and a generous dash of "his deeply religious feeling" thrown in for good measure. And a snappy title, Williams believed, was absolutely essential. Although *I Shall Not Want* and *My Three Lives* won early support, *It's Good to Be Alive* was the consensus pick. "I think the title is superb," Williams wrote Campy that April. "IT'S GOOD TO BE ALIVE seems to me to carry just the right balance between the joy of living and your deep respect for life itself."

Released on September 30, 1959, *IGTBA* was an immediate critical success. "Don't think this is just another ghost-written book about baseball by a player," raved the *Herald Tribune*'s Herbert Kupferberg. "He tells the story of these last months . . . straightforwardly, without self-pity, sanctimony or phony cheerfulness." The celebrated poet and Dodger fan Marianne Moore was even more effusive. "I read to chapter SIXTEEN, unable to lay it down," she wrote Williams. "This book is more persuasive—inherently—as emphasizing the injustice, indeed hatefulness, of race prejudice, than any book I know; and what an incentive to accept grief and disability, not just stoically but with joy."

With its glowing reviews and special selection in the Book-of-the-Month Club, Campy's autobiography sold briskly, although perhaps not quite as briskly as Williams had hoped. A year after publication, Little, Brown reported sales of about twenty-six thousand copies, not enough to earn back the hefty advance. But unlike most books, *IGTBA* remained in print for years, eventually reaching hardcover sales of fifty thousand by the early 1970s. Its continued commercial appeal was hardly surprising. Reichler and Camerer had served up an irresistible feast for the reading public: an undeniably inspirational story larded with a recurrent yet easily digestible strain of spirituality (Little, Brown even mailed free copies to 125 ministers as a marketing ploy).

As a historical document, however, *IGTBA* has only limited value. Even overlooking its numerous inaccuracies and annoying chronological errors, the 306-page book offers surprisingly little that is new, particularly in its coverage of Campy's baseball years. Instead, his ghosts generally performed a classic cut-and-paste job, shamelessly appropriating massive chunks verbatim from Dick Young's biography, old magazine and newspaper articles, and even a recent juvenile work by Milton Shapiro.

The public seemed not to notice or care. Nor did Roy. Despite his limited contributions, *IGTBA* more than succeeded in presenting an idealized image of himself that he very much wanted the world to see: an always optimistic racial gradualist who deeply loved God, his family, and baseball, not necessarily in that order. This polished image endured in the public's mind over the next fifty years, thanks to future writers and historians who uncritically accepted Roy's autobiography as fact.

THAT FALL, Jackie Robinson was putting the final touches on his own long-awaited autobiography. Unlike Campy, Jackie had consciously chosen to collaborate with a black writer, Carl Rowan, determined to avoid a "pollyanna" portrait.

Both Rowan and Robinson agreed that the Campanella issue needed to be addressed, although Jackie remained somewhat uneasy. "Suppose I go into that," he remarked to Roger Kahn. "I'm hitting a cripple." Nevertheless, Rowan wrote a strongly worded chapter on the particulars of the feud (loftily compared to the celebrated conflict between W.E.B. Du Bois and Booker T. Washington). Jackie, however, soon had second thoughts, especially when his friend Dan Mich at *Look* expressed serious reservations after reading the draft. "I would like to see you . . . admit that your resentment of him was at least partially due to the fact that you were just two entirely different kinds of people," Mich advised. Campy's courageous rehabilitation fight, Mich suggested, had actually "done the cause of the Negro . . . a lot of good. . . . I feel that you will come out bigger and do more good if you make this acknowledgment."

Rowan, though somewhat miffed by Jackie's concern over the opinion of "some white person," was forced to rethink his approach. "Frankly I believe we should refer briefly to the relationship," Jack wrote him in July 1959, "only to point out that I recognize what Roy and others say about not being a crusader but they don't really understand the entire situation." A decision was finally made to excise a good deal of the most inflammatory Campanella material (the 1949 barnstorming incident, Campy's 1956 "son of a bitch" comment) and integrate the rest into other chapters.

Despite the considerable edits, most critics and readers saw in the May 1960 publication of *Wait Till Next Year* yet another salvo in the ongoing Campanella/Robinson feud. "Jackie describes Campanella as a great ballplayer," wrote L. I. Brockenbury, "but possessed of an 'Uncle Thomas' attitude." But Campy, his long-ingrained dislike of controversy even more acute in his current condition, offered no public rebuttal. As far as he was concerned, his old roommate could have the last word.

19

A DIFFERENT KIND OF LIFE

IF THE WARM, FUZZY FINAL PAGES of *It's Good to Be Alive* were any indication, Roy seemed optimistic about his future as the new decade dawned. He not only talked of perhaps walking "again with my youngsters" but also of moving to Los Angeles, where a Dodger job awaited. And a pair of exciting television opportunities fell into his lap in early 1960: a fifteen-minute interview show with Mel Allen between Yankee doubleheaders on WPIX and a weekly, half-hour, televised version of *Campy's Corner.* Syndicated in several major markets, the program attracted a surprisingly impressive array of guests, ranging from comic icons Jack Benny and George Burns to Gump Worsley, one of the NHL's last maskless goalies.

Roy's triumphs—the TV shows, the benefit, the book—all helped keep the worrisome "bad thoughts" under control. But painful reminders of his past glories and current limitations were inescapable. The demolition of Ebbets Field in February brought back a flood of memories, as did his locker, uniform, and a pot of dirt from the ballpark that had been saved for him. Like the other old Dodgers gathered on February 23, 1960, he couldn't help but feel a little sick as he watched the wrecking ball ("painted white to resemble a baseball," complete with seams) begin its grisly work.

His second trip to spring training as a quad a few weeks later was just as depressing. After only a few days, the bladder problems so common in spinal-cord injuries forced him to be hospitalized, transferred back to the institute, and eventually required surgery.

Try as he might to recapture even the tiniest speck of his old life, it was gone forever. That he intensely mourned its passing was hardly surprising, although Campy would later claim his depression lasted only a few months. His son Roy tells a very different story. "He went through a drinking problem. And I know because I mixed the drinks for him. And he went through periods of talking about baseball and crying." His friend Vin Dacquino once asked him whether he ever considered suicide. "He looked at me and he laughed the way only he could. . . . 'Dacquino, Dacquino . . . I was paralyzed. How was I supposed to reach the pills? . . . And I wanted to live more than I wanted to die.' "

His deteriorating relationship with Ruthe only added to his despair. As Dr. Leonard Diller explains, a newly quadriplegic spouse creates enormous stress in a marriage. For men, "there is a total change in the role. . . . Aside from the sexuality factor, there is someone who no longer can feel he is masculine and feel like he's the head of a household. You also have someone where you're put into a situation of physical dependence." In an already shaky marriage kept intact solely by Roy's incapacitation ("He was planning to leave me when the accident occurred," Ruthe later admitted), the chance of weathering such constant emotional tensions was almost nil.

Ruthe initially tried her best to stand by the husband who no longer wanted her. Sportswriters marveled at her devotion, and Campy himself praised her "tireless care and consideration" in *IGTBA*. But the signs of Ruthe's growing inability to cope never made it into print: the frantic calls to Dr. Sengstaken's home, the "shouting" scenes at the institute, and a "very demanding" attitude toward the staff. Her unwavering loyalty to her troubled son David created additional strains unrelieved by his exile to his grandmother's home in the Bronx.

With his marriage self-destructing, Campy finally filed for separation in August 1960. Among the sordid charges (some made public, others not) were claims that a boozing Ruthe openly cheated (at times with an attendant), smacked a helpless Campy, shoved a used tampon in his face, and brazenly neglected their children. "She wants to get rid of me," Roy told reporters. "She told me I'm of no use to her any longer. She complained that she was tied down to me."

Although Campy was never shy about stretching the truth, at least two eyewitness accounts confirm the disturbing degree of Ruthe's hostility. Raymond Ormand, Roy's manager and travel companion in the early 1960s, remembered getting a desperate call one summer evening. "She had locked him in the bedroom. . . . The poor guy was just sitting in the wheelchair in the bedroom and he couldn't get out." Meanwhile, Glen Cove policeman Frank Heenan recalled local law enforcement was no stranger to Salt Spray. "They would get into arguments and she'd end up calling the cops and we'd go down there." At one point, a near-hysterical Ruthe demanded they arrest Campy for threatening her, only to be told, "There's no way he's going to get locked up."

Ruthe, her husband now airing the dirtiest of family laundry, found herself in a hopeless situation. The battle lines, as far as the public was concerned, were all too clear: the beloved paralyzed baseball hero versus the abusive, insensitive, cheating wife. Still, she vehemently denied the charges while presenting Roy as abnormally suspicious, unable to adjust to his condition, and constantly undermining her household authority, even cutting off her expense money and car. "We feel," her attorney Hubert Delany announced, "that Roy is so physically and mentally ill that he is merely making a jackass of himself." Delany cryptically hinted that more "damaging things" might surface in any court proceeding. "He's just not the angel that he has always been painted to be."

Ruthe had plenty of ammunition at her disposal. She knew Campy was with another woman on the night of his accident. And Roy had hardly been a passive victim in the breakup of their marriage, fighting Ruthe tooth and nail every step of the way and reportedly even running into her with his wheelchair. The late Ruth Bowen, singer Dinah Washington's manager and a close confidant of Ruthe's, insisted that Campy "drove her away. He was the most evil person after he had the accident. . . . He got bitter with everybody and took everything out on her like it was her fault." Even Barbara Brannen, loyal friend to both Campanellas, agrees that Roy was a very different, almost "self-destructive" man during those years. "He was bitter and he was angry. His whole personality changed. Like day and night."

Why Ruthe did not leak Campy's unseemly side to the press remains a mystery, although Bowen cited a desire to protect the children from further embarrassment. And Roy seemed to sense that a courtroom drama was the last thing that the family needed. After preliminary peace talks, he agreed in September to drop the separation action. "She's been very good," Campy admitted. "She's been leaning over backwards to be a good wife and mother."

The troubled relationship could not be salvaged for long. Six months later, Roy moved out of Salt Spray for good and into the fashionable Lenox Terrace apartments near his liquor store. "He's an unhappy man," Ruthe told the *Mirror.* "He just doesn't want any peace. . . . If he doesn't want to live with me, why can't he just sit down with me and settle it peacefully?" But Roy was now intent on exacting revenge. He again cut off most of her charge accounts, halted payments on her car (forcing his children to be driven to and from school by taxi), and offered a measly $150 per week in support until a Domestic Court judge persuaded him to increase it by $50 in early 1962.

For Ruthe, $800 a month was not nearly enough to keep her household of four afloat. But Campy refused to budge, even for the sake of the children he now saw on alternating weekends. He desperately wanted a divorce and was willing to smoke his wife and kids out of Salt Spray to get it. Bills for the mortgage, milk delivery, and utilities now went unpaid. "She had no lights out there," recalled Ruth Bowen.

Campy's increasingly ugly war of attrition continued. In the fall of 1962, he initiated a motion, ultimately unsuccessful, to cut her already skimpy weekly support in half. "He has a liquor store, an apartment house, and he isn't on television for nothing, yet he is allowing his children to be put out in the street," Ruthe bitterly complained. He also went public with more infidelity charges, alleging she had an affair with the well-known saxophonist Willis "Gator Tail" Jackson. Although the evidence was rather flimsy (an affidavit signed by a chauffeur buddy from the barnstorming wars), he hoped this was the smoking gun he needed to score a New York divorce, then obtainable only by proof of adultery.

By this time, Harlem gossips knew exactly why Roy was so hell-bent on divorce and not just a legal separation, which many Gothamites settled for. He had begun seeing a neighbor at the Lenox named Roxie Doles, although courtship as a quad was not always easy. "How do you hit on this beautiful lady from a wheelchair?" he asked himself after first spotting her in an elevator. Things had already grown quite serious, so serious that the press began asking questions about Roy's new lady love. "I don't even know the woman," he insisted. "If I ever get out of this one, I want no more of marriage."

Ruthe was not about to go away quietly, although her situation grew more dire by the day. She was now reduced to pawning items for quick cash while relying on her mother and the Brannens to cover some of her bills. Her home, sold at a foreclosure auction, would need to be vacated in the coming weeks. Still, she remained determined to slug it out in the courts. "The question is whether he can provide for his children," she told a reporter, "and if he doesn't have it, that's one thing, but in his case, he has it, and I will fight to see that these children are provided for in the manner their father can afford."

As 1963 dawned, Campy's worst nightmare loomed: a year almost certain to be filled with courtroom dates and intimate details of his private life exposed. Ruthe's tough new lawyer, Joseph Tanenbaum, had already begun to grill Roy in court about Roxie Doles, and the withering cross-examination left him squirming more than once. "I said to him, 'Mr. Campanella, you're virtually a folk hero to millions of kids.' . . . And he was sitting there and he was kind of deadpan, didn't say anything. And I said, 'What do you think would happen if these kids were here in court today and they heard this testimony? Would they think you're a hero or a bum?' "

Tanenbaum's questions, Roy knew, might get even more embarrassing if his wife decided to increase the mudslinging. For now, Ruthe was more concerned with determining Campy's true worth. In an attempt to dig into his tax returns, she called the IRS shortly after noon on Friday, January 25. During the conversation, the IRS representative was alarmed by the sound of a sudden "dull thud . . . and then silence" on the line. She alerted the Glen Cove police, who arrived at Salt Spray to find Ruthe on the bedroom floor, the phone still off the hook. At 12:55 p.m., she was pronounced dead, the cause either a heart attack or cerebral hemorrhage, at age forty.

Campy did his best to play the part of weeping widower. "I knew my wife had a heart condition," he told a reporter, "but I never knew it was this serious. . . . I can't believe she's dead." In a move that raised more than a few eyebrows, he ordered a massive "heart-shaped wreath of red roses" sent to the funeral home with the inscription TO MY DEAR WIFE. He also took control of the funeral arrangements, preferring a private ceremony, although Ruthe's mother insisted on a public viewing.

Monday, January 28, was a frigid day in Harlem, but there was no shortage of mourners gathered at the Griffin-Peters Funeral Home near Campy's liquor store. Among them was David, whose late arrival from a Puerto Rico honeymoon temporarily delayed the funeral. The sight of Campy piously overseeing the proceedings proved more than he could take. "David leaped from his seat," wrote Gerri Major of *Jet*, "and, with the veins swelling on his forehead and neck, lunged toward his stepfather screaming: 'You killed my mother.' "

Campy said nothing. He did not wish to acknowledge his share of the blame in the marital turmoil, nor would he ever, and he still wanted the world to see him as Lovable Old Campy. "I'll be at this grave many a day when people won't know where I am," he told his mother-in-law after the services. "Ruthe is the only one who knows what's in my heart."

THE BRUTAL separation might well have plunged an already depressed Roy into a permanent abyss of despair. But his new lady, Roxie Doles (née Joynes), was not about to let that happen.

Roxie, then forty-six (mysteriously, she always claimed to be ten years younger, even at the time of her death), had spent her early years in Cape Charles, Virginia, before moving to New York. Attractive and vivacious, she soon drew the attention of Harlem's movers and shakers, including hotshot lawyer John T. Doles, whose firm represented her in a discrimination suit. With her 1948 marriage to Doles (ironically a candidate for NNL president a year earlier), she gained entry to the crème de la crème of African-American society so lavishly covered in the black press. Thanks to her ongoing publicized involvement with the Sigma Wives, an offshoot of the elite black fraternity Phi Beta Sigma, her name and photograph were familiar to most well-connected locals in the 1950s.

Campy had crossed paths with John Doles at least once in 1953, but the date of his first meeting with Roxie remains a mystery. In one interview, he claimed to have met her in the winter of 1957 at a basketball game at the Renaissance Casino (perhaps the benefit game twelve days before his accident?). In another, he concocted a fairy tale about meeting her *after*

Ruthe died. In any event, their relationship blossomed once Roy moved into the Lenox Terrace in 1961. Roxie, now separated with two kids of her own, found herself drawn to Campy. "He was really, really down. Because he felt he was all alone in the world and had nobody. He had left his home and his family. And I just let him talk. As he talked, I could see a lot of really good things in this man."

With Ruthe gone, Roy was finally free to tie the knot with Roxie, although the marriage did not occur for another fifteen months. Campy's eagerness to avoid the slightest whiff of impropriety partly explained the delay, but Roxie's unsettled situation with her former husband may also have played a role. No one seemed to be entirely sure whether she was truly divorced from John Doles or legally separated, at least to judge from the conflicting press reports. The newlyweds, however, claimed their wedding just fifteen days after Doles's death was merely a coincidence, as they had applied for a marriage license several weeks earlier.

The third Mrs. Campanella proved to be exactly what Roy needed. Thanks to her earlier nursing training, she was unfazed by his quadriplegia, and her attentiveness was nothing short of phenomenal. "Roxie was the greatest thing that ever happened to him," says Vin Dacquino. "No one could love a man the way she loved him." Carl Erskine agrees: "She saved his life. . . . She extended it." But Roxie's greatest gift may have been the stability she provided. No longer did Roy have to face the "bad thoughts" on his own. Like a rock, Roxie was always there by his side, morning, noon, and night. He came to adore her two children, Joni and John, as much as his own.

For the first time in years, Campy had attained a sense of inner peace. With peace came maturity and a greater awareness of the world around him, particularly on matters of race. Like much of black America, the recent dramatic and sometimes violent struggles on the civil rights front—the sit-ins, the Freedom Riders, the disturbing scenes of fire hoses and dogs in Birmingham—had radicalized him, and in a way that surprised those who remembered his "don't make waves" days with the Dodgers. Wendell Smith was shocked to hear Campy at a Milwaukee banquet politely yet firmly condemn continued spring training segregation. "If you play like a major leaguer, you should be permitted to live like one."

Within a few years, Roy was signing his name to petitions calling for

South Africa's ban from the Olympics, openly supporting Charles Rangel's first campaign for Congress, and even tolerating his son Roy's recordings of Malcolm X's speeches. Though far from a fire-breathing extremist, Campy now understood that waiting was not the answer to America's racial dilemma. "We thought we were accomplishing a lot when we integrated baseball," he admitted. "We never thought it would be like this. I didn't think this would go on for years and years and years. I thought this would gradually change."

Jackie Robinson, thrilled with Campy's apparent change of heart, now reached out to his old adversary. "I know from Jack's point of view he began to understand what the press was doing to them," Rachel Robinson says, "and how they had gotten played by the press." In 1963, Jackie invited Roy to participate in *Baseball Has Done It*, a forthcoming book of mostly firsthand accounts of black ballplayers, past and present, and their experiences since integration. Campy not only agreed to be interviewed but again demonstrated a forcefulness inconceivable even five years earlier:

> It's a horrible thing to sit here and realize what a situation like this means to an individual—to be born an American and have to go to court to find out how much of an American he is. It's a horrible thing to be born in this country and go along with all the rules, laws and regulations and have to battle in court for the right to go to the movies—to wonder which store my children can go in in the South to try on a pair of shoes or sleep in a hotel. I am a Negro and I am part of this. I don't care what anyone says about me. . . . I feel it as deep as anyone, and so do my children. . . . This struggle has mushroomed into something much more powerful than the hydrogen bomb. This is the biggest explosive the United States has. They can't put it in a blanket and tie a knot around the head of it. It's in the open and it'll never be closed up again.

Once Jackie read those words, he knew their feud was over. The symbolic end occurred shortly following the book's publication in the spring of 1964 when Al Duckett, Jackie's friend and newspaper-column ghost, arranged a publicized meeting of the minds at Campy's liquor store. A crowd of reporters watched intently as Roy "greeted Robinson warmly," graciously accepted his signed copy of *Baseball Has Done It*, and then engaged in a freewheeling two-hour discussion with Jackie about race in America. Jackie, listening to Campy dismiss talk of antiwhite "hate gangs" in Harlem and denounce George Wallace and "other preachers of hate," couldn't have been happier. "Roy's contribution to the cause can be as vital as anybody's I know of," he announced, "and what he is saying here today is an inspiration to kids all over the nation." Jackie's only disappointment was the meager local coverage of the reunion. The press, he believed, simply wasn't "interested in letting the world know that two black major leaguers . . . had the maturity and the understanding to forget their differences and to advise all blacks to do the same—and to unite in a common cause."

The two old Dodgers were back on the same team. Campy even had the Robinsons over for a cookout at his new brick home in Hartsdale, New York, although the old annoyances still occasionally resurfaced. When a 1968 Jim Murray column dared to repeat the claim that Roy might have been the barrier breaker "had he known what Mr. Rickey was offering," Robinson dashed off one of his trademark angry letters to the hapless writer. But the crucial issue of civil rights no longer divided them. Jackie's stance, viewed by many in the timid fifties as overly aggressive, was now comfortably mainstream and more than acceptable to Campy. Ironically, Jackie now found himself being labeled an Uncle Tom by a new generation of militant young blacks, who dismissed his integrationist philosophy and viewed his outspokenness as hopelessly tame, at least when compared to the likes of Muhammad Ali. "Jesse Owens and Jackie Robinson belonged to a controlled generation," remarked Harry Edwards, a key figure in the black athletic revolt of the late 1960s. "We don't."

REGARDLESS OF his current respectability, Jackie had always suspected that his earlier quarrels with the white media might keep him out of the Baseball Hall of Fame. But the writers proved not to be vindictive. In 1962, his first time on the ballot, Jackie received 124 of 160 possible votes, good enough for enshrinement at Cooperstown.

Campy's turn came two years later in 1964 (the Hall of Fame had biennial elections through 1966), but he would have to wait much longer to earn his plaque. On his first try, he finished third, prompting black sportswriter Doc Young to launch an all-out "Let's Get Roy Elected" campaign. Though pulling for Campy, Jackie warned Young that the effort might backfire, and Roy would again fall short in 1966 and 1967. After another near miss a year later, Campy had every reason to be frustrated, if not furious. Still, he maintained his usual calm and unperturbed exterior. "I sort of learned not to count on things until I have them. . . . I do hope I get in . . . but I don't want a sympathy vote." Anyway, he was certain that his fifth bid would be the charm. "The good Lord will take care of me next year," he confidently told Jack Lang, secretary-treasurer of the Baseball Writers Association of America.

The 1969 election followed Roy's prediction perfectly. When Lang called on January 21 with the news that Campy had polled 270 votes, 15 more than necessary for election, he was so elated that he could barely listen to the specifics. "It don't make no difference how many votes I got as long as I got enough," he said, grinning. "This is the climax of my baseball career." Fighting a bad cold, his voice nevertheless rose to its trademark squeak as he excitedly accepted congratulations, gave thanks to the now deceased Mr. Rickey, and fielded the media's questions.

The formal induction ceremony at Cooperstown came six months later. He was a bit disappointed when he took a look at his plaque, hardly one of the Hall's better efforts. "This plaque doesn't look nothing like me," Campy later complained. "The face ain't like mine. It's got curly hair coming out from under my cap." Still, the botched sculpture failed to tarnish what he called "the greatest day of my life," culminating with an almost perfect five-minute acceptance speech. Included were all the vintage Campanella themes—gratitude, humor, and a fervent love of the game—but the loudest applause came when he dusted off a familiar chestnut. "To be good you have to have a little boy in you. Because when you see one of these fellows—for instance, Ted Williams, Willie Mays—hit a home run, and you see a grown adult running around the bases, jumping and hopping, and at home plate, some of your teammates would greet you with a kiss and a hug, you have to have a little boy in you to do these things."

The genuine outpouring of affection for Roy that afternoon overshadowed a disturbing reality. At the moment of his greatest baseball triumph, he had no formal affiliation with the game. His annual trips to Vero Beach stopped after 1963, and no other sufficiently lucrative job offers materialized from the Dodgers or any other team. "I really don't have time to return to it," he insisted in 1964. "My big goal is to help others like myself realize they have something to live for."

But when his television gigs dried up and his store became less profitable following changes in state liquor laws, Campy itched to return to the game. He sounded out the commissioner's office about doing some public relations work and even met with O'Malley about a full-time scouting job. "I told him not to let my wheelchair bother him," Roy explained. "The only thing affected by that crash was my body, not my brain."

What he really wanted was a crack at managing, a job he once considered too full of "headaches" to consider. As early as August 1964, Campy wrote O'Malley about "becoming a manager of a major league ball club, preferably the Los Angeles Dodgers," then floundering in seventh place. "Healthwise I feel as though I can manage this task and baseball wise I have no doubts." Although O'Malley's reply is not available, it seems safe to say that he was not interested in dumping Alston, who bounced back to win another World Series a year later.

O'Malley, whose soft spot for Campy was considerable, did try to use his influence to make his friend's dream a reality. In 1969, he championed Roy to Bob Short, who had recently purchased the Washington Senators. Indeed, the move might have been a stroke of genius for a new owner of a failing franchise desperate to make a splash in a heavily African-American city. But Short politely sidestepped O'Malley's lobbying effort. He not only doubted that "Campy could do the job in a wheel chair," but he found an even more famous name for manager: Ted Williams.

Roy's hopes would be raised again a year later when O'Malley's son Peter, now calling the shots in the Dodger front office, told Doc Young that he "wouldn't be surprised at all to see Campy managing a major league club very soon." And Roy seemed to believe he was on the short list of potential candidates to become major league baseball's first black manager, perhaps with one of the new expansion teams. The dreadful San Diego Padres, currently headed by former Dodger coach Preston Gomez, seemed the obvious destination. Buzzie Bavasi, who left the O'Malleys in 1968, was team president, and he had placed his old Brooklyn pals in coaching and announcing jobs.

Bavasi dumped Gomez in 1972, replacing him with another ex-Bum,

Don Zimmer, the man Roy famously dubbed Popeye years earlier. When Zim and his successor, John McNamara, failed to turn the Padres around, rumors surfaced in August 1974 that Campy's time had finally come. Bavasi, Roy told Dick Young, had already spoken to him about the job in February. "I told him not right now. . . . He mentioned it again when I saw him two weeks ago. I told him I'd think about it. I have thought about it and I'm ready."

If Campy was ready, Bavasi was not. Campy was soon forced to admit that his conversations with Buzzie had mainly dealt in "generalities." (A few reporters claimed that Campy had actually misunderstood Bavasi's invitation to manage in an upcoming old-timers' game.) Years later, Bavasi emphatically denied that he had ever offered the Padres job to Roy. "The only ex-Dodger that I talked to was Pee Wee, and he decided it was too late for him to take over a club. Had Campy not been injured he would have been with me in 1968. He would have been a good one."

Such words were no consolation for Roy, who watched ex-teammates such as Gil Hodges and Dick Williams develop into successful big league pilots in the late 1960s while he was reduced to running baseball clinics around New York for the Housing Authority. And the only genuine managerial opportunities that fell his way were one-shot ceremonial occasions such as a Martin Luther King, Jr., benefit at Dodger Stadium or the periodic old-timers' games that fans seemed to love in those days. He did get a nibble from the Global League, an attempt to develop a third major league with worldwide franchises, but the organization did not entice him.

The long-awaited call to manage a major or even minor league club never came. "If you've got a heart," observed Doc Young, "it gets wrenched when Roy Campanella . . . talks about managing." But Campy, despite his trademark faith and optimism, never really had a chance to land his dream job or any substantial employment in baseball. There were simply too many doubts about his disability and perhaps even more about his race.

The baseball establishment had long made its peace with black players. It was not, however, about to admit them into the backslapping good-old-boys network that filled the managing or front-office positions after retirement. "There's all types of jobs," sighed Campy. "Of course, none of the men holding them is a Negro." Jackie Robinson, as usual, worded his displeasure more strongly, engaging in a heated debate with Bob Feller in

1969 about baseball's pathetic minority-hiring practices. When a reporter tried to lure Campy into the fray following his Hall of Fame induction, he was reluctant to criticize the game he loved or "get into other people's arguments." Still, he knew Jackie wasn't wrong, not when old friends such as Larry Doby virtually had to beg "on . . . hands and knees" to get a crumb of any kind from Organized Baseball. "I'd say there was room for improvement," Roy admitted.

Roy never doubted he could do the job if baseball would only give a black man a chance. As a C5/6 quadriplegic, Campy functioned remarkably well as he approached fifty. Anyone spending any time with him was astounded by his ability to lift a glass to his lips using his wrists, work an adding machine with a special "wooden dowel" strapped to his hand, and even sign checks at his store with a similar device. Bob Considine once devoted an entire column to describing Roy's unbelievable feat of somehow getting a key stuck on a sixteenth-floor window ledge to his locked-out housekeeper. The resourceful Campy recovered an aluminum-foil cylinder from the trash, flattened it with his teeth so it would fit in his wrist device, bent it at the appropriate angle, then successfully nudged the key off the ledge. But Raymond Ormand was most impressed by Roy's steadfast refusal to wallow in much-deserved self-pity. "He never, never complained. It was unbelievable."

For all his undeniable mastery of the wheelchair, he was still utterly dependent out of it. Each morning began with a two-hour ordeal of being lifted out of bed, bathed, shaved, and dressed by an attendant whose devotion to the job was often suspect. Campy went through as many as six different attendants a year, although the worst may have been a Harlem man named Junior. "He just stole and stole and stole from him," recalled Ormand. "It broke Campy's heart really, because he took such good care of this young kid. . . . And that's how he thanked him. He took advantage of Campy. It was a damn shame." At those unhappy moments, Roy was doubly grateful for Roxie. "At nightfall when my attendant comes to put me to bed, I always fear that if he didn't come back the next morning, I couldn't get out of bed," Roy explained. "But my wife is always there."

Magnifying his limitations was a 1960s America that too often lacked even the most basic accommodations for the disabled. And if the considerable architectural barriers were discouraging, the public's unenlightened attitude was not much better. Bobbi Wailes remembered the discrimination that she and her able-bodied husband faced at restaurants. "They'd look at me and say, 'Well, you can come in to eat but she can't. . . . Because if anybody looks at her, they'll get nauseous.'" Although Campy was too big a name to be turned away so cruelly, he heard more than his share of ignorant comments. "I had a lady—she walked up to me on the side of the car I was sitting in—'Gee, you look so well to be so sick.' I'm not sick—I'm paralyzed but I'm not sick."

But as the years went on, his continued visibility as perhaps America's only wheelchair celebrity helped undermine long-held stereotypes. And Campy was more than willing to use his unique position as a soapbox for the cause. Fans who came to hear Roy talk baseball at his frequent appearances were often surprised when he also launched into a more serious discussion about the need for ramps in new construction.

His understated activism reflected a strong sense of kinship with the disabled community that had only deepened as he grew older. "The handicapped people," he once observed, "consider me 'one of the gang.'" He seldom turned down their requests, whether it was merely showing up at the National Wheelchair Games (where he met Wailes, a remarkably skilled archer), helping out a Bronx paraplegic trying to get a job as a cabbie, or simply giving a pep talk to a recently diagnosed quad. "Roy would be dead tired, feeling his own pain, but he'd put down that phone or letter and say, 'Roxie, I think we'd better go on over there and help,'" his wife later recalled. "And we did, hundreds of times. I've got the memory burned in my mind—Roy just sitting in some room alone with a boy, talking to him, trying to get to him."

Admittedly, with his name, wealth, and high-tech wheelchair, he was more fortunate than most, but he understood the often painful realities of their world all too well. "Today, my life is either in bed or in this chair," he conceded. "There is no in-between. So you have to brainwash yourself to acceptance of a lot of things. You got to make a different kind of life."

20

BOY OF SUMMER

IN EARLY 1972, the New York publisher Harper & Row authorized a conservative twelve-thousand-copy first printing of a new book about the Brooklyn Dodgers by Roger Kahn. Although already chosen as a featured selection of the Book-of-the-Month Club, Harper was not quite sure what it had on its hands. Kahn's editor, Buz Wyeth, thought the title—*The Boys of Summer*, taken from a Dylan Thomas poem—might be a bit too "gay" for its intended male audience and pushed hard for the more nondescript *The Team*.

But three days after publication, the first print run was already sold-out. Critics and the public were immediately captivated by Kahn's gracefully written yet frank narrative tracing his own personal story and his experiences as a twentysomething newbie on the Dodger beat in '52 and '53 for the now defunct *Herald Tribune*. But what attracted most readers were the poignant "Where are they now?" profiles of the Bums and the often divergent paths their lives had taken since retirement. For every Gil Hodges managing the Mets, there was a Carl Furillo installing elevators at the World Trade Center, a Billy Cox tending bar at the Owls Club, and a George Shuba leading the humdrum existence of a post-office clerk-typist.

By late May, *The Boys of Summer* was a national sensation, topping the *New York Times* nonfiction bestseller list and earning a program-length discussion on ABC's *Dick Cavett Show.* But not every former Dodger was grateful for the attention. Duke Snider later complained that Kahn "seemed to grope for the sad side, for pathetic tales of what happened to those boys when they were forced out into the cruel world of reality." Bavasi, meanwhile, insisted that the book took questionable factual "liberties" in discussing his relationship with O'Malley, while Red Barber disliked the "overly profuse use of four letter words." Kahn had even stripped some of the veneer off Roy, portraying him as a moody, second-guessing, and somewhat shallow figure during his Dodger days.

Though always a ferociously loyal Jackie Robinson partisan, Kahn was far from a Campy hater. "Part of me loved Campanella, and part of me says, 'You could have been more,' " he observes. While working on the book, he found Roy eager to participate and a "gracious" host when Kahn visited. As usual, Campy was not the most revealing of interview subjects. He did not want to talk about Ruthe (and was annoyed that Kahn had dug up some of the splashier newspaper accounts), instead preferring to spin his pat, tried-and-true anecdotes, many of which eventually found their way into *The Boys of Summer.* Still, Kahn came away from their meeting with more than enough material to create a sympathetic and nuanced portrait of a "Manchild at 50" who had not only survived a near-fatal tragedy but had evolved remarkably as a person.

The phenomenal popularity of *The Boys of Summer* (sales of three million copies to date) ensured that Campy's 1950s-era Brooklyn Dodgers would be recognized and lionized like no other team before or since, Casey Stengel's Yankee dynasty notwithstanding. But at the very moment that Roy and his teammates were being so enthusiastically rediscovered and celebrated, the book's pervasive theme of "time and what it does to all of us" became impossible to ignore in their own lives. On April 2, 1972, the Dodger family received the stunning news that Gil Hodges, only forty-seven, had dropped dead of a massive heart attack in spring training. "It's hard to imagine," sadly observed Jackie Robinson. "First Campy, now this. It came as such a shock."

Robinson, only five years older than Hodges, had long been certain he would be the first to go. Once a magnificent physical specimen, he was now ravaged by diabetes. He had already suffered a heart attack, he was virtually blind in one eye and rapidly losing vision in the other, and he was facing amputation of both legs. His son Jackie Jr.'s drug addiction, recovery, and recent death in a car accident had been another devastating blow. Nevertheless, Robinson was on hand for Hodges's funeral in Brooklyn, as were Reese, Erskine, and other old Dodgers.

Campy was not among the mourners at Our Lady Help of Christians church that April morning. His own health was only marginally better than Jackie's and had recently taken a turn for the worse. In an era when quads were lucky to live a decade or so, Campy's fourteen years in the chair were an eternity, and he was now entering a critical period when serious complications flared all too frequently. Years of sitting motionless in a wheelchair left him increasingly susceptible to the pressure sores that still remain a serious threat today, even with the improved cushions now available. As Janet Jeghelian explains, infection often occurs, "and they get septicemia in their bloodstream," the exact course of events that led to Christopher Reeve's death nine years after his spinal-cord injury.

It was not a pressure sore that forced Campy to miss the Hodges funeral. A week earlier, he had been rushed unconscious to Grasslands Hospital following a pulmonary embolism (blood clot in the lung), the inevitable result of the impaired circulation common in quadriplegics. So dire was his condition that he was transferred to the ICU, underwent another tracheostomy, and teetered dangerously between life and death throughout much of April. Campy managed to escape the grim reaper once again, although he would endure an exhausting series of hospital stays in the years to come.

The doctors had chosen to keep Hodges's death from Campy until he stabilized. Like Robinson, he was deeply shaken when he finally overheard a TV report of his friend's passing. As he recuperated at home in May, his thoughts seldom strayed from Hodges and the other Boys of Summer he hoped to see at the Dodgers' second annual old-timers' game in a few weeks. He knew he was in no shape to manage one of the squads, as he had done last year, but nothing short of an act of God was going to keep him from attending. It was not simply to see his old pals, although that was usually reason enough for Campy, who loved nothing more than a good-natured session of reminiscing and tall-tale telling. The Dodgers, at long last, were retiring his number 39, Koufax's 32, and Jackie's 42. Roy simply had to be there.

Robinson, his relationship with the O'Malleys distant at best, was not quite so eager to participate. Disgusted by major league baseball's feet-dragging minority-hiring practices, Jackie had made it a point to boycott old-timers' games in recent years. Only a personal plea from Don Newcombe got him to show up, but he was glad he made the trip. He was especially encouraged by a chat with Peter O'Malley, who appeared genuinely receptive to Jackie's concerns about the lack of postretirement opportunities for black players. Still, Jackie remained cynical about the prospects for any substantial sea change in attitudes anytime soon. "I don't think we'll see a black manager in my lifetime. I don't think that's the black man's loss as such, but baseball's loss and America's loss."

The 43,818 lucky fans at Dodger Stadium on Sunday, June 4, experienced sheer baseball bliss that afternoon. Elderly Casey Stengel was there, babbling and capering in his special multiemblem uniform ("All the places I was fired from," he cracked), as were Joe DiMaggio, Stan Musial, and Mickey Mantle. But the most poignant sight were the three Dodger icons gathered together—Koufax, fit as ever; Campy, paunchy, mustachioed, and still smiling; and Jackie, who looked every bit a senior citizen with his horn-rimmed glasses and snow white hair. "I'm still a Dodger," Roy told the cheering crowd, "and I always will be."

Traveling was now increasingly difficult for Campy, and the trip to the coast took a heavy toll. Less than three weeks later, he was back in the ICU, this time for lung congestion. Jackie, meanwhile, went home to Stamford and put the finishing touches on his latest book, *I Never Had It Made*. In October, he made another surprising high-profile appearance, throwing out the first ball of game two of the World Series in Cincinnati, while again prodding baseball to hire a black manager. But just as Robinson had predicted, he would not live to see a black man make out the lineup card. Nine days later, he suffered a heart attack and died at the age of fifty-three.

For the second time that year, the Boys of Summer gathered to honor one of their fallen comrades. Campy, though recovering from two hospitalizations, had no intention of missing this one ("the last funeral I was at," he later claimed), and parked his wheelchair near the first row at Riverside Church. Onlookers saw him sadly stare at Jackie's casket while "humming softly as the organ played 'Precious Lord.'" At the end of the services, he watched an almost surreal scene unfold: Reese, Branca, Newk, Gilliam, Doby, and basketball great Bill Russell hoisting the coffin of a man who had been yin to his yang for almost thirty years.

In a piece published shortly after Robinson's death, Campy shared his feelings, some still unresolved, about their relationship. "I'll miss him quite a bit, not only as a crusader, and as the first black player to get into the major leagues, but as a person. Somebody else might have been first, but maybe they couldn't do the job like he did it. Jackie accomplished things. He had a way."

THE DEATHS of two teammates and his own health scares forced Roy to think not only about his own mortality but also his legacy. Although *It's Good to Be Alive* had perfectly presented an idealized Campanella to the world, it seemed a bit out-of-date in a far more cynical 1970s America. At one point, Campy approached Roger Kahn about collaborating on a new book. Kahn, still remembering a nightmarish experience trying to ghost Mickey Rooney's autobiography, was not interested, particularly when he doubted Roy's willingness to spill his guts for publication. Kahn tried to steer him toward Ed Linn, who had worked with Bill Veeck among others, but it was Kahn or no one for Campy. Annoyed by his friend's rejection, he zoomed away in his wheelchair in a huff.

Campy's second book would never get written. Instead, the public would be reintroduced to Roy Campanella through a film version of *It's Good to Be Alive*. Although the book's generous helpings of tragedy and triumph seemed to be a perfect fit for the big screen, Hollywood producers had done little more than kick the tires a few times without a serious offer materializing. The combination of a heavily black cast and a baseball theme seemed too daunting for Hollywood.

By the 1970s, Roy was so discouraged by the false starts and half-baked proposals that he stopped talking to producers altogether. But one, Larry Harmon, better known as Bozo, the world's most famous clown, got an audience with Campy. Bozo was no longer happy just being Bozo and wanted to do bigger things, such as produce films. "My kids grew up on Bozo," Roy said, smiling. "If I didn't see you, how could I face them?" Within a short time, Harmon, Campy, and Metromedia worked out a deal for a made-for-TV version of *It's Good to Be Alive* to be shot in late 1973 with Michael Landon (of *Bonanza* and later *Little House on the Prairie* fame) directing.

First telecast on February 22, 1974, on CBS as a special General Electric Theater presentation, the film attracted a sizable audience (this author, then eight years old, among them), ranking #16 in the weekly Nielsens. But like most TV movies, *It's Good to Be Alive* suffers from the genre's usual melodrama, manipulative music (courtesy of *Brian's Song*'s Michel Legrand), and cringe-inducing dialogue (Ruthe: "Will he ever walk again?" Dr. Rusk: "No. But there's a good chance he'll smile again"). And Paul Winfield bore not the slightest resemblance to Roy in build or face (painfully obvious every time the film interjected a clip of the "real" Campy).

In the course of roughly 104 minutes, the surprisingly slender TV Campanella manfully struggles through rehabilitation amid plenty of tough love from his assistant Sam Brockington (a figure never once mentioned in the book) and a bizarre, mawkish confrontation with David. But the unquestionable villain of the piece is Ruthe, played to the hilt by Ruby Dee (the same actress cast as Jackie's wife in his 1950 biopic) as nothing less than a boozing, negligent monster. Not surprisingly, Ruthe's cartoonishly sinister depiction appalled her friends, who quickly dubbed the film "It's Great to Be a Lie." The most surprising criticism came from within the Campanella clan itself. Roy, Jr., now twenty-five, not only denied that his mother ever had a "drinking problem" but condemned her entire portrayal as "completely fictional," distorted to make his dad "into a more sympathetic figure. He's being made to look as good off the field as he was on."

Campy, who briefly appeared at the beginning and end of the film, fatuously insisted the script was "one hundred percent accurate." At an advance screening, he told reporters, "It does justice to me." More important, the film, like the book, succeeded in fixing an overwhelmingly positive portrayal of Campy in the public's mind.

AS CAMPY saw the strides made by blacks in the early 1970s, he now better understood his own role in breaking down societal barriers and stereotypes, although he knew too many still remained. "I don't see the day that people will look at an athletic star and rate him on his talent and not be conscious of his skin. Color, I'm afraid, is going to be with us awhile."

He sometimes found himself puzzled by the attitudes of younger blacks. Why, he wondered, did some of them want separate dorms and tables? "I want to feel free to eat where I want to," Roy griped. "A damn fool wants to go back thirty years to sit at a table of his own."

His own children kept him closely in touch with the pulse of the current generation. As they grew older, he was proud to share in their milestones, whether it was Roy Jr.'s graduation from Harvard or Joni's outdoor wedding at their home in Hartsdale. But his two oldest girls by Bernice—Beverly and Joyce—were no longer part of his life. He would never mention them again in interviews, nor would they be acknowledged as his daughters at the time of his death.

As Beverly died in 1999 and Joyce declined to be interviewed, the cause of the estrangement remains uncertain. Like many family quarrels, it may have been about money. Campy, according to Bernice's brother George Ray, had provided only minimal child support for the girls. Roy, meanwhile, was not thrilled with Joyce's choice of a husband, who just happened to be a talented high school catcher.

In the late 1970s, Joyce's daughter Gale Muhammad attempted to reach out to the grandfather she barely knew. On a college field trip to New York, she left her class behind at a museum and headed straight for the hospital where Campy was enduring yet another prolonged stay. "I said, 'Hi, Granddaddy,' " she remembered. "His eyes lit up." The visit went so well that Roy gave her his phone number and told her to stay in touch.

Encouraged, Muhammad later called Roy to tell him about her younger brother Derek Williams, a catcher who not only resembled his grandfather but was good enough to be drafted and signed by the Phillies. In the past, Bernice had enlisted Campy's help to give their grandson a boost, only to encounter a stone wall. Now that Derek had been released by the Phils and was trying out with the Blue Jays in spring training, Muhammad thought perhaps Campy might be able to help her brother or at least see him in Florida. But when she took Roy's return call (collect), she was shocked by the ungrandfatherly voice on the other end. "The first thing he said was 'I don't have any money. What do you want? I don't have any money.' . . . I was so hurt that he said that to me." His change in demeanor, she believed, happened because he was "back with that family."

Derek, undaunted, nevertheless sought out Roy in spring training. The meeting with his grandfather did not go as he hoped. "He told him there was nothing he could do for him [and] turned his wheelchair around," a still angry Muhammad remembers. There would also be no reconciliation with Gale and Derek's mother, Joyce, her letters to Campy unanswered. Whether Roy's decision to permanently disown his two oldest daughters and their families was justified is impossible to say without knowing the full details. But Muhammad believes that he was merely a puppet of "other people" by this time, and a man not fully "in control of his life."

WITH JOYCE and Beverly excommunicated and his other kids grown and out of the house, an aging Campy had every reason to feel a bit isolated out in Hartsdale. Roxie was always there for him and the liquor store still kept him busy, but at times he craved the companionship that had come so much easier to him as an able-bodied man. "He needed a buddy," says Vin Dacquino. "He needed a friend. He needed somebody he could complain to. Not that he complained much. He needed to talk about those things."

Dacquino, a Westchester County English teacher in his late twenties who didn't much care for baseball, became Campy's unlikely bosom pal in the mid-1970s after they met through a mutual acquaintance. Like many others before him, Dacquino almost immediately succumbed to Roy's still intact charisma, optimism (even about his own condition), and affability. Now a published author, Dacquino credits Campy for starting his writing career ("I'm so tired of you being wishy-washy," an exasperated Roy barked. "Just write a book"). "You'd never ever have a friend like him, if you met him even one day," Dacquino recalled. "One day is all it would have taken. He had a heart of gold. . . . He understood and appreciated life like no one else could."

But Dacquino also gave Roy a precious gift: the chance to lead something resembling a "normal" life. He soon mastered the ins and outs of transporting and caring for Campy, so much so that the two were able to take off anywhere in Dacquino's Firebird without the need for an attendant. "We'd be able to go and look for hot dog trucks and we'd go have a hot dog together or an ice cream. We were able to do things that he was never able to do for years. . . . He really just wanted to be a regular guy."

Dacquino witnessed firsthand just how desperately Roy desired to be a "regular guy" again. One day, he taught Campy a "trick" that would allow him to reach the operator by hitting the phone switch a certain number of times. "He was so excited by the fact that he could call a buddy. . . . He was going to surprise me in the middle of the night and call me." But when Dacquino's phone eventually rang the next day, it was not Roy's trademark high-pitched voice on the line. "Oh, Vinnie, oh, Vinnie," Roxie moaned. "He tried all night long to hit that phone." Campy's hand, she told Dacquino, had grown redder by the hour but he refused to give up. "He beat that hand so badly trying to make that call. And he was brokenhearted that he just couldn't do it."

At those times Dacquino saw the true depth of the emotional pain that Campy almost always hid from the world. "He kept the disappointments to himself. He didn't want to share the negative side of who he was. He wanted people to understand that he appreciated the positive side." But as the two grew closer, Campy began to open up more and more about the daily frustrations of a quadriplegic's life. "You don't know what it's like to be in bed and awake," he once told Dacquino. "That's the hardest part of being me. . . . Sometimes I lay in bed for hours and hours. . . . Whatever position they put me in, that's the position you'll find me in in the morning."

Dacquino only rarely saw Campy succumb to much-deserved self-pity. "He didn't have bad days. He had bad moments. And he got over them. He didn't wear them like a helmet." But in the midst of Roy's blossoming friendship with the young man, yet another serious medical crisis proved almost more than Roy could bear. Pressure sores again forced him back into the institute in the summer of 1976, and his stay would not be brief. Over the next year, he would endure a series of skin-graft procedures and blood transfusions, all while remaining flat on his stomach.

Eighteen years after his accident, Campy had seemingly come full circle: back with Howard Rusk and once again a prisoner of the Stryker bed that turned him like a rotisserie chicken every two hours. The "bad thoughts" that he had shooed away for so long now haunted him. Alarmed about Roy's lack of appetite, Rusk enlisted the help of Dacquino, who wheeled Campy to the roof of the institute and plied him with the hot dogs and beer that he loved so much. His mood, however, remained despondent. "He used to talk to me that this was the lowest point," says Dacquino. "They [his doctors] were so afraid that we were going to lose him."

By the summer of 1977, Roy's condition had stabilized enough for discharge. His mental state had also improved, thanks to a stern lecture from Roxie. "I told him that he had lived two great lives but that some of the young children in this hospital never had one life, that he should be ashamed of himself and snap out of it. And he has. I think being back here helped." On July 15, two days after a major New York blackout (Campy's liquor store was spared, perhaps intentionally, in the ensuing looting), Roy's grueling year at the institute ended. With his depression now lifting, flashes of the old Campy reappeared. "The main thing is, I can think right," he told the gathered reporters. "I've got a lot to be thankful for."

BASEBALL, AS USUAL, was one of the few things that had brought him solace during the long, demoralizing hospital stay. Lying on his stomach for hours on end, he was grateful for the Mets' radio broadcasts, which he found more appealing than trying to watch the games on TV. Even at his lowest point, he still followed the game closely and offered his thoughts on Tom Seaver's shocking trade and his old nemesis Billy Martin's third-place Yankees to the writers covering his discharge.

He still wanted to be part of the game, even if baseball could not seem to find a place for him. Throughout the 1970s, he faithfully showed up at the old-timers' games and made an annual pilgrimage to Cooperstown for the induction of the latest Hall of Fame class. The Hall had finally begun to make an effort to recognize Negro League players, thanks to Campy and nine others who served on a new committee to select deserving blackball candidates. "The thing that I feel sorry about," he once observed, "is that so many of the men with whom I played came along too late." He was genuinely thrilled to see Satchel Paige and his boyhood hero Josh Gibson be the first two enshrined, despite Hall officials who preferred a separate wing for Negro League inductees. Later as a member of the Veterans' Committee, he continued to push the candidacy of outstanding black stars such as Ray Dandridge and Leon Day, both of whom eventually won election.

Though a committed champion of his blackball colleagues, Campy was far from the typical fuddy-duddy, aging ex-ballplayer, unable and unwilling to relate to the modern game. Baseball, he believed, was still "a wonderful game today" with no shortage of talented players. He thought Seaver the best pitcher in the midseventies and later expressed admiration for Ozzie Smith and Wade Boggs. But he was somewhat ambivalent at times about the new era of expansion, one-handed catchers, AstroTurf, and players who seemed to lack the intensity and "enthusiasm we had for the game." Free agency and million-dollar contracts, he suspected, might have something to do with it. "All they think about is money," he once griped, although he refused to take the easy position of blaming so-called "greedy" players. "I don't think any man is overpaid today because someone else has to agree to that figure before the contract is signed."

The one change that Campy welcomed most was the continued progress of African-Americans in major league baseball. The hiring of Frank Robinson as the first black manager heartened him, as did the numerous African-Americans now on major league rosters. "Every team has some black faces on it," he marveled in 1980. "This to me means more than just about anything I've ever done." He was especially delighted that black players no longer had to adopt a squeaky-clean persona to gain acceptance and could speak out freely without being "crucified for it." Relatively few, he knew, recognized the debt they owed to Jackie Robinson and the other pioneers, but that did not concern him. Rickey's Great Experiment had succeeded in ways that neither Campy nor Jackie could have foreseen thirty years earlier, changing baseball and America for good.

EXCEPT FOR appearances at old-timers' games at Dodger Stadium and an occasional trip to Vero Beach, Campy's connection with his old club was virtually nonexistent in the early 1970s. But the O'Malleys' loyalty and affection for Roy remained as strong as ever. While Campy recuperated during his yearlong institute stay, Peter O'Malley urged him to move out to California, where a Dodger job would be waiting. "They refused to let him recede into emptiness," observed Vin Scully. "They made sure Roy knew he was needed, and that helped keep the spirit in him."

Roy was not quite ready to leave New York. After years of waiting, a baseball job had finally come through: a public relations position with the Mets and a radio show between doubleheaders. Though grateful for the work, he never stopped thinking about O'Malley's offer. The kids were grown, and the liquor store was now a drain rather than an asset. Campy had even been forced to install bulletproof glass in recent years to cope with the neighborhood's rising crime and drug problems. "I remember him telling me that those who came in and stole . . . were the ones who should be pitied, not him," recalls Philip Ketover, then a young catcher who often visited Campy at his store for baseball tips.

Soon to be fifty-seven, Roy decided it was now or never. In 1978, he put his store and his house up for sale, purchased a four-bedroom home in the Los Angeles suburb of Woodland Hills, and bade farewell to Dacquino and his other New York friends. Just as he'd promised, Peter O'Malley found a job for Roy, working in the Dodgers' community relations department with Newk, now stable and sober after battling alcoholism and bankruptcy. Campy's new position was formally announced in early November, just weeks after the early death of yet another teammate, Jim Gilliam. Asked about a possible Boys of Summer curse, Campy was scornful. "Bosh. People die every day."

The shift to sunny Southern California more than agreed with Roy. "In New York, in the wintertime, he couldn't get out, and that could get depressing," noted Roxie. "This was definitely the right move." His job was also a perfect fit, utilizing his formidable speaking skills, honed further by years on the banquet circuit. Seldom using notes, he spoke slowly but emphatically, and the attention of the audience, be they elementary-school kids or executives, never wavered. "You could hear a penny drop," recalled one Dodger employee. "He made everyone else realize that there's more to life than just throwing a baseball."

His role with the club soon grew beyond goodwill ambassador. During spring training in 1980, Campy's old teammate and current Dodger manager Tom Lasorda pulled him aside. The young Dodger catchers, he informed him, needed help. "I've told these guys to listen to you. . . . You've got a total free hand. You see something, you say so. . . . And that goes for any of the hitters." Other than walking again, nothing could have made Roy happier. For the first time in years, he was part of a team, actually contributing to their success on the field. More important, Lasorda's simple gesture gave him a renewed sense of purpose, a reason to get up in the morning. Carl Erskine believed it may have actually saved his life.

His prize pupil at Vero Beach in the early 1980s was a young catcher named Mike Scioscia, who also hailed from the Philadelphia area. For hours at a time, Roy tirelessly drilled him in the finer points of blocking the plate, calling a smart game, and stopping errant pitches and foul tips. Scioscia took it all in, eventually developing into an outstanding receiver.

"Roy Campanella, I think, has helped me as much as anyone with the mental aspect of the game," he later admitted. "You just have to pay attention to what he says."

Roy's involvement with the team continued far beyond Vero. During the regular season, he was a permanent fixture at every Dodger home game until the last out, immaculately dressed as always with Roxie by his side. Curious fans who reluctantly approached soon found that he was always more than willing to talk baseball or give them one of his autographed photos that he kept handy in a wheelchair pouch. But what he loved most of all was just being around the team and imparting his wisdom, whether it was telling Steve Sax to "master the bat. Don't let it master you," preaching patience and plate discipline to Dusty Baker before the final game of the '81 World Series, or encouraging Orel Hershiser when he rehabbed from shoulder surgery. Campy even had the ear of front-office officials such as Fred Claire, who heeded his suggestion to keep the veteran catcher Rick Dempsey, a nonroster spring training invitee in 1988. Dempsey not only proved to be a solid backup to Scioscia that year but caught the final out of the World Series in October. "I thought it was very appropriate," remarked Claire. "I thought of Roy."

No longer contending with Northeastern winters, Campy also found plenty to keep him busy during the off-season. The advent of fantasy camps in the early eighties was a godsend: a twice-yearly excuse to reminisce with his old Brooklyn teammates while schmoozing with a captive audience of mostly middle-age men who had shelled out $2,395 for the privilege of spending six days in Dodgertown with their heroes. "Every morning of that week," one camper later recalled, "there he was, in full Dodger uniform, moving his chair around the field as he greeted and talked to the campers . . . offering a tip, sharing a story. And smiling . . . always smiling. . . . We could hear his high-pitched voice from across the field, and when we approached him, his smile drew us in."

Besides the camps, there were media requests, and Campy was only too happy to oblige, whether it was the *Los Angeles Times* or a more obscure publication such as *Sports Collectors Digest*. "I like being interviewed," he admitted. By now, he seldom deviated from a script in his dealings with journalists: a heavy dose of his tried-and-true, folksy stories, many less than accurate, laced with his wry sense of humor. "If I had my life to live all over again, I would have done it all the same way," he told more than one interviewer. "Except run into the pole that I did and turned over. That's the only thing I'd eliminate." The media of the 1980s, like their predecessors, ate it up.

With the interviews, fantasy camps, and close relationship with the Dodgers, Campy was a baseball man again, and happy. "Mentally, baseball has helped me tremendously," he remarked in 1980. "I don't think about the bad things that have happened to me because I have too many good things to think about." Even as he slept, his thoughts often turned to the game he still loved so much. "Many times, I dream I'm back in Ebbets Field belting a home run. With dreams like those, I almost hate waking up."

BASEBALL, THOUGH a welcome respite as always, could only temporarily distract him from the day-to-day struggles of a quadriplegic's existence. His life remained limited to the bed or the wheelchair, an especially cruel punishment for a man who had once loved nothing more than taking off at a moment's notice.

With the exception of a new van equipped with a wheelchair lift to ease his travel burden, Campy's daily routine had changed little in three decades. To avoid a recurrence of the near-fatal buttocks ulcers, he spent a good amount of time in bed, watching television, reading, or listening to the radio, usually KABC, the Dodgers' flagship station. Moving from bed to chair or in and out of cars when the van was unavailable still required male attendants, each seemingly more inept than the last. In 1980, he fell and broke both legs after an attendant rammed his chair into a curb on a poorly lit Beverly Hills street. Six years later, he had a near miss, this time at Cooperstown following the induction ceremonies. One of his aides slipped, and Campy and his wheelchair helplessly began tumbling down the steps. "Somehow, the rear attendant regained control and the runaway vehicle was stopped," recalled Bill Deane, then employed at the Hall. "Poor Campy was shaken up, but O.K."

Such incidents horrified Roxie, but she knew they had no choice. "If only I could get him out of bed, everything would be fine," she observed. "I can put him down, but I can't pick him up. So we are at the mercy of other people. And he hates that." Desperate to find competent help, she even used Bill Plaschke's widely read *Los Angeles Times* column as a recruiting tool.

"The job pays well, you travel with Roy, you may only have to work two to three hours a day, which pays the same as ten hours a day," she told Plaschke. "I don't know what it is with young people today, but we just can't find anybody reliable."

If attendants remained a frustrating yet essential part of Campy's life, his doctors had become even more important. As he aged, the intervals between hospital stays for quadriplegic complications and infections grew briefer. He was admitted to Northridge Hospital for more skin grafts in 1980, and three years later for another infected ulcer. By the late 1980s, he was also contending with diabetes and breathing difficulties. But somehow he pulled through again and again. "Roy was a strong believer in willpower," his wife later observed, "and the mind being a very powerful thing, more powerful than the body."

Sheer willpower and a burning desire to survive, however, could take him only so far. In late December 1989, Campy caught a cold that quickly turned into pneumonia. A lengthy ICU stay at Northridge followed, as doctors fought to somehow simultaneously control his diabetes and heart failure, keep him breathing with a tracheostomy and respirator, and remove troublesome gallstones. For the first time in more than a decade, there would be no trip to Vero Beach that spring, although plenty of Dodgers, young and old, flocked to his bedside. Mike Scioscia and Franklin Stubbs both donated blood, as did Newk, who stopped by to encourage his old pal. "A doctor was in there, adjusting a tube, and Roy is jumping every time the doctor adjusts it," he recalled. "I say, 'Roomie, I know how you feel.' But then I think a minute, and I say, 'I'm sorry, I don't know how you feel. Damn it, I can't know how you feel. Nobody knows how you feel, you tough SOB.' "

Tough SOB was an understatement. Just three days after he was released, he somehow made it to Dodger Stadium for the home opener, although his ongoing breathing problems soon landed him right back in the hospital for three more weeks that summer. To the shock of almost everyone, he still insisted after his discharge on making his annual summer trek to Cooperstown for the new crop of Hall of Fame inductees. "Being in the Hall of Fame is very important to me," he explained.

A month later, he flew back to the East Coast to do an autograph signing at a card show at Hofstra University. The exploding market in baseball memorabilia had convinced him, like other old-timers, to set aside any moral objections to charging for autographs, especially when he could command a whopping $225 per signature on the card circuit. Using a Sharpie pen "taped and gauzed to a brace that begins at his elbow and goes to his wrist," he signed four hundred items that day, "his wife by his side, whispering encouragement."

Those lucky enough to get an autograph saw a man sadly ravaged by age and illness. His weight had dropped to 175, he was often short of breath, and his voice seldom exceeded a whisper. *New York Post* columnist Pete Hamill was shocked when he encountered Campy "bundled up, wearing a hat, a blanket over the legs . . . looking small and frail" at a Dodger fantasy camp in early 1991. "This was a man who once was built like Mike Tyson. . . . Now you wanted to hold him tight and tell him everything was all right." Hamill asked Campy why he was in Vero Beach. "'Cause it's beautiful," he responded. "It really is beautiful." Baseball? asked Hamill. "No . . . the whole damned world."

THOUGH WEARY from the blows of life, Campy still had one last project to complete: the transformation of a shaky young Dodger catcher named Mike Piazza, yet another receiver from the Philadelphia area. Drafted in the sixty-second round of the 1988 draft, some said as a favor to Lasorda, a close friend of Piazza's father, Vince, Piazza was thought by many to be destined for the lower minor leagues. Although Dodger officials soon recognized that the kid could certainly swing the bat, he was at best a work in progress behind the plate.

As Piazza advanced through the Dodger system, he began working with Campy in spring training. At first, their discussions were mostly technical, as Roy tried to smooth the rough edges off his latest protégé. "I can still hear him telling me to relax, to not rush my throws, to keep the ball in front of me," Piazza later observed. "You wouldn't believe how comprehensive he still was. He could observe and critique as well as anyone." But as the relationship deepened, their conversations often dealt with other topics, ranging from Campy's old Negro League days to the demands and pitfalls of stardom. "Michael, you're going to be reading a lot of things in the paper, people are going to be talking about you, you're going to be seeing things, other players are going to be talking about you," Roy warned

Piazza. "Just go out and play baseball." For Piazza, no stranger to controversy during his major league career, it would prove to be "the best advice I've ever gotten."

After watching Piazza terrorize AA and AAA pitching, the Dodgers decided it was time to give him a shot in 1992. As a September call-up, he caught sixteen games down the stretch, hitting an unimpressive .232 while throwing out only four of fourteen runners. Still, he was expected to be in the mix next year to replace the aging Scioscia, whom the last-place Dodgers did not re-sign in the off-season.

When Piazza reported to Vero Beach the following spring, Campy, now seventy-one, his health ever precarious after thirty-five years in the chair, was there to lend his usual support. Although exceptionally proud of the youngster's progress, he was not ready to release Piazza from the rigors of his Catching 101 clinic. "He told me how important it is to emphasize repetition, so things become second nature," noted Piazza after a Dodgertown session with Roy that February. "You don't want to get into a situation where you ask, 'What do I have to do?' You just want to do it." Even after earning the starting job thanks to a sensational spring, Piazza continued to consult with the master regularly. "He was still coming down to the locker room after the first home series this year and telling me things he had seen that I wasn't aware of," Piazza later remarked.

Piazza's immediate success at the major league level and the improvement of the Dodgers in the early weeks of the season heartened Campy. But his body, medical marvel that it was, finally gave out that summer. At approximately 7:00 p.m. on Saturday, June 26, 1993, he suffered a heart attack and was dead by the time paramedics arrived. One hour earlier, he had reportedly asked his attendant to call Peter O'Malley "and tell him I love him." Fittingly, it was Piazza who was at bat when the news of Campy's death was announced in the eighth inning at Dodger Stadium that evening. Somehow managing to keep his emotions in check, Piazza singled to start a game-winning rally that would snap a four-game Dodger losing streak.

Campy's body was cremated and a private memorial service held at Forest Lawn–Hollywood Hills. "I tried so hard to keep him here as long as I could," a distraught Roxie sadly observed. "But God took him away. But now he's walking, something he always wanted to do." In the days and weeks that followed, nearly every media outlet weighed in with laudatory tributes, predictably recounting his Dodger triumphs, his inspirational life after the accident, and his passionate love of the game. But a few choice quotes from his old Brooklyn mates succeeded in conveying his greatness far more effectively than any sportswriter could. "Maybe the only person in baseball history in which absolutely no one had a bad thing to say," remarked Pee Wee Reese. "Campy can never be truly gone," noted Vin Scully, "because of the way he touched the lives of all of those around him."

Carl Erskine's impressions of his old batterymate remain indelible. "He had gratitude. . . . His heart was full of thanksgiving for what he had been able to accomplish and his ability. . . . If you said anything to him that even smacked of pity, he would say, 'Wait a minute. Yeah, I lost a little bit here and there but look what I got left. I got a good mind. All these great years we had together. No, man, I'm happy.' And he was. That was amazing."

When asked in 2008 to share his remembrances of Roy Campanella, Don Zimmer couldn't help but think of how few of the Boys of Summer remained. "I wish they were all alive today so you could ask all of them," he sighed. But Zim's own simple words eloquently spoke for his long-departed Brooklyn teammates. "He was like a little Santa Claus. Everybody loved Campy. . . . This guy was just one happy, great, lovable baseball person. And that's about the way I can describe him."

ACKNOWLEDGMENTS

WRITING AND RESEARCHING may be solitary endeavors, but no historian works alone.

I am particularly indebted to the late Jules Tygiel, a professor at San Francisco State University and renowned Jackie Robinson scholar, who suggested that the time was ripe for a new Campanella biography. Thanks, also, to my agent, Heather Schroder at ICM, for her support and wise counsel from the moment I first met her in 2004. Special thanks to my editor, Bob Bender at Simon & Schuster, for his continued patience and encouragement while the manuscript took shape over three years.

Laurie Chin and Brady Higa photocopied and scanned research materials for me. David Smith at Retrosheet.org never failed to answer even my most obscure Campanella inquiry. Larry Lester at NoirTech Research helped to fill in some of the statistical gaps of Campy's Negro League career. My siblings Diane, Marc, and Cathy all read and commented on earlier drafts of the manuscript. My sister Nancy didn't, but only because she was too busy with her new baby girl, Summer, who brightened all of our lives at a difficult time.

Finally, this book could not have been written without the cooperation of numerous Campanella friends, associates, and scholars who graciously agreed to be interviewed. Unfortunately, some of Campy's surviving teammates proved difficult to talk to. For every Carl Erskine who patiently answered questions for an hour and offered a fresh perspective on the Campanella/Robinson relationship, there was a former Dodger whose son informed me that his father now charges $5,000 for an hour-long interview. Another well-known Dodger declined to participate, explaining that he had been "misquoted too many times" in the past. And Clem Labine, Preacher Roe, and Johnny Podres died before I was able to arrange interviews.

From the onset of this project, I sought the cooperation of Roy Campanella's surviving children. After two years of futile attempts, I was advised by Roy, Jr., that they would not participate.

Still, it was not difficult to find others eager to share their Campanella memories in person or by telephone or e-mail. Big thanks to Bob Addis, Dave Anderson, Ahmad Baabahar, Allen Ballard, Bob Bartlett, Buzzie Bavasi, Howard Baynard, William Benswanger, Jr., Henry Betts, Ruth Bowen, Bobby Bragan, Al Brancato, Barbara Brannen, Rocky Bridges, Helen Brino, Joseph Brino, Jr., Craig Callan, Clayborne Carson, Donald Chartier, Pedro Treto Cisneros, Daniel Cohen, Frank "Tick" Coleman, Donald Connery, Anna Covalt, George Crowe, Evelyn Cunningham, Vincent T. Dacquino, Pam Jacquet Davis, Ross "Satchel" Davis, Bill Deane, George DeLemos, Jorge Colón Delgado, William DeLury, Billy DeMars, Dr. Leonard Diller, George Dixon, Maxine Dixon, Mahlon Duckett, Lester Dworman, Robert González Echevarría, Alan E. Ericksen, Carl Erskine, Dan Evans, Terry Finn, Gus Galipeau, Herb Goldberg, Frank Graham, Jr., Harriet Hamilton, Eric Hayden, Leslie Heaphy, Frank Heenan, Gene Hermanski, Lyndon Hill, Jack Hofkosh, Sonia Hofkosh, Monte Irvin, Stan Isaacs, Randy Jackson, Janet Jeghelian, Estelle Jones, George Kafcos (Kafcopoulos), Roger Kahn, Philip Ketover, Clyde King, Jim Kreuz, Raymond Krupka, Valerie Lanyi, Dorothy Lee, Gwen Lehr, Lawrence Luongo, Sr., Robert Marsden, William Marsden, Morris Martin, Bill McCracken, Pat McGlothin, Glenn Mickens, Bobby Mitchell, James "Red" Moore, Bobby Morgan, Gale Muhammad, Raymond Ormand, Andy Pafko, Lynn Parrott, Dave Patchell, Jr., Delores Patterson, Wilson Pettus, Judy Poe, Joseph Pontarelli, Andy Porter, Arnold Rampersad, Steve Rand, George Ray, Paul Reichler, Bernard Reinertsen, Rachel Robinson, Lester Rodney, Edmund Rosner, John Rutherford, Mike Sandlock, Elwood Sandrow, Johnny Schmitz, John Sengstaken, Elmer

Sexauer, Larry Shepard, William Staas, Jr., Skip Steloff, Ed Stevens, Joseph Tanenbaum, Jean Taylor, Dick Teed, Patrick Therriault, Donald Thompson, Wally Triplett, John Van Cuyk, Tom Van Hyning, Tom Villante, Roberta "Bobbi" Wailes, Louis Welaj, Roger Welden, Thomas Williams, Butch Woyt, Jim Zapp, and Don Zimmer.

ROY CAMPANELLA BATTING RECORD

NEGRO LEAGUES

		G	AB	H	2B	3B	HR	AVG
1937	Bacharach Giants	5	20	6	0	0	0	.300
1937	Washington							
	League	7	19	4	2	0	0	.211
	Nonleague	9	30	12	1	0	0	.400
1938	Baltimore							
	League	12	37	11	1	1	1	.297
	Nonleague	7	25	1	1	0	0	.040
1939	Baltimore							
	League	22	70	15	1	0	2	.214
	Nonleague	15	57	19	5	1	0	.333
1940	Baltimore							
	League	28	93	26	5	1	5	.280
	Nonleague	12	41	9	2	0	2	.220
1941	Baltimore							
	League	32	113	39	10	5	4	.345
	Nonleague	22	81	23	5	2	0	.284
1942	Baltimore							
	League	38	138	42	6	3	1	.304
	Nonleague	5	18	6	1	0	0	.333

		G	AB	H	2B	3B	HR	AVG
1944	Baltimore							
	League	53	210	85	26	4	6	.405
	Nonleague	7	28	6	1	0	2	.214
1945	Baltimore							
	League	65	234	85	16	4	8	.363
	Nonleague	14	46	13	2	1	0	.283
Total								
	League	257	914	307	67	18	27	.336
	Nonleague	91	326	89	18	4	4	.273

These statistics, based entirely on my compilation of published box scores from the regular season and playoffs, represent only a fraction of Campanella's Negro League career, much of which remains unrecorded or undiscovered. For the thirty-two box scores that did not provide at bats, I estimated the number of at bats based on the score and length of the game. Preseason and East-West games were excluded.

MEXICAN LEAGUE

		G	AB	R	H	2B	3B	HR	RBI	BB	SO	HBP	SH	SF	GDP	SB	CS	AVG	OBP	SLG
1942	Monterrey	20	81	15	24	6	2	2	15	9	8	0	0			2		.296	.367	.494
1943	Monterrey	90	342	74	99	24	5	12	54	46	28	1	0			4		.289	.375	.494
Total		110	423	89	123	30	7	14	69	55	36	1	0			6		.291	.374	.494

WINTER LEAGUES

PUERTO RICO

		G	AB	R	H	2B	3B	HR	RBI	BB	SO	HBP	SH	SF	GDP	SB	CS	AVG	OBP	SLG
1940–41	Caguas		171	36	45			8										.263		
1941–42	Caguas		156	22	46	11	2	0	18									.295		
1944–45	Santurce		85	20	25			1	14									.294		
1946–47	Santurce		45	8	10			2	7									.222		
Total			457	86	126			11										.276		

CUBA

		G	AB	R	H	2B	3B	HR	RBI	BB	SO	HBP	SH	SF	GDP	SB	CS	AVG	OBP	SLG
1943–44	Marianao		128	15	34	9	3	0	27							2		.266		

VENEZUELA

		G	AB	R	H	2B	3B	HR	RBI	BB	SO	HBP	SH	SF	GDP	SB	CS	AVG	OBP	SLG
1946	Vargas	12	53	11	19	3	2	2	13							0		.359		.604
1947–48	Vargas	40	134	31	45	12	1	5	21							8		.336		.552
Total		52	187	42	64	15	3	7	34							8		.342		.567

MINOR LEAGUES

		G	AB	R	H	2B	3B	HR	RBI	BB	SO	HBP	SH	SF	GDP	SB	CS	AVG	OBP	SLG
1946	Nashua	113	396	75	115	19	8	13	96	64	28	3	5			16		.290	.393	.477
1947	Montreal	135	440	64	120	25	3	13	75	66	41	3	4			7		.273	.371	.432
1948	St. Paul	35	123	31	40	5	2	13	39	23	23	0	0			0		.325	.432	.715

MAJOR LEAGUES

		G	AB	R	H	2B	3B	HR	RBI	BB	IBB	SO	HBP	SH	SF	GDP	SB	CS	AVG	OBP	SLG
1948	Brooklyn	83	279	32	72	11	3	9	45	36		45	1	5		3	3		.258	.345	.416
1949	Brooklyn	130	436	65	125	22	2	22	82	67		36	3	1		11	3	2	.287	.385	.498
1950	Brooklyn	126	437	70	123	19	3	31	89	55		51	2	0		17	1		.281	.364	.551
1951	Brooklyn	143	505	90	164	33	1	33	108	53		51	4	0		19	1	2	.325	.393	.590
1952	Brooklyn	128	468	73	126	18	1	22	97	57	12	59	3	5		22	8	4	.269	.352	.453
1953	Brooklyn	144	519	103	162	26	3	41	142	67	13	58	4	0		13	4	2	.312	.395	.611
1954	Brooklyn	111	397	43	82	14	3	19	51	42	6	49	2	4	1	13	1	4	.207	.285	.401
1955	Brooklyn	123	446	81	142	20	1	32	107	56	9	41	6	5	9	14	2	3	.318	.395	.583
1956	Brooklyn	124	388	39	85	6	1	20	73	66	15	61	1	4	2	20	1	0	.219	.333	.394
1957	Brooklyn	103	330	31	80	9	0	13	62	34	6	50	4	6	6	11	1	0	.242	.316	.388
Total		1215	4205	627	1161	178	18	242	856	533	61i	501	30	30	18i	143	25	17i	.276	.360	.500

i - incomplete

WORLD SERIES BATTING RECORD

		G	AB	R	H	2B	3B	HR	RBI	BB	IBB	SO	HBP	SH	SF	GDP	SB	CS	AVG	OBP	SLG
1949	Brooklyn	5	15	2	4	1	0	1	2	3	1	1	0	0	0	0	0	0	.267	.389	.533
1952	Brooklyn	7	28	0	6	0	0	0	1	1	0	6	0	0	0	1	0	1	.214	.241	.214
1953	Brooklyn	6	22	6	6	0	0	1	2	2	1	3	1	0	0	0	0	0	.273	.360	.409
1955	Brooklyn	7	27	4	7	3	0	2	4	3	0	3	0	1	0	0	0	0	.259	.333	.593
1956	Brooklyn	7	22	2	4	1	0	0	3	3	1	7	0	0	2	0	0	1	.182	.259	.227
Total		32	114	14	27	5	0	4	12	12	3	20	1	1	2	1	0	2	.237	.310	.386

Sources: Author's compilations; Larry Lester/NoirTech; Retrosheet.org; Jorge Colón Delgado, official historian, Puerto Rico Baseball League; *La enciclopedia del béisbol en Venezuela* (1997); Jorge Figueredo, *Cuban Baseball: A Statistical History, 1878–1961* (2003); Pedro Treto Cisneros, *Enciclopedia del Béisbol Mexicano* (2007); *Sporting News Official Baseball Guide,* 1947, 1948, 1949.

NOTES

EPIGRAPH

vii *No one had more courage*: *Newsday*, June 28, 1993.

PROLOGUE

2 *"I felt like some sad"*: Roy Campanella, *It's Good to Be Alive* (Boston: Little, Brown, 1959), 241. (Hereafter, *IGTBA*.)

2 *"Hi, Slugger!"/"Attaboy, Campy!"*: *Salt Lake Tribune* (Associated Press account), October 5, 1958.

2 *"you got it licked"*: *New York Herald Tribune*, October 5, 1958.

2 *"tan Bebop cap"*: *Baltimore Afro-American*, October 11, 1958.

2 *"By some sort of mental"*: *New York Journal-American*, October 5, 1958.

3 *"a clenched fist"*: *Baltimore Afro-American*, October 11, 1958.

3 *"wasn't going to cry"*: *San Antonio Light*, October 5, 1958.

3 *"kept looking back"*: *New York Times*, October 5, 1958.

3 *"It's hard to explain the feeling"*: *IGTBA*, 242.

CHAPTER 1: NICETOWN BOY

5 *leaving the old country*: 1900 United States Federal Census, Ancestry.com.

5 *4201 North Fifth Street*: *Gopsill's Philadelphia city directory* (Philadelphia: J. Gopsill, 1893).

6 *"It takes 100 percent"*: *New York Times*, March 6, 1905.

6 *moved to St. George's Hundred*: 1900 United States Federal Census.

6 *who died in infancy or childhood*: Don Connery, "Take Two," June 22, 1955,

Time, Inc. Dispatches from *Time* magazine correspondents: first series, 1942–55, Houghton Library, Harvard University. (Hereafter, *Time* dispatches.)

7 *"Everybody always laughs"*: *New York Journal-American*, May 6, 1957.

7 *Twelve of the other twenty-three dwellings*: 1930 United States Federal Census.

8 *"Now you can stay down here"*: Interview with Thomas Williams, September 13, 2008.

8 *"Yes, your daddy's white"*: *Saturday Evening Post*, June 5, 1954.

8 *"Remember, your daddy has"*: *IGTBA*, 36.

9 *"Whatever the sport"*: *IGTBA*, 46.

9 *"sawed-off broomsticks"*: *IGTBA*, 30.

10 *"My hero was Bill Dickey"*: *New York Journal-American*, January 3, 1952.

11 *"I don't think I went"*: Transcript, Rod Roberts interview with Roy Campanella, July 24, 1987, National Baseball Hall of Fame Library. (Hereafter, NBHOFL.)

11 *"If I wondered at all about"*: Connery, "Take Two," June 22, 1955, *Time* dispatches.

11 *"You know we'd get just"*: Transcript, *Person to Person*, CBS Television, October 2, 1953, reel 40, Edward R. Murrow papers.

12 *"Roy should be made"*: *Philadelphia Tribune*, September 29, 1956.

12 *"The other kids didn't want to"*: *New York Post*, June 29, 1955.

12 *"in on every pitch"*: *New York Journal-American*, September 20, 1953.

13 *"Campanello"*: *Philadelphia Tribune*, May 30, 1935.

13 *Dusty Ballard later claimed*: *Philadelphia Tribune*, August 10, 1946.

13 *"big for his age"*: Ed Fitzgerald, "Roy Campanella—Mr. Catcher," *Sport*, March 1952, 46.

13 *"Sitting on the bench"*: *Complete Baseball*, December 1953.

14 *"scuffling and playing"*: *IGTBA*, 30.

14 *"totally color-blind"*: Interview with Gwen Lehr, December 17, 2006.

14 *"Don't get involved in gangs"*: Interview with Dave Patchell, Jr., December 14, 2006.

14 *"keep it in its place"*: *IGTBA*, 48.

14 *"the good Lord will"*: *New York Post*, July 5, 1966.

14 *"be happy for"*: *New York Post*, June 3, 1985.

14 *"It was the only way"*: *New York Daily Mirror*, July 8, 1952.

15 *"that's how I became a catcher"*: Roger Kahn, "Roy Campanella," *TV Guide*, February 16–22, 1974, 19.

15 *"a pretty good idea"*: Unsigned document, July 1969, Roy Campanella file, NBHOFL.

16 *"Campanello"*: *Philadelphia Inquirer*, June 21, 1936.

16 *"great progress"/"not uncommon"*: *Philadelphia Independent*, July 19, 1936.

CHAPTER 2: THE BIG LEAGUE OF COLORED BASEBALL

18 *now in college at Tuskegee*: *Philadelphia Tribune*, February 25, 1937.

19 *shipped to the Homestead Grays*: *Pittsburgh Courier*, March 27, 1937.

20 *Dixon might bring home $100*: *Philadelphia Independent*, August 27, 1939.

20 *"Somebody had told me"/"a short, wide-chested"*: *Philadelphia Tribune*, June 30, 1973.

21 *"go places"*: Dick Young, *Roy Campanella* (New York: Grosset & Dunlap, 1952), 72.

21 *"eat good food"*: *IGTBA*, 50.

22 *had left the Bacharachs*: *Norristown Times-Herald*, May 25, 1937; *Camden Morning Post*, May 29, 1937.

22 *"Cantenella"*: *Norristown Times-Herald*, June 3, 1937. The box score for a May 31 game in Camden lists a "Campbell" catching for the Bacharachs. See *Camden Morning Post*, June 1, 1937.

22 *"had a lot of patience"*: Interview with George Dixon, April 24, 2007.

22 *"never more scared"*: *IGTBA*, 51.

23 *"tore a fingernail loose"*: *IGTBA*, 52.

24 *Louis Armstrong had just finished a stint*: *New York Amsterdam News*, May 29, June 5, 1937.

24 *peppering 24 hits*: *Mount Vernon Daily Argus*, June 7, 1937.

25 *pitching for his uncle's team*: *Pittsburgh Courier*, June 29, 1957.

25 *"Biz Mackey was one of the great catchers"*: Interview with Monte Irvin, April 17, 2007.

25 *"was the cog"*: *Pittsburgh Courier*, April 10, 1937.

25 *"cracked finger"*: *Philadelphia Afro-American*, May 22, 1937.

26 *"Campanella looked like Mackey"*: John Holway, *Blackball Stars* (Westport, CT: Meckler Publishing, 1988), 228.

26 *"This is only a start"*: Young, *Roy Campanella*, 77.

28 *"on somebody's front porch"*: *Norristown Times-Herald*, June 15, 1937.

28 *"big league of colored baseball"*: Young, *Roy Campanella*, 81.

29 *"We hesitate about taking"*: *Sporting News*, July 14, 1948.

30 *managed a hit in four at bats*: *Chester Times*, June 16, 1937.

30 *"at least six men over six feet tall"*: *Asbury Park Evening Press*, June 18, 1937.

30 *"I came to Newark"*: Interview with Monte Irvin, April 17, 2007.

32 *"Roy Campinelli [sic] A Future Great"*: *Philadelphia Tribune*, June 24, 1937.

CHAPTER 3: MACKEY'S PROTÉGÉ

35 *"speed, power"*: *Pittsburgh Courier*, June 29, 1963.

35 *"just about the best"*: *Baltimore Afro-American*, October 21, 1939.

35 *"Bill Wright"*: Interview with Mahlon Duckett, April 20, 2007.

35 *"mean"*: Interview with Monte Irvin, April 17, 2007.

36 *"fastest ball in colored"*: *Pittsburgh Courier*, February 8, 1941.

36 *"He was a little"*: Interview with Andy Porter, January 11, 2007.

36 *"always try to keep"*: Holway, *Blackball Stars*, 228.

36 *"You're going"/"Well, he ain't"/"You got to say"*: *Saturday Evening Post*, May 26, 1956.

37 *"It took me a long while"*: *New York World-Telegram and Sun*, February 14, 1957.

37 *"You never did see him"*: Holway, *Blackball Stars*, 230.

38 *"We had so many games"*: Don Connery, "Take Three," June 22, 1955, *Time* dispatches.

38 *"They just carried him"*: John Holway, *Voices from the Great Black Baseball Leagues* (New York: Da Capo, 1992), 266.

38 *an impressive five hits*: *Long Island Daily Press*, July 8–9, 1937; *Asbury Park Evening Press*, July 10, 1937; *Chester Times*, July 22, 1937.

38 *"behind some construction"*: *Paterson Morning Call*, June 28, 1937.

39 *"The players must understand"*: See Posey to Effa Manley, July 17, 1941, Newark Eagles papers, Newark Public Library.

40 *"The bus"*: *IGTBA*, 66.

41 *"They were the only ones"*: *Sports Collectors Digest*, April 22, 1994.

41 *"Negroes and whites frequenting"*: *Pittsburgh Courier*, September 27, 1930.

41 *"a special section"*: *Nashville Tennessean*, August 8, 1937.

42 *"I thought you gave him"*: Young, *Roy Campanella*, 90.

42 *"I had this explained"*: *New York Amsterdam News*, July 28, 1979.

43 *"Josh is unquestionably a great hitter"*: *Baltimore Afro-American*, July 29, 1939.

43 *"Biz was tops in catching"*: *Pittsburgh Courier*, February 6, 1943.

43 *"was very adequate"*: Interview with Monte Irvin, April 17, 2007.

43 *connected for two doubles*: *Cumberland Times*, July 25, 1937.

43 *"Big, strong, could run"*: *New York World-Telegram and Sun*, July 20, 1957.

43 *"a likeable big lug"*: *Baltimore Afro-American*, May 27, 1944.

43 *"little boy" and "little kid"*: Peter Golenbock, *Bums: An Oral History of the Brooklyn Dodgers* (New York: G. P. Putnam's Sons, 1984), 200.

44 *"And I caught"*: *New York Post*, July 25, 1951.

44 *"I wasn't tired"*: Tom Meany, "Campanella—King of Catchers," *Sport*, August 1950, 88.

44 *Local newspapers reveal*: *Cincinnati Enquirer*, August 13, 1937; *Middletown Journal*, August 13, 1937.

45 *"What do I want with"*: *New York Journal-American*, May 11, 1953.

45 *"routine check of official records"*: *Saturday Evening Post*, June 5, 1954.

45 Evening Bulletin *subsequently publicized*: *Philadelphia Evening Bulletin*, June 2, 1954.

45 *furious when the story surfaced*: Frank Graham, Jr., "What Campy Means to All of Us," *Sport*, September 1958, 84.

46 *"He has an amazing memory"*: *Chicago Defender*, May 30, 1953.

46 *"could have gone to college"*: *Montreal Herald*, June 6, 1947.

46 *"I was gonna be an architect"*: Roger Kahn, *The Boys of Summer* (New York: Harper & Row, 1972), 366.

46 *"honor medal in draftsmanship"*: *Roy Campanella—Baseball Hero* (Fawcett Publications, 1950).

47 *"I think that if I"*: *Pittsburgh Courier*, June 23, 1956.

CHAPTER 4: ELITE GIANT

48 *"exhibited much promise"*: *Philadelphia Tribune*, April 14, 1938.

49 *"reads at least"*: *Baltimore Afro-American*, May 1, 1948.

49 *"dirty, dilapidated seats"*: *Pittsburgh Courier*, December 11, 1937.

49 *"The ordinary procedure"*: *Philadelphia Tribune*, April 22, 1950.

50 *"just like being in the South"*: Interview with Ross Davis, November 9, 2006.

50 *"really noted for pretty"*: Interview with Monte Irvin, April 17, 2007.

50 *"not suited for"*: *Pittsburgh Courier*, April 17, 1937.

51 *"In the colored leagues"*: *Sporting News*, July 18, 1951.

52 *"We saw different pitchers"*: *Los Angeles Times*, June 17, 1985.

52 *"high leg kick"*: Warren Corbett, "George Earnshaw," SABR Biography Project.

52 *losing end*: *Brooklyn Eagle*, June 6, 1938.

52 *"He cheated"*: John Holway, *Black Diamonds* (Westport, CT: Meckler Publishing, 1989), 8.

52 *"not a hitter, living or dead"*: *Philadelphia Tribune*, August 5, 1944.

53 *"We used to cross him up"*: *Pittsburgh Courier*, July 2, 1955.

53 *"They'd fire at you"*: *New York Post*, April 30, 1957.

53 *"nasty slider"*: Holway, *Voices*, 224.

53 *"ready to fight"*: *Washington Tribune*, April 2, 1938.

53 *"Baseball ain't the old folks home"*: *New York Post*, March 2, 1954.

54 *A single, double*: *Philadelphia Tribune*, September 22, 1938.

54 *"look after"*: Brent Kelley, *The Negro Leagues Revisited* (Jefferson, NC: McFarland & Company, 2000), 56.

54 *"They were neighborhood kids"*: Interview with George Ray, December 21, 2006.

55 *"center for unwed expectant mothers"*: *Chicago Defender*, February 19, 1938.

55 *wed on January 3, 1939*: In *IGTBA*, Campanella states his marriage to Bernice occurred in 1939 without providing a specific date. During his major league career, however, reporters were told that Campy married Ruthe Willis (his then wife) on January 3, 1939. The bride may not have been correct, but I suspect the date is.

55 *"I had a job"*: *IGTBA*, 81.

55 *"They weren't harsh"*: Interview with Andy Porter, January 11, 2007.

56 *got himself tossed*: *Baltimore Afro-American*, June 3, 1939.

56 *Nearly seventy years later, Moore still remembered*: Interview with Red Moore, November 30, 2006.

56 *"goes to the right"*: *Detroit Tribune*, August 9, 1941.

56 *"the best two"*: *New York World-Telegram and Sun*, March 20, 1953.

57 *"'Come on, Pee Wee'"*: Holway, *Voices*, 329.

57 *"beat out a slow roller"*: *Chester Times*, August 24, 1939.

57 *"youthful Leroy Campanello"*: *Baltimore Afro-American*, September 16, 1939.

58 *Only 462 fans*: Newark Eagles papers.

59 *"fiery bingle to left"*: *Philadelphia Tribune*, September 28, 1939.

59 *"proceeded to return"*: *Philadelphia Independent*, September 8, 1940.

60 *fateful radio interview*: Neil Lanctot, *Negro League Baseball: The Rise and Ruin of a Black Institution* (Philadelphia: University of Pennsylvania Press, 2004), 220–23.

60 *"autograph six balls"*: *New York Amsterdam News*, September 23, 1939.

61 *"drilled a single to right"*: *New York Amsterdam News*, September 30, 1939.

61 *"This is what you'd call"*: *New York Age*, September 30, 1939.

62 *"put in an appearance"*: *Baltimore Morning Sun*, October 9, 1939.

62 *could play in the major leagues*: *Daily Worker*, July 16, 1942; *PM*, July 28, 1942.

CHAPTER 5: A RISING STAR

64 *"Ray Camponella"*: *Philadelphia Independent*, August 11, 1940.

64 *"He had the snap"*: Interview with Ross Davis, November 9, 2006.

64 *"He'd throw all the balls"*: Holway, *Voices*, 329.

64 *"no one in organized baseball"*: *Pittsburgh Courier*, June 29, 1963.

64 *"He was a hard swinger"*: Holway, *Voices*, 330.

65 *his average of .359 was second*: *Baltimore Afro-American*, August 10, 1940.

65 *reduced to running exhibitions*: *Philadelphia Tribune*, April 11, 1940.

65 *make a desperate leap*: *Philadelphia Tribune*, June 13, 1940.

66 *"We was kids"*: Kelley, *Negro Leagues Revisited*, 90.

66 *had secretly been carrying on*: Monte Irvin with James A. Riley, *Nice Guys Finish First: The Autobiography of Monte Irvin* (New York: Carroll & Graf, 1996), 44–45.

66 *"Most of us will be glad"*: *Baltimore Afro-American*, January 11, 1941.

67 *"We would fish"*: Interview with Monte Irvin, April 17, 2007.

67 *"The fact that the league"*: *Baltimore Afro-American*, February 14, 1942.

67 *ranked last in the league*: *Puerto Rico World Journal*, January 25, 1941.

67 *"Dude, I see you're in a slump"/"Campy was jumping around back"/"That's what kept me"*: Irvin, *Nice Guys Finish First*, 87.

68 *became one of four players*: E-mail from Jorge Colón Delgado, official historian, Puerto Rico Baseball League, May 29, 2008.

68 *The entire park went berserk*: Thomas E. Van Hyning, *Puerto Rico's Winter League* (Jefferson, NC: McFarland & Company, 1995), 85; *Puerto Rico World Journal*, April 7, 1941.

68 *The inscription had the wrong year*: Lot 844, Hunt Auctions, August 22 and 23, 2003.

68 *"gets a warm feeling"*: *Baltimore Afro-American*, February 18, 1956.

69 *"You're growing up"*: Golenbock, *Bums*, 200.

69 *Selective Service Department preferred*: George Q. Flynn, "Selective Service and American Blacks during World War II," *Journal of Negro History* 69 (Winter 1984): 14–25.

69 *making $175 per month*: Kelley, *Negro Leagues Revisited*, 100.

69 *3822 North Smedley Street*: Passenger list, SS *Seminole*, San Juan to New York, March 1, 1942, Ancestry.com.

70 *"despite his name"*: *Pittsburgh Courier*, June 21, 1941.

71 *headed to Parkside Field*: *Philadelphia Tribune*, June 26, 1941.

71 *held him hitless*: *New York Amsterdam News*, July 12, 1941; *Baltimore Afro-American*, July 12, 1941; *Chester Times*, July 10, 1941.

71 *stroke began to return*: *Washington Post*, July 20, 1941; *Brooklyn Eagle*, July 21, 1941; *Baltimore Afro-American*, July 22, 1941.

72 *"It gives you the giggles"*: *Philadelphia Tribune*, July 17, 1941.

72 *"juggling votes"*: Cum Posey to Effa Manley, January 11, 1943, Newark Eagles papers.

72 *"overtook the veteran"*: *Pittsburgh Courier*, July 19, 1941.

72 *"It was felt in many"/"unable to throw well"*: *Baltimore Afro-American*, August 2, 1941.

72 *"According to gossip in diamond circles"*: *Philadelphia Independent*, July 20, 1941.

72 *a new song by Count Basie*: *Philadelphia Tribune*, July 24, 1941; *Sports Illustrated*, July 19, 1993.

73 *"the largest crowd"*: *Chicago Defender*, August 2, 1941.

73 *"Only Marcus Garvey"*: *New York Amsterdam News*, August 2, 1941.

73 *"race problem address"*: *Chicago Defender*, August 2, 1941.

73 *"lost his copy"/"stranded on the first base line"*: *Chicago Defender*, August 9, 1941.

74 *"It's up to the catcher"*: *New York World-Telegram and Sun*, February 14, 1957.

74 *"The players who have been in South America"*: *Chicago Defender*, August 2, 1941.

74 *"had to be worked over"*: *Baltimore Afro-American*, August 9, 1941.

75 *"pretty gal picturetaker"*: *Baltimore Afro-American*, August 2, 1941.

75 *"You know what he wants"*: Irvin, *Nice Guys Finish First*, 42.

75 *"swinging bunt"*: Interview with Monte Irvin, April 17, 2007.

75 *"the folly of having women"*: *Baltimore Afro-American*, August 2, 1941.

76 *"What you need"*: Irvin, *Nice Guys Finish First*, 87.

77 *pondering his plate approach*: *El Mundo*, December 8, 1941.

CHAPTER 6: WAR AND A TRYOUT

78 *"Man, the war scared"*: *New York Amsterdam News*, January 17, 1942.

79 *"Let's Put the Axe to the Axis"*: *Los Angeles Times*, March 22, 1942.

79 *refused to hire African-Americans*: Walter Licht, *Getting Work Philadelphia, 1840–1950* (Cambridge: Harvard University Press, 1992), 45.

79 *"I was given the job of operating"*: *IGTBA*, 88.

79 *"I remember what I was doing"*: *Baltimore Afro-American*, March 11, 1950.

80 *"it would be best for the country"*: *New York Times*, January 17, 1942.

81 *"refused to pose for pictures"/"hovered around menacingly"*: A. S. (Doc) Young, "The Black Sportswriter," *Ebony*, October 1970.

81 *"We are powerless to act"*: *Pittsburgh Courier*, March 21, 1942.

81 *"keep his trap closed"*: *Pittsburgh Press*, July 27, 1942.

82 *"rule-making power"/"If he had had any such power"*: *Study of Monopoly Power: Hearings before Subcommittee on Study of Monopoly Power of the Committee on the Judiciary*, House of Representatives, Eighty-second Congress, first session, serial no. 1, Part 6, "Organized Baseball" (Washington, DC: Government Printing Office, 1952), 687.

82 *"spreading disunity"/"sick and tired"*: *PM*, July 17, 1942.

82 *"Negroes are not barred"*: *Milwaukee Journal*, July 17, 1942.

83 *"this ruling will usher in a new era"*: *Daily Worker*, July 18, 1942.

83 *"Landis' statement was hypocritical"*: Quoted in *New York Amsterdam News*, July 25, 1942.

83 *"colored people should develop"*: *Baltimore Afro-American*, July 25, 1942.

83 *"play professional baseball"*: MacPhail to the Reverend Raymond Campion, July 28, 1942, cited in *Chicago Defender*, August 8, 1942.

83 *"I'm sure I could do OK"*: *Daily Worker*, July 16, 1942.

83 *"told to wait"*: *Daily Worker*, July 16, 1942.

84 *"I never worked out"/"colored man and his wife"*: *Pittsburgh Courier*, August 1, 1942.

84 *land him in a psychiatric ward*: *Pittsburgh Courier*, January 9, 1943.

85 *made an unfortunate statement*: *Pittsburgh Press* (United Press) and *Pittsburgh Post-Gazette* (Associated Press), August 7, 1942.

85 *"Speed" (!) Campanella*: *Washington Post*, August 1, 1942.

85 *"It might be a good thing"*: *Pittsburgh Sun-Telegraph*, July 17, 1942.

85 *"I will be glad"*: *Daily Worker*, July 26, 1942.

85 *"thundering roar of approval"*: *Daily Worker*, July 28, 1942.

85 *"scathing denunciations"*: *Daily Worker*, August 24, 1942.

85 *"So far as colored boys"*: *Pittsburgh Sun-Telegraph*, July 28, 1942.

86 *"I've been playing baseball"*: *Daily Worker*, August 4, 1942.

86 *"had no idea at the time"*: *IGTBA*, 97.

86 *a scolding from the rabid anticommunist*: *New York Post*, March 8, 1955.

86 *"I don't believe there is a thing"*: *Pittsburgh Sun-Telegraph*, July 26, 1942.

86 *"The furor gets under Campanella's skin"*: *Cleveland Plain Dealer*, August 6, 1942.

86 *"I called and I insisted"*: Interview with Lester Rodney, November 26, 2007.

87 *later claim that he was swayed*: *Sporting News*, January 11, 1950; *Pittsburgh Courier*, February 24, 1962; interview with William Benswanger, Jr., May 3, 2007.

87 *"Plenty of Negro players are ready"*: *Daily Worker*, September 19, 1942.

88 *Campy still had time to collect a couple of hits*: *Cleveland Plain Dealer* and *Cleveland Press*, August 10, 1942.

88 *"They deserve no sympathy"*: *Pittsburgh Courier*, August 15, 1942.

88 *the press reported that Josh Gibson*: *Baltimore Afro-American*, August 15, 1942.

89 *Mexican League had already tried*: *Baltimore Afro-American*, February 14, 1942.

CHAPTER 7: MEXICO

90 *"one of the crummiest"*: Robert Dallek, *Lone Star Rising: Lyndon Johnson and His Times, 1908–1960* (New York: Oxford University Press, 1991), 77.

90 *"no Mexican"*: *IGTBA*, 92.

91 *"George Steinbrenner of Mexico"*: John Virtue, *South of the Color Barrier: How Jorge Pasquel and the Mexican League Pushed Baseball Toward Racial Integration* (Jefferson, NC: McFarland & Company, 2008), 1.

91 muy americanizado: *New York Times*, April 25, 1943.

91 *"When the fans whistle"*: *Sporting News*, March 31, 1948.

92 *"He'd lose fifteen or sixteen pounds"*: Holway, *Voices*, 330.

92 *"Why, after you hit a double down"*: *People's Voice*, April 20, 1946.

92 *"Every afternoon the train"*: *New York Journal-American*, May 3, 1953.

92 *In 20 games for Monterrey*: Correspondence with Pedro Treto Cisneros, author of *The Mexican League, Comprehensive Player Statistics, 1937–2001* (Jefferson, NC: McFarland & Company, 2002), April 2007.

92 *delayed payment on a performance bonus*: *New York Daily News*, August 22, 1958.

92 *"Quincy, don't expect me"*: Virtue, *South of the Color Barrier*, 107.

93 *"Jorge called me over"*: Interview with Monte Irvin, April 17, 2007.

93 *"stay in essential"*: P. E. Schwahm to Emanuel Millman, April 3, 1943, Newark Eagles papers.

93 *"cussing out"*: *Pittsburgh Courier*, July 24, 1943.

93 *a deal was reached*: Roy Campanella to Art Carter, July 29, 1943, Art Carter Papers, Manuscript Division, Moorland-Spingarn Research Center, Howard University, Washington, DC.

94 *"This is a very fine country"*: Roy Campanella to Art Carter, May 14, 1943, Art Carter Papers.

94 *"leading the league in home runs"/"I hear that the Elites aren't"*: Roy Campanella to Art Carter, July 29, 1943, Art Carter Papers.

94 *12 of his team's 27 homers*: Correspondence with Pedro Treto Cisneros, April 2007.

95 *went after three of Roy's*: *Sporting News*, August 22, 1964.

95 *so-called Mexican Babe Ruth*: *Sporting News*, July 3, 1941.

95 *"I knew I could make it"*: *Baltimore Sun*, May 1, 1990.

95 *Landis had again publicly stated*: *Philadelphia Tribune*, December 11, 1943.

96 *no qualms about refusing to sign Bob Berman*: Charles J. Sanders, "In Search of the Great American Baseball Dream," *Baseball Digest*, February 1985, 39.

96 *"We are going to beat the bushes"*: Arthur Mann, *The Jackie Robinson Story* (New York: Grosset & Dunlap, 1963), 11.

96 *"good Mexican players"*: Branch Rickey to Tom Greenwade, April 29, 1943, courtesy of Jim Kreuz, author of "Tom Greenwade and His '007' Assignment," *National Pastime*, 2007.

96 *"If the first word of his message"*: Tom Meany, *The Artful Dodgers—New Revised Edition* (New York: Grosset & Dunlap, 1963), 87.

97 *"Informants state they have"*: Alfonso L. Fors memo, April 12, 1943, courtesy of Jim Kreuz.

97 *"I kill him"*: *Philadelphia Daily News*, April 9, 1997.

97 *couldn't pull the ball*: *Sporting News*, October 3, 1956.

97 *Quincy Trouppe would assert*: Quincy Trouppe, Sr., *20 Years Too Soon: Prelude to Major League Integrated Baseball* (St. Louis: Missouri Historical Society Press, 1995), 78.

97 *stories surfaced that Greenwade had scouted*: *Atlanta Constitution*, December 3, 1953.

97 *denied ever hearing of Campy*: Branch Rickey to Carl Rowan, May 8, 1959, Correspondence, folder Jackie Robinson correspondence, 1957–60, box 1, Carl T. Rowan Papers, Series II, *Minneapolis Tribune* Files 2, Oberlin College Archives, Oberlin, OH.

97 *"good Mexican boys"*: Branch Rickey to Tom Greenwade, May 10, 1943, courtesy of Jim Kreuz.

98 *"light mulatto"*: Roberto González Echevarría, *The Pride of Havana: A History of Cuban Baseball* (New York: Oxford University Press, 1999), 186.

98 *four appeared with Marianao that season*: Jorge S. Figueredo, *Cuban Baseball: A Statistical History, 1878–1961* (Jefferson, NC: McFarland & Company, 2003), 255–56.

98 *Treadway and Burnett were both Southerners*: Both appeared in the lineup with Campy on December 11, 1943. See Jorge S. Figueredo, *Beisbol cubano: A un paso de las grandes Ligas, 1878–1961* (Jefferson, NC: McFarland & Company, 2005), 223.

98 *"taught Campy how to get along"*: *At Nightfall: The Roy Campanella Story*,

Brooklyn Dodgers: The Original America's Team, directed by Mark Reese, ESPN, 1996.

99 *"Our league seems to be in fine shape"*: J. B. Martin to Effa Manley, February 8, 1944, Newark Eagles papers.

100 *brief notation in an unpublished preliminary outline*: *It's Good to Be Alive* file, Little, Brown records, Houghton Library, Harvard University. (Hereafter, Little, Brown records.)

100 *"showed up dressed to kill"*: *Pittsburgh Courier*, March 11, 1944.

100 *"I think she loved him"*: Interview with Gale Muhammad, May 1, 2007.

100 *"Campy was one of the few guys"*: Don Connery, "Take Three," June 22, 1955, *Time* dispatches.

101 *"Well, I'm only seventeen"*: Ron Fimrite, "Triumph of the Spirit," *Sports Illustrated*, September 24, 1990, 101.

101 *"didn't get it in enough"*: Golenbock, *Bums*, 235.

101 *"the first pitch right over his head"*: Fimrite, "Triumph of the Spirit," 101.

101 *box score provides an accurate snapshot*: *Harrisburg Evening News*, August 23, 1944.

101 *slammed twenty-three hits in his first fifty-four at bats*: *Pittsburgh Courier*, July 1, 1944.

101 *"He was really fast"*: Connery, "Take Three."

101 *"was always something less"*: *New York Amsterdam News*, October 18, 1952.

102 *"I don't put Josh Gibson"*: *New York Amsterdam News*, July 15, 1944.

102 *"I felt pretty funny on third"*: Fitzgerald, "Roy Campanella—Mr. Catcher," 74.

102 *"removed from Bugle Field"*: *Philadelphia Tribune*, June 10, 1944.

102 *"if it is true that Josh has lost his mind"*: Bill Yancey to Effa Manley, June 14, 1944, Newark Eagles papers.

103 *"This year I rate the young Philadelphia receiver"*: *Philadelphia Tribune*, October 7, 1944.

103 *"We placed Campanella over Gibson"*: *Pittsburgh Courier*, December 16, 1944.

103 *"hiding in the mountains"*: *Baltimore Afro-American*, November 17, 1945.

103 *tried to interest the Elites*: *Philadelphia Tribune*, August 11, 1945.

103 *"Everything I could do"*: *Washington Post*, February 9, 1972.

104 *"Snow did the best"*: *Baltimore Afro-American*, November 4, 1944.

104 *"I took a big ribbing"*: Interview with Lawrence Luongo, Sr., October 15, 2006.

104 *slam five straight hits*: *Philadelphia Tribune*, June 24, 1944.

104 *"needed seasoning"*: *Philadelphia Tribune*, April 14, 1945.

104 *"sure-fire"*: *Philadelphia Tribune*, September 2, 1944.

CHAPTER 8: MR. RICKEY

106 *median income*: U.S. Bureau of the Census, current population reports, consumer income, March 1948, "Family and Individual Money Income in the United States: 1945."

106 *introduced to him by the Pittsburgh Crawfords' batboy*: *IGTBA*, 110.

106 *the original meeting at the 1939 World's Fair*: Fitzgerald, "Roy Campanella—Mr. Catcher," 46; Lee Allen, "Roy Campanella: The Dodger That Everybody Likes," *Baseball Magazine*, May 1956, 17.

106 *play tennis*: Dick Wimmer, *Baseball Fathers, Baseball Sons* (New York: William Morrow & Company, 1988), 90; *New York Age*, January 28, 1939.

106 *"Ruthe was not an outgoing person"*: Interview with Barbara Brannen, November 8, 2007.

106 *"Not very expressive"*: Interview with Rachel Robinson, January 16, 2008.

106 *married in 1942*: *New York Age*, May 23, 1942.

107 *"They had a wonderful love affair"*: Interview with Barbara Brannen, November 8, 2007.

107 *"The law is on our side now"*: Carl T. Rowan with Jackie Robinson, *Wait Till Next Year* (New York: Random House, 1960), 102.

108 *"went berserk almost"*: Jules Tygiel, *Baseball's Great Experiment: Jackie Robinson and His Legacy*, expanded ed. (New York: Oxford University Press, 1997), 45.

108 *"punctuated with spicy epithets"*: *People's Voice*, April 14, 1945.

108 *squeaky-clean background*: Lanctot, *Negro League Baseball*, 254–55.

109 *contacting Sam Jethroe*: *Pittsburgh Courier*, April 14, 1945.

109 *"We are now up"*: Roy Wilkins to Mary Van Dyke, May 16, 1945, Part 15, Segregation and Discrimination, Complaints and Responses, 1940–1955, Series A: Legal file, Negroes in Sports, 1942–1952, reel 9, Papers of the NAACP, University Publications of America, Frederick, MD.

109 *"a colored man to make"*: *Baltimore Afro-American*, February 28, 1948.

110 *"discrimination against Negroes in the big leagues"*: *Michigan Chronicle*, May 12, 1945.

110 *"I don't believe in barring"*: *Chicago Defender*, May 12, 1945.

110 *" 'coached' by some one"*: *Pittsburgh Courier*, September 1, 1945.

110 *"Negro baseball officials and players"*: *Philadelphia Inquirer*, May 4, 1945.

110 *"establishment and operation"*: Larry MacPhail to A. B. Chandler, April 27, 1945, cited in Joseph Thomas Moore, *Pride Against Prejudice: The Biography of Larry Doby* (Westport, CT: Greenwood Press, 1988), 30.

110 *"A decent, strong Negro League"*: Branch Rickey to Mel Jones, May 2[4?], 1945, box 15, Correspondence, Thomas Melville "Mel" Jones, 1942–63, Branch Rickey papers, Library of Congress.

111 *"to enable me to do open"*: Rowan with Robinson, *Wait Till Next Year*, 106.

111 *"mythical team"*: Jackie Robinson with Charles Dexter, *Baseball Has Done It* (Philadelphia: J. B. Lippincott, 1964), 42.

111 *ample evidence of the existence*: See Lanctot, *Negro League Baseball*, 263–70.

112 *"I've never had any real coaching"*: *People's Voice*, April 20, 1946.

112 *"liked to sit on the back wheel"*: Interview with Jim Zapp, February 26, 2008.

112 *"how easy their work was"*: *York Dispatch*, June 15, 1945.

113 *show his curve*: Fitzgerald, "Roy Campanella—Mr. Catcher," 74.

113 *"brilliant demonstration of pitching"*: *York Dispatch*, June 15, 1945. Campy had beaten a Camden semipro team in an earlier start in 1944, striking out fourteen hitters. See *Camden Morning Post*, August 25, 1944.

113 *"The other teams in the NNL"*: *Baltimore Afro-American*, September 15, 1945.

113 *"official" league stats*: *Philadelphia Tribune* and *Baltimore Afro-American*, September 22, 1945.

114 *slamming six hits*: *Baltimore Afro-American*, October 6, 1945.

115 *10,424 hardy souls*: *Philadelphia Tribune*, October 13, 1945.

115 *rumored to be lurking*: *New York Amsterdam News*, October 13, 1945.

115 *middle-age white man named Clyde Sukeforth*: Multiple versions of the story exist, but see *Baltimore Afro-American*, October 15, 1949; *Saturday Evening Post*, April 8, 1950; *Sports Illustrated*, August 22, 1955; Danny Peary, *We Played the Game: 65 Players Remember Baseball's Greatest Era, 1947–1964* (New York: Hyperion, 1994), 9.

116 *"stage fright"*: Effa Manley to Vernon Green, October 20, 1945, Newark Eagles papers.

116 *"chased a foul"*: *Philadelphia Tribune*, October 13, 1945.

116 *"almost unhittable"*: Interview with Monte Irvin, April 17, 2007.

116 *"He was the best"*: *Sporting News*, July 14, 1948.

117 *"That would bring in a lot of problems"*: *Pittsburgh Courier*, September 1, 1945.

117 *"other and possibly better players"*: Branch Rickey to Arthur Mann, October 7, 1945, box 1, 1901 May 8–1946 December 27 folder, Arthur Mann papers, Library of Congress.

117 *"fierce-looking pirate"*: *Brooklyn Eagle*, May 21, 1951.

117 *"He spoke in a profound manner"*: Interview with Lynn Parrott, October 30, 2007.

118 *"Do you want to get married?"*: Interview with Clyde King, September 27, 2007.

118 *"three to four inches thick"/"He read it"*: Golenbock, *Bums*, 200.

118 *"Our general opinion"/"That boy's not too old"*: *Sporting News*, July 18, 1951.

118 *ask to see a birth certificate*: Connery, "Take Four," June 22, 1955, *Time* dispatches.

118 *"I told him right off"*: Fitzgerald, "Roy Campanella—Mr. Catcher," 74.

119 *"on the string"*: Connery, "Take Four."

119 *"election football"*: Mann, *Jackie Robinson Story*, 124.

119 *"Leftwich"*: *Baltimore Afro-American*, September 15, 1945.
120 *crossed in August*: *Baltimore Evening Sun* and *Baltimore News-Post*, August 11, 1945; *Sporting News*, July 14, 1948.
120 *a game of gin rummy*: Young, *Roy Campanella*, 13.
121 *"a biting tongue"*: *Baltimore Afro-American*, November 28, 1953.
121 *7 straight hits*: *Washington Star*, June 25, 1945.
121 *Bavasi claimed*: Buzzie Bavasi and John Strege, *Off the Record* (Chicago: Contemporary Books, 1987), 32.
122 *"war nerves"*: *Newsday*, March 2, 1997.
122 *Gus Greenlee pushed Rickey*: Charles Greenlee interview, June 18, 1980, Black Sport in Pittsburgh Collection, Archives of Industrial Society, Hillman Library, University of Pittsburgh.
122 *"some scouts raved"*: Rowan with Robinson, *Wait Till Next Year*, 109. A similar quote can be found in Meany, *Artful Dodgers*, 103.
122 *"Campanella was never mentioned"*: Branch Rickey to Carl Rowan, May 8, 1959, Carl T. Rowan Papers.
122 *"was probably far"*: Arnold Rampersad, *Jackie Robinson: A Biography* (New York: Alfred A. Knopf, 1997), 292.
122 *"C'mon you, Roy"*: Connery, "Take One," June 22, 1955, *Time* dispatches.
123 *"handled white pitchers"*: Donn Rogosin, *Invisible Men: Life in Baseball's Negro Leagues* (New York: Atheneum, 1983), 31.
123 *"I knew I was right"*: *Pittsburgh Courier*, November 3, 1945.
123 *"It was a pleasant shock"*: Interview with George Crowe, February 29, 2008.
123 *"I knew I could play"*: *IGTBA*, 118.
123 *document in the Branch Rickey Papers*: Brooklyn Baseball Club, "The Case Against Jimmy Powers," 1946, box 34, Baseball File/Brooklyn Dodgers/James Powers, 1942–1946, Branch Rickey Papers.
123 *"for the Brooklyn Brown Dodgers"*: Harold Rosenthal, "He Made the Difference for the Dodgers," *Saturday Evening Post*, April 8, 1950, 155.
124 *"Campy said that someone"*: Carl Rowan interview with Jackie and Rachel Robinson, 1957, box 15, Jackie Robinson Papers, Library of Congress.

CHAPTER 9: NASHUA

125 *"several other Negroes"*: *Philadelphia Evening Bulletin*, October 25, 1945.
126 *"I would like to see"*: *Chicago Defender*, December 8, 1945.
126 *"Campanella was just living"*: Trouppe, *20 Years Too Soon*, 88.
126 *"I remember one day"*: Ibid., 87.
126 *"coming along swell"*: *Pittsburgh Courier*, December 22, 1945.
126 *"good pitcher"*: Jules Tygiel interview with Roy Campanella, November 15, 1980, NBHOFL.
127 *"the happiest person in the hotel"*: Trouppe, *20 Years Too Soon*, 88.
127 *farm system of nineteen clubs*: *Sporting News*, April 28, 1946.
128 *"some inexperienced youngster"*: E-mail from Buzzie Bavasi, January 6, 2007.

128 *selling stock at $10 a share*: *Danville Commercial News*, February 8, 1946.
128 *decision appears to have been made*: E-mail from Buzzie Bavasi, January 6, 2007.
128 *"always buzzing around"*: Bavasi and Strege, *Off the Record*, 9.
128 *"pretty good reputation"*: *Newsday*, May 5, 2000.
128 *$185 a month*: Brooklyn Baseball Club, "The Case Against Jimmy Powers."
128 *"It's been practically your life's dream"*: *IGTBA*, 122.
129 *"they gave us two beautiful"*: *Nashua Telegraph*, April 16, 1997.
129 *"kept saying things"*: *USA Today*, July 2, 1990.
129 *"Hey, Newk"*: *Nashua Telegraph*, April 16, 1997.
130 *"You didn't fool with him"*: Interview with Larry Shepard, January 11, 2007.
130 *"Campy was one of my favorites"*: E-mail from Buzzie Bavasi, December 30, 2006.
130 *"My first impression"*: E-mail from Buzzie Bavasi, January 6, 2007.
130 *"They had a lot of talent"*: Interview with Bernard Reinertsen, January 11, 2007.
131 *Roy's backup, Gus Galipeau*: Interview with Gus Galipeau, December 3, 2006.
131 *"You couldn't find a nicer guy"*: Interview with Donald Chartier, February 6, 2007.
131 *"He was a great person"*: Interview with Billy DeMars, February 6, 2007.
131 *"Everything is swell here"/"We're going to make"*: *New York Amsterdam News*, May 11, 1946.
131 *discouraging distances of at least 450 feet*: *Sporting News*, July 10, 1946.
131 *"I have my mind set"*: *Philadelphia Tribune*, August 13, 1946.
132 *"I don't ask for the sensational kind"*: *Pittsburgh Courier*, May 18, 1946.
132 *"whaled a whistling single"*: *Pittsburgh Courier*, May 11, 1946.
132 *3,939 fans*: *Lynn Daily Item*, May 9, 1946.
132 *"a typical New England town"*: *Pittsburgh Courier*, May 18, 1946.
133 *"We used to put Campanella's kid"*: Interview with Billy DeMars, February 6, 2007.
133 *"too much publicity"*: *Philadelphia Tribune*, August 13, 1946.
133 *"Campy kind of looked after"*: Interview with Larry Shepard, January 11, 2007.
133 *"We had never seen black people"*: Steve Daly, "Dodgers still have a place in local hearts," *Sunday Telegraph* (Nashua), August 11, 1996.
133 *"Who should I see sitting right"*: *Baltimore Afro-American*, April 8, 1950.
133 *"They just about own the town"*: Scott C. Roper and Stephanie Abbot Roper, " 'We're Going to Give All We Have for This Grand Little Town': Baseball Integration and the 1946 Nashua Dodgers," *Historical New Hampshire* 53, nos. 1/2 (Spring/Summer 1998): 15.
134 *"Sure they're Negroes"*: *Philadelphia Tribune*, August 13, 1946.
134 *"When Rufus Raised the Roofus"*: *Los Angeles Times*, May 26, 1958.

134 *"reluctant to assert himself"*: *Saturday Evening Post*, June 4, 1954.
134 *"We were losing by one run"*: Fitzgerald, "Roy Campanella—Mr. Catcher," 75.
134 *the* Nashua Telegraph *indicates*: *Nashua Telegraph*, June 17, 1946.
135 *"I doubt if things will ever change"*: *Chicago Defender*, July 31, 1948.
135 *"I thought they were going"*: *Philadelphia Tribune*, August 13, 1946.
135 *"I called time right"*: Fitzgerald, "Roy Campanella—Mr. Catcher," 75.
135 *had actually thrown dirt on Campy twice*: *Sport*, July 1959, 65.
135 *"Yvars was a dirty goddamn"*: Peary, *We Played the Game*, 15.
136 *"drive those two colored boys"*: *Philadelphia Tribune*, August 13, 1946.
136 *"They had some real"*: *Boston Globe*, March 28, 1997.
136 *"Wanted to know"*: *Los Angeles Times*, March 9, 1967.
136 *"Don't you talk"*: Bavasi and Strege, *Off the Record*, 24.
136 *"The guy told Buzzie"*: *Los Angeles Times*, March 9, 1967.
137 *"Why don't you say"*: *Boston Globe*, March 28, 1997.
137 *"We had no more"*: Bavasi and Strege, *Off the Record*, 24.
137 *Mr. Murder*: *Nashua Telegraph*, September 10, 1946.
137 *"Here he is"*: Daly, "Dodgers still have a place in local hearts."
137 *"You know, people expect"*: *Philadelphia Tribune*, August 13, 1946.
138 *"From all appearances"*: *Baltimore Afro-American*, July 20, 1946.
138 *"He wasn't comfortable"*: Interview with Monte Irvin, April 17, 2007.
138 *tipped off his pitches*: Don Bell, "The Wright Stuff," *MVP Magazine*, June 1984?, 46, in John Wright file, NBHOFL.
138 *a recent secret preliminary report*: Lanctot, *Negro League Baseball*, 296–99.
138 *"The young boy Gilliam"*: *Washington Post*, December 26, 1952.
138 *thought about little else*: Jackie Robinson as told to Ed Fitzgerald, "You Play Bolder in the Series," *Sport*, November 1956, 64.
138 *"Very good receiver"*: "Scout Report Card," September 9, 1946, Roger Kahn Papers, box 19, folder 5, NBHOFL.
138 *"Roy is much too good"*: *Baltimore Afro-American*, August 24, 1946.
138 *"first Negro regular"*: Cited in *Nashua Telegraph*, January 7, 1947.
139 *"I just left everything"*: Tygiel interview with Campanella, November 15, 1980.
139 *"new fellows"*: Rowan with Robinson, *Wait Till Next Year*, 173.
139 *a place so disgusting*: *Los Angeles Daily News*, February 16, 1997.
139 *"a room sans sunlight"*: *Baltimore Afro-American*, March 13, 1948.
139 *"specifically requested"*: Roy Campanella II, "Roy Campanella," in Danny Peary, ed., *Cult Baseball Players: The Greats, the Flakes, the Weird, and the Wonderful* (New York: Simon & Schuster, 1990), 257.
140 *"He didn't want"*: Ibid.
140 *use of a drinking cup*: *Sporting News*, May 21, 1947.
140 *"Don't throw him out"*: *Pittsburgh Courier*, March 15, 1958.
141 *"I'm convinced now"*: *Baltimore Afro-American*, April 5, 1947.

141 *"today purchased the contract"*: *New York Times*, April 11, 1947.
142 *"Gosh, Homey"*: *Baltimore Afro-American*, May 17, 1947.
142 *"troublesome"*: Branch Rickey memo, April 23, 1947, box 3, folder 8, Jackie Robinson Papers.
142 *"He can take it with a smile"*: *Chicago Defender*, March 22, 1947.
142 *heaped racist insults*: *Baltimore Afro-American*, May 24, 1947.
142 *"It was just as bad"*: Interview with Butch Woyt, May 1, 2007.
143 *"Hey, pal, give me one"*: *Baltimore Afro-American*, August 9, 1947.
143 *"Some of those older players"*: Interview with Ed Stevens, May 3, 2007.
143 *"If some guys think"*: *Pittsburgh Courier*, May 24, 1947.
143 *took his postgame shower*: Interview with Ed Stevens, May 3, 2007.
144 *"Jackie always struck us"*: *Montreal Gazette*, September 16, 1947.
144 *"about some of the pranks"*: *Pittsburgh Courier*, July 19, 1947.
144 *"one of the best"*: *Sporting News*, May 5, 1948.
144 *"We used to walk"*: Interview with Mike Sandlock, May 7, 2007.
144 *"had me do nothing"*: "Baseball's Best Catcher," *Ebony*, June 1950.
144 *"I have improved a lot"*: *Baltimore Afro-American*, April 26, 1947.
145 *cut down an impressive*: *Sporting News*, December 17, 1947.
145 *"His judgment is great"*: *Baltimore Afro-American*, August 9, 1947.
145 *"has to make people like him"*: Robinson with Dexter, *Baseball Has Done It*, 83.
145 *"He's gonna give out"*: *Baltimore Afro-American*, May 31, 1947.
145 *"I don't find the pitching"*: *Pittsburgh Courier*, May 24, 1947.
145 *"What else has he"*: *Montreal Star*, June 28, 1947.
146 *"best catcher in baseball"*: *Montreal Gazette*, June 30, 1947.
146 *"the best in the league"*: *Montreal Gazette*, May 17, 1947.
146 *"Maybe Campanella is"*: *Montreal Gazette*, June 30, 1947.
146 *"a troubled boy"*: *Brooklyn Eagle*, April 3, 1948.
147 *"held the ball in a vise-like grip"*: *Montreal Star*, September 8, 1947.
147 *tearful Kehn*: *Montreal Herald*, September 8, 1947.
147 *"Every once in a while"*: Young, *Roy Campanella*, 47.
148 *"I regard him"*: *Baltimore Afro-American*, March 27, 1948.
148 *"definitely won't be brought up"*: Unidentified clipping (*Brooklyn Eagle*?), October 1947, Roy Campanella file, NBHOFL.
148 *"He is a real worker"*: *Pittsburgh Courier*, July 19, 1947.

CHAPTER 10: BROOKLYN

150 *"All of a sudden"*: Frank Graham, Jr., "What Campy Means to All of Us," 83.
150 *"Wait a minute, Luke"*: Connery, "Take Four," June 22, 1955, *Time* dispatches.
150 *divorce proceedings against Bernice*: "Certificate of decree in divorce issued Dec-1 1947," City Hall, Philadelphia, Pennsylvania.
150 *received her divorce a week*: Divorce decree, Ruthe Willis and David B.

McKenzie, Jr., December 8, 1947, Commonwealth of Virginia, Department of Health, Bureau of Vital Statistics.

150 *on April 30*: Although I was unable to locate a marriage license, April 30, 1948, appears the most likely date. See *New York Amsterdam News*, January 12, 1963; *IGTBA*, 294.

151 *"a better chance to make"*: Young, *Roy Campanella*, 47.

151 *"He has a great arm"*: *Pittsburgh Courier*, January 17, 1948.

151 *"They know their own business"*: *Pittsburgh Courier*, January 24, 1948.

151 *discussing Edwards*: *Chicago Defender*, April 11, 1948.

152 *"Did you ever hear"*: *Sporting News*, March 31, 1948.

152 *"a slightly more impressive"*: *New York Times*, March 2, 1948.

152 *"undercurrent of white superiority"*: *Baltimore Afro-American*, March 20, 1948.

153 *"stuck his neck out"*: *Chicago Defender*, July 31, 1948.

153 *"you don't talk back"*: Connery, "Take Five," June 23, 1955, *Time* dispatches.

153 *tried to present his own ideas*: Young, *Roy Campanella*, 53.

153 *"I've requested Clay Hopper"*: *Sporting News*, March 17, 1948.

154 *"I wouldn't trade Hodges"*: *Sporting News*, April 7, 1948.

154 *hotel swimming pool with Sandlock*: *Baltimore Afro-American*, March 20, 1948.

154 *arranged for Barrett*: *Baltimore Afro-American*, March 27, 1948.

154 *"I kept looking down"*: *Pittsburgh Courier*, April 10, 1948.

154 *"the happiest . . . of my life"*: *Saturday Evening Post*, August 2, 1958.

155 *close to thirty pounds overweight*: *Sporting News*, January 23, 1957.

155 *"Robinson seemed indifferent"*: *Baltimore Afro-American*, April 3, 1948.

155 *"mess"*: *New York Times*, March 4, 1950.

155 *"take it upon themselves"*: *Pittsburgh Courier*, March 27, 1948.

155 *a roped-off segregated section*: *Baltimore Afro-American*, April 10, 1948.

155 *"sent the Negro portion"*: *New York Times*, April 1, 1948.

156 *black fans let out*: *Chicago Defender*, April 17, 1948.

156 *"racial epithets"*: *Pittsburgh Courier*, April 17, 1948.

156 *"It would be bad"*: *Sporting News*, April 21, 1948.

156 *"Why not Roy Campanella?"*: Quoted in *New York Amsterdam News*, April 10, 1948.

156 *"As things now stand"*: *Baltimore Afro-American*, May 1, 1948.

157 *roughly 50 percent of the population*: *New York Times*, October 28, 1953.

157 *"I like Brooklyn"*: Lee Lowenfish, *Branch Rickey: Baseball's Ferocious Gentleman* (Lincoln: University of Nebraska Press, 2007), 328.

157 *"Around their battered standard"*: *New York Times*, September 29, 1963.

159 *"long cream-colored"*: *New York Herald Tribune*, April 21, 1948.

159 *"This is the first"*: *New York Journal-American*, April 21, 1948.

160 *"one of those big"/"got along wonderfully"*: Rowan interview with Jackie and Rachel Robinson, 1957.

160 *"If he didn't want"*: *At Nightfall: The Roy Campanella Story.*
160 *promptly drilled him*: *Brooklyn Eagle*, April 21, 1948.
160 *"let the ball talk"*: Stephen Banker, *Black Diamonds: An Oral History of Negro Baseball* (Washington, DC: Tapes for Readers, 1978).
160 *"I told you not"/"You better not play"*: Tygiel interview with Campanella, November 15, 1980.
161 *"I just want to play"*: *Baltimore Afro-American*, May 15, 1948.
161 *meal money on the road*: *Sporting News*, January 18, 1950.
161 *"the best thing"*: *Pittsburgh Courier*, December 5, 1964.
161 *"get along like two brothers"*: *Chicago Defender*, October 16, 1948.
161 *teased Campy*: *Chicago Defender*, May 15, 1948.
162 *"Everyone's wondering"*: *New York Daily News*, May 6, 1948.
162 *"What is all this mystery"/"If you should put it"*: *Brooklyn Eagle*, May 12, 1948.
162 *"I hated to see him go"*: *Pittsburgh Courier*, May 29, 1948.
162 *707 Rondo*: *St. Paul Dispatch*, June 30, 1948.
163 *"There was a colored man out here"*: *Minneapolis Spokesman*, June 4, 1948.
163 *"I keep one thing in mind"*: *Minneapolis Morning Tribune*, June 3, 1948.
163 *covering the Campanella story*: *Minneapolis Spokesman*, June 18, 1948.
164 *cursed out*: *New York Daily Mirror*, May 25, 1948.
164 *placed on waivers*: *Sporting News*, June 2, 1948.
164 *"Hey, Hollywood"/"He masterminds"/"fodder for radio comics"*: *Sporting News*, June 2, 1948.
164 *last in the league in hitting*: *New York Times*, July 4, 1948.
165 *"Campanella's here"*: Golenbock, *Bums*, 202.
165 *"How can you keep a fellow"*: *New York Journal-American*, July 1, 1948.
165 *had worn number 56*: *Baltimore Afro-American*, April 3, 1948.
165 *HILDA IS HERE*: *New York Times*, September 3, 1955.
166 *fondness for liquid lunches*: *Los Angeles Times*, September 24, 2007.
166 *requests from the players*: *Sporting News*, May 10, 1950.
166 *"a metal bridge chair"*: *Sporting News*, August 31, 1955. Fans and writers often misspelled his last name as *Rickard*. See *Sporting News*, October 8, 1952.
166 *"sounds like a train-caller"*: *Sporting News*, October 12, 1955.
166 *"Don't throw nuthin' "*: *Brooklyn Eagle*, July 9, 1948.
166 *hurled his spikes*: *Sporting News*, September 22, 1948.
167 *"greatest . . . of my life"*: Young, *Roy Campanella*, 111.
167 *"region untouched"*: *Sporting News*, July 14, 1948.
167 *"The Negro is by far"*: *New York Journal-American*, July 6, 1948.
167 *"They're gonna have to cut"*: *Pittsburgh Courier*, May 21, 1955.
167 *cereal ad*: *New York Amsterdam News*, October 2, 1948.
168 *"Dick Young was a great reporter"*: Interview with Dave Anderson, May 6, 2008.

168 *"They let him do it"*: Interview with Lynn Parrott, October 30, 2007.

168 *unqualified support to the first generation*: *New York Times*, September 2, 1987.

168 *"I had always respected Dick"*: Rowan interview with Jackie and Rachel Robinson, 1957.

168 *"will use you to attack"*: Peary, *Cult Baseball Players*, 258.

168 *"Hell, no, I won't resign"/"That's horrible"/"Durocher was too much"*: *New York Journal-American*, July 17, 1948.

169 *"I want to let bygones be bygones"*: *New York Times*, July 18, 1948.

169 *"If you missed a signal"*: Interview with Gene Hermanski, August 13, 2007.

169 *"I don't say a fellow"*: *New York Daily Mirror*, May 18, 1948.

169 *"like an embalmed cucumber"*: *New York Journal-American*, October 10, 1949.

169 *"I tell 'em what"*: *Sporting News*, July 20, 1949.

169 *"When I have players"*: *Sporting News*, July 19, 1950.

170 *"crabbed and hostile"*: *New York Post*, March 8, 1955.

170 *"best friend"/"a great manager"*: *New York Journal-American*, July 17, 1948.

170 *"Mr. Rickey's puppet"*: Interview with Bobby Morgan, September 30, 2007.

170 *"nigger rich"*: Rowan interview with Jackie and Rachel Robinson, 1957.

170 *"great young catcher"*: *Brooklyn Eagle*, July 17, 1948.

170 *"stay ready for a pitcher's fast pitch"*: Roberts interview with Campanella, July 24, 1987.

170 *"It is not difficult to sense"*: Jack Sher, "Jackie Robinson: The Great Experiment," *Sport*, October 1948, 137.

171 *"Barney was always afraid"*: Connery, "Take Six," June 23, 1955, *Time* dispatches.

171 *Cavarretta promptly rifled*: *Chicago Tribune*, September 20, 1949.

171 *"Don't you ever shake me off again"*: Golenbock, *Bums*, 219.

171 *"Negro ace threw his cap"*: *New York Times*, August 3, 1948.

171 *"It's good!"*: *Baltimore Afro-American*, September 4, 1948.

172 *"It may take ten years"*: Connery, "Take Five," June 24, 1955, *Time* dispatches.

172 *"I would like to take five"*: Rowan interview with Jackie and Rachel Robinson, 1957.

172 *"no such conversation ever occurred"*: Rowan with Robinson, *Wait Till Next Year*, 327.

173 *"Everything we did stood out"*: Tygiel interview with Campanella, November 15, 1980.

173 *"They just weren't aggressive"*: *Sporting News*, November 3, 1948.

173 *"I like my team"*: *Sporting News*, November 17, 1948.

CHAPTER 11: OUT OF THE SHADOWS

174 *"A lot of the younger"*: *Daily Worker*, January 20, 1949.
174 *"Those kids seeing"*: *New York Amsterdam News*, November 20, 1948.
175 *"I've always thought"*: *IGTBA*, 155.
175 *successful lawsuit*: *New York Times*, February 14, 1947.
175 *up to $8,800*: *Baltimore Afro-American*, February 12, 1949.
175 *"You're always going to be"*: *IGTBA*, 160.
176 *Lena Horne*: *Baltimore Afro-American*, April 9, 1949; *Chicago Defender*, January 22, 1949; *Pittsburgh Courier*, August 27, 1949.
176 *"He was wonderful"*: Interview with Barbara Brannen, November 8, 2007.
176 *"I don't think he was all that close"*: Interview with Delores Patterson, April 15, 2008.
176 *"enjoyed being a big wheel"*: E-mail from Buzzie Bavasi, January 6, 2007.
176 *"dreamed about having everybody"*: Red Barber, *The Rhubarb Patch: The Story of the Modern Brooklyn Dodgers* (New York: Simon & Schuster, 1954), 91.
177 *"assembly line baseball"*: *New York Times*, March 10, 1949.
177 *"police whistles"*: *Sporting News*, March 16, 1949.
177 *"new-fangled batting tees"/"Buck Rogers gadgets"*: *New York Times*, March 10, 1949.
177 *"We do not claim"*: *New York Journal-American*, March 11, 1949.
177 *"one of the worst"*: *Long Beach Independent*, October 26, 1972.
177 *"keep on the alert"*: *Baltimore Afro-American*, March 11, 1950.
177 *standard tale of Campy*: Golenbock, *Bums*, 197.
177 *"I spoke up the first time"*: Robinson with Dexter, *Baseball Has Done It*, 85–86.
178 *"go around back"*: Morton Puner, "An All-American Lineup," *Baseball Digest*, August 1950.
178 *"had a colored boy"*: Roscoe McGowen, "Baseball's Best Catcher—Roy Campanella," *Baseball Magazine*, September 1950.
178 *"It is practically impossible"*: Connery, "Take Two," June 22, 1955, *Time* dispatches.
178 *"Publicly, there was always"*: Interview with Dave Anderson, May 6, 2008.
179 *"Roy is a Coke addict"*: *Baltimore Afro-American*, March 19, 1949.
179 *"I'd be willing to bet"*: *New York Post*, March 15, 1949.
179 *"Sure, he made"*: *Sporting News*, March 30, 1949.
179 *"somehow gave the impression"*: Meany, "Campanella—King of Catchers," 87.
179 *"I couldn't hear what they were saying"*: Connery, "Take Six," June 23, 1955, *Time* dispatches.
180 *"in the midst of seven"*: *Baltimore Afro-American*, February 18, 1950.
180 *"Kill that nigger!"*: *Sports Illustrated*, March 14, 1983.
180 *"attacked a white man"*: Robinson with Dexter, *Baseball Has Done It*, 75.

180 *"I think he can pitch"*: *Pittsburgh Courier*, May 21, 1949.
180 *"fine records"*: *Baltimore Afro-American*, April 2, 1949.
180 *"blue-eyed bitches"*: John Roseboro with Bill Libby, *Glory Days with the Dodgers, and Other Days with Others* (New York: Atheneum, 1978), 122.
180 *"a little belligerent"*: Interview with Carl Erskine, April 8, 2008.
181 *"this is the most backward"*: *Baltimore Afro-American*, April 9, 1949.
181 *"a black family would get"*: Interview with Lynn Parrott, October 30, 2007.
181 *"a young smart aleck"*: *Baltimore Afro-American*, April 16, 1949.
181 *"As long as they stay"*: *Sporting News*, January 26, 1949.
182 *"shoot you out on"*: Golenbock, *Bums*, 222.
182 *"When we got to Atlanta"*: Ibid., 224.
182 *"We are lodged"*: *Baltimore Afro-American*, April 16, 1949.
182 *"had come out there well"/"to head right"*: Rowan interview with Jackie and Rachel Robinson, 1957.
182 *"You've got it made"*: Golenbock, *Bums*, 224.
182 *"It should prove"*: *Sporting News*, April 20, 1949.
182 *"the center of every eye"*: *Pittsburgh Courier*, April 16, 1949.
183 *a local reporter remarked*: *Baltimore Afro-American*, April 16, 1949.
183 *"He has become the Babe Ruth"*: *Sporting News*, April 20, 1949.
183 *use of amphetamines*: *New York Daily News*, June 30, 1957.
183 *"cathode ray oscillograph"*: *Sporting News*, September 30, 1953.
183 *"electron calculator"*: *Long Island Daily Press*, March 19, 1955.
183 *"That doesn't exist"*: Interview with Dave Anderson, May 6, 2008.
184 *$500,000-plus annual payroll*: *Sporting News*, July 3, 1957.
184 *"communist tendencies"*: *New York Journal-American*, April 14, 1949.
184 *"The strange thing to me"*: *Sporting News*, November 30, 1955.
184 *"Sign it or stay home"*: Interview with Dick Teed, February 26, 2008.
184 *"We were like kids"*: *Los Angeles Times*, October 10, 1983.
184 *"We cannot get the owners"*: *New York Times*, August 30, 1953.
185 *"phony fences"*: *Sporting News*, May 14, 1952.
185 *"jack rabbit"*: *Brooklyn Eagle*, August 24, 1951.
185 *"two platoon system"*: *New York Daily Mirror*, October 8, 1949.
185 *"The way the game"*: *Long Island Daily Press*, July 29, 1955.
185 *"babied too much"*: *Sporting News*, March 26, 1952.
185 *"Today, eighty percent"*: *Saturday Evening Post*, September 13, 1952.
185 *"A slider is"*: *Sporting News*, September 7, 1949.
185 *"the slider has made"*: *Sporting News*, February 22, 1956.
185 *"It ruins your whole"*: Connery, "Take Eight," June 24, 1955, *Time* dispatches.
186 *all but abandoned*: *Sporting News*, August 29, 1956.
186 *airing over a hundred games*: *New York Times*, March 27, 1955.
186 *highest TV/radio rights*: *New York Times*, March 22, 1957.
186 *a 1955* New York Times *piece*: *New York Times*, June 19, 1955.

186 *"security-conscious"*: *New York Times*, March 30, 1958.
186 *"and I grabbed it"*: Interview with Gene Hermanski, August 13, 2007.
186 *appearance on Ed Sullivan's*: *Long Island Daily Press*, May 21, 1955.
186 *Topps baseball card*: *New York Times*, June 18, 1958.
187 *built a stable*: *Sporting News*, April 18, 1956.
187 *full-page ads*: *New York Times*, October 1, 1952.
187 *a suggestion by team statistician*: Harold Rosenthal, *Baseball Is Their Business* (New York: Random House, 1952), 142.
187 *"But what we need"*: *New York Journal-American*, March 15, 1949.
188 *"We need his bat"*: *New York Journal-American*, April 14, 1949.
188 *"I discovered there"*: *Pittsburgh Courier*, May 7, 1949.
188 *moved his legs*: *Baltimore Afro-American*, April 30, 1949; Connery, "Take Six," June 23, 1955, *Time* dispatches.
188 *"The Lord"*: "Burt's Catcher," *Time*, May 16, 1949.
188 *"should be able to play"*: *Baltimore Afro-American*, March 19, 1949.
188 *"How do you like"*: *Sporting News*, May 4, 1949.
189 *"one more word"*: Unidentified clipping, April 28, 1949, Roy Campanella file, NBHOFL.
189 *"I've played in leagues"*: *Baltimore Afro-American*, May 14, 1949.
189 *"I didn't curse"*: *New York Journal-American*, May 2, 1949.
189 *"not to take anything"*: *Calhoun Times and Gordon County News*, April 30, 1988.
189 *"The big Philadelphian"*: *New York Amsterdam News*, May 14, 1949.
189 *"I think he has decided"*: *St. Louis Argus*, May 20, 1949.
189 *"giant Negro"*: *New York Journal-American*, May 15, 1949.
189 *"What are you talking"*: Golenbock, *Bums*, 239.
189 *"This kid's going"*: *Pittsburgh Courier*, June 25, 1949.
190 *mistaken for the Nat King Cole*: *Baltimore Afro-American*, May 28, 1949.
190 *"What would happen if"*: *Boston Traveler*, July 1949, NBHOFL.
190 *"spread out"*: *Sport*, July 1959, 61.
190 *"Sometimes, the guys"*: *Los Angeles Times*, March 15, 1977.
190 *"I didn't socialize"*: Peary, *We Played the Game*, 90.
190 *"Judas Priest, Roy"*: *Baltimore Afro-American*, September 3, 1949.
190 *"Roy was always very sociable"*: Peary, *We Played the Game*, 90.
191 *"Kingdom Brown wants"*: *New York Amsterdam News*, June 18, 1949.
191 *"It seems to me"*: *Sporting News*, July 20, 1949.
192 *"I want my kid"*: *New York Times*, July 9, 1949.
192 *his son would claim*: Peary, *Cult Baseball Players*, 258.
192 *"When Paul Robeson said"*: *Baltimore Afro-American*, July 12, 1949.
192 *"and I feel someday"*: *Daily Worker*, July 21, 1949.
192 *"reject such an invitation"*: Jackie Robinson as told to Alfred Duckett, *I Never Had It Made* (New York: G. P. Putnam's Sons, 1972), 96.
192 *"loud-speakers are blaring"*: *Chicago Defender*, July 30, 1949.

192 *"slight trace"*: *Baltimore Afro-American*, July 9, 1949.
192 *"They just don't do"*: *Sporting News*, August 31, 1949.
193 *"every player should be"*: *Sporting News*, October 12, 1949.
193 *"they're better hurt"*: *New York Post*, September 1, 1949.
193 *"swollen to twice"*: *Baltimore Afro-American*, August 6, 1949.
193 *"I've just washed my face"*: *New York Times*, August 24, 1949.
193 *"You're some man"/an unapologetic bigot*: *Baltimore Afro-American*, September 24, 1949.
194 *"If a player needed"*: *Atlantic City Press*, August 15, 1999.
194 *Reese pulled out the letter*: *Baltimore Afro-American*, September 24, 1949.
195 *"Roy! How are you"*: Connery, "Take Six," June 23, 1955, *Time* dispatches.
195 *"This was the worst"*: *New York World-Telegram*, September 17, 1949.
195 *"He was crouching"*: *New York Journal-American*, September 17, 1949.
195 *Jackie was certain was deliberate*: *New York Daily News*, August 2, 1951.
195 *ran to Campy's side*: *Baltimore Afro-American*, September 24, 1949.
195 *"two plastic strips"*: *Pittsburgh Courier*, August 1, 1953.
195 *"You can't hit much"*: *New York Sun*, September 17, 1949.
196 *"It's bound to take away"*: *Pittsburgh Courier*, August 1, 1953.
196 *"I'm not trying"*: *Pittsburgh Courier*, September 24, 1949.
196 *"constantly-screeching"*: *Baltimore Afro-American*, April 1, 1950.
197 *"not to let Newcombe choke up"*: *Baltimore Afro-American*, October 1, 1949.
197 *"He accused me"*: *New York Journal-American*, September 22, 1949.
197 *"got very loud"*: *St. Louis Argus*, September 30, 1949.
198 *roughed up the Phillies*: *Sporting News*, February 1, 1950.
198 *"before I even showed"*: *New York World-Telegram*, September 26, 1949.
198 *"unsolicited"*: *New York Daily Mirror*, September 27, 1949.
198 *"lost his stuff"/"if he doesn't like"*: *New York Journal-American*, September 27, 1949.
198 *"I choose to believe"*: *New York World-Telegram*, September 27, 1949.
198 *"This is the first time"*: *Baltimore Afro-American*, October 1, 1949.
198 *"several different versions"*: *Baltimore Afro-American*, October 8, 1949.
199 *"just keep pitching"*: *New York Post*, September 30, 1949.
199 *"Cancel those"*: *New York Post*, October 4, 1949.
199 *"A week ago"*: *New York Times*, October 1, 1949.
200 *"which would only go"*: *New York Daily Mirror*, September 7, 1949.
200 *"Well, if we win"*: *Philadelphia Inquirer*, October 2, 1949.
200 *On the sixth pitch*: *Baltimore Afro-American*, October 8, 1949.
201 *"Hysterical Brooklyn rooters"*: *Philadelphia Inquirer*, October 3, 1949.
201 *"Pinch me"/"I could sit down"*: *New York Daily Mirror*, October 3, 1949.
202 *"That was the hardest"/"The Yankees might be"*: *Pittsburgh Courier*, October 8, 1949.
202 *"looking more like a scarecrow"*: *Philadelphia Inquirer*, October 11, 1949.

202 *"This is the worst-looking"*: *New York World-Telegram*, October 7, 1949.
202 *"The crowd is noisier"*: *New York Journal-American*, October 8, 1949.
203 *"all kinds of filth"*: *People's Voice*, October 11, 1947.
203 *"most prejudiced"*: *Pittsburgh Courier*, February 25, 1950.
203 *"where Negroes can't even"*: *Philadelphia Tribune*, August 12, 1950.
203 *"The Yankees should only"*: *New York Times*, October 5, 1949.
203 *"had someone hold his place"*: *New York World-Telegram*, October 5, 1949.
203 *At Sing Sing*: *New York Daily Mirror*, October 4, 1949.
203 *A Long Island junior high*: *New York World-Telegram*, October 6, 1949.
203 *Beth-El Hospital took*: *New York Journal-American*, October 4, 1949.
203 *"Television has grown up"*: *New York Daily Mirror*, October 11, 1949.
204 *"a dog picture"*: *New York World-Telegram*, October 6, 1949.
204 *at least two of them spitters*: *New York World-Telegram and Sun*, January 2, 1959.
204 *"I never kissed"*: *New York World-Telegram*, October 7, 1949.
204 *"groining"*: Roger Kahn, *The Era: 1947–1957, When the Yankees, the Giants, and the Dodgers Ruled the World* (New York: Ticknor & Fields, 1993), 228.
204 *"There have been pennants"*: *Sporting News*, October 19, 1949.
204 *"The Yankees are a lucky team"/"You know, I'm beginning"*: *New York Daily Mirror*, October 10, 1949.
205 *"I was nervous before"*: Roy Campanella, "Series Pressure Is Unbearable," *Complete Sports—World Series 1962*, 22.
205 *"amazing pickup"*: *New York Daily Mirror*, October 8, 1949.
205 "Que pasa?": *New York Daily Mirror*, October 10, 1949.
205 *"A graceful and solid"/"stood out like"*: *Sporting News*, October 19, 1949.
205 *"Brooklyn showed me"*: *Sporting News*, October 26, 1949.
205 *"From what he showed"*: *Baltimore Afro-American*, April 8, 1950.
205 *"He's easily one"*: *Baltimore Afro-American*, April 22, 1950.

CHAPTER 12: THE SPLIT

207 *$3,500 guarantee*: Roy Campanella to Lester Dworman, July 1949, in *Lester J. Dworman and Ted Worner vs. A. Pompez, Roy Campanella, Donald Newcombe, and Larry Doby*, State of New York, County of New York, 1950 (16828).
207 *"The first week"*: Rowan interview with Jackie and Rachel Robinson, 1957.
208 *Doby had cut*: Larry Doby to Lester Dworman, August 18, 1949, in *Dworman vs. A. Pompez.*
208 *"If you guys feel"*: Rowan interview with Jackie and Rachel Robinson, 1957.
208 *"fantastic"/"Jackie and I were partners"*: Interview with Lester Dworman, December 6, 2007.
208 *"unapproachable"/"Campanella played hard"*: *Baltimore Afro-American*, October 29, 1949.
209 *"by holding out"*: *Los Angeles Times*, July 25, 1969.

209 *"Where he plays"*: *New York Post*, September 20, 1949.
209 *"Roy instituted everybody"*: Interview with George Crowe, February 29, 2008.
210 *would reportedly forbid*: *Jet*, October 9, 1952.
210 *"barely on speaking"*: *Baltimore Afro-American*, April 15, 1950.
210 *"sensationalizing"*: *Baltimore Afro-American*, February 2, 1957.
210 *"ignored their questions"*: *New York Amsterdam News*, November 27, 1948.
210 *"He took my hand"*: *New York Age*, October 15, 1949.
210 *his usual enthusiastic manner*: *Philadelphia Tribune*, October 15, 1949.
210 *"I can excuse"*: *New York Age*, October 15, 1949.
211 *"overly raucous"*: Sher, "Jackie Robinson," 148.
211 *"He plays just as hard"*: *Baltimore Afro-American*, April 21, 1956.
211 *watched Robinson inform Doby*: *New York Amsterdam News*, October 15, 1949.
211 *"Being able to excel"*: Irvin, *Nice Guys Finish First*, 110.
211 *"Jackie spoke like"*: *The Boys of Summer*, VCA Programs, Inc., and Thorn EMI Video Programming Enterprises, Inc., 1983.
211 *"was more business"*: Interview with Lynn Parrott, October 30, 2007.
212 *"You don't find companionship"*: Ed Linn, "The Last Days of Brooklyn's Old Gang," *Sport*, October 1956, 55.
212 *"The sooner I can get out"*: *Pittsburgh Courier*, November 26, 1949.
212 *"self-respecting person"*: *Daily Worker*, December 29, 1949.
212 *"He was the quintessential"*: Luke Ford interview with Roy Campanella, Jr., June 18, 2002, www.lukeford.net/profiles/profiles/roy_campanella.htm.
212 *"just can't play ball"*: *Daily Worker*, July 21, 1949.
212 *"For the most part"*: *Baltimore Afro-American*, July 29, 1969.
212 *"I never saw one thing"*: Interview with Carl Erskine, April 8, 2008.
213 *"They were so respectful"*: Interview with Rachel Robinson, January 16, 2008.
213 *"That's about what"*: *Pittsburgh Courier*, July 13, 1957.
213 *the same as that of Andy Seminick*: "Philadelphia National League club and its wholly owned subsidiaries—Treasurer's Report, 1950," box 4, Philadelphia Phillies papers, Hagley Museum and Library.
214 *"Maybe they aren't paying"*: *Baltimore Afro-American*, March 11, 1950.
214 *"Three times around Campanella"*: *Pittsburgh Courier*, March 18, 1950.
214 *"How are you gonna get"*: *Baltimore Afro-American*, March 18, 1950.
214 *found no car waiting*: *Baltimore Afro-American*, April 1, 1950.
214 *"highly secret meeting"*: *New York Age*, August 27, 1949.
214 *"any suggestion"*: *New York Age*, September 17, 1949.
215 *"He doesn't have the friendly"*: *Baltimore Afro-American*, March 11, 1950.
215 *"slave complex"*: *New York Post*, August 5, 1953.
215 *"miniature bats"*: *Sporting News*, May 3, 1950.
215 *"He has less privacy"*: *Chicago Defender*, May 7, 1950.

215 *might be headed for a breakdown*: *Baltimore Afro-American*, April 15, 1950.
215 *"indifference toward training"/"open flare-up"*: *Baltimore Afro-American*, April 1, 1950.
216 *"best liked guy"*: *Chicago Defender*, June 10, 1950.
217 *"a jackrabbit—with Benzedrine"*: *New York Post*, June 23, 1950.
217 *Spalding people*: *Sporting News*, August 16, 1950.
217 *"If you had ever seen"*: Interview with Don Zimmer, December 4, 2008.
217 *"Not long ago"*: McGowen, "Baseball's Greatest Catcher."
217 *"I didn't hear"*: Roberts interview with Campanella.
218 *"Roe and Newcombe"*: *Sporting News*, July 12, 1950.
218 *"Things just aren't"*: *Pittsburgh Courier*, July 22, 1950.
218 *"tossing his bat"*: *New York Daily Mirror*, July 29, 1950.
218 *"guess we better write off"*: *New York Herald Tribune*, July 22, 1950.
218 *"They're not hungry"*: *New York Post*, June 30, 1950.
218 *"Dissension?"*: *New York World-Telegram and Sun*, September 5, 1951.
218 *"There's going to be more hustle"*: *New York Daily Mirror*, July 29, 1950.
219 *"He has developed a contempt"*: *New York Post*, October 10, 1949.
219 *"If I managed the Dodgers" contest*: *New York Journal-American*, August 2, 1950.
219 *"a star player"*: *New York Daily News*, August 4, 1950.
219 *"He has done a magnificent"*: *New York Daily News*, August 3, 1950.
219 *"The Dodgers of a year ago"*: *Sporting News*, August 16, 1950.
219 *"The Brooks are playing"*: *New York Daily News*, August 13, 1950.
220 *"Jackie's not the only one"*: *Philadelphia Evening Bulletin*, August 16, 1950.
220 *"Right now, we are"*: *New York Journal-American*, August 16, 1950.
220 *"I'd get up at five"*: *New York Post*, August 6, 1951.
220 *onto the roof of a nearby laundry*: *New York Daily Mirror*, August 27, 1950.
220 *estimated by one observer*: *Baltimore Afro-American*, September 2, 1950.
221 *"against a screen"*: *New York Daily News*, August 27, 1950.
221 *"Love that boy"*: *New York Daily News*, September 13, 1951.
221 *"His total is somewhat amazing"*: *New York Journal-American*, August 28, 1950.
222 *"would appear to be a pretty difficult"*: *Los Angeles Times*, September 6, 1950.
222 *needing only 106 pitches*: *New York Post*, September 7, 1950.
222 *"a big, strong boy like Don"*: *New York Times*, October 1, 1949.
222 *"That's the only day"*: Unidentified clipping, July 22, 1956, Roy Campanella file, NBHOFL.
223 *"They wrote us off"*: *New York Post*, September 7, 1950.
223 *"as big as a delicatessen"*: *Brooklyn Eagle*, September 9, 1950.
223 *"They're shivering"*: *New York Post*, September 8, 1950.
223 *"Each day, now"*: *New York Daily News*, September 8, 1950.
223 *sat in the same row*: *New York Journal-American*, September 10, 1950.

224 *"It doesn't hurt too much"*: *New York Post*, September 18, 1950.
224 *"It was different"*: *New York Post*, September 20, 1950.
225 *for $1.025 million*: *New York Times*, October 26, 1950. Some sources list the sale at $1.05 million.
225 *turned over her voting rights*: Michael D'Antonio, *Forever Blue: The True Story of Walter O'Malley, Baseball's Most Controversial Owner, and the Dodgers of Brooklyn and Los Angeles* (New York: Riverhead, 2009), 123.
225 *teamed up with the Mulvey family*: Barber, *Rhubarb Patch*, 98.
226 *he later saw Rickey's signature*: *Sports Illustrated*, April 18, 1966.
226 *"should be a little"/"I'm losing"*: *New York Daily News*, September 25, 1950.
226 *"It seemed that Mr. Rickey was playing"*: Tygiel interview with Campanella, November 15, 1980.
226 *"They're through"*: *New York Post*, September 25, 1950.
227 *Showers were forecast*: *New York Journal-American*, September 29, 1950.
227 *"jumbo-sized"*: *New York Times*, September 26, 1950.
228 *"your six-year-old son"*: *New York Daily News*, September 30, 1950.
229 *"Hello, Mama"*: *Long Island Daily Press*, September 30, 1950.
229 *taunted the Ebbets fans*: *Philadelphia Daily News*, April 7, 1986.
229 *"If you snap me again"*: *New York Times*, September 30, 1950.
229 *"It's better that we win"*: *Philadelphia Inquirer*, September 30, 1950.
229 *"One defeat"*: *New York Times*, September 30, 1950.
229 *"I'll take the first"*: *New York Times*, October 1, 1950.
229 *"had more stuff"*: *New York Daily News*, July 26, 1950.
230 *"an old-fashioned Brooklyn"/"look mighty sick"*: *New York Journal-American*, October 1, 1950.
230 *"bobby-soxer"*: *New York Times*, October 1, 1950.
230 *On a 1-0 count*: *New York Post*, October 1, 1950.
231 *Fizz Kids*: *Brooklyn Eagle*, October 1, 1950.
231 *A boy who had caught*: *New York Times*, October 1, 1950.
231 *Campy had been given one*: *Lester J. Dworman . . . vs. A. Pompez.*
231 *blackboard in the clubhouse*: *New York Daily News*, October 1, 1950.
232 *another 10,000 were turned away*: *Sporting News*, October 11, 1950.
232 *"just a foot in front of"*: *Long Island Daily Press*, October 2, 1950.
232 *"looping slice"*: *Sporting News*, October 11, 1950.
232 *"risked life and limb"*: *New York Times*, October 2, 1950.
233 *"I've heard it said"*: *Philadelphia Daily News*, April 7, 1986.
233 *"would uncork"*: *New York Daily News*, October 2, 1950.
233 *bounced off his chest*: Peary, *We Played the Game*, 122.
234 *"fine"*: *Los Angeles Times*, October 2, 1950.
234 *"Only one girl ever"*: *New York Daily News*, October 15, 1950.
234 *"Keep the ball"*: Golenbock, *Bums*, 255.
234 *"Campy just stood there"*: *Philadelphia Daily News*, June 28, 1993.
234 *"The place was a deathly"*: *New York Daily News*, October 2, 1950.

234 *"That's a hell"*: *New York Post*, October 2, 1950.
235 *"I never saw a guy"*: *Brooklyn Eagle*, October 2, 1950.
235 *"halfheartedly waving me"*: *Baseball Digest*, September 1992, 74.
235 *his decision to hold Furillo*: *New York Post*, September 26, 1949.
235 *"The way Roberts was pitching"*: *New York Post*, October 2, 1950.
235 *"Whitey Ashburn just wasn't playing"*: *New York Journal-American*, October 2, 1950.
235 *"superb handling"*: *New York Daily News*, September 28, 1950.
236 *"It's a marvelous club"*: *New York Daily News*, October 2, 1950.

CHAPTER 13: A YEAR TO REMEMBER

237 *"The undersigned citizens"*: *Pittsburgh Courier*, November 25, 1950.
238 *"He [O'Malley] had a rule"*: E-mail from Buzzie Bavasi, November 15, 2007.
238 *"portly, jowly, florid"*: Frank Graham, Jr., *A Farewell to Heroes* (Carbondale/Edwardsville: Southern Illinois University Press, 2003), 234.
238 *"great man"*: *Pittsburgh Courier*, August 27, 1983.
238 *"Nobody who ever"*: Dick Young, "The Dodgers Are Due for a Collapse," *Sport*, July 1958, 87.
238 *slashed major league gates*: J. G. Taylor Spink, *Baseball Guide and Record Book—1951* (St. Louis: Sporting News Publishing Company, 1951), 111.
238 *"Dick Young was a guy"*: Rowan interview with Jackie and Rachel Robinson, 1957.
238 *"Fans like to see"*: *Sporting News*, March 7, 1951.
238 *"good, sound baseball"*: Rowan interview with Jackie and Rachel Robinson, 1957.
239 *"ear piercing whistle"*: *New York Times*, November 29, 1950.
239 *"no incubator baby could go nine"*: Golenbock, *Bums*, 305.
239 *"ate onion sandwiches"*: *Los Angeles Times*, August 11, 1966.
239 *"fancy stuff"*: *New York Times*, November 25, 1953.
239 *"egotism is more"*: *Sporting News*, October 28, 1953.
240 *"Dressen and Campanella"*: Robinson, "You Play Bolder in the Series," 64.
240 *"to see if I can't"*: *Pittsburgh Courier*, December 9, 1950.
240 *came home around*: *New York Times*, January 11, 1951.
240 *"I'm burned!"*: Young, *Roy Campanella*, 128.
241 *"I sure was lucky"*: *New York Daily News*, January 11, 1951.
241 *"I was scared"*: *Sporting News*, January 2, 1952.
241 *"I prayed to God again"*: *IGTBA*, 158.
241 *already been thinking*: *Baltimore Afro-American*, March 11, 1950.
241 *"I told Mr. Rickey"*: *Pittsburgh Press*, September 23, 1956.
242 *"my people drink"*: *IGTBA*, 13.
242 *"eight liquor stores"*: *New York World-Telegram and Sun*, June 29, 1955.
242 *up to 90 percent*: *Philadelphia Evening Bulletin*, June 29, 1955.
242 *"There were no payoffs"*: *New York Post*, June 29, 1955.

242 *Wilkins, had once operated*: *New York Amsterdam News*, July 13, 1940.
242 *"gleaming structure"*: Fitzgerald, "Roy Campanella—Mr. Catcher," 43.
242 *"The bronze trimming"/"So long as they"*: Connery, "Take Ten," June 24, 1955, *Time* dispatches.
243 *couldn't help but be impressed*: *Philadelphia Tribune*, November 14, 1972.
243 *"lucrative liquor business"*: *Sporting News*, January 23, 1957.
243 *"It just didn't work"*: Interview with Rachel Robinson, January 16, 2008.
243 *grossing close to $400,000*: *New York Journal-American*, June 30, 1955.
243 *"He got fat"*: *New York World-Telegram and Sun*, April 3, 1952.
244 *"I want you like"*: *Pittsburgh Courier*, March 3, 1951.
244 *"This is a game"/"I see why"*: *Baltimore Afro-American*, March 3, 1951.
244 *"Eight eggs a day"*: *Sporting News*, May 2, 1951.
244 *ran out and purchased*: *Sporting News*, April 25, 1951.
244 *appeared together*: *Chicago Defender*, June 30, 1951.
245 *"I just want to stay in"*: *Pittsburgh Courier*, April 14, 1951.
246 *"Are you wearing your wife's"*: *New York Post*, June 28, 1950.
246 *"stick it in his"*: Golenbock, *Bums*, 284.
246 *ready to square off*: *New York Daily News*, July 5, 1950.
246 *resented that Durocher*: *New York Daily Compass*, August 7, 1951.
247 *"I've been hit"*: *New York Post*, April 23, 1951.
247 *"Jockeying"*: *Sporting News*, May 9, 1951.
247 *publicly scorned his fastball*: *Long Island Daily Press*, March 11, 1955.
247 *"step in"*: *Washington Post*, May 3, 1951.
247 *"Then you're a bush league"*: *Baltimore Afro-American*, May 26, 1951.
248 *"shouldn't try to take"*: *Baltimore Afro-American*, May 12, 1951.
248 *"God complex"*: *New York Post*, May 4, 1951.
248 *"Stop, Look and Listen"*: *Sporting News*, May 2, 1951.
248 *"I'm not blind"*: *Baltimore Afro-American*, April 28, 1951.
248 *his first boos*: *New York Post*, May 1, 1951.
248 *"Jackie talks entirely"*: *Baltimore Afro-American*, May 12, 1951.
248 *"He'll snap out"*: *Pittsburgh Courier*, May 19, 1951.
249 *"That's the first one"*: *Pittsburgh Courier*, May 26, 1951.
249 *restraining Jackie*: *Brooklyn Eagle*, June 1, 1951.
249 *"nigger motherfucker"*: Golenbock, *Bums*, 340.
249 *"Anytime I want"*: *New York Times*, May 9, 1951.
250 *"It was the worst"*: *New York Post*, July 2, 1951.
250 *"the worst trade ever"*: *Sporting News*, June 27, 1951.
250 *often called by other general managers*: *Brooklyn Eagle*, May 28, 1952.
250 *"they won't draw"*: *Sporting News*, June 27, 1951.
250 *"without spending a cent"*: *Baseball Digest*, November 1951.
250 *"I've been on some good clubs"*: *Pittsburgh Courier*, June 23, 1951.
250 *"rumors that both Robinson"/"but some scout"*: *New York Times*, June 28, 1951.

250 *"the scout they sent down"*: Graham, Jr., "What Campy Means to All of Us," 84.
251 *Birmingham official, Eddie Glennon*: *New York Post*, July 31, 1951.
251 *"What do you say, Willie?"*: Irvin, *Nice Guys Finish First*, 148.
251 *"That's nothing"*: Young, *Roy Campanella*, 155.
251 *"I don't believe in that"*: *Saturday Evening Post*, May 26, 1956.
251 *"When I was his age"*: *Sporting News*, September 5, 1951.
252 *.287 average and 6 homers*: Retrosheet.org.
252 *"Oh, Donald!"*: *Baltimore Afro-American*, July 14, 1951.
252 *"The Dodgers will win"/"couldn't stay unquoted"*: *Baltimore Afro-American*, July 21, 1951.
252 *"You can order"*: *Chicago Defender*, July 21, 1951.
252 *"He's a better hitter"*: *New York Post*, August 8, 1951.
253 *"Maybe my methods are different"*: *New York Post*, July 27, 1951.
253 *"We took a shower"*: *Brooklyn Eagle*, July 21, 1951.
253 *"Ice up the beer"*: *Pittsburgh Courier*, August 4, 1951.
254 *"Eat your hearts out"*: *Brooklyn Eagle*, August 27, 1951.
254 *boasted of the brilliance*: *New York Post*, August 10, 1951.
254 *"the hardest I was ever hit"*: *New York Post*, January 8, 1952.
254 *"It was like taking a punch"*: *Brooklyn Eagle*, August 10, 1951.
254 *"now gets the biggest ovation"*: *Long Island Daily Press*, August 14, 1951.
254 *"Look at him"*: *New York Post*, August 13, 1951.
254 *felt secure enough*: *Sporting News*, January 23, 1957.
254 *"We've still got"*: *Long Island Daily Press*, August 20, 1951.
254 *"Sure we got a chance"*: *New York Daily Compass*, August 23, 1951.
255 *an elaborate sign-stealing scheme*: See Joshua Prager, *The Echoing Green: The Untold Story of Bobby Thomson, Ralph Branca and the Shot Heard Round the World* (New York: Pantheon, 2006).
255 *Milton Gross accurately alluded*: *New York Post*, May 7, 1952.
255 *Giants actually hit better on the road*: David W. Smith, "Play by Play Analysis of the 1951 National League Pennant Race," July 12, 2001, courtesy of Retrosheet.org.
255 *"Stealing signs is dangerous"*: Interview with Don Thompson, December 20, 2007.
255 *unable to bend his left elbow*: *Long Island Daily Press*, August 23, 1951.
255 *received an advance from Bavasi*: Prager, *Echoing Green*, 109.
256 *"I wish folks would stop"*: *New York Daily News*, August 31, 1951.
256 *"Every game we win"*: *New York Daily News*, August 29, 1951.
256 *the tape he often applied*: Prager, *Echoing Green*, 99.
256 *"anywhere from two to three"*: Joan F. Dreyspool, "Conversation Pieces: Yogi and Campy," *Sports Illustrated*, April 9, 1956.
256 *"Sometimes with a runner on"*: Roger Kahn interview with Pee Wee Reese, box 8, folder 6, Roger Kahn Papers, NBHOFL.

256 *lock up at inopportune moments*: *New York Daily News*, September 4, 1951.
256 *"joint mice"*: *New York Times*, September 4, 1951.
256 *"Superman Campanella"*: *New York Post*, September 4, 1951.
256 *"He seems indestructible"*: *New York World-Telegram and Sun*, September 5, 1951.
257 *amid cries of "choker"*: *New York Daily News*, September 3, 1951.
257 *"He's just a kid"*: *New York Daily Compass*, September 3, 1951.
257 *"They seemed to suspect a phone"*: *New York World-Telegram and Sun*, September 10, 1951.
257 *"feeling fine"*: *New York Daily News*, September 12, 1951.
257 *"We've got to make sure"*: *New York Daily News*, September 11, 1951.
257 *"Players who never before"*: *New York Daily News*, September 13, 1951.
257 *match Dressen move for move*: *New York Journal-American*, September 13, 1951.
258 *"the baddest man"*: *New York Journal-American*, September 9, 1952.
258 *two hits in thirty-two lifetime at bats*: Retrosheet.org.
258 *"You've got the pennant"*: *Long Island Daily Press*, September 16, 1951.
258 *"We deliver anywhere"*: *Sporting News*, September 26, 1951.
258 *"Clem's got a sinker"*: Connery, "Take Nine," June 24, 1955, *Time* dispatches.
259 *Sam Lacy wondered*: *Baltimore Afro-American*, September 29, 1951.
259 *"my first real fright"*: *Sporting News*, November 28, 1951.
259 *"I ate a big breakfast"*: *New York Daily News*, September 19, 1951.
259 *"His equilibrium suffers"*: *New York World-Telegram and Sun*, September 22, 1951.
260 *"I wanted him to throw"*: *Long Island Daily Press*, September 22, 1951.
260 *"It was so bad"*: *New York Journal-American*, September 24, 1951.
260 *"It's a funny game"*: *New York Post*, September 24, 1951.
261 *"the pressure is all on the Giants"*: *Los Angeles Times*, September 26, 1951.
261 *"It will be Roe"*: *Boston Globe*, September 27, 1951.
261 *Dressen would not use Roe*: *New York Journal-American*, September 24, 1951.
261 *"Campy spun him off"*: Interview with Carl Erskine, April 8, 2008.
261 *"off to the right"*: *Sports Illustrated*, April 13, 1959.
261 *"Campy jumped up and down"*: *Sporting News*, August 23, 1961.
261 *"cowboy actor"*: *Sporting News*, August 21, 1957.
262 *"feeble hopper"*: *Sporting News*, October 10, 1951.
262 *"Everybody was hollering"*: Rowan interview with Jackie and Rachel Robinson, 1957.
262 *"Gutless incompetent"*: *New York Daily Compass*, September 30, 1951.
262 *"TV umpire"*: *Sporting News*, March 21, 1956.
262 *"I thought I went underneath"*: Interview with Bob Addis, August 1, 2007.
262 *"It was close"*: *New York Daily News*, September 28, 1951.
262 *"I didn't cuss him"*: *New York Post*, September 28, 1951.

262 *"I never said anything"*: *New York Journal-American*, September 28, 1951.
262 *led the majors in ejections*: Retrosheet.org.
263 *"If I don't throw him out"*: *Boston Globe*, September 28, 1951.
263 *"for having been 'too hasty'"*: *New York Daily News*, September 29, 1951.
263 *"just like nothing happened"*: Martin Cohen, "Roy Campanella Today," *Sport*, June 1967, 93.
263 *his friend's ejection confirmed*: Thomas Kiernan, *The Miracle at Coogan's Bluff* (New York: Thomas Y. Crowell, 1975), 244.
263 *"The Dodgers now must win"*: *New York Daily News*, September 28, 1951.
263 *"The bravado they displayed"*: *Baltimore Afro-American*, October 6, 1951.
263 *"I just can't believe it"/"I'm a believer in prayer"*: *Long Island Daily Press*, September 30, 1951.
264 *"Hum that pea"*: *New York Daily News*, September 30, 1951.
264 *some fans went to their church*: *Brooklyn Eagle*, October 3, 1951.
264 *would later suggest he trapped*: *Sporting News*, April 3, 2000.
264 *dodged tin cans*: *Baltimore Afro-American*, October 6, 1951.
264 *Roy led the team*: Smith, "Play by Play Analysis of the 1951 National League Pennant Race."
265 *"greater seating capacity"*: *Washington Post*, February 26, 1955.
265 *"be able to walk"*: *New York Daily News*, October 2, 1951.
265 *"Any other runner"/"We've beaten them before"*: *Long Island Daily Press*, October 2, 1951.
265 *"Wotta year"*: *New York Daily News*, October 3, 1951.
266 *"Sink, you devil"*: Young, *Roy Campanella*, 143.
266 *"begged Charlie Dressen"*: *New York Times*, June 28, 1993.
266 *"in an atrocious moment"*: *New York Daily News*, October 4, 1951.
266 *prodded and scolded*: *Saturday Evening Post*, September 13, 1952; Kahn, *Era*, 274; Bobby Thomson with Lee Heiman and Bill Gutman, *"The Giants Win the Pennant! The Giants Win the Pennant!"* (New York: Citadel Press, 2001), 239–40.
267 *"might bring Roy Campanella in"*: *Pittsburgh Courier*, February 23, 1952.
267 *"I think if he envisioned a wild pitch"*: Interview with Carl Erskine, April 8, 2008.
267 *"If Roy Campanella is healthy"*: *Long Island Daily Press*, October 18, 1951.
267 *"Campy was the brains"*: Cohen, "Roy Campanella Today," 51.

CHAPTER 14: ACHES, PAINS, AND A COMEBACK

268 *"Lemme talk to"*: *Sporting News*, May 23, 1956.
268 *"It was the biggest disappointment"*: *Brooklyn Eagle*, October 4, 1951.
268 *believed Campy's late-season injuries*: *New York Post*, January 14, 1952.
268 *"I guess the good Lord"*: *Sports Illustrated*, March 31, 1958.
268 *"voluntarily fostering"*: *Baltimore Afro-American*, October 27, 1951.
269 *"He was practically yelling"*: *Baltimore Afro-American*, November 10, 1951.

269 *"deserves every honor"*: *Sporting News*, November 7, 1951.
269 *"had done a fantastic job"*: Draft, *I Never Had It Made*, box 11, folder 9, Jackie Robinson Papers.
269 *"If you ask any impartial"*: Rowan with Robinson, *Wait Till Next Year*, 242.
269 *"small-minded hypocrisy"/"I had made a vow"*: Draft, *I Never Had It Made*.
270 *"I remember once when"*: E-mail from Frank Graham, Jr., June 18, 2008.
270 *players called Fatso*: *Long Island Daily Press*, September 4, 1951.
270 *"grippy beeswax"*: Dreyspool, "Conversation Pieces: Yogi and Campy."
270 *"a kid in gang fights"*: *New York Post*, January 14, 1952.
270 *"I never saw a guy"*: Interview with Glenn Mickens, February 28, 2008.
270 *"He always scored from second"*: Fay Vincent, *We Would Have Played for Nothing: Baseball Stars of the 1950s and 1960s Talk about the Game They Loved* (New York: Simon & Schuster, 2008), 122.
271 *"firm glove"*: Dreyspool, "Conversation Pieces: Yogi and Campy."
271 *"He's the one and only guy"/"He did things"*: Interview with Dick Teed, February 26, 2008.
271 *"dusky, whiskerless Santa Claus"*: Graham, Jr., "What Campy Means to Us All," 83.
271 *"Why don't you catch"*: *Sporting News*, April 4, 1951.
271 *"I don't want to miss"*: *Saturday Evening Post*, June 5, 1954.
271 *"public enemy number one"*: *Anchorage Daily News*, August 25, 1987.
271 *"jelly leg"*: *Los Angeles Times*, July 6, 1971.
271 *"long left leg"*: *Sporting News*, July 31, 1957.
271 *"a baseball doesn't have any sense"*: *New York Times*, October 6, 1951.
271 *"You have to be a man"*: "Big Man from Nicetown," *Time*, August 8, 1955.
271 *"Hey, Campy"*: Graham, Jr., "What Campy Means to Us All," 83.
272 *"We just hooked him"*: *Baltimore Afro-American*, May 9, 1953.
272 *"As long as I live"*: *Sporting News*, February 10, 1960.
272 *"give you that extra moment"*: Interview with Lester Rodney, November 26, 2007.
272 *"consciously created a role"/"a lot of ham"*: Graham, Jr., "What Campy Means to Us All," 12.
273 *"Bible Belter"*: *New York Times*, June 14, 1953.
273 *"a true Christian"/"A man doesn't have"/"He just does what comes"*: Connery, "Take One," June 22, 1955, *Time* dispatches.
273 *"all-wise"*: Ed Linn, "The Last Days of Brooklyn's Old Gang," *Sport*, October 1956, 62.
273 *"is probably the least liked"*: Ibid., 61.
273 *"Roy Campanella was much more competitive"*: Peary, *We Played the Game*, 185.
273 *"though many think"*: *Sporting News*, August 29, 1951.
273 *"a terrific dresser"*: Interview with Tom Villante, June 24, 2008.
274 *"He'd talk baseball"*: *Los Angeles Times*, April 26, 1976.

274 *"Roy was pretty much a loner"*: E-mail from Buzzie Bavasi, January 16, 2007.
274 *"You want to be a ballplayer"*: *New York Journal-American*, January 31, 1958.
274 *"A kid on a big league"*: *New York Post*, June 29, 1955.
274 *"They really made my children"*: *New York World-Telegram and Sun*, February 15, 1957.
274 *"When I tell my kids"*: *Sporting News*, July 29, 1953.
274 *"He could work with concrete"*: *Roy Campanella—ESPN SportsCentury*, ESPN, 2001.
274 *"one of the most approachable"*: E-mail from Paul Reichler, February 4, 2008.
275 *"That was a tough break"*: *Pittsburgh Courier*, September 6, 1952.
275 *"Why have your arm cut"*: *New York Post*, January 8, 1952.
275 *"There's no sense"*: *New York Daily News*, January 8, 1952.
275 *"He had a month"*: *Baltimore Afro-American*, January 19, 1952.
275 *"It also was learned"*: *New York Herald Tribune*, January 13, 1952.
275 *"I don't see how in the world"*: *New York Post*, January 14, 1952.
275 *"I don't care how much money"*: *New York Daily News*, January 14, 1952.
276 *"If that mayor wants"*: Roger Kahn interview with Campanella, box 8, folder 6, Roger Kahn Papers.
276 *"the worst the tan Dodgers"/"red caps"/"flies"/"The salary"*: *Baltimore Afro-American*, April 19, 1952.
276 *"Hit him in the head"*: *Sporting News*, April 16, 1952.
276 *"Campy is all business"*: *Baltimore Afro-American*, April 19, 1952.
276 *"Hello, Charlie"*: *New York Times*, April 13, 1952.
276 *"I hear the Giants"*: *Washington Post*, March 31, 1952.
277 *"ten feet"*: *New York Herald Tribune*, May 4, 1952.
277 *"with a Bronko Nagurski charge"*: *Long Island Daily Press*, May 4, 1952.
277 *"so hard"*: *Sporting News*, May 28, 1952.
278 *"You'd be surprised"*: *Brooklyn Eagle*, May 24, 1952.
278 *"too darn polite"*: *Long Island Daily Press*, May 24, 1952.
278 *"Me polite?"*: *Sporting News*, June 18, 1952.
278 *"he didn't block the plate"*: Kahn interview with Reese.
278 *"He should step up"*: *New York World-Telegram and Sun*, October 1, 1955.
279 *"If Willie gets any better"*: *New York Post*, May 15, 1952.
279 *"I knew I was doing the wrong"*: *New York Post*, July 17, 1952.
279 *"in tears"*: *New York Herald Tribune*, July 15, 1952.
279 *"A lot of people"*: *Saturday Evening Post*, September 13, 1952.
280 *"Like to see one of you"*: Kahn, *Boys of Summer*, 358.
280 *"I can't clap"*: Golenbock, *Bums*, 336.
280 *"You shouldn't rile"*: Kahn, *Boys of Summer*, 143.
280 *"tore off his glove"*: *New York Times*, July 2, 1952.
280 *"happiest man in baseball"*: Connery, "Take One," June 22, 1955, *Time* dispatches.

280 *Prager has suggested*: Prager, *Echoing Green*, 277.
280 *"something funny went on"*: *Sporting News*, October 15, 1952.
280 *"If they lose the pennant"*: *New York Post*, September 9, 1952.
281 *"I know one thing"*: *Sporting News*, September 10, 1952.
281 *"the most incompetent man"*: Rowan interview with Jackie and Rachel Robinson, 1957.
281 *"He told me to shut up"*: *New York Post*, September 5, 1952.
281 *"not a great club"/"As I told my players"*: *New York Journal-American*, September 29, 1952.
281 *"We are ready for them"*: *New York Journal-American*, September 30, 1952.
281 *THIS IS NEXT YEAR*: *Sporting News*, October 15, 1952.
281 *"neglected hangnail"*: *New York Herald Tribune*, September 17, 1952.
282 *"The hand is bad"/"I want to play"*: *New York Herald Tribune*, October 2, 1952.
282 *"Campy's smart"*: *Baltimore Afro-American*, September 20, 1952.
282 *"I told him, relax"*: *New York Post*, October 2, 1952.
282 *"I killed them both"*: *New York Herald Tribune*, October 2, 1952.
282 *"I was kidding Larry Doby"*: *Baltimore Afro-American*, October 11, 1952.
283 *"I'll cheer all"*: *New York Times*, October 6, 1952.
283 *"I didn't want to see"*: *New York Journal-American*, October 6, 1952.
283 *publicly predicted that the Yankees*: *New York Post*, October 7, 1952.
283 *"I wish I was making two hundred dollars"*: *New York Post*, March 3, 1954.
283 *"Billy may not be a genius"*: *New York Post*, September 17, 1954.
283 *"the sun blinded me"*: *New York Journal-American*, October 6, 1952.
283 *"Whatever possessed you"*: *New York Times*, October 7, 1952.
284 *"that fresh kid"*: *New York Times*, October 9, 1952.
284 *"Why do the Dodgers"*: *New York Post*, October 8, 1952.
284 *"They'll come through"*: *New York Journal-American*, October 12, 1952.
285 *"the fans are no longer"*: *New York World-Telegram and Sun*, May 1, 1953.
285 *"I want him to set an example"*: *New York Times*, October 11, 1952.
285 *"didn't improve his rest"*: *Chicago Defender*, February 21, 1953.
285 *"Mr. O'Malley has offered me"*: *Philadelphia Evening Bulletin*, October 10, 1952.
285 *"When I played with the trains"*: *New York Herald Tribune*, February 22, 1953.
286 *"I was crazy about Campy"/"I got to work"/"If anything happened"*: Interview with Bobby Mitchell, November 13, 2007.
286 *not quite slim enough to win*: *Sporting News*, February 25, 1953.
286 *served as batboy*: *Long Beach Press-Telegram*, April 17, 1959.
286 *for $10,000*: *Sporting News*, April 8, 1953.
287 *heaved his duffel bag*: *Los Angeles Times*, July 27, 1972.
287 *"Some of the white players"*: *Baltimore Afro-American*, January 29, 1955.
287 *"taking over"/"Pretty soon now"*: *Sporting News*, April 1, 1953.

287 *"We have never had any dissension"*: *New York Post*, March 22, 1953.
287 *"Negro baiting remarks were made"*: *New York Post*, March 23, 1953.
287 *"Unlike what was often reported"*: Peary, *We Played the Game*, 90.
287 *"If Buzzie saw something coming"*: *New York Daily News*, January 2, 1958.
287 *"He and Jackie got along fine"*: Irvin, *Nice Guys Finish First*, 172.
288 *"Brooklyn will never"*: *New York Times*, February 27, 1953.
288 *"that boy"/"I'm just praying"*: *Sporting News*, April 29, 1953.
288 *"My hands"*: *New York Post*, May 11, 1953.
288 *"They don't pitch me"*: *New York World-Telegram and Sun*, May 11, 1953.
289 *"I'm just trying to meet"*: *New York Post*, May 11, 1953.
289 *"And that's exactly what Hearn"/"Didn't I"*: Golenbock, *Bums*, 305.
289 *"They shot pictures of me"*: *Pittsburgh Courier*, June 13, 1953.
289 *"You sound so rugged"*: *What's My Line*, September 6, 1953, episode.
289 *recorded a song*: *Pittsburgh Courier*, August 1, 1953.
289 *"guys with the greatest personal"*: *Sporting News*, July 1, 1953.
290 *"I see no reason"*: *New York Post*, January 29, 1952.
290 *impressed by a young minor*: *Philadelphia Independent*, March 6, 1954.
290 *"Cobb once told me"*: *Chicago Defender*, January 29, 1962.
290 *"impressed him the most?"/"That fella's"*: *Pittsburgh Courier*, August 8, 1953.
291 *exchanged harsh words with Johnny Antonelli*: *Sporting News*, August 5, 1953.
291 *"black bastard"*: *Pittsburgh Courier*, August 15, 1953.
291 *"adolescent sense of humor"*: Michael Shapiro, *The Last Good Season: Brooklyn, the Dodgers, and Their Final Pennant Race Together* (New York: Doubleday, 2003), 205.
291 *revenge with brushbacks*: *Sport*, April 1954, 66.
291 *worked the count to 2-2*: *New York World-Telegram and Sun*, August 4, 1953.
291 *"Black nigger bastard"*: *New York Post*, August 4, 1953; *Pittsburgh Courier*, August 15, 1953.
292 *tossed aside by the mighty*: *Baltimore Afro-American*, August 15, 1953.
292 *"Why did you call him that"*: *Milwaukee Sentinel*, August 4, 1953.
292 *"near riot"*: *Milwaukee Sentinel*, August 6, 1953.
292 *"I never said a word to the man"/"No, I wouldn't"*: *New York World-Telegram and Sun*, August 4, 1953.
292 *"My head ain't"*: *Pittsburgh Courier*, August 15, 1953.
292 *"would like to have killed me"*: *New York Journal-American*, August 4, 1953.
292 *hurling cushions and eggs*: *Baltimore Afro-American*, August 15, 1953.
292 *"It seems funny"*: *Milwaukee Journal*, August 7, 1953.
292 *his "smile" following the strikeout*: Peary, *We Played the Game*, 390.
293 *"the term Giants refers"*: *Sporting News*, September 2, 1953.
293 *"We'll worry about that"*: *New York Post*, August 21, 1953.
294 *"I'd pay a thousand dollars"*: *Sporting News*, September 16, 1953.

294 *"I shoulda had that order"*: *Baltimore Afro-American*, September 19, 1953.
294 *scoffed at the televised Brooklyn celebration*: *New York Times*, September 14, 1953.
294 *"If those Dodgers couldn't beat us"*: *Sporting News*, September 30, 1953.
294 *"This is the Dodgers' best club"*: *Sporting News*, September 9, 1953.
294 *"If we don't win it"*: *Pittsburgh Courier*, September 26, 1953.
294 *"they can be beaten"*: *Pittsburgh Courier*, October 10, 1953.
294 *"I think the members"*: *New York Times*, December 1, 1952.
295 *"Robinson Should Be Player"*: *Sporting News*, December 10, 1952.
295 *"just trying to give an honest opinion"*: Draft, *Wait Till Next Year*, box 14, folder 4, Jackie Robinson Papers.
295 *"The pain was almost unbearable"*: *Pittsburgh Courier*, October 10, 1953.
295 *Kahn says Reynolds always believed*: Interview with Roger Kahn, June 1, 2009.
295 *"If it's broken"*: *Baltimore Afro-American*, October 10, 1953.
295 *"You scuffle all year"*: *New York Post*, October 2, 1953.
296 *"indistinguishable"*: *New York World-Telegram and Sun*, October 2, 1953.
296 *"Thank you, Mr. Reynolds"*: *New York Post*, October 2, 1953.
296 *"Don't tell the sportswriters"*: *Sporting News*, October 14, 1953.
296 *"pleasing personality"*: *Baltimore Afro-American*, October 8, 1955.
296 *"Bury it, Carl"*: Interview with Carl Erskine, April 8, 2008.
296 *"Stick one in that nigger's ear"*: Banker, *Black Diamonds*.
297 *"Now this is really an ordinary studio"*: Transcript, *Person to Person*, October 2, 1953.
297 *"Imagine them crying"*: *New York Herald Tribune*, October 4, 1953.
297 *"He threw him"*: Interview with Don Thompson, December 20, 2007.
297 *"What the hell was he thinking"*: *New York Herald Tribune*, October 4, 1953.
298 *"close in"*: *Sporting News*, February 10, 1954.
298 *"It is almost incredible"*: *Sporting News*, October 14, 1953.
298 *"The Dodgers are the Dodgers"*: *Sporting News*, October 21, 1953.
298 *"It was a wonderful season"*: *New York Post*, October 6, 1953.

CHAPTER 15: IT HURTS UP HERE

299 *"His going to the major"*: Holway, *Voices*, 350.
299 *"That's why some of us turned"*: *Sporting News*, November 25, 1953.
300 *"beat my brains out"*: *Baltimore Afro-American*, December 5, 1953.
300 *"Some claim Robinson"/"willing [but] not happy"*: *Baltimore Afro-American*, November 28, 1953.
300 *"What more can a man ask?"*: *New York Times*, November 20, 1953.
300 *"Just couldn't say 'Yankee'"*: *Chicago Defender*, December 26, 1953.
300 *considering a biopic*: *Sporting News*, March 10, 1954.
301 *"Holy jumping jeepers"*: *Roogie's Bump*, directed by Harold Young, Republic Pictures, 1954.

301 *"I don't know why I can't go on"*: *New York Journal-American*, September 22, 1953.
301 *"It was nerve-racking"*: *Sporting News*, November 4, 1953.
301 *"All I can say is that it was a pip"*: *New York World-Telegram and Sun*, October 16, 1953.
301 *"didn't realize that Walter"*: E-mail from Buzzie Bavasi, November 15, 2007.
302 *"I feel a good manager"*: *New York Post*, October 15, 1953.
302 *"He didn't hesitate to tell"*: *Los Angeles Times*, August 11, 1966.
302 *"If the team was going badly"*: E-mail from Roger Kahn, August 11, 2009.
302 *"What are you doing"/"What has Cholly"*: *Sporting News*, December 9, 1953.
302 *"recently guided a neighborhood team"*: *Sporting News*, October 28, 1953.
302 *"get tough with his friends"*: *Sporting News*, November 4, 1953.
302 *"crazy not to take it"*: *Sport*, June 1957, 62.
303 *been to Ebbets Field exactly twice*: *Sporting News*, December 9, 1953.
303 *"Dis guy is gonna"*: *New York World-Telegram and Sun*, November 24, 1953.
303 *"antithesis"*: *New York Post*, May 27, 1954.
303 *"trade ten feet"*: *Sporting News*, January 25, 1956.
303 *"Real square"*: *Sporting News*, March 10, 1954.
303 *"He's a great guy"*: *New York World-Telegram and Sun*, November 24, 1953.
303 *dip into the diet pills*: *Baltimore Afro-American*, January 23, 1954.
303 *"I'm going to beat out some"*: *New York Post*, February 24, 1954.
303 *"Skip, don't worry"*: Golenbock, *Bums*, 372.
303 *"When I get started talking"*: *Chicago Defender*, March 27, 1954.
303 *"tall, taciturn"/"He seems to be suffering"*: *New York Daily Mirror*, March 20, 1954.
304 *"He wanted to play"*: *Long Island Daily Press*, April 27, 1954.
304 *"I never heard such filth"*: Robinson with Dexter, *Baseball Has Done It*, 132.
304 *"Russ leaped out"*: *Baltimore Afro-American*, July 17, 1954.
305 *"Look out, Babe Ruth"*: *Philadelphia Daily News*, April 18, 1990.
305 *"getting him angry"*: *Sporting News*, April 21, 1954.
305 *a stint at Harlem Hospital*: Interview with Lyndon Hill, December 26, 2007.
305 *"It was the first time"*: *New York Post*, May 5, 1954.
306 *"I don't care"*: *Long Island Daily Press*, April 28, 1954.
306 *"juggled the ball"*: *New York Herald Tribune*, April 29, 1954.
306 *"You can't minimize"*: *New York Daily News*, April 29, 1954.
306 *"It's my own fault"*: *New York Daily News*, May 4, 1954.
306 *"I couldn't 'break my wrist' "*: *New York Herald Tribune*, May 4, 1954.
306 *"had become so entangled"*: *New York Times*, May 13, 1954.
306 *"The doctors can cut"*: *Daily Worker*, May 13, 1954.
307 *alluded to a near fistfight*: *Toledo Blade*, December 25, 1982.
307 *"I guess I'm now qualified"*: *New York Times*, March 19, 1954.
307 *"a certain Negro star"*: *Pittsburgh Courier*, January 23, 1954.

307 *"The antis still hate"*: *New York Amsterdam News*, September 11, 1954.

307 *several major league hotels*: *Baltimore Afro-American*, May 29, 1954; *Sporting News*, May 5, 1954.

308 *a slew of conditions*: Monte Irvin as told to Ed Linn, "This Is Where the Negro Ballplayer Stands Today," *Sport*, April 1957, 65.

308 *Sam Lacy announced*: *Baltimore Afro-American*, March 27, 1954.

308 *supposedly discouraged the Giants*: *St. Louis American*, May 6, 1954.

308 *"A lively argument"*: *Sporting News*, January 23, 1957.

308 *"He checked in"*: Interview with Don Thompson, December 20, 2007.

308 *Curtis Roberts made the mistake*: *Pittsburgh Courier*, May 8, 1954.

308 *"They didn't want us"*: *Baltimore Afro-American*, May 8, 1954.

309 *Robinson had employed similar reasoning*: *Chicago Defender*, April 30, 1949.

309 *"We felt that if we were to be Jim Crowed"*: *Baltimore Afro-American*, May 29, 1954.

309 *"Everybody knows that Campy is right"/"in his strange role"/"It's so clear"*: *Baltimore Afro-American*, May 22, 1954.

309 *"If no colored players"*: *Baltimore Afro-American*, May 15, 1954.

309 *the Shoreham insisted*: *Baltimore Afro-American*, April 18, 1953.

309 *"On our arrival"*: E-mail from Buzzie Bavasi, January 6, 2007.

309 *fat, juicy steaks to enjoy*: *Chicago Defender*, August 28, 1954.

309 *"Everybody on the avenue"*: *St. Louis Argus*, May 14, 1954.

310 *"to beat the curfew"*: *Sporting News*, January 23, 1957.

310 *"The things they've written"*: *Baltimore Afro-American*, May 29, 1954.

310 *the bar and the pool remained off-limits*: Irvin as told to Linn, "This Is Where the Negro Ballplayer Stands Today," 65.

310 *"Baseball was the main thing"*: Interview with Lester Rodney, November 26, 2007.

310 *"Supreme Court made the right decision"*: *Mike Wallace Interviews*, December 11, 1959, audio courtesy of Mike Wallace Papers, Syracuse University Library.

310 *member of the executive board*: *New York Amsterdam News*, December 26, 1953; *Baltimore Afro-American*, August 11, 1951.

310 *"Where else could I have gotten"*: *Sporting News*, November 21, 1956.

310 *"At times I have felt"*: Rowan with Robinson, *Wait Till Next Year*, 331.

311 *"Through the early and middle fifties"*: *Baltimore Afro-American*, July 29, 1969.

311 *"We weren't concerned"*: Robinson with Dexter, *Baseball Has Done It*, 91.

311 *"I don't believe in going"*: Connery, "Take Six," June 23, 1955, *Time* dispatches.

311 *"When I play Campy"*: *Long Island Daily Press*, May 29, 1954.

312 *"He was in the way"*: Connery, "Take Nine," June 24, 1955, *Time* dispatches.

312 *one pitch after the Cardinals' lefty*: *Sporting News*, July 7, 1954.

312 *belief that a well-placed brushback*: *Sporting News*, April 28, 1954.

312 *a letter to O'Malley on July 8*: www.walteromalley.com.
312 *"Why doesn't he learn"*: *New York Post*, July 2, 1954.
312 *"It is obvious"*: *New York Post*, July 9, 1954.
312 *"the worst play"*: *New York Daily News*, July 2, 1954.
313 *"It is much worse"*: *Long Island Daily Press*, July 10, 1954.
313 *"worried, almost terrorized expression"*: *New York Daily News*, July 10, 1954.
313 *"That was a helluva"*: *Chicago Defender*, July 17, 1954.
313 *"I just want to find out"*: *Long Island Daily Press*, July 12, 1954.
313 *"It's time"/"I feel so great"*: *New York Daily News*, July 13, 1954.
313 *"sad-looking single"*: *New York Daily News*, July 18, 1954.
313 *"It doesn't appear to be as numb"*: *New York Post*, July 20, 1954.
313 *"prayers, good luck charms"*: *Long Island Daily Press*, July 28, 1954.
314 *criticized the front office for waiting*: *New York Daily News*, July 26, 1954.
314 *"You've got to admire him"*: *Long Island Daily Press*, July 28, 1954.
314 *"that's over a half a year!"*: *New York Post*, July 29, 1954.
314 *"was barely able to abduct"*: *Samuel Shenkman v. Roy Campanella*, Supreme Court, State of New York, County of New York, 1955 (6925).
314 *"to prevent any further atrophying"*: *Samuel Shenkman v. Walter O'Malley*, Supreme Court, State of New York, County of New York, 1955 (8686).
314 *"looked worse today"*: *Long Island Daily Press*, August 3, 1954.
314 *"has not only prevented recovery"*: *Shenkman v. O'Malley*.
315 *"like a toothache"/"I read where"*: *New York Post*, August 4, 1954.
315 *"If you used statistics"*: *Pittsburgh Courier*, August 25, 1956.
315 *"He could make me think"*: Interview with Clyde King, September 27, 2007.
315 *"Nobody doubts your pain"*: *New York Post*, August 6, 1954.
315 *"electro-impulse treatments"*: *New York Daily News*, July 30, 1954.
316 *"Both the Giants and Braves"*: *New York Post*, August 16, 1954.
316 *"All of a sudden he would see"/convinced that Alston was threatened*: Rowan interview with Jackie and Rachel Robinson, 1957.
316 *"The first year Jackie"*: *Saturday Evening Post*, August 17, 1957.
316 *"If that son of a bitch"*: Rowan interview with Jackie and Rachel Robinson, 1957.
317 *"publicity seeker"*: *Washington Post*, September 6, 1954.
317 *waiter overheard five Dodgers*: *Sporting News*, September 22, 1954.
317 *Alston apologized to Jackie/"This is a business"*: *Baltimore Afro-American*, September 25, 1954.
317 *"Robby, even if he can't"*: *Sporting News*, October 6, 1954.
317 *"In four months"*: *Sporting News*, September 15, 1954.
317 *"I might fool"*: *Long Island Daily Press*, September 14, 1954.
317 *September 20 at 10:40 p.m.*: *Sporting News*, September 29, 1954.
317 *"It hurts up here"*: *Long Island Daily Press*, September 21, 1954.
318 *"This was more than"*: *New York Post*, September 21, 1954.

318 *"It is an entirely different"*: *New York Daily News*, September 18, 1954.
318 *"Hey, Chuck, give us"/"We win 110"*: *Long Island Daily Press*, September 25, 1954.
318 *"No one can be certain"*: *Sporting News*, September 29, 1954.
318 *"How can a grown man"*: Connery, "Take Eight," June 24, 1955, *Time* dispatches.
318 *"They're not going to pay"*: *New York Daily News*, September 5, 1954.
319 *some sensation in his pinkie*: *New York Times*, October 16, 1954.
319 *"They cannot guarantee me"*: *New York Journal-American*, October 9, 1954.
319 *"I have made up my mind"*: *Washington Post*, October 13, 1954.
319 *"unless something could"/"He became a little indignant"/"cut across, badly contused"*: *Shenkman v. Campanella.*
319 *"I've been trying it"*: *Philadelphia Tribune*, November 2, 1954.
319 *"This . . . is the Most Valuable Player"*: *New York Times*, November 2, 1954.

CHAPTER 16: REDEMPTION

320 *"It feels* good*"*: *Sporting News*, March 2, 1955.
320 *in a letter to his sister*: *New York World-Telegram and Sun*, January 25, 1956.
320 *dangled catchers Ed Bailey*: *Long Island Daily Press*, April 26, September 17, 1955.
320 *"They ain't gonna need"*: *Sporting News*, January 26, 1955.
321 *"I honestly don't believe"*: *Sporting News*, February 23, 1955.
321 *"You're just sore"*: Dick Young, "The Burden of Proof Is on Alston," *Sport*, May 1955, 93.
321 *informed reporters*: *Long Island Daily Press*, March 23, April 16, 1955.
321 *"Roy's the best catcher"*: *New York Post*, March 1, 1955.
321 *"There's no pain"*: *New York Post*, March 2, 1955.
322 *"happiest guy in camp"*: *Long Island Daily Press*, March 5, 1955.
322 *"Everything I saw at Vero"*: *Long Island Daily Press*, March 10, 1955.
322 *"the greatest young prospect"*: *Long Island Daily Press*, September 23, 1954.
322 *"Camp, what do I have to do"*: *Philadelphia Inquirer*, June 28, 1993.
322 *"has more natural speed"*: *New York Journal-American*, September 1, 1959.
322 *refused to face him*: *Long Island Daily Press*, June 17, 1955.
322 *"I want you to know"/"Go ahead and make it"*: *Sporting News*, August 24, 1955.
323 *"if he'll take off fifteen pounds"*: *Sporting News*, October 27, 1954.
323 *"get back in the good graces"*: *Sporting News*, December 1, 1954.
323 *"He's been working hard"*: *Pittsburgh Courier*, March 19, 1955.
323 *"I can't sit around"*: *Long Island Daily Press*, March 18, 1955.
323 *spread the controversy*: *New York Daily News*, April 4, 1955.
323 *"I'm sure if I had said"/"I think Campanella too"*: Rowan interview with Jackie and Rachel Robinson, 1957.
323 *"The guy who stepped in"*: Golenbock, *Bums*, 387.

324 *"cleared a lot of air"*: *Sporting News*, January 23, 1957.
324 *"bush league"*: *Baltimore Afro-American*, April 16, 1955.
324 *"He could be the strongest"*: *Sporting News*, August 31, 1955.
324 *hit only .235*: *New York Times*, April 8, 1955.
324 *"I'm just waiting to hit"*: *Jet*, April 21, 1955.
324 *"I don't care what I hit"*: *New York Post*, April 14, 1955.
324 *"I ain't no fucking"*: Interview with Roger Kahn, June 1, 2009.
324 *"I got no right hitting"/"The only thing worse"*: *New York Post*, April 14, 1955.
324 *"Let him show me"*: *New York Journal-American*, April 14, 1955.
325 *"I've been playing"*: *New York Post*, April 21, 1955.
325 *"If they can't draw them now"*: *Long Island Daily Press*, April 20, 1955.
325 *"I can't understand this town"*: *New York Post*, April 22, 1955.
325 *"They can hardly avoid"*: *Sporting News*, May 4, 1955.
325 *"You know what the announcement"*: *New York Post*, April 22, 1955.
325 *"low-bridged"*: *Long Island Daily Press*, April 24, 1955.
325 *"let someone else do it"*: *Sporting News*, February 1, 1956.
326 *"his own version of a football block"*: *New York Times*, April 24, 1955.
326 *"Damn, Jackie"*: *Long Island Daily Press*, April 24, 1955.
326 *"You've got to be serious"*: *Long Island Daily Press*, March 2, 1955.
326 *"I won't argue"*: *Long Island Daily Press*, May 6, 1955.
326 *"I was under the impression"*: *Sport*, July 1959, 64.
326 *"I don't know what your problems are"*: *Long Island Daily Press*, May 6, 1955.
327 *"That's your bread"*: *Pittsburgh Courier*, May 21, 1955.
327 *he apologized to Alston*: *Baltimore Afro-American*, May 14, 1955.
327 *"mostly by his roomie"*: *Long Island Daily Press*, May 7, 1955.
327 *"We were all a bit shocked"*: *Baseball Digest*, June 2005, 66.
327 *"will be glad"*: *New York Daily News*, September 2, 1954.
327 *"That man must be out"*: *Baltimore Afro-American*, June 11, 1955.
327 *contradicted by his own doctor*: *Washington Post*, February 16, 1956.
328 *had to pay that bill*: *Shenkman v. O'Malley*.
328 *"thought he was operating"*: *Time*, June 6, 1955.
328 *"How's your $9,500 hand?"*: *New York Times*, May 30, 1955.
328 *161 to 117*: *Sporting News*, June 29, 1955.
328 *"What difference does it make?"*: *Sporting News*, October 4, 1993.
328 *"Campy became extremely upset"*: Connery, "Take Ten," June 24, 1955, *Time* dispatches.
329 *"Tell me one thing"*: *Sporting News*, October 26, 1955.
329 *"Don't confuse this"*: *New York Journal-American*, June 30, 1955.
329 *"I just can't take"*: *New York Times*, July 10, 1955.
329 *"showing no desire"*: *Sporting News*, July 6, 1955.
329 *"My players and I appreciate"*: *Long Island Daily Press*, June 30, 1955.

329 *"They want to nail"*: Connery, "Take Eight," June 24, 1955, *Time* dispatches.

329 *"special foam rubber insert"*: *New York Post*, July 13, 1955.

329 *"The knee doesn't hurt"/"I doubt if that knee"*: *New York Daily News*, July 14, 1955.

330 *still unable to move*: Connery, "Take Eight," June 24, 1955, *Time* dispatches.

330 *boos had grown increasingly persistent*: *Long Island Daily Press*, June 7, 1955; Connery, "Take Six," June 23, 1955, *Time* dispatches.

330 *"The phone's always ringing"*: *Sporting News*, August 10, 1955.

330 *"Campy would answer the phone"*: *Sports Illustrated*, March 31, 1958.

331 *"You all know what happened"*: *Sporting News*, September 7, 1955.

331 *"The Dodgers will finally"*: *New York Post*, July 25, 1955.

331 *a day after O'Malley was again rebuffed*: Shapiro, *Last Good Season*, 71.

331 *"It is only a matter of time"/"If you expect"*: *New York Post*, August 17, 1955.

331 *"I wish to hell"/"They're the worst fans"*: *Long Island Daily Press*, August 26, 1955.

332 *"Time and again"*: *Long Island Daily Press*, August 27, 1955.

332 *"Finally, he asked me"*: *Sporting News*, April 9, 1966.

332 *"I don't figure"*: *New York Post*, August 31, 1955.

333 *"He hits you"*: *New York Post*, April 5, 1956.

333 *"But, man, I sure"*: *New York Post*, September 9, 1955.

333 *later gave him a year's supply*: *Pittsburgh Courier*, October 15, 1955.

333 *"It was about the only thrill"*: *IGTBA*, 190.

334 *"always take care"*: *Long Island Daily Press*, September 27, 1955.

334 *"There is no getting around"*: *Pittsburgh Courier*, July 17, 1954.

334 *"They used to murder us"*: *Baltimore Afro-American*, October 1, 1955.

334 *he told Ruthe they would buy*: *Pittsburgh Courier*, October 8, 1955.

334 *"How can I get ready"*: *Long Island Daily Press*, September 16, 1955.

334 *discreetly placed him on waivers*: *Sporting News*, January 23, 1957.

334 *"very favorable"*: *New York Post*, September 26, 1955.

335 *"Why, in St. Louis"/"stock of salami"*: *New York Post*, September 27, 1955.

335 *"Watch that boy"*: *New York Post*, October 3, 1956.

335 *"spike shy"*: *Philadelphia Evening Bulletin*, September 29, 1955.

335 *Reese himself thought*: Kahn interview with Reese.

335 *"I was worried"*: Robinson, "You Play Bolder in the Series," 14.

336 *"Watching the opener"*: *New York Post*, September 29, 1955.

336 *"Anytime that"*: *Washington Post*, September 29, 1955.

336 *"might have punched"*: *Philadelphia Evening Bulletin*, September 29, 1955.

336 *"The goat's horns"/"I think some guys"*: *Long Island Daily Press*, September 30, 1955.

337 *"sponsor's sombrero"/"Why aren't you hitting"*: *New York Times*, October 1, 1955.

337 *"He threw a changeup"*: *Long Island Daily Press*, October 1, 1955.

337 *"slow stuff"*: *Baltimore Afro-American*, October 8, 1955.
337 *"I had to break out"*: *Long Island Daily Press*, October 1, 1955.
338 *"The Yankees now have"*: *Sporting News*, October 12, 1955.
338 *"He talked about the Yankee"*: *Pittsburgh Courier*, February 25, 1956.
338 *"really had the Yankees"*: Maury Allen, *Brooklyn Remembered: The 1955 Days of the Dodgers* (Champaign, IL: Sports Publishing, LLC, 2005), 186.
338 *"deserve a world championship"*: *Sporting News*, October 12, 1955.
338 *"rat trap"*: *New York Times*, October 3, 1955.
338 *Dressen now providing Stengel*: *Sporting News*, October 12, 1955.
338 *"They don't swing"*: *Long Island Daily Press*, October 4, 1955.
339 *"On a bright afternoon"*: *Sporting News*, October 12, 1955.
339 *"Just get that changeup"/"I'll get it"*: *New York Post*, October 5, 1955.
339 *"the biggest base hit"*: *Washington Post*, July 18, 1982.
339 *"Throw hard now"/"Shake me off"*: *New York Post*, October 5, 1955.
339 *"He's got good stuff"*: *Saturday Evening Post*, January 21, 1956.
339 *"He'll be all right"*: *New York Post*, October 5, 1955.
340 *"because it was high enough"*: Roberts interview with Campanella.
340 *"Campanella was calling"*: *Brooklyn Dodgers: The Ghosts of Flatbush*, HBO, 2007.
340 *"Those Podres games"*: *Sporting News*, February 8, 1956.
340 *"Dammit, let him"*: *Saturday Evening Post*, May 26, 1956.
340 *"He was trying to throw"*: *New York Post*, October 5, 1955.
341 *"I wasn't the only Dodger"/"I pray"*: *Long Island Daily Press*, October 5, 1955.
341 *passing out bottles*: *Chicago Defender*, October 15, 1955.
341 *"What do I care?"*: *Newsday*, October 30, 1997.
341 YANKEE FANS, GET OUT: *Long Island Daily Press*, October 5, 1955.
341 *"We're giving out"*: *Sporting News*, October 19, 1955.
341 *"The Dodgers won the title"*: *Sporting News*, October 12, 1955.
341 *"I sure hope"*: *Long Island Daily Press*, October 5, 1955.

CHAPTER 17: THE LUCKIEST MAN IN THE WORLD

342 *"So many great things"*: *Baltimore Afro-American*, December 17, 1955.
343 *purchase the entire building*: *Sporting News*, October 19, 1955.
343 *"buxom damsel"*: *Sporting News*, January 18, 1956.
343 *closer to $50,000*: *IGTBA*, 192; *Los Angeles Times*, January 31, 1963.
343 *pulling in $60,000 to $70,000 annually*: *Shenkman v. Campanella.*
343 *"Next year I hope"*: *Sporting News*, February 1, 1956.
343 *did not sit well*: Interview with Eric Hayden, January 7, 2008.
343 *"I can see there"*: Cohen, "Roy Campanella Today," 94.
343 *$58,000 offer*: Property card, 1 Eastland Drive, Nassau County Department of Assessment.
344 *"I play harder"*: Dreyspool, "Conversation Pieces: Yogi and Campy."

344 *"To me"*: *New York Amsterdam News*, June 2, 1956.
344 *"I'm the luckiest man"*: *New York Post*, February 6, 1956.
344 *"He's the most important thing"*: *Philadelphia Tribune*, September 29, 1956.
344 *"He was like a god"*: Interview with Wilson Pettus, Jr., March 6, 2007.
344 *"Ruthe was a fine young lady"*: E-mail from Buzzie Bavasi, January 16, 2007.
345 *"We called the girls"*: Peary, *We Played the Game*, 94.
345 *known as the Varsity*: *New York Times*, September 27, 1974.
345 *began to pursue Joe Black*: Graham, Jr., *Farewell to Heroes*, 254; e-mail from Frank Graham, Jr., June 18, 2008.
345 *"I just want to be"*: Interview with Vincent T. Dacquino, August 19, 2008.
345 *"not a very good idea"*: Cohen, "Roy Campanella Today," 94.
345 *"Jolly and juvenile"*: *Pittsburgh Courier*, November 10, 1956.
345 *"It seems Campy has a girl"/"The more you see"*: Rampersad, *Jackie Robinson*, 292.
346 *"Robinson would be the first son of a bitch"/"if this thing"/"forget it"/"forgotten it"/"I talked to Newcombe"/"My being the first"*: Rowan interview with Jackie and Rachel Robinson, 1957.
346 *"gutless draft boards"*: *Sporting News*, March 21, 1956.
347 *"Everywhere baseball is played"*: *Sporting News*, June 6, 1956.
347 *"You can have this South"*: *Long Island Daily Press*, April 5, 1956.
347 *"If I knew why"*: *Sporting News*, May 2, 1956.
347 *"Our situation"*: Sid Offit, "Jersey City's (Brooklyn) Dodgers," *Baseball Magazine*, May 1956.
348 *"you can't let a park"*: *New York Post*, April 20, 1956.
348 *"I can't understand"*: *Long Island Daily Press*, May 5, 1956.
348 *a guess hitter*: *Sporting News*, September 28, 1955.
348 *sharing barbecued ribs*: *Sporting News*, June 27, 1956.
349 *"strangest sight"*: *Los Angeles Times*, April 23, 1959.
349 *"get him mad"*: *Long Island Daily Press*, June 21, 1956.
349 *"I'm pressing"/"Don't you worry"*: *Sports Illustrated*, July 2, 1956.
349 *"Thank God"*: *New York Post*, June 22, 1956.
349 *"never healed properly"*: *New York Journal-American*, August 12, 1956.
349 *"They don't know"*: *Milwaukee Journal*, September 14, 1956.
349 *believed it cost them*: Shapiro, *Last Good Season*, 164.
350 *"There's only one answer"*: *New York Times*, July 27, 1956.
350 *"a clump of twisted"*: *Milwaukee Journal*, September 14, 1956.
350 *"Campy's trying to do"*: *New York Post*, September 5, 1956.
350 *"gutless"*: *Long Island Daily Press*, July 16, 1956.
350 *"look of the leper"*: *Sporting News*, October 17, 1956.
351 *"Dressen was often disliked"*: *New York Post*, July 17, 1956.
351 *breaking two false teeth*: *Long Island Daily Press*, July 18, 1956.
351 *"Every time we have"*: *Sporting News*, October 10, 1956.
351 *"They want me in"*: *New York Post*, September 5, 1956.

351 *"There just isn't"*: *Milwaukee Journal*, September 14, 1956.
351 *one of the few*: *Los Angeles Examiner*, January 26, 1958.
351 *"We jollied him"*: *Baseball Digest*, October–November 1959, 41.
352 *"whooped"*: *New York Post*, October 2, 1956.
352 *"Thank God"*: *New York Post*, October 1, 1956.
352 *"practicin' for Campanella"*: *New York Post*, October 3, 1956.
353 *"It was a good pitch"*: *Sporting News*, October 17, 1956.
353 *"had real good control"*: *New York Post*, October 9, 1956.
353 *"gutless"*: *New York Times*, November 22, 1956.
353 *a wild brawl*: *Chicago Defender*, November 3, 1956.
354 *"it was not a foul"*: Interview with Carl Erskine, April 8, 2008.
354 *"definitely"*: *New York Amsterdam News*, October 6, 1956.
354 *Sam Lacy claimed*: *Baltimore Afro-American*, October 20, 1956.
354 *bombed on scotch*: *New York Times*, November 6, 1975.
354 *"Nipponese"*: *Sporting News*, November 7, 1956.
354 *"We went over there"*: Vin Scully, "The Dodgers in Japan," *Sport*, April 1957, 92.
354 *"remember Pearl Harbor"*: Duke Snider with Bill Gilbert, *The Duke of Flatbush* (New York: Zebra Books, 1988), 187.
354 *"Those Japs treated"*: *Baltimore Afro-American*, March 23, 1957.
354 *"Back in the States"/"in one little"*: *Sports Illustrated*, March 31, 1958.
355 *"favorite player"*: *Los Angeles Times*, April 15, 1981.
355 *Monte Irvin suggests*: Irvin, *Nice Guys Finish First*, 111.
355 *"I thought the blowup"*: Interview with Rachel Robinson, January 16, 2008.
355 *"He and Walter never"*: E-mail from Buzzie Bavasi, January 16, 2007.
355 *"Just say that Jackie"*: E-mail from Buzzie Bavasi, January 17, 2007.
356 *"That's typical"*: *New York Daily News*, January 6, 1957.
356 *"But Jack is grown"*: *New York Amsterdam News*, January 10, 1957.
356 *"I think he's about done"*: *New York Post*, January 21, 1957.
356 *"I'd be surprised if Jackie"*: *New York Daily News*, January 26, 1957.
357 *"You can play with a guy"*: *New York World-Telegram and Sun*, January 26, 1957.
357 *"He's always been envious"/"I could say why"*: *Washington Post*, January 27, 1957.
357 *"regret . . . shock"*: *New York Post*, January 28, 1957.
357 *"talks entirely too much"*: *Baltimore Afro-American*, February 2, 1957.
357 *"That oughta"*: *New York Amsterdam News*, February 2, 1957.
357 *"discreetly placed"*: *Pittsburgh Courier*, February 16, 1957.
358 *"I don't like that stuff"/"believed much"/"You can't make"*: *New York Daily News*, March 3, 1957.
358 *"To me this was Uncle Tomism"*: Draft, *Wait Till Next Year.*
358 *"I never made such a statement"*: *Baltimore Afro-American*, March 9, 1957.
358 *"change out of their"*: Connery, "Take Six," June 23, 1955, *Time* dispatches.

358 *"It's been all right"*: *Mike Wallace Interviews*, December 11, 1959.
358 *"I'm a colored man"*: *New York Post*, March 29, 1957.
358 *specifically requested/bothered to attend*: Draft, *Wait Till Next Year.*
359 *"refusal to turn my tennis"*: *Baltimore Afro-American*, November 22, 1958.
359 *fifty-five blacks in spring training*: *New York Post*, March 26, 1957.
359 *"There isn't a single Negro"*: Fred Down, United Press article, March 14, 1957, box 1, folder 23, Jackie Robinson Papers.
359 *posing in photographs*: *IGTBA*, 8.
359 *"There ain't no cause"*: *New York Post*, March 7, 1957.
359 *"If Campy can have"*: *New York Times*, January 11, 1957.
360 *"Get your rear end moving"*: *Los Angeles Times*, May 29, 1983.
360 *"He was like a godfather"*: *Roy Campanella—ESPN SportsCentury.*
360 *"telling them the truth"/"Kid, you're"*: Roseboro, *Glory Days*, 108.
360 *"Campy is washed-up"*: *New York Amsterdam News*, April 20, 1957.
360 *"if they'd signed"*: *Washington Post*, June 28, 1993.
361 *"We haven't got to the point"*: *New York Post*, May 26, 1957.
361 *instead offering the old World's Fair*: D'Antonio, *Forever Blue*, 239–40.
361 *"I think they're goners"*: *New York Post*, May 31, 1957.
361 *"Up to now"*: *New York Times*, May 30, 1957.
361 *"If they go"*: *New York Post*, May 29, 1957.
362 *"would see a lot more"*: *New York Post*, July 21, 1957.
362 *"I knew if we put Campy on"*: *New York Post*, July 7, 1957.
362 *"Ol' Camp may not be"*: *New York Post*, July 28, 1957.
362 *"That Cuban blankety-blank"*: *New York Post*, July 12, 1957.
362 *"peacemaker"/"didn't punch nobody"*: *Sporting News*, July 24, 1957.
362 *"even a frown"*: *Chicago Defender*, September 16, 1958.
362 *"taking over"*: *New York Post*, March 27, 1957.
363 *"Slowly, stubbornly"*: *New York Post*, August 26, 1957.
363 *spitting angrily*: *New York Daily News*, August 8, 1957.
363 *"The team needs"*: *New York Post*, August 6, 1957.
363 *"I too have given up"*: Jackie Robinson to Caroline Wallerstein, August 9, 1957, box 15, folder 14, Jackie Robinson Papers.
363 *"completely paralyzed"*: *New York Post*, August 16, 1957.
363 *"The ball don't care"*: *New York Post*, August 30, 1957.
363 *"I don't know why"*: *New York Daily News*, July 2, 1957.
363 *"Man, this is awful"*: *Sports Illustrated*, March 31, 1958.
364 *"Campy has the best potential"/"If Robinson weren't"*: *New York Post*, March 31, 1957.
364 *"perfectionist"*: E-mail from Buzzie Bavasi, January 7, 2007.
364 *"It's baseball"*: *New York Daily News*, January 2, 1958.
364 *served crab fingers*: *New York Times*, September 25, 1957.
364 *"Lord, how he loved"*: Roseboro, *Glory Days*, 108.
365 *"He can still help us"*: *New York World-Telegram and Sun*, October 22, 1957.

365 *"I don't think he could"*: Interview with Don Zimmer, December 4, 2008.
365 *"six others would pick"*: *Sports Illustrated*, September 16, 1957.
365 *"As long as I have"*: *Jet*, November 7, 1957.
365 *"From a business standpoint"*: *Sporting News*, February 26, 1958.
365 *"If I had owned"*: *Sporting News*, May 21, 1958.
365 *"Nobody's played"*: *Sporting News*, January 29, 1958.
366 *"The batter will have"*: *New York Journal-American*, January 21, 1958.
366 *Victoria Park section*: *Sporting News*, December 4, 1957.
366 *lucky fans at the Renaissance Casino*: *New York Amsterdam News*, January 25, 1958.
366 *"I'm looking forward"*: *Los Angeles Examiner*, January 26, 1958.
366 *"As a Democrat"*: *New York Journal-American*, January 28, 1958.

CHAPTER 18: DOSORIS LANE

368 *approaching forty-two degrees*: *New York Times*, January 28, 1958.
368 *Ruthe's brother had banged up*: Kahn, *Boys of Summer*, 359.
368 *he didn't budge*: *IGTBA*, 18; *Saturday Evening Post*, July 26, 1958.
369 *actually left*: *New York World-Telegram and Sun*, January 28, 1958; *New York Journal-American*, January 28, 1958; *Newsday*, January 29, 1958.
369 *Art Rust*: *New York Amsterdam News*, July 3, 1993.
369 *drive the blind singer Al Hibbler*: *New York Post*, January 29, 1958.
369 *"strict confidence"*: E-mail from Buzzie Bavasi, January 7, 2007.
369 *"was visiting a friend"*: E-mail from Buzzie Bavasi, January 17, 2007.
369 *other interviews confirm*: Interviews with Ruth Bowen, November 28, 2006; Delores Patterson, April 15, 2008; Roger Kahn, June 1, 2009; William Marsden, October 1, 2009.
369 *thirty miles an hour*: *New York World-Telegram and Sun*, May 26, 1959.
369 *"big ice patches"/"I tried furiously"/"hitting the pole"*: *IGTBA*, 19.
370 *"Maybe he went to sleep"*: *Long Island Daily Press*, January 28, 1958.
370 *"fell asleep"*: E-mail from Buzzie Bavasi, January 17, 2007.
370 *"artillery-like"*: *Long Island Daily Press*, January 29, 1958.
370 *"dented right fender"*: *New York World-Telegram and Sun*, May 26, 1959.
370 *"doubled up like a pretzel"*: *New York Journal-American*, January 28, 1958.
370 *"his chin striking"*: *New York World-Telegram and Sun*, May 26, 1959.
370 *"Roy, could you"/"I don't seem"*: Interview with Roger Welden, January 24, 2009.
371 *there seemed to be no alternative*: *Newsday*, January 29, 1958.
371 *"straighten him out"*: *New York Herald Tribune*, January 29, 1958.
371 *arrived at 3:45*: *Glen Cove Echo*, January 30, 1958.
371 *"This is Roy Campanella!"/"She couldn't have"*: Interview with Roger Welden, January 24, 2009.
371 *"The canal of the spinal"*: Interview with William Staas, Jr., September 10, 2009.

371 *"My back hurts"*: *New York Post*, January 29, 1958.
371 *"Car skidded"*: *New York Journal-American*, January 29, 1958.
371 *"Doc, what happened"*: *New York Post*, January 29, 1958.
372 *"a sad strained"*: *Philadelphia Evening Bulletin*, January 22, 1969.
372 *"You never know"*: *New York Post*, January 29, 1958.
372 *"Campy is alive"*: *Long Island Star-Journal*, January 29, 1958.
372 *"I'll have something"*: *New York Post*, January 29, 1958.
372 *"Campanella is one"*: *Long Island Star-Journal*, January 29, 1958.
372 *"He suffered"/"reduced the fracture"*: *New York Journal-American*, January 28, 1958.
372 *"too early"*: *Long Island Star-Journal*, January 29, 1958.
372 *"He won't be able"*: *New York Journal-American*, January 28, 1958.
372 *"I don't think"*: *Long Island Star-Journal*, January 29, 1958.
373 *"everything is going"/"He's in such pain"/"Hello, boss"*: *Long Island Star-Journal*, January 29, 1958.
373 *"I knew I was in trouble"*: Interview with Eric Hayden, January 7, 2008.
373 *"I thought I was"*: *IGTBA*, 202.
374 *"cheerful"*: *New York Times*, February 4, 1958.
374 *"no new improvement"*: *New York Times*, February 6, 1958.
374 *"Dodgers Fear"*: *New York Journal-American*, February 14, 1958.
374 *"never heard"*: *Chicago Tribune*, February 15, 1958.
374 *"Campanella's progress"/"He may still"*: *Newsday*, February 17, 1958.
374 *"How can they"*: *Long Beach Independent-Press-Telegram*, March 23, 1958.
374 *"make a liar"*: *Baltimore Afro-American*, March 1, 1958.
374 *"rack"*: *Los Angeles Herald-Express*, April 28, 1959.
374 *"like a piece of ham"*: *New York Daily News*, February 28, 1958.
374 *"Why did it have"/"I think if Campanella"*: *Roy Campanella—ESPN SportsCentury*.
374 *"They told me"*: *New York Post*, February 21, 1958.
375 *"Maybe he was thinking"*: *New York Journal-American*, March 19, 1958.
375 *"lying prone"*: *At Nightfall: The Roy Campanella Story*.
375 *"let the club down"*: *New York Daily Mirror*, March 19, 1958.
375 *"I'm still with you"*: *New York World-Telegram and Sun*, April 15, 1958.
375 *"I've had a tough"*: *Los Angeles Times*, April 18, 1958.
376 *"essentially a quadriplegic"*: *New York Times*, May 6, 1958.
376 *"unresponsive as stone"*: *Reader's Digest*, October 1978.
376 *"It's hopeless"*: Phil Jensen, "Can Campy Come Back?" *Inside Story*, October 1958, 27.
376 *"They would simply"*: Howard A. Rusk, *A World to Care For: The Autobiography of Howard A. Rusk, M.D.* (New York: Random House, 1972), 58.
376 *"terrible bedsores"*: Ibid., 56.
376 *"emotional, social"*: Ibid., 85.
377 *"It was an incredible"*: Interview with Janet Jeghelian, May 25, 2009.

377 *"strapped to his left"*: *New York Times*, August 2, 1951.
377 *"We have one rule"*: Transcript, *Person to Person*, CBS Television, February 27, 1959, Edward R. Murrow papers.
377 *"If it wasn't"*: Interview with Bobbi Wailes, January 12, 2008.
377 *"I'm all right"/"I don't want"*: *Jet*, May 22, 1958.
378 *"a little ball"*: Interview with Janet Jeghelian, May 25, 2009.
378 *"Rusk was the type"*: Interview with Pat Therriault, September 9, 2008.
378 *"Can't you give me"*: Jensen, "Can Campy Come Back?" 51.
378 *"independence through"*: "Spinal cord injury-rehabilitation costs and results and follow-up in thirty-one cases," *Journal of the American Medical Association* 164, no. 14 (August 3, 1957): 1553.
378 *"If I could sit"*: *IGTBA*, 216.
378 *"life . . . is"*: Harriet Hentz Houser, *Hentz, Of Things Not Seen* (New York: Macmillan, 1955), 120.
378 *"It always amazed me"*: Interview with Bob Bartlett, August 26, 2008.
379 *"to try to strengthen"*: Interview with Janet Jeghelian, May 25, 2009.
379 *"They lose the musculature"*: Interview with Pat Therriault, September 9, 2008.
379 *"He was a gracious"/"One of the things"*: Interview with Bob Bartlett, August 26, 2008.
380 *"I honestly believe"*: *New York Daily News*, September 11, 1958.
380 *"Things just aren't"*: *New York Post*, March 24, 1958.
380 *"He was the team's"*: *Los Angeles Times*, May 28, 1958.
381 *"Skip, they can't be"*: *New York Post*, May 18, 1958.
381 *"When we saw"/"I can visualize"*: Interview with Carl Erskine, April 8, 2008.
381 *"like a corny movie"*: Kahn, *Boys of Summer*, 260.
382 *"don't ever gripe"*: *New York Post*, November 13, 1958.
382 *"I was in his room"*: Interview with Pat Therriault, September 9, 2008.
382 *"I know they're feeling"*: *Saturday Evening Post*, July 26, 1958.
382 *"looks away"*: *New York Daily News*, August 29, 1958.
382 *"Whether I liked him"*: *New York Journal-American*, January 28, 1958.
382 *"I don't know how"*: Interview with Rachel Robinson, January 16, 2008.
383 *"has done a tremendous"*: *Pasadena Star-News*, January 30, 1958.
383 *Reichler's Associated Press feature*: See, for example, *Elmira Sunday Telegram*, February 2, 1958.
383 *"racial matters"*: *New York Post*, February 3, 1958.
383 *"Roy always has looked"*: Joe Reichler to Jackie Robinson, February 17, 1958, box 2, folder 21, Jackie Robinson Papers.
384 *"Over those weeks"*: Interview with Eric Hayden, January 7, 2008.
384 *"phenomenal functional improvement"*: *New York World-Telegram and Sun*, September 10, 1958.
384 *"ashamed to have"*: *IGTBA*, 250.
384 *"look as neat"*: *Los Angeles Times*, June 17, 1985.

385 *Dick Young claimed*: *Sporting News*, October 15, 1958.
385 *"like one big family"*: *IGTBA*, 240.
385 *"The public"*: *New York Journal-American*, November 26, 1958.
385 *"They want help"*: *New York Post*, January 3, 1959.
385 *"wouldn't let me"/"They don't feel"*: Transcript, *Person to Person*, CBS Television, January 2, 1959, reel 39, Edward R. Murrow papers.
386 *insurance coverage had*: Cohen, "Roy Campanella Today," 93.
386 *"Ersk, you're our"*: Interview with Carl Erskine, April 8, 2008.
386 *$42,000 salary*: Roy Campanella 1958 player contract, Lot 877, Hunt Auctions, August 22 and 23, 2003.
386 *"hoping the game"*: *Person to Person*, January 2, 1959.
386 *"You wonder"*: *Philadelphia Evening Bulletin*, November 16, 1958.
386 *"Things like this"*: *Mike Wallace Interviews*, December 11, 1959.
386 *"If you don't believe"*: *New York Post*, August 28, 1958.
387 *"Once in a while"*: *Philadelphia Evening Bulletin*, November 16, 1958.
387 *"get such thoughts"*: *New York Herald Tribune*, November 27, 1958.
387 *"sort of a nonverbal"*: Interview with Leonard Diller, July 10, 2009.
387 *"By next year"*: *New York Daily News*, January 5, 1959.
387 *"carry on"*: *Person to Person*, January 2, 1959.
388 *"with the impact"*: *New York World-Telegram and Sun*, May 27, 1959.
388 *"Get me out!"*: *Philadelphia Evening Bulletin*, January 25, 1959.
388 *"by far"*: *New York World-Telegram and Sun*, May 27, 1959.
388 *Harlem's gambling folk*: *Chicago Defender*, January 28, 1959.
388 *"I just don't know"*: *New York Post*, January 20, 1959.
388 *did not learn the truth*: Interview with Ahmad Baabahar, August 24, 2010.
388 *"There was no difference"*: Interview with Barbara Brannen, November 8, 2007.
388 *"he was going to be"*: *New York Journal-American*, February 26, 1959.
388 *"He was a guy"*: Interview with Eric Hayden, January 7, 2008.
388 *"People would come up"/"He was very nice"*: Correspondence with George Kafcos (Kafcopoulos), September 25, 2008.
389 *"grabbed a bunch"*: Interview with George DeLemos, March 16, 2008.
389 *"This is the worst"*: *New York Journal-American*, February 25, 1959.
389 *"My first reaction"*: *New York Amsterdam News*, February 28, 1959.
389 *"Dave says"*: *Baltimore Afro-American*, February 28, 1959.
390 *"looked haggard"*: *Chicago Tribune*, March 1, 1959.
390 *"winked slyly"*: *Los Angeles Times*, March 1, 1959.
390 *"John was scared"*: *Long Beach Independent*, March 3, 1959.
390 *"I get the feeling"*: *Los Angeles Examiner*, March 13, 1959.
391 *a possible draw of one hundred thousand fans*: *New York Daily News*, March 28, 1959.
391 *"As much as we"*: *Long Beach Independent*, May 7, 1959.
391 *"I'm really"*: *Pasadena Independent-Star-News*, April 12, 1959.

391 *"I know I'm crying"*: *Los Angeles Examiner*, April 15, 1959.
391 *"There have been three"*: *Los Angeles Sentinel*, May 14, 1959.
392 *"gaily florid"*: *Pasadena Star-News*, May 12, 1959.
392 *Clark Gable to Frank Sinatra*: *Los Angeles Herald-Express*, May 8, 1959.
392 *"I want to thank"*: *Roy Campanella—ESPN SportsCentury.*
392 *"lighting candles"*: *Chicago Defender*, May 16, 1959.
392 *"like swarming fireflies"*: *Los Angeles Times*, May 8, 1959.
393 *"I wondered if"*: *Los Angeles Sentinel*, May 14, 1959.
393 *"My parents"/"My father's"*: Peary, *Cult Baseball Players*, 259.
393 *"It really gets"/"Whatever a father"*: *Sporting News*, May 20, 1959.
393 *Bavasi's 1960 explanation*: *Los Angeles Times*, June 29, 1960; *Long Beach Independent*, June 29, 1960.
393 *"The city was good"*: E-mail from Buzzie Bavasi, December 31, 2007.
394 *"Fans, judging"*: *Long Beach Independent*, May 12, 1959.
394 *"Wheelchair embarrasses"*: *Los Angeles Examiner*, May 13, 1959.
394 *"I don't know if"*: *New York Herald Tribune*, August 17, 1959.
394 *"Having read"*: J. Randall Williams memo to A. H. Thornhill, Jr., September 12, 1958, Little, Brown records.
394 *"never mention"*: Memo to "All Salesmen," Little, Brown records.
394 *"spirit of Campy's talk"*: Copyediting form, Little, Brown records.
394 *"his deeply religious"*: J. Randall Williams memo to Edwin Seaver, November 26, 1958, Little, Brown records.
394 *"I think the title"*: J. Randall Williams to Roy Campanella, April 13, 1959, Little, Brown records.
395 *"Don't think"*: *New York Herald Tribune*, October 11, 1959.
395 *"I read to chapter"*: Marianne Moore to J. Randall Williams, October 10, 1959, box 132, Little, Brown records.
395 *hardcover sales of fifty thousand*: J. Randall Williams memo to "Mr. Devereux," February 15, 1974, box 132, Little, Brown records.
396 *"pollyanna"*: Carl Rowan to Jackie Robinson, April 3, 1959, Carl T. Rowan Papers.
396 *"Suppose I go"*: Kahn, *Boys of Summer*, 390.
396 *"I would like to see"*: Daniel D. Mich to Jackie Robinson, January 8, 1959, box 1, folder 15, Jackie Robinson Papers.
396 *"some white person"*: Carl Rowan to Jackie Robinson, April 3, 1959, Carl T. Rowan Papers.
396 *"Frankly I believe"*: Jackie Robinson to Carl Rowan, July 1959, Carl T. Rowan Papers.
396 *"Jackie describes"*: *Los Angles Sentinel*, June 2, 1960.

CHAPTER 19: A DIFFERENT KIND OF LIFE

397 *"again with"*: *IGTBA*, 305.
397 *"painted white"*: *New York Times*, February 24, 1960.

398 *"He went through"*: *At Nightfall: The Roy Campanella Story.*
398 *"He looked at me"*: Interview with Vincent T. Dacquino, August 19, 2008.
398 *"there is a total"*: Interview with Leonard Diller, July 10, 2009.
398 *"He was planning"*: *New York Amsterdam News*, April 8, 1961.
398 *"tireless care"*: *IGTBA*, 248.
398 *calls to Dr. Sengstaken's home*: Interview with John Sengstaken, January 5, 2008.
398 *"shouting"*: E-mail from Sonia Hofkosh, June 7, 2008.
398 *"very demanding"*: Interview with Janet Jeghelian, May 25, 2009.
398 *shoved a used*: Interview with Joseph Tanenbaum, July 28, 2009.
398 *"She wants to get"*: *Milwaukee Journal*, August 12, 1960.
399 *"She had locked him"*: Interview with Raymond Ormand, June 14, 2009.
399 *"They would get into"/"There's no way"*: Interview with Frank Heenan, January 20, 2009.
399 *"We feel"*: *New York Daily News*, August 12, 1960.
399 *"damaging things"/"He's just"*: *New York World-Telegram and Sun*, August 12, 1960.
399 *"drove her away"*: Interview with Ruth Bowen, November 28, 2006.
399 *"self-destructive"/"He was bitter"*: Interview with Barbara Brannen, November 8, 2007.
400 *"She's been very good"*: *New York Journal-American*, September 14, 1960.
400 *"He's an unhappy"*: *New York Daily Mirror*, April 5, 1961.
400 *driven to and from school*: Allan Morrison, "The Heartbreak of Campanella's Lonely Wife," *Jet*, March 15, 1962, 22.
400 *"She had no lights"*: Interview with Ruth Bowen, November 28, 2006.
400 *"He has a liquor store"*: *New York Amsterdam News*, November 3, 1962.
400 *more infidelity charges*: *Baltimore Afro-American*, January 19, 1963.
400 *"How do you hit"*: *Roy Campanella—ESPN SportsCentury.*
401 *"I don't even know"*: *Jet*, January 3, 1963.
401 *"If I ever get out"*: *Baltimore Afro-American*, January 19, 1963.
401 *"The question is whether"*: *New York Amsterdam News*, December 1, 1962.
401 *"I said to him"*: Interview with Joseph Tanenbaum, July 28, 2009.
401 *"dull thud"/"I knew my wife"*: *Philadelphia Tribune*, January 29, 1963.
401 *"heart-shaped wreath"*: *New York Amsterdam News*, February 2, 1963.
402 *"David leaped"/"I'll be at this grave"*: *Jet*, February 14, 1963.
402 *then forty-six*: Roxie Joynes, application for Social Security card, March 15, 1938, Social Security Administration; 1920 United States Federal Census, Ancestry.com.
402 *firm represented her*: *New York Amsterdam News*, July 7, 1945.
402 *Campy had crossed paths*: *New York Amsterdam News*, January 17, 1953.
402 *met her in the winter*: Fimrite, "Triumph of the Spirit," 100.
402 *fairy tale*: *Los Angeles Times*, January 28, 1988; March 15, 2004.

403 *"He was really": At Nightfall: The Roy Campanella Story.*
403 *"Roxie was the greatest"*: Interview with Vincent T. Dacquino, August 19, 2008.
403 *"She saved his"*: Interview with Carl Erskine, April 8, 2008.
403 *"If you play like"*: *Pittsburgh Courier*, February 25, 1961.
404 *"We thought we were"*: Robinson with Dexter, *Baseball Has Done It*, 85.
404 *"I know from Jack's"*: Interview with Rachel Robinson, January 16, 2008.
404 *It's a horrible thing*: Robinson with Dexter, *Baseball Has Done It*, 80–81, 86.
404 *"greeted Robinson warmly"/"other preachers"/"Roy's contribution"*: *New York Amsterdam News*, May 16, 1964.
405 *"interested in letting"*: Draft, *I Never Had It Made.*
405 *had the Robinsons over*: Cohen, "Roy Campanella Today," 94.
405 *Jim Murray column*: *Los Angeles Times*, February 25, 1968.
405 *"had he known what"*: *Los Angeles Times*, November 28, 1969.
405 *"Jesse Owens and Jackie Robinson"*: *New York Times*, May 12, 1968.
406 *"I sort of learned"*: *Sporting News*, January 18, 1969.
406 *"The good Lord"*: *Baseball Digest*, September 1997, 84.
406 *"It don't make"*: *Sporting News*, February 1, 1969.
406 *"This plaque"*: *New York Times*, July 16, 1977.
406 *"the greatest day"*: *Chicago Defender*, August 2, 1969.
406 *"To be good"*: Recording of 1969 induction ceremony, NBHOFL.
406 *"I really don't"*: *Philadelphia Evening Bulletin*, March 10, 1964.
407 *"I told him"*: *New York Post*, July 5, 1966.
407 *"headaches"*: *Person to Person*, January 2, 1959.
407 *"becoming a manager"*: Roy Campanella to Walter O'Malley, August 28, 1964, www.walteromalley.com.
407 *"Campy could do the job"*: *Los Angeles Sentinel*, February 27, 1969.
407 *"wouldn't be surprised"*: *Los Angeles Sentinel*, March 26, 1970.
408 *"I told him not"*: *New York Daily News*, August 12, 1974.
408 *"generalities"*: *Washington Post*, August 13, 1974.
408 *"The only ex-Dodger"*: E-mail from Buzzie Bavasi, January 16, 2007.
408 *"If you've got a heart"*: *Chicago Defender*, March 13, 1969.
408 *"There's all types"*: Cohen, "Roy Campanella Today," 93.
409 *"get into other"*: *Chicago Defender*, August 2, 1969.
409 *"on . . . hands"*: *Los Angeles Times*, July 23, 1969.
409 *"I'd say there"*: *Chicago Defender*, August 2, 1969.
409 *"wooden dowel"*: Cohen, "Roy Campanella Today," 92.
409 *Bob Considine once*: *Philadelphia Inquirer*, May 11, 1962.
409 *"He never"/"He just stole"*: Interview with Raymond Ormand, June 14, 2009.
409 *"At nightfall": At Nightfall: The Roy Campanella Story.*
410 *"They'd look at me"*: Interview with Bobbi Wailes, January 12, 2008.

410 *"I had a lady"*: Transcript, "Man with a Mission: Dr. Howard A. Rusk," *The Twentieth Century*, CBS television, March 29, 1964, Howard Rusk papers, Western Historical Manuscript Collection, Columbia, University of Missouri, Columbia, Missouri.

410 *"The handicapped people"*: *Bridgeport Post*, October 27, 1964.

410 *"Roy would be dead tired"*: *Los Angeles Daily News*, January 6, 1994.

410 *"Today, my life"*: Cohen, "Roy Campanella Today," 92.

CHAPTER 20: BOY OF SUMMER

411 *Buz Wyeth, thought*: E-mail from Roger Kahn, August 11, 2009.

412 *"seemed to grope"*: Snider, *Duke of Flatbush*, 134.

412 *"liberties"*: Buzzie Bavasi to Roger Kahn, March 17, 1972, box 9, folder 6, Roger Kahn Papers.

412 *"overly profuse"*: Red Barber to Buz Wyeth, October 28, 1971, box 9, folder 6, Roger Kahn Papers.

412 *"Part of me"/"gracious"*: Interview with Roger Kahn, June 1, 2009.

412 *"time and what"*: *Sports Illustrated*, March 30, 2009.

412 *"It's hard"*: *Chicago Tribune*, April 3, 1972.

413 *"and they get septicemia"*: Interview with Janet Jeghelian, May 25, 2009.

414 *"I don't think"*: *Los Angeles Times*, June 5, 1972.

414 *"All the places"/"I'm still"*: *Los Angeles Times*, June 5, 1972.

414 *"the last funeral"*: *Boys of Summer* (video).

414 *"humming softly"*: *Chicago Defender*, October 30, 1972.

415 *"I'll miss him"*: *St. Petersburg Times*, October 25, 1972.

415 *approached Roger Kahn*: Interview with Roger Kahn, June 1, 2009.

415 *Hollywood producers had done*: Rogers Terrill to J. Randall Williams, December 30, 1959, box 132, Little, Brown records.

415 *"My kids grew up"*: *Los Angeles Times*, February 18, 1974.

416 *ranking #16*: *Long Beach Independent*, March 4, 1974.

416 *"Will he ever walk"*: *It's Good to Be Alive*, directed by Michael Landon, Larry Harmon Pictures/Metromedia, 1974.

416 *"It's Great to Be a Lie"*: *New York Amsterdam News*, March 9, 1974.

416 *"drinking problem"*: *New York Amsterdam News*, March 2, 1974.

416 *"one hundred percent"*: *San Francisco Chronicle*, February 9, 1974.

416 *"It does justice"*: *Chicago Defender*, February 12, 1974.

416 *"I don't see the day"*: Associated Press story, December 12, 1974.

417 *"I want to feel free"*: Kahn interview with Campanella.

417 *provided only minimal child support*: Interview with George Ray, December 21, 2006.

417 *"I said, 'Hi' "/"The first thing"/"back with that family"/"He told him"/"in control"*: Interview with Gale Muhammad, May 1, 2007.

418 *"He needed"/"I'm so tired"/"You'd never ever"/"We'd be able"/"He was so excited"/"Oh, Vinnie"/"He beat that"/"He kept the disappointments"/"You*

don't know"/"He didn't have bad"/"He used to talk to me": Interview with Vincent T. Dacquino, August 19, 2008.

420 *"I told him"/"The main thing"*: *New York Times*, July 16, 1977.

420 *"The thing that"*: *Pittsburgh Courier*, June 29, 1963.

420 *Hall officials*: *Sporting News*, June 28, 1982.

420 *"a wonderful game"*: *Los Angeles Times*, June 17, 1985.

421 *"enthusiasm we had"*: *Pasadena Star-News*, August 24, 1975.

421 *"All they think about"*: Fimrite, "Triumph of the Spirit," 98.

421 *"I don't think any man"*: *Los Angeles Times*, February 15, 1979.

421 *"Every team has"*: Tygiel interview with Campanella, November 15, 1980.

421 *"crucified for it"*: Robinson with Dexter, *Baseball Has Done It*, 86.

421 *"They refused to let"*: *Long Beach Press-Telegram*, July 2, 1993.

421 *"I remember him"*: E-mail from Philip Ketover, July 10, 2010.

422 *"Bosh"*: Associated Press, October 10, 1978.

422 *"In New York"*: *Los Angeles Times*, January 28, 1988.

422 *"You could hear"*: Interview with Craig Callan, February 6, 2007.

422 *"I've told these guys"*: *Los Angeles Times*, March 4, 1980.

423 *"Roy Campanella, I think"*: *Los Angeles Daily News*, May 3, 1987.

423 *"master the bat"*: *Los Angeles Times*, March 4, 1985.

423 *preaching patience*: *Los Angeles Times*, October 29, 1981.

423 *"I thought it was"*: *Torrance Daily Breeze*, June 28, 1993.

423 *shelled out $2,395*: *Miami Herald*, October 27, 1983.

423 *"Every morning of that week"*: Posting by shlevine42 on Brooklyn Dodgers forum, www.baseball-fever.com, January 29, 2008.

423 *"I like being"*: *Los Angeles Times*, June 17, 1985.

423 *"If I had my life"*: *Boys of Summer* (video).

424 *"Mentally, baseball"*: *Los Angeles Times*, July 6, 1980.

424 *"Many times, I dream"*: *Jet*, August 31, 1972.

424 *broke both legs*: *Sporting News*, May 24, 1980.

424 *"Somehow, the rear"*: E-mail from Bill Deane, January 14, 2007.

424 *"If only I could"/"The job pays"*: *Los Angeles Times*, February 26, 1990.

425 *"Roy was a strong believer"*: *Los Angeles Daily News*, November 1, 1998.

425 *donated blood*: *USA Today*, July 2, 1990.

425 *"A doctor was"*: *Los Angeles Times*, February 26, 1990.

425 *"Being in the Hall"*: *Newsday*, August 5, 1990.

426 *"taped and gauzed"*: *Newsday*, March 31, 1991.

426 *"bundled up"*: *New York Post*, February 22, 1991.

426 *"I can still hear"*: *Riverside Press-Enterprise*, June 28, 1993.

426 *"Michael, you're going"*: *New York Times*, July 12, 1993.

427 *"Just go out"/"the best advice"*: *New York Post*, August 9, 2003.

427 *"He told me how important"*: *USA Today*, February 23, 1993.

427 *"He was still coming"*: *Riverside Press-Enterprise*, June 28, 1993.

427 *"and tell him"*: *Los Angeles Sentinel*, July 8, 1993.

427 *Piazza who was at bat*: *Los Angeles Daily News*, June 27, 1993.
427 *"I tried so hard"*: *Los Angeles Daily News*, July 17, 1993.
428 *"Maybe the only person"*: *Long Beach Press-Telegram*, July 1, 1993.
428 *"Campy can never"*: *Torrance Daily Breeze*, June 28, 1993.
428 *"He had gratitude"*: Interview with Carl Erskine, April 8, 2008.
428 *"I wish they were"*: Interview with Don Zimmer, December 4, 2008.

INDEX